The Painter IX Wow! Book

BOOK

Cher Threinen-Pendarvis

 Peachpit Press

The Painter IX Wow! Book

Cher Threinen-Pendarvis

Peachpit Press
1249 Eighth Street
Berkeley, CA 94710
(510) 524-2178
(800) 283-9444
(510) 524-2221 (fax)

Find us on the World Wide Web at: http://www.peachpit.com/wow.html

Peachpit Press is a division of Pearson Education.

Series Editor: Linnea Dayton
Peachpit Press Editor: Karyn Johnson
Cover design: Mimi Heft
Cover illustration: Cher Threinen-Pendarvis
Book design: Jill Davis
Art direction and layout: Cher Threinen-Pendarvis
Editors: Carol Benioff, Jennifer Eberhardt, Beth Meyer
Proofreader: Jessica McCarty
Indexer: Joy Dean Lee
Peachpit Press Production Editor: David Van Ness
Production and Prepress Manager: Jonathan Parker

This book was set using the Stone Serif and Stone Sans families. It was written and composed in Adobe PageMaker 6.52. Final output was computer to plate at CDS, Medford, Oregon.

ISBN 0-321-30532-9

0 9 8 7 6 5 4 3 2 1
Printed and bound in the United States of America.

CREDITS

Cher Threinen-Pendarvis is the originator of *The Painter Wow! Books*. In addition to being the author of this book, she is a fine artist, designer, educator and author of *The Photoshop and Painter Artist Tablet Book: Creative Techniques in Digital Painting*. A California native, she lives near the coast with her husband, Steve, who is an innovative surfboard designer.

Exercising her passion for Painter's artist tools, Cher has worked as a consultant and demo-artist for the developers of Painter. Her artwork has been exhibited worldwide and her articles and art have been published in many books and periodicals. Cher holds a BFA with Highest Honors and Distinction in Art specializing in painting and printmaking, and she is a member of the San Diego Museum of Art Artist Guild and the Digital Art Guild. She has taught Painter and Photoshop workshops around the world, and is principal of the consulting firm Cher Threinen Design. To learn more about Cher, please visit her web site at www.pendarvis-studios.com.

Carol Benioff helped to develop and illustrate several techniques for Chapters 3, 4, 6 and 13, and she edited portions of Chapters 8, 10, 11, 12 and 13. A native San Franciscan, she is an award-winning artist and illustrator currently living in Oakland. Carol loves combining Painter with her printmaking, drawing and painting tools, which is an ongoing experiment that she uses in all her work. When she puts down her brush, she loves to garden, accompanied by her cats, and take long walks in the wood with her companion, Heinz. You can see more of Carol's art and illustrations on her website, www.carolbenioff.com.

Please see the Acknowledgments for a more thorough listing of the *Painter Wow!* team contributors.

To my husband, Steven,
for his friendship,
encouragement and understanding;
and to our Creator
from whom all inspiration comes. . .

— Cher Threinen-Pendarvis

John Derry, co-creator of Painter

Capitola Woodcut *was created by John Derry using Painter's Woodcut features.*

FOREWORD

Ten years ago, back in the twentieth century, Cher's *Painter Wow!* book made its debut, filled with step-by-step techniques detailing the features of the recently released Painter 3. Six editions later, we now find ourselves at *The Painter IX Wow! Book* (which you are obviously holding in your hands!). The original edition was just over two hundred pages; this edition is almost five hundred. Like this book, Painter's audience has grown and matured.

In looking through these pages, what particularly strikes me is the stylistic diversity demonstrated by the contributing artists' gallery examples. The capacity to express a broad range of style is what makes Painter so unique as a graphics application. Painter does not impose a signature upon the artist's creative vision and, as a result, imagery and art created with Painter clearly articulates personal expression.

As you thumb through this edition, you can't help but be impressed by the variety of the imagery. Imagery that was all spawned from the same application! Book illustration, game board design, editorial cartooning, magazine illustration, motion picture storyboards, multimedia design, web graphics, and medical illustration are just a sampling of the areas of usage in which Painter has found a home.

Another interesting facet of the examples presented is how Painter has found its way into traditional art-making environments. Artists are integrating Painter with intaglio printmaking, glass sculpture, ceramics, photography, animation and film. This demonstrates how digital tools like Painter are no longer seen as the new kids on the block and are now accepted tools within the art-making world.

John Derry created Painted Flowers *using Painter IX.*

Thanks to Cher's creativity, diligence and hard work, you have in your hands an exhaustive compendium of Painter's multifaceted abilities. Cher begins each chapter by introducing you to a specific aspect of Painter's broad toolset. After a thorough explanation, a series of practical projects are presented illustrating the use of these tools. Every step is clearly explained and is accompanied by images of the artists' work, allowing you to follow along. In effect, you learn by example. As a finishing touch, a gallery of art by expert users is presented, utilizing the tools highlighted in the chapter.

Whether you are an aspiring student or a seasoned professional, you are sure to find invaluable inspiration in Cher's personable teaching style. Cher's enthusiasm for Painter is infectious and will have you eager to begin—or continue—your personal creative expedition.

A journey of a thousand miles begins with a single step. Likewise, a masterpiece begins with a single stroke. May it be yours!

John Derry
Overland Park, Kansas
March, 2005

Tomato and Basil *is a packaging illustration created by Michael Bast.*

High Flyer *was created by Chet Phillips using the Scratchboard Tool variant of Pens and Pastels and Airbrushes variants.*

PREFACE

Over the years, The Painter Wow! books have been an important entry point into digital painting for artists worldwide.

The first time I picked up *The Painter Wow! Book*, I was immediately inspired by all of the incredible art inside. More importantly, it provided me with invaluable insight into how to get the most out of Painter. With every new edition released, Cher continued to inspire and I continued to learn new ways to use Painter.

The Painter IX Wow! Book is no exception. Filled with tips and techniques from many Painter masters and from Cher herself, this book will help you unlock the secrets of Painter and give you the confidence to try new ways to express your creativity. From complete coverage of the basics to advanced techniques employed by masters of the digital medium, *The Painter IX Wow! Book* is the key to taking your art to the next level.

As the Program Manager for Corel Painter IX, I have had the unique opportunity to travel the globe to meet with artists in almost every industry. Whether it's gaming, comic books, manga, anime, automotive and industrial design, photography, movies and television, graphic design, illustration or fine art, *The Painter IX Wow! Book* is *the* preeminent resource for learning and mastering Painter. In fact, many artists have confided that the style they are now famous for resulted from having had spent time with Cher's books. With Painter's rapidly growing presence in art schools and design colleges, *The Painter IX Wow! Book* has also become required reading for their students.

Not only is Cher the author of The Painter Wow! books, but she also has a long history of working with Painter's developers to create new mediums including Watercolor and Painter IX's brand

Gecko on Ti Leaf was created for the Kona Brewing Company by Delro Rosco. The art is used on printed materials to promote the beer product. Rosco painted with various Airbrushes and Watercolor brushes.

new Artists' Oils. This is one of the many reasons why there is no one more qualified to help you master these mediums than Cher. *The Painter IX Wow! Book* features an expanded painting chapter that includes exciting new techniques for both Artists' Oils and Digital Watercolor, helping you to integrate them smoothly into your paintings.

Much of Painter's content that you and I use every single day, has also been created by Cher. She has literally created hundreds of brushes that the world's best digital artists use to bring their ideas to life. It's very possible that the next movie you see or car you buy was conceptualized using one of Cher's brushes! In *The Painter IX Wow! Book,* Cher includes an entire chapter that demystifies this fine art of brush creation, giving you the ability to customize brushes to a finite level of detail. The CD-ROM at the end of the book also includes new brushes and content that you will not find anywhere else.

Regardless of the type of art you are creating, author, educator, and Painter icon Cher Threinen-Pendarvis has created yet another invaluable resource for both learning *and* inspiration.

Rick Champagne
Program Manager, Corel Painter
Corel Corporation
April, 2005

Mark Zimmer created the original Paint Can *image for the Painter 1.0 program.*

Pouring it on with Painter *was created for the Painter 3 poster by John Derry.*

ACKNOWLEDGMENTS

The Painter IX Wow! Book would not have been possible without a great deal of help from some extraordinary people and sources.

First of all, I am grateful to each of the talented Painter artists who contributed their work and techniques; their names are listed in Appendix D in the back of the book.

Heartfelt thanks go to my friend and colleague Carol Benioff for collaborating with me to create new art and lessons for the book and for helping to edit chapters. Sincere thanks go to my inspirational friend John Derry, for collaborating with me to create two new lessons for the book. His inspiration and encouragement have been motivating factors during all editions of *The Painter Wow!* book.

Warmest thanks go to Linnea Dayton, the *Wow!* Series Editor and a longtime friend and colleague. Thank you, Linnea, for your encouragement and helpful advice. Special thanks go to Jill Davis for her brilliant book design, to Jennifer Eberhardt for her excellent advice, to my special friend Elizabeth Meyer for her support and diligent technical editing, to Joy Dean Lee for her careful indexing, and to longtime friend and colleague Jonathan Parker, for his careful attention to the production issues. Jonathan's calm assurance during the deadlines of all seven editions of this book was much appreciated!

Sincere thanks go to my friends at Peachpit Press, especially Ted Nace for his inspiration, Nancy Ruenzel for guidance, Karyn Johnson for her helpful advice, David Van Ness for his production advice, Victor Gavenda for his work on the CD-ROM and the rest of the Peachpit publishing team for their support. Thank you, Peachpit, for giving me the opportunity to write this book.

John Derry created this illustration for the Painter 4 poster.

John Derry created this illustration for the Painter 6 poster.

© COREL CORPORATION

Phoenix and Painter at Mount Fuji was created for the Painter 7 poster by Cher Threinen-Pendarvis.

A big "thank you" goes to the creators of Painter: Mark Zimmer, Tom Hedges and John Derry, for creating such a *Wow!* program with which we artists can enjoy limitless creativity.

My warmest thanks go to Rick Champagne and Sean Young, the Program Manager and Product Manager for Painter products, for their support. I'm also grateful to the Painter IX development team: Christopher Tremblay, Vladmir Makarov, Max Kuzmin, Dan Jette, Valentin Ivanov, Philippe Casgrain, and to the QA folks—Kerry Liberty and Tom Watts.

I'd also like to thank the companies who supplied the *Wow!* book team with supporting software and hardware during the development of the book. I'm grateful to Adobe Systems for supplying me with Photoshop, so that I could demonstrate how nicely the program works with Painter.

Thanks to Wacom for their great pressure-sensitive tablets and Cintiq pressure-sensitive LCD, and to Epson for color printers for the testing of printmaking techniques.

Thanks to Corbis Images, PhotoDisc and PhotoSpin for their support during all editions of the book; these "stock on CD-ROM and Web" companies allowed us to use their photos for demonstration purposes in the book. I am also grateful to the other companies who provided images or video clips for *The Painter IX Wow!* CD-ROM; they are listed in Appendix A in the back of the book.

My warm thanks go to Carol Benioff for sharing her expertise in traditional and digital printmaking and Steven Gordon for his experience with terrain maps. Special thanks go to Dorothy Krause, Bonny Lhotka and Karin Schminke for sharing their knowledge of experimental printmaking; Jon Lee and Geoff Hull of Fox Television for sharing their experience in designing for broadcast television; Cindy and Dewey Reid of Reid Creative, and John and Joyce Ryan of Dagnabit! for sharing their expertise in animation and film; and Lynda Weinman for sharing her knowledge about designing graphics for the Web.

A heartfelt thank you to these special "co-workers": to my husband, Steve, for his encouragement, humor, healthy meals and reminders to take surfing breaks during the project; and to our cats, Soshi, Pearl, Sable and Marika, the close companions who entertain us and keep me company in the office and studio. Warm thanks go to dear friends Lisa Baker, Susan Bugbee, Julie Klein, Donal Jolley and Beth Meyer, who shared sincere encouragement and prayers. Thanks for checking in with me while I worked!

Finally, I would like to thank all the other family, friends and colleagues who have been so patient and understanding during the development of seven editions of this book.

— Cher Threinen-Pendarvis

CONTENTS

WELCOME TO *PAINTER IX WOW!*

SOME PEOPLE EMPHASIZE THE DIFFERENCES between traditional and digital art tools—almost as if "real" art and the computer are not compatible. But during the early development of this book, we discovered many working artists who had bought computers specifically because they were thrilled by the promise of Painter. It seemed logical that *The Painter Wow! Book* should become a bridge connecting conventional tools and techniques with their electronic counterparts. Early chapters of the book, in particular, touch on color theory, art history and conventional media, and explain how to translate foundational art theory using Painter's tools.

This book addresses the needs of a wide variety of creative professionals: artists making the transition from traditional to digital media; photographers looking to expand their visual vocabulary; screen or print graphic designers hunting for special effects to apply to type and graphics; even creative explorers out for some fun. For those of you with a long history in a traditional art form and a short history with computers, we've done our best to guide you through Painter's interface, making it as simple as possible for you to achieve the results you want. And if you've spent more time with a keyboard and mouse than you have with an artist's palette and paintbrush, you may learn a lot about conventional art terms and techniques as you read the book.

The creative team that invented Painter—Mark Zimmer, John Derry and Tom Hedges—are famous for their creativity. John Derry of the original team consulted with the innovative Corel development team during the creation of Painter IX. Along with exciting new natural-media tools such as the Artists' Oils medium and other useful features such as the helpful Brush Controls palette, Corel has made significant changes to the interface that make Painter more streamlined and much easier to use.

The Artists' Oils brushes in Painter IX let you paint with luscious wet oil paint, as show here in Quiet Moment at Schwetzingen.

CHER THREINEN-PENDARVIS

Hillside Lake was created using the Liquid Ink brushes and layers with which you can create images with thick, sticky ink.

CHER THREINEN-PENDARVIS

Carol Benioff used the Digital Watercolor medium to create Pupa, shown here as a detail.

WHAT'S NEW IN PAINTER IX?

To make *The Painter IX Wow! Book* complete and up-to-date for Painter IX, we've revised every page. And we've expanded the book—adding brand-new techniques, new real-world tips, and galleries that specifically profile features added in version IX. Here's a quick overview of some of Painter's exciting new features and a description of where in this book you can find information about them.

Among the changes that make Painter easier to use are these: Painter IX features an **improved speed and stability**. The Corel development team worked closely with Apple, Intel and AMD to improve Painter and help it run more efficiently. Some brushes, for instance, Liquid Ink and Watercolor, are up to ten times faster!

The new **Brush Controls palette** mirrors the settings in the Brush Creator and allow you to make changes to brushes, on the fly, as you work. The new **Boost** slider, found in the General section of Brush Controls, allows you to speed up the performance for brushes that employ the continuous-stroke model; for instance, the Soft Runny Wash variant of Watercolor.

The improved **Tracker** palette remembers brush categories and variants, making it easy to return to a brush you recently used by choosing it in the Tracker palette. Favorite brushes can be locked so that they are easily accessible.

Painter IX boasts exciting new natural-media features, including the **Artists' Oils Painting System**, with dozens of brushes to use with the medium. The Artists' Oils brushes can pick up a mixture of colors from the Mixer palette, and then apply the multiple colored paint directly to an image. The Artists' Oils paint is luscious and wet, and you can integrate the Artists' Oils with other media on the Canvas or on default layers. See "A Painter Artists' Oils Primer" on page 98, "Painting with the Artists' Oils" on page 101 and "Illustrating with the Artists' Oils" on page 105 for information about using these new tools in a creative way.

Digital Watercolor has been dramatically improved with Painter IX. Digital Watercolor is an easy-to-use, transparent medium you can use to paint on the Canvas or on a default layer. You can brush on washes that are smooth, diffused, or grainy. Several step-by-step techniques feature Digital Watercolor; for instance, "Painting with Digital Watercolor" on page 90 and "Digital Watercolor with Custom Brushes" on page 166.

Illustrators will love using **Snap-to-Path Painting** to create precise brushstrokes that follow the edges of a path or shape, while retaining the richness of the famous Painter brushes.

An area of the program that's most likely to change the way you work is Painter IX's **improved Photoshop compatibility**, including the ability to import and preserve layers, layer sets, layer masks and channels from Photoshop files. Painter's industry-standard **masks and layers** model will be familiar to users of Adobe Photoshop. With Painter IX, new layers are now added

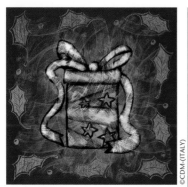

©CDM-(ITALY)

Athos Boncompagni used Painter IX's Chalk, Pastels and Oils brushes while creating this wrapping paper design.

You'll learn real applications for Painter's tools in the Basics sections of each chapter.

The Primers include detailed information about Painter's more complex media.

above the selected layer and layers with different Composite Methods can now be collapsed.

Animators will be enthusiastic about the new **Frames-per-Second Control** which allows them to preview their animations using different frame rates. Artists will appreciate the new **Interactive Save** feature which allows you to quickly save sequentially numbered versions of an image and photographers will enjoy the new **Quick Clone** feature, which streamlines the image-cloning process.

Painter IX features **enhanced support** for the new Wacom **Intuos3** tablets, the **Cintiq pressure-sensitive LCD** and the **Wacom 6D Art Pen**, which allows you to express a more complete range of natural hand movements.

DO YOU USE MAC OR WINDOWS?

Painter works similarly on Macintosh and PC/Windows platforms. We've taken the path of least resistance by using primarily Macintosh OS X screen shots. (Just to make sure of our techniques, though, we've tested them under Windows 2000, and we've included key commands for both Mac and Windows users.) The few differences between running Painter on Mac and PC are covered in Chapter 1.

ARE YOU A BEGINNER OR A POWER USER?

If you're new to Painter, welcome! We've worked very hard to make this edition of *Painter Wow!* more friendly to beginners by adding more cross-references and by including complete, unabbreviated directions to the techniques in the book. We've also added more basics to the chapter introductions. For intermediate and advanced users, we've included new power-user tips throughout and added many new techniques and inspiring galleries.

We've assumed that you're familiar with the basic Mac or Windows mouse functions and that you know how to open and save files, copy items to the clipboard and navigate through the Mac's hierarchical file system or through Windows directories. We suggest reading Chapter 1, "Getting To Know Painter," Chapter 5, "Selections, Shapes and Masks," and Chapter 6, "Using Layers," before jumping into the more advanced techniques. It's also a good idea, though it isn't essential, to have worked with the *Painter IX Help* and to have completed tutorials that come with the program.

HOW TO USE THIS BOOK

In Chapters 2 through 13, the information we're presenting generally progresses from simple to complex. We've organized these chapters into six types of material: "Basics" sections, "Primers," techniques, practical tips and galleries. In addition, useful hardware, software and other resources are listed at the back of the book.

1 The **Basics** sections teach how Painter's tools and functions work, and give real-world applications for the tools. *The Painter IX Wow! Book* wasn't designed to be a replacement for the *Painter*

You can temporarily switch to the Dropper tool and sample colors by holding down the Ctrl/⌘ key while you're using many of Painter's other tools.

Each chapter includes step-by-step technique sections.

Each chapter includes an inspiring gallery of professional work.

Help that comes with the program. We've focused on the tools and functions that we think are most useful. In some cases we've further explained items addressed in the manual, and, where important, we've dug deeper to help you understand how the tools and functions work. In other cases, we've covered undocumented functions and practical applications, either shared by contributing artists or uncovered in our own research.

2 Several of Painter's media types (for instance the Artists' Oils, Impasto, Liquid Ink and Watercolor), are rich and complex, so we've written detailed, inspirational **Primers** to help you unlock their power.

3 The **Tips** are easily identified by their gray title bar. We've placed them in the Basics and Technique sections where we thought they'd be the most helpful. But each tip is a self-contained tidbit of useful information, so you can learn a lot very quickly by taking a brisk walk through the book, reading only the tips.

4 Within each **Technique** section, you'll find step-by-step, real-world methods that give you enough information to re-create the process yourself. In the *Wow!* format, pictures illustrating the stages of the process are positioned alongside the appropriate step in the project. Browse the pictures in the art column within a technique for a quick overview of the development of an image. We've done our best to give you enough information so you won't have to refer to the manual to follow the steps.

5 The **Galleries** are there for inspiration, and one appears at the end of every chapter. With each gallery image, you'll find a short description of how the artwork was produced.

6 No book is an island, so in the **Appendixes** in the back of this one, we've included lists of other resources for your use. If you want to contact a vendor, an artist, or a fine art print studio, or locate an art-related book or other publication, you'll find the information you need there.

The Painter IX Wow! Book was created to share useful techniques and tips and to provide creative suggestions for using the program. We hope that you'll use it as inspiration and a point of departure for your own creative exploration. Above all, don't be overwhelmed by Painter's richness. . . . Just dig in and enjoy it!

—Cher Threinen-Pendarvis

Painter Wow! Web site: www.peachpit.com/wow/painter

Cher Threinen-Pendarvis's Web site: www.pendarvis-studios.com

GETTING TO KNOW PAINTER

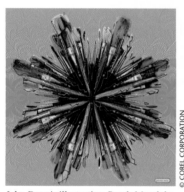

John Derry's illustration, Brush Mandala, was inspired by the artist Peter Max. Derry created it for the promotion of Painter using a variety of brushes and special effects such as Effects, Esoterica, Blobs and Apply Marbling. To create the mirrored group of paintbrushes, he used Painter's Kaleidoscope dynamic plug-in. Derry also painted spontaneous brush strokes using the Smeary Flat variant of Oils and the Smooth Ink Pen variant of Pens.

© COREL CORPORATION

SIT RIGHT DOWN AND POWER UP! This chapter explores Painter's basic needs and functions, as well as its unique strengths. If you're new to Painter, you'll benefit the most from this chapter if you've already spent some time with the *Painter IX Help* that ships with the program.

PAINTER'S REQUIREMENTS FOR MAC AND PC

Here are Painter's *minimum* requirements: If you use a Macintosh you'll need at least a G3 running System OS X (version 10.2.8 or later) with a minimum of 128 MB of application RAM. To run Painter on Windows 2000, or Windows XP, you'll need a Pentium II or higher processor with at least 128 MB of application RAM. For both platforms, a 1024 x 768 display with 24-bit color is recommended, and a hard disk with approximately 395 MB of free space is required to perform an installation.

When you open an image in Painter—for example, a 5 MB image—and begin working with it, Painter needs three to five times that file size in RAM in order to work at optimal speed—in our example, that would be 15–25 MB of RAM. Opening more than one image, adding layers or shapes, or increasing the number of Undos (under Edit, Preferences, Undo, in Windows, and under Corel Painter IX on Mac OS X) adds further demands on RAM. When Painter runs out of RAM, it uses the hard disk chosen under Edit, Preferences, Memory & Scratch in Windows and under Corel Painter IX on Mac OS X as a RAM substitute. This "scratch disk" holds the

ABOUT LAYERS AND SHAPES

Layers and *shapes* are image elements that are "stacked" above the Painter image canvas. Both layers and shapes can be manipulated independently of the image canvas—allowing for exciting compositing effects.

This Wacom 6 x 8 Intuos3 pressure-sensitive tablet with stylus is versatile and easy to use. The Intuos3 tablets offer pressure-sensitivity, as well as tilt and bearing, and allow you to paint more expressive strokes with Painter's brushes that can sense the pressure you apply, and the rotation of your hand, as you draw. You will find detailed information about using a tablet with Painter in The Photoshop and Painter Artist Tablet Book, *published by Peachpit Press (www.peachpit.com/tabletbook).*

Painter Temp file you may have seen. Since hard disks operate much slower than RAM, performance suffers—even if you have a fast hard disk.

Ideally, to work with Painter, you would use a computer with a speedy processor; a large, fast hard disk; and lots of RAM. In addition, you'll want a large, 24-bit color monitor—probably no less than 17 inches—and perhaps a second monitor on which to store palettes. Also

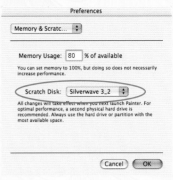

The Scratch Disk pop-up menu with a Volume chosen

highly recommended—some would say *essential*—is a pressure-sensitive drawing tablet with a stylus. Not only is it a more natural drawing and painting tool than a mouse, but many of Painter's brushes have a lot more personality with a pressure-sensitive input device.

Memory allocation. Both Windows and Mac OS X allow Painter to use as much RAM as it needs. Windows users go to the Edit menu and then choose Preferences, Memory & Scratch. Mac OS X users go to the Corel Painter IX menu and then choose Preferences, Memory & Scratch. You can specify a larger percentage of available RAM for Painter; however, this may not increase performance. The default is 80% and the maximum is 100%. The minimum that you can specify is 5%. If you type a number in the dialog box to change it, quit all applications, and then relaunch Painter.

FILE SIZE AND RESOLUTION

If you're new to the computer, here's important background information regarding file sizes: Painter is primarily a *pixel-based* program, also known as a *bitmap*, *painting* or *raster* program, not a *drawing* program, also known as an *object-oriented* or *vector* program. Drawing programs use mathematical expressions to describe the outline and fill attributes of objects in the drawing, while pixel-based programs describe things dot-by-dot. Since mathematical expressions are more "compact" than dot-by-dot descriptions, object-oriented files are generally smaller than pixel-based files. Also, because its components are mathematically described, object-oriented art can be resized or transformed with no loss of quality. Not so with Painter, Photoshop and other pixel-based programs. Increasing the size of most images in these programs means that additional pixels must be created to accommodate the larger size by filling in spaces as the existing pixels spread apart. As a result of these interpolated (manufactured) pixels, resized images can lose their crispness.

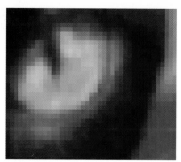

This scan of a photograph is a pixel-based image. Enlarging it to 1200% reveals the grid of pixels.

GENERATING A "SKETCH"

Using Painter's cool new Sketch effect, you can generate a black-and-white sketch from a photo. Open an image with good contrast, and then choose Effects, Surface Control, Sketch. In the dialog box, move the Grain slider to the right to add more grain and leave the Sensitivity slider at a lower range if you'd like to pick up primarily the edges.

We increased the Sensitivity to 1.40 to pick up lines from the photo background. We set the Grain setting at 1.40 to add richer paper grain to the sketch.

The black-and-white "sketch" image

There are ways of working around this "soft image" dilemma. One solution is to do your early studies using a small file size (for instance, an 8 x 10-inch image at 75 pixels per inch), and then start over with a large file to do final art at full size (for instance, an 8 x 10-inch file at 300 pixels per inch). Another approach is to block in the basic form and color in a small file, and then scale the image up to final size (using Canvas, Resize) to add texture and details (textures seem particularly vulnerable to softening when enlarged). You'll notice that many of the artists whose work is featured in this book use another efficient method: They create the components of a final piece of art in separate documents, and then copy and paste (or drag and drop) the components into a final "master" image. Painter offers yet another solution for working with large file sizes—composing with reference layers (small "stand-in" versions of larger images that are kept outside the document). Because data for the large image is not kept in the working file, performance improves. "Using Reference Layers" on page 224, tells more about this feature.

Painter's vector capabilities. Although it's primarily a pixel-based program, Painter does have some object-oriented features—type, of course, and shapes, shape paths and outline-based selections. Painter's shapes exist as layers above the image canvas; they are mathematically described outlines with stroke and fill attributes. And Painter's selections (areas of the image designated for work) are versatile; they can be used as pixel-based selections (similar to Photoshop's selections), or they can be transformed into outline-based selections or converted into shapes. (Other elements in Painter—the image canvas, masks and image layers—are pixel-based.) Chapters 5 and 6 tell more about selections and shapes.

Pixels and resolution. There are two commonly used ways of describing file sizes: in terms of their pixel measurements, or in a unit of measure (such as inches) plus a resolution (pixels per unit of measure). An image is a fixed number of pixels wide and tall—like 1200 x 1500—or a measurement combined with a resolution—4 x 5 inches at 300 ppi (4 x 300=1200, and 5 x 300=1500), so both files are these dimensions. (Either way it's expressed, this flat full-color file is 7 MB.) If you use pixels as a measurement for Width and Height in the New dialog box, notice that changing the numbers you type into the Resolution box doesn't change the file

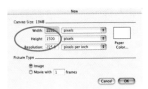

Expressing width and height in pixels in the New dialog box keeps the file size the same, regardless of how you change the resolution.

Whether the Constrain File Size check box in the Canvas, Resize dialog box is checked or unchecked, if you're using pixels as the units, the file size stays the same, regardless of how you change the resolution.

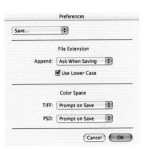

In the Preferences, Save dialog box, you can choose to have Painter ask if you want to Append a File Extension when you save the file, and to prompt you to check the Color Space when saving as well.

Click the Browse button in the Open dialog box to preview all of the images in a folder. The watercolor studies in Mary Envall's "Lilies" folder are shown here. (Some files may not have a preview—for example, some PICT or JPEG files created by other programs.)

size. But increasing or decreasing the number of pixels in the Width and Height fields in the New dialog box or the Canvas, Resize box will add (or reduce) pixel information in the picture.

OPENING FILES

Images in Painter are 24-bit color, made up of RGB (red, green and blue) components consisting of 8 bits each of color information. Painter will recognize and open CMYK TIFF and grayscale TIFF images as well as layered Photoshop format files in CMYK, but it will convert both CMYK and grayscale files to Painter's own RGB mode. CIE LAB, Kodak Photo CD format and other color formats will need to be converted to RGB in a program such as Adobe Photoshop or Equilibrium's Debabelizer before Painter can read them.

SAVING FILES

Painter offers numerous ways to save your image under File, Save or Save As. If you've created an image with a mask to hide some parts of the image and reveal others (Chapter 5 tells about masks), some of the formats will allow you to preserve the mask (by checking the Save Alpha box in the Save or Save As dialog box), while others won't. Here's a list of the current formats that includes their "mask-friendliness" and other advantages and disadvantages:

RIFF. Thrifty (files are saved quite small) and robust (allows for multiple layers), RIFF (Raster Image File Format) is Painter's native format. If you're using elements unique to Painter, such as Watercolor Layers, Liquid Ink layers, reference layers, dynamic layers, shapes, or mosaics, saving in RIFF will preserve them. (Watercolor Layers, Liquid Ink layers, reference layers, dynamic layers and shapes are described in depth in Chapter 6; mosaics are described in Chapter 8.) If you have *lots* of free hard disk space, check the

You can preserve layers in files by saving in either RIFF or Photoshop format, but RIFF (even uncompressed) is usually significantly smaller. Rick Kirkman's 663 x 663-pixel image with 150 layers weighs in at 1.7 MB as a compressed RIFF, 6.1 MB as an uncompressed RIFF and 7.1 MB when saved in Photoshop format.

To create Zorro's Gone, Janet Martini used several of Painter's brushes and effects, including Shells sprayed with the Image Hose and a fill using the Flying Blackbirds pattern. She colored the birds white using the Graphic Paintbrush variant of F-X. To complete the image, she added a Woodcut look by choosing Effects, Surface Control, Woodcut.

Uncompressed box in the Save dialog box when you're saving in RIFF: Files will become many times larger, but will save and open much more quickly. Few other programs recognize RIFF, so if you want to work with a Painter image in another program, save a copy in a different format.

Photoshop format. Saving files in Photoshop format gives you nearly all the flexibility of RIFF, and is ideal if you frequently move data between Painter and Photoshop. When you use Photoshop to open a file saved in this format, Painter's layers become Photoshop layers (Chapter 10, "Using Painter with Photoshop," contains more information about working with Painter and Photoshop); Painter's masks (explained in depth in Chapter 5) become Photoshop channels; and Painter's Bézier paths translate perfectly into Photoshop's paths and subpaths, appearing in Photoshop's Paths palette.

TIFF. Probably the most popular and widely recognized of the bitmap file formats, TIFF allows you to save a mask with your image (check the Save Alpha check box). Unfortunately, unlike Photoshop, Painter's Save As dialog box gives you no option to compress the TIFF file—the Uncompressed check box is checked and grayed-out.

PICT. PICT is the format of choice for many Mac multimedia programs and other onscreen displays. Painter's PICT format lets you save a single mask (but not layers), and save a Painter movie as a sequence of numbered PICT files to export and animate in another program (described in Chapter 11, "Animation and Film with Painter"). Painter also opens PICT files very quickly.

JPEG. When you save a file in JPEG format, a dialog box will appear with four choices: Excellent, High, Good and Fair. You'll get the best-looking results by choosing Excellent. The advantage of saving a file in JPEG format is that you get superb space

Here are some hints for working with Painter in a CMYK production environment. If you're starting with scanned images, scan them in RGB instead of CMYK—RGB has a significantly broader color gamut. If possible, avoid importing your image into another program (like Photoshop) to convert it to CMYK until you're ready to print, since you lose colors when you convert from RGB to CMYK. And, it's a good idea to save a copy of the RGB image before converting in case you want to convert it again with different RGB-to-CMYK conversion settings.

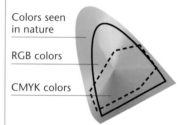

Colors seen in nature

RGB colors

CMYK colors

Relative sizes and extents of color gamuts

Janet Martini began Crane Crashes into Chip *by scanning a copyright-free drawing of a crane from a Dover clip art book. She copied the scan and pasted it into her image, and then she used Painter's Image Hose to spray a few poker chips onto the illustration. Next, she pasted in her signature, a "chop" image, which she drew using a Pens variant. To paint the bright pink, yellow and green areas, she used the Graphic Paintbrush variant of F-X. Finally, to create a higher-contrast look, she used the Effects, Surface Control, Woodcut feature.*

The Save As GIF Options dialog box includes GIF Animation Options. To learn about creating a GIF animation step-by-step, turn to "Making a Slide Show Animation" on page 412.

savings: A JPEG file is usually only one-tenth as large as a TIFF file of the same image if you choose Excellent, and only one-hundredth the size if you choose Fair. The drawbacks: no mask, layers or paths are saved, and the compression is a lossy compression—which means that some data (color detail in the image) is lost in the compression process. While JPEG is a good way to archive images once they're finished (especially images that have no sharp edges), many artists prefer not to use JPEG because it alters pixels. Don't save a file in JPEG format more than once—you'll lose more data every time you do so.

JPEG is also useful for preparing 24-bit images with the tiny file sizes that are needed for graphics used on the World Wide Web. (See Chapter 12 for more information on using JPEG in projects created for the Web.)

GIF. GIF is the graphics format of choice for most non-photographic images on the World Wide Web. Like TIFF, PICT or JPEG, saving in GIF format combines layers with the background. It also reduces the number of colors to a maximum of 256, so remember to Save As in a different file format first if you want to be able to access the original image structure again. When you save in GIF, a dialog box appears that gives you a number of options for saving your file. Check the Preview window to see how your choices will affect your image. For more information about using Painter's GIF format, turn to Chapter 12, "Using Painter for Web Graphics."

EPS. Saving in this format drops layered elements into the background and ignores masks, so it's best to choose Save As in another format if you'll want to make changes to your document at a later time. Saving in EPS format also converts the file into a five-part DCS file: four separate files for the four-process printing colors, and a fifth file as a preview of the composite image. Check the Painter Online Help for a complete explanation of the EPS Options dialog box.

PC formats. BMP, PCX and Targa are formats commonly used on DOS and Windows platforms. BMP (short for "bitmap") is a Windows-based graphics file format, and PCX is the PC Paintbrush native format. Neither of these two formats supports shapes or masks. Targa is a popular format used for creating sophisticated 24-bit graphics. The Targa format is often used (in place of PICT) when preparing numbered files for import into Windows animation applications.

Yellow Orchid, a detail of which is shown here, was painted with several of Painter's Artists' Oils brushes, including the Tapered Oils and the Dry Brush. The final illustration appears on the front cover of this book.

Movie formats. Movies in Painter (described in Chapter 11, "Animation and Film with Painter") are saved as frame stacks, but you can choose Save As to export the current frame of your movie, export the entire frame stack as a QuickTime or AVI (on the PC) movie or export the entire Frame Stack as numbered PICT files. See Chapter 11 for more about multimedia formats.

PAINTER BASICS

Here's a guide to some of Painter's basic operating procedures:

Navigating the Painter Workspace. The Painter IX workspace is easy to use. The Content Selectors in the Toolbox and the context-sensitive Property Bar allow you to choose tools and change settings quickly.

Painter's Menus, Palettes and Document Window

Painter's **Property Bar** is a context-sensitive palette that offers controls for the Tool that's active.

The **Brush Selector Bar** is where you choose Brush Categories and Variants.

Menu Bar

Toolbox

Color Rectangles

The six **Content Selectors** allow you to choose Papers, Gradients, Patterns, Weaves, Nozzles and Looks.

Colors Palette

Layers Palette

Canvas

Document Window

Drawing Mode Icon

Navigation Icon

Zoom Slider

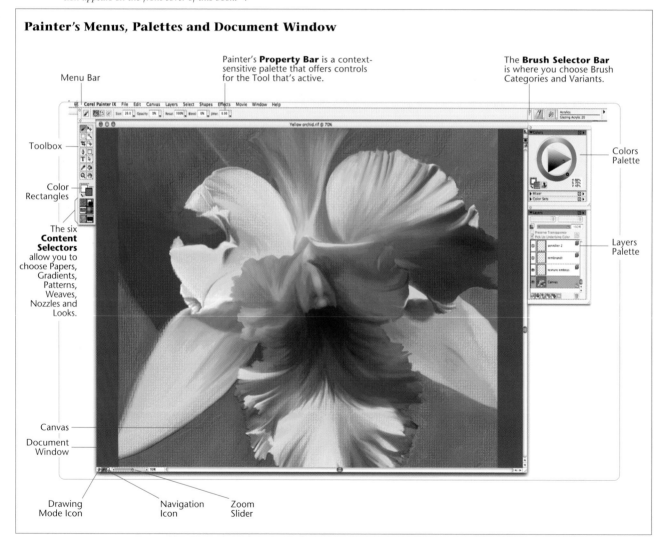

You can change settings in the Property Bar for the Brush tool using your keyboard. Press **b** to navigate to the Brush tool, and then press **v** to paint straight lines; press **b** to toggle back to freehand operation.

*In this detail of the Property Bar, Freehand Strokes mode is chosen. To paint Straight Line Strokes, click the button to the right, or press **v** on your keyboard.*

LAYER ADJUSTER TOOL TOGGLE

Painter's Layer Adjuster tool is analogous to the Move tool in Adobe Photoshop. You can use the Ctrl/⌘ key to switch temporarily to the Layer Adjuster tool when you are using the following tools: the Magnifier, Rotation Page, Crop, Lasso, Magic Wand, Brush, Paint Bucket, Dropper, Rectangular Selection, Oval Selection, Selection Adjuster and Shape Selection.

Using the Toolbox. Painter's slick, redesigned Toolbox features mark-making tools, and tools with which you can draw and edit shapes, view and navigate a document and make selections. In addition to the Color Rectangles, you'll also find the Content Selectors near the bottom of the Toolbox.

Painter's Toolbox

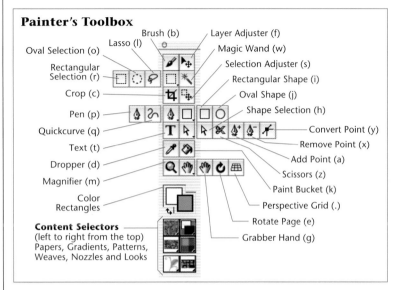

Brush (b)
Lasso (l)
Layer Adjuster (f)
Magic Wand (w)
Oval Selection (o)
Selection Adjuster (s)
Rectangular Selection (r)
Rectangular Shape (i)
Crop (c)
Oval Shape (j)
Pen (p)
Shape Selection (h)
Quickcurve (q)
Convert Point (y)
Text (t)
Remove Point (x)
Dropper (d)
Add Point (a)
Magnifier (m)
Scissors (z)
Color Rectangles
Paint Bucket (k)
Perspective Grid (.)
Rotate Page (e)
Grabber Hand (g)

Content Selectors
(left to right from the top)
Papers, Gradients, Patterns, Weaves, Nozzles and Looks

Accessing art materials using the Content Selectors. Previous versions of Painter used a drawer-like container to hold materials. In Painter, swatches for Papers, Gradients, Patterns, Weaves, Looks (a combination of a brush and a paper, for instance) and Nozzles (images that are sprayed using the Image Hose) are easy to choose from the Toolbox. Each Content Selector has a triangle menu that pops out a menu with which you can access commands, like launching a full palette or loading an alternate library of materials.

Choosing Art Materials

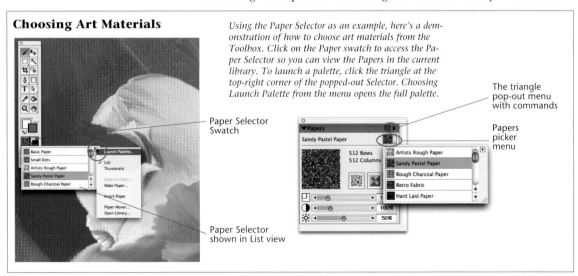

Using the Paper Selector as an example, here's a demonstration of how to choose art materials from the Toolbox. Click on the Paper swatch to access the Paper Selector so you can view the Papers in the current library. To launch a palette, click the triangle at the top-right corner of the popped-out Selector. Choosing Launch Palette from the menu opens the full palette.

Paper Selector Swatch

The triangle pop-out menu with commands

Papers picker menu

Paper Selector shown in List view

Using the Brush Selector Bar. The Brush Selector Bar, which is located to the right of the Property Bar at the top of the Painter workspace, offers an open list of thumbnails for both brush categories and their variants. (For more information about using the Brush Selector Bar, turn to the beginning of Chapter 3.)

The Brush Selector Bar

In the Brush Selector Bar, click the Brush Category icon to open the picker, and then click on the tiny triangle to the far right of the Brush Category menu to open the pop-out menu, which will allow you to switch from List view (shown here) to Thumbnail view. Click on a name in the list to choose a new Brush Category.

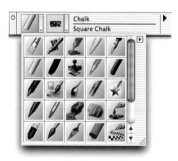

The Brush Selector Bar, showing the Brush Category picker open, to display the Brush Category Thumbnails. Click on a Thumbnail to choose a Brush Category.

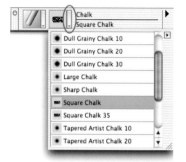

Clicking on the triangle to the right of the Brush Variant icon in the Brush Selector Bar will open a pop-out menu, which allows you to choose a variant—in our case, the Square Chalk variant of Chalk. The Brush Variant menu can be displayed using the List view (shown here), or Stroke view.

Menus

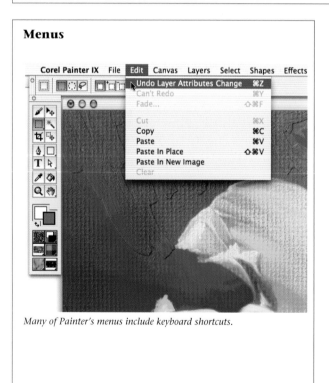

Many of Painter's menus include keyboard shortcuts.

Palettes

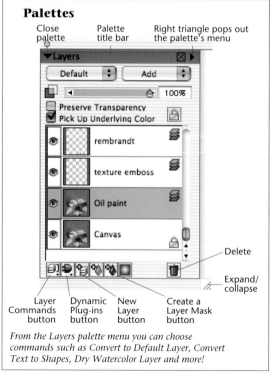

Close palette

Palette title bar

Right triangle pops out the palette's menu

Delete

Expand/collapse

Layer Commands button

Dynamic Plug-ins button

New Layer button

Create a Layer Mask button

From the Layers palette menu you can choose commands such as Convert to Default Layer, Convert Text to Shapes, Dry Watercolor Layer and more!

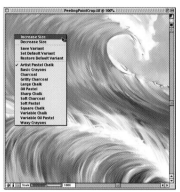

By right-clicking a two-button mouse in Windows, or by pressing the Control key and clicking on a Mac with a one-button mouse, you can access helpful, context-sensitive menus like this one, which appears when a Brush is chosen.

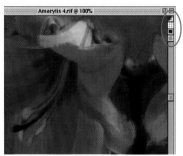

Toggle Tracing Paper, Toggle Overlay, Toggle Color Correction and Toggle Impasto Effect icons reside at the top of Painter's vertical scroll bar.

A. Rafinelli Vineyard *by Cher Threinen-Pendarvis. The Drawing Mode icons will pop up if you click the icon in the lower-left corner of the image window. They are, from left to right: Draw Anywhere, Draw Outside and Draw Inside. To read more about them, turn to Chapter 5.*

Screen management shortcuts. Like other programs, Painter offers lots of shortcuts designed to cut down on your trips to the menus, palettes or scroll bars. To *scroll* around the page, press and hold the spacebar (a grabber hand appears), and then drag on your image. To *zoom in* on an area of your image at the next level of magnification, hold down Ctrl/⌘-spacebar (a magnifier tool appears) and click in your image. Add the Alt/Option key to *zoom out*. (You can also use Ctrl/⌘-plus to *zoom in* one magnification level and Ctrl/⌘-minus to *zoom out*.) These are the same zooming shortcuts used in Photoshop and Adobe Illustrator.

To *rotate the page* to better suit your drawing style, press spacebar-Alt (Windows) or spacebar-Option (Mac) until the Rotate Page icon (a pointing finger) appears, and click and drag in your image until the preview shows you the angle you want. (The Rotate Page command rotates the view of the image only, not the actual pixels.) Restore your rotated image to its original position by holding down spacebar-Alt or spacebar-Option and clicking once on the image.

Another frequently used screen-management shortcut is Ctrl/⌘-M (Window, Screen Mode Toggle), which replaces a window's scroll and title bars with a frame of gray (or toggles back to normal view).

Context-sensitive menus. Painter boasts context-sensitive menus that make it easier to change the settings for a brush, or even quickly copy a selection to a layer. Context-sensitive menus are available for all of Painter's tools and for certain conditions, such as for an active selection when a Selection tool is chosen. To access a context-sensitive menu, right/Ctrl-click.

Helpful icon buttons. Just outside the Painter image window are two sets of very helpful icon buttons. At the top right on the Painter Window scroll bar are four toggle buttons: the Toggle Tracing Paper icon (allowing you to turn Tracing Paper on and off), the Toggle Grid icon (which turns the Grid View on and off), the Toggle Color Correction icon (to toggle between the full-color RGB view and a preview of what your image will look like when printed) and the Toggle Impasto Effect icon (which you can click to hide or show the highlights and shadows on thick paint). For a step-by-step technique using Tracing Paper, see "Cloning, Tracing and Painting" on page 110; see page 15 for information about using Grid Overlay. Turn to Chapter 13, "Printing Options," for

SEEING THE WHOLE PICTURE

If you're working with an image too large to fit within your screen, choose Window, Zoom to Fit, or double-click on the Grabber tool in the Toolbox. Painter will reduce or enlarge the magnification to fit the window size.

HIDE AND SHOW PALETTES

To hide all of Painter's open palettes, press the Tab key. The key command works as a toggle—press the Tab key to show the palettes again.

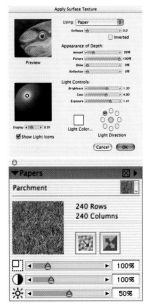

The Apply Surface Texture dialog box Preview window, shown here Using Paper (top), updates when a new choice is made in the Papers palette (bottom).

VARIABLE ZOOM

The continuous, variable zoom function in the left corner of the Painter image window includes a Scale slider, and you can also specify an exact zoom factor using the text field. Click the binocular icon to its left to access the Navigator, and pan around your image.

Clicking the Navigation icon (the binoculars) opens a window, in which you can see the area you are viewing in relationship to the entire image.

information about Painter's Output Preview; Impasto is covered in Chapter 3, "Painting with Brushes."

In the left corner of Painter's window frame is an icon that pops up the three Drawing Mode icons, which allow you to control where you paint—anywhere in the image, outside of a selection, or inside of a selection. Turn to the beginning of Chapter 5, "Selections, Shapes and Masks," to read more about the Drawing Modes.

Interactive dialog boxes. In most programs, clicking to make choices outside of a dialog box will reward you with an error beep, but Painter's interactive dialog box design encourages you to continue to make the choices you need. As an example, you can open a piece of artwork or a photo, and then choose Effects, Surface Control, Apply Surface Texture and click and drag in the Preview window until you see a part of the image that you like. If you then choose Paper in the Using pop-up menu you can go outside the dialog box to choose a different paper (even a paper in another library) from the Paper Selector (in the Toolbox) or from the Papers palette. You can even move the Scale, Contrast and Brightness sliders in the Papers palette and watch as the Preview image in the Apply Surface Texture dialog box updates to reflect your choice. When you've arrived at a result that you like, you can click OK in the Apply Surface Texture dialog box. The Effects, Surface Control, Color Overlay dialog box and the Effects, Surface Control, Dye Concentration dialog box behave in a similar way, allowing you to choose different papers like the Apply Surface Texture dialog box, or you can choose Uniform Color in the pop-up menu and test different colors from the Colors palette before you click OK. The Effects, Fill dialog box (Ctrl/⌘-F) is also interactive, giving you the ability to preview your image before it's filled with the current color, a pattern, a gradient or a weave.

ALIGNING SHAPES AND LAYERS AUTOMATICALLY

The Align dialog box (Effects, Objects, Align) is helpful for lining up shapes or layers (or a combination of the two). To align a series of items, start by selecting the Layer Adjuster tool, pressing the Shift key and clicking on each item's name in the Layers palette. When all the items are selected, go to the Effects menu and choose Objects, Align, and choose your settings. The dialog box preview will update to show you how your choice of Horizontal and Vertical options will affect alignment of the objects, and you can click OK to accept or cancel. The elements (below in the center) are aligned using Horizontal: Center and Vertical: None. The elements (below on the right) were aligned using their tops. The settings were Horizontal: None and Vertical: Top.

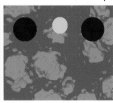

The Objects, Align dialog box with settings for the shapes in the center illustration above

Positioning the baseline of text with the help of the Ruler and Horizontal Guides created by clicking the Vertical ruler. The circled items here are the Ruler Origin field (top) and a triangular guide marker (bottom).

Using the Grid Overlay to help when positioning text

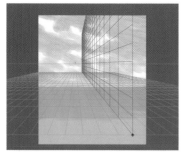

The Perspective Grid feature enables you to set up a one-point Perspective Grid, which is useful as a guide while drawing.

Measuring and positioning elements. The Ruler, Guides, Grid Overlay and Perspective Grid can help you measure and position shapes and layers. The commands for these features reside in the Canvas menu. They are especially helpful for aligning text and selections.

To set up a guide using precise measurements or to change the default guide color, double-click on the Ruler to access the Guide Options. Double-click on a triangular marker on the Ruler to access options for an individual guide. Delete guides by dragging their triangles off the document window or by pressing the Delete All Guides button in Guide Options.

To easily measure the exact *width* of an item, try moving the Ruler Origin. Press and drag it from the upper-left corner of the Ruler, where the horizontal and vertical measurements meet, to the left end of the item you want to measure. Then see where the right end falls on the ruler.

The Grid Overlay is useful for aligning items. Choose Canvas, Grid, Show Grid or click on the checkered Grid icon above the scroll bar. To change the grid's appearance (for example, to create a grid of only horizontal lines), choose Canvas, Grid, Grid Options and adjust the settings.

The Perspective Grid is useful both for aligning items and for setting up a grid that is helpful when drawing. Choose Canvas, Perspective Grids, Show Grid to display a grid. You can adjust the grid using the Perspective Grid tool from the Toolbox by dragging the vanishing point and horizon line or the forward edge of the grid. Choose Canvas, Perspective Grids, Grid Options to adjust the settings and to save your own presets.

The Colors palette showing a custom grouping including the Mixer and Color Sets palettes

When you make a brushstroke in the Preferences, Brush Tracking dialog box, Painter adjusts the range of pressure-sensitivity based on your stroke.

THE GHOST OF A BRUSH

To view Painter's brush footprint cursor, turn on the Enable Brush Ghosting check box in the Preferences, General dialog box.

The Opaque Acrylic 20 variant of Acrylics shows the "brush ghost" or footprint of its static bristle dab.

CUSTOMIZING YOUR WORKSPACE

Painter makes it easy to customize your workspace. To move a palette grouping to another part of the screen, drag the title bar at the top of the palette. You can also move up or down within a palette group, and remove or add palettes to a group. To see this work easily, click on a blank area of a palette title bar and drag it up or down. For instance, we rearranged our Colors palettes in this order: Colors, Mixer and Color Sets, eliminating the other palettes from the group by clicking the white "x" box near the right end of the title bar.

To save your palette layout permanently, choose Window, Arrange Palettes, Save Layout, and when the Save Layout dialog box appears, name your palette grouping and click OK. As your needs change, it's easy to rearrange the palette group. Then to restore a saved layout, choose Window, Arrange Palettes and choose the saved layout from the menu. To delete a layout, choose Window, Arrange Palettes, Delete Layout and choose the layout you want to remove from the list. To return to Painter's default palette arrangement, choose Window, Arrange Palettes, Default.

SETTING PREFERENCES

Painter's Preferences (under the Edit menu, in Windows, or the Corel Painter IX menu in Mac OS X) go a long way in helping you create an efficient workspace. Here are a few pointers:

Brush Tracking. Before you begin to draw, it's important to set up the Brush Tracking so you can customize how Painter interprets the input of your stylus, including parameters such as pressure and speed. Windows users choose Edit, Preferences, Brush Tracking (OS X users choose Corel Painter IX, Preferences, Brush Tracking) and make a brushstroke with your stylus using typical pressure and speed. Painter accepts this as the average stroke and adjusts to give you the maximum amount of range and pressure sensitivity based on your sample stroke. Previous versions of Painter did not remember Brush Tracking settings when you quit the program, but Painter IX will remember your custom settings until you change them.

Multiple Undos. Painter lets you set the number of Undos you want under Edit, Preferences, Undo. (OS X users choose Corel Painter IX, Preferences, Undo.) The default number of Undos is set to 32. It's important to note that this option applies cumulatively across all open documents within Painter. For example, if the number of Undos is set to 5 and you have two documents open, if you use 2 Undos on the first document, you'll be able to perform 3 Undos on the second document. And, since a high setting for the number of Undos can burden your RAM and scratch disk—because the program must perform a save for each Undo—unless you have a good reason (such as working on a small sketch

You can open alternate libraries using each of the six Content Selectors in the Toolbox. For instance, click the Paper Selector in the Toolbox and when it opens, click the right triangle to open the pop-out menu and choose Open Library.

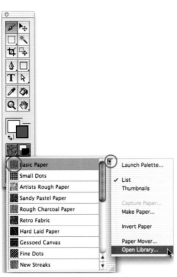

The open Papers Selector showing Painter's default Paper Textures library, and the path to the menu where the Open Library command is chosen

The open Papers palette showing the path to the menu where Open Library is chosen

where you'll need to make many changes), it's a good idea to set the number of Undos at a low number, such as 5.

Palette Preferences. You can choose which palettes are displayed by choosing their names from the Window menu, which makes it easy to configure Painter to save valuable screen real estate. The Preferences, Palettes dialog box offers controls for Autoscroll (lets you automatically scroll through a palette with several elements), Snapping Behavior (how palettes in a group are laid out) and Snapping Tolerance (how close one palette needs to be to another before it's snapped into the group).

The General Preferences dialog box lets you specify default libraries, cursor type and orientation, Temp File Volume (location of the scratch disk) and Units, among other features.

Painter IX's General Preferences dialog box, with the Drawing Cursor set for our right hand and Brush Ghost enabled

ORGANIZING WITH LIBRARIES AND MOVERS

Painter uses *libraries* and *movers* to help you manage the huge volume of custom textures, brushes and other items that the program can generate. Libraries are the "storage bins" for those items, and movers let you customize those bins by transferring items into or out of them.

How libraries work. Every palette that includes a resource list of materials has an Open Library (or Load Library) command. Let's use the Papers palette as an example. Choose Window, Show Papers. Click the right triangle on the palette title bar to access the pop-out menu, and choose Open Library to display a dialog box that lets you search through folders on any hard disk until you find the library you want; then double-click to open it. (Although you can load libraries directly from a CD-ROM—like the Painter IX CD-ROM or the *Painter IX Wow!* CD-ROM—it's more reliable to copy the libraries from the CD-ROM into your Painter application folder.) Fortunately, Painter is smart enough to show only libraries that can be opened in the palette you're working from. For instance, if you choose the Open Library command from the Papers Selector or from the Papers palette, you'll see Papers libraries only, not the Gradients or Patterns libraries.

Using movers to customize your libraries. If you find that you're continually switching paper texture libraries, it's probably time to use the Paper Mover to compile several textures into a single custom library for your work. For instance, you can create a Paper texture library containing favorite textures that work well

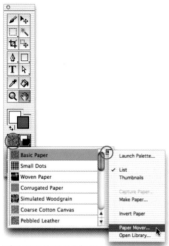

The open Papers Selector showing Painter's default Paper Textures library, and the path to the menu where the Paper Mover choice is located

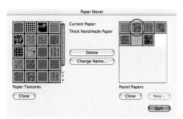

Dragging an item from the default Paper Textures library into the newly created Pastel Paper Textures library

Painter's helpful context-sensitive Info palette (Window, Show Info) offers an image-size preview, document dimensions, X and Y cursor position and unit information, such as pixels, inches and resolution. The Info palette also displays the RGB and HSV information. To see these values, choose the Dropper tool and click in the image.

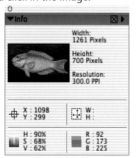

with Painter's grain-sensitive Chalk and Pastel brushes and the Wow! Chalk Brushes library on the Painter IX Wow! CD-ROM—such as Basic Paper, Thick Handmade Paper, Rough Charcoal Paper (from Painter's default Paper Textures library), Ribbed Deckle, Rough Grain and Light Sand (from the Drawing Paper Textures library) and Coarse Pavement (from the Relief Textures library). The Drawing Paper Textures and Relief Textures libraries can be found in the Paper Textures folder, on the Painter IX CD-ROM.

Here's how to build this custom paper library: In the Toolbox, click the Papers Selector, and open its pop-up menu. Choose Paper Mover. (You can also access the Paper Mover via the pop-up menu on the Papers palette.) In the Paper Mover, create a new, empty Papers library by clicking on the New button on the right side of the mover, and then name your new Papers file and save it. (We named ours Pastel Paper Textures.) To copy a texture from the left side of the mover (your currently active library) into the new library, select a texture's icon on the left side of the mover. The name of the selected texture will appear in the center of the mover window; drag the texture icon from the original library (left side) and drop it into the new library (right side).

Continue adding textures to the new library in this fashion. We selected the three textures from the default Paper Textures library and dropped their icons into the new Pastel Paper Textures library. Next, we added the Ribbed Deckle, Rough Grain and Light Sand textures from the Drawing Paper Textures library. To add a texture from another library to your new library, click on the left Close button, and then click again when it changes to an Open button and open the next

You can make new script libraries to store some of your automated special effects (and reduce the size of the Painter Script Data file, where the default scripts are stored). In the Scripts palette, click the right triangle to open the menu and choose Script Mover. The Painter Script Data file will open on the left side of the mover. Click the New button on the right side of the mover to make a new library and name it and save it when prompted. Select the scripts you want to copy, and drag and drop them into the new library. When you've finished copying, delete the items you've copied from the Painter Script Data file (by clicking on them and pressing Delete) to keep file size trim. (For more information about effects scripts, see Chapter 11.)

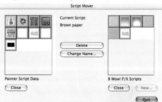

Using the Script Mover to import scripts saved in the Painter Script Data file (left side) into a custom library of special effects scripts (right side)

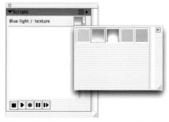

The Scripts library containing special effects "macros" that can be applied to images

For this illustration of a Queen Parrotfish, we laid in color for an underpainting with the oil-painting brushes (including the Round Camelhair variant of Oils), and then we added texture to areas of the image by painting with grain-sensitive brushes (the Square Chalk variant of Chalk, for instance) over the Laid Pastel Paper loaded from our custom Pastel Paper Textures library.

library that you want to draw from. (Don't forget the libraries on the Wow! and Painter IX Application CD-ROMs!) We selected the Coarse Pavement texture from the Relief Textures library and dragged and dropped it to our new library. When you've finished, click Quit. Now open your new library by choosing Open Library from the pop-up menu on the right side of the Papers Selector's list menu. Your custom paper library will remain loaded even after you quit the program.

All movers work in the same way, so you can follow the above procedure to create a new Patterns library that contains the only five patterns that you ever use. (See "Creating a Seamless Pattern" on page 304 to read about building a pattern using the Pattern Mover.)

LOADING AN ALTERNATE BRUSH LIBRARY IN PAINTER IX

To load a different brush library in Painter IX, first copy it into the Brushes folder within the Painter application folder, and then click the triangle menu on the right side of the Brush Selector Bar and choose Load Library. When the Brush Libraries dialog box appears, navigate to the brush library and click Open. (We chose the Wow! Chalks.) When the Brush Libraries dialog box reappears, click the Load button. The new brushes will now be visible in the Brush Selector Bar.

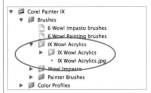

The open Corel Painter IX application folder (shown in Mac OS X), with the Brush Libraries organized in the Brushes folder; choosing Load Library from the Brush Selector Bar pop-up menu; selecting the IX Wow! Acrylics library in the Brush Libraries dialog box, and then clicking the Load button. **Note:** *To be read as a brush library, the brush category folder and category JPEG must be inside a folder with the same name as the category.*

IMPORTING OLDER BRUSHES

In Painter IX you can import favorite brushes that were created in earlier versions of Painter. These brushes must first be converted to the new brush model, and this is done by choosing Import Brush Library from the pop-up menu on the Brush Selector Bar. Early Watercolor brushes were not built to work with Painter IX's Watercolor layers or Digital Watercolor. They can be imported, but will not perform the same as in the earlier version because they were designed to work with the old Wet Paint layer on the Canvas.

The open Corel Painter IX application folder (shown in Mac OS X), with the 6 Wow! Chalk brushes library (created in Painter 6) copied into the Brushes folder. After choosing Import Brush Library from the Brush Selector Bar's pop-up menu, we selected the 6 Wow! Chalk brushes library in the Select Brush Library dialog box and clicked the Open button, which opened the Brush Libraries dialog box. Then we chose the newly converted 6 Wow! Chalk brushes 1 library from the list and clicked the Load button.

3RD-PARTY FILTERS & PAINTER

You can use third-party filters with Painter by installing them in the Painter application folder within the Plugins folder. Painter will automatically load them the next time you launch the program. To use third-party filters that are stored outside the Painter application folder, you can set up a Shortcut (Windows) or an Alias (Mac) for the plug-in folder to access it: To create a Shortcut, choose the folder containing the plug-in in My Computer or Windows Explorer. Then choose File, Create Shortcut. To create an Alias on the Mac, select the folder on the desktop and choose File, Make Alias. Move the Shortcut or Alias into the Plug-ins folder in the Painter application folder and restart Painter to see the new filters, which will appear at the bottom of the Effects menu.

■ With a background as a psychiatric counselor and as an experimental artist, **Kramer Mitchell** is interested in the field of art therapy, in which art techniques are used to work toward healing and personal development.

"Painter, Photoshop and my Epson 2200 printer with its archival inks have allowed me to bring my various interests together in this latest form of experimental art," says Mitchell.

Historically, dolls have been used for healing, prayer, magic, fertility, as fetishes, for personal development and more. By drawing from the rich history of dolls, Mitchell found a vehicle to express her artistic passion.

For *Untitled Frac Talisman Doll 1* (above left), Mitchell began by creating a fractal fabric pattern in Painter. (For detailed information about creating patterns, see Chapter 8.) Then, she sketched the design for the doll. After printing the design, she traced it on the back side of the fractal fabric. Then, she cut it out, sewed it by hand, stuffed it with polyfill and embellished it with beaded embroidery.

To begin *Untitled Art Doll* (above right), Mitchell painted the head and face using a variety of Painter IX's Artists' Oils brushes. Then, she sketched a design for the body of the doll. She resized the head and face in Painter and printed it onto a fabric sheet that had an adhesive backing. When the design for the body shape was complete, she printed it and then traced it onto a piece of interesting fabric. She cut out the doll, sewed it on her sewing machine and then stuffed it. As a final touch, she added the nose bead and emu feather.

To print her fabric designs, Mitchell used an Epson 2200 and specially prepared materials that she purchased at craft stores and quilting shops. Mitchell also recommends the Dharma Trading Company as an excellent resource for specially prepared materials. Find them on the Web at www.dharmatrading.com. For information more about printing, see Chapter 13, "Printing Options."

■ A longtime practicing potter and clay artist, **Brian Gartside** uses Painter as his sketchbook and to keep himself visually fit. During his career as an artist, he has moved from painting, woodcuts, etching and silkscreen before finding his current medium—clay. Gartside is internationally renowned for developing a unique system of ceramic glazes. "There is so much to know about color. To use it well is a real skill," says Gartside. Colors and shapes are the building blocks of his imagery, and he uses Painter to loosen up visually and to experiment with color. *Virtual Pots* (left), are examples of pots he has painted using Painter. The examples in the photograph above show his glazing technique and imagery on the actual clay pots. His abstract imagery is often inspired by the land and sky forms of his current home in New Zealand.

Since the very first version of the program, Gartside has used Painter to see and mix color combinations quickly and freely. *Seeing* color in this way and being able to make dramatic changes quickly gave Gartside a more profound understanding of color and composition. Gartside expanded his original color experiments with later versions of Painter and now finds the new creation and manipulation of shapes, use of transparency, layers and other improved tools give him new ways to visualize. As mentioned above, Gartside uses Painter to keep himself visually fit. With his Wacom tablet, pen and monitor, he does daily visual exercises, or warm-up exercises, and this results in a free-flowing, unrestricted feeling in all that he creates. There is no analysis, no thinking and no hesitation, but simply alertness of experience as he creates his imagery.

When Gartside approaches the surface of the clay, he maintains the same intuitive, open attitude. He works the clay and glaze with as much ease as possible, without trying to emulate his Painter sketches. However, he does keep the freedom and free-flowing hand movements he gained during the computer drawing experience when he paints with the ceramic glazes on the clay surface. He loves the contrast of the two mediums—Painter which is all light, and clay which is grounded in earth and fire. Gartside feels that the two mediums, Painter and clay, feed one another. Each activity reflects on the other, yet has its own inherent characteristics. The color and shapes he works with during the visual exercises in Painter provide him with a fresh visual dialog that keeps him working.

■ These two festive Christmas paper designs were created by Italian illustrator **Athos Boncompagni**.

To begin the illustrations, Boncompagni created a rich background texture. Using a conventional brush with coarse bristles, he painted thick black acrylic paint on a square piece of white illustration board, leaving a smooth border around the edges. When the paint was dry, he scanned the painted board and opened the scan in Painter.

Then, to enhance the contrast of the scanned brush work, Boncompagni used Painter's versatile Effects, Surface Control, Express Texture feature with Image Luminance. When the texture was as he liked it, he captured it as a custom texture by choosing Capture Paper from the pop-up menu on the right side of the Papers palette (Window, Library Palettes, Show Papers).

Next, Boncompagni opened a new square file that matched the dimensions of his scanned brush work. First, he used Chalk brushes to create black-and-white drawings of the ornament and star to work out their values and design. When he was satisfied with the design, he added a new layer and then painted in color using smeary Pastels and Chalk brushes.

When most of the red brushstrokes were complete, he added a new layer and then painted with bright yellow and gold colors.

Boncompagni sketched the small star and package elements in separate files. He pasted them into his working images as layers, and then positioned them with the Layer Adjuster. He used the seamless Pattern features in Painter to preview his paper designs. (You will find detailed information about patterns in Chapter 8.) However, to create his final layered pattern files, he used Photoshop's compositing features. He appreciates the precise pixel-based offset feature in Photoshop (Filter, Other, Offset) that allows him to precisely move a layer that includes repeating border elements.

©CDM-(ITALY)

©CDM-BBS-(ITALY)

Belgian Diamonds
Los Gatos
By Tom Tilney

■ **Tom Tilney** is a manufacturing jeweler and designer who specializes in designing with platinum and 18K gold. When Tilney is commissioned to create a new piece of jewelry for a client, he uses Painter to develop the design and to create a full-color presentation to show the client before he begins the manufacturing process. First, Tilney interviews the client to get a basic idea for the design, and for the stones and metals that are desired.

For the example in gold, Tilney wanted to make a setting that complemented the client's beautiful Tanzanite stone. After photographing the stone, he opened the photo in Painter. Then, he used the Pen tool to draw a shape for the border around the stone. (Later, during the manufacturing process, he would use the shape to cut a bezel to hold the stone in place.) Next, he drew the shapes that would become the yellow-gold outer portion of the pendant. To keep the shape perfectly symmetrical, he drew half of the form, duplicated it and flipped it horizontally. He moved the new segment so that the endpoints lined up with the original segment and then joined the end points. (For detailed information about working with shapes and layers, see Chapters 5 and 6.) For the diamonds along the top, Tilney used a photograph of a 10 mm stone from his Image Portfolio. He dragged the stone image from the Image Portfolio (Window, Show Image Porfolio) and dropped it into his working image, and then he scaled it using the Effects, Orientation, Free Transform function. Then, he duplicated it to create the diamonds around the top of the piece.

Next, Tilney converted the larger shape to a layer (Shapes, Convert to Layer), and then he filled it with a custom gold gradient. To achieve a shiny appearance, and to add dimension to the gold, he used Painter's versatile Effects, Surface Control, Apply Surface Texture effect to apply a custom gold environment map to the layer. (For information about making and applying environment maps, see Chapter 8.)

For the diamond and platinum pendant, Tilney used many of the same techniques. He used the Pen tool to draw intricate, curved shapes for the platinum and bevels. After converting the shapes to layers, he applied a custom platinum gradient to them. To achieve the look of shiny white metal, he used special environment maps that complemented the platinum-colored metal.

To complete both presentations, Tilney added artistic, textured backgrounds by choosing Effects, Surface Control, Apply Surface Texture, Using Paper and subtle settings. Then, he used the Create Drop Shadow effect to apply a soft offset shadow to each background.

■ Artist **Mary Ann Rolfe** was commissioned to create these two translucent window panels for the home of Kris and Hans Campestrini in Green Valley, Arizona. Rolfe built each panel with a front and back layer with different imagery on each panel. The layering of the imagery adds depth and movement to the panels. Rolfe developed her images in Painter and transferred the images to translucent panels using her unique transfer process.

To build the color scheme for this project, Rolfe took digital photographs of the interior of the Campestrini's home. She opened several of the photographs in Painter, cut and pasted elements from each of the photographs into a new file,

and saved the new file. Rolfe built a custom color set from the new composite image that matched the color scheme of her client's home. To make the color set, she chose New Color Set from Image in the pop-up menu of the Color Sets palette. Rolfe loves Painter's capability to easily generate custom color sets that she can use when painting a commission.

Working in Painter, Rolfe opened the scans of the motif drawings that she planned to incorporate into the panels. She painted on top of the scanned drawings with variants of the Oil Pastels using the colors from the custom color set. To add depth, Rolfe applied surface texture by choosing Effects, Surface Control,

Apply Surface Texture and a shadow by choosing Effects, Objects, Create Drop Shadow. For more detailed information about Rolfe's process, see "Creating Art for Glass Sculpture" in Chapter 8, on page 321. For the final piece, Rolfe arranged the painted motifs in two new Painter files, and then filled the background with custom Gradient fills using her custom Color Set.

To complete the window panels, Rolfe used an Epson 2000P to print the two panels onto a speciality paper that she uses in her unique transfer process. For more information about her printing process visit Rolfe's Web site at www.digitalstretch.com.

■ Artist **Donal Jolley** created *Flower Girl* as an exercise to merge traditional pencil, Painter and Photoshop in one continuous work. He started by shooting a digital photograph, which he printed on legal size paper on his laser printer. He laid a transparent sheet of vellum over the photograph and traced the basic lines where the composition would merge. Removing the vellum, he continued to use his soft graphite pencil to complete the loose composition on the vellum.

When the drawing was complete, Jolley scanned the vellum and saved it as a Photoshop file. Then he opened the original photo and scan in Photoshop. He scaled the drawing to fit the photograph, cropped the piece and then masked the unwanted background elements using layer masks. Next, he deleted the background by applying the layer mask to the image. Jolley then copied the photo layer to a new document, saved the Photoshop file and then closed it. He saved the layered file with the sketch and edited photo in Photoshop format, named it *Flower Girl 1* and then closed the file.

Next, Jolley opened the *Flower Girl 1* file in Painter, and cloned it by choosing File, Quick Clone. (The Quick Clone command cloned the image, deleted the clone Canvas and enabled Tracing Paper.) He saved the clone image by choosing File, Save As, and renamed the file *Flower Girl 2*. He kept the *Flower Girl 1* file open. Next, Jolley added a new layer to the *Flower Girl 2* image, on which he would rough in the composition. He sketched in color on the layer using the Square Chalk variant of Chalk, varying the size and opacity as he worked. To smooth areas, he used the Just Add Water variant of Blenders. When the figure and room were laid in, Jolley toggled off Tracing Paper (Ctrl/⌘-T). He arranged his reference photo next to his painting on the screen so that he could refer to it while he developed the values of the forms on the figure and clothing.

Next, Jolley added a new layer to his image and set its Composite Method to Multiply in the Layers palette. The Multiply method allowed Jolley to create rich color and depth in the shadows. As he painted, he used several brushes, including the Round Camelhair variant of Oils, and he varied the size and opacity of the brushes as he worked. When the basic composition was complete, he added another new layer (leaving this one set at the Default Composite Method) and he used low-opacity brushes to paint glazes over the entire image to brighten color and add more contrast. Then he added a few accents to the image with the Smeary Round variant of Oils.

Jolley dropped all layers by choosing Drop All from the Layers palette menu, and then he saved the *Flower Girl 2* file in Photoshop format. Next, he opened both the *Flower Girl 2* Painter image and the previously created *Flower Girl 1* image that included the sketch layer and the photo layer. He selected the *Flower Girl 2* image and copied it using the Layer, Duplicate Layer command, designating the *Flower Girl 1* file as the target. With the updated *Flower Girl 1* file active, he moved the Painter layer to the bottom, and then he used Photoshop masking techniques to compose all three layers into a seamless composition. To read more about using Painter with Photoshop, turn to Chapter 10.

THE POWER
OF COLOR

Susan LeVan used saturated colors on the focal point, and monochromatic dark values to create the ominous presence in Behind You. *To see more of her work, turn to the gallery in Chapter 5.*

Colors bar	
Color (Hue) ring	
Saturation Value triangle	
Color rectangles	
HSV/RGB color readout	

The Standard Colors picker with Hue ring, opened by expanding the Colors palette bar

Hue Indicator Bar

The Colors picker command menu opens so you can switch between the Standard and Small Colors pickers.

INTRODUCTION

"COLOR, THE FRUIT OF LIGHT, is the foundation of the painter's means of painting—and its language." Abstract painter Robert Delaunay's observation mirrors our own appreciation of color as an expressive and essential element of the visual arts. Getting the most out of Painter's powerful color tools is an important first step for those of us who work with "the fruit of light."

HUE, SATURATION AND VALUE

Painter's interface for choosing color is built around a model that uses *hue, saturation* and *value* (HSV) as the three basic properties of color. The program is designed so that you'll typically first choose a hue, then alter it by changing its saturation or value. Painter's Standard Colors picker and Small Colors picker are designed to work with these properties, but the program also allows you to work in RGB (red, green, blue) color space if you prefer. Clicking the triangle on the left end of the Colors palette bar (Window, Show/Hide Color Wheel) opens the HSV Colors. To switch between Standard and Small Colors pickers, click the triangle at the top right of the Colors bar to access the pull-down menu. To view RGB values rather than HSV, choose RGB Color by clicking the triangle on the Colors bar. To open the Color Info palette where you can specify color using RGB sliders, click the triangle at the top right of the Color Info palette bar.

Hue. The term *hue* refers to a predominant spectral color, such as red or blue-green. Hue indicates a color's position on the

QUICK SWITCH TO RGB

Click on the HSV color readout on the Standard or Small Colors picker to show color readings in RGB mode. Click again to switch back to HSV.

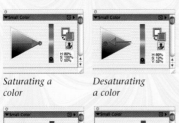

The Color Info palette with Red, Green and Blue sliders. (We moved the Color Info palette nearer to the Colors picker in the nested palette. To move it, drag the Color Info title bar.)

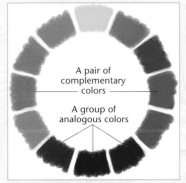

A pigment-based color wheel

MAIN/ADDITIONAL COLORS

Two overlapping rectangles display the current Main and Additional colors. To exchange the Main and Additional colors in the Colors picker, click the "Swap" icon, or press the Shift-X keys.

Saturating a color

Desaturating a color

Creating a shade of a color

Creating a tint of a color

color wheel or spectrum, and also tells us the color's temperature. A red-orange hue is the warmest color; a blue-green hue is the coolest. (Keep in mind, though, that temperatures are relative. Blue-violet is a cool color, but it warms up when it's placed next to blue-green.)

In the traditional pigment-based color system, red, yellow and blue are *primary* hues—colors that cannot be obtained by mixing. *Secondary* hues—green, orange and violet—are those colors located midway between two primary colors on the color wheel. Yellow-green, blue-violet and red-orange are examples of *tertiary* hues, each found between a primary and a secondary color.

Analogous hues are adjacent to each other on the color wheel and have in common a shared component—for instance, blue-green, blue and blue-violet. *Complementary* hues sit opposite one another on the color wheel. Red and green are complements, as are blue and orange. (Painter's Hue ring and bar are based on the RGB components of the computer screen; they don't exactly match a traditional pigment-based color wheel.)

To change hues in Painter's Standard Colors picker, drag the little circle on the Hue ring or click anywhere on the ring. Dragging and clicking also works with the Hue bar in the Small Color picker.

Saturation. Also known as *intensity* or *chroma*, *saturation* indicates a color's purity or strength. The most common way of changing a color's saturation is by adjusting the amount of its gray component. In the Color triangle, move the little circle to the left to desaturate a color, or to the right to saturate it. Fully or very saturated colors—those at or near the tip of the Color triangle—won't print the way they look on the screen. If you want to see colors closer to their printed equivalents while you paint, the Canvas, Color Management command can help. (See the "Color Management" tip on page 34 of this chapter and the *Painter IX Help Menu.*)

USING THE MIXER

The Mixer allows you to mix color as an artist would mix paint on a palette. Begin by clicking on one of the Color Wells at the top of the palette (or choosing a color in the Color picker), and dab the colored paint onto the Mixer Pad using the Brush tool in the Mixer palette. Add a second color and use either the Mix Color tool (selected in the illustration) to mix the two colors as we did here. The tools at the bottom of the Mixer are from left to right: the Dirty Brush Mode, Mix Color (chosen), Sample Color, Sample Multiple Colors, Zoom, and Pan.

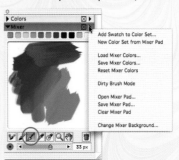

We mixed colors using the Mix Color tool in the Mixer. The pop-up menu allows you to save Mixer Colors, add them to a Color Set, and more.

As you can see in this detail of Decoys, *Richard Noble used saturated color and strong value contrast to paint a bright morning light on his subject. To see more of Noble's work, turn to the galleries at the end of this chapter and Chapter 3.*

An example of atmospheric perspective. The illusion of distance is enhanced in Along Tomales Bay *because the distant hills are painted with reduced saturation and less value contrast.*

A study in value contrast, based on a drawing by Michelangelo

Value. A color's lightness or darkness is its *luminance* or *value*. To create a *tint* of a color (lightening it, or increasing its value), move the little circle higher in the Color triangle. To create a *shade* of a color (darkening it, or decreasing its value), move the little circle lower in the Color triangle.

PUTTING HSV TO WORK

Here are several practical suggestions and creative solutions for solving artistic problems using hue, saturation and value.

Reduce saturation and value to indicate distance. Artists have been creating *atmospheric* (or *aerial*) *perspective* in their work for thousands of years. The wall paintings of Pompeii in the first century B.C. show this technique. Hills we see in the distance have less intensity than nearer hills, and they also have less variation in value. This effect increases in hazy or foggy conditions. To depict this in your art, you can reduce the color saturation and value range as the landscape recedes from the foreground.

Use saturation to indicate time of day. At dawn or dusk, colors appear to be less saturated, and it becomes more difficult to distinguish colors. At noon on a bright sunny day, colors seem saturated and distinct.

Use color temperature to indicate distance. The eye puts warm colors in front of cool colors. For example, orange flowers in the foreground of a hedge appear closer than blue ones.

Create drama with light-to-dark value contrast. Baroque and Romantic period artists as diverse as Caravaggio, Zurbarán, Géricault and Rembrandt are known for their use of extreme light-to-dark contrast. They accomplished this by limiting their palette to only a few hues, which they either tinted with white or shaded by adding black. A close look at the shadows and highlights that these artists created reveals complex, modulated tone. Digital artists can use Painter's Apply Lighting feature (from Effects, Surface Control) to add a dramatic splash of contrast to an image and also to unify a painting's color scheme, although achieving genuine tonal complexity requires additional painting.

Use complementary colors to create shadows. The Impressionists, Monet, Renoir and Degas frequently avoided the use of black in the shadow areas of their paintings. They embraced a more subjective view of reality by layering complementary colors to create luminous shadows.

Neutralize with a complement or gray. One way to tone down a hue is to paint on top of it with a translucent form of its complement. El Greco painted his backgrounds in this manner to draw attention to more saturated foreground subjects. Try painting with a bright green hue, and then glaze over it with a reduced opacity of red. The result will be an earthy olive. You can also

To paint dramatic billowing clouds in Path to Water West, *we blended color by using the Smeary Palette Knife variant of Palette Knives, and the Grainy Water variant of the Blenders.*

Simultaneous contrast at work. Notice how the gold looks brighter next to the dark blue than it does next to pink.

A landscape with figures, based on Mahana no atua (The Day of the God) *by Paul Gauguin*

neutralize a hue using shades of gray, as did the French artist Ingres. Although he often limited his palette to red, blue, gold and flesh tones, he created the illusion of a larger palette by adding varying proportions of gray and white.

Blending, pulling and thinning colors. Subtle changes in hue and saturation take place when colors are blended in a painting. You can use the Just Add Water, Grainy Water or Smudge variant of the Blenders brush (from the Brush Selector Bar) to blend, for instance, two primary colors (red and blue) to get a secondary color (violet). For a more dramatic blending, you can pull one color into another by using the Smeary Palette Knife variant of the Palette Knives. Artists using traditional tools often thin paint by mixing it with an extender. In Painter, you get a similar effect by reducing a brush's Opacity in the Property Bar.

Draw attention with simultaneous contrast. If two complementary colors are placed next to one another, they intensify each other: Blue looks more blue next to orange, and white looks more white next to black. In the 1950s, Op artists used the principle of simultaneous contrast to baffle the eye. Advertising art directors understand the power of simultaneous contrast and use it to gain attention for their ads.

Use a family of colors to evoke an emotional response. You can create a calm, restful mood by using an analogous color theme of blues and blue-greens. Or develop another family of hues using reds and red-oranges to express passion and intensity. You can also use a color family to unite the elements of a composition.

Create your own color world. Post-Impressionist Paul Gauguin (among others) created a powerful, personal color language by combining several of the above techniques. He used warm, bright colors to bring a subject forward in his composition, and used cool, dark colors to convey distance and mystery. He also made the bright foreground colors seem brighter by surrounding them with darker, more subdued colors.

COLOR FROM A CLONE SOURCE

In addition to choosing color from the Color pickers, you can sample color from an image by clicking with the Dropper tool, or, you can paint with color from another image (or clone source). To see how cloning color works, begin by making a clone. Open a file and choose File, Clone. In the Brush Selector Bar, choose the Impressionist Cloner variant of the Cloners. You can paint over the imagery, or you can delete the contents of the file and clone onto the blank canvas from the original. To read more about cloning, turn to "Cloning, Tracing and Painting" in Chapter 3.

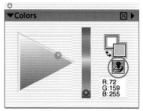

When the Clone Color box is checked, the Standard and Small Colors pickers are disabled.

These brushstrokes were painted with the Round Camelhair variant of the Oils with the following settings in the Color Variability palette: top brushstroke, Hue slider only set to 50%; middle, Saturation slider only set to 50%; bottom, Value slider only set to 50%.

These brushstrokes were painted with the Diffuse Grainy Camel (top) and the Wash Bristle (bottom) variants of Water Color with a Hue variability of 10%.

These brushstrokes were painted with the Scratchboard Rake variant of the Pens with an increased Hue variability of 10% (top) and 50% (bottom). Each "tine" of this Rake brush can carry a different color.

PAINTING WITH MULTIPLE COLORS

Painter's Brush Selector has several brushes that can paint with more than one color at a time if you use the settings in the Color Variability palette (Window, Brush Controls, Show Color Variability). Brushes with the Rake or Multi stroke type or the Bristle Spray, Camelhair or Flat dab types have the capability to paint with multiple colors. The Van Gogh variant of the Artists brush and the Round Camelhair variant of the Oils are examples.

Randomize colors with Color Variability. To see how multicolor works, open the Color Variability palette by clicking the triangle on the Color Variability bar. (Make sure that "in HSV" is chosen in the pop-up menu.) From the Brush Selector, choose the Round Camelhair variant of the Oils; its Camelhair dab type has the potential to carry a different color on each brush hair. Choose a color in the Color picker and begin painting. Then experiment by adjusting the Hue (±H), Saturation (±S) or Value (±V) slider in the Color Variability palette and painting again.

For transparent Watercolor washes with variable color, try the Diffuse Grainy Camel and the Wash Bristle. Both of these brushes have the potential to carry a different color in each brush hair.

Also try the Scratchboard

COLOR VARIABILITY CAUTION

Painter remembers the changes when you try out Color Variability, and this may cause confusing results later. After you've finished using Color Variability, set the Color Variability pop-up menu to "in HSV" and restore the Hue, Saturation and Value sliders to 0.

Rake variant of the Pens. The Scratchboard Rake incorporates the Rake stroke type; each "tine" of a Rake brush can paint with a different color. In the Color Variability palette, set Hue to 10% (for a subtle variation) or much higher (for a rainbow-like effect) and make brushstrokes on your image.

Use Color Variability based on a gradient. With Painter, you can paint with multiple colors from a gradient instead of using completely random Color Variability. To begin, set all the Color Variability sliders to 0; open the Color picker and set up the colors for a two-point gradient by clicking on the front color rectangle and selecting a color, and then clicking on the back color rectangle and selecting a color. Open the Gradients palette by choosing Window, Show Gradients. In the Gradients palette, choose Two-Point from the pop-up menu. From the Brushes Selector Bar, select the Oils category and the Opaque Bristle Spray variant. In the Color Variability palette, choose From Gradient from the pop-up menu, and then make brushstrokes on your image. If the brush does not immediately paint using the Color Variability from the gradient, click the little circle in the Color picker to help it to update.

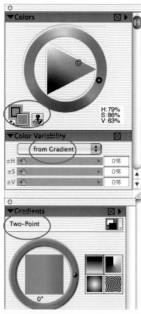

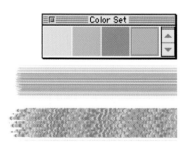

Brushstroke painted with the Opaque Bristle Spray variant of the Oils using Color Variability based on the current gradient

Brushstrokes painted with the Smeary Flat (above) and the Dry Ink (below) variants of the Oils using Color Variability based on the Color Set shown here

Use Color Variability based on a color set. You can create a special Color Set containing a few colors and then use those colors when painting. Begin by opening the Color Variability palette (Window, Brush Controls, Show Color Variability); set Color Variability to "in HSV" and the ±H, ±S, and ±V sliders to 0. Open the Color Set palette (Window, Color Palettes, Show Color Sets) and choose the Library Access button (the one with the picture of the Grid). The Color Sets palette will now be empty; it's ready for you to begin adding colors. Choose a color in the Color picker. Click on the Add Color to Color Set button (the "Plus") to add the chosen color to the Color Set. Continue to select and add more colors by using the Colors picker and clicking the "Plus" button. Choose the Smeary Flat variant of the Oils, and in the Color Variability palette, set Color Variability to "from Color Set." Paint brushstrokes on your image. To learn more about color sets, turn to "Keeping Colors in Color Sets," on page 35 and to "Capturing a Color Set," later in this chapter.

Change colors with stylus pressure. Use your pressure-sensitive stylus to paint in two colors. Start by choosing the Acrylics category and the Captured Bristle variant. In the Color Expression palette, choose Pressure from the Controller pop-up menu. In the Colors picker, click on the front color rectangle and choose a bright blue color. Click the back color rectangle and select a rose color. If you paint with a light touch, you'll be painting in rose. If you press heavily, the stroke turns blue. (If the balance between the two colors seems uneven, choose Corel Painter IX, Preferences, Brush Tracking. Make a typical brushstroke in the Scratch Pad area, click OK, and then try the graduated version of the Captured Bristle variant again.)

MORE COLOR VARIABILITY

Painter's Color Variability controls include RGB variability and variability based on the current Gradient or Color Set. These options are chosen from the pop-up menu in the Color Variability palette.

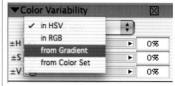

Choosing Color Variability from Gradient

MORE COLORFUL STROKES

To paint with two colors using criteria other than pressure, open the Color Expression palette (Window, Brush Controls, Show Color Expression) and move the Controller pop-up menu to Velocity. Once you get started, if you move slowly, you paint using the color in the front Color rectangle; speeding your strokes paints with the back color. Now change the Controller menu to Direction. Start drawing horizontal brushstrokes (front color) and then gradually turn the strokes vertical (back color).

Before and after: Sampling in the image with the Dropper to determine the color cast of a bright highlight on the aluminum foil reveals these values: Red: 227, Green: 241, and Blue 213 (left); the corrected image (right) with pure white highlights shows Red, Green and Blue values of 255.

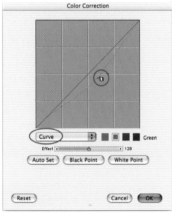

Pull the Green color curve in the Color Correction dialog box to lessen the green cast in the image above. Light colors are represented at the upper right and dark colors in the lower left. The biggest change in color occurs at the point where you pull the curve. If you pull the dot, the color you sampled will be affected most. The Effect slider controls how much of the curve will change when you pull on it. Move the slider to the right to affect a broad range of tones. Move the slider to the left to affect a narrower range of tones.

MAKING COLOR ADJUSTMENTS

Painter offers several ways to modify color in scanned photos or in your artwork *after* you have created it. To see the results of your choices in many of the dialog boxes that are involved in color adjustments, you'll need to click and drag in the Preview window.

Correct Colors. Do you see an unnatural color cast in your image? The Correct Colors, Curve feature can help you fix this problem. This feature is especially useful when working with scanned photos, for instance.

To adjust an image so that the brightest highlights are pure white, begin by analyzing the color cast. (To ensure that the front Color rectangle in the Color picker will show the color you are about to sample, make sure that "in HSV" is chosen from the menu in the Color Variability palette.) Use the Dropper tool to sample a bright highlight in your image. In the Color picker, click on the HSV values box to toggle to RGB val-

ues. Check the RGB values in the Color picker. In our example (shown at the left), the color and numbers show that the unwanted color cast is green, because the G value is higher than the R and B values. A bright white should have R, G and B values of 255 in the Color picker. Choose Effects, Tonal Control, Correct Colors and choose Curve from the pop-up menu in the Color Correction dialog box. Curve will allow you to adjust the individual RGB values. Click on the small square icon for the color that you want to adjust. (We clicked on the Green color icon—to constrain the adjustment to *only* the green values in the image.) Then, position the crosshair cursor over the diagonal line, and when you see the hand cursor appear, pull down and to the right. Pulling down (as shown) will decrease the selected color in the image. Click the Reset button to try out another adjustment without leaving the dialog box.

Adjust Colors. To change the hue, saturation or value of all of the colors in an image, choose Effects, Tonal Control, Adjust Colors. Experiment with the sliders and view the changes in the Preview window. Adjust Colors is also useful for quickly desaturating a full-color image—making it look black-and-white. To desaturate an image, move the Saturation slider all the way to the left.

Adjust Selected Colors. You may want to make color adjustments—in particular, color ranges of your image. Painter's Adjust Selected Colors feature lets you make dramatic changes (turning a

Using Adjust Selected Colors to neutralize a bright blue

blue sky yellow) or more subtle ones (removing the red cast from a subject's face). Choose Effects, Tonal Control, Adjust Selected Colors. When the dialog box opens, click in your image (*not* in the Preview window) on the color you want to change. Adjust the Hue Shift, Saturation and Value sliders at the bottom of the dialog box. When the targeted color is changed to the color you want, use low settings on the Extents sliders to limit the range of colors that are adjusted. Use the Feather sliders to adjust transitions between colors: 100% produces soft transition; 0% gives abrupt ones.

Color Overlay. Found under Effects, Surface Control, the Color Overlay dialog box lets you tint an image with a color using either a Dye Concentration model (which applies *transparent* color) or a Hiding Power model (which covers the image with the *opaque* color). With either model you can add texture by choosing Paper in the pop-up menu, as we did in the illustration at the left. When using the Dye Concentration model, adjust the Amount slider to control the density of the color from 0% for no effect to 100% or –100% for full transparent coverage. The Hiding Power model operates differently. You can add color using a plus value, or pull color out of an image using a minus value. Try this to see how it works: Open a new image and use the Rectangular Selection tool to make a selection. Choose a yellow-green in the Color picker (approximately H 58%, S 92%, V 43%). Fill the selection using Effects, Fill, Current Color. Choose yellow in the Color picker (ours was H 50%, S 94%, V 70%) and then choose Effects, Surface Control, Color Overlay, Using Uniform Color and Hiding Power. Move the Opacity slider to 100% to see the yellow completely cover the yellow-green. Finally, move the Opacity slider to –100% to the see some of the yellow disappear from the original green.

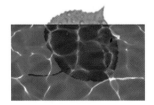
Dye Concentration. With Effects, Surface Control, Dye Concentration you can add or remove pigment from your image. Setting the Maximum slider above 100% increases the density of the existing pigment. When you choose Paper in the Using menu, the Maximum slider controls the amount of dye on the peaks and the Minimum slider controls the amount of dye in the valleys of the texture.

We added colored texture to this photo with Color Overlay.

PHOTO: PHOTODISC

Susan LeVan used Effects, Tonal Control, Negative on the left side of the background of Guardians as shown in this detail. After creating the negative side of the image, she drew over portions of the left side to make the character unique.

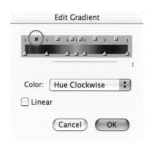

Here is the Edit Gradient dialog box with Painter's Jungle Neon gradient, and the Linear box is unchecked. When you click a square hue box above the Gradient, the Color hue pop-up menu appears. Here it's set to Hue Clockwise, resulting in a tiny spectrum below the square hue box.

Click on a color control point triangle, and the Color Spread slider will appear. Adjust it to control the smoothness between the colors.

Negative. Creating a negative of all or part of an image can have dramatic, artistic purposes—such as in the detail of Susan LeVan's illustration, at left. Choose Effects, Tonal Control, Negative to convert your image or a selected part of it.

Output Preview and Video Colors. Your monitor can display more colors than can be reproduced in the four-color printing process, and if you are creating images for video, some highly saturated colors will not make the transition from computer to video. It's a good idea to convert your out-of-gamut colors while you're in Painter so there won't be any surprises. Choose Canvas, Color Management or Effects, Tonal Control, Video Legal Colors, depending on whether your image is destined for paper or video. For more information about output for printing, turn to Chapter 13, "Printing Options."

MORE COLOR TOOLS

Adding color with Gradients. Painter's powerful Gradients palette lets you fill selected areas with preset gradations or ones that you've created. (See "Adding Color and Gradations to Line Art" later in this chapter.) You can also colorize an image with a gradation using Express in Image from the pop-up menu at the right side on the Gradients palette. To see an example of this technique, turn to "Creating a Sepia-Tone Photo" in Chapter 7.

The gradient editor is a powerful tool for creating custom color ramps. You can't use this tool to alter all of Painter's existing gradations. However, it is used primarily for creating new ones. Choose Window, Show Gradients to open the palette; then click the right triangle, and choose Edit Gradient from the pop-up menu to bring up the gradient editor. Select one of the triangular color control points and choose a color from the Color picker. The color ramp will update to reflect your choice. Add new color control points by clicking directly in the color bar; the triangular control points are sliders that can be positioned anywhere along the ramp. To delete a control point, select it and press the Delete

Linda Davick uses gradient fills to give her illustrations depth, as shown here in Mice. *Read about Davick's technique in "Adding Color and Gradations to Line Art" on page 36 of this chapter.*

key; click on the gradient bar to add a new control point. Clicking on any of the squares above the gradient displays the Color menu; experiment with the options available there to get quick rainbow effects in the section of the gradient indicated by the square. To store the new gradient in the Gradients palette, choose Save Gradient from the pop-up menu on the right end of the Gradients palette.

Coloring images. You can color images or selected parts of images using either Effects, Fill (Ctrl/⌘-F) or the Paint Bucket tool. The Fill command lets you fill your image with a color, a gradient, a clone source (if one is available), a pattern (if no clone source is available) or a weave. The Paint Bucket gives you the same fill options. (The Paint Bucket options appear on the Property Bar when you select the Paint Bucket tool.) Cartoonists and others who fill line art with color will want to explore the Lock Out Color feature (to preserve black line art, for example) made available by double-clicking on the Paint Bucket tool icon in the Tools palette. For more information about Lock Out Color and Cartoon Cel fills, see the *Painter IX Help Menu.*

Keeping colors in Color Sets. Painter can store your most frequently used colors in a Color Set. Painter Colors is the default set. Switch Color Sets by clicking on the Library Access button (the grid) in the Color Sets palette. You'll find more Color Sets (including several Pantone sets) in the Color Sets folder on the Painter IX application folder. For more about Color Sets, turn to "Capturing a Color Set" on page 44.

CONSTRAINING BUCKET FILLS

You can use the Paint Bucket to fill an entire area of your image by clicking the Paint Bucket within the area, or you can constrain the fill into a rectangle. To create a rectangular filled area, press, hold and drag a marquee with the Paint Bucket. When you release the mouse or lift up on your stylus, the area will fill with color.

In H is for Hell-bent Haddocks *(shown here as a detail), Keith MacLelland used the Paint Bucket to create a background of filled squares. To see more of MacLelland's work, turn to the galleries in this chapter and Chapter 4.*

SAMPLING PAINT

While you're using many of Painter's other tools, you can temporarily switch to the Dropper tool and sample colors by holding down the Alt/Option key.

NAMING AND FINDING COLORS

To name your colors so you can search for them by name, double-click on the color in the Color Set palette that you want to name, type a name and click OK. To view color names, click the right triangle on the Color Set bar and choose Display Name. To search for a named color in a set, click the Find Color in Color Set button (the binoculars near the top of the Color Set section).

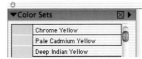

A Set with names displayed

RESTORING DEFAULT COLORS

To restore the default Color Set (called Painter Colors) after you've used or created another Color Set, choose Open Color Set from the pop-out menu and find the Painter Colors file in your Painter 8 folder on your hard disk.

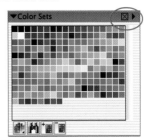

The Color Sets palette with Painter Colors as the current color set

Adding Color and Gradations to Line Art

Overview *Draw line art with the 1-Pixel Pen variant; use the Paint Bucket to fill areas with flat color and gradations; add highlights with the Airbrushes.*

LINDA DAVICK

Line art created with the 1-Pixel variant of the Pens brush, shown here as a detail

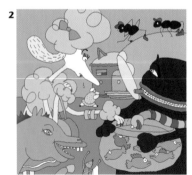

Filling the drawing with flat color

FILLING LINE ART WITH COLOR AND GRADATIONS is slick and efficient in Painter, using what children's book illustrator Linda Davick calls "the coloring-book technique." Davick employed the Paint Bucket tool when creating the illustration *Fish Fry* for Debbie Smith's *Beauty Blow-Up.*

1 Creating a black-and-white line drawing. From the Brush Selector Bar palette, choose the Pens, 1-Pixel variant. Choose Window, Brush Controls, Show General and in the General section of the Brush Controls choose the Flat Cover subcategory. Flat Cover lets you draw a solid-color line, creating the necessary barriers for this technique that fills all neighboring pixels of the same color. Choose black in the Color picker and draw your line art, making sure all your shapes are completely enclosed with black lines. If you need to correct your work, switch the color to pure white in the Color picker and erase.

2 Filling with flat color. To test color choices and tonal values, you can fill areas of your illustration with flat color. So the color is flat and not affected by settings in the Color Variability palette, choose Window, Brush Controls, Color Variability to open the Color Variability palette, and choose "in HSV" from the pop-up menu. Set the ±H, ±S and ±V sliders to 0. Now choose the Paint Bucket tool, and in the Property Bar, click the Fill Image button and under the Fill menu, Current Color. Turn off Anti-Alias. Choose a color, and then click in the area of your drawing that you want to fill. Since the Paint Bucket fills all neighboring pixels of the same color, you can refill by choosing another color and clicking again. If you're filling small areas, it's important to know that the Paint Bucket's "hot spot" (where it fills from) is the tip of the red paint in the icon. Davick filled all areas except Zuba's (the pink poodle) face using this method.

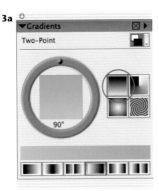

Setting up the Two-Point linear gradient for the sky behind Zuba

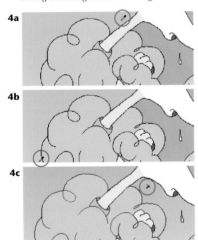

Filling the background with the gradient

Sampling the gradient across from the top of the area to be filled (a); sampling across from the bottom of the area to be filled (b); filling the area with the gradation (c). Repeat this process for each flat color (negative) area to be filled.

Adding dimension to Zuba's hair using the Digital Airbrush inside a selected area

3 Adding color ramps. To fill the background with a gradation, open the Gradients palette (Window, Library Palettes, Show Gradients). Choose Two-Point from the pop-up menu (top right of the palette) and click the Linear Gradient button (from the four Types buttons to the right of the direction ring), and set an angle for your fill by rotating the red ball around the direction ring. In the Color picker, choose colors for both the front and back Color rectangles. (Click on the front Color rectangle and select a color; then click on the back Color rectangle and select a color.) With the Paint Bucket chosen, in the Property Bar, click the Fill Image button, and from the Fill menu, choose Gradient. Finally, to apply the gradation, click in the area that you want to fill. Davick filled the largest background sky area with a linear gradation.

4 Duplicating color ramps. To duplicate the large background gradation in each of the smaller background shapes—to the right of Zuba, and under the ants—Davick created a new gradation using color sampled from areas in the background gradation. She then filled the smaller background shapes with the new gradation. If you need to do this on the "negative" shapes in your image, first check the Color picker to make sure that the Color rectangle that contains the starting color of your original gradation is selected. Choose the Dropper tool and position it over the gradation in your image at approximately the same height as the top of the negative area that you want to fill. Click in the gradation to sample the color. To sample the bottom portion of the gradation, select the other Color rectangle; then position and click the Dropper at about the same height as the bottom of the area to be filled. Click in the negative area using the Paint Bucket to fill with the new sampled gradation. (If you need to refill, undo the fill—Edit, Undo Paint Bucket Fill—before you fill again.)

5 Painting airbrush details. Davick finished the piece by painting with the Digital Airbrush variant of the Airbrushes within roughly circular selections to add details to Zuba's face and fur. You can make roughly circular selections using the Lasso tool by choosing the Lasso tool and dragging in your image. (To read more about selections, turn to the beginning of Chapter 5, "Selections, Shapes and Masks.") Now use the Digital Airbrush to add dimension. Paint along the edge of the animated selection marquee. Davick used the same Airbrush with unrestricted strokes to add other details in other areas, such as on the cat's face and paws.

Coloring a Scanned Illustration

Overview *Scan a traditional black-and-white pen drawing; clean up the scanned line art; use the Paint Bucket to fill areas with flat color; create texture and energy with a variety of brushes.*

WENDY MORRIS

The raw scan of the Rapidograph pen drawing

WENDY MORRIS'S WHIMSICAL DRAWING STYLE appears to be a quick, spontaneous expression, but her illustrations begin by drawing carefully with traditional pen and ink. In Morris's *Beeman*, the sky is vibrant and charged with frenetic bee energy. *Beeman* was colored with Paint Bucket fills and a variety of brushes.

1 Creating a pen drawing and scanning. Morris chose a bright white recycled drawing paper with a smooth finish and created a black-and-white line drawing using a conventional Rapidograph pen. She intended to use the *Beeman* illustration for a 6 x 8-inch greeting card design that would be printed with off-set lithography so she scanned the line drawing using grayscale mode at 100% magnification with a resolution of 300ppi. She saved the scan as a TIFF file and opened it in Painter, which automatically converted the grayscale art to RGB. To learn more about scanning and resolution, see Chapter 1, "Getting to Know Painter" and Chapter 13, "Printing Options."

2 Cleaning up the scan. Morris adjusted the contrast of the scanned line work using Brightness/Contrast. To make the adjustment on your scan, choose Effects, Tonal Control, Brightness/

2a

Contrast. When the dialog box appears, you can thicken or thin the line work by moving the Brightness slider (the bottom one of the two) to the left or to the right, respectively. Then, to get rid of any fuzziness ~~...~~

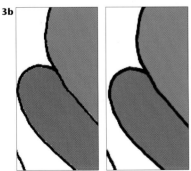

Cleaning up specks of black on the scan

3a

Setting up the Property Bar and the Lock Out Color dialog box to make Cartoon Cel fills

3b

Color fills with halos (left), and color fills made with the Cartoon Cel method, showing no halos (right)

~~...~~ bucket fills that follow in step 3.)

3 Filling areas with flat color. After Morris had adjusted the contrast of the line art, to establish the color theme, she used the Paint Bucket tool to fill the flower petals, stems and sky with flat color. When the Paint Bucket is used to fill areas within scanned black-and-white line art, halos (partially unfilled areas) can appear along the edges of the anti-aliased black lines. In Painter there are at least two ways to prevent these halos: One approach involves layering a copy of your original line work over a thinned version of the lines and filling the thinner version with color. This way any halos that develop on the layer below will be hidden by the original, thicker lines in the layer above. This method is easy to understand and carry out, and it makes it easy to change colors later if you want to. The technique is described in the "Trapping Fills Using a Transparent Layer" tip on page 41. However, if you feel that using extra layers would get in the way of the "painterly" experience of applying color to a single layer of canvas, the Cartoon Cel method may be the technique for you. It works by allowing the fill color to "seep into" the anti-aliasing pixels at the edge of the line work, leaving no halo. This method is described next.

There are three essential parts to the Cartoon Cel fill method: (1) making a selection based on luminance, (2) setting the Paint Bucket's Mask Threshold and filling criteria and (3) choosing a color and filling.

First select the black lines in the image using Select, Auto Select, Using Image Luminance, and click OK.

Second, in the Tools palette, double-click the Paint Bucket to open the Lock Out Color dialog box and set the Mask Threshold low—moving the slider to a point between 7% and 14% usually works well. Click OK to close the dialog box. In the Property Bar, click the Cartoon Cel button, and under the Fill menu, choose Current Color.

3c

The petals and stems filled with color

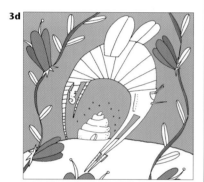

3d

After filling the sky with a flat color fill

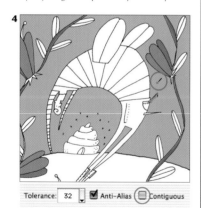

4

Tolerance: 32 ☑ Anti-Alias ⬜ Contiguous

Using the Magic Wand to select the sky. This detail of the Property Bar shows the Contiguous box unchecked.

Third, open the Color Variability palette (Window, Brush Controls, Show Color Variability), choose "in HSV" from the pop-up menu and set the (±H), (±S) and (±V) sliders to 0. This will allow you to choose a flat color in the Color picker. After choosing a color, click with the Paint Bucket in one of the white spaces enclosed by the black lines. Then examine the resulting color fill. (To get a better look at the edge, you can choose Select, Hide Marquee. You can also zoom in by clicking on the image with the Magnifier tool.) If the fill has overrun the lines, the Mask Threshold is set too low. On the other hand, if you see a halo at the edge, the setting is too high. If you need to refill, first undo the fill—Edit, Undo—and then change the Mask Threshold setting and fill again. Once you have a satisfactory fill, you should be able to use the same Mask Threshold setting throughout your drawing.

Morris filled the flower petals with three shades of a purple-pink color. Then she filled the stems and sky with other colors.

4 Making a selection with the Magic Wand. In preparation for the next step, when she planned to paint lively brushstrokes across the sky, Morris isolated the entire sky area (based on its color) by making a selection using the Magic Wand. To select all of the blue sky areas at once, she chose the Magic Wand in the Tools palette, unchecked the Contiguous check box on the Property Bar, and clicked on a blue sky area in her image. To read more about the Magic Wand and selections, turn to the beginning of Chapter 5, "Selections, Shapes and Masks."

5 Painting with brushes. Morris used the Dropper tool to sample sky color in her image; then she used the Variable Flat variant of the Oils to paint "helter-skelter style" brushstrokes across the sky. The Variable Flat incorporates enhanced Color Variability, which allowed the value of the color to change subtly as she painted. For more subtle brushstrokes, she lowered the opacity using the Opacity slider on the Property Bar.

6 Adding texture and details. After completing the flat color fills and the brushwork in the sky, Morris used the Dirty Marker variant of the Felt Pens to modulate color in the plant stems; then she used a low-opacity Digital Airbrush variant of the Airbrushes to paint soft shadows on the leaves and stems. To add texture to the ground, she used the Scratchboard Rake variant of the Pens.

Next, Morris added movement and energy to the bee swarm and the beeman's stinger. She chose black in the Colors section and used the Pixel Dust variant of the Pens to paint spiraling strokes behind the bee's stinger and above the hive. (The Pixel Dust pen is located in the Painter 5 Brushes library, within the Extras, Brushes folder, on the Painter IX CD-ROM.)

5

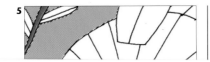

Morris finished the piece using the Digital Airbrush to add more highlights and shadows to the bee, plants and flowers. She airbrushed a soft drop shadow along some of the edges on the beeman and the flowers. For more subtle brushstrokes, she low-

6a

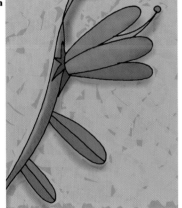

Morris airbrushed soft shadows along edges of the foliage.

6b

The image with fills and brushwork texture, prior to adding Pixel Dust to the bee swarm

copy) and choose Select, the line art. (Layer 1 will appear in the Layers section of the Objects palette.) In the Layers section, turn off the visibility of Layer 1 by clicking its eye icon off; then target the Canvas layer by clicking on its name. Make the lines thinner on the canvas by choosing Effects, Tonal Control, Brightness/Contrast, and moving both sliders to the right enough to thin the lines but not enough to make breaks in them (you may have to experiment with settings, depending on the thickness of your lines).

Now choose the Paint Bucket tool, and in the Property Bar, click the Image button and from the Fill menu choose Current Color. In the Colors picker, choose a new color; then click the Paint Bucket in a white area of the canvas. To complete the "trap" on your fill, toggle Layer 1's visibility back on by clicking its eye icon, and choose Multiply in the pop-up Composite Method menu at the top of the Layers section. You can inspect the result with the Magnifier tool. (To read more about Layers, turn to Chapter 6, "Using Layers.")

The Layers palette

Image canvas showing the flat color fills with "halos"

Image with Layer 1 in Multiply mode and with its visibility turned on

Coloring a Woodcut

Overview *Create black-and-white art; float it and apply the Gel Composite Method; view the black-and-white art as you add colored brush work and texture to the original canvas layer.*

The black-and-white drawing

The Layers palette showing the active line drawing layer

HERE'S A CREATIVE WAY TO ADD COLOR to black-and-white art, a favorite technique of artist Chet Phillips. To paint *Flame Throwing His Voice*, Phillips used the Gel Composite Method, which makes the white areas of a layer appear transparent. He colored the image using a brilliant palette of blues, reds and greens, with accents of orange, purple and gold. Then, to add a variety of colored textures to elements (for instance, the dragons' clothing and the background), Phillips used Effects, Surface Control, Color Overlay.

"This play-on-words image of a dragon ventriloquist and his flame-throwing dummy started with a sketch that addressed both the composition and the details of the dragons," Phillips says.

1 Creating black-and-white art. Phillips creates a black-and-white drawing in Painter as follows: Start a new document with a white background. Choose black for the Main color (front color square) in the Color picker; then choose Effects, Fill, (Ctrl/⌘-F), Fill with Current Color. Click OK. Use white and the Scratchboard Tool variant of the Pens to "etch" into the black fill, with the look of a detailed woodcut in mind.

2 Making a layer with transparent white areas. Select All (Ctrl/⌘-A), choose the Layer Adjuster tool and click once on the image. The image is now floating over a white background. In the

3a

The Canvas layer is selected.

3b

The masks in the Channels palette

4

Using the Digital Airbrush and Pastels to paint colorful strokes on the dragon's head. The active selection limits the paint.

5a

Using Color Overlay to apply the Retro Fabric paper within the little suit selection

5b

The colored texture added to the little suit. The drawing layer is hidden.

Layers palette, choose Gel from the Composite Method pop-up menu. This method makes the white areas of the layer transparent, which allows any color you add to the background in steps 3 and 4 to completely show through without affecting the black in the layer.

3 Making freehand selections to limit paint. In preparation for painting the background, Phillips used the Lasso tool to draw freehand selections for the curtains, backdrop, dragon head, and the suits of both characters. As he built each selection, he saved it as a mask in the Channels palette for safekeeping.

Before beginning to work on the background Canvas, click the Canvas layer's name in the Layers palette. Choose the Lasso tool in the Toolbox, and press, hold and drag to create an irregular selection boundary on your image. Then save the selection as a mask in the Channels palette. You will find more detailed information about selections and masks in Chapter 5, "Selections, Shapes and Masks."

4 Painting on the background. To render the background, Phillips used a rich color palette. He used the Digital Airbrush and Fine Spray variants of the Airbrushes to lay in basic color within selected areas. Choose a color in the Color picker. For smooth airbrushed strokes, choose the Digital Airbrush variant of Airbrushes in the Brush Selector Bar. Begin painting. For a fine-grained look, switch to the Fine Spray variant. Next, using the Artists Pastel Chalk variant of Pastels, you can take advantage of the brush's texture-sensitive capability to brush on textured strokes in a few areas of your image.

5 Overlaying colored texture. Next, to add more richness to his image, Phillips loaded individual selections, and he applied transparent colored textures to the clothing and other areas. Begin by using the Color picker to choose a color that will contrast with your image. (Phillips chose

5c

The paint and texture are complete on the Canvas. The drawing layer is hidden in this example.

white to contrast with the brown and blue suits.) Now, choose a texture in the Paper Selector. (Phillips used the Retro Fabric texture for the little suit and the Tweedy texture from the Fabric-inspired library on the *Painter IX Wow!* CD-ROM for the big suit.) To apply the texture, choose Effects, Surface Control, Color Overlay. In the Using menu choose Paper, click the Hiding Power button and set the Opacity to about 15%. Click OK.

Capturing a Color Set

Overview *Capture color from a reference image using the Dropper; build and customize a Color Set; use the Color Set to paint a new image.*

1a

The reference photograph

PHOTO: PHOTODISC

1b

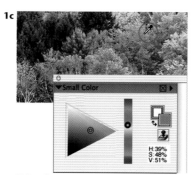

The Color Variability palette showing ±H, ±S and ±V set to 0

1c

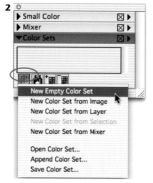

Using the Dropper to sample color from the image

2

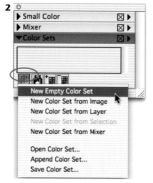

Choosing Create New Empty Color Set in the Color Sets palette

CHER THREINEN-PENDARVIS

IF YOU'RE PLANNING A SERIES OF ILLUSTRATIONS based on the same color theme, you'll find Painter's Color Sets invaluable. Use this technique of sampling color from a photo or painting to quickly build a selective palette of colors as we did here prior to creating the pastel painting *Tienda Verde*.

1 Sampling the color. Open the image that contains the color range you want. Before you begin to sample the color, open the Color Variability palette (Window, Show Color Variability), choose "in HSV" from the pop-up menu and set the (±H), (±S) and (±V) sliders to 0. (This will ensure that the colors sampled will be pure color instead of variegated.) Now choose the Dropper tool and click it on a colored pixel in the image. The Color picker will display the color. If the displayed color isn't the one you want, you can click or drag the Dropper around your image. The Color picker will update to show the new color.

2 Creating a Color Set. Now click on the Color Sets section name to open the Color Sets palette, and click on the Library Access button (the Grid). From the pop-up menu choose Create New Empty Color Set. The Color Sets palette will now be empty. Click on the Add Color button (the "Plus" in the Color Set section) to add the selected color to the Color Set. Continue to sample and add more colors by clicking the Dropper and the Plus button. To save your colors, click on the right triangle on the Color Sets palette bar and choose Save Color Set from the menu, navigate to the Painter IX application folder, or wherever you want to store your set, name the set and click Save. To use the new Color Set it can be reopened by selecting it in the Painter application folder and clicking the Open button. We named ours "Autumn Color."

3 Arranging the Color Set display. You can change the layout of your colors in the Color Set to fit your drawing environment. To change the shape of the individual color squares, click

3a

on the right triangle on the Color Sets bar and choose Swatch Size to display choices. If you don't see a size that you like, choose Customize. We built our Color Set of 32 x 24-pixel-wide

4

The completed Autumn Color Set

Applying colored brushstrokes with the Square Chalk using the Autumn Color Set

Chalk brush.

AUTOMATIC COLOR SET TOOLS

Painter offers four automatic color set building features: New Color Set from Image, New Color Set from Selection, New Color Set from Layer and New Color Set from Mixer. Using these tools, you can quickly build a color set by extracting every color from an image, selection, layer or the Mixer. (These features are useful if you want to sample every color, but they don't offer quite the same control as sampling individual colors with the Dropper.) To make a color set based on a selected area of your image, begin by opening the Color Sets palette by clicking the Color Sets palette bar name. Open an image, and make a selection (as we did here with the Rectangular Selection tool). In the Color Sets palette, click the Library Access button (the Grid) to display the pop-up menu and choose New Color Set from Selection. Painter will generate the color set. After our color set was made, we displayed the colors in dark-to-light order by clicking the right arrow on the Color Sets palette bar and choosing Sort Order from the pop-up menu, and then choosing LHS (Light, Hue and Saturation) from the menu. Automatically generated color sets often have several colors that are very similar. To remove a color, click on it in the working Color Sets and then click the Delete Color from Color Set button (the "Minus") in the Color Sets section. To save your colors, click on the right triangle on the Color Sets palette bar and choose Save Color Set from the menu, navigate to the Painter IX application folder (or wherever you want to store your set), name the set and click Save. To use the new Color Set it can be reopened by navigating to where you saved it, and clicking the Open button.

CHER THREINEN-PENDARVIS

An active rectangular selection shown on Forked Path *(top left). Choosing New Color Set from Selection in the Color Sets palette (top right); choosing LHS in the Sort Order menu; Show Grid is enabled in the pop-out menu; and the brightly colored color set (bottom left).*

■ **Dennis Orlando's** sensitive use of light combined with layered color in the shadowed areas in his paintings has earned him the name "The Modern Impressionist."

Inspired by the work of the Impressionist master Claude Monet, Orlando began **Monet's Branch of the Seine** with the Artist Pastel Chalk variant of Pastels. To establish a mood of late day, he used soft colors and a varied palette with deep shadow colors and subtle highlights. He laid in color with the Artist Pastel Chalk, using increased Color Variability (Window, Brush Controls, Show Color Variability) to create activity in the color. Then he pulled and blended colors into one another using a Grainy Water variant of the Blenders brush. In areas where he wanted to preserve more of the modulated color, he reduced the Opacity of the Grainy Water variant, and then continued to blend and pull the color. For the look of wet paint, he used a modified Round Camelhair variant and the Smeary variants of Oils. These brushes allowed him to add color and blend as he painted. Finally, for the look of wet oil paints, he painted using low-opacity Smeary brushes and a light touch on his stylus to paint soft, gently curved brush strokes. This brushwork is most evident in the highlights on the water and in the foliage on the trees.

■ For *Monet's Oat Fields,* **Dennis Orlando** used a similar process to *Monet's Branch of the Seine,* but this time he used a more luminous color palette, and he preserved more of the grainy pastel strokes.

Orlando began the painting by making a sketch with the Thick and Thin variant of Pencils. Then he loosely laid in broad strokes of color using the Artist Pastel Chalk variant of Pastels. To establish the mood, he used a brighter palette with deep shadow colors and more saturated highlights. To achieve activity in the color, Orlando increased the Color Variability for the Artist Pastel Chalk, and then he laid in more brush strokes. He pulled and blended colors into one another using the Grainy Water variant of the Blenders.

For the look of wet paint, he used his favorite modified Round Camelhair variant and the Smeary variants of Oils, which allowed him to add color and blend as he painted. To finish the painting, he added a few grainy strokes using the Artists Pastel Chalk. This brushwork is most noticeable on the right of the painting, in the foreground grass and on the trees.

■ **Fiona Hawthorne** creates wild and imaginative illustrations with a strong graphic feel and vibrant, saturated color.

Shots magazine commissioned Hawthorne to create ***Breaking China*** (left) and ***Advertising in Korea*** (below) for articles that focused on creativity moving forward with technology. She began the illustrations by sketching with the Pens, Pencils and Oils variants. Then she added graphic details.

Keeping in mind the theme of the article (China finding a new creative foundation in a very fast-moving economy), Hawthorne created the bold, expressive illustration *Breaking China*. For the bright-colored strokes on the buildings, she used the Retro Dots variant of the Graphic Design brushes (loaded from the Extras, Brushes folder on the *Painter IX* CD-ROM). Then to add more texture, she pasted in a few bits of images (for instance, for the image on the TV sets, she scanned her own Deng Xiaoping watch and photos of a TV). She selected the watch element layer and increased its saturation using Effects, Tonal Control, Adjust Colors, and then she duplicated it several times. Finally, she drew over the scanned elements with the Thick and Thin variant of Pencils so that they matched the brushwork in the illustration.

For *Advertising in Korea*, Hawthorne was inspired by the fact that broadband Internet access at home, the latest mobile phones and 15-second TV commercials are mainstream in South Korea. She created an image that suggested a link to the new products, ideas and the freedom of youth. She used a large Scratchboard Tool (Pens) to lay in the face, and then she sketched a few loose brushstrokes using the Retro Dots variant to suggest the hair and chest. Next, she used the Pen tool to draw shapes for the stars, which she duplicated and scaled. Then she downloaded a picture of the Korean flag to use as a graphic in the necklace. She copied and pasted the flag image into her file as a layer and duplicated it, and then positioned the flags using the Layer Adjuster tool.

■ "I want people to see the intricacies of lines, color variations, and the subtle texture patterns that inhabit my paintings," says illustrator **Keith MacLelland**. In his illustrations he communicates the fun he has when creating his art. He began both images by making a sketch in Painter with the Flattened Pencil and 2B variants (Pencils), then refined the drawings using the Scratchboard Tool variant of the Pens, Oils, Blenders and Oil Pastels.

MacLelland created *IT Carnival* for *Philly Tech Magazine*. "The illustration depicts a time when the IT industry was taking hard hits," says MacLelland, "and while some folks kept taking hits, they just would not stay down. There was hope." MacLelland used a palette of pastel colors accented by brighter pink, yellow, red and green colors to help communicate the theme of hope.

To create the feeling of an old carnival poster that showed a history of years of use, MacLelland incorporated a custom texture that he had made from a scan of a piece of furniture he had crackle-painted. To bring out the texture in specific areas (for instance, the clothing), he used a texture-sensitive brush, the Square Chalk variant of Chalk.

■ Artist **Richard Noble** successfully re-creates the look of traditional watercolor and acrylic using Painter. "I have always tried to keep a feeling of freshness in my work and to stay away from the overworked syndrome," Noble says.

For a look similar to conventional watercolor, in *Decoys* (above) and *Geese* (right), Noble used favorite brushes such as the Broad Water Brush variant of Digital Watercolor, the Smooth Runny Bristle variant of Watercolor to lay in washes, and then he added details using the Airbrushes, Gouache brushes and the Artist Pastel Chalk variant of Pastel. Noble generally begins by importing a reference photograph into Painter to use as a template.

For *Decoys*, Noble used a warm palette of earth tone colors, including warm greens and olives, reddish-browns and golden ochres. To begin the work, Noble set up the decoys on an old table in the morning sun and photographed them. He wanted to capture strong lights and darks while also interpreting the texture of the old working decoys. After opening his reference photo, he chose File, Quick Clone to create a clone copy of the image with a black canvas and Tracing Paper turned on. Then, he roughed in large brush strokes using the Broad Water Brush. Noble kept the colors warm with the exception of the colors on the actual decoys. To retain a fresh, spontaneous feeling, he painted the background and forms of the decoys quickly. For a sense

of drama, Noble painted strong shadows on the decoys and foreground. Then he rendered a few areas like the eyes, neck areas and some of the old textures in the sides of the decoys using smaller brushes. For these details he used a combination of Digital Watercolor, Artist Pastel Chalk (Pastels) and the Fine Detail variant of the Airbrushes.

All of these brushes that Noble used can be used with color from the Color palette, or with color imported from the clone source, using the Clone Color button (the stamp) on the Colors palette. Noble enjoys alternating between using color he mixes using the Color palette, and color imported from the clone source.

■ **Richard Noble** depicted the bright, almost directly overhead light—of midday—in *Geese.* He painted most of the work with the Broad Water Brush variant of Digital Watercolor using one of his digital photographs for reference. After opening the photo, he chose File, Quick Clone to create a clone copy of the photo, but with a blank canvas and Tracing Paper turned on in the clone image. Noble planned to use elements from the photo, and to create a more simplified, elegant image. After choosing the Broad Water Brush, he enabled Clone Color in the Color palette so that he could pick up color from the photo while he made the first loose, broad brushstrokes. As he painted, he toggled the Clone Color button off when he wanted to paint with a color he mixed using the Color palette and on when he wanted to use color from the reference. He used the Digital Watercolor brushes for smoother wash areas and the Watercolor brushes on Watercolor layers for more textured brush work. The textured brush strokes are most noticeable in the warm-colored reflections near the geese.

When Noble had the overall image blocked in, he added the lighter colors and details using the Gouache brushes. To marry the look and texture of the gouache strokes with the background watercolor strokes, he used the Confusion brush variant of the F-X brush. Noble refined the important detail areas, while leaving the larger areas rough.

■ **Athos Boncompagni** used Painter's Tinting brushes to add luminous color to his black-and-white drawing for *Regina 1*. To begin, Boncompagni drew a detailed cross-hatched line drawing on the Canvas using the Scratchboard Tool variant of Pens and black ink. Then he added vibrant color to his illustration with the Tinting brushes. He created a new empty layer by clicking the New Layer button on the Layers palette, and set its Composite Method to Multiply so that the color to be applied would appear as a clear overlay over the black and white illustration. Then he used various Tinting brushes (including the Basic Round and Soft Glazing Round), to add color to the illustration. To blend areas, Boncompagni used the Diffuser 2 and Blender variants of the Tinting brushes.

■ For *Dreaming Venezuelan*, fine artist **Ileana Frometa Grillo** was inspired by feelings and perceptions of her home country, Venezuela. In the painting, Grillo used color and subject matter as symbols to tell a story. For instance, each woman's dress represents a color in the Venezuelan flag, and the orchid is the national flower of Venezuela. Gifted with wonderful natural resources and creative, loving people, her country has also been plagued with corrupted politics that threaten its progress. So she chose to portray the woman in blue, looking out the window, pondering the future. The woman in yellow is portrayed in a more introspective stance to reflect on the past. The woman in red, gazing toward the freshly-cut flowers in the waterless vase, illustrates the beauty of Venezuela's natural resources.

Ileana began her painting by making a loosely drawn pencil sketch. After scanning the drawing, she opened it in Painter, and blocked in broad areas of color using the Chalk variants. To blend, she used the Blenders brushes. For more texture over the blended areas, she brushed lightly with a Soft Chalk, which was based on the Large Chalk variant of Chalk.

■ Artist and teacher **Steve Rys** began *Katchina* by sketching from life. When he was happy with his drawing, he created a monochromatic study to work out the values.

Rys established a palette of five values ranging from white to black. If the study works in five values, it gives him the confidence to build color within the values. Working with a cover brush (similar to the Opaque Round variant of Oils), he laid in a medium gray value and then began to mass the light and dark values using the values on either side of the medium value.

When he was satisfied with the value study, Rys worked out interesting shapes by making a hard-edged study with mid-value orange (warm) and blue (cool) colors. The warm-cool study established the pattern of light and shadow. At this point, he saved the file.

Working over the top of a copy of his warm-cool study, Rys began painting local colors onto the subject. He usually left the cool colors at mid-value and darker and the warm colors at mid-value and lighter. When the colors were blocked in, he blended some of the edges with the Just Add Water variant of Blenders. When he was satisfied with the small color study, he developed the final painting using his value and color studies for reference.

Rys is currently experimenting with a limited palette, based on the palette that he uses with conventional acrylic paints, to create a more unified color appearance without a formula or routine. All of the color and blending is done from a limited palette. "For me, working within boundaries is freeing. Instead of looking at millions of colored pixels, I am working with eight and blending them," says Rys.

■ Based in Holland, artist and educator **Ad Van Bokhoven** works both traditionally and digitally. To paint *Poppies*, he used Painter to emulate the brush work and color that he achieves with traditional oil paints on location. Van Bokhoven appreciates the realistic effects that can be achieved with the Acrylics, Oils, Impasto and Blenders variants in Painter.

Van Bokhoven began *Poppies* by taking photographs to use for reference. Back at his studio, he opened a new file, and then he used the custom Oils brushes to block in a vibrant color theme that

included reds, blues and greens. To take advantage of being able to apply paint and blend it as he worked, he worked directly on the Canvas, without the use of layers. To mix and pull color, he used various custom Blenders, similar to the Round Blender Brush and the Grainy Blender variant of Blenders.

As he worked, Van Bokhoven focused on preserving the vibrant color theme and the play of the colors against one another—the hot reds against the cool turquoise-blues. Intuitively, he added accents of cool and warm greens. He kept his brush work loose and dynamic as

he painted. He did not paint a lot of detail, but instead massed large areas of color for impact.

To achieve the subtle layering of color in the sky, he sampled color from his image and used the Colors picker to subtly change the color, which he then applied using a lower opacity brush.

As a final touch, Van Bokhoven added a subtle canvas texture to the painting. He chose a canvas texture in the Paper Selector and then chose Effects, Surface Control, Apply Surface Texture, Using Paper, with subtle settings.

3

PAINTING
WITH
BRUSHES

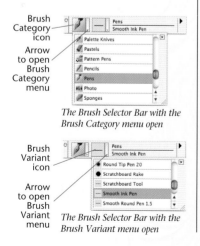

This detailed illustration for the National Museum of American History shows Karen Carr's refined digital oil painting technique, achieved by using Charcoal, Blenders and Oils variants. See the entire illustration Washington's Camp *in the gallery at the end of this chapter.*

Brush
Category
icon

Arrow
to open
Brush
Category
menu

The Brush Selector Bar with the Brush Category menu open

Brush
Variant
icon

Arrow
to open
Brush
Variant
menu

The Brush Selector Bar with the Brush Variant menu open

INTRODUCTION

PAINTER'S BRUSHES ARE THE PROGRAM'S HEART: Without them, Painter would be a lot like other image editors. What sets Painter apart is the way it puts pen to paper and paint to canvas—the way its brushes interact with the surface below them and with the paint that you've already applied. Here's a primer on getting the most from Painter's brushes.

Brush basics. Located in the Brush Selector Bar, Painter's brushes are organized into *categories* and *variants*. Brush *categories* are shown as the mark-making tool icons on the Brush Selector Bar. To choose a brush category, you can click on the small arrow to the right of the Brush Category icon to display a pop-up list and then choose a new category, such as the Pens. Brush categories are at the top level of organization for mark-making tools in Painter; they are like the *containers* or *drawers* that hold the individual brushes, pens, pencils, pastels and other painting and drawing implements.

Every brush *category* has its own *variants* or varieties, so every time you choose a different brush category, the list of variants changes. Brush variants appear in the pop-up menu to the *right* of the brush category menu in the Brush Selector Bar. For instance, within the Pens are several variants, such as the Smooth Ink Pen, Thick n Thin Pen and Coit Pen. To choose the Smooth Ink Pen variant of the Pens, click the variant pop-up menu and choose Smooth Ink Pen. For detailed information about other aspects of brushes, including custom brushes, see Chapter 4, "Building Brushes."

Getting started with painting. If you're new to Painter, follow these steps to jump right in and begin painting. Create a new file (File, New). If the Brush Selector Bar is not open, choose Window, Show Brush Selector Bar to open it or double-click the Brush tool in the Toolbox. (For more brush choices, you can click the

Strokes drawn with the Smooth Ink Pen (left) and the Coit Pen (right)

Strokes drawn with the Square Hard Pastel (left) and the Tapered Pastel (right)

Strokes painted with the Flat Oils (left) and the Round Camelhair (right)

Strokes drawn with the Grainy Variable Pencil (left) and the Sketching Pencil (right)

CHER THREINEN-PENDARVIS

A lower-opacity brush will allow you to build up color slowly with more sensitivity. This technique was used to paint the coastal hills in Punta San Antonio.

small arrow to the right of the Brush Category icon to choose a new brush from the pop-up menu.) Choose Pastels—a texture-sensitive brush—from the Brush Category pop-up menu, and then choose the Square Hard Pastel. Then to select a color, choose Window, Show Colors. Click in the Colors picker's Hue ring or bar and in its triangle to choose a color for your painting (we chose a blue). When you launched Painter, Basic Paper, a versatile medium-grained texture, was automatically loaded. (For information about changing paper textures, see "Switching papers" on page 58.)

With your stylus in hand, sketch loose circles to get the feel of the brush. This simple exercise will help you get to know the Painter brushes and become more comfortable with your tablet and stylus. Experiment by trying out more brushes, for instance, the Flat Oils and Round Camelhair variants of Oils and the Grainy Variable Pencil and Sketching Pencil variants of Pencils. (You can find detailed information about drawing and painting with a tablet and stylus and Painter in *The Photoshop and Painter Artist Tablet Book: Creative Techniques in Digital Painting*, published by Peachpit Press.)

In addition to painting on the Canvas, it's also possible to paint on a layer or mask. Painting on masks is covered in Chapter 5, "Selections, Shapes and Masks," and painting on layers is covered in Chapter 6, "Using Layers."

SAVING AND RESTORING VARIANTS

Many artists are content to use just a few of the many brush variants that come standard with the Painter, whereas others like to create their own. In-depth information for creating your own brushes can be found in Chapter 4, "Building Brushes," on page 152.

When you make modifications to a brush, Painter remembers the custom settings. Still, it's a good idea to save your custom brushes under their own names and to preserve Painter's default brushes. If you've changed settings and want to switch back to the default, choose Restore Default Variant from the pop-up menu at the right side of the Brush Selector Bar. (To restore all brushes to their default settings, choose Restore All Default Variants from the pop-up menu.) To *replace* a default brush with your custom settings, choose Set Default Variant from the triangle menu. **A word of caution:** After this choice, to restore Painter's original default variant, you will need to remove the variant you saved and relaunch Painter. To navigate to where your custom variants are stored, look for Users, User Name, Library, Application Support, Corel, Corel Painter IX, Brushes, Painter Brushes and remove the variant you saved from the category folder you used when you chose Set Default Variant. After relaunching Painter, you will have the original, default brush.

If you've made changes to a brush variant and you'd like to store it in the Brush Selector Bar, choose Save Variant from the pop-up menu on the Brush Selector Bar, name the variant and click OK. The variant that you made changes to will still be selected. Choose Restore Default Variant, and then click on the new brush variant name that you saved. Your new variant will stay there until you remove it by selecting it and then choosing Delete Variant from the pop-up menu. Custom variants that you save are also stored in the Application Support folder, as described above.

Athos Boncompagni added interest to Casa 1—*maximizing the interaction between brush and virtual texture in Painter—by exaggerating the size of the texture. Before painting with Chalk variants, he adjusted the Paper Scale slider in the Papers palette.*

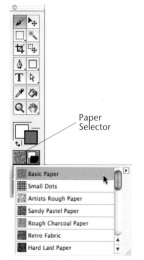

Paper Selector

The pop-up menu in the Paper Selector

Controls on the Papers palette allow for the adjustment of Paper Scale, Paper Contrast and Paper Brightness. There are also buttons for toggling Directional Grain and Invert Paper on and off. (Paper Contrast is adjusted here, and the Invert paper box is circled.)

Paper interaction. When you draw with a texture-sensitive brush (such as the Grainy Variable Pencil variant of Pencils or the Square Hard Pastel variant of Pastels), the paper texture will be revealed in the stroke as you draw. When you launched Painter, Basic Paper was loaded automatically. (At this time, Painter does not remember the last paper you might have chosen.) Not all brushes are sensitive to the paper texture in the Papers palette. For instance, many of the default Acrylics, Gouache and Oils variants paint beautiful strokes that have bristle marks but do not show paper textures. Although these default brushes do not interact with the paper textures, they can create interesting textures of their own.

Switching papers. Here's how to switch paper textures. Click the Paper Selector icon near the bottom of the Toolbox. (It's the top-left button in the group of six buttons at the bottom of the Toolbox.) Now, click the Papers icon to open the Papers list and click a new paper swatch (such as Rough Charcoal Paper) to change the texture from Painter's default. Experiment by choosing different textures and making brushstrokes using a grain-sensitive brush such as one of the Chalk or Pastels brushes.

GRAIN PENETRATION

For almost all of Painter's grain-sensitive brushes (such as the Chalk and Pastel brushes), the lower the Grain setting, the "grainier" your strokes will look. That's because the Grain setting actually describes *grain penetration*. A lower Grain setting means that less of the color will penetrate into the valleys of the grain. The paint is hitting only the "peaks" of the paper surface. However, with Digital Watercolor, the controls are reversed. A higher setting will reveal more Grain.

The Grain setting and pop-up slider are visible in the Property Bar when the Brush tool is selected in the Toolbox.

INVERTING THE GRAIN

Painter allows you to paint on both the "peaks" and the "valleys" of paper textures. To demonstrate this, choose the Fine Dots texture in the Papers Selector. Open the Papers palette by clicking the tiny arrow on the top right of the Paper Selector and choose Launch Palette. Now choose the Square Chalk variant of Chalk in the Brush Selector Bar and a blue color in the Colors picker. Use the Square Chalk to brush over the "peaks" of the texture. To paint in the "valleys" of the texture, turn on the Invert Paper check box in the Papers palette and brush lightly to apply a gold color.

Applying Surface Texture to an empty canvas is a good way to give an entire surface a texture, but it will be covered as you paint if the brush you're using doesn't show grain (doesn't have the word "grainy" in its subcategory). Some artists apply Surface Texture before *and* after they paint.

Painter's Tracker palette remembers the most recent brushes that you've used, and it's also useful for keeping your favorite brushes close at hand while you're working. To open the Tracker palette, choose Window, Show Tracker. To choose a brush from the palette, click on it. The Tracker palette can store up to 25 variants. New with Painter IX, brushes are now stored in the Tracker palette after the document is closed and in-between work sessions. Painter IX also allows you to clear a selected brush variant and save a brush variant into the palette. To clear a brush variant, select the brush and then choose Clear Selected from the palette menu. To save a brush variant with the Tracker, select the brush variant that you want to save and then choose Save Variant from the palette menu. Give the variant a name and click OK. The variant will appear in the Tracker palette, and it will also appear in the variant list under the current brush category on the Brush Selector Bar. If you have a few brushes that you regularly use, you can lock them on to the Tracker palette, so that they will appear at the top of the Tracker every time you launch Painter. To lock a brush, click on it and then choose Lock Variant from the Tracker palette menu. The locked brush will appear at the top of the list. To unlock it, select it and choose Unlock Variant from the palette menu. You can also click the Lock button at the bottom of the palette to lock and unlock brushes.

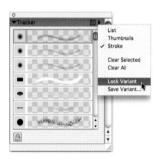

EMULATING TRADITIONAL TECHNIQUES

Here's a brief description of favorite traditional art techniques and how to re-create them in Painter. One or two techniques for each medium are outlined as a starting point for your own experimentation, but there are a number of ways to obtain similar results.

Pencil. Pencil sketches using traditional materials are typically created on location. Tools include soft-leaded graphite pencils (HB to 6B), various erasers and white paper with a smooth to medium grain. To create a pencil sketch in Painter, select an even-grained paper texture such as Basic Paper and choose the Pencils category, 2B Pencil variant. Select a black or dark gray and begin sketching. To paint a light color over dark—for instance, to add highlights—choose a white color and draw with the Cover Pencil variant. For more about working in pencil, see "Sketching with Pencils" on page 70.

Colored pencil. Conventional colored pencils are highly sensitive to the surface used. Layering strokes with light pressure on a smooth board will create a shiny look, whereas a rougher surface creates more of a "broken color" effect (strokes that don't completely cover the existing art). To closely match the grainy, opaque strokes of a soft Prismacolor pencil on cold-pressed illustration board with Painter, select a fine- or medium-grained paper such as Plain Grain (found in the Drawing Paper Textures library in the Paper Textures folder on the Painter Application

These quick sketches of Little Doll were drawn using the Cover Pencil variant on Italian Watercolor Paper with a Wacom pressure-sensitive tablet and stylus and a laptop.

The Artist Pastel Chalk variant of Pastels and the Large Chalk variant of Chalk were used on a rough texture to paint Coastal Meadow.

For this Harp Shell *study, a Conté variant was used to draw on custom-made Laid Pastel Paper.*

This charcoal study inspired by Raphael Sanzio was drawn with the Hard Charcoal and Soft Charcoal variants (Charcoal), and then blended with the Just Add Water variant (Blenders).

CD-ROM). Choose the Colored Pencil variant of Colored Pencils. Open the General section of Brush Controls and switch the Method from Buildup to Cover and then change the Subcategory to Grainy Edge Flat Cover. See "Drawing with Colored Pencils" later in this chapter for a full description of this technique.

Pastel. Pastels encourage a bold, direct style. Edgar Degas preferred pastels for his striking compositions because they simultaneously yield tone, line and color. A great variety of hard and soft pastels are used on soft- or rough-grain papers. Pastel artists often use a colored paper stock to unify a composition.

Use Painter's Chalk, Pastels and Oil Pastels brushes to mimic traditional hard or soft pastels, and if you want to use a colored paper, click on the Paper Color box (in the New dialog box) as you open a new document and choose a color. The Chalk and Pastels variants are among Painter's most popular. For a step-by-step technique, turn to "Blending and Feathering with Pastels" later in this chapter.

Conté crayon. Popular in Europe since the 1600s and used today for life drawing and landscapes, Conté crayons have a higher oil content than conventional chalk or pastel; as a result, they work successfully on a greater variety of surfaces.

To get a realistic Conté crayon look in Painter, choose the Conté category and the Tapered Conté variant. Reveal more paper grain in the brush work by moving the Grain slider in the Property Bar to 8%. Begin drawing. This Conté variant works well over the Hard Laid Pastel Paper. To blend color while revealing the paper texture, choose the Smudge variant of the Blenders brush.

Charcoal. One of the oldest drawing tools, charcoal is ideal for life drawing and portraiture in *chiaroscuro* (high-value contrast) style. Renaissance masters frequently chose charcoal because images created with it could be transferred from paper (where corrections could be made easily) to canvas or walls in preparation for painting. To create a charcoal drawing in Painter, select a rough paper (such as Charcoal Paper) and a Hard Charcoal Pencil variant of Charcoal. Create a gestural drawing and then blend the strokes—as you would traditionally with a tortillion, a tissue or your fingers—with the Smudge variant of the Blenders. For a smoother result with less texture, try blending with the Just Add Water variant of Blenders. Finish by adding more strokes using the Gritty Charcoal variant of Charcoal.

Pen and ink. Many artists use Painter's Pens variants to draw editorial and spot illustrations. To create a black-and-white pen-and-ink drawing in Painter, choose the Fine Point variant of the Pens and choose 100% black in the Colors picker. Sketch your composition. To draw with lines that are expressively thick and thin based on the pressure you apply to your stylus, switch to the Smooth Ink Pen. To etch white lines and texture into black areas

To draw Crab, *a spot illustration, Mary Envall used the Smooth Ink Pen and Scratchboard Tool variants of the Pens. Both of these Pens use Painter's rendered dabs.*

Kathleen Blavatt created Heart *using Painter's Liquid Ink brushes.*

In Tiger Kitty, *Chet Phillips used the Scratchboard Tool variant of the Pens.*

of your drawing, select pure white in the Colors picker and draw with the Fine Point or Smooth Ink Pen. For a sense of spontaneous energy try drawing with the Nervous Pen.

Thick ink and resists. When you start to paint with Painter's Liquid Ink, a special Liquid Ink layer is created. With Liquid Ink you can use the thick, viscous ink to paint graphic, flat-color art or to paint thick, impasto-like brushstrokes. For smooth-edged strokes try the Smooth Camel variant. To paint textured brushstrokes, experiment with the Sparse Bristle and Coarse Camel variants. To erode Liquid Ink you've already laid down, choose a Resist variant, such as the Graphic Camel Resist. Brush over the area of ink you want to erode. You can also apply a resist and then paint over it. The resist will repel brushstrokes made with a regular Liquid Ink variant, until repeated strokes scrub the resist away. To see how to add volume to a Liquid Ink drawing, click on the Liquid Ink layer in the Layers palette (Window, Show Layers) and press the Enter key. Move the Amount slider to 50%, and click OK. For more information about using Liquid Ink, turn to "A Painter Liquid Ink Primer" later in this chapter.

Scratchboard illustration. Scratching white illustrations out of a dark (usually black) background surface became popular in the late 1800s. Illustrations created in this manner often contained subtle, detailed tone effects, making them a useful alternative to photographic halftones in the publications of that era. Modern scratchboard artists use knives and gougers on a variety of surfaces, including white board painted with India ink. To duplicate this look in Painter, start with the Flat Color variant of the Pens and increase its size in the Property Bar. Choose black from the Colors picker and rough out the basic shape for your illustration. To "scratch" the image out of the shape with hatch marks, switch to white and change to the Scratchboard Tool variant. Use the Scratchboard Rake to draw several lines at once. Turn to the gallery in Chapter 6 to see Painter-generated scratchboard work by Chet Phillips.

Calligraphy. With the exception of "rolling the nib" and a few other maneuvers, you can imitate nearly all conventional calligraphic strokes in Painter.

BRUSH RESIZE SHORTCUT

To resize your brush on the fly, press Ctrl-Alt (Windows) or ⌘-Option (Mac). You will see the cursor change to a crosshair. Drag to create a circle the size of the brush you want.

Brushstrokes made using the Opaque Acrylic 30 variant of Acrylics. In the upper left, its default size; upper right, the resized brush "ghost" cursor; lower right, a stroke made with the resized brush.

Script drawn with a pressure-sensitive stylus using the Calligraphy variant of Calligraphy

(If you have a Wacom 6D Art Pen you can emulate those as well. See page 68 for more information about the 6D Art Pen and the Art Pen Brushes.) To create hand lettering similar to the example on the left, choose the Calligraphy variant of Calligraphy and begin your brush work. To make guides for your calligraphy, select Canvas, Rulers, Show Rulers and drag guides out from the rulers, or use Painter's Grid overlay (choose Canvas, Grid, Show Grid). If you want a rougher edge to your strokes, try switching to the Thin Grainy Pen 10 variant of Calligraphy, which has a flatter "nib."

See page 68 for more information about the 6D Art Pen and the Art Pen Brushes.

WET FRINGE PREVIEW

When you use Digital Watercolor variants with Wet Fringe set to 10% or higher (such as the Broad Water Brush variant), your image preview will change as illustrated below. As soon as you change to a brush without Wet Fringe (such as the Coarse Water variant), your view will go back to normal. If you dry the image, you may have to close and reopen the file to see the change.

No Wet Fringe   Wet Fringe 50%

CHER THREINEN-PENDARVIS

Cloudy Day on Kauai *was painted with the Runny Wash Bristle, Wash Camel, Fine Camel and Diffuse Camel variants of Watercolor. On the trees, highlights were brought out using the Eraser Dry variant, and foreground texture was added with the Eraser Salt.*

Watercolor. Landscape artists such as Turner and Constable helped popularize watercolors in the nineteenth century. The medium's portability lends itself nicely to painting on location. Traditional watercolor uses transparent pigment suspended in water, and the paper is often moistened and stretched prior to painting.

Painter lets you achieve many traditional watercolor effects— without paper-stretching! There are *two* watercolor mediums in Painter: Watercolor and Digital Watercolor. Painters who have worked with traditional watercolors may find themselves more at home with Watercolor, even though it's a bit more challenging to use. In contrast to Digital Watercolor, Watercolor employs a special Watercolor media layer. Here, the pigments can realistically blend, drip and run. To paint with Watercolor, choose the Wash Bristle variant of Watercolor, a rough paper (such as French Watercolor Paper) and a light-to-medium color and then begin painting. (If the color painted is too intense, reduce the Opacity in the Property Bar.) To remove only the color painted with Watercolor variants, use the Eraser Dry variant of Watercolor. For more about Watercolor, turn to "A Painter Watercolor Primer" on page 78.

For more about Watercolor, turn to "A Painter Watercolor Primer" on page 78.

Digital Watercolor. Digital Watercolor operates like most of Painter's other painting tools—you can choose a brush and begin to paint on a standard layer or on the canvas. (Users of Painter 6 and previous versions will recognize similarities between the earlier watercolor and the new Digital Watercolor.) Many beautiful transparent painting effects can be achieved with Digital Watercolor, which is easier to use and correct than Watercolor. Choose the New Simple Water variant of Digital Watercolor and make brushstrokes on your image. To blend color, stroke over the area with a low opacity New Simple Water brush. For strokes that

CHER THREINEN-PENDARVIS

Glazing techniques were used for this watercolor portrait of Sabina Gaross.

Study of a Nude *after Rembrandt van Rijn. We sketched with the Fine Point variant of Pens, and then added translucent washes using the Wash Brush variant of Digital Watercolor.*

reveal bristle marks, try the Coarse Dry Brush or the Coarse Mop Brush. Turn to pages 90–93 and 166–168 for step-by-step techniques using Digital Watercolor.

Pen and wash. Tinted, translucent washes over pen work has been a medium of choice of Asian painting masters for many centuries. Painter's Digital Watercolor lets you add a wash to any drawn (or scanned) image without smearing or hiding the original image. Choose the Dry Brush or Wash Brush variant of Digital Watercolor and pick a color (it works best to build up color beginning with very light-colored washes). Choose an even, medium-textured paper (such as Basic Paper) and begin painting on top of line work.

Airbrush. The trademark of most traditional airbrush work is a slick, super-realistic look; photo retouching is a more subtle use of the tool. A traditional airbrush is a miniature spray gun with a hollow nozzle and a tapered needle. Pigments include finely ground gouache, acrylic, watercolor and colored dyes, and a typical support surface is a smooth illustration board. Airbrush artists protect areas of their work from overspraying with pieces of masking film or flexible friskets cut from plastic.

In Painter, choose one of the Airbrushes variants and begin sketching or retouching. To get the most from the tool, make selections with the Lasso tool and use them to limit the paint, just as you would with traditional airbrush friskets.

Several of Painter's Airbrushes (such as the Fine Spray, Pixel Spray and Graffiti variants) spray paint onto the image Canvas differently from earlier Airbrushes such as the Digital Airbrush. These Airbrushes take advantage of input technology available from tablet-and-stylus manufacturers such as Wacom. They respond to angle (tilt) and bearing (direction). For instance, as you paint, particles of color land on the image Canvas, reflecting the way the

> **HIGH-RESOLUTION PAINTING**
>
> If you are working with large, high-resolution files, consider increasing your brush size and scaling up paper textures. Choose a brush, and in the Property Bar adjust the Size slider, or type in a new value. To scale up a paper texture, use the Paper Scale slider in the Papers palette or type in a new percentage.

artist tilts the stylus. And with Painter's Fine Wheel Airbrush variant, you can adjust the flow of paint by adjusting the wheel on a special Airbrush stylus. For those accustomed to the Airbrushes in earlier versions of Painter, the Digital Airbrush variant is most similar to these. Turn to "Selections and Airbrush" in Chapter 5 and the gallery in Chapter 9 to see John Dismukes' masterful airbrush work using selections and layers.

To paint Porcelain Morning Glory, *Kathleen Blavatt used several Airbrushes variants.*

Gouache. Rouault, Vlaminck, Klee and Miró were a few of the modern artists who experimented with this opaque watercolor, used most frequently in paintings that call for large areas of flat color. Gouache contains a blend of the same type of pigment

This detail of Nancy Stahl's *Sappi Portrait* shows her gouache technique. To see the full image and read about her illustration, turn to "Painting with Gouache," later in this chapter.

used in transparent watercolor, a chalk that makes the medium opaque and an extender that allows it to flow more easily. For an expressive, opaque color painting brush, try the new Flat Opaque Gouache variants; for a more subtle semi-transparent look, use the Wet Gouache Round variants.

USING SETTINGS IN THE PROPERTY BAR

You can quickly check settings for the current brush variant by using the Property Bar (Window, Show Property Bar). Settings for the Tapered Flat Oils variant of the Oils category are displayed below. To change brush settings (such as Size) without opening the Brush Controls or the Brush Creator, click on the tiny arrow to the right of the field to access the setting pop-up and then drag the slider to the right to increase the setting or drag to the left to decrease it.

The default settings for the Tapered Flat Oils variant of Oils

Oil paint and acrylic. These opaque media are "standards" for easel painting. Both can be applied in a thick impasto with a palette knife or stiff brush. (Impasto is a technique of applying paint thickly.) They can also be *extended* (thinned) with a solvent or gel and applied as transparent glazes. They are typically applied to canvas that has been primed with paint or gesso. Try the following methods to get the look of acrylic in Painter.

This detail from Amaryllis *was painted with the Opaque Bristle Spray and Smeary Bristle Spray variants of Oils, and then blended with the Smudge variant of Blenders.*

For a technique that incorporates the texture of brush striations and a palette knife, begin by choosing the Gessoed Canvas paper texture from the Paper Selector (located near the bottom of the Toolbox) and an Opaque Acrylic variant of the Acrylics, and then start painting. Blend colors using short strokes with a Round Blender Brush variant of Blenders. To subtly bring out the Gessoed Canvas texture, try blending with the Grainy Water variant of Blenders. To scrape back or move large areas of color on the image canvas, use a Smeary Palette Knife variant of the Palette Knives. When working on smaller areas of your image, adjust the size of the Palette Knife variant using the Size slider on the Property Bar.

For an oil painting technique with the feel of wet paint on canvas, use the Sargent Brush variant of the Artists brush. The Sargent Brush allows you to move color as well as apply it. As you pull the Sargent Brush through pools of color on the image canvas, the brush carries some of the neighboring color with it as you paint.

Coast *by Richard Noble is an example of the artist's digital acrylic technique.*

For a painting method that emphasizes the texture of canvas, begin by choosing the Coarse Cotton Canvas texture from the Paper Selector. Now choose the Opaque Bristle Spray variant of the Oils and lay color into your image. To smear existing paint as you add more color, switch to the Smeary Bristle Spray variant. To reveal the texture of the image canvas, while you blend colors, switch to the Smudge variant of Blenders. For yet another digital oil method, see Dennis Orlando's version of a traditional oil look in "Painting with

This detail from Agaves on the Edge, Summer *was painted with the Artists' Oils brushes. See the entire image on page 101.*

This detail of Sax *by Nancy Stahl shows her use of the Impasto and Gouache brushes. You can see the entire image in the gallery at the end of this chapter.*

Chelsea Sammel used Impasto brushes to add thick paint to Dying Orchids, *a detail of which is shown here. To see the entire image and read about her painting process, turn to page 127.*

Pastel and Oils," in Chapter 4; to see more examples of Richard Noble's digital acrylic paintings, turn to the gallery in Chapter 2, "The Power of Color," and to the gallery at the end of this chapter.

To get textured brushstrokes (a "3D paint" look) with any of these methods when you're finished, choose Effects, Surface Control, Apply Surface Texture. Choose Image Luminance from the pop-up menu and an Amount setting of 20%–30%. If you want to mimic the look of acrylic paint extended with a glossy gel medium, drag the Shine slider to 100%. To get a semi-matte finish, move the Shine slider to between 20% and 30%.

Painting with wet Artists' Oils paint. New in Painter IX, the Artists' Oils medium feels just like viscous, wet oil paint. With this new medium, you can apply paint and blend paint to your heart's content. The brushes are also exciting to use for loose gestural work and for working over photographs. For more information about the Artists' Oils see "A Painter Artists' Oils Primer" on page 98, and "Painting with the Artists' Oils" on page 101.

Painting with realistic Impasto. Impasto gives you the power to show the texture of brushmark striations and the thickness of paint itself with realistic highlights and shadows as you paint. Impasto brings thick paint to the tip of your stylus! When you choose a variant of the Impasto brush (such as the Thick Wet Round) in the Brush Selector Bar, the Impasto effect is automatically enabled. You can use Impasto on the image Canvas or on added layers.

Here's an Impasto primer: Create a new, blank file (File, New). To activate Impasto, choose an Impasto brush (such as the Thick Wet Round variant) from the Brush Selector Bar. Make brushstrokes on the image canvas. To toggle the Impasto effect on and off, you can click the small paint splat icon in the upper-right corner of Painter's scroll bar. (This toggle does not affect the dimensionality created with the Apply Surface Texture command described on the "Oil paint and acrylic" section above.) To read more about painting with Impasto, turn to "A Painter Impasto Primer," "Brushing Washes Over 'Live' Canvas" and "Working with Thick Paint," later in this chapter.

IMPASTO COMPOSITE DEPTH

You can paint Impasto on layers and then set Composite Depth on each layer (in the Layers palette) to raise or excavate the paint, as described in the Impasto Primer on pages 123–124. (The Composite Depth option will have no effect if you've used Impasto on the Canvas instead of on added layers.)

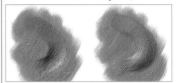

We painted each rust brushstroke on a separate layer with the Opaque Round variant of Impasto. Then, we used Composite Depth controls, Subtract (left) and Add (right), to excavate the left stroke and raise the right stroke.

In Three Trees, *Chelsea Sammel mixed media while painting. As shown in this detail, she used modified Chalks and Oils brushes: the Smeary Bristle Spray; Blenders, the Coarse Smear; and finally the Oil Pastels and a modified Sharp Chalk variant (Chalk) to define details.*

To complete Speedy Persimmon, *Janet Martini mixed media using the Calligraphy variant of the Calligraphy on top of Watercolor variants and Oil Pastel strokes.*

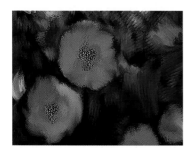

For Zinnias, *we painted over a photo with Pastel variants, completely covering it with colored strokes. Then, we used Distortion and Blender variants to distort the flowers, add texture and emphasize the focal point.*

Mixed media. You can create media combinations in Painter that would be impossible (or at least very messy!) in traditional media. Try adding strokes with a Watercolor or Pencils variant atop Oils, or use a Pens variant on a base you've painted using the Chalk or Gouache variants. See how artists Chelsea Sammel and Janet Martini combined media in the two paintings at the left.

Mixed media painting with a liquid feel. Painter offers several brushes that are reminiscent of wet paint on canvas—for instance, the Sargent Brush variant of the Artists brush, which can both lay down color and smear it, and the Palette Knives variants, which can move large areas of color. Painting with these new brushes is a very tactile experience, as you learned if you experimented as described on page 64.

In the *Paths to Water 4* study shown on page 67, we sketched in color with the Square Chalk (Chalk) and a Round Soft Pastel (Pastels) on a rough paper. Then, we switched to the Sargent Brush variant of the Artists brushes to apply more painterly strokes. To blend areas of the foreground and midground, we used the Grainy Water variant of Blenders, and then we used the Smeary Palette Knife and Subtle Palette Knife variants of the Palette Knives to expressively pull color in the sky. To paint and blend using these brushes, choose the Sargent Brush and a color, and begin painting. When you are ready to pull and blend paint, switch to the Palette Knife. Try reducing its Opacity in the Property Bar for a more subdued effect.

The Blenders and Distortion variants are also helpful blending tools. To create *Zinnias*, we used the Bulge variant of the Distortion category to enlarge the pink flowers, and the Coarse Smear variant of Blenders to pull pixels and add diffused texture to the edges. Then we used the Marbling Rake variant of Distortion to add linear texture and to pull pixels up and around the image to create a sense of movement.

Erasing techniques. Painter provides several ways to simulate traditional erasing and scratch-out techniques. *Lighten* an area of an image by using the Bleach variant of the Erasers, lowering the Opacity slider in the Property Bar to 5% for improved control. (You can also use the Dodge variant of the Photo brush to lighten color.) Use the Thin Grainy Pen 10 variant of the Calligraphy brush and white (or a light color) to *scratch out* pigment from a pastel or oil painting; to create strokes with more subtle texture, switch to the Thin Smooth Pen 10 variant of Calligraphy. Use the Eraser Dry variant of the Watercolor brush to pull up pigment from a "wet" painting done with Watercolor variants (similar to *sponging up* a

LIQUID BRUSH STRENGTH
To control the strength of the Bulge, Pinch, Smear and Turbulence variants of the Distortion brush, adjust the Strength (or Opacity) slider in the Property Bar.

In this detail from a study for Paths to Water 4, *Palette Knife variants were used to pull and spread color in the clouds and sky.*

traditional watercolor). For a more subtle result, lower the Opacity slider (in the Property Bar) to 40%. Try the Bleach Runny variant of Watercolor to leach color from an area, while creating a drippy texture. To pull color out of areas when using Digital Watercolor, use the Wet Eraser, and for picking color out of smaller areas, try the Pointed Wet Eraser variant of Digital Watercolor.

Painting with texture. The Add Grain variant of the Photo brush is just as useful for painting as it is for photo manipulation, because it literally puts texture on the tip of your brush. You can switch textures at any time during the painting process by changing the selection in the Papers palette. For best results, use very light pressure on the stylus. Make a few marks in the document to preview the effect. For a more subtle look, try lowering the Strength and Grain settings in the Property Bar.

Painting with special effects. Painter offers intriguing special-effects brushes that allow you to paint with fire, glows, fur, sparkly fairy dust, hair spray, neon, striped strokes, shattered glass and more! In the detail of *Creative Journey* shown on the left, Brian Moose used the Glow variant of the F-X brush to make the paintbrush tips in his image smolder with a fiery glow.

Painting with the Fire and Glow variants works best on a dark area of your image. To paint semi-transparent flames, choose the Fire brush variant of the F-X brush. For a subdued fire effect that you can build up gradually, with a light pressure on the stylus, choose a very dark orange color with a value (V) of 10%–15% in the Colors picker. Make short strokes in the direction you want the

Brian Moose used the Glow brush variant of the F/X brush to make the brush tips burn in his painting Creative Journey, *a detail of which is shown here.*

When you work with Impasto, the depth and lighting information is stored in a way that allows you to change it for the entire image—as many times as you like, for both past and future Impasto brushstrokes. To demonstrate this flexibility, select an Impasto variant (such as Texturizer-Heavy) and a color, and paint on your image. Next, choose Canvas, Surface Lighting and when the dialog box opens, increase the Shine (for more glossy paint). Increase the Amount (to make the paint look thicker) and experiment with other settings in the Appearance of Depth and Light Controls sections. Also try toggling Impasto off and on using the Enable Impasto check box. To clear (delete) the effect entirely, choose Canvas, Clear Impasto. Clearing Impasto is useful if you want to completely start over with new Impasto. Also, if you decide not to keep the Impasto effects in your image, clearing can save memory.

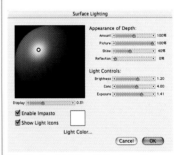

The Surface Lighting dialog box allows you to dynamically set Appearance of Depth and Light Controls for Impasto brushstrokes in the entire image.

Calligraphy drawn with the 6D Art Pen and the Thin Smooth Calligraphy pen from the Art Pen Brushes

Expressive brush strokes painted with the 6D Art Pen and the Soft Flat Oils brush from the Art Pen Brushes

CHER THREINEN-PENDARVIS

To paint this study for Cutting Back at Rincon, *we used the Pens, Gouache and Airbrushes variants to paint on transparent layers. After drawing the line sketch on its own layer, we created a second layer for the color work. Using low-opacity color, we painted on the "color" layer to build up brushstrokes without altering the image canvas or the layer with the line sketch. We finished by dragging the line sketch layer to the top of the Layers palette, placing it on top of the color layer.*

flames to go. For realism, vary the size of the brushstrokes. Change the size of the brush by using the Size slider in the Property Bar; then paint more brushstrokes by using a light pressure on the stylus.

USING THE EXPRESSIVE ART PEN BRUSHES

The Art Pen Brush Pack is available for download at www.corel.com/painter. The Art Pen Brushes were designed by Cher Threinen-Pendarvis to work with the Wacom 6D Art Pen and to allow you to tap into more expression in Painter IX. The 6D Art Pen and Painter IX support rotation, which until now was a missing dimension for artists using a Wacom tablet. The brushes are as follows: Thin Smooth Calligraphy, a broad pen that changes stroke thickness and character as you rotate the pen; Grainy Calligraphy, a tapered pen that responds by changing the character of the stroke as you rotate your hand; the Soft Flat Oils, a flat brush whose soft bristles respond subtly as you move your hand in a natural way while painting; the Tapered Gouache, a round brush whose bristles also respond as you rotate your hand and the stroke thickness also changes as you apply pressure to the stylus; and the Square Grainy Pastel, a brush that is similar to a hard square pastel that shows a lot of paper grain. Its strokes also change as you move your hand in a natural rotation while drawing.

PAINTING ON LAYERS

Painter lets you paint (and erase) not only on the program's Canvas but on transparent layers above it. A *transparent layer* is similar to a piece of clear acetate that hovers above the image canvas. When you paint on a transparent layer with a brush, in the clear areas you can see the Canvas underneath, as well as color on other layers that you may have stacked up. You can also change the stacking order of the acetate sheets. If you work with Adobe Photoshop, you'll find Painter's transparent layers familiar.

To add a new layer to an existing file, open the Layers palette (Windows, Show Layers) or click the left triangle on the Layers section bar to open this section. Click the right triangle on the section bar to access the Layers palette's pop-up menu and choose New Layer. To paint on the new layer, choose any brush except a Watercolor or Liquid Ink variant, target the layer in the Layers palette and begin painting.

Layers offer great flexibility to digital illustrators. Some artists prefer to draw each item in an image on its own layer, which isolates the item so that it can be repositioned or painted on as an individual element. Transparent layers are also useful when creating *glazes*—thin, clear layers of color applied over existing color. (Turn to Chapter 6, "Using Layers" to read more about painting and compositing techniques.)

PICKING UP COLOR

To bring color from underlying layers into an upper layer that you're painting on (and mix color on the active layer), turn on Pick Up Underlying Color in the Layers section.

The default Shapes Preference settings for the Align Brush to Path

The Align to Path button in the Property Bar

Selecting the Canvas layer, with the Oval shape layer visible

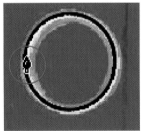

Painting on the Canvas with an Artists' Oils brush using Snap-to-Path function. The Oval Shape layer is visible.

PAINTING ALONG A PATH

When you want to paint a precise curve or shape, the new Snap-to-Path Painting feature in Painter IX will save you time. Using Snap-to-Path, you can constrain a brushstroke to a path by clicking the Align to Path button on the Property Bar. The brush stroke will reflect the sensitivity that Painter brushes are famous for, such as pressure, tilt and bearing.

To use the Snap-to-Path feature, begin by choosing the Oval shape tool in the Toolbox. In the Property Bar, enable Stroke and disable Fill, and then choose a color in the Colors picker. From the Shapes menu, choose Set Shape Attributes and set the Width of your stroke to 2. As your draw the shape, constrain the oval to a circle by holding down the Shift key. With the Oval shape layer visible, click on the Canvas layer in the Layers palette to select it. Choose a brush in the Brush Selector Bar. In the Property Bar click on the Align to Path button to activate the Snap-to-Path function. (Note: In Preferences, Shapes you can set the Align Brush to Path tolerance and enable Paint hidden shapes. For this example, we used the default preference settings of 20 for Tolerance with Paint hidden shapes unchecked.)

As you paint, your strokes will follow the path of the circle. To create concentric circles, select the Layer Adjuster tool, and then Shift-drag one of the corner handles of the shape to proportionally reduce the size of the circle. Now, move the smaller circle shape inside of one of your painted circles and paint with Snap-to-Path active around the smaller circle. Experiment by trying out more brushes with the Snap-to-Path feature. To read about how Carol Benioff uses the Snap-to-Path feature turn to "Illustrating with the Artists' Oils" on page 105 later in this chapter.

THE LOOKS YOU LIKE

If you like the look of a particular brush-and-paper combination (for instance, a Square Soft Pastel variant of Pastels on Rough Charcoal Paper), save the combo as a *Brush Look* so that you can quickly call it up when you want to use it again. Before you can save a new Look, in Painter it's necessary to select an area of an image that can be used as an icon for the Brush Look. In the Toolbox, choose the Rectangular Marquee tool and drag in the image to make a selection. Select the texture from the Paper Selector (near the bottom of the Toolbox) and the

brush variant from the Brush Selector Bar. In the Toolbox, click the Looks Selector and choose New Look from the triangle pop-up menu. Naming your New Look saves it to the current Brush Look library, which is located in the Look Selector in the Tools palette. Open the Look Selector by clicking the Look icon. To paint with your new Brush Look, select it from the pop-up menu.

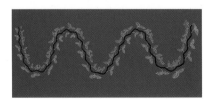

A brushstroke painted with the Pattern Pen brush, Pattern Pen Masked variant (over a blue background) using the Jungle Vines pattern as the Source. This look can be accessed by clicking the Looks Selector (near the bottom of the Toolbox) and choosing Jungle Vine Pen.

Sketching with Pencils

Overview *Draw a loose sketch with Pencils variants; scribble and crosshatch to develop tones; brighten highlights with an Eraser.*

CHER THREINEN-PENDARVIS

Making a stroke in the Brush Tracking window

The loose composition sketch

Adding tones to the background and values to the faces

Darker tones and more texture have been added to the background and the faces.

LOOSE, EXPRESSIVE SKETCHES CAN BE DRAWN with the Painter's Pencils variants, with a look that's similar to traditional tools, as shown in this drawing of *Soshi and Pearl.*

1 Setting Brush Tracking. Pencil sketching often involves rapid, gestural movements with the stylus so it's important to set up Brush Tracking before you begin to sketch. With Brush Tracking you can customize how Painter interprets the input of your stylus, including parameters such as pressure and how quickly you make a brushstroke. Choose Edit, Preferences/Corel Painter IX, Preferences, Brush Tracking and make a representative brushstroke in the window.

2 Beginning to sketch. Create a new image file (File, New). (Ours measured 1100 x 600 pixels.) Click OK. Click on the Paper Selector icon in the Toolbox and select an even-textured paper such as Basic Paper and then select the Pencils category, 2B Pencil variant in the Brush Selector Bar. The default 2B Pencil uses the Buildup method, which means that color you draw is semitransparent and will darken to black, just like when you draw with a conventional 2B graphite pencil. Select a dark gray in the Colors picker and draw a line sketch that will establish the negative and positive shapes in your composition.

3 Building tones and modeling form. To bring the subjects forward in the picture frame, add dark values behind them. Make crosshatched strokes with the 2B Pencil to create the darker tones. Keep your strokes loose and gestural. Lively stroke patterns will add texture interest to your drawing. To model the faces and bodies of the cats, we used the Oily Variable Pencil, which smeared the pencil slightly as we scribbled and crosshatched. The Oily Variable Pencil incorporates the Cover method, which means that the color you draw is opaque; a lighter color will paint over a darker color.

For highlights, choose white in the Colors picker and switch to the Cover Pencil variant in the Brush Selector Bar. The Cover Pencil is ideal for adding highlights because it covers previous strokes without smearing. To clean up areas, choose the Eraser variant (Erasers). A tiny Eraser also works well for brightening highlights.

Drawing with Colored Pencils

Overview *Create a sketch with the Sharp Colored Pencil variant; use the Cover Colored Pencil to further develop the drawing; adjust Color Variability settings for a more active color effect.*

CHER THREINEN-PENDARVIS

The line sketch drawn with Colored Pencils

2a **2b**

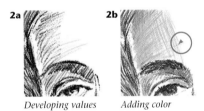

Developing values   *Adding color*

3

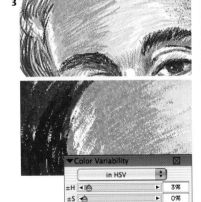

Building dimension using increased settings in the Color Variability section of the Brush Controls, and strokes that follow the form

YOU CAN MODIFY THE COLORED PENCIL variant and get a broken color effect (where the color only partially covers the background or underdrawing) by brushing lightly across a textured surface.

1 Starting with a sketch. To work at the same size we did, open a new 883-pixel-wide file with a white background. Click the Paper Selector near the bottom of the Toolbox, choose Basic texture and select a dark brown color in the Colors picker. From the Brush Selector Bar, choose the Colored Pencils category and the Sharp Colored Pencil variant, and then draw a portrait sketch.

2 Developing value and adding color. Now choose the Cover Colored Pencil 5 variant of Colored Pencils from the Brush Selector Bar. Use this brush and a lighter brown to develop values throughout the sketch. Choose a skin color (we chose a tan for this portrait of Steve Pendarvis) and apply strokes with a light touch to partially cover some of the brown sketch. Follow the form with your strokes, switching colors and brush sizes as you draw.

3 Building dimension. To give a shimmery look to the color as it's applied, drag the Hue (±H) and Value (±V) sliders in the Color Variability section of Brush Controls to 3%. Using a light touch to allow the underpainting to show through, apply a fresh layer of strokes in the areas of strongest color (in our drawing, the forehead and nose shadows and the hair). 🖌

COLORED PENCIL WASHES

If you're using Colored Pencils on rough paper, you can create a wash effect. Choose the Grainy Water variant of the Blenders, reducing Opacity and Grain penetration in the Property Bar to 40% or less. Stroke over your pencil work to blend colors while maintaining texture on the "peaks" of the paper grain.

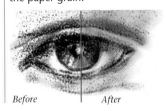

Before   *After*

Making Sketchbook Studies Using Pens

Overview *Start with gestural drawing; build the forms with crosshatching; clean up with an Eraser.*

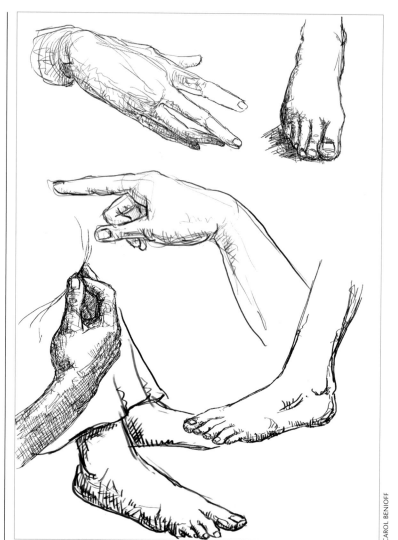

CAROL BENIOFF

Drawing the first gestural lines with the Croquil Pen variant

Adding defining lines to the gesture drawing and removing some of the lines with an Eraser variant

USING THESE SIX DIFFERENT PEN VARIANTS, it's easy to create quick studies with a variety of looks. The Pens resemble their traditional counterparts, but unlike the conventional pens they emulate, Painter's Pens do not spatter, and you can erase their ink. Carol Benioff used the Pens to draw these black-and-white studies.

Studies from Leonardo da Vinci. Benioff began by finding good reproductions of Leonardo da Vinci's drawings to use as a reference. Then she created a new 7 x 9-inch image in Painter at 300 pixels-per-inch.

1 Making a gesture drawing. She chose the Croquil Pen 5 and she sketched a gestural drawing, mapping out the shape of the hand.

2 Defining lines. Benioff drew over the gesture drawing with more definitive lines. She removed lines that she no longer

3

Completing the study with crosshatch and gestural strokes

4

Study of a hand drawn with a Smooth Round Pen in short curving strokes

5

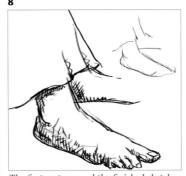

Hand drawn with the Thick n Thin Pen

6

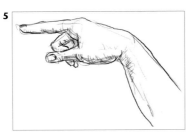

Study of a foot using the medium weight line of the Ball Point Pen 1.5

needed using a Pointed Eraser variant of Erasers. Next, she built up the tones and form with short, quick strokes.

3 Completing the study. Using a combination of crosshatching and curving lines, she created the highlights and shadows that gave the hand its definition. The study had the scratchy feel of the traditional croquil pen without the splatters.

4 Using the Smooth Round Pen. Turning to another drawing by Leonardo to use as her model, Benioff then selected the Smooth Round Pen 1.5 variant of Pens. It had the delicate quality that she wanted to create thin expressive lines. She drew this study using long gestural strokes.

5 Using the Thick n Thin Pen. For her fifth study, Benioff selected the Thick n Thin Pen 3. The bold quality of line the pen produces helped to create a clean and simple drawing. She added a suggestion of shading, which she sketched using short squiggles and a bit of crosshatching.

6 Using the Ball Point Pen. For this study of a foot, Benioff chose a Ball Point Pen variant. This gave her an even-weighted medium line. She built up the form using overlapping scribbles and crosshatching.

7

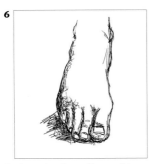

The beginning gesture drawing and the completed sketch of a foot using the Reed pen variants

8

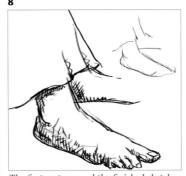

The first gestures and the finished sketch of two feet, using the Bamboo Pen 10 resized to about 5 pixels using the Size slider on the Property Bar

7 Using the Reed Pen. In this drawing of a foot Benioff selected the Reed Pen 5 for its strong, thick-to-thin lines. First she drew a quick gestural outline. Then she used long, smooth strokes to define the contours. Sizing the pen nib down to 3.7 from 7 pixels in the Property Bar, she continued to draw short, curving strokes to indicate the form and shadow.

8 Using a Bamboo Pen. For a strong, clear line Benioff chose the Bamboo Pen 10, sizing it down to about 3 pixels. Again she started with a simple gestural outline, and then used short, smooth lines to add the contours. She finished the sketch with short straight lines to add definition to the form and to indicate shadows.

Expressive Drawing with Pens

Overview *Create a line sketch using a Thick n Thin Pen; modify the Leaky Pen for more expression; add spotted and linear accents.*

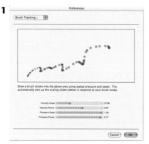

Setting up Brush Tracking

Drawing the line sketch with the Thick n Thin Pen 5 variant of Pens

PAINTER IX IS THE ULTIMATE DIGITAL ART STUDIO, with literally hundreds of brushes to choose from. For *Today's Suit,* a fashion illustration sketch, we drew with several expressive Pens variants in Painter, including the Thick n Thin Pen, the Coit Pen, and the Leaky Pen. Additionally, we modified the Leaky Pen so that it would paint even more random spots.

1 Setting Brush Tracking. For the most responsive strokes during your work session, it's important to set up Brush Tracking. Brush Tracking allows you to customize how Painter interprets the input of your stylus, including parameters such as pressure and speed. From the Edit/Corel Painter IX menu, choose Preferences, Brush Tracking and make a representative brushstroke in the window. For instance, if you plan to use both light and heavy pressure while sketching slowly and then quickly, make a brushstroke that includes these factors.

2b

Drawing a few squiggly accents on the line sketch with the Thick n Thin Pen

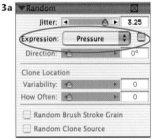

3a

Changing the Jitter Expression pop-up menu to Pressure

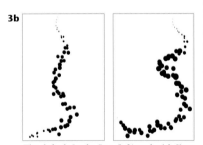

3b

The default Leaky Pen (left) and with Jitter Expression set to Pressure (right)

3c

Leaky Pen spots on the hat and jacket

2 Creating a line sketch. Open a new file that is 1500 x 2000 pixels. In the Brush Selector Bar, choose the Pens category from the Brush Category pop-up menu; then choose the Thick n Thin Pen 5 variant from the Brush Variant pop-up menu. It's a good idea to make some practice marks with the pen. Choose black in the Colors picker and press lightly on your stylus to sketch a thinner line and press more heavily to draw a thicker line. When you've finished practicing, delete your practice strokes by choosing Select, All and then pressing the Delete/Backspace key.

For this illustration, we chose to sketch the basic shapes using the Thick n Thin Pen because it allows you to draw smoothly, while varying the thickness of the lines. To sketch a graceful, tall model, use your stylus to make sweeping, curved vertical strokes, which will suggest the outline of the model and emphasize her height. As you sketch, keep in mind the motion of her walk and the sweeping curves of her clothing. Then, add a few details and accents with shorter, squiggly strokes.

3 Adding more expression to the Leaky Pen. In preparation for adding texture with the Leaky Pen, we modified its settings to make it even more expressive. Choose Window, Brush Controls, Show Random and set the Jitter Expression pop-up menu to Pressure. Save your variant by choosing Save Variant from the pop-up menu on the Brush Selector Bar and give it a name. For good Painter housekeeping, restore the default variant to its original settings by choosing Restore Default Variant from the same menu.

4 Adding texture with unusual Pens. Next, we added whimsical texture to the line work using two unusual Pens variants. To add interesting textured spots, we used both the default Leaky Pen and the custom Leaky Pen from step 3. Choose your modified Leaky Pen. Make a practice stroke using light pressure to begin the stroke, and then gradually apply heavier pressure at the end

3d

Detail showing the Coit Pen strokes on the jacket and skirt

of the stroke. You'll notice that the spots will become larger and more random with heavier pressure. Now, draw a few textured accent strokes on your model using the modified Leaky Pen. We loosely drew in a few accents.

Next, we used the Coit Pen to draw textured line accents. When you have the spotty texture as you like it, switch to the Coit Pen variant of Pens and draw a few gently curved linear accents, as we did here along the sides of the jacket and skirt in the illustration.

Blending and Feathering with Pastels

Overview *Set up a still life; sketch from life with pastels; build color and form; blend the painting; add feathered brushstrokes to finish.*

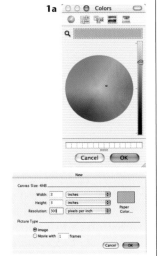

1a

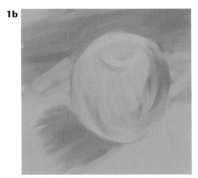

Choosing a paper color

1b

Loosely sketching with the Square X-Soft Pastel 20 variant of Pastels

FEATHERING—THIN, PARALLEL STROKES over a blended underpainting—is a traditional pastel technique that yields texture and freshness. Because the feathered finishing strokes remain unblended on the painting's surface, the viewer's eye must work to blend the colors. Here is an example of optical color blending.

1 Starting with a sketch on colored paper. We set up a still life on a table next to a window. We arranged the subject so that the shadow would help to lead the eye into the composition and give the painting more depth.

When we were happy with the still life design, we opened a new file (File, New: 4 x 5 inches x 300 ppi) with a light brown-colored background. To set the Paper Color, click the Paper Color preview in the New window and choose a color in the Colors dialog box. To select a new hue or adjust its saturation, click or drag in the color wheel. To make the color darker or lighter, adjust the value slider on the right side of the window. When you have a

2a

Painting curved and angled strokes of varied color on the foreground and apple

2b

Adding hatched strokes to sculpt the form of the apple and build values

3

Blending with the Grainy Water and Smudge variants of Blenders

color that you like, click OK. Now click the Paper Selector near the bottom of the Toolbox and select Sandy Pastel Paper texture. Pick a color to sketch with from the Colors picker (we began with a warm yellow). Select the Square X-Soft Pastel 20 variant of Pastels from the Brush Selector Bar. For a more sensitive response when using your stylus, choose Edit Preferences/Corel Painter IX, Preferences, Brush Tracking, make a representative brushstroke in the window and click OK. Begin to roughly sculpt the shape of the apple and suggest a horizon line (in our case, an angled table top) and then rough in the background, choosing new colors as needed.

2 Blocking in color over the sketch. Still working with Square X-Soft Pastel 20, lay in more color over your sketch, allowing your strokes to follow the direction of the form.

Now, choose the Artist Pastel Chalk variant, and add more color and value to your sketch. To smear existing paint as you add new color, try one of the Soft Oil Pastel variants of Oil Pastels. As we worked, we also used the Grainy Water variant of Blenders to selectively blend areas. Layer the color and blend the underpainting until you're pleased with the form. We also added rust and gray colors to the background by using angled brushstrokes. Then, we painted varied gray and brown colors on the table and background to give the simple composition more interest.

3 Softening the brush work. Select the Grainy Water variant of Blenders, and blend areas of color, again following the direction of the form. To blend while revealing more paper texture, blend colors with the Smudge variant of Blenders.

4 Adding feathered strokes and detail. To create thin, textured strokes on top of the blended forms, choose the Tapered Pastel 10 variant. If you need to reduce its Size, use the Size slider in the Property Bar. Stroke with this brush in the direction of the form. In our example, feathering is most noticeable in the highlights of the apple—in the red and orange colors overlaid over the apple's gold and light green colors, and on the foreground shadow. Finish the piece by using the Grainy Water variant to soften the feathering in the shadow areas. (To do the final blending touches, we lowered the Grainy Water variant's Opacity to 40% using the Opacity slider in the Property Bar.) We also used a tiny Soft Pastel Pencil to add detail to the stem on the apple.

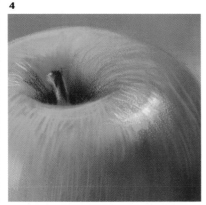

4

Using feathered strokes to bring out highlights and color variations on the apple

A Painter Watercolor Primer

Overview *Here you'll find the basics for painting with Painter's Watercolor brushes and layers.*

CHER THREINEN-PENDARVIS

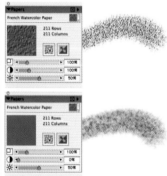

Two brushstrokes painted with the Diffuse Grainy Camel variant of Watercolor: 100% Contrast, the default (top), and painting with 0% Contrast (bottom)

PAINTER FEATURES TWO KINDS OF WATERCOLOR: Watercolor layers and Digital Watercolor. This primer covers Watercolor Layers. Digital Watercolor, which is simpler to use and doesn't require a special layer, is covered on pages 90–93.

Watercolor media layers provide artists with an experience that's surprisingly like traditional watercolor. The Watercolor Layer is a simulation of a transparent wet medium containing suspended pigment. This makes it possible to create smooth, transparent washes and then diffuse color into existing wet paint to blend, as a traditional watercolorist would.

Laelio Cattleya Orchid (above), is one of a series of flower studies painted using a technique similar to the one presented step-by-step in "Combining Wet-into-Wet and Glazing on Layers" on page 86. But before you start using Watercolor, reading these four pages will help you to understand how to achieve the results you desire.

Controlling Watercolor. With Painter, you can control the wetness, drying time, direction in which your wash will run and many other techniques that you're able to achieve using conventional watercolor tools. The most important settings for Watercolor are in the Brush Controls (the General, Size and Water sections—these windows are also located in the Stroke Designer tab of the Brush Creator); the Papers palette and the Layers palette. When you make a brushstroke with a Watercolor brush, a Watercolor

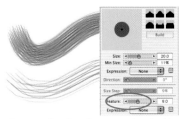

These two brushstrokes were painted with the Dry Bristle brush. The top stroke uses the default brush settings. For the bottom stroke, the Feature size was increased to 8.0 in the Size section of the Brush Controls, which resulted in a brushstroke with fewer brush hairs.

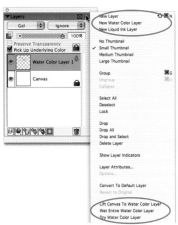

The Water section of the Brush Stroke Designer (Brush Controls) contains controls for modifying Watercolor brushes.

The menu on the right side of the Layers palette bar offers useful options for working with Watercolor layers: New Watercolor Layer, Lift Canvas to Watercolor Layer, Wet Entire Watercolor Layer and Dry Watercolor layer.

Layer is automatically generated in the Layers palette. Watercolor Layers can be targeted in the Layers palette and edited like other layers. Chapter 6 tells about working with layers.

In the General section of Brush Controls, the Watercolor dab types are displayed in the Dab Type pop-up menu. A dab type determines the shape of the brush—for instance, Watercolor Flat and Watercolor Camel Hair (round). Most of the Watercolor brushes use continuous-stroke technology, which means that brushstrokes are painted using brush hairs that are a set of anti-aliased 1-pixel lines. You'll find more information about dab types in the "Building Brushes" chapter on page 152.

In the Size section of Brush Controls, you'll find the Feature slider, which determines the density of the brush hairs in the continuous-stroke brushes.
Note: A very low Feature setting (producing more densely packed brush hairs) takes greater computing power, which can slow down the performance of a Watercolor brush.

In the Water section of the Brush Controls, *Wetness* works with Evaporation Threshold to control the amount and spread of the *water* and *dye*. A low Evaporation Threshold will allow more spread; higher values will cause less spread. A high Wetness setting will blur the individual bristle marks and (with a high Diffusion Amount setting) increase the spread of the stroke, but it may make the performance of the brush lag. *Pickup* controls the amount of existing paint that gets moved when a new brush-stroke paints over existing pigment. High Pickup rates cause wet edges or puddles, which can be desirable. The *Dry Rate* controls the length of time the water and pigment take to settle. A high Dry Rate will keep a brush with high Diffusion Amount settings from spreading as far, because the stroke will dry before it has had time to diffuse. A low Dry Rate value will allow more time for spread. *Evaporation Threshold* controls the amount of *water* that can diffuse. (In traditional watercolor, evaporation is the rate in which liquid is sublimated into the atmosphere.) *Diffuse Amount*

TURN ON ACCURATE DIFFUSION

With Accurate Diffusion off in the Water section, larger cells are visible when a brushstroke is made. Accurate Diffusion allows finer detail and a more natural-looking diffusion of pigment into the Watercolor Layer. But it may cause a slight decline in brush responsiveness.

Two brushstrokes painted with the Diffuse Camel variant of Watercolor (brushstrokes shown at 200%). Accurate Diffusion was turned off when the top stroke was painted and turned on for the bottom stroke.

A smooth wash (top), and thick and thin flower petal shapes (bottom), painted with the Wash Camel variant of Watercolor

A smooth stroke painted The Wash Bristle (top) and diffused strokes with wet edges, painted with the Wet Bristle (bottom). The variation in color is caused by pigment buildup.

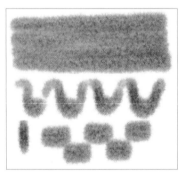

These soft-edged washes and brushstrokes were painted with the Diffuse Flat.

These crisper, expressive strokes were painted with the Wash Pointed Flat.

controls the amount of *pigment* that can diffuse. *Capillary Factor* and *Grain Soak-In* affect the amount of pigment that settles in the valleys of the paper grain. Setting both of these controls to 0 will minimize grain effects. Also, very low Capillary Factor and Grain Soak-In settings will allow a runny wash to spread more smoothly. A high Capillary Factor (with a low Grain Soak-In setting) will create a "stringy" drip texture in the runny wash.

GETTING TO KNOW THE WATERCOLOR BRUSHES

Here are some suggestions for how to paint traditional-looking brush work using Painter's Watercolor brushes. Even if you're familiar with using a stylus and Painter's other brushes, try these exercises and experiment with all of the Watercolor brushes. You may enjoy discovering a new kind of expressive brushstroke!

Versatility with Camel brushes. The most versatile of all the Watercolor brushes, the Camel brushes, are round. In addition to painting various kinds of washes, most Camel brushes allow you to paint brushstrokes that can be thick and thin, depending on the pressure applied to the stylus. Other Camel brushes allow you to apply drippy washes (Runny Wash Camel and Runny Wet Camel), while the Diffuse Camel paints strokes that have soft, feathery edges.

Choose the Wash Camel variant and paint a smooth wash area. Apply even pressure to your stylus, and make a horizontal stroke; then carefully paint a second horizontal stroke below it, just slightly overlapping the first stroke. The diffusion in the stroke edge will help make a smooth transition between the strokes. Before painting thick to thin strokes, choose Edit, Preferences/Corel Painter IX, Preferences, Brush Tracking, make a representative brushstroke in the window and click OK. Using the Wash Camel, press harder to paint the thicker area of the shape; then gradually reduce pressure on the stylus, finally lifting your stylus as you complete the stroke.

Expressive brush work with Bristle brushes. These Watercolor brushes paint just like brushes with real bristles because they're sensitive to tilt and rotation of the stylus. As you tilt your stylus, the bristles of the brush spread or splay out as you rotate your hand through the stroke. To paint a wash that has the texture of soft bristle marks, try the Wash Bristle brush. For a wet-into-wet effect with subtle bristle marks and pools at the stroke edges, experiment with the Wet Bristle.

Thick and thin strokes with the Flat brushes. Look for brushes with the word Flat in their name; the Diffuse Flat and Wash Pointed Flat are examples. With Flat-tipped brushes, you can paint wide or narrow strokes, depending on the way you hold the stylus and how much pressure you apply. When trying the strokes that follow, position your stylus with the button facing up (away from you). To paint a fuzzy wash with the Diffuse Flat (as in the image on the left), pull the brush straight across your image using even pressure. To make the thin lines, pull down. To

The Fine variants are useful when painting expressive, linear brushstrokes, as in the sketches of the eye and grasses shown here.

We painted this cloud study using the Runny Wash Bristle and Runny Wet Camel to paint the clouds, the Wash Camel and Fine Camel variants to paint the water and the Diffuse Camel to soften a few edges.

For this foliage study we created texture in the foreground with a small Splatter Water brush.

As a final touch to Pink Orchid, we used the Eraser Salt variant of Watercolor to sprinkle light speckles on the tops of the petals.

make a curved, thin-to-thick wavy line, use light pressure on your stylus for the thin top areas, and more pressure as you sweep down and rotate the brush.

For flat brushstrokes with crisper edges and more thin-to-thick control, try the Wash Pointed Flat. For a thin-to-thick sweeping curved stroke, begin the thin portion with very light pressure on your stylus, and as you sweep downward rotate your stylus slightly (changing the button orientation) and apply more pressure. To make a thick, even stroke, pull the stylus sideways relative to the button, using even pressure. For the thin lines, apply even pressure and pull in a direction toward or away from the button.

Adding detail with the Fine brushes. The Fine variants of the Watercolor brush are good for painting details, and for calligraphic line work. The Fine Bristle and Fine Camel are similar to "rigger" or "line" brushes, which are used to paint expressive line work in traditional watercolor.

Painting runny washes using the Runny brushes. The *Runny* variants (the Runny Wash Bristle and the Runny Wash Camel, for instance), are useful for painting drippy wet-into-wet washes, where the colors run together and blend, but they don't displace the underlying color. The *Runny Wet* variants, however, will run and move existing color as the new pigment travels. The Runny Wet brushes are useful if you want to add a darker wet-looking edge to the bottom of a cloud, for instance.

For all of the Runny Wash and Runny Wet brushes, the Wind Direction and Force settings determine the direction of the run and how far a wash will run, much like tipping your watercolor board when working in the field. To paint a Watercolor Runny wash that moves only a little, lower the Force setting.

While painting the clouds in the illustration on the left, we laid varied sky colors in using the Runny Wash Bristle and Runny Wet Camel. To soften some of the runny edges, we dotted in more color using the Diffuse Camel, applying color with short dabbing strokes. Then we painted the water with the Wash Camel and Fine Camel variants, again softening areas with the Diffuse Camel.

Adding spatter effects. With the Splatter Water variant, you can add dots of diffused color to your paintings. This is especially effective when painting foliage. Paint some wash areas using the Wash Camel or Wash Flat, and varied colors of green. Now choose the Splatter Water variant and a slightly different color. Paint a few dots of color; then change the color slightly in the Colors picker and add a few more diffused color dots, changing the size of the brush as you work.

Also, you can add varied, light speckles to your images (as we did in the image on the left), with the Eraser Salt variant of Watercolor. To follow a step-by-step technique similar to the one used for painting the orchid, turn to "Wet-into-Wet Watercolor" on page 82.

Wet-into-Wet Watercolor

Overview *Make a "pencil sketch"; loosely paint smooth washes with Watercolor brushes to build up varied color; add subtle wet-into-wet bristle marks; add details to the image and create a speckled texture using Salt.*

CHER THREINEN-PENDARVIS

Starting a new file for the African Violet painting

The pencil sketch drawn in Painter using the Grainy Cover Pencil variant of Pencils

AFRICAN VIOLET, A LOOSE WATERCOLOR STUDY, was painted from life using Painter and a Wacom Intuos pressure-sensitive tablet and stylus. Watercolor wet-into-wet techniques were used; then details and texture were added. *Wet-into-wet* is a traditional technique that can be simulated using Painter's Watercolor layers. Wet-into-wet is the most fluid way to apply color, as it involves keeping the paper wet while new color is applied, so that new colors blend with existing moist paint. With Watercolor layers, you can paint with Watercolor brushes that apply pigment that percolates and diffuses into the paper grain and paint washes that actually run and blend into existing wet paint, and you can paint transparent glazes. More texture effects are possible with Watercolor layers than with Digital Watercolor, which is described on pages 90–93.

1 Setting up and opening a new file. Begin by creating a new file with a white background (File, New). In the New dialog box, click the Image button. For a square format, set the Width and Height at 1500 x 1500 pixels. Click OK. (The brush sizes that you'll use will depend on the pixel size of the document.)

2 Making a pencil sketch on a new layer. Select a natural-looking grain (such as French Watercolor) by clicking the Paper Selector near the bottom of the Toolbox and choosing from the menu. Choose a dark gray color in the Colors picker and select

3a

Painting smooth washes using the Wash Camel variant

3b

An active Watercolor layer shown in the Layers palette. The sketch layer is also visible.

3c

Adding light, varied washes of color using the Wash Camel and Diffuse Camel variants

SETTING BRUSH TRACKING

It's a good idea to set up Brush Tracking before you begin a Watercolor session because it will increase expressiveness in Painter's brushes and make smoother strokes. With Brush Tracking you can customize how Painter interprets the input of your stylus, including parameters such as pressure and how quickly you make a brushstroke. You'll notice the more sensitive control of the Watercolor brushes, especially with brushes such as the Diffuse Camel and Fine Camel variants. From the Edit/Painter IX menu, choose Preferences, Brush Tracking, make a representative brushstroke in the window and then click OK.

Making a brushstroke in the Brush Tracking window

the Grainy Cover Pencil variant of Pencils (in the Brush Selector Bar) to draw your line sketch. Make a new layer by clicking the New Layer button on the Layers palette. Drawing your sketch on a new layer will give you the flexibility to adjust its opacity and composite method. We set up our blooming violet plant next to the computer and sketched from life.

3 Painting the first washes. The brush work in the *African Violet* study is fresh and loose. As you prepare to begin adding color, make a few practice brushstrokes. (You can always undo the brushstrokes by pressing Ctrl/⌘-Z, or you can delete your practice Watercolor layer by selecting it in the Layers palette and clicking the Delete button on the palette.)

Plan to work from light to dark as you add color washes to your painting. Choose a light color in the Colors picker (we chose a warm light green). In the Brush Selector Bar, choose the Wash Camel variant of Watercolor. (When you select a Watercolor brush and make a brushstroke on your image, Painter automatically creates a new Watercolor layer in the image.) When you apply a light, even pressure on your stylus, the Wash Camel allows you to lay in the wash areas smoothly. The slight bit of diffusion built into the brush will help the brushstrokes to blend subtly as you paint. When you make a new stroke, place it next to the previous stroke so that it barely overlaps. Try not to scrub with the brush or paint over areas too many times, unless you want to darken the area. Painter's Watercolor operates like traditional transparent Watercolor. Paint with strokes that follow the direction of the forms in your subject. Complete the lighter wash areas, leaving some of the "white of the paper" showing through for the highlights. If the paint seems to build up too fast, reduce the opacity of the brush using the Opacity slider in the Property Bar. (We used opacities between 10%–20% for the light washes on the flowers and leaves.)

4a

The violet study in progress showing the light and midtone washes

4b

Painting darker greens on the leaves to help focus more attention on the flowers. The sketch layer is viewed at 50% opacity in this example.

5

The soft runny washes on the leaves were painted with the Runny Wash variants of Watercolor. The sketch layer is hidden in this example.

4 Building up the midtones.

Using medium-value colors, begin to develop your midtones, painting lighter colors first and then adding darker tones to continue to develop the form. Keep your light source in mind and let your strokes follow the direction of the forms. To resize the brush or change its Opacity as you work, use the sliders on the Property Bar. We gradually built up deeper golden-yellows and greens, while keeping the brush work loose.

As we completed the midtones stage, we switched to the Dry Camel variant of Watercolor, which allowed us to add a little more brushstroke texture over some of the wash areas and at the ends of the strokes, while still allowing the new strokes to blend as wet-into-wet.

5 Painting wet-into-wet runny washes.

Painter offers dynamic brushes that allow you to emulate various traditional Watercolor *run* effects. For a smooth, runny wash that will not displace the underlying color, use one of the Runny Wash variants. Choose a slightly different color in the Colors picker and dab the new color onto areas with existing color. Using the Runny Wash Camel and Runny Wash Bristle, we applied brighter orange, pink and magenta colors (using short dabbing strokes) on the deeper colored areas of the flower lip. Then, we added deeper green colors to the leaves. The Runny Wash variants allowed the new color to mix with existing color without moving the existing color.

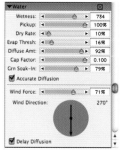

The default Runny Wet Bristle variant of Watercolor paints strokes that run vertically down the image and move existing color. The Dry Rate is set at 10%, allowing lots of time for the pant to run; the Wind Direction is set to 270°, and the Wind Force setting (71%) makes the washes drip a long way. The high Pickup rate allows the brushstrokes to move existing color. Notice that the Delay Diffusion check box is enabled for better performance.

6

Painting a soft, modulated background using the Diffuse Grainy Camel variant

7

The crisp detail on flower stamens painted with the Fine Camel variant, and the softened shadows on the petals painted with the Diffuse Camel variant

8

Sprinkling a little "salt" on the leaves and flower using the Eraser Salt variant of Watercolor

6 Painting the background. Using the Diffuse Grainy Camel variant to paint short, dabbed strokes of varied color, we added a soft, modulated background with darker values that would help to bring the subject forward in the composition.

7 Adding details. If you want very crisp details, it's a good idea to paint detail work on a separate layer, but in this case we stayed on the same Watercolor layer because we wanted to preserve the softer wet-into-wet look. Add crisper edges to areas that need definition by using a small Fine Camel variant (6–8 pixels). To reduce the Size of the Fine Camel variant, use the Size slider in the Property Bar. If the Fine Camel seems too saturated for your taste, lower the Opacity to about 20%, using the Opacity slider in the Property Bar. If you'd like softer edges, experiment with the Wash Camel and the Diffuse Camel variants, using a small size (about 6–8 pixels). For expressive strokes, vary the pressure on the stylus. To paint details, we used the Fine Camel variant to add curved brush strokes and to paint small areas of color on the interior of the flowers. We also added a little more color to the shaded areas under the flowers using the Runny Wash Camel. To break up some of the crisper strokes, we chose a light color in the Colors picker and then used the Diffuse Camel variant to dab and pull color out from the linear strokes that we had painted using the Fine Camel.

It's not possible to use a variant of the Erasers brush on a Watercolor layer, and you can't use a Watercolor Eraser or Bleach variant on the Canvas, or on an image layer. To softly remove color on a Watercolor layer, choose the Eraser Dry variant of Watercolor and choose white in the Colors picker. In the Layers palette, click on the name of the Watercolor layer you wish to edit and brush over the area you'd like to lighten. We used the Eraser Dry variant to brighten the highlights on the flower petals and the stamen.

8 Adding speckled texture. Finally, we added a light speckled texture using the Eraser Salt variant of Watercolor, in various sizes. To add bleached speckles on your image, choose the Eraser Salt variant and scrub the brush over the area you want to add speckles to. To keep a spontaneous hand-finished look, we retained the lower opacity version of the original sketch drawn with the Grainy Cover Pencil in the image. 🖌

Combining Wet-into-Wet and Glazing on Layers

Overview *Draw a tight pencil sketch; brush in soft wet-into-wet washes; paint glazes on separate layers; add texture and crisp details.*

1

The pencil sketch drawn using the 2B Pencil variant of Pencils

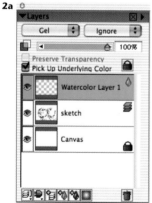

2a

The Layers section showing the "sketch" layer and the active new Watercolor layer

TWO COMMON TRADITIONAL WATERCOLOR techniques that can be simulated with Painter are *wet-into-wet* and *glazing*. Wet-into-wet creates a softer-edged look—the painting surface is kept wet as new color is applied, so new paint blends easily with old. Glazing involves applying transparent washes of watercolor; colors are usually built up in layers from light to dark.

Before beginning *Two Green Apples*, we arranged the apples in the natural light of a window near the computer, and chose a close-up view of our subject to emphasize subtle details. We began the painting with a tight pencil sketch in Painter and used transparent glazes to build layers of color and value, progressing from light to dark. As the painting progressed, we added more Watercolor layers so that we could edit the wet-into-wet brush work separately without disturbing underlying color.

1 Drawing a tight pencil sketch. Create a new file with a white background by choosing File, New. (Our image measured 1200 x 850 pixels.) Before beginning your sketch, choose an even-textured paper (such as French Watercolor or Basic Paper) from the Paper Selector (near the bottom of the Toolbox) and choose a dark gray in the Colors picker. Now select the 2B Pencil variant of Pencils from the Brush Selector Bar and begin sketching. While drawing, we carefully explored the shapes and forms of the apples and we established the light source. (Turn to "Sketching with Pencils" on page 70 to read more about working with Pencils in Painter.)

Because we planned to use the sketch as a guide, we wanted to be able to turn its visibility on and off and adjust its opacity as needed, so we decided to float the sketch onto a layer. To put your

2b

The background showing the in-progress wash painted with the Diffuse Bristle

3

The first very light washes

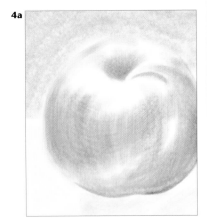

4a

The left apple, showing brushstrokes that wrap around its form

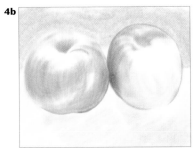

4b

The apples with light washes established and midtones in-progress

sketch onto a layer, choose Select, All (Ctrl/⌘-A), and Select, Float. To lower the opacity of the layer, click on the layer name in the Layers palette; then adjust the Opacity slider to about 25%. If the Layers palette is not open, choose Window, Show Layers. (For more information about layers, turn to Chapter 6, "Using Layers.")

2 Painting the background. When you choose a Watercolor brush and touch your stylus to the tablet, a Watercolor Layer will automatically appear in the Layers palette. You can choose to paint your entire painting using only one layer (which is beneficial if you want a natural wet-into-wet look). Or you can choose to paint different stages of the painting on separate layers as we did. When creating a tight illustration (such as the apples shown here), using several layers can give you better control over separate brush work, but some of the effect of overall wet-into-wet may be sacrificed.

When painting the background, we carefully painted around the shapes of the apples. Choose the Diffuse Bristle variant of Watercolor in the Brush Selector Bar. When you apply a light pressure on your stylus, the Diffuse Bristle will allow you to smoothly lay in soft-edged washes. The Diffuse Bristle incorporates diffusion, which helps overlapping brushstrokes to subtly blend. Try not to cover every inch of your background with color. Leaving areas of white will add texture and interest to your painting. (We left some white paper showing in the top areas of the painting.)

3 Painting the first light washes. Add a new Watercolor Layer by choosing New Watercolor Layer from the menu that pops out from the upper-right corner of the Layers palette. As you add color washes to your painting, plan to work from light to dark as much as you can. Choose a very light color in the Colors picker and use the Diffuse Bristle variant of Watercolor. Using the light color, block in large areas and begin to establish the roundness of the forms. Establish the cast shadows and foreground also by painting light washes.

4 Adding richer color and tonal values. For the deeper tones, add another new Watercolor Layer, as you did in step 3. Working on the new layer, build up medium-value colors, and then gradually add darker tones that will sculpt volume. Keep your light source in mind as you paint, and let the brushstrokes follow the direction of the forms. Resize the brush, or change its Opacity as needed using the sliders on the Property Bar. Remember to preserve the white areas that will be kept as bright highlights. To render the volume of the left apple, we painted curved vertical strokes in the shadowed areas. Then we added a few curved horizontal brushstrokes. We also used medium tones of brown to begin to paint the stems.

4c

The midtones and some darker tones in the shadows

5

The speckled texture is visible in this detail of the two apples

6

The fine details on the apple stems and their cast shadows added

7a

Setting up the custom two-point gradient

7b

In this example, the painted blue background layer is hidden. The gradient is applied to the Canvas (left); the texture is applied (right).

5 Adding subtle wet-into-wet texture. Working on the Watercolor layer that contains the midtones, we used a grain-sensitive brush to paint subtle texture in the shadow areas of the apples. The Diffuse Grainy Camel paints soft-edged washes while bringing out the texture chosen in the Paper Selector. Choose the Diffuse Grainy Camel. Now sample color from the image by pressing the Alt/Option key to temporarily switch from the Brush to the Dropper; then paint using short dabbing strokes to "bleed" color variation and subtle values into the shadows. We sampled color several times while we painted over the shadow areas. For the light-colored speckles on the apples, we used a small Splatter Water variant of Watercolor.

6 Painting details. To keep detail crisp, add a separate layer for your detail work (as described in step 3). In areas that need more definition, paint crisper edges using a small Fine Camel brush (4–5 pixels). If the Fine Camel seems too saturated for your taste, lower its Opacity to about 20% using the slider in the Property Bar. For more subtle edge effects, try experimenting with the Soft Camel and the Diffuse Camel variants, using a small size (about 6–8 pixels). To complete the study, we used the Fine Camel variant to darken the edges of the shadows under the apples.

7 Adding a gradient with Watercolor texture. Our painting needed more depth. To quickly add deeper color to the image background, as detailed below, we filled the Canvas with a blue-to-white gradient, then we floated it to a Watercolor Layer and applied a Watercolor texture effect.

To fill the Canvas with a gradient, target the Canvas by clicking on its name in the Layers palette. Choose the Dropper and click on a rich blue in the background area behind the apples. Open the Gradients palette by choosing Window, Library Palettes, Show Gradients and choose Two-Point from the resource list menu. To edit the gradient so that the blue is concentrated near the top of the image, with white below, choose Edit Gradient from the menu that pops out from the right side of the Gradients palette bar. In the Edit Gradient dialog box, click on the colored ramp to add another color control point where you'd like it. With the new control point active, choose white in the Colors picker. Click OK. For more information about gradients turn to Chapter 2, "The Power of Color." In the Gradients section, drag the Gradient Ring to position the Gradient Preview with the blue at the top. When the gradient is the way you like it, choose Effects, Fill, Fill with Gradient.

To give the gradient on the Canvas a Watercolor texture, lift it to a Watercolor layer by choosing Lift Canvas to Watercolor Layer from the menu on the right side of the Layers palette. You can now apply a Watercolor-like texture to the new layer that is based

7c

Choosing Wet Entire Watercolor Layer from the Layers palette menu

8a

Blocking in the cast shadows using the Wash Bristle

8b

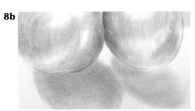

The in-progress cast shadows showing some of the brush work added with the Grainy Wash Bristle

8c

The final cast shadows after the Wet Entire Watercolor Layer effect was applied

on the characteristics of the Watercolor brush chosen in the Brushes palette. If the brush chosen is texture-sensitive, the paper texture chosen in the Paper Selector will also contribute to the effect. Select the Grainy Wash Camel variant. With the new Watercolor layer active, choose Wet Entire Watercolor Layer from the menu on the right side of the Layers palette bar.

8 Completing the cast shadows. We carefully studied the subtle graduated tones in the cast shadows created by the light from the window. In areas where they overlapped, darker-toned curved shapes were created. The shadows gradually became lighter as they progressed toward the foreground.

Working on a new Watercolor Layer so that we could edit the shadows separately from the rest of the image, we gradually developed the deeper tones in the cast shadows as follows: Add a new Watercolor Layer using the process in step 3. Choose the Wash Bristle variant and a blue-gray color in the Colors picker, which will work well with the blue you've chosen for your background. Block in the basics shapes, then to add more texture in the deeper-colored areas, switch to the Grainy Wash Bristle and gradually add to the deeper tones.

To melt the new work into the old, wet the cast shadow layer: With the Grainy Wash Bristle still selected, choose Wet Entire Watercolor Layer from the menu on the right side of the Layers palette bar.

LIFTING ART ON THE CANVAS TO A WATERCOLOR LAYER

With Painter's Watercolor technology, any existing artwork or photograph on the Canvas layer can be turned into Watercolor, as follows:

1 Open an image that contains artwork on the Canvas layer. From the pop-out menu on the right side of the Layers palette bar, choose Lift Canvas to Watercolor Layer.

2 Choose a texture in the Paper Selector. Some brushes (such as the Grainy Wash variants) are grain-sensitive and apply nice texture effects.

3 In the Brush Selector Bar, choose a Watercolor brush with characteristics you'd like to apply to your image.

4 Choose Wet Entire Watercolor Layer from the pop-out menu on the right side of the Layers palette, and watch as Painter applies Watercolor effects to your image! In the Layers palette, when the animated water drop to the right of the Watercolor layer name stops dripping, the effect is complete.

After lifting this pastel drawing to a Watercolor Layer, we added to the texture on the image by using the Grainy Wash Camel variant of Watercolor to "wet" the Watercolor Layer.

Painting with Digital Watercolor

Overview *Scan a pencil sketch; use it as a guide while painting contours using a brush; apply colored washes to the sketch with brushes; add final highlight detail to the dried image with an Eraser.*

CHER THREINEN-PENDARVIS

The sketch made using pencils and paper

The contours painted using the Pointed Simple Water variant

Light washes painted with the New Simple Water variant

WITH PAINTER'S DIGITAL WATERCOLOR, you can paint wet-into-wet and add smooth glazes of thin transparent color on the Canvas or on a standard layer. For wet-into-wet, the painting surface is kept wet as new color is applied, so new paint blends easily with existing paint. The process of layering washes using Digital Watercolor is similar to using Painter's Watercolor layers (covered on pages 78–89). The pigment colors are usually built up in layers from light to dark, but the effects are not as realistic as those that can be achieved with Painter's special Watercolor media layers. Digital Watercolor is simpler and quicker to apply, and thus it's ideal for quick studies.

1 Sketching and scanning. We began *Aloe Medusa*, one in a series of plant studies, by sketching with conventional pencils in our sketchbook. We carefully observed the subject while making the drawing, and added such details as the shadow lines along the edges of the leaves. Then we scanned the pencil drawing at 300 ppi, a resolution suitable for offset printing.

2 Setting up and painting contours. Because we planned to remove the pencil sketch after the painting was roughed out, we painted a contour drawing using a color that would appear in the final image. The contours would help to define the edges of some of the forms in the study. Before beginning to paint, put your scanned sketch on a layer by choosing Select, All (Ctrl/⌘-A) and Select, Float. So the white areas in the sketch will appear transparent, set the Composite Method for this layer to Multiply in the Layers palette. Now target the Canvas by clicking on its name in the Layers palette. Choose a color that will appear in the light-to-midtone areas of your painting (we chose a rich golden color) and select the Pointed Simple Water variant of Digital Watercolor in the Brush Selector Bar. When you paint using a Digital Watercolor brush, the layer's Composite Method will automatically change from

Building up tones using slightly darker washes

Painting soft, diffused washes behind the leaves for a background

Painting crisper washes on the leaves and beginning to build up the forms

Adding deeper tones to the interior of the aloe using the New Simple Water variant

Adding detail to the edges of the leaves

Default to Gel to give the look of transparent washes. Sketch the contours with the brush expressively, applying more pressure to your stylus when you want a thicker line and less for a thinner line. When wet-into-wet washes are added in the next step, the colors will mix at the edges of the contour lines.

3 Adding the first washes. We used highlight colors for the first washes. Choose very light colors and block in the large areas with the New Simple Water variant of the Digital Watercolor. (This brush will allow you to add color and will subtly smear it into existing pigment.) After the lightest washes are laid in, use the New Simple Water variant to add a slightly darker series of washes with more detail, as we did before developing the midtones in the next step. We also began to layer deeper blues for the background behind the leaves. We pulled the strokes out from the center of the plant to accentuate the focal point. (At this point, we removed the pencil sketch by selecting its name in the Layers palette and clicking the Delete button at the bottom of the Layers palette.) To paint a soft, diffused background, choose the Coarse Water brush and use light pressure on your stylus as you apply the strokes to gradually build up the deeper tones. For a smoother effect, try the Soft Diffused Brush.

4 Building form and midtone values. Choose medium-value colors and develop your midtones, applying lighter colors first, and then darker ones to create form. Keep your light source in mind and let your strokes follow the direction of the forms. We added the larger intermediate-value shapes and some of the shadows. Then we added deeper greens and teals to the interior of the aloe to enhance the focal point, while remembering to leave areas of the "paper" white to preserve the highlights.

5 Adding texture, details and blending. Next, we used the Coarse Mop Brush (Digital Watercolor) to paint soft, striated strokes onto the background. To softly blend areas of the background, we used a lower-opacity New Simple Water variant. After completing the blending, we dried the painting by choosing Dry Digital Watercolor from the pop-up menu on the right side of the Layers palette. Then we used a small Pointed Simple Water variant to brighten the green and golden yellow details on the interior of the aloe. We added linear details to the leaves and deepened shadows, adjusting the Opacity and Size of the brush in the Property Bar as we worked. We worked carefully to develop subtle layers of color and contrast. To bring the aloe forward more in the composition, we used the New Simple Water variant to paint loose strokes of deeper blues behind the plant. Then we diffused the paint on the layer by choosing Diffuse Digital Watercolor from the pop-up menu on the Layers palette. To finish, we sharpened areas of the painting that needed definition using a tiny Pointed Simple Water brush. Finally, we defined the highlights along the edges of the leaves with a tiny Pointed Eraser variant of the Erasers.

Coloring a Drawing Using Digital Watercolor

Overview *Create a drawing using traditional pencils and paper; scan the drawing; put the drawing on a layer; use Painter's Digital Watercolor brushes to hand-color the drawing.*

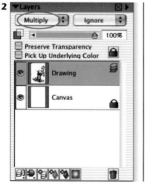

The scanned drawing along with Benioff's custom color set

The drawing on a layer with its Composite Method set to Multiply in the Layers palette

CAROL BENIOFF

CAROL BENIOFF TAKES ADVANTAGE of the quick and fluid qualities of the Digital Watercolor brushes in *On the Beach*, one of a continuing series of prints and drawings using shoes as the motif.

1 Preparing to paint. Benioff drew the two shoes on the beach with a 2B pencil on acid-free bristol board. Then she scanned the drawing at 300 pixels-per-inch and opened the image in Painter. Next, she opened one of her custom color sets by choosing Window, Show Color Sets, clicking on the right arrow of the Color Set palette and choosing Open Color Set. For the paper texture, Benioff chose Thick Handmade Paper from the Paper Selector near the bottom of the Toolbox.

2 Putting the drawing on a layer. After she opened her scanned pencil drawing, Benioff selected the entire image (Select, All), and then put the drawing onto a layer by choosing Select,

For painting the sky, Benioff chose the variants Wash Brush, Soft Broad Brush, Soft Round Blender and the Pure Water Brush.

Using short quick strokes, Benioff painted the shoe using the Broad Brush, Fine Tip Water and Fine Mop Brush variants of Digital Watercolor.

Benioff mixed colors in the Mixer palette.

Float. To make the white areas of the drawing appear transparent in the next step, she set the Composite Method for the layer to Multiply in the Layers palette. Then she clicked on the Canvas in the Layers Palette to make it active so she could begin her painting.

3 Painting the sky and the beach. To add the first washes of color, she chose the Brush Tool in the Toolbox and chose the Wash Brush variant of Digital Watercolor in the Brush Selector Bar. Using large sweeping strokes she began painting the sky, resizing the brush from 50 to 90 pixels in the Property Bar as she worked. She also used the Soft Broad Brush sized to 40 pixels, the Soft Round Blender with its Wet Fringe set to 0% in the Property Bar (with its Size ranging from 40 to 70 pixels) and the Pure Water Brush sized to 40 pixels. These combinations of brushes gave her the smooth translucent look that she wanted. As she was painting, she chose varying hues of blues, greens, ochres and pinks from her custom Color Set.

4 Painting the shoes. For the shoes, Benioff wanted to add the textured brushstrokes of more intense color. So she chose the Broad Water Brush and set its Wet Fringe to 0% in the Property Bar. She likes this brush's capability to lay down color and blend with underlying colors. She painted with short, quick strokes, resizing the brush from 9 to 15 pixels and changing its percentage of Opacity in the Property Bar. For fine detail in the image, Benioff used the Fine Tip brush with its Opacity set to 6%. She selected the Fine Mop brush to add a more watery feel.

5 Mixing colors. When Benioff's Color Set did not have the color she wanted, she switched over to the Color Mixer palette (Window, Show Mixer). With her current color selected she chose the Apply Color tool in the Mixer palette, painted a stroke, and then selected another color from her custom Color Set and mixed them on the palette. Clicking on the Sample Color tool in the Color Mixer palette, she then could select a new color from her mix. Another option she uses is the Eye Dropper from the Toolbox (the Alt/Option key) to pick up newly mixed colors in the image.

The final watercolor image without the pencil drawing layer

6 The final touches. For the last washes of translucent color in the figure, beach and sky, she used the Wash Brush with its Opacity turned down to 2%.

Painting with Acrylics

Overview *Paint a rough sketch; build up form and color; enrich the final colors with glazing.*

The beginning sketch with the Dry Brush

Using and adjusting a custom Color Set to define the color palette

The Wet Soft Acrylic brush both paints and blends the colors

CAROL BENIOFF

PAINTING THIS *PORTRAIT OF HEINZ*, Carol Benioff was pleased to be able to use the Acrylics brushes straight out of Painter's box. She used a direct method of painting on the canvas with no preliminary drawings. This enabled her to finish the portrait in one sitting, even though Heinz has difficulty sitting still for long.

1 Roughing out the painting. Create a new document with a white background color. (Benioff created a 7 x 9-inch image at 300 pixels-per-inch.) Starting with the Dry Brush 10 variant of Acrylics, Benioff began to draw out the shapes using a neutral green. Then, she switched to the Wet Acrylic 20 variant, varying the size from 10 up to 62 pixels in the Property Bar as she roughly laid out the shapes and colors.

2 Selecting the colors. To ensure she is using colors that will print the way she wants them, Benioff makes her own custom Color Sets. (For information about making a Color Set that includes printable colors, see Chapter 13.) From the start, she

4

Adding depth and detail with the Dry Brush and Wet Acrylic variants

5a

The final painting before the translucent glazes of color were added

5b

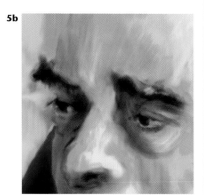

Detail of the face before glazing

opened her own Color Set by choosing Window, Color Palettes, Show Color Set. Then she clicked on the right arrow of the Color Sets palette and selected Open Color Set. To quickly modify the colors as she painted, she also opened the Color Info palette, where you can adjust the current selected color with RGB sliders.

3 Working with the paint. Benioff continued to work with a combination of Dry Brush and Wet Acrylic variants. She selected soft hues of blue so the back wall would sit behind Heinz's face and the back of the chair. She used the Wet Soft Acrylic brush in various sizes to push and smear the paint to a greater degree. She found that Dry Brush variants worked best for the details, and also provided her with the ability to scumble. To scumble, use a light pressure on the stylus and brush lightly across the peaks of the paper texture. With scumbling, colors blend optically and texture is added.

4 Defining form. Switching between the Dry Brush and the Wet Acrylic brush, she built up the form with contrasting colors both in the highlights and shadows. Benioff helps keep the painting lively with the push and pull of contrasting colors, strong lights and darks and loosely drawn paint strokes.

5 Tying it all together. With the three variants of the Acrylic brushes Benioff was able to quickly complete her painting. She enlarged a Wet Acrylic variant to more than 60 to do more work on the background. She deepened the shadows, creating more contrast. Benioff then moved in close and painted with the smaller Wet Acrylic and Dry Brush, bringing out the details of the face. She then concentrated on the lights and darks of the shirt to create the illusion of it draping around his neck.

6 Glazing to add richness and depth. Benioff loves the depth and richness that happens with laying thin washes of translucent color over an existing painting. This technique, called

6

Detail of the face after multiple glazes of blues and deep purple were applied

glazing, is one that she has used in traditional mediums and in most of the work that she has created with Painter. The brush category of Acrylics comes with its own built-in glazing variants called Glazing Acrylic. She used these variants in varying sizes up to 60 to glaze in the shadows, adding richness to the color and helping the shadows recede.

Painting with Gouache

Overview *Create a finely grained surface; begin with a scanned sketch; sculpt highlights and details using Oils, Gouache and Impasto variants; pull color with a Palette Knife.*

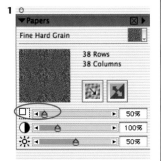

Scaling the Fine Hard Grain texture to 50%

Stahl's sketch drawn with the Smooth Ink Pen variant

ARTIST NANCY STAHL HAS WORKED WITH TRADITIONAL gouache on illustration board since 1976. When she began to work with the computer, her clients would accept her digital art only if the quality matched her conventional style. After much experimentation with Painter's brushes and surfaces, she has been able to fully re-create the effects in her traditional work, evident in *Sappi Portrait*, above.

1 Emulating a traditional gouache surface. Stahl's favorite traditional gouache support is a Strathmore kid finish illustration board. The kid finish is soft and allows for a smooth application of paint. To create a surface for gouache similar to Stahl's, begin by choosing Window, Library Palettes, Show Papers to open the Papers palette. Choose the Fine Hard Grain texture. To make the

3a

Sculpting the forms of the eye and brow area using the Camelhair Medium

3b

The completed color study

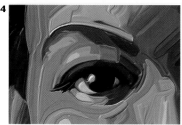

4

The Impasto painting of the eye and brow area is shown in this example

5

Using a tiny Palette Knife (Impasto) to pull color in the hair and background

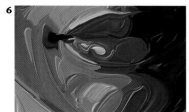

6

Using the Palette Knife (Impasto) to add linear accents and paint texture on the lips and chin

surface even smoother, scale it to 50%. This finely textured surface is most noticeable when used for painting the hair in step 3.

2 Beginning with sketches. Stahl began by using traditional pencils and paper to draw a black-and-white study to establish the composition and work out values.

In Painter, she created a new file that measured approximately 1200 x 1900 pixels. Stahl drew an expressive sketch with the Smooth Ink Pen variant of Pens. Begin by creating a new file similar to the size of Stahl's, select the Smooth Ink Pen variant and set the Size to 4.0 in the Property Bar. Choose a dark color and begin sketching.

3 Painting teardrop shapes. For the color study, Stahl used two brushes, a fast, sensitive brush with grainy edges to rough in color (the Broad Cover Brush 40 variant of Gouache sized to 25 pixels) and a modified Round Camelhair variant, to paint teardrop shapes suggesting highlights in the hair and to sculpt the facial features. The controls needed to build Stahl's modified Round Camelhair brush are located in the Property Bar.

In the Brush Selector Bar, choose the Round Camelhair variant, and in the Property Bar, set Feature to 1.3. (Lowering the Feature setting "tightens" the bristles in the brush, giving the strokes a smoother, crisper edge with fewer bristle marks, similar to using a soft traditional brush loaded with paint on a smooth surface.) In the Property Bar, set Resat to 65% and Bleed to 8% (increasing the Resat setting allows the brush to paint with more of the current color, with less mixing of colors on the image canvas). From the Brush Selector Bar's triangle pop-up menu, choose Save Variant, name your variant (Stahl named hers Camelhair Medium) and click OK. Stahl varied the size of her brush while she worked.

4 Building up thick paint. For the look of thicker paint, Stahl used Impasto brushes. To quickly make a copy of her color study, she chose File, Clone. She saved the clone image using a new name, to preserve the color study, then she painted directly over the copy of the color study using various Impasto brushes, including the Opaque Flat and Round Camelhair. When she wanted to reveal bristle marks, she used the Opaque Bristle Spray (Impasto). To pull color with a flat-sided tool that would give the features a sculpted look, she used a small Palette Knife variant (Impasto).

5 Pulling and blending. Stahl used varying sizes of the Palette Knife variant of Impasto to blend and pull colors in the background and on the shoulders. To paint curls in the hair and achieve an oily look, she used the Distorto variant of Impasto.

6 Finishing touches. To finish, Stahl added linear accents on the model's eyes, lips, nose and chin using a small Palette Knife (Impasto) and she painted a few thick bristle marks on the background and hair using Opaque Bristle Spray (Impasto).

A Painter Artists' Oils Primer

Overview *Here you'll find the basics for painting with the Artists' Oils medium and brushes.*

CHER THREINEN-PENDARVIS

The fluid blending of wet Artists' Oils paint can be seen in this detail of the in-progress trees and sky.

The Mixer palette with the Sample Multiple Colors tool chosen, ready to pick up paint and apply it to an image

WITH THE REVOLUTIONARY ARTISTS' OILS medium and brushes in Painter IX, you can paint expressive, gestural strokes. Like traditional oils, Artists' Oils paint is malleable and viscous. As you paint, the brush will run out of pigment just like a traditional brush. When you paint a new stroke, you can mix the new paint with the existing paint on the canvas just as you can with conventional media.

Quiet Moment at Schwetzingen (above) was painted with the Dry Brush, Blender Brush and Blender Palette Knife variants of Artists' Oils. Before you start an Artists' Oils painting of your own, reading this Primer will help you to achieve the results you desire.

The Artists' Oils and the Mixer. The Artists' Oils work in conjunction with the Mixer (Window, Color Palettes, Show Mixer). You can load a brush (the Dry Brush, for instance) with colors from the Mixer and paint with them. You can blend colors in the Mixer palette and apply the multi-colored mix directly to your painting. The Sample Multiple Colors tool allows you to sample a color mix, load your brush and then apply the mix to your image. (This feature works only with the Artists' Oils at this time.) To learn more, see the "Artists' Oils and Mixer" tip on page 102.

Controlling the Artists' Oils. When you choose an Artists' Oils brush, the Canvas is filled with oil, making it very easy to lay down color and blend. You can choose the amount of paint and oil that you load into a brush, and how the new paint interacts with the existing paint. The most important settings for the Artists' Oils are

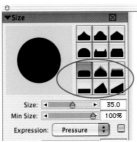

The six new Artists' Oils Brush Tip profiles are located in the Size window. The top three work best with the Artists' Oils brushes; the bottom three work best with the Artists' Oils Palette Knife variants.

Strokes painted using the Tapered Oils variant of Artists' Oils. This variant uses the Pointed Rake Brush Tip Profile. Leaning the stylus paints a more pointed stroke.

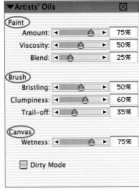

The Artists' Oils section of Brush Controls

in the Property Bar and in the Brush Controls. They are the General, Size and Artists' Oils sections. (You will find these same controls in the Stroke Designer window of the Brush Creator.)

In the General section of the Brush Controls, the Artists' Oils dab type is displayed in the Dab Type pop-up menu. A dab type determines the character of the brush. You'll find more information about dab types in Chapter 4, "Building Brushes," on page 153.

In the Size section of the Brush Controls, you'll find the six new *Artists' Oils Brush Tip Profiles* that were designed specifically to work with the Artists' Oils. The Soft Round, Pointed Rake Profile and Flat Rake Profile work best with the brushes (the Dry Brush and Impasto Oil, for instance), and the Flat Profile, Chisel Profile and Wedge Profile were built for the Artists' Oils palette knives (such as Blender Palette Knife and Dry Palette Knife). Depending on how you hold the stylus, the beginning of a stroke will change. Hold the stylus vertically and the start of the stroke will be flatter. Hold the stylus at an angle, and the start of the stroke will reflect the brush tip profile. The effect is subtle.

The Artists' Oils window in Brush Controls is organized into the Paint, Brush and Canvas areas. The seven sliders in the Artists' Oils section work in conjunction with each other to create the character of the oily brushstrokes. These controls are complex and interdependent. Dig in and try out the Artists' Oils variants, while keeping an eye on the controls in the Artists' Oils section.

In the Paint area, the *Amount* slider controls the amount of oil that is loaded when you make each new stroke. The *Viscosity* slider allows you to control the flow of the paint through the brush and how fast the brush will run out of paint. The *Blend* slider controls how easily new strokes will mix with the existing paint.

In the Brush area, the *Bristling* slider allows you to design how subtle or prominent the bristles look. This pertains to both the head and tail of the stroke. The *Clumpiness* slider allows you to

Strokes painted with the Dry Brush (top) and custom Smooth Dry Brush (bottom)

Strokes painted with the Clumpy Brush (top). For more subtle striations (bottom), adjust the Clumpiness and Blend sliders.

Strokes painted with the Oily Bristle and blended with the Grainy Blender

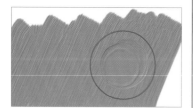

Thick strokes painted with the Wet Oily Impasto. Notice the excavated paint.

Strokes painted with the Dry Clumpy Impasto brush. Notice the graininess in the brush trails.

adjust the randomness of the brush hairs and to make them fine or coarse. For a good example of a clumpy brush, check out the Dry Clumpy Impasto variant. With the *Trail-off* slider, you can adjust the length of the brush trail.

In the Canvas area, you'll see the *Wetness* slider. With the Wetness slider, you can adjust the Wetness of the paint on the Canvas (or layer) and how this paint interacts with new strokes that you apply.

The *Dirty Mode* allows you to intermix colors as you pick them up from the Mixer and apply them to your image. When you choose a new color, you'll notice that some of the previous color remains in the brush.

CANVAS VERSUS LAYERS

When you choose an Artists' Oil brush, the Canvas is loaded with oil. The oil on the Canvas makes it easier to blend between colors. When painting on a layer, the oil exists only where you apply Artists' Oils brushstrokes.

WORKING WITH THE ARTISTS' OILS BRUSHES

Here are some suggestions for how to paint using the Artists' Oils brushes. Even if you're familiar with Painter's other brushes, try out these ideas and experiment with all of the Artists' Oils variants.

Making smooth strokes. Brushes with low Bristling and Clumpiness settings will allow you to paint strokes with smooth, soft beginnings, with less striated tones. Sample a single color from the Mixer using the Sample Color tool (not the Sample Multiple Colors tool) and paint a stroke with the Dry Brush variant. To make it smoother, in the Artists' Oils window, reduce the Bristling to 0 and the Clumpiness to 0.

Painting striated strokes. Brushes with a high Clumpiness setting will paint strokes with variation in color and value. Experiment with the Clumpy Brush. For more subtle striations, decrease the Clumpiness setting to 20% and reduce the Blend setting to 10%.

Mixing color with blender brushes. Any Artists' Oils variant with Blender in its name will allow you to blend as you lay down new paint, just like a brush loaded with very wet paint. Choose the Grainy Blender and use light pressure on your stylus to make strokes that pull color up, blending while revealing the grain.

Artists' Oils thick paint. The Artists' Oils Impasto brushes paint strokes of thick paint with realistic highlights and shadows. Choose the Wet Oily Impasto brush. Using a light pressure on your stylus, and lay down several strokes on top of one another to build up thick paint. Then use heavy pressure to dig into the existing paint. You can adjust the lighting in the Canvas, Surface Lighting menu. To adjust Impasto settings, use the Impasto section of Brush Controls. (To learn more about working with Impasto, see "A Painter Impasto Primer" on page 123.)

Painting with the Artists' Oils

Overview *Plan a composition; build a color palette using the Mixer; use the Artists' Oils to create a colorful underpainting; sculpt forms; paint glazes to build richer color and values; paint details.*

CHER THREINEN-PENDARVIS

1a

The conventional pencil sketch

1b

The sketch on a layer, with the Composite Method set to Multiply

Agaves on the Edge, Summer is one in a series of seascapes of the spectacular cliffs in San Diego, California. The inspiration for this painting was a bright sunny morning on a day when there was a brisk wind. To begin the painting, we made conventional sketches on location in a sketchbook. Back at the studio, we assembled the sketches and used them for reference as we developed the painting by using the Artists' Oils medium in Painter.

1 Sketching and planning the composition. Observe your subject and decide where your focal point will be. After choosing the viewpoint, we made composition sketches of the landforms and lighting in pencil and pastel. We also made a more detailed drawing of a few of the plants in our sketchbook.

Back at the studio, we scanned the composition pencil sketch at full size, at 300 ppi and saved it as a TIFF file. (The scan of the composition sketch measured 2500 x 2700 pixels.)

Open your sketch in Painter, and for added flexibility, cut it to a layer by choosing Select, All and Select, Float. To make the white areas of the layer appear transparent, set the Composite Method to Multiply in the Layers palette. Then, to stay organized, name your layers (we named our layer "sketch"). It's a good idea to save your working file in RIFF format under a new name so

2

The Mixer palette with the basic colors. The Brush tool is chosen.

3a

Using large brushes to lay in the basic shapes and structure. The sketch layer is hidden in the example.

3b

Detail of the blocked-in cliffs. The sketch layer is hidden in the image.

that your original sketch is not accidentally replaced. RIFF format preserves media that is native to Painter—such as the Artists' Oils—which you'll be using later in the development of your painting.

2 Mixing the base colors.

For the painting, we used the Mixer palette to create a color palette based on the colors in nature, but more saturated.

If the Mixer is not open, choose Window, Color Palettes, Show Mixer. Apply color with the Add Color tool (the brush) at the bottom of the Mixer. You can blend between colors using the Mix Color tool (the palette knife). Just like an artist's palette, you can pick up color from the Mixer Pad with the Sample Color tool (Eyedropper in the Mixer palette) and then use the color and brushes to apply the paint to your image.

3 Making an underpainting.

We used large brushes to create an underpainting to work out the basic values and colors in the composition. While referring to location sketches, we blocked in simple colored shapes, just as we would when painting on location using watercolor, acrylics or oil paint.

Working on layers will allow you to enjoy added flexibility as you develop your painting. To add a new layer, click the New Layer button on the bottom of the Layers palette. With the new layer selected, begin by blocking in the darker values using broad brushstrokes. Don't focus on the details at this stage. Use your sketch as a guide, but develop the shapes in your scene expressively, without worrying about staying within the lines of your drawing.

THE ARTISTS' OILS AND MIXER

The Mixer palette works in conjunction with the Artists' Oils. With the Artists' Oils, you can load your brush with multiple colors from the Mixer and apply them to your image. If the Mixer is not open, choose Window, Color Palettes, Show Mixer. To apply color to the Mixer, you can choose a color from the Colors picker or from the color wells at the top of the Mixer, or you can sample color from an image using the Dropper tool from the Mixer. Apply color using the Add Color tool (the brush, second from the left at the bottom of the Mixer Pad). You can blend between colors using the Mix Color tool (the palette knife). Just like an artist's palette, you can pick up color from the Mixer using the Sample Color tool (Eyedropper in the Mixer) and then use brushes to apply the paint to your image.

The Sample Multiple Color tool (the eyedropper in a circle) works in conjunction with Artists' Oils (but not with other brushes at this time) to allow you to load your brush with more than one color and then apply it to your image.

Using the Sample Multiple Colors tool

3c

Establishing the light on the forms

4a

Adding more color to the foreground

4b

Pulling color on the cliff face using the Wet Oily Palette Knife

5a

Dabbing with short strokes to sculpt the cliffs

As we began to apply color on the new layer using the Oily Bristle variant of the Artists' Oils, we focused on the design of the landscape and the natural light. We laid in the darker values first to establish the light on the forms—the purple-gray shadows at the base of the cliffs and the darker browns on the cliff faces. Then, we roughed in the foliage by using loose strokes of warm greens, golds, oranges and browns. For the ocean, we painted cool turquoise blues, and we used warmer blues in the sky.

When your composition is established, delete the sketch layer from the file by selecting it and pressing the Delete (trash can) button on the Layers palette. When your underpainting is complete, save the file.

4 Refining the color study. Next, we added more complex color areas on another new layer. This way, we could adjust the opacity or the Composite Method if we chose to, or remove the information on the layer and start over without harming the underpainting below.

Click the New Layer button to add a new layer to your image and enable the Pick Up Underlying Color button on the Layers palette. This will allow you to pick up color from the underlying layer when you work with brushes such as the Blender Brush or Oily Blender Brush, that blend and smear color. Switching between the Blender Brush and the Oily Bristle variants, we painted, pulled and blended colors, rendering the forms using expressive strokes.

When you want to move and blend paint without applying more color, switch to the Wet Oily Palette Knife variant of Artists Oils. To move small areas of paint, we reduced the size of the Wet Oily Palette Knife to about 9–12 pixels. The palette knife work is most visible on the broad cliff faces. When you are happy with your color study, save your file—including its layers—in RIFF format.

5 Sculpting forms and building more complex color. At this point, we wanted to take advantage of the oilier feel of the Artists' Oils medium on the Canvas, so we dropped all of the layers to the Canvas and then saved a new version of the file with a new name. To drop your layers to the Canvas, choose Drop All from the Layers palette menu. As we sculpted and refined the forms of the landscape, we worked new color into existing color.

For the foreground grass, we used the Sample Multiple Color tool to pick up mixtures of green and gold colors from the Mixer palette and loosely painted the grass using short, curved strokes.

When you choose an Artists' Oils brush (such as the Oily Bristle) and begin to paint on the Canvas layer, the Canvas will be loaded with the Artists' Oil medium, and you will notice an oily feel that allows you to effortlessly blend paint. The brush will run out of paint if you attempt to paint a long stroke. For best results, paint using short strokes to keep the brush loaded with paint. If you paint on a layer, the oil will exist only where you have applied Artists' Oil brushstrokes. Additionally, when painting on a layer, it will take longer for a brush to run out of paint.

5b

Refining the foreground cliff forms

6a

Painting the crevices in the foreground cliffs and finessing the highlights and shadows

6b

Details of the loosely painted foreground plants and grass, and the reflected light painted on the lower cliff face

6 Finessing the foreground. Then, we added more color interest and light to the cliffs using lighter reddish browns and purples that were based on the colors from the Mixer. To bring the foreground cliff into clearer focus, we used a tiny Wet Oily Palette Knife to sharpen some of the edges on the cliff tops and define the smaller crevices on the cliffs. To help the distant cliffs recede, we mixed a light blue-gray and used a low-opacity Oily Bristle brush to apply a glaze of the lighter colored paint.

To refine the agave plant forms, we defined the exterior shapes of the leaves, and then we used tints and shades of the same color to model the highlights and shadows. We also used the Dry Bristle variant of Artists' Oils to add accent color to the leaf edges. Next, we switched to the Wet Oily Palette Knife and pulled and blended color, making sure to let our strokes follow the forms of the leaves.

7 Painting glazes and final details. We wanted to paint the choppy, active ocean that we remembered on the windy day. So when adding more color to the water, we chose the Wet Oily Bristle. Starting with a medium value blue that had a little green in it for the turquoise water, we painted short, curved strokes. Then, we added white to mix lighter tints and added darker blues to create shades of the color, and again painted short, curved strokes.

If you want to paint a calmer sea, use the Wet Oily Bristle to paint longer brushstrokes and blend them to create a smoother surface, still varying the color for interest. To smooth the transitions between the colors in the water, use the Blender Brush or the Wet Oily Palette Knife.

As a last step, we zoomed in to 100% and took a closer look at the brush work. Then, we used the Dry Bristle brush to add small areas of warmer color to the foreground water and beach. 🖌

7

The glazes of paint on the water and the subtle color transitions on the beach

Illustrating with the Artists' Oils

Overview *Scan a rough pencil sketch for the template; fill the canvas with a colored ground; build color and form with the Artists' Oils brushes; use the Snap-to-Path feature when painting the frame; add paper texture and lighting.*

CAROL BENIOFF

The scan of the rough sketch that Benioff used as a template

Benioff filled the canvas by using the Rectangle Selection tool and the Paint Bucket.

WHEN DEVELOPING AN IMAGE for her ongoing series *The Price of Silence,* Carol Benioff maximized the fluid capabilities of the Artists' Oils. Because she planned to combine the image with an intaglio print or use it as part of another illustration, she kept her Painter composition simple and the background open. (To read about Benioff's creative printmaking process turn to "Combining Digital and Intaglio Printmaking" on page 424 in Chapter 13.

1 Setting up. To begin, Benioff scanned a rough sketch of her image and opened it in Painter. She selected the image (Select, All), lifted the drawing to a new layer by choosing Select, Float and then she set the Composite Method to Multiply in the Layers palette. Next, she created a custom color set from a scan of one of her paintings. (See "Capturing a Color Set" on page 44 for how to create a Color Set.) Click on the Canvas layer in the Layers palette to select it.

Roughly painting the colors of the face with the Dry Brush

Blocking out the lights and darks in the glove with neutral tones

Painting into the background with deep purples and oranges

To save time while building the colored frame, Benioff used the Paint Bucket tool and selections. To make the outer frame, select the Rectangle Selection tool (Toolbox) and draw a rectangle selection. Select the Paint Bucket tool, choose Fill with Current Color in the Property Bar, select a color in the Colors picker and then click inside the selection to fill it with color. Repeat the process to build the inside of the frame, but this time use a smaller rectangular selection and a yellow-ochre color. Leave the area outside the larger frame white.

2 Picking brushes. When working with the Artists' Oils, Benioff was drawn to these brushes: Dry Brush, Dry Bristle, Wet Brush, Wet Oily Brush, Tapered Oils and Grainy Blender. To extend the possibilities within this group of variants, she made subtle changes to a few of the brushes. Benioff's Soft Tapered Brush (described in the tip on this page) has soft bristles that are filled with paint that easily blends with the underlying colors. (See "A Painter Artists' Oils Primer" on page 98 for information about the Artists' Oils brush settings. To learn more about making your own custom brushes, see Chapter 4, "Building Brushes" on page 152.)

3 Working with Artists' Oils. Benioff kept the Sketch layer visible to use as her template, but painted on the active Canvas layer. (Click on Canvas in the Layers palette to select it.) Working with a light hand and short strokes, quickly rough out the values and tones in your image using the Dry Brush. Pick a mix of cool and warm colors to build rich hues. When you'd like to soften transitions, use the Grainy Blender variant to smooth the strokes that wrap around the forms. Continue to add layers of paint to the image using a mix of cool and warm colors.

Benioff painted neutral tones for the lights and darks of the glove using the Tapered Oils, Dry Brush, Dry Bristle and Wet Oily brushes. With short, curved overlapping strokes of dark purples and oranges, she began to paint the background area. She continued painting, adding depth and color to the face and glove. She did not paint over the frame at this stage.

Painting with Artists' Oils required Benioff to work with slower, shorter strokes and a lighter hand than usual. She found that by adjusting her technique, she maximized the fluidity and gestural capabilities of these brushes.

A SOFT TAPERED BRUSH

This version of the Tapered Oils will give you a soft brush that is loaded with paint that moves easily around the canvas. Choose the Tapered Oils variant of Artists' Oils in the Brush Selector Bar and from the pop-up menu choose Restore Default Variant. Now choose Window, Brush Controls, Show Size. In the Size section, reduce the Minimum size to 30%; in the Artists' Oils section increase the Amount to 86%, reduce the Viscosity to 35%, increase the Blend to 75% and increase the Wetness to 35%. Save your new variant by choosing Save Variant from the pop-up menu on the Brush Selector Bar and give your new custom brush a name.

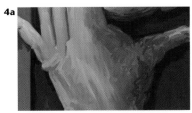

4a

Adding ochres and greens to the glove

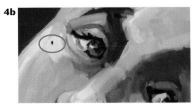

4b

Painting a highlight on the cheek using the Dry Bristle brush variant

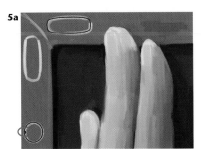

5a

Painting with her Skinny Tapered brush on the Canvas with the Oval shape layer visible using the Snap to Path function

5b

Detail of the completed decorative pattern that was painted using Snap to Path

6

Detail of the final image before Benioff applied texture using the Dye Concentration effect (top) and afterwards (bottom)

4 Adding color, details and highlights. Benioff used the Wet Oily and Dry Bristle brushes to paint a variety of ochres and greens (from her color set) onto the glove. She continued to move around the image, pushing and pulling the paint to refine the forms. She used a small version of the Tapered Brush to add gestural lines and detail. To punch out the highlights, choose the Dry Bristle brush from the Brush Selector Bar. Pick a warm white color in the Colors picker. To paint as Benioff did, use short strokes that follow the contour of the cheek, nose and forehead. Use a light touch to let the bristles of each stroke show at the start and end of each stroke. To deepen the shadows, Benioff painted broad translucent glazes by using a low opacity version of the Wet Oily Brush.

5 Painting the frame using Snap-to-Path. To paint the decorations and the edges of the frame, Benioff used the Snap-to-Path function, which constrains your brushstrokes to the path of a visible shape, making it easy to paint concentric circles and straight edges. (See "Painting Along a Path" in Chapter 3, page 69 for more information about using Snap-to-Path.) First, she drew shapes with the Pen, Oval Shape and Rectangular Shape tools. (For information about working with Shapes, see Chapter 6.) She selected the small Tapered Brush, clicked on the Align to Path button in the Property Bar, and then clicked on the Canvas Layer in the Layers Palette to make it active. As she painted multiple strokes of light and dark yellow, the strokes were automatically constrained to the visible path. With the Layer Adjuster tool active, Benioff moved, rotated and scaled the shapes as needed while she painted along the transformed shapes to complete her decorative border. When it was complete, Benioff disabled the Align to Path button in the Property Bar and painted the details and shadows of the decorations by using small versions of the Tapered Brush and Dry Brush.

6 Adding texture. Benioff wanted to add a subtle texture to the image. To apply the effect that she used on the painted areas only, select the Magic Wand tool, click in the white area around the image, choose Select, Invert and then Select, Save Selection. To open the Paper palette, choose Window, Library Palettes, Show Paper and select French Watercolor Paper. Increase the Paper Scale to 140% and increase the Paper Brightness to 65%. Now, choose Effects, Surface Control, Dye Concentration, Using Paper and set the Maximum to 159% and the Minimum to 22%. Click OK.

7 Applying lighting for drama. Finally, Benioff added drama to her image using a custom lighting effect. She lit the face and top of the glove with a custom yellow and pink Soft Globe light, dropping the rest of the image into shadow. She loaded the selection from step 6 (Select, Load Selection), and then she chose Effects, Surface Control, Apply Lighting and applied the light. (The Warm Globe light will give a similar effect.) See "Adding Dimension with Lighting" on page 298 for more information about the Apply Lighting feature.

Mixed Media Painting

Overview *Lay in background colors; build a custom Felt Pen; draw a sketch; create form and dimension with Felt Pens and the Artists' Oils; refine details with Felt Pens and Palette Knives.*

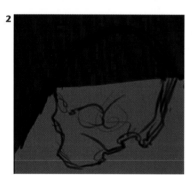

The background is established.

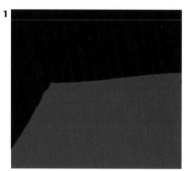

Sketching the skull using a custom Felt Pen

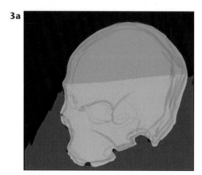

The base color for the skull is laid in.

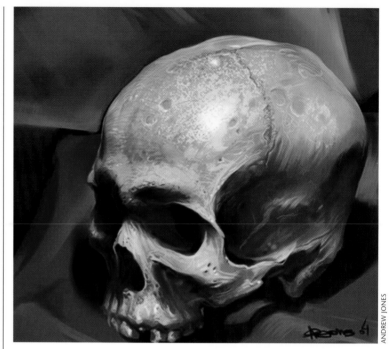

ANDREW JONES

WHEN PAINTING *SKULL*, ANDREW JONES painted from direct observation. Working in Painter, he used a variety of tools, including Felt Pens, Artists' Oils brushes and Palette Knives.

Jones is passionate about drawing from observation and imagination. He has worked for Industrial Light and Magic, Black Isle Studios and is the Senior Concept Artist at Retro Studios. Jones created the concepts for Nintendo's *Metroid Prime* games.

1 Roughing in the background. Because Jones designs for the screen, he usually works with small file sizes, under 1500 pixels. Jones opened a new image. He chose a warm red and a cool green that would reflect interesting lighting onto the subject as he worked. Then he began to block in warm and cool background colors. He filled the Canvas with a dark green using the Paint Bucket. Next, he used the Lasso tool to quickly make a selection for the tabletop, and then he used the Paint Bucket to fill it with a rich rust color. (See Chapter 5, "Selections, Shapes and Masks" to read about selections.)

2 Sketching the skull with a custom Felt Pen. Next, Jones used a custom Felt Pen (that incorporated the Cover method) to sketch the outline of the skull and to suggest a few of its basic forms, including the eye sockets and cheek bones. To build his custom Felt Pen, choose the Felt Pens category and the Medium Tip Felt Pens variant in the Brush Selector Bar. Choose Window, Brush Controls, General and change the Method to Cover and the Subcategory to Soft Cover. Now, open the Size section of Brush Controls, and in the Brush Tip Profile area, click on the Linear Profile,

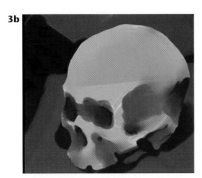

3b

Roughing in the shadows

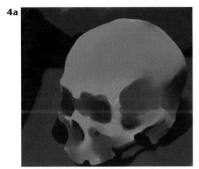

4a

Adding warmer color

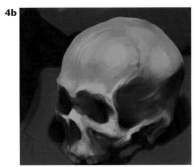

4b

Beginning to refine the forms

4c

Painting deeper shadows and brighter highlights

and then save your new variant by choosing Save Variant from the pop-up menu on the Brush Selector Bar. Give it a name such as *Felt Pen Cover*. To stay organized, it's a good idea to return the default Medium Tip Felt Pens to its original settings by choosing Restore Default Variant from the pop-up menu on the Brush Selector Bar.

Carefully observe your subject and use the Felt Pen Cover to sketch the basic shapes and forms. Jones drew around the outside of the skull loosely from one direction, and then he sketched again, this time starting from the other direction and drawing over his original lines. "It's like getting a second opinion of the forms," says Jones.

3 Laying in color and shadows. At this point, Jones added a new layer by clicking the New Layer button on the Layers palette. He set the layer to the Screen Compositing Method. Then, he chose a cream color in the Colors picker. He made a Lasso selection of the shape of the skull and laid a cream color into the area using the Paint Bucket. Then, he dropped the layer to the Canvas by choosing Drop from the pop-up menu on the Layers palette.

Next, Jones increased the Size and lowered the Opacity of the Felt Pen Cover to about 50%, using the sliders in the Property Bar. Using a medium umber-ochre color, he laid in the big shadow masses on his subject. When they were in place, he added lighter colors to the areas that were catching more light.

To apply glazes, Jones added a new layer. He set this layer to Multiply, and then, using a lower opacity Felt Pen, he gradually painted glazes of light and dark umber colors to build the dimension of the forms. Then he dropped the layer. At this point, he switched to the Artists' Oils category and used a variety of the Artists' Oils brushes (including the Wet Oily Palette Knife) to move and blend areas of paint and to add more color and tone. When you use an Artists' Oils brush, the entire Canvas is covered with oil, and this makes the paint on the Canvas very malleable. Jones used the blending capabilities of the Artists' Oils brushes to smooth and refine areas.

4 Refining the forms and adding details. Jones chose a darker value of the umber-ochre and, using a varied pressure on his stylus, he developed the deeper shadow areas using the Artists' Oils and his custom Felt Pen. Then, using a light cream color, he added the brightest highlights to the top of the skull, its brow and a few other areas. Jones also refined the reflected light that was bouncing from the table and wall onto the subject.

As a last step, Jones refined the details on the skull (for instance, the crevices above the brow and the indentations in the top of the head) using the Felt Marker Cover. To achieve harder edges (such as along the top of the brow), he switched to the Loaded Palette Knife variant of Palette Knives, and then he applied more color and tightened up edges. 🖌

Cloning, Tracing and Painting

Overview *Open a reference image; make a Quick Clone; use tracing paper to aid in drawing the original image; paint brushstrokes using default and custom cloning brushes.*

CHER THREINEN-PENDARVIS

The original photo

PHOTO: © COREL CORPORATION

The reference image with irregular border

The Quick Clone area of General Preferences

IF YOU DON'T HAVE TIME TO PAINT an illustration from scratch, Painter's cloning and tracing paper features make it easy to use a photo or other existing art as a reference for a new illustration. Using these tools in a thoughtful manner can also help you improve your observation and your drawing and painting skills.

1 Selecting and preparing the reference image. Start by opening a reference image in Painter (such as a painting or photo). Before we began the cloning process, we gave the photo a soft, irregular border that would add interest to the final image. Choose the Lasso tool and draw a freehand selection inside the border of the image. Now, choose Select, Feather and give the selection a feather of about 20 pixels. Choose Select, Invert (to reverse the selection). Then press Backspace/Delete to remove the image portion of the image outside the feathered border.

2 Using Quick Clone and Tracing Paper. New in Painter IX, the Quick Clone feature can save you several steps. You can set up its Preferences to your liking. Choose Corel Painter IX, Preferences, General, and in the Quick Clone area, turn off the Switch to Cloner Brushes check box. Click OK to exit the Preferences dialog box and choose File, Quick Clone. A clone of your reference will be created—the contents of the clone image will be deleted and Tracing Paper will be turned on. The default name of our clone was *Clone of lady bugs_painter.riff*. Choose File, Save As and rename your clone. We named our clone *1 lady bugs sketch.riff*. After saving the clone, leave the original image open because Painter needs it for a reference. Working with Tracing Paper in Painter is similar to using

USING CLONE COLOR

To paint brushstrokes on an image using color from another image, check the Clone Color button (the rubber stamp) on the Colors picker.

The clone image with Tracing Paper active. Notice the Toggle Tracing Paper button in the upper right of the image window.

Choosing the Grainy Pencil 3

A detail of the in-progress pencil sketch, showing Tracing Paper enabled

These loose, expressive clone strokes will be a basis for more detailed brushwork.

This close-up detail of the in-progress image shows more detail on the ladybugs.

a conventional light table. Art directors and designers will find Painter's Tracing Paper helpful when drawing thumbnails and design comps. The original image will appear "screened back," ready to be traced with a brush.

SOURCE AND DESTINATION

The new clone will be linked to the original file—its clone source. The cloning process maps the clone (the destination image) directly to the original (the source image), pixel-by-pixel.

3 Drawing a sketch. Begin by choosing a brush, a paper texture and a color. Click on the Paper Selector in the Toolbox and choose a paper texture from the pop-up list. (We chose Basic Paper.) To simulate a conventional graphite pencil, choose a dark gray in the Colors picker and then choose the Grainy Pencil 3 variant of Pencils from the Brush Selector Bar.

Now, make a new layer by clicking the New Layer icon in the Layers palette. Drawing your sketch on a transparent layer will give you the flexibility of adjusting the opacity and Composite Method and editing it apart from the rest of the image. We renamed our layer *sketch* by double-clicking the name of Layer 1 in the Layers palette and entering the new name.

Begin sketching on the new layer using the clone source image as a guide. To toggle Tracing Paper off and on as you work, press Ctrl/⌘-T. We sketched the ladybugs and the two flowers—focusing on the main elements—with only a suggestion of the background leaves. The Grainy Pencil allowed us to sketch thick to thin lines while revealing the paper texture. When the sketch was complete, we reduced the opacity of the sketch layer to 20% so that it would not distract us as we painted.

4 Cloning and painting with brushes. Next, we targeted the Canvas (background) layer and painted loose strokes over the image Canvas using the Camel Oil Cloner variant of Cloners. The Camel Oil Cloner will pull color and imagery from the source image and allow you to apply it to the clone in a painterly way. You can apply imagery and blend and smear with this brush, depending on the pressure that you apply to your stylus.

Carefully study your subject. Don't simply brush in a scrubbing or angled pattern, but instead let your brushstrokes follow the forms and shapes that you see in the photo. We used very dynamic brush work for a painterly look. Try to avoid working in a tight photo-realistic manner at this stage. For more interest and spontaneity, we brushed out near the edges to create an uneven border. Next, we used a smaller version of the Camel Oil Cloner to paint more detailed brush work on the flowers and ladybugs. Then, we added a few more graceful brushstrokes to the foliage.

5 Restoring details. To restore details from the original image, we used the Soft Cloner variant of Cloners. This brush is similar to a soft airbrush and it imports imagery directly from the

The Clone Color button is turned on in the Colors palette

Painting details on the flower and ladybugs using the new Oily Cloner brush

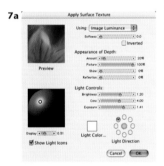

The settings in the Apply Surface Texture dialog box

The paint texture and the low-opacity sketch can be seen in this detail.

original image without smearing paint like the Camel Oils Cloner. We used this brush only on areas where we wanted to enhance the focal point—the ladybugs and the flower.

6 Painting with a new custom Oily Cloner brush. We wanted to use one of the Smeary Oils brushes as a cloning brush. You can do this by assigning Clone Color to the brush. Begin by choosing the Smeary Bristle Spray variant of Oils. This brush smears paint in a way similar to traditional wet oil paint. In the Colors picker, enable the Clone Color option. Save your new Oily Cloner by choosing Save Variant from the pop-up menu on the Brush Selector Bar. Then, to preserve the settings in the original brush, choose Restore Default Variant from the same menu on the Brush Selector Bar. Now, choose your new Oily Cloner from the variant menu and paint some practice strokes. To slowly build up the paint, we lowered its opacity to 30% using the Opacity slider in the Property Bar. Then we zoomed in on the image and used our new Oily Cloner to paint with clone color and smear the new color with existing paint. To add painterly details to the bugs and flower, we used a small size (about 15 pixels). We continued to use this lower opacity brush in various sizes to paint over the expressive strokes applied earlier.

7 Adding texture and completing the image. Next, we gave the brushstrokes three-dimensional highlights and shadows by choosing Effects, Surface Control, Apply Surface Texture, Using Image Luminance. We chose an Amount setting of 20%. (For a realistic look when using Surface Texture, we always recommend using subtle settings.) We set Shine at 0% for a matte look and left the other settings at their defaults. So that the effect would be more natural and look less like a filter, we used the Oily Cloner to paint back into some areas; for instance, the lady bugs and flower. The texture and touch-up strokes can be seen in illustration 7b.

To complete the image, we experimented with the opacity of the sketch layer, settling on 25%. We liked the combination of the subtle hand-drawn sketch lines and the cloned and painted imagery. We also added soft brush work to the border by using the low opacity custom Oily Cloner and the Round Blender Brush variant of Blenders. You can see the complete, final image on page 110.

You can see the complete, final image on page 110.

CLONING FROM ONE UNRELATED IMAGE TO ANOTHER

To clone from one unrelated image to another (to map pixel for pixel or to use the Tracing Paper function), the two images must have exactly the same pixel dimensions. Open two images that are the same size and choose one image for your destination image. (You can use Canvas, Resize to check the size of the source image, if needed.) Choose File, Clone Source and designate the second image as the clone source. Use a cloning brush to bring imagery into the destination image, in exactly the same position as in the source. To continue to clone or use Tracing Paper, the source image must be left open.

Coloring
and Cloning

__Overview__ Scan a pencil sketch; clone it, tint it and add texture; restore from the original by cloning; add color with the Airbrush, Chalk and Watercolor brushes.

PHILIP HOWE

The original pencil illustration, scanned

Adding a tint and a texture to the clone

Using a Cloning method brush to partially restore the gray tones of the original

MUCH OF THE BEAUTY of illustrator Philip Howe's work lies in his seamless, creative blending of the traditional with the digital. In a spread for *Trailblazer* magazine—a detail of which is shown here—Howe combined hand-drawn calligraphy, a photo of two slides, a photo of a watercolor block (for the background), and his own pencil sketches, colored to simulate traditional watercolor.

1 Starting with a sketch. Howe began by sketching the various birds in pencil on watercolor paper. He scanned the images on a flatbed scanner, saving them as grayscale files in TIFF format. Each bird image was 4 to 5 inches square and 300 ppi.

2 Modifying a clone. Open a grayscale scan in Painter. Choose File, Clone to clone your scan, giving you an "original" and a clone. Keep the original open—you'll want to pull from it later. Howe added a color tint and a texture to the clone of the scanned bird. To add a tint, choose a color in the Colors picker (Howe chose a reddish brown); then choose Effects, Surface Control, Color Overlay. Select Uniform Color from the Using pop-up menu, set Opacity to 30%, click the Dye Concentration button and click OK. To add texture, select a paper texture (Howe chose Basic Paper) from the Paper Selector near the bottom of the Toolbox, and choose Effects, Surface Control, Apply Surface Texture. Select Paper from the Using menu, set Amount to 50% and set Shine to 0%. Click OK.

3 Restoring from the original. Howe used Painter's cloning capabilities to replace most of the tint and texture in the bird's body with the light gray tones of the original. In the Brush Selector Bar, choose the Cloners category, and the Soft Cloner variant. In the Property Bar, try lowering this cloning brush's Opacity for more sensitivity. (The Soft Cloner sprays soft color, similar to an airbrush.) Once you've arrived at the opacity you like, paint on the portion of your image that you want to restore. The original will automatically be revealed in the area covered by your strokes.

4 Adding color tints with an Airbrush. To achieve the effect of traditional airbrushing with transparent dyes or watercolor

Applying color tints with the Digital Airbrush in Buildup method

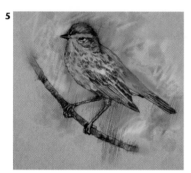

Using a Large Chalk variant to add color to the background

Applying watercolor accents with the Splatter Water variant

Another spot illustration from the Trailblazer *spread. Howe used the same brushes and technique for all illustrations.*

pigments, Howe used two versions of the Digital Airbrush variant of Airbrushes. The first Digital Airbrush (using the default Cover method) allowed a light color to cover a darker one. In the Property Bar, he reduced the Opacity setting to between 5% and 10%. He used this low-opacity brush to carefully lay in the golden brown tones on the bird's back. Howe's second airbrush used the Buildup method, which applied color transparently. The Buildup method allowed him to use a slightly higher Opacity (between 10% and 20%) to achieve richer color while preserving the intensity of the pencil sketch. To make a "transparent" airbrush similar to Howe's, choose the Digital Airbrush variant of Airbrushes in the Brush Selector Bar. To change its method from Cover to the Buildup Method, open the Brush Controls. (Choose Window, Brush Controls, Show General.) In the General section, change the Method pop-up menu to Buildup, and the subcategory pop-up menu to Soft Buildup.

5 Cloning again and brushing with Chalk. Howe uses the Clone feature like a flexible "Save As" command. When he's ready to move on to the next phase of an illustration, he often makes a clone and uses the original as "source material." Here, when he had colored the bird to his satisfaction, he chose File, Clone. If he over-worked an area in the new clone, he restored it by cloning in imagery from the previous version by opening that version and designating it as the "source" by choosing File, Clone Source. Then he painted with a cloning brush to restore the area.

Howe switched to the Large Chalk variant of Chalk and began to paint loose, gestural strokes on the image background around the bird using two similar green hues. He changed the size of the brush as he worked by making adjustments in the Property Bar.

6 Adding tints and texture. To add a finishing touch without muddying his existing color work, Howe used transparent washes to add more depth to the color on the bird's head and other areas. To paint washes, use the Wash Camel variant of Watercolor. (As you paint, a Watercolor layer will be generated in the Layers palette, keeping these brushstrokes separate from the Canvas.) Now, sample color from the bird and background using the Dropper tool, switch to the Splatter Water variant and paint a "water drop" effect on the background. To combine the selected Watercolor layer with the Canvas, click the Layer Commands button at the bottom of the Layers palette and choose Drop.

Merging the files. Using the Lasso, Howe drew a loose selection around the bird; then he chose Select, Feather and feathered it 30 pixels. Then he opened the 17 x 11-inch main image and used the Layer Adjuster tool to drag and drop the bird into the main image. To blend the bird layer with the background, he set its Composite Method in the Layers palette to Multiply.

Combining Oil Pastels, Texture and Blending

Overview *Start from a pencil sketch; build a drawing using Oil Pastels variants combined with different paper textures; blend them with Blenders variants.*

CAROL BENIOFF

The scan of the pencil sketch

Drawing with the Chunky Oil Pastel on Pebbled Leather texture for the stuffed dog

Benioff clicked the Invert Paper button in the Papers palette, and then she painted the texture for the flooring.

THE OIL PASTELS ARE A VERY VERSATILE set of tools—their strokes, blending capability and responsiveness to paper textures all add to the tactile feel of this illustration of toys painted by artist Carol Benioff. She also used Blenders variants, to smear, ripple, add texture and blend the drawing.

1 Starting with a pencil sketch. Benioff started by drawing a simple composition of toys with traditional pencils and paper. Then, she scanned the drawing at 300 pixels per inch and opened it in Painter. To load a new paper library, open the Paper palette (Windows, Library Palettes, Show Papers), and in the pop-up menu, select Open Library. (The message "Loading a new Paper Texture will overwrite your current Paper Textures, and any changes that you have made will be lost" will appear. If you have saved custom paper textures in the default Paper Textures library, choose Cancel and then use the Paper Mover to create a new library for them before you open a new library. For information about libraries and movers, see Chapter 1.) Next, navigate to the Painter IX application folder, Extras, Paper Textures and select Painter 8 Textures.

2 Picking different papers. Benioff began sketching the stuffed dog. She selected the Pebbled Leather texture from the Painter 8 Textures library that she had loaded in the Papers palette. The paper emulates the dog's nubby blue fabric. Using the Chunky Oil Pastel variant of Oil Pastels, she drew colored strokes, which revealed the pebbly paper and blended with the underlying colors. For the floor, she switched to the Simulated Wood Grain texture and a Soft Oil Pastel variant. To reveal more texture,

3a

She drew the jacks on Smooth Handmade Paper and the ball on Coarse Cotton Canvas.

3b

Benioff used Oil Pastels variants and 1954 Graphic Fabric texture to paint the jack-in-the-box and the wallpaper.

4

Drawing the bear with the Chunky Oil Pastel on Corrugated Paper, with the paper texture inverted and lighter colors

5

Using the Grainy Water variant of Blenders on the stuffed bunny

she adjusted the Grain slider to 10% in the Property Bar. Then, she painted dark blue color. To reverse the value of the paper, Benioff clicked on the Invert Paper button in the Papers palette and then she selected a light blue and again drew on the floor with quick strokes. With the inverted paper texture, you can now draw into the recesses of the paper with the lighter color. Vary the pressure on the stylus as you paint to control how much of the paper texture is revealed or covered by the pigment. The Soft Oil Pastel is built so the amount of resaturation and bleed are controlled by the amount of pressure you apply.

3 Using smooth and coarse textures. To achieve the dull metal sheen on the jacks, Benioff chose the Oil Pastel 10 variant, reduced its size to 4 pixels and then she chose the Smooth Hand-made Paper for a more subtle paper texture effect. To paint the ball and simulate the rough-textured rubber, she picked the Coarse Cotton Canvas texture in the Paper Selector, and then she switched to the Chunky Pastel, which reveals the paper texture as well as blends with the colors underneath.

Next, Benioff chose the 1954 Graphic Fabric texture for the box, the jack-in-the-box's clothing and the striped wallpaper. For the wallpaper and the jack-in-the-box's clothing, Benioff used the Variable Oil Pastel brush in a variety of sizes. Before drawing the straight lines for the wallpaper, she clicked the Straight line strokes button on the Property Bar. Then, she painted the box with the Round Oil Pastel.

4 Using inverted texture. To paint the stuffed bear's well-worn fur, she used a Chunky Oil Pastel over Corrugated Paper texture. First, she mapped out the lights and darks of the forms. Then, she clicked on the Invert Paper button in the Papers palette and selected lighter shades of browns to draw into the recesses of the paper. By varying the colors, pressure and strokes, she was able to paint mottled textures on the bear.

5 Blending and smearing color. To complete the study, Benioff used a variety of the Blenders brushes on different areas of her drawing as follows: For the dog, she chose an Oily Blender, and pushed and pulled the existing color. For the ball, she switched to a Coarse Oily Blender, with the Coarse Cotton Canvas paper selected. This pushed and pulled the paint and blended the strokes, while still revealing subtle paper texture. For the jacks, she used a Detail Blender, which maintained their dull metallic shine. For the jack-in-the-box's clothing, she used a Coarse Smear blender. She used Just Add water to bleed and blur the rough-edged strokes on the box. To soften the transitions from light to dark while keeping the texture on the bear and rabbit, she used a Grainy Blender and the same paper texture that she had used with the oil pastels. Finally, Benioff used the Runny variant of Blenders to create a rippling effect on the floor. ✏

Applying Paper Textures

Overview *Scan textured paper and fabric; open the file in Painter and capture the texture; use grain-sensitive brushes and Painter's special effects to paint and apply texture.*

Scanned lace texture (left) and Japanese paper (right)

Capturing a selected area of the lace scan

Saving and naming the new paper texture

Selecting Make Paper in the Papers palette

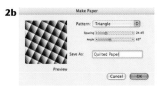

Using the Triangle Pattern in the Make Paper dialog box to build the Quilted Paper

CAROL BENIOFF

WHILE PAINTER OFFERS A LARGE ASSORTMENT of ready-made paper grains, it also offers many ways to create your own unique surfaces. You can capture textures from video grabs, scanned photos, texture collections on CD-ROM, scans of paper, patterns, natural objects (leaves, flowers, wood grains) or images drawn in Painter. The Make Paper and Make Fractal Pattern features in Painter provide another way to generate custom paper textures. With *Parked Boot*, Carol Benioff took full advantage of Painter's capability to apply paper textures with effects and brushes as she painted with variants of the Chalk and Oil Pastels.

1 Scanning and capturing paper textures. Benioff scanned decorative papers, cork, lace and flowers on her flatbed scanner at 300 ppi in grayscale mode. If you are scanning a translucent sheet, or lace, like Benioff used for this piece, you may want to place a black sheet behind it to create greater contrast. For maximum flexibility when applying the texture, make sure the scan has good contrast and a broad tonal range.

Use the Rectangular Selection tool to isolate an area of your image. The repetition of your paper pattern may be too obvious if you select an area that is smaller than 200 x 200 pixels. Open the Papers palette (Window, Library Palettes, Show Papers). Choose

3

Detail of textures applied with the Color Overlay effect to the background surfaces

4a

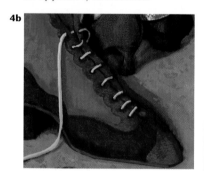

Detail of Quilted Paper texture painted onto the top portion of the brown boot

4b

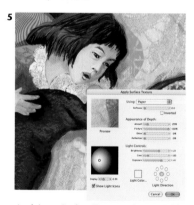

Benioff used Painter's Pebble Board texture with Oil Pastels to paint the dark brown leather of the boots.

5

Applying a Surface Texture using Benioff's captured Japanese Paper texture

Capture Paper from the pop-up menu on the Papers palette. For the smoothest results, use a Crossfade setting between 16–30. Name your paper and click OK. A picture of the texture will appear in your current Paper library.

2 Making papers. To build the Quilted Paper, Benioff opened the Make Paper dialog box. (To choose Make Paper, click on the right triangle of the Papers palette and choose Make Paper.) In the Patterns pop-up menu, Benioff selected Triangle, adjusted the spacing and angle and then named her paper and clicked OK.

3 Filling selections with textured color. Benioff built broad areas of color and texture by selecting portions of her drawing with the Magic Wand and Lasso tools, and then filling the selections with color and texture using the Color Overlay effect. To paint as Benioff did, choose a color in the Colors picker and a paper in the Papers palette. Then choose Effects, Surface Control, Color Overlay. In the Using pop-up menu, select Paper. Next, set your desired Opacity and click the Dye Concentration button for a transparent tint *or* the Hiding Power button for a semi-opaque look. On the background wall, Benioff applied the Japanese Paper texture and the Lace texture using Color Overlay. For more depth, she applied the Lace texture again using the Dye Concentration effect.

4 Applying paper grain with brushes. Benioff brushed the Quilted Paper texture on the ankle-high boot using the Square Chalk variant of Chalk and a yellow ochre color. Then, for the shadow areas, she reversed the Quilted Paper by checking the Invert Paper box in the Papers palette and painted dark brown strokes. (See "Inverting the Grain" on page 58 to learn more about inverted textures.) Next, she used the Pebble Board texture in Painter IX and the Oil Pastels to create the leather grain on the red boot. She painted reds and browns. As she worked, she adjusted the Grain slider on the Property Bar to vary the amount of texture revealed in the strokes. Choose Pebble Board texture in the Papers palette and the Soft Oil Pastel variant of Oil Pastels. Using gentle pressure on your stylus, brush textured strokes onto your image using the Soft Oil Pastel.

5 Applying paper grain with effects. For more warmth and depth on the background wall, Benioff overlaid more texture and a warm yellow light. She began by selecting the captured Japanese Paper texture in the Papers palette. Then she chose Effects, Surface Control, Apply Surface Texture and used these settings: Using, Paper; Amount, 25%; Shine, 0%. Benioff adjusted the Brightness, Exposure and Color of the Light, and then she clicked OK. 🖌

EXCITING TEXTURED EFFECTS

Here's how selected special effects apply paper textures to your images with exciting results. *Surface Texture* applies texture by simulating a paper surface with lighting and shadows, *Color Overlay* applies texture as a transparent or semi-opaque tint and *Dye Concentration* applies texture by darkening (or lightening) pixels in the image that fall in recesses of the paper grain.

Painting Rich Textures with Brushes

Overview *Scan a traditional pencil sketch; modify brushes to include enhanced grain settings; paint rich color with varied textures using the Digital Watercolor and Chalk brushes.*

DON SEEGMILLER

The scanned pencil sketch

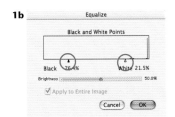

Using Equalize to give the sketch more contrast. The sliders are adjusted.

BY SKILLFULLY USING COLOR WHILE PAINTING with several brushes and textures, Don Seegmiller created a mysterious atmosphere for *Griffin*, which began as a book cover sketch that he had developed for *The Oathbound Wizard*. He developed a rich layering of textures, which he applied, using brushes that included enhanced grain settings.

Seegmiller, whose traditional oil paintings can be found in both private and public collections, has worked as an art director for innovative gaming development companies. He also teaches illustration at Brigham Young University.

1 Sketching, scanning and equalizing. Seegmiller began by sketching with conventional pencil on paper. He scanned the pencil drawing at 300 ppi, a resolution suitable for offset printing. Because he likes working with a high-contrast version of the sketch, he removed the grays from the scan. To increase the contrast in your sketch, as Seegmiller did, choose Effects, Tonal Control, Equalize. When the Equalize dialog box appears, move the black point marker and the white point marker under the histogram closer

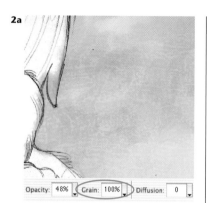

2a

Opacity: 48% | Grain: 100% | Diffusion: 0

A close up of the texture that is revealed when using the New Simple Water brush and the Grain setting in the Property Bar

2b

The first washes are laid in on the background. Starting to brush color onto the figure.

3a

Adding deeper value and color to the illustration by applying thin glazes

together to eliminate the gray tones. Move them right or left to affect the line thickness and quality. You'll be able to preview the adjustment in your image before you click OK to accept.

CHALK, DIGITAL WATERCOLOR AND PAPER GRAIN

The Grain setting in the Property Bar describes *grain penetration*. With most of Painter's grain-sensitive brushes (such as the Chalk brushes), the lower the Grain setting, the "grainier" your strokes will look. A lower Grain setting allows less of the color to penetrate into the valleys of the grain, and the paint hits only the "peaks" of the paper surface. However, with Digital Watercolor, the controls are reversed. A *higher* setting will reveal more Grain.

2 Painting the first washes. Prior to painting with color, Seegmiller made a quick duplicate of his sketch to preserve the original. Choose Select, All, and then copy and paste the sketch back into your file. Now change the composite method of the newly pasted layer to Gel, so that all of the white in the image becomes transparent, leaving the drawing to use as a guide later, if you need it. Seegmiller used a custom texture that is similar to the Pavement texture from the Painter 6 library on the Painter IX CD-ROM. To load the Pavement texture, open the Papers palette (Windows, Library Palettes, Show Papers) in the pop-up menu, select Open Library, navigate to the Painter IX application folder, Extras, Paper Textures and select Painter 6 Textures.

Next, he used the New Simple Water variant of Digital Watercolor to lay in light washes onto the background. Seegmiller likes the New Simple Water brush because of the way that it interacts with the paper texture. To paint as Seegmiller did, from the Brush Selector Bar choose the New Simple Water variant of Digital Watercolor and a light color in the Colors picker. Begin by painting light values of color on the background. When the background is as you like it, dry the wet Digital Watercolor paint so that subsequent strokes do not mix with the existing paint on the Canvas. Choose Dry Digital Watercolor from the pop-up menu on the Layers palette.

When the background was laid in, Seegmiller began to add color to his character. As he worked, he varied the look of the textures by changing the scale using the Paper Scale slider in the Papers palette. To open the Papers palette, choose Window, Library Palettes, Show Papers. He continued to build up thin layers of color over the entire image. Part of the beauty of using Digital Watercolor is its capability to slowly build up rich areas of color with great textural effects.

3 Building up thin glazes of color. Seegmiller gradually painted three glaze layers of Digital Watercolor and dried the washes between each application of paint. The washes are subtle applications of digital paint, similar to the glazes that you would apply with traditional watercolor.

As Seegmiller finished his last Digital Watercolor washes, he added richer, darker colors where he wanted more contrast.

3b

Applying final Digital Watercolor washes

The trees with sketch and Digital Watercolor (left) and with the Variable Chalk brush work (right)

5

Defining the Griffin's forms

6

The darker wing on the Griffin helps to bring the hand forward

Notice that there is still a lot of texture visible throughout the image. When the washes were complete, again, he dried this final watercolor glaze. He painted the next stage using a different brush.

4 Painting with a grainy chalk. At this point, Seegmiller wanted to cover areas of the original sketch and achieve a more painterly feeling—so he switched to a favorite brush—the Variable Chalk variant of Chalk and he chose Basic Paper in the Paper Selector in the Toolbox. Now, set the Grain very low in the Property Bar: Move the Grain slider to about 8% to allow the Chalk to reveal more grain. (Seegmiller used varied Grain settings between 9%–17% when using the Chalk.) To keep your chalk strokes separate from your Digital Watercolor, make a new layer by clicking the New Layer button on the Layers palette and begin to paint with the Variable Chalk. Seegmiller painted over the background trees, leaving only hints of the sketch. Then, he began to develop the foreground texture and details using the Variable Chalk, changing the size and opacity of the brush as he worked.

5 Adding definition with a custom brush. Next, to add more definition and form to the Griffin, Seegmiller switched brushes again, this time to *Don's Brush*, a custom variant that he had created. He worked from dark to light and, for the most part, across the form. His brush has a fairly low opacity setting of about 30%.

For information about building a brush that is similar to Seegmiller's, see the custom Soft Captured Oil Brush that is described on page 159 in the introduction of Chapter 4, "Building Brushes." Seegmiller's brush has some similar qualities, but he uses the Grainy Soft Cover or the Grainy Hard Cover Subcategory in the General section of Brush Controls. *Don's brush* can be found on the *Painter IX Wow!* CD-ROM in the Don Seegmiller folder.

6 Darkening the shaded wing. The shadow side of the character's right wing was too light, so he wanted to darken it by duplicating a portion of the chalk layer. To use his method, select the area of the layer that you want using the Lasso tool, copy the selection and then paste the selection back over the same areas using Edit, Paste in Place (Shift-Ctrl/⌘-V). Then change the Composite Method to Multiply in the Layers palette. The Multiply method can make the area very dark, but you can adjust the Opacity

A USEFUL ITERATIVE SAVE

When working on a detailed illustration, saving multiple versions will provide great versatility. If you don't like a change that you've made, it's easy to go back to an earlier version and then continue on from the previous stage. When you make a major change, save a new version of the file using a new name. Iterative Save is a useful feature that quickly saves sequentially numbered versions of the image. Choose File Iterative Save (Ctrl/⌘-Alt/Option-S). Each time you use the Iterative Save command, a new file is created with sequential numbering.

7

The grass blades and toadstools are added.

8

The reptile skin texture on the chest

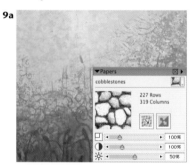

9a

Painting rich textures on the foliage and midground

9b

Making the flame flicker

9c

Painting light shining from the flame

slider to get the effect that you want. Next, Seegmiller cleaned up the edges of this new layer with an Eraser variant. He saved his image and combined the two layers into one. To merge the layers, Shift-select their names in the Layers palette, group the two layers (Ctrl/⌘-G) and then collapse them together by choosing Collapse from the Layer Commands menu on the Layers palette. After collapsing the layers, he saved a new version of his image using Iterative Save. It is not uncommon for Seegmiller to have as many as 50 saved versions when a project is complete.

7 Adding elements to the character and foreground. He continued to work on the foreground. Although it's not a good idea to try to paint every blade of grass, sometimes there is no other way to get a realistic look. Using your stylus and *Don's brush*, quickly paint a number of blades of grass in the foreground. Vary the direction of the blades of grass to create a random, natural look. At this point, Seegmiller also painted the red toadstools.

8 Painting the reptile skin on a layer. Next, he added another new layer so that he could work freely as he painted the skin. This method is more flexible than carefully painting textured strokes around elements, such as the feathers on the arms, because he could easily touch up areas or erase on the layer without disturbing the underlying paint. Switching to a custom paper texture that he had created to imitate reptile skin, he used the Variable Chalk to add texture to the torso and legs of the Griffin on the new layer. When the skin textures were laid in, they looked too harsh, so he softened them slightly by applying Effects, Focus, Soften to the layer, using subtle settings.

9 Painting details, texture and the flame. Next, Seegmiller added small bits of texture to the foreground foliage. He continued to work from dark to light as he refined the highlights on the grassy areas. He also used the Variable Chalk to paint a subtle crescent moon in the lightest sky area. Seegmiller added another new layer and painted the flame above his character's paw. Then, he used the Turbulence variant of the Distortion brush to add a flickering look to the flame. He painted the lighting on the paw of the figure, and he added light to the deep shadow areas that were catching the light from the flame. He added all of his final detail work on the new layer to make the corrections easy. ✍

A Painter Impasto Primer

***Overview** Here you'll find the basics for painting with the Impasto medium and brushes.*

CHER THREINEN-PENDARVIS

The Toggle Impasto Effect button in the image window

Brushstrokes made with the Thick Tapered Flat variant of Impasto

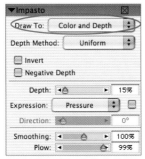

The Impasto section of Brush Controls, with the Draw To pop-up menu set to Color and Depth

WITH IMPASTO, LUSCIOUS THICK PAINT is available at the tip of your digital brush. Painter's Impasto brushes and Impasto depth layer give you the ability to paint with exciting, realistic, three-dimensional brushstrokes that leave bristle marks and paint texture on the surface of the image. Impasto brushes are found in the Impasto category and in other categories in the Painter Brushes library such as the Acrylics, Gouache, Oils and Cloners. Look for brushes with the word *Thick* in their name, such as the Thick Opaque Acrylic variant of Acrylics and the Thick Wet Camel variants of Oils. A few brushes in the Cloners category include Impasto settings; the Oil Brush Cloner and the Thick Camel Cloner variants of Cloners are examples.

Impasto properties. Impasto has two properties: the *color* of the paint and the *depth* of the paint. The Impasto depth medium is a grayscale bump map that is part of the Painter image Canvas. It is similar to a layer, but it does not appear in the Layers palette. Choose the Thick Tapered Flat variant of Impasto and make a brushstroke. You will see a brushstroke with the realistic highlights and shadows of thick paint. To view your Impasto brushstrokes with their color only (without the depth), use the Toggle Impasto Effect button to turn the depth on and off. The Toggle Impasto Effect button is the paint splat icon located in the upper right of the Painter image window.

Controlling Impasto. There are two types of controls for Impasto. The first affects the appearance of individual Impasto brushstrokes and is located in the Impasto section of Brush Controls. Choose Window, Brush Controls, Show Impasto to open the Impasto section. (The Impasto section is also located in the Stroke Designer section of the Brush Creator.) The Impasto section controls affect the performance of the Impasto brushes and the depth of individual brushstrokes as you paint them. In the Draw To menu, Color applies only color; Depth applies three-dimensional highlights and shadows but with no color; Color and Depth applies both color and

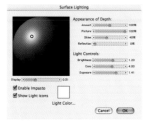

The choices in the Draw To pop-up menu in the Impasto section

The Surface Lighting dialog box settings apply to the entire image.

The Composite Depth is set to Subtract.

three-dimensional highlights and shadows of thick paint. Depth applies the depth layer only. (For an example of an Impasto brush that uses Draw To Depth, try out the Thick Clear Varnish.) The Depth slider controls the amount of depth the brush will apply; Smoothing allows you to adjust the texture of the strokes and Plow controls how much a new stroke will displace existing paint. Under the Depth Method menu, Uniform applies depth evenly; Erase removes depth and Paper applies depth using the current paper texture. (For *Lilies* on page 123, we used the Paper Depth Method to achieve the grainy strokes.) Original Luminance applies depth based on a Clone Source, and Weaving Luminance applies depth using the current weave.

The second way you can control Impasto is by adjusting lighting that shines onto the brushstrokes. Surface Lighting, which is located under the Canvas menu, is a global control, which means that it affects the entire document, including all of its layers. Surface Lighting is dynamic, which means that you can continue to adjust the appearance of the Impasto brushstrokes, until you're satisfied with the look.

Building up, or excavating paint. The Thick Tapered Flat and Thick Round are examples of brushes that will build up thick Impasto paint. To excavate, or dig into the paint, use the Palette Knife variant of Impasto. You can also customize a brush to dig into existing Impasto paint. Choose the Thick Round variant of Impasto, and in the Impasto section, enable the Negative Depth box.

Impasto, layers and Composite Depth. When creating *On Golden Hill*, we painted Impasto on layers so that we could adjust the Composite Method and the Composite Depth. We built up paint and excavated paint. The Composite Depth settings on the Layers palette allowed for interesting paint interaction. We painted brushstrokes on two layers with the Thick Acrylic Round variant of Acrylics. Then, we used the Composite Depth controls, Subtract (to excavate) and Add (to raise) the brushstrokes. For more Impasto painting tips and techniques, see pages 125 and 127, "Brushing Washes over Live Canvas" and "Working with Thick Paint."

For On Golden Hill, *we painted Impasto brushstrokes on layers so that we could use the Composite Depth for more complexity in the overlapping, thick brushstrokes.*

LIVE, DYNAMIC IMPASTO

If you save your file in RIFF format to preserve the "live" Impasto qualities, you can use Canvas, Surface Lighting to change the light direction, or to increase or decrease the depth of the Impasto paint, even after you open and close the image.

ERASING IMPASTO DEPTH

If you're not satisfied with the look of the relief after you've applied depth, you can erase Impasto with one of these two methods. To erase the entire depth effect, choose Canvas, Clear Impasto. To use a brush to decrease depth from an area, choose the Depth Equalizer variant of Impasto and brush over the area you want to smooth. To completely erase a portion of the depth layer, use the Depth Eraser. However, use the Depth Eraser with care, as it can make an indentation in the depth layer.

Brushing Washes over "Live" Canvas

Overview *Open a new file and use an Impasto brush to emboss texture into the image canvas; paint color washes over the canvas with brushes.*

STANLEY VEALÉ

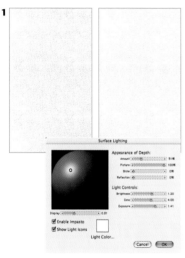

The canvas with the default Impasto Lighting settings (left) and with the reduced Amount and Shine (right), as set in the Impasto Lighting dialog box.

2a

Choosing the Wet Bristle variant of Impasto in the Brush Selector Bar

ON TRADITIONAL CANVAS YOU CAN USE OIL PAINT mixed with linseed oil and turpentine to brush washes over the surface without obliterating the canvas grain. With Painter's Impasto feature you can do something very similar, with the added advantage of being able to emphasize or de-emphasize the grain by changing the angle or intensity of lighting on the canvas. Using the Impasto feature to "emboss" the canvas will keep the grain "live" and changeable throughout the painting process. To paint *Ashanti,* a still-life study of an African wood carving, artist and designer Stanley Vealé used a unique method that allows the canvas texture to always show through the brushstrokes.

1 Embossing the canvas. Begin by creating a new file the size and resolution you need. (Vealé's file was 800 pixels square.) In the Papers Selector, choose the Coarse Cotton Canvas texture. (Considering the 800-pixel file size, Vealé left the Scale of the Coarse Cotton Canvas texture at 100% in the Papers palette.)

Vealé used the Grain Emboss variant of Impasto to "emboss" the Raw Silk texture values into the image canvas without adding color. Select the Grain Emboss variant of Impasto and paint wide strokes all over the image so that the paper texture is embossed into the image. You can reduce or increase the effect of the texture by choosing Canvas, Surface Lighting, and adjusting the Amount slider to your liking. Because the default Impasto Lighting settings seemed too coarse and shiny, Vealé reduced the Amount to 51%, and for a matte finish on the canvas, he set the Shine at 0.

2 Customizing a brush. Vealé likes the Wet Bristle variant of Impasto because of its bristle marks and how it scrubs existing paint when you apply pressure on the stylus. However, if he used the

2b

Changing the Impasto settings in the Stroke Designer tab of the Brush Creator for the Wet Bristle variant copy

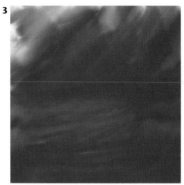

3

Applying glazes to the image canvas

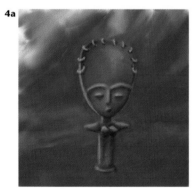

4a

The figure study in progress

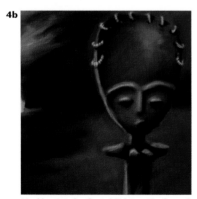

4b

Vealé painted reflected light on the face of the Ashanti figure.

default Impasto Wet Bristle, the brush would paint with depth as well as color, eventually covering the embossed texture applied in step 1. So he modified a copy of the Wet Bristle so that it would apply only color to his image, as follows: Select the Wet Bristle variant of Impasto and copy it to the Oils category by choosing Copy Variant from the triangle pop-up menu on the right side of the Brush Selector Bar. When the Copy Variant dialog box appears, choose the Oils category from the pop-up menu and click OK. Now choose the Wet Bristle copy from the Oils category. Open the Brush Creator (Ctrl/⌘-B), and its Stroke Designer tab. In the Impasto section, change the Draw To pop-up menu to Color. Then choose Set Default Variant from the Variant menu in the Brush Creator to make the change permanent for the new Wet Bristle variant.

3 Painting colored washes. Using a light touch on the stylus, and the new Wet Bristle brush, Vealé freely brushed loose washes of color over the image canvas, suggesting a subtle horizon line and a glowing campfire in the background.

Choose your new Wet Bristle variant and paint brushstrokes on the image. The brush applies paint when you press lightly, but scrubs underlying paint when you press hard. (You can also achieve good washes with other brushes, such as the Smeary Round and the Variable Flat variants of the Oils.)

4 Setting up a still life and painting the figure. Vealé set up a conventional light to shine from behind the figure that served as his model and another to reflect light onto its face. Then he carefully studied the Ashanti figure's form, and painted it directly on the image canvas with a smaller version of the Wet Bristle variant. He built up values slowly, gradually adding more saturated, darker tones to the still life study. Vealé brought out orange tones that were reminiscent of firelight in the background. He added deeper red and brown colors to the sky, and brighter colors and more detail to the bonfire in the background. Then he added stronger highlights and cast shadows to the foreground and to the carving. Finally, to relieve some of the rigidity of the centered composition, he repainted areas of the background to move the horizon up.

Variations. A slightly different effect (shown at right) can be achieved if you choose the new Wet Bristle, and in the General section of the Stroke Designer (Brush Creator), reduce the Opacity of the brush to between 20%–40% and set the Opacity Expression pop-up menu to Pressure. 🖌

Figure study by Stanley Vealé

Working with Thick Paint

Overview *Paint a color study; use Impasto brushes to add 3D brushwork to the study; use Surface Lighting to adjust the appearance of the highlights and shadows on the thick paint.*

CHELSEA SAMMEL

Sammel's black-and-white pencil study

IMPASTO BRINGS THE TEXTURE OF THICK, LUSCIOUS PAINT to the tip of your stylus. When painting *Dying Orchids,* artist Chelsea Sammel used Impasto brushes in Painter to add the texture of brush marks with realistic highlights and shadows to a color study. Then she scraped back and added more expressive brushwork, bringing more texture and activity to the painting.

1 Designing the still life and making a sketch. Sammel envisioned a composition with strong side lighting in which the orchids appeared to be suspended in space. She designed an airy, asymmetrical flower arrangement with interesting negative space, set up in the natural light of a window.

To begin the sketch, she created a new file that measured 1200 x 1600 pixels. In the Brush Selector Bar, she chose the Colored Pencil variant of the Colored Pencils, and in the Paper Selector, she chose Basic Paper. Then she drew a tight, black-and-white sketch. To sketch as Sammel did, select the Colored Pencil variant

The color underpainting

A detail showing scraped back canvas

Adding texture to the background with the Loaded Palette Knife variant of Impasto

and choose Restore Default Variant from the triangle pop-up menu on the right side of the Brush Selector Bar to make sure that the Colored Pencil uses the default settings.

2 Creating the color underpainting. She began to lay color directly over the sketch using the Round Camelhair variant of the Oils. She painted using warm autumn colors—browns, burnt sienna, golds—and other rich hues.

Traditional artists often add texture and complexity to the surface of their paintings by scraping areas of paint off the canvas. To scrape back areas, Sammel chose the Loaded Palette Knife variant of the Palette Knives. To make a smaller version of the brush, she reduced its size using the Size slider in the Property Bar. Switching between the Round Camelhair and Loaded Palette Knife variants, she painted and scraped back, pulled and blended colors, creating an expressive painting with a lot of movement.

3 Adding textured brushwork. Then Sammel added more interest and activity to the composition by adding textured brushstrokes that did not necessarily follow the lines of the colored paint. She modified the Loaded Palette Knife variant of Impasto, so that it would paint with negative depth, but not color, and she made it smaller. To make Sammel's custom palette knife, choose the Loaded Palette Knife variant of Impasto and set the Size slider in the Property Bar to 11.0. Open the Brush Creator by pressing Ctrl/⌘-B. Click the Stroke Designer Tab to open the Stroke Designer; then click the Impasto section bar to open the Impasto section. In the Impasto section, set the Draw To menu to Depth and the Depth slider to 35%, leaving other settings at their defaults: Smoothing, 77% and Plow, 100%. Save the variant by choosing Save Variant from the Brush Creator's Variant menu, giving it a new name. Then, to preserve the original variant, choose the original Loaded Palette Knife and restore its default settings by choosing Variant, Restore Default Variant.

When she wanted the new palette knife to paint with both color and depth, she modified it to pick up and smear underlying colors. To make this modification, select the new palette knife, and in the Impasto section of the Stroke Designer (Brush Creator), set the Draw To menu back to Color and Depth. To pick up and mix underlying colors more, click on the Well section bar to open the Well section and set Resat to 20%. Save and name the new variant; then reselect the first modified palette knife.

Using warm, creamy colors, Sammel painted loose, gestural brushstrokes over the background. At this point, she exaggerated the strong side lighting and enhanced the negative space in the painting by using the Variable Flat Opaque variant of Impasto with Draw To set to its default Color and Depth to apply more white brush work to the right side of the image.

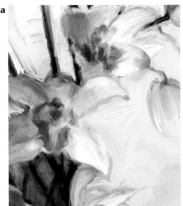

4a

Painting details on the orchids

4b

Pulling and blending paint on the flowers with a small Variable Flat Opaque brush (Impasto)

5a

Adding more texture to the foreground using the Texturizer-Fine (Impasto)

4 Painting details on the flowers, vase and table.

Once the background was painted in, Sammel painted over the orchids using the Variable Flat Opaque (Impasto). She added bright highlights to the right side of the orchids and deeper, richer colors to areas in shadow on the flowers, vase and table. As she worked, she frequently modified settings in the Impasto section of the Brush Controls for the Variable Flat Opaque variant. To paint with color and texture, she left the Draw To menu set at Color and Depth; to add textured brushstrokes without adding color, she chose the Draw to Depth setting. To paint brushstrokes with texture based on the current paper texture, she kept the Depth Method set to Paper.

5 Refining the painting.
Sammel used a small Loaded Palette Knife (Impasto) to drag color through the image (especially in the vase), then she added more colored paint using the Dry Ink vari-

5b

Painting final details on the vase and flowers using the Loaded Palette Knife (Impasto) and Dry Ink (Sumi-e) variants

ant of Sumi-e. To allow the Dry Ink to mix and pull colors on the canvas, she made changes to the Well controls using the Property Bar. She lowered the Resat (to about 20%) and raised the Bleed setting (to about 80%).

She added spattery Impasto texture to the image foreground with the Texturizer-Fine variant of Impasto. Then Sammel brushed over areas that were too "impastoed" using the Depth Equalizer variant (Impasto) at a low Opacity. She lowered the Opacity using the Opacity slider in the Property Bar. Finally, she reduced the overall effect of the Impasto by choosing Canvas, Surface Lighting. For a more subtle Impasto look she reduced the Amount to 75%. 🐾

A Painter Liquid Ink Primer

Overview *Here you'll find the basics for painting with the Liquid Ink brushes and layers in Painter.*

CHER THREINEN-PENDARVIS / CREATED FOR COREL CORPORATION

We began this Liquid Ink study of Little Doll *by creating a black line drawing with the Fine Point variant of Liquid Ink on a Liquid Ink layer. Then we added a new layer (by choosing New Liquid Ink Layer from the Layers palette menu), dragged it below the sketch layer in the Layers palette and added color to the table and background with the Graphic Camel variant. For the cat's fur we created another new layer between the two we already had, and painted using gold and tan colors. For the look of thicker paint on the fur, we double-clicked the layer's name in the Layers palette and adjusted the Amount slider in the Liquid Ink Layer Attributes dialog box. Then we painted with the Coarse Camel Resist to erode some of the colored ink.*

WITH THE LIQUID INK BRUSHES AND MEDIA LAYERS in Painter, you can paint bold, graphic brushstrokes of flat color, and then erode ink with resist brushes or build up thick ink that has three-dimensional highlights and shadows. Like traditional viscous media (printer's ink or the enamel used in jewelry making, for example), Liquid Ink is sticky.

Yellow Pitcher (above), one in a series of studies of 1930s California pottery, was created with the Graphic Camel and Graphic Camel Resist variants on several Liquid Ink layers, so that each color could be kept separate without mixing. Before you start a Liquid Ink painting of your own, reading the next five pages will help you to understand how to achieve the results you desire.

Controlling Liquid Ink. The most important settings for Liquid Ink are in the Property Bar and in several sections of the Brush Creator's Stroke Designer window: the General, Size and Liquid Ink sections of the Stroke Designer; the Layers palette; and the Surface Lighting dialog box, found under the Canvas menu. Painting with a Liquid Ink brush automatically generates a Liquid Ink Layer, which is then listed in the Layers palette. Liquid Ink layers can be targeted in the Layers palette and edited like other layers. (Chapter 6 tells more about working with layers.)

RESOLUTION-INDEPENDENT INK

A graphic medium, Liquid Ink is resolution-independent. It's possible to create a Liquid Ink illustration at half size, and then double the resolution of the file and retain the crisp edges on the brush work.

In this example, the "e" was drawn after the "S," and the new Liquid Ink stroke melted into the existing ink. The lettering was drawn using the Smooth Flat variant of Liquid Ink. The rough strokes were added using the Graphic Camel.

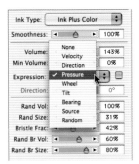

The Volume settings in the Liquid Ink section of the Stroke Designer allow you to specify which factor controls the Volume of a stroke.

The Liquid Ink section, showing the Ink Type pop-up menu

The Liquid Ink section, showing the default settings for the Graphic Camel

In the General section of the Stroke Designer (Brush Creator), the Liquid Ink dab types are displayed in the Dab Type pop-up menu. A dab type determines the shape of the brush tip—for instance, Liquid Ink Flat and Liquid Ink Camelhair (Camel brush tips are round). The Liquid Ink brushes use continuous-stroke technology, which means that brushstrokes are painted using brush hairs that form a set of antialiased 1-pixel lines. You'll find more information about dab types in Chapter 4, "Building Brushes" on page 152.

In the Property Bar (and in the Size section of the Stroke Designer, and in the Size section of Brush Controls), you'll find the Feature slider, which determines the density of the brush hairs in the continuous-stroke brushes. **Note:** A very low Feature setting (producing more densely packed brush hairs) takes greater computing power, and this can slow down the performance of a Liquid Ink brush.

In the Liquid Ink section of Stroke Designer (Brush Creator), if the Volume Expression controller is set to Pressure, the height of the brushstroke will increase as pressure is applied to the stylus.

Liquid Ink has two basic components: Ink and Color. *Ink* consists of the shape and dimension of the Liquid Ink, giving the medium its sticky, plastic quality and form. The *Color* component is independent of the ink form. In the Liquid Ink section of the Stroke Designer (Brush Creator), the Ink Type pop-up menu includes nine important Color-and-Ink options that dramatically affect the performance of the Liquid Ink brushes. The Ink Type settings themselves are complex and are also affected by slider settings in the Liquid Ink section (described below). A brush of the *Ink Plus Color* type adds new ink using the current color in the Color picker. While the *Ink Only* type affects only the shape of the brushstroke, the *Color Only* type affects only the color component. *Soften Ink Plus Color* alters existing brushstrokes so that the ink changes shape and the colors blend into one another. The *Soften Ink Only* reshapes the ink without changing its color, and *Soften Color Only* blends the Color without reshaping.

Painting with a *Resist* type brush will cause brushstrokes applied over the resist to be repelled. (Scrubbing with a non-resist brush can erode the resist until it is eventually removed.) Using the *Erase* type will remove existing ink and color. *Presoftened Ink Plus Color* works in conjunction with the Volume control settings to build up height as additional brushstrokes are applied.

INK AND COLOR COMPONENTS

Liquid Ink has two basic components: Ink and Color. *Ink* controls the shape and dimensionality of the strokes and gives the medium its sticky, plastic quality. *Color* controls color without affecting the shape.

INTERACTIVE SETTINGS

Many of the various settings that control Liquid Ink interact with one another in complex ways. This is what produces the magic of this medium, but mastering the complexity can present quite a challenge. It's a good idea to experiment with the different brushes and types until you get a feel for how Liquid Ink performs.

An active Liquid Ink layer as it appears in the Layers palette. To create a new Liquid Ink layer, click the right triangle on the Layers palette bar and choose New Liquid Ink Layer or click the Create New Liquid Ink Layer button at the bottom of the Layers palette.

For Ocean Waves, *the Coarse Bristle variant of Liquid Ink was used to draw curved strokes with a thick, bristly texture. We used the Coarse Airbrush Resist to add a foamy texture to the water and to suggest atmosphere in the sky.*

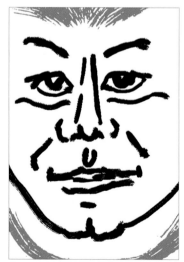

Sumo Ink Man. *We drew this study using a Wacom pressure-sensitive tablet and stylus on a laptop (while watching Sumo wrestlers on TV), with the Graphic Camel and Graphic Bristle variants of Liquid Ink.*

The eight sliders in the Liquid Ink section work in conjunction with each other to create many kinds of Liquid Ink brushstrokes. Because these controls are very complex and interdependent, they're difficult to clearly define. Experiment—dig in and try out the Liquid Ink variants, while keeping an eye on the Liquid Ink section controls. The *Smoothness* slider controls how sticky the ink is. Lower values will create coarser brushstrokes with less self-adhesion. A high Smoothness setting will help to hide the individual bristle marks and will increase adhesion, but it may make the performance of the brush lag. *Volume* controls the height of the brushstroke. Use this setting in conjunction with the Volume Expression in the Liquid Ink section to add height to brushstrokes. (**Note:** To view volume on your image, the Amount setting must be adjusted in the Liquid Ink Layer Attributes dialog box. See the "Turning on 3D Highlights and Shadows" tip below.) The *Min Volume* controls the amount that the volume can vary. (This slider is used in conjunction with the Volume Expression in the Liquid Ink section.) *Rand Vol* controls the randomness of the volume in a stroke. A low value will create a smoother, less variable stroke. *Random Size* controls randomness of brush hair size within the stroke; again, a lower value will help to create a smoother stroke. *Bristle Frac* controls the density of the bristles. *Rand Bristle Vol* controls the variation in volume of ink laid down by individual bristles, and a low value will make the bristle marks a more even thickness. *Rand Bristle Size* controls variation in the widths of individual bristles. A very low setting will make the bristles more similar in width.

TURNING ON 3D HIGHLIGHTS AND SHADOWS

To view Liquid Ink brush work with three-dimensional highlights and shadows, double-click the name of the Liquid Ink Layer in the Layers palette and increase the Amount (thickness) setting. Click OK. The Liquid Ink medium has no thickness limit. After you have increased the Amount setting, you can use your stylus to paint more Liquid Ink onto the layer, continuing to build up the pile of ink. You can adjust the thickness at any time using the Amount slider in the Liquid Ink Layer Attributes dialog box. (There is no preview in this dialog box. You have to adjust the slider and click OK, and then observe the effect on the image.) To change the direction, intensity or other properties of the lighting, choose Canvas, Surface Lighting and adjust the settings in the Surface Lighting dialog box.

Increasing the Amount setting (left) increased the thickness of the brushstrokes (right). We left the settings in the Surface Lighting dialog box at their defaults.

After drawing black line work using the Fine Point variant, John Derry created a new Liquid Ink layer and dragged it below the line work layer in the Layers palette. Working on the new layer, he used the Smooth Knife variant to paint broad areas of color onto the background. He created interesting texture by eroding paint with the Coarse Airbrush Resist. For the smooth-edged highlights on the stool, he painted with the Smooth Camel variant.

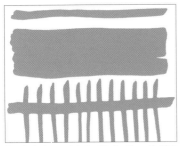

Brushstrokes painted with the Smooth Flat variant of Liquid Ink

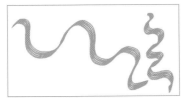

Thin-to-thick sweeping curved strokes painted with the Pointed Flat variant of Liquid Ink

WORKING WITH THE LIQUID INK BRUSHES

Here are some suggestions for how to paint using the Liquid Ink brushes in Painter. Even if you're familiar with Painter's other brushes, try out these ideas and experiment with all of the Liquid Ink variants.

Painting coarsely textured brushstrokes. To paint brushstrokes with a coarse, bristly texture, choose the Coarse Bristle variant. You can control the paint coverage by applying more or less pressure to the stylus—a lighter pressure will create a stroke with less paint. The Graphic variants also paint coarsely textured brushstrokes and with better performance, for more spontaneous painting. The Graphic Camel is one of our favorites because it paints expressive, thin-to-thick strokes, with finer texture on the edges of the brushstrokes.

Blended color with smooth brushes. Any Liquid Ink variant with Smooth in its name has a high smoothness setting and will paint just like a brush loaded with very thick, sticky ink or paint. The Smooth Bristle variant's bristles will spread or splay out as you rotate your hand through the stroke, while the Smooth Camel performs like a big, round brush with longer bristles. As you press harder on the stylus, the Smooth Camel will paint a broader stroke. As you paint a new color over existing ink with a Smooth brush, the edges of the colors will subtly blend.

Thick and thin strokes with the Flat brushes. Look for brushes with the word Flat in their name; the Coarse Flat and Pointed Flat are examples. With Flat-tipped brushes, you can paint wide or narrow strokes, depending on how you hold the stylus relative to the stroke direction and how much pressure you apply. When trying the strokes below, position your stylus with the button facing up (away from you). To paint a broad flat area of color with the Smooth Flat (as in the example on the left), pull the brush straight across your image using even pressure. To make the thin lines, pull down. To make a curved, thin-to-thick wavy line, use light pressure on your stylus

MOUSE ALERT!

Liquid Ink brushes are very responsive to the pressure applied to a stylus. Because of the importance of pressure, many of the brushes do not perform as described here when a mouse is used. For instance, the brushes will not paint the expressive thick-to-thin brushstrokes that are possible with a pressure-sensitive tablet and stylus. Also, the Volume settings that are enhanced by pressure will not perform identically.

for the thin top areas, and more pressure as you sweep down and rotate the brush. For flat brushstrokes with sensitive thin-to-thick control, try the Pointed Flat. With this brush, bristle marks will be more visible when heavy pressure is applied to the stylus. For a thin-to-thick sweeping curved stroke, begin the thin portion with

We drew the sketch for Yellow Pitcher *using the Velocity Sketcher variant.*

The Graphic Camel Resist variant was used to erode ink and create highlights in Yellow Pitcher. *A detail is shown here.*

very light pressure on your stylus, and as you sweep downward rotate your stylus slightly and apply more pressure. To make a thick, even stroke, pull the stylus sideways relative to the button, using even pressure. For the thin lines, apply even pressure and pull in a direction toward or away from the button.

Sketching and line work. You can also sketch or draw line work with Liquid Ink. Quick performance makes the Velocity Sketcher ideal for spontaneous sketching. On the edges of the brushstrokes, you'll notice grainy texture.

The *Fine* variants of Liquid Ink are good for painting details and for calligraphic line work. The Fine Point draws like a steel pen with a pointed nib, and the Fine Point Eraser is ideal for cleaning up edges and for removing small patches of ink.

Painting resists. A *resist* is a substance that can be painted onto a Liquid Ink layer with a Liquid Ink Resist-type brush. A resist is capable of repelling ink when the area is painted over by a standard Liquid Ink brush. You can also "scrub away" existing Liquid Ink using a Resist type brush. The Coarse Bristle Resist and the Graphic Camel Resist, for instance, are useful for painting coarse, eroded areas on a Liquid Ink painting. For a smoother resist, try the Smooth Bristle Resist, Smooth Camel Resist or Smooth Flat Resist variant. To erode existing ink and create an interesting speckled texture, use the Coarse Airbrush Resist.

SOFTENING EDGES

Using the Soften Edges and Color variant of Liquid Ink, you can subtly blur areas of ink and color.

Detail of Hillside Lake. *We used Soften Edges and Color to blend the top edge of the purple hill in the midground.*

ADJUSTING LIQUID INK EDGES

You can nondestructively make Liquid Ink brushstrokes appear to expand or contract by adjusting the Threshold slider in the Liquid Ink Layer Attributes dialog box. To see how Threshold works, in the Layers palette, target the layer that you'd like to change and access the Liquid Ink Layer Attributes dialog box by double-clicking the layer's name in the Layers palette (or press the Enter key). To thicken the appearance of the brushstrokes, lower the Threshold value by moving the slider to the left. To give the ink a thinner appearance, raise the Threshold value by moving the slider to the right.

Adjusting the Threshold slider very low (to –49%) thickened the blue ink.

Adjusting the Threshold very high (to 160%) dramatically thinned the blue ink on the sugar bowl.

Encaustic Painting with Liquid Ink

Overview *Use a Liquid Ink brush to paint textured color on a layer; duplicate the layer; make a custom coloring brush; recolor the layer and erode areas; add more layers with new color and texture.*

JOHN DERRY

1a

Painting the yellow square with the Sparse Camel variant of Liquid Ink

1b

The new active Liquid Ink layer shown in the Layers palette

ENCAUSTIC PAINTING INCORPORATES PIGMENTS suspended in wax. It was used by the ancient Greeks who painted the brightly colored statues in the Acropolis and by the Romans for wall murals in Pompeii. Traditional encaustic technique involves heating the wax-based medium and then painting quickly while the wax is still malleable. Delicate layering of transparent color as well as heavy Impasto techniques are possible. In Painter, you can create the look of encaustic painting with the new Liquid Ink brushes and media layers.

To create *Chess*, John Derry used Liquid Ink brushes and media layers to emulate encaustic painting. He painted bright colors on Liquid Ink layers, and then eroded and scratched out areas to reveal the color and textured brush work on the underlying layers. For the look of thick encaustic paint, he added subtle three-dimensional highlights and shadows to the layers.

1 Creating textured brush work. Begin your Liquid Ink painting by opening a new file with a white background (File, New). To work at the scale of this painting, set the Width and Height at 800 x 800 pixels and click OK.

To paint a background consisting of large, textured strokes, choose the Sparse Camel variant of Liquid Ink in the Brush Selector Bar and choose a bright yellow color in the Colors picker. When you've chosen a Liquid Ink brush and you touch your

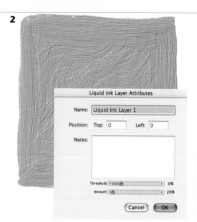

The completed first layer, showing the highlights and shadows on the brush work and the settings in the Liquid Ink Layer Attributes dialog box

The active, duplicate layer in the Layers palette

Choosing Color Only for the Type setting in the Liquid Ink Section of the Stroke Designer

The square reddish areas added to the image on the duplicate layer, and then partially eroded using a resist brush; shown with both layers visible (left) and with the yellow layer hidden (right)

stylus to the tablet, a Liquid Ink layer will automatically be generated and will be listed in the Layers palette. Loosely block in a square shape using the Sparse Camel. Derry purposely painted an irregular edge and left part of the white background as an informal border, which would add to the textural contrast in his image.

2 Turning on thick paint. To add realistic highlights and shadows to the brush work on the yellow layer, double-click its name in the Layers palette. When the Liquid Ink Layer Attributes dialog box appears, increase the Amount setting to about 20% and click OK.

3 Duplicating a Liquid Ink layer. Derry wanted to add different colors while keeping the brushstroke pattern that he had already created. So he duplicated the active yellow layer by choosing the Layer Adjuster tool in the Toolbox, pressing the Alt/Option key and clicking once on the layer in the image. (To read more about working with layers, turn to Chapter 6, "Using Layers.") Once you've duplicated the layer, choose the Brush again in the Toolbox.

4 Making a custom brush for coloring. With some Liquid Ink brushes, you can recolor elements without disturbing the ink (shape, volume and lighting) component that you've painted on a layer. After the layer duplicate was created, Derry modified the Sparse Camel brush so that it would change the color without changing the shape and thickness of the existing strokes. To modify the Sparse Camel as Derry did, open the Brush Creator palette by choosing Window, Show Brush Creator, or by pressing Ctrl/⌘-B. Click the Stroke Designer tab, and open the Liquid Ink section by clicking on the Liquid Ink section bar. (The Liquid Ink section can also be found in the Brush Controls.) In the section's Ink Type pop-up menu, choose Color Only. To save this custom Sparse Camel brush, choose Save Variant from the Variant menu in the Brush Creator, name the new brush and click OK to save it. In addition to saving your new brush, Painter will remember the changes that you've made to the default Sparse Camel brush, so it's a good idea to restore it to its default settings. To return the original Sparse Camel variant to its default, choose Restore Default Variant from the Variant menu in the Brush Creator.

5 Coloring and eroding the duplicated layer. With the duplicate layer active in the Layers palette, choose a new color (Derry chose a bright reddish-pink) and paint over the areas that you want to

6a

The smaller blue squares are added to the image, breaking each of the original four squares into four.

6b

The small green squares are added, so that now each of the four original squares has 16 parts.

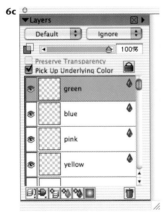

6c

The Layers palette showing the renamed Liquid Ink layers

recolor. To scrape away areas of the layer so that the color from the underlying layer will show through, you can use a Resist-type variant or an Eraser-type variant of Liquid Ink. Because he likes the texture it creates, Derry scrubbed with the Sparse Camel Resist variant to scrape away the pink upper-right and lower-left areas to reveal the yellow. Then, to add an eroded texture into areas within the pink squares that he planned to keep, he brushed lightly over them using the Sparse Camel Resist variant.

6 Adding the blue and green squares. To add the blue and green colors to his image, Derry repeated the duplicating, revealing and eroding process in steps 2 and 3. The blue squares were smaller, so the effect was to break each pink square into four. The green squares were even smaller; the effect was to break up each original square into 16.

7 Painting the chess piece. So the castle would look as if it were thicker paint sitting on top of the painted chess board, Derry wanted the direction of the brushstrokes to be different. He created a new Liquid Ink layer by clicking the New Liquid Ink Layer at the bottom of the Layers palette bar. On the new layer, he blocked in the basic shape of the chess piece with the default Sparse Camel using white color, and then used the Sparse Camel Resist to erode some of the white paint. For the black areas on the chess piece, Derry duplicated the white layer as he had done for the yellow in step 3. Then he chose his custom Sparse Camel brush (which used Color Only) and painted black onto the right half of the castle. To finish, he used the Sparse Camel Resist to erode areas of the black layer to expose the white underneath.

7a

The white shape was painted on a new Liquid Ink layer.

7b

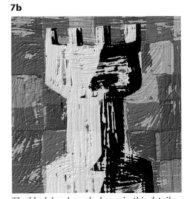

The black brush work shown in this detail was painted on a duplicate of the white layer.

American Soldier

French Soldier

British Soldier

Hessian Soldier

British Sailor

■ "I approach painting in Painter the same way I paint conventionally," says **Karen Carr**, an accomplished, award-winning illustrator who often creates natural history illustrations for educational publishers. Carr was commissioned by the National Museum of American History to create the illustrations on these two pages.

Soldiers (above) was created in collaboration with her father, **Bill Carr**, who is also an award-winning illustrator. The Carrs began by sketching with the Charcoal variants, and then laying in color using Oils variants. Carr painted glazes of color over the top of her underpainting just as she does with oil paints. She prefers to keep the use of layers to a minimum, because she likes the tactile feel of moving paint around on the Canvas. After blocking in basic color using a modified Charcoal variant, she used the Just Add Water variant of Blenders to smoothly blend and sculpt the figures. She worked back and forth, adding color and blending as she refined the volume of their forms. When she wanted to smudge paint and reveal texture, she used the Coarse Smear and Smudge variants of Blenders.

■ **Karen Carr** was commissioned by the National Museum of American History to paint this illustration representing George Washington's camp during the Revolutionary War.

To begin *Washington's Camp*, Carr chose a light brown color in the Colors picker and then chose Effects, Surface Control, Color Overlay to establish the color theme for the painting. Then, using Charcoal variants, she sketched the composition. To paint transparent glazes, she used the Digital Watercolor brushes and a variety of textures, and she changed the size and opacity of the

brushes as she worked. She dried the Digital Watercolor so that she could merge it with brushstrokes she had applied with the Charcoal brushes. As Carr began to build up elements in the landscape, she used the Just Add Water (and other Blenders variants) to blend and pull color. This blending is most evident in the sky and on the distant trees. To create the texture on the rocks and ground, she blended and pulled paint by using the Distorto variants of the Distortion category and she also used her own custom Blenders variants.

■ Inspired by memories of a favorite art teacher's home, artist **Kramer Mitchell** painted *Woman Reading*.

Mitchell began the image by scanning a photograph, and then retouching and cropping the scan in Photoshop. Then she opened the photograph in Painter. She also opened a new file exactly the same size as the cropped photo. She chose the Sketching Pencil 3 variant of Pencils and created a rough composition sketch. She put the sketch on a layer (Edit, Copy and then Edit, Paste in Place) to use it as a guide while she painted the base colors. Mitchell reduced the opacity of the sketch layer so that she could see the Canvas. She laid in color using a custom Oils brush, and as she worked, she sampled colors from the photograph using the Eyedropper tool. The custom Oils brush worked similarly to the Round Camelhair variant of Oils, which smears paint as you apply it.

After blocking in the color, she set the sketch aside. Then, Mitchell chose the photograph again and created a clone by choosing File, Clone. Using the Wet Oils Cloner variant of Cloners, she painted onto the cloned photo image, creating a painterly look. Then, she saved this file in RIFF format. At this point, she made the sketch file active and removed the sketch layer. She chose File, Clone Source and designated the cloned photo image as the Clone Source. Working on her sketch image, she began painting with the Smeary Flat variant of Oils. As she worked, she alternated between two brushes: the Smeary Flat (Oils) to apply and smear paint and the Wet Oil Cloner (Cloners) to bring back areas. Mitchell created a vibrant, painterly look. To bring detail back into the woman's face, she used the Soft Cloner variant of Cloners at a very low opacity.

Mitchell added more saturation to a few areas by making selections and then using Effects, Surface Control, Color Overlay, Dye Concentration. To paint final details (such as the highlights on the woman's blouse), she used the Detail Oils 10 variant of Oils.

■ Concept designer **Andrew Jones** has created concepts for films and video games. Jones founded the online community conceptart.org. He created *Final Thunder Sarah* for a conceptart.org art challenge. To read more about Jones's work, see "Mixed Media Painting" on page 108.

To begin, Jones opened a new file and used the Paint Bucket to fill the background with gray. Then, he drew a composition sketch of his friend Sarah—a roller derby racer—dressed in a *Thunderdome*-inspired costume. In preparation for adding color, he used the Lasso tool to select the figure's skin. Then, he applied a peach color to the selected areas using the Paint Bucket. He

proceeded to select and fill other areas with flat base colors.

Jones built a custom cover Felt Pen that was based on the Medium Tip Felt Pen variant of Felt Pens. In the General section of Brush Controls, he changed its Method to Cover and the Subcategory to Soft Cover. In the Size section, he set Size Expression to Pressure, and he also decreased the Min Size so that the size would change gradually with the pressure he applied.

Using his custom Felt Pen, he modeled the forms on the figure and clothing, and he painted the background. He varied the size and opacity of the Felt Pen as he worked. To paint the linear textured strokes on

the boots and to paint a glow around the woman's shoulders, Jones used a modified Loaded Palette Knife that included an increased Feature setting in the Property Bar. With this brush he was able to apply linear strokes of color and to achieve optical color mixing and textures. He used a low-opacity version of the custom Palette Knife to complete the modeling on the woman's skin and boots. Using brushes and effects, Jones applied several custom paper textures to the painting, for instance, the cracked texture in the foreground and the woven texture on Sarah's skirt. As a final touch, Jones used the Glow variant of F-X to paint a blue glow at the tip of Sarah's guitar.

■ **Dennis Orlando** is well known for his Impressionist-style landscape and still-life paintings. To create the vibrant look of pastel in *Flowers Pastel,* he layered color using the Artist Pastel Chalk variant of Pastels.

Orlando chose the Artists' Canvas texture from the Paper Selector in the Toolbox. Using a palette of luminous colors, he roughed out a study for the composition using Chalk and Pastels variants, and then he layered more color. Switching back and forth between the Artist Pastel Chalk and the Grainy Water variant of Blenders, he continued to add color and smudge it. To help to modulate color, Orlando increased Color Variability for the Artist Pastel Chalk variant, moving the ±H (hue) slider to about 10% in the Color Variability palette. His use of enhanced Color Variability is most easily seen in the foreground tabletop and on the vase. To build rich texture, he used a Large Chalk variant of Chalk and a light pressure on the stylus. This scumbled texture is most noticeable in the foreground and on the upper portion of the bird-of-paradise flowers. Finally, Orlando used a tiny Grainy Water variant of Blenders to blend and finesse the highlights on the flowers and leaves.

■ **Richard Noble** has been an accomplished traditional painter and designer for many years. Today, he paints most of his fine artwork in Painter, using techniques that simulate traditional acrylic painting. He typically begins a painting by shooting reference photos and making sketches on location.

"I have always tried to keep a feeling of freshness in my work and to stay away from the overworked syndrome. In the traditional world of watercolor and acrylics, that means laying in large areas quickly and getting them right, and then by following up by working in the detail areas and leaving the large areas alone. This gives the eye the detail while retaining a fresh, immediate look," says Noble.

For *Foothills*, Noble roughed in vibrant, saturated color using the Gouache variants and the Round Camelhair variant of the Oils. The Round Camelhair allowed Noble to move paint around on the Canvas as he worked. To blend and move paint while adding a subtle texture, Noble used the Coarse Oily Blender variant of Blenders. Then, using an Opaque Smooth Brush variant of Gouache, he painted fine details in the shady areas of the foreground foliage, as well as in the sunlit areas of the trees. To add a few textured strokes to the foliage, he used a small Artist Pastel Chalk brush.

Noble usually prints his paintings on canvas with light-fast inks and finishes them with touches of acrylic paint.

■ **Susan Thompson** was commissioned
to create *Cookies for Santa* as part of a
triptych for the Disneyland 1st Annual
Christmas Collectibles Festival. The theme
of the three pieces is *The Childhood
Dreams of Christmas*. Prior to shooting
photographs and painting, Thompson
made butter cookies and then hand-
painted each one with baker's dyes.
Then, she photographed the still life with
an sx70 camera and hand-manipulated
the emulsion layers to give it an impres-
sionistic look. The edition of 500 pieces
was printed as ultra high-gloss Fuji Crystal
Archive prints, and it sold out. Thompson
decided to rework the image using
Painter. This version of *Cookies for Santa*
is shown here.

Thompson opened a scan of the
manipulated sx70 print, and then she
cloned it by choosing File, Clone. To add
expressive brushstokes to the image, she
used the Oil Cloner variant of Cloners,
but without the thick Impasto paint. To
turn off the Impasto, she opened the
Impasto section of Brush Controls and
changed the Draw To pop-up menu to
Color. Then, Thompson painted the
background areas, changing the Size and
Opacity of the brush as she worked. For
the fabric and plates, she used custom
Oil brushes. Next, she switched to the
Wet Acrylic 30 variant of Acrylics. To
paint with the brush using color from the
Clone Source, she enabled the Clone
Color button on the Colors palette, and

then she painted the window, wreath
and cookies.

To bring back details from the original
image, Thompson used the Soft Cloner
variant of Cloners. To build up the density
in a few areas, such as Mickey's face and in
the white lines of the poinsettia, she used
the Burn variant of the Photo brush. To
brighten highlights on the candle flames,
presents and candelabra, she used the
Glow variant of F-X. Finally, to add the
magic sparkles to areas, she used a custom
variant similar to the Fairy Dust variant of
F-X. As a last step, she added more size to
her image (Canvas, Canvas Size), and then
she painted border effects using the Oil
Cloner, the Wet Acrylic and her custom Oil
brushes.

■ Artist **Donal Jolley** usually begins his paintings by shooting reference photos. He roughs in color using the Chalk and Pastels variants, and then he uses the Oils variants for more developed brush work and the Pens variants for tiny details.

Jolley began *Saturday Morning Watering* by shooting photos of his young daughter in their flower garden. He opened the photos in Painter and made a clone of the photo by choosing File, Clone, and then deleted the contents of the clone image by selecting All (Ctrl/⌘-A) and pressing Backspace/Delete. He saved the clone image by choosing File, Save As, giving it a new name. Jolley kept the original photo open and turned on Tracing Paper in the clone by pressing Ctrl/⌘-T. Next, he added a new layer on which he would rough in the composition and develop the color theme. Working on the new layer, he used the Sharp Chalk to sketch the composition and the Square Chalk to paint the larger shapes and broad colored areas. As he worked, he constantly changed the sizes of his brushes. He added more layers as he worked on certain areas (for instance, the child and water) so that he could build up highlights and shadows, and then adjust their opacity. After the composition was developed, he dropped the layers to the Canvas. Then, using the Smeary variants of the Oils he applied new color and blended it with the existing pigment, for a painterly feeling. This work is especially evident in the spray of water, in the trees, and also on the girl's helmet and skin. To blend and smooth areas, he used the Just Add Water variant of the Blenders.

■ Artist **Nancy Stahl** has created award-winning illustrations using gouache and other traditional materials since 1976. Using Painter's brushes and surfaces, she's been able to re-create the effects she achieved in her traditional work, as shown here in *Sax* (above) and *Workbook Man* (right). To learn more about her painting techniques, turn to "Painting with Gouache," on page 96.

Stahl began *Sax* by roughing in a cream-colored background using a modified Broad Cover Brush variant (Gouache). Using a darker color, she sketched the forms of the sax using the Smooth Ink Pen variant of the Pens.

Using custom-made brushes she had built to imitate her favorite gouache brushes, Stahl added color and began to render the forms of the musical instrument. For the look of thicker paint on her study, Stahl used the Opaque Flat and Round Camelhair variants of Impasto to paint expressive linear strokes on the instrument and behind it. To move the paint around while carving into the existing thick paint, she switched to a small Palette Knife variant of Impasto. To finish, she chose the Opaque Bristle Spray (Impasto) and brightened the highlights in a few areas.

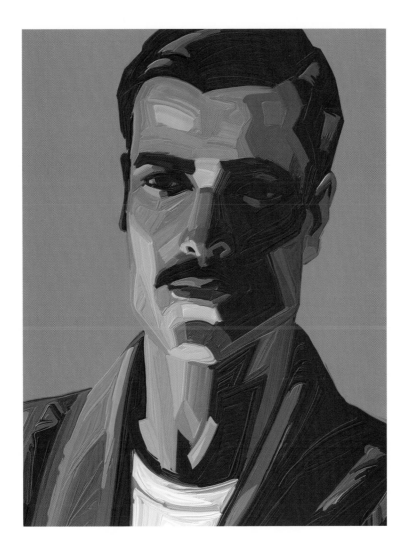

■ For *Workbook Man*, **Nancy Stahl** used Painter brushes that imitate her favorite traditional tools.

Stahl began the study by setting up a colored background for her image. She chose File, New and in the New dialog box, she clicked in the Paper Color square and chose a dark tan paper color. Then she chose a darker color in the Colors picker. She used the Smooth Ink Pen variant of Pens to draw a line sketch for the portrait. To block in the basic color theme, while beginning to sculpt the forms of the head, Stahl used a modified version of the Round Camelhair variant (Oils). To add brushstrokes with thicker paint, she switched to the Opaque Flat variant of Impasto. Then, to scrape into the thick paint and move it around while enhancing the expressive, angular look of the painting, she switched to a small Palette Knife variant of Impasto and made straighter, angled brushstrokes on the neck and shoulders. To complete her painting, she brightened a few of the highlights on the shirt, nose and chin using the Opaque Flat variant of Impasto.

■ Based in Normandy, France, **Kathy Hammon** is an accomplished artist and educator who works both traditionally and digitally. Hammon's current work with traditional media consists of very large oil paintings on canvas. Her digital paintings also give the viewer the feeling of vast spaces. When she uses Painter, she paints directly onscreen, without the use of photographs or scans. Hammon loves the realistic textures that can be achieved with the Chalk, Pastels, Oil Pastels, Oils, Sumi-e and Blenders variants.

The Whale was inspired by the beautiful whale she saw while sailing in Ecuador. She interpreted this vision as a dream of a whale swimming and jumping during the night. Hammon began the painting by using Oil Pastels variants to paint sweeping brushstrokes and large areas of color. When she wanted to blend one color into another, she used the Just Add Water variant of Blenders. Spontaneously painting, and then blending, she worked back and forth, changing the sizes of the brushes as she worked. For the coastline,

she used deeper colors to enhance the dreamy nighttime scene. To add details to the coastline (the palm trees and volcanoes), she used lighter colors and a small Artist Pastel Chalk variant (Pastels). Then she added more coarse brushstroke details to the hills and trees using the Dry Ink (Sumi-e). To complete the seascape, Hammon used a modified Artist Pastel Chalk variant to add texture and redefine the edge of the whale's tail. She also added a few small highlights to the distant hills.

■ **Cher Threinen-Pendarvis** often makes several studies for a painting on location, carefully observing how light and atmosphere affect color in highlights and shadows.

An isolated, cherished view and a forth-coming weather change provided the inspiration for *Downstream Weather*. For this painting, Pendarvis began by making several colored pencil sketches (details in the cliffs and the overall seascape) in a conventional sketchbook that she'd carried in her backpack. Later, back at the studio, she created a new file in Painter. Using the 2B Pencil and the Sketching Pencil variants of the Pencils, she sketched the composition. Then she loosely blocked in color directly over the sketch with a Round Camelhair variant of Oils, which she had modified to include a small amount of Color Variability to help to modulate the color. To build up layers of color interest on the hills, cliffs and water, she dabbed small strokes of paint on top by using the Fine Bristle variant of Gouache, and then she blended areas of the cliffs, hills and water using the Round Blender Brush and the Grainy Water variants of Blenders. Pendarvis added soft clouds to the sky using the Square Soft Pastel variant of Pastels, and then smoothed and blended color using the Grainy Water. To add textured highlights to the beach and color interest to the cliffs, she used the Square Hard Pastel and the Artist Pastel Chalk (Pastels). To balance the composition, she reworked the path along the cliff using the Artist Pastel Chalk and then added softer brushstrokes to the path using the Round Camelhair variant. She also used the Art-ist Pastel Chalk to feather colored strokes over the foliage above the cliffs, and to add color complexity and movement. Finally, she applied highlights to a few areas using a small Artist Pastel Chalk brush.

■ In preparation for painting *Paths to Water 4,* **Cher Threinen-Pendarvis** made several loose color studies on location. She observed how light and atmosphere affect the color in highlights and shadows on the seascape.

Pendarvis' *Paths* series (of which *Path to Water 4* is a member) is inspired by favorite paths that lead to breathtaking coastal views and surf spots in California. For this painting, Pendarvis began by making pastel sketches of the hillside, plant life and seascape, using Canson paper and pastels that she'd carried in her backpack. Later, back at the studio, she created a new file in Painter and set her onsite sketch beside the computer as a reference. Using the Square Chalk variant of Chalk and a Round Soft Pastel variant of Pastels over the Charcoal

Paper texture, she loosely sketched the composition, first blocking in larger areas of color. Then, she gradually focused on areas that she wanted to define with crisper details. To build up layers of color interest on the hillside and water, she dabbed small strokes of subtle color on top using a small Soft Oil Pastel variant of Oil Pastels. Then, she blended distant areas of the hillside and trees using the Grainy Water variant of Blenders. To move and pull paint in the sky, she used a Subtle Palette Knife variant of Palette Knives. Pendarvis added lighter areas to the water using the Square Chalk, and then smoothed and blended color using the Grainy Water. To add textured color to the path and tonal interest to the hills, she lightly scumbled using a Square Chalk and a Round Hard Pastel. To

enhance the serpentine path, which was the focal point of the composition, she added brighter color using a Soft Oil Pastel. Then, to bring the foreground closer, she reworked the nearest foliage with the Round Camelhair variant of Oils using dynamic, curved strokes. She also added a few strokes of brighter color to the shadows on the path using a small Round Camelhair brush. Finally, Pendarvis used expressive, quick strokes to paint the foreground grasses using the small Round Camelhair brush and the Soft Oil Pastel. She wanted to print the mixed media work on even-textured paper with light fast inks, so she chose 13 x 19-inch Epson Archival Matte paper and printed the final image on an Epson 2200 printer using Epson's seven-color UltraChrome ink set.

■ *Animal Watch Magazine* commissioned **Carol Benioff** to create *Elk,* an illustration about a hunter's change of heart. Benioff combined a pen-and-ink drawing with a painting that she created in Painter. She began by making pencil sketches of the elk and the hunter. When the drawings were as she liked them, she scanned the two sketches and opened them in Painter. She copied and pasted the sketch of the hunter onto a layer over the elk, and set the Composite Method for the layer to Multiply in the Layers palette. Benioff experimented with the size and positioning of the two drawings until they worked well together.

To develop the image of the elk, Benioff painted with the Acrylic brushes, and then she added details using Chalk variants. To give the image more depth, she painted translucent glazes using a low-opacity brush and then added a lighting effect. To apply the lighting effect, she chose Effects, Surface Control, Apply Lighting. The completed elk painting is shown on the left.

Benioff replaced the pencil sketch of the hunter with a scan of the pen-and-ink drawing. To tint the pen-and-ink drawing, she added a new layer under the hunter. With the new layer's Composite Method set to Multiply, Benioff painted light washes of color using the Digital Watercolor brushes.

4

BUILDING
BRUSHES

Vase of Flowers, shown here as a detail, was painted using the custom brushes described in "Painting in Pastel Using Custom Brushes" on page 162.

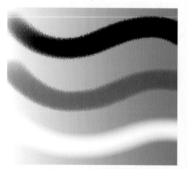

Switch methods to make dramatic changes in brush characteristics. Here we've applied the Waxy Crayons variant of Crayons over a gradient using the default Buildup method (top), Cover method (center) and Eraser method (bottom).

INTRODUCTION

IF YOU ARE AN ARTIST who does not rest until you get exactly the brush stroke that you want, then this chapter is for you.

Painter offers many features for customizing brushes, including the Brush Creator's Stroke Designer (described on pages 158–159) and the Transposer and Randomizer functions (described on pages 160–161). The Stroke Designer is where the individual controls for building unique custom brushes reside. The Transposer allows you to blend components of two existing Painter brushes and choose which blend you want. With the Randomizer you can choose a brush and have Painter create 12 variations.

If you like trying new brushes but don't want to build them, check out the Brush libraries on the Wow! CD-ROM in the back of this book—you'll find the brushes shown on these pages and more. But if you enjoy creating your own brushes, read on.

METHODS

Methods are the backbone of many brush variants, including brushes that users of earlier versions of Painter know and love. A brush variant's Method setting controls how the paint will interact with the background and with other paint. For instance, by default the Felt Pens variants use the Buildup method, meaning that overlapping strokes will darken. The Chalk variants use the Cover method by default, which means that strokes—even light-colored ones—will cover other strokes. You can, however, switch the method for the variant that you design. For example, you can save a Cover method variant of the Felt Pens. To see the method for a specific brush variant, such as the Square Soft Pastel, open the Brush Controls palette's General section by choosing Window, Brush Controls, Show General.

The Gritty Charcoal variant of Charcoal was applied using various Subcategory settings: the anti-aliased default Grainy Hard Cover (top); the pixelated Grainy Edge Flat Cover (middle); and the soft-edged Soft Cover (bottom).

Strokes painted with the default Square Hard Pastel that uses a Grain setting of 10% (left), and with the grain reduced to 6% (right)

You will find the Dab Type, Stroke Type, Method, and Subcategory in the General section of the Stroke Designer in the Brush Creator (and in the General section of the Brush Controls).

SUBCATEGORIES

While each method gives a radically different effect to a brush, the *subcategories*, or submethods, make more subtle changes, affecting the edges of brush strokes. Subcategories that include the word *Flat* produce hard, aliased strokes with pixelated edges. Those that include the word *Hard* give smoother strokes. Strokes made using *Soft* subcategories appear with feathered edges. Strokes with the word *Grainy* in their subcategory setting will be affected by the active paper texture. Strokes that contain the word *Edge* give a thicker, stickier look; *Variable* refers to strokes that are affected by tilt and direction.

Paper textures. "Grainy" brush methods will reveal the paper texture you've selected in the Paper Selector. Adjust the Grain slider on the Property Bar to vary the intensity of the grain revealed by your brushstrokes. For most of Painter's brushes, a lower Grain setting means that *less of the color will penetrate the grain*, so your strokes will look grainier.

DAB TYPES

In Painter, brushstrokes are built from *dabs*. Painter has 24 dab types (all located under the Dab Type menu); however, they fall into two general classifications: *dab-based* brushes (such as the brushes in earlier versions of Painter) and brushes created with *continuous-stroke* dab types. The main difference lies in how brushstrokes are created from the dabs as described in "Dab-Based Brushes" and "Continuous-Stroke Brushes" on page 154. You can switch dab types by opening the Brush

THE BRUSH CREATOR

When building new brushes, you'll spend most of your time using the Stroke Designer tab of the Brush Creator (described on pages 158–159). The Brush Creator offers more useful features for customizing brushes including the Transposer and Randomizer functions (described on pages 160-161).

BRUSH CONTROLS ARE BACK!

Users who are familiar with the Brush Controls in Painter 6 and 7 will be pleased to see that the set of palettes has returned with Painter IX. The Brush Controls mirrors the functions in the Stroke Designer section of the Brush Creator. To open it, choose Window, Brush Controls, Show General. Click a section name to open that section.

General
Size
Spacing
Angle
Bristle
Well
Rake
Random
Mouse
Cloning
Impasto
Image Hose
Airbrush
Water
Liquid Ink
Digital Watercolor
Artists' Oils
Color Variability
Color Expression

The Brush Controls palette with sections closed

Choosing the Circular dab type in the General section of the Stroke Designer within the Brush Creator

Four examples of dab-based brushes. Top, from left to right: Soft Round Pastel 40 variant of Pastels (Circular), Square Hard Pastel 40 variant of Pastels (Captured). Bottom, from left to right: Spatter Water variant of Digital Watercolor (Circular) and Dry Ink variant of Sumi-e (Static Bristle).

Four examples of continuous stroke-based brushes. Top, from left to right: Flat Oils 40 variant of Oils (Flat), Smeary Bristle Spray variant of Oils (Bristle Spray). Bottom, from left to right: Texturizer-Variable variant of Impasto (Airbrush) and Pixel Spray variant of Airbrushes (Pixel Airbrush).

Creator (Ctrl/⌘-B), selecting the Stroke Designer, and in its General section, selecting a new dab from the Dab Type pop-up menu. You can also access the Dab Type menu using the Brush Controls by choosing Window, Brush Controls, Show General.

Dab-Based Brushes

For brushes that are *dab-based,* you can think of the dab as the footprint for the brush—a cross-section of its shape. The brush lays down a series of dabs of color to make a stroke. If the spacing is set tight the stroke will appear to be a continuous mark. If the spacing is loose, the stroke will be a series of footprints with space between them.

Circular. Many of Painter's brushes use this round dab type. Don't be fooled by the term *Circular*; even if you change a brush's Squeeze setting in the Angle section of the Brush Controls palette so that its footprint looks elliptical, it's still a Circular brush.

Single-Pixel. Just as it sounds, this is a 1-pixel-wide brush.

Static Bristle. Because Static Bristle brushes are made up of several "hairs," they have a rich potential. You can make adjustments in Bristle Thickness, Clumpiness and other settings in the Bristle section of the Stroke Designer tab (Brush Creator).

Captured. You can capture any area of a document to act as the footprint for a Captured brush. Use the Rectangular Selection tool and draw a marquee (press the Shift key if you want to constrain the selection to a perfect square) around a mark or group of markings. With the Brush Creator open, choose Brush, Capture Dab; the brush footprint will appear in the Size section of the Brush Creator's Stroke Designer tab.

Continuous-Stroke Brushes

Brushes using *continuous-stroke* dab types produce smoother-edged, more responsive brushstrokes because these brushes render brushstrokes using a bundle of continuous, anti-aliased one-pixel lines. Because the stroke is composed of continuous lines instead of overlapping dabs, the brushes can produce smoother, more realistic brushstrokes than dab-based brushes can. Additionally, each brush hair has the capability to carry its own well of color. When an artist uses a traditional brush, the bristles often get contaminated by the colors of wet paint on the canvas. When the brush touches a neighboring color, it affects the paint along the edges of the new brushstroke.

Camel Hair. With Camel Hair dabs, you can build round brushes that paint brushstrokes with obvious bristle marks.

<table>
<tr><th>THINNING BRUSHES</th></tr>
<tr><td>For many brushes with continuous-stroke dab types (Camel Hair, Flat, Palette Knife and Bristle Spray) you can control how many bristles apply paint. Simply move the Feature slider in the Property Bar. High Feature settings have a thinning effect.</td></tr>
</table>

Click on the brush footprint in the Size section's Preview window to switch the view between "hard" (showing the maximum and minimum sizes) and "soft" (showing bristles).

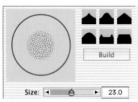

The Size section of the Stroke Designer (Brush Creator) palette showing a "soft" view of a Static Bristle dab used to create the Feathering Brush described on page 159

When you paint a stoke with a brush that has an airbrush-like conical spray (Airbrush, Pixel Airbrush or Line Airbrush dab type), you can tilt the stylus to apply paint more densely along the edge closest to the stylus. To switch the direction of the spray without changing the tilt of the stylus, hold down the Control-Alt/Option keys as you paint.

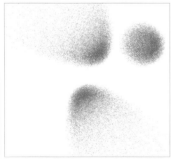

The Fine Spray variant of the Airbrushes is sensitive to the amount of tilt and to the bearing (which direction the stylus is leaning) and sprays conic sections—similar to a beam of light projected onto the canvas—just like a traditional airbrush. Holding the stylus upright sprays a smaller, denser area of color (top right). Tilting the stylus sprays color wider and farther (top left). And holding down Control-Alt/Option redirects the spray (bottom).

Brushes using the Camel Hair dab type (the Round Camelhair variant of Oils, for example) are capable of painting very smoothly, and they can carry a different color on each brush hair.

Flat. Like it sounds, a flat dab is used to create a flat-tipped brush. With brushes using the Flat dab type, you can paint wide or narrow strokes, depending on the way you hold and move the stylus. The Opaque Flat variant of Oils is an example.

Palette Knife. With Resaturation set low in the Well section of the Stroke Designer (Brush Creator), you can use brushes with Palette Knife dabs to scrape paint or move it around on the canvas. The Loaded Palette Knife and Smeary Palette Knife variants (Palette Knives) are examples.

Bristle Spray. With many brushes that use Bristle Spray dabs (such as the Opaque Bristle Spray variant of Oils), the bristles will spread out on one side of the brushstroke as you tilt the stylus.

Airbrush. Like Bristle Spray, Pixel Airbrush and Line Airbrush dab types, Airbrush dabs spray conic sections, and they "understand" Bearing (which direction the stylus is leaning) and Angle (amount of tilt). (See "Redirecting the Spray" on the left.)

Pixel Airbrush. Brushes using this dab type work like brushes using the Airbrush dab type. With the Pixel Airbrush dab type, however, the individual droplets *cannot* be adjusted using the Feature slider.

Line Airbrush. Brushes using the Line Airbrush dab type (such as the Furry Brush variant of F/X) spray lines instead of droplets.

Projected. The Projected dab-type brushes spray conic sections, similar to the Airbrush dab type, but without the responsiveness. For now, we recommend constructing brushes with the Airbrush and Pixel Airbrush dab types rather than a Projected dab type.

Rendered. In addition to painting with color, brushes built using Rendered dabs can contain a pattern or gradation as a Source. The Graphic Paintbrush

For brushes with Airbrush dab types, you can use the Feature slider in the Property Bar to control the size of droplets. With a higher Feature setting, Airbrush dabs spray larger droplets, like those shown on the right.

Several of Painter's Airbrushes—the Coarse Spray, the Fine Spray and the Graffiti variants, for example—allow media to pool when the stylus (or mouse) is held down in one position. In contrast, the Digital Airbrush and Inverted Pressure variants must be moved before they apply color to the image. To enable these two variants to apply color at the first touch, turn on Continuous Time Deposition in the Spacing section of the Stroke Designer tab (Window, Show Brush Creator).

We painted this Portrait Study *from life using the Grainy Wash Bristle, Runny Wash Bristle and Fine Camel variants of Watercolor.*

When painting Chess, *John Derry used Liquid Ink brushes and media layers to emulate encaustic painting. Turn to "Encaustic Painting with Liquid Ink" on page 135 to read about his technique.*

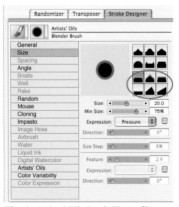

The six Artists' Oils Brush Tip profiles allow for expressive strokes, depending on how you hold your stylus.

variant of F/X is an example. To change the Source used by a Rendered dab brush, use the Source pop-up menu in the General section of Brush Controls (or Brush Creator).

Watercolor dab types. The five Watercolor dab types were created for painting on Watercolor media layers. These dabs are based on several of the rendered dab types discussed earlier—the Camel Hair, Flat, Palette Knife, Bristle Spray and Airbrush. For more information about working with Watercolor, turn to "A Painter Watercolor Primer" on page 80 of this chapter.

Liquid Ink dab types. Designed for painting on Liquid Ink media layers, there are five Liquid Ink dab types. They're based on several of the rendered dab types: the Camel Hair, Flat, Bristle Spray, Palette Knife and Airbrush. To read more about Liquid Ink, turn to "A Liquid Ink Primer" on page 130.

Artists' Oils dab type. The Artists' Oils dab type is unique in that it is designed only for painting with the new Artists' Oils medium. This dab type works in conjunction with the six new Artists' Oils Brush Tip profiles (in the Size section) and Bearing (Tilt/Direction) that is applied to the stylus, to vary the appearance of a stroke. To read more about the Artists' Oils, turn to "An Artists' Oils Primer" on page 98.

STROKE TYPES

The *stroke* is the way a dab is applied over a distance. You can switch Stroke Types using the pop-up menu in the General section of the Stroke Designer (Brush Creator).

QUICKER CUSTOM BRUSHES

When you want to design and capture a brush, start by opening a variant that's close to the effect you want. That way you'll have fewer adjustments to make.

BRUSHES THAT SMEAR

Do you want a brush to pull and smear color? A low Resaturation and a high Bleed setting (in the Well section of the Stroke Designer) will work with Brush Loading to allow the brush to smear pigment while applying it. Choose the Variable Flat variant of the Oils, and in the Well section, set Resat at 5% and Bleed at 80%. To see the colors mix, choose a new color in the Colors picker and drag the brush through existing color on your image.

SCRUBBING EXISTING COLOR

To make a brush that applies color when you use a light touch and scrubs underlying color when you use heavier pressure, choose the Fine Camel variant of Oils. Go to the Well section of the Stroke Designer, and set Resat low. Also, next to the Resaturation Expression pop-up menu, turn on the Invert box.

AN ANGLE ON CALLIGRAPHY

If you'd like to adjust the orientation of a Calligraphy pen for right- or left-handed work, open the Angle pane of the Stroke Designer within the Brush Creator. Drag the Angle slider to set the angle you want, and make a test stroke in the Preview window.

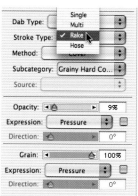

Choosing the Rake stroke type in the General section of the Stroke Designer (Brush Creator)

When changing settings for a brush, sometimes typing numerals into the fields is easier than trying to hit a point on the slider.

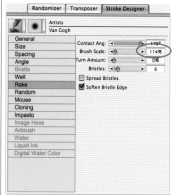

Most of the settings in the Stroke Designer's windows (and Brush Controls windows) can be typed in, as shown here in setting Brush Scale in the Rake section.

Using Impasto, you can add brushstrokes that have 3D texture but that don't alter the color in the image—like painting with thick, clear varnish. Select any Impasto variant and in the Draw To pop-up menu in the Impasto section of the Stroke Designer, select Depth.

Single. Just as it sounds, Single stroke-type brushes have only one stroke path. Because of this, they're fast. If you use a Static Bristle, a Camel Hair or a Flat dab type, you can create a fast Single stroke-type brush with a lot of complexity. Most Painter brushes incorporate the Single stroke type.

Multi. Painter's power hungry Multi stroke-type brushes can paint sensitive multicolored strokes, but are the least spontaneous of the program's brushes. (The Continuous-Stroke dab-type brushes on page 154 provide a much more responsive way to paint with multiple colors.) Try drawing a line with the Gloopy variant of the Impasto. Instead of a stroke, you'll see a dotted "preview" line that shows its path; the stroke appears a moment later. Multi brushes are built from several randomly distributed dabs that may or may not overlap. The Gloopy variant of Impasto is an example of a Multi-stroke brush in the Painter IX default brush library. But lovely, variable strokes can be made using custom Multi brushes. To spread the strokes of a Multi-stroke brush, increase the Jitter setting in the Random section of the Brush Creator's Stroke Designer tab.

Rake. The Rake stroke type is like a garden rake; each of the evenly spaced tines is a bristle of the brush. Painter gives you control over the bristles; for instance, you can make them overlap, which makes it possible to create wonderfully complex, functional brushes. And you can change the number of Bristles (keeping in mind that fewer bristles make faster brushes). In the Rake section of the Stroke Designer, you can also adjust the way the bristles interact. To try out an existing Rake brush, paint with the Van Gogh variant of the Artists brush.

Hose. The Hose stroke type sprays a variety of images when you paint each stroke. To read about painting with the Image Hose, turn to "Building an Image Hose" and to "Creating a Tidepool" in Chapter 8 of this book.

Brush Loading enables a brush to carry a unique color in each brush hair. Many of Painter's brushes have this capability already built into them—for instance, the Variable Round variant of the Oils. (When Brush Loading is built into a brush, the Brush Loading check box is grayed out in the Well section of the Brush Controls.) To allow a static bristle brush (such as the Opaque Acrylic variant of the Acrylics) or a dab-based brush from an earlier version of Painter to use Brush Loading, open the Well section of the Brush Controls and turn on Brush Loading. With Static Bristle and earlier dab types, Brush Loading works in conjunction with the Resaturation and Bleed sliders in the Well section to allow the brush to paint with multiple colors.

Overlaying paint with the Opaque Acrylic without Brush Loading (left) and with Brush Loading (right)

The Brush Creator preview may not reveal all of the delicate nuances of certain brushes (for instance, the Liquid Ink variants), so it's a good idea to also try out your brushes on the image canvas as you're making finer adjustments to them.

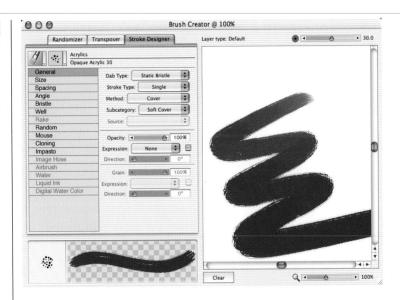

BUILDING AN IMPASTO BRUSH

You can add settings to any brush that will allow it to paint with thick Impasto paint. To set up a brush for Impasto, begin by choosing a brush (such as a Bristle Oils variant of the Oils). We used these settings in the Impasto section of the Brush Controls to build a Bristle Oils Impasto brush: Draw To, Color and Depth; Depth Method, Uniform; Depth, 180%; Smoothing, 120%; and Plow, 100%. To save your variant, from the Brush Creator's Variant menu, choose Save. To read more about Impasto turn to "A Painter Impasto Primer" on page 123 and to "Working with Thick Paint" on page 127.

Painting thick Impasto brushstrokes with the custom Bristle Oils Impasto brush

MAKING BRUSHES USING THE STROKE DESIGNER

For the custom brushes that follow, we used the Stroke Designer window of the Brush Creator. Open it by choosing Window, Show Brush Creator, or by pressing Ctrl/⌘-B and clicking the Stroke Designer tab.

For each of the custom brushes, we started with an existing Painter brush, and we radically modified its character by making adjustments that affect brush behavior. After you've created the brush (and perhaps made further modifications on your own), you can save your variant. Choose Variant, Save Variant from the Brush Creator's menu at the top of your screen to save the variant under a new name into your current palette. After saving your custom variant, restore the default settings for the Painter brush by selecting the variant you began with and choosing Variant, Restore Default from the menu.

Try these brushes on images of 1000 pixels square or less. If you work with larger files, you'll want to proportionally increase the Size slider settings that we list here. When a Circular or Static Bristle dab type is used, you'll also want to optimize the Spacing and Min Spacing in the Stroke Designer's Spacing section to accommodate the larger size. If you have trouble setting exact numbers with the sliders, try typing the number into the field to the right of the slider. Press the Enter key to accept the number you've typed. And don't think your computer has crashed if nothing happens for a while when you try to paint: Painter is working away, building a very complex brush.

To make room for more brushes, we've shortened our descriptions of how to make the brushes. For instance, "*Well:* Resat, 80%" means, "In the Stroke Designer's Well section set Resaturation to 80% but leave all other sliders at their default settings." The

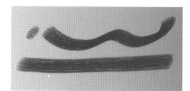

Brushstrokes made with the Soft Dry Flat

Selecting a painted dab with the Rectangular Selection tool so that it can be captured

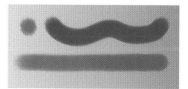

Brushstrokes made with the Captured Oils Brush

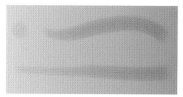

Brushstrokes made with the Feathering Brush

Using the Camelhair Blender Brush to blend strokes made with the Captured Oils Brush

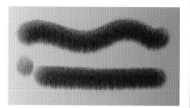

Brushstrokes made with the Soft Runny Wash Watercolor

palette sections you will use are found in the Stroke Designer. For a full description of the functions of the controls in each of the sections, you can refer to Painter's *Online Help*, although painting with the brush after you make each adjustment will teach you a lot, too. **Caution:** Before starting a brush recipe, restore the default settings for the starting brush by choosing Variant, Restore Default from the main menu above the Brush Creator.

Soft Dry Flat. This Single stroke Flat brush was created to feel like a traditional soft, flat brush with dry bristles.

Start with the default Opaque Flat variant of the Oils. *Size:* Size, 31.2; Min Size, 42%; Size Expression, Pressure; Feature, 4. *General:* Opacity, 100%; Opacity Expression, Pressure. *Well:* Resaturation, 70; Bleed, 40. *Random:* Jitter, 0.05. *Color Variability:* ±H, 1; ±V, 3.

Soft Captured Oils Brush. This captured dab type brush is built to feel like a soft brush with fine bristles. Begin by choosing the Coarse Spray variant of Airbrushes and black paint; then click once in your image to paint a dab. Choose the Captured Bristle variant of the Acrylics. *(Although this default brush is titled Captured Bristle, it has a Static Bristle dab type.)* Capture the painted dab by making an unconstrained selection using the Rectangular Selection tool and then choosing Capture Dab from the pop-up menu on the Brush Selector Bar. *Size:* Size, 38.0; Min Size, 30%; Size Expression, Pressure. *General:* Opacity, 26. *Spacing:* Spacing, 30; Min Spacing, 1.5. *Well:* Resaturation, 79; Bleed, 30. *Color Variability:* ±V, 3.

Feathering Brush. Created for feathering over existing color to add interest and texture, this Single-stroke, Bristle brush paints tapered strokes quickly. Increase pressure to widen the stroke.

Start with the default Captured Bristle variant of the Acrylics. *Size:* Size, 23.0; Min Size, 30%. *Size:* Size Expression, Pressure. *General:* Opacity, 9. *Spacing:* Spacing, 9. *Well:* Resaturation and Dryout, maximum; Bleed, 0. *Bristle:* Thickness, 40; Clumpiness, 0 (for smooth strokes); Hair Scale, 515%. *Color Variability:* ±H, 1; ±V, 2.

Camelhair Blender Brush. The *Well* section settings for this Single-stroke, Camelhair brush let you pick up existing color and blend with it. The brush hairs spread with more pressure, because Feature is set to Pressure in the Expression section.

Start with the default Round Camelhair variant of the Oils. *Size:* Size, 23; Min Size, 37%; Feature, 4.1; Feature Expression, Pressure. *Well:* Resat, 4%; Bleed, 96%.

Soft Runny Wash Watercolor. This round Watercolor brush paints smoother runny washes with soft edges.

Start with the default Runny Wash Bristle variant of Watercolor. *Water:* Pickup, 11%; Dry Rate, 10%; Evap Thresh, 83%; Cap Factor, 0. Turn on Accurate Diffusion.

To create a custom brush category icon from scratch, first select a square area of an image using the Rectangular Selection tool. From the Brush Selector Bar choose Capture Brush Category. Name your brush category and click OK. You'll see your selection appear in the Brush Selector Bar with the variant you chose below it. You've just created an empty "variant holder," ready to be filled with your own custom variants.

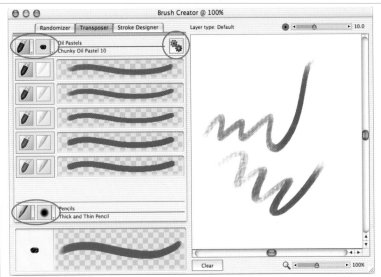

The Transposer window of the Brush Creator allows you to blend the components of two existing Painter brushes. Settings for the Oil Pastel Pencil are shown.

MAKING BRUSHES USING THE TRANSPOSER

The Transposer allows you to create a set of variations based on two brush variants that you choose. The Transposer has two Brush Selector bars, one at the top and one at the bottom of the window. In the illustration above, the Chunky Oil Pastel 10 is chosen in the *From* Brush Selector, and the Thick and Thin Pencil is chosen in the *To* Brush Selector. Painter will calculate new brush variations based on these two brushes when you click the Transpose Current Selection button (the Gears button). The variations that are nearest to the Chunky Oil Pastel 10 will be most like this original, and as you move down toward the Thick and Thin Pencil the variations will begin to resemble the pencil. If you want a 50% blend between the two variants, click the center choice.

You can also continue to transpose variants by clicking on a brushstroke in the window. This choice will be the next variant that will be transposed.

For the three custom brushes that follow, we used the Transposer window of the Brush Creator. Open it by clicking the Transposer tab.

Oil Pastel Pencil. This pencil allows you to sketch while smearing color and revealing grain. In the Transposer's top category pop-up menu choose Oil Pastels, and in the variant pop-up menu choose Chunky Oil Pastel 10. In the Transposer's bottom category pop-up menu choose Pencils, and choose Thick and Thin Pencil as the variant. Next, click the Transpose Current Selection button (the Gears button) and then click the center choice. Save the variant.

Grainy Charcoal. This charcoal allows you to softly sketch with Charcoal while revealing more grain. In the Transposer's top category pop-up menu choose Charcoal and also choose Charcoal

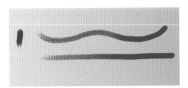

Brushstrokes made with the Oil Pastel Pencil

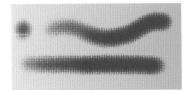

Brushstrokes made with the Grainy Charcoal

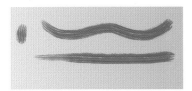

Brushstrokes made with the Wet Bristle Oils

for the variant. In the Transposer's bottom category pop-up menu choose Chalk, and choose Blunt Chalk 10 as the variant. Next, click the Transpose Current Selection button (the Gears button) and then click the center choice. Save the variant.

Wet Bristle Oils. This brush allows you to paint while subtly smearing color. In the Transposer's top category pop-up menu choose Acrylics, and choose Wet Soft Acrylic 20 as the variant. In the Transposer's bottom category pop-up menu choose Oils, and choose Bristle Oils 20 as the variant. Next, click the Transpose Current Selection button (the Gears button), and then click the center choice. Save the variant.

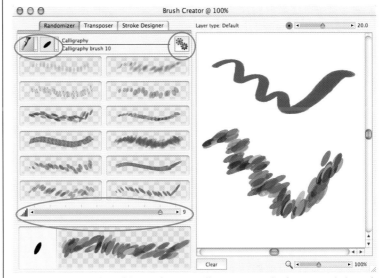

The Randomizer window of the Brush Creator allows you to randomly create variations of a brush. The Calligraphy brush 10 is shown here.

MAKING BRUSHES USING THE RANDOMIZER

While it doesn't offer the control of the Stroke Designer or Transposer, the Randomizer is fun to use. It allows you to choose a brush (such as the Calligraphy brush 10 shown here) and have Painter randomly create 12 variations of the brush for you to choose from. To create your own randomization, click on the Randomizer tab of the Brush Creator. Painter will automatically generate the variations for the brush you have chosen. You can adjust the Amount of Randomization slider below the choices to make the randomizations more alike or more varied. If you want to create another set of variations adjust the Amount of Randomization slider or choose another brush from the Brush Selector bar at the top of the window; then click the Randomize Current Selection button (the Gears button).

Brushstrokes made with the Calligraphy 10 (top), and with one of the choices from the Randomizer (bottom)

Painting in Pastel Using Custom Brushes

Overview *Build a palette of colors; make a drawing; add layers of color with custom Pastels; blend colors with custom Blenders brushes; add "scumbling" for texture and details to finish.*

CHER THREINEN-PENDARVIS

Using the Mixer to create a palette of colors. The Mix Color tool is chosen.

Sketching in color with the Soft Pastel Pencil 3 variant of Pastels

INSPIRED BY THE SOFT LIGHT on a late afternoon, *Nani Waianae,* a pastel study of a favorite location on the west side of the island of Oahu in Hawaii, was painted using custom Pastels and Blenders variants. For inspiration, we referred to colored pencil sketches drawn on location. To achieve the soft atmosphere, we painted layers of color with modified Pastels variants, blended color using our Blenders brushes, and then added details and broken color to finish the painting.

1 Setting up. Choose a photo or a landscape sketch to use for reference. Open a new file. We started with a 14 x 10-inch file at 300 ppi. Set Brush Tracking for a more sensitive response when using your stylus. Choose Corel Painter IX, Preferences, Brush Tracking, make a representative brushstroke in the window, and click OK.

Next, use the Colors palette and Mixer (Window, Color Palettes) to create a palette of colors for your painting. We chose a range of earthy greens, browns and oranges, including a few more saturated hues of green, turquoise and purple. The Waianae Coast is on the leeward (western) shore of Oahu, and has a drier climate than some other areas of the island, hence the earthy palette. To apply paint to the Mixer, use the Brush tool in the Mixer to apply colors to the Mixer Pad. To blend colors, use the Mix Color tool. (Turn to page 27 in Chapter 2 for more information about using the Mixer.)

2 Making a drawing. Next, choose a color from the Colors picker or your Mixer palette. Click the Paper Selector icon (near the bottom of the Toolbox) and choose a medium-grained paper, such as Charcoal Paper. Select the Pastels category in the Brush Selector Bar, choose the Soft Pastel Pencil variant and begin sketching. To keep the freshness and energy of your sketch while you draw, don't get bogged down with details.

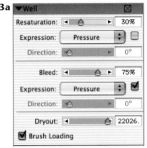

3a

The Well section of Brush Controls with the settings for the Soft Smeary Pastel

3b

Strokes painted with the Soft Smeary Pastel

4

Blocking in the sky using the custom Soft Smeary Pastel variant. Blending the clouds with the Grainy Water (Blenders).

5a

The General section of Brush Controls with the settings for the Grainier Water

5b

Blending the top of a pastel stroke using the new Grainier Water variant

3 Building a custom Pastel variant. When you've finished sketching your composition and you're ready to layer color in the underpainting, create a soft Pastel variant that will allow you to apply color and smear it as you vary pressure on your stylus. (So that you begin with the same settings discussed here, before beginning to build the brushes, choose Restore All Default Variants from the pop-up menu on the Brush Selector Bar.) Now, choose the Square Soft Pastel 30 variant of Pastels. In the Property Bar, lower its Opacity to 70%. Open the Well section of the Brush Controls (Window, Brush Controls, Show Well). Set Resaturation to 30%, Bleed to 75% and then check the Invert box next to the Expression pop-up menu. (Make sure that the Expression menu is set to Pressure.) A lower Resaturation setting, coupled with a high Bleed setting, allows you to blend color as you apply it. Enabling the Invert check box to the right of the Expression pop-up menu allows you to apply more color with lighter pressure and blend more with medium pressure. A lower opacity will allow you to build up color slowly, with more sensitivity. To save this custom brush, choose Save Variant from the pop-up menu on the right side of the Brush Selector Bar. Name your variant and click OK. (We named ours *Soft Smeary Pastel*.) The new name will appear in the Brush Selector Bar under the Pastels category. For good Painter housekeeping, it's a good idea to restore the original Square Soft Pastel to its default settings: Choose Restore Variant from the pop-up menu on the Brush Selector Bar while the Square Soft Pastel is chosen.

4 Blocking in color for an underpainting. With your custom pastel in hand, choose a color and begin laying in broad areas of color over your entire painting. At this point, don't focus on details, but paint larger shapes to establish values and the general color scheme. We adjusted our new variant's size and opacity as we worked, switching to a 50% opacity, for instance, when layering color to show the warm light shining onto the hills.

Blending colors. To achieve a smooth look with traditional pastels, you rub them with precise blending tools such as a tortillion or a blending stump. Use the Just Add Water, Grainy Water and Smudge variants of the Blenders brush to mimic these traditional tools. A few hints about these blenders: The Just Add Water uses the Soft Cover subcategory and blends smoothly without texture; Grainy Water uses Grainy Flat Cover and blends showing a hint of texture; Smudge uses Grainy Hard Cover and reveals more texture as it blends color. Begin blending, and experiment with these brushes and various brush sizes while you work.

5 Building a custom Grainier Blender. We layered color using our new custom Pastel and other Pastels variants, and blended using the Grainy Water and Just Add Water variants of Blenders. We also wanted to blend while revealing more texture in certain areas than the default variants would allow, so we built a new custom

6a

The basic colors are blocked in over the entire painting to create a soft atmosphere.

6b

Defining the subtle shadows on the distant hills using the Artist Pastel Chalk

6c

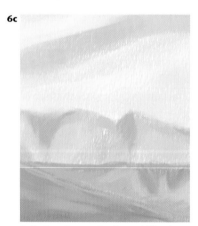

Softening edges on the distant hills using the custom Grainier Water

7a

Brush strokes painted using the default Square Hard Pastel (left) and the custom Square Grainy Pastel (right)

blender based on the Grainy Water 30 variant. To build the new blender, choose the Grainy Water 30 variant of Blenders. Open the General section of Brush Controls and set the Subcategory pop-up menu to Grainy Edge Flat Cover, and then move the Grain slider to 15% (for less paint penetration). Save your new blender by choosing Variant, Save Variant from the pop-up menu on the Brush Selector Bar. Name your variant and click OK. (We named ours *Grainier Water.*) The new name will appear in the Brush Selector Bar under the Blenders category. To restore the Grainy Water 30 to its default settings, choose Restore Default Variant from the pop-up menu on the Brush Selector Bar.

6 Achieving a soft atmosphere. Select the Soft Smeary Pastel variant you created in step 3. Imagine soft afternoon light shining over your landscape, and apply light strokes over the hills in your painting. For aerial perspective (where the hills seem to recede into the distance), use lower contrast values and less saturated colors in the more distant areas. We added gold, warm green and blue strokes to the midground hills and lighter blues, soft purples and grays to the more distant hills. We alternated between using our new Soft Smeary Pastel and a default Square Soft Pastel, and covered most of the coastal hills with soft brushstrokes. We also used the Artist Pastel Chalk variant of Pastels to strengthen values in a few areas and to define edges in the midground and faraway hills. To soften a few of the edges on the most distant hills (where the hills met the sky), we used the new custom Grainier Water brush.

7 Making a Grainier Pastel for "scumbling." Artists using traditional media will often add more texture to a painting by brushing the side of the pastel lightly along the peaks of the rough art paper. This technique, called *scumbling*, causes colors to blend optically and adds texture. A few Pastel variants that ship with Painter are useful for scumbling: for instance, the Square Hard Pastels and the Round Hard Pastels. However, we wanted a new brush that would not penetrate into the paper grain, but instead would paint color only onto the peaks of the paper surface. To build this special grainy Pastel variant, begin with the Square Hard Pastel 40 variant of Pastels. In the Property Bar, set the Grain slider to 6% (to reduce grain penetration) and set Opacity to 100%. Save your new pastel by choosing Save Variant from the pop-up menu on the Brush Selector Bar, and name your variant. (We named ours *Square Grainy Pastel.*) The new name will appear under the Pastels category. To restore the original Hard Square Pastel 40 to its default settings, choose Restore Variant from the pop-up menu on the Brush Selector Bar.

To scumble electronically, select your new Square Grainy Pastel variant from the Brush Selector Bar and brush lightly using a contrasting color. We scumbled to add texture interest to the sky and to suggest sunlight on the hills, beach and path.

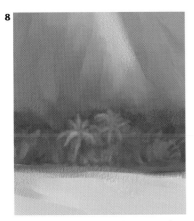

Scumbling on the hills and sky using the custom Square Grainy Pastel variant

Adding definition to the palm trees and other foliage using the Artist Pastel Chalk and the Tapered Pastel brushes

8 Defining the midground. After scumbling, we added important details to the midground: for instance, we added more definition to the palm trees and other foliage, and defined the edges and shadows on the closer hills using the Artist Pastel Chalk. In keeping with our color palette, we painted with warm greens and browns and cooler blues. Then, we softened areas using a Grainy Water variant or our custom Grainier Water brush, depending on the amount of texture that was needed.

9 Painting final details and adding more texture. During the painting process, we had created an underpainting by blocking color over the entire image (step 4). Then, as we defined areas, we worked mostly from the background to the foreground. Before we began to paint the foreground, we chose the Tapered Pastel 10, and opened the Color Variability palette (Window, Brush Controls, Show Color Variability) and adjusted the Value (±V) to 5% so that the color would vary slightly as we painted. To sketch the foreground plants, we used an Artist Pastel Chalk and greenish-gold and rusty colors. Then we painted thin, slightly curved strokes for the grass using a Tapered Pastel. To enhance the path, we scumbled and painted brighter highlights onto the areas that were catching the sunlight by using our custom Square Grainy Pastel, and then we blended using the custom Grainier Water.

As a last step, we strengthened the small cliff on the nearest hill-top that towered above the trees. So that the hill would stand out more in the composition, we also painted deeper color onto the sky above the hill and repainted some areas of the clouds.

A CUSTOM PASTEL PAINTING PALETTE

So that you can have easy access to your new Pastel brushes, favorite default Pastels, Blenders and textures, it's a good idea to make a custom palette for them. Begin by choosing a Pastel variant in the Brush Selector Bar. Click on the variant thumbnail and drag it out of the Brush Selector Bar and onto your desktop. A new custom palette will appear. To enlarge it, grab its lower-right corner and drag it out into a horizontal shape that will easily fit at the bottom of your screen. Continue to choose variants, and drag and drop them into your new palette. To reposition an icon, press Shift-Ctrl/⌘ and drag it to a new position. We organized our palette with larger pastels on the left and smaller variants in the center with a space in-between so that we could grab them quickly. To make our palette complete, we added favorite Blenders and paper textures. To add a texture, select it in the Paper Selector in the Toolbox and drag and drop it into your palette. To name your custom palette, choose Window, Custom Palette, Organizer, select its default name (Custom 1, etc.) and then click on Rename. Give your palette a name and click OK.

The custom Pastel painting palette with Pastels, Blenders and favorite paper textures. To view the name of an art material using Tool Tips, hover the cursor over its icon.

The loosely painted foreground foliage and the scumbling on the path

Digital Watercolor with Custom Brushes

Overview *Quick Clone a scan of a rough pencil sketch; refine the sketch with the 2B Pencil; build custom Digital Watercolor brushes; apply color washes using default and custom Digital Watercolor brushes.*

CAROL BENIOFF

1a

The final drawing that Benioff used as a guide for her Digital Watercolor painting

1b

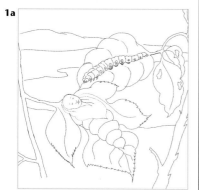

Selecting New Color Set from Image in the Color Set palette pop-up menu

THE DIGITAL WATERCOLOR MEDIUM IN PAINTER IX ALLOWED Carol Benioff to build up rich tones and luminous colors in her illustration, *Pupa*. Benioff created six custom brushes that were based on the variants that ship with Painter IX. As she painted, she alternated between painting color washes with wet-into-wet paint and drying the wet paint. Then, she added more washes without disturbing the dried color underneath, just like glazing in conventional watercolor. Digital Watercolor offers the richness of watercolor, with more flexibility.

1 Preparing to work. Benioff began by scanning a rough pencil sketch, opening the scan in Painter and making a Quick Clone. (Quick Clone allows you to see the rough sketch underneath, like drawing on a light table.) To sketch as Benioff did, open a scanned drawing, choose File, Quick Clone and leave the original file open. Select the 2B Pencil variant of Pencils. Using the rough sketch as a guide, draw cleaner lines and reshape the forms in your drawing. Then, save the Quick Clone file with a new name in the RIFF format, which will preserve the Digital Watercolor wet paint that you will use in future stages.

After cleaning up her drawing, Benioff created a custom color set based on one of her conventional watercolor images. She opened a scan of the watercolor image; then she clicked on the right triangle on the Color Set palette to access the pop-up menu and chose New Color Set from Image. She chose Save Color Set

2a

Brush stroke samples of Benioff's custom Dry Grainy Brush variant

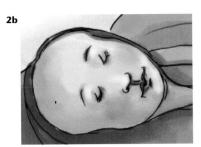

2b

Painting with the Dry Grainy Brush to build up the shadows on the face

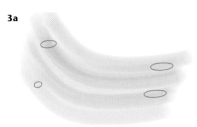

3a

Strokes painted with the Glaze Brush. The circles show the overlapping areas.

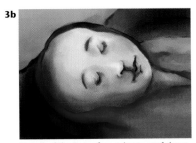

3b

Detail of the Pupa face prior to applying a wash with her Glaze Brush

3c

Detail of the Pupa face after applying a wash with her Glaze Brush

from the palette menu, named her set and saved it in the same location as her new Painter file.

2 Building a Dry Grainy Brush. Next, Benioff built six custom brushes that were based on the default Digital Watercolor variants that ship with Painter IX. Two of them are described in detail here; four more are described in the tip that follows this story. (So that you begin with the same settings that Benioff did, before beginning to build the brushes, choose Restore All Default Variants from the pop-up menu on the Brush Selector Bar.)

Benioff built a brush that she named *Dry Grainy Brush.* She liked the softness of Soft Broad Brush, but wanted a thicker, bristly brush that would lay down a bit more paint and bleed into the underlying colors. Her Dry Grainy Brush puts down soft grainy washes of color with the bristle marks visible at the end of each stroke. To build the Dry Grainy Brush, choose the Soft Broad Brush variant of Digital Watercolor in the Brush Selector Bar and open the Brush Controls palette by choosing Window, Brush Controls, Show General. In the General section, change the Dab Type from Circular to Static Bristle (for the bristle look) and increase the Opacity from 4% to 39%. To make the brush look dry, decrease the amount of Grain to about 25%. The lower the percentage of Grain, the less the paint will penetrate the paper, revealing more paper texture. In the Size section of the Brush Control palette, increase the Size to 26. To keep the brush size constant, set the Expression pop-up menu to None. In the Digital Watercolor section of Brush Controls, set the Wet Fringe to 20% to help the color to pool at the edges of each stroke. (When using a brush with Wet Fringe settings, the preview of the wet paint strokes can change temporarily until you switch to a brush with a Wet Fringe setting below 10%.) In the Well section of the Brush Controls, reduce the Resaturation from 40% to 32% and in the Expression pop-up menu choose Pressure (leaving the Invert box disabled) so that the pressure you apply will affect how much color the brush applies. Next, increase the Bleed from 21% to 80% and set the Expression pop-up menu to Pressure. This will ensure that the brush will blend with the underlying color, depending on the pressure that you apply with each stroke. Save the variant by choosing Save Variant from the pop-up menu on the Brush Selector Bar.

3 Building a brush for glazing. Benioff frequently uses a custom *Glaze Brush* in her work, which is based on the Simple Water variant. She wanted a soft, even brush that painted smooth translucent washes, without grain. To build this brush, begin by choosing the Simple Water variant of Digital Watercolor in the Brush Selector Bar. In the Brush Controls, General section, reduce the Opacity to 1% and the Grain to 0. In the Size section, increase the Size to 32.2. The Spacing will need to be adjusted to accommodate the larger size. In the Spacing section of the Brush Controls,

4

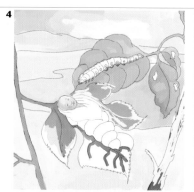

Blocking in the basic colors on the canvas

5a

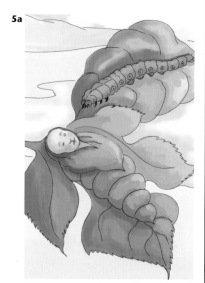

Adding layers of color with the Soft Broad Brush and Dry Grainy Brush

5b

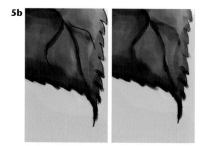

Before Benioff blended the pencil lines (left) and after she blended the pencil lines with the Just Add Water brush (right)

reduce the Spacing to 13% and set the Minimum Spacing to 0.1. The tighter spacing will create a smoother stroke with no circular dab artifacts. In the Well section of Brush Controls, reduce the Resaturation to 5%. To ensure that this brush will *not* pick up any of the existing color, set the Bleed to 0%. Save the variant. Benioff continued to build the four other custom brush variants that she used in the piece. With all her brushes in hand, she was ready to paint.

4 Blocking in colors. For each new Painter session, you have to select the paper you have been using because Painter does not remember this setting. To paint as Benioff did, choose the French Watercolor Paper from Paper Selector in the Toolbox. Begin by painting broad, loose strokes that quickly cover the canvas. She used her new custom variants, the Dry Grainy Brush, Soft Wash Brush, Extra Fine Tip Water and the default variants Fine Tip Water and Gentle Wet Eraser to paint the first washes. (The Soft Wash Brush and Extra Fine Tip Water are described in the tip on page 169.) When you have completed your first washes, choose Dry Digital Watercolor from the Layers palette menu to prevent the subsequent layers of Digital Watercolor from mixing with the first washes.

5 Adding layers of color and tone. Benioff built up the color and tonalities of the pupa and caterpillar by painting washes using the Soft Broad Brush. Then, she used the Dry Grainy Brush to build up the shadow tones. Benioff painted the smaller details with the Extra Fine Tip Water brush (described in the tip on page 169). Then she dried the wet paint by choosing Dry Digital Watercolor from the Layers palette menu. To add more depth and richness to the shadows, Benioff painted thin washes of complementary colors using her Glaze Brush. Again, she dried the wet paint.

Benioff continued to build up the richness of her colors by painting smooth wash strokes with the Soft Broad Brush on the leaves and stems. When her brush strokes overlapped onto the dried paint on the pupa or caterpillar, Benioff used the Gentle Wet Eraser to remove the unwanted wet Digital Watercolor. She could easily erase the wet Digital Watercolor strokes with any of the *wet* erasers without disturbing the previously dried Digital Watercolor strokes. She painted with her custom variants Thick Clumpy Dry Brush and the Dry Grainy Brush in various sizes to deepen the tones and color of the leaf. She dried the paint on the leaf and then added thin washes using her Glaze Brush. Once again, she dried the watercolor to protect it from the next wet washes of paint. When the first leaf was completed and dried, Benioff repeated the same steps for the remaining leaves and stems. She continued this process until she was pleased with the varied tonalities and colors of the foreground. Then, she dried the entire image. At this point, Benioff felt that the pencil lines were too prominent, so to soften some of the lines and to integrate them into the image, she used the Just Add Water and the Grainy Water

5c

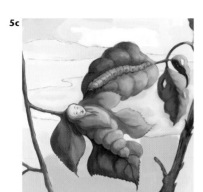

The painting on the foreground completed

6

Adding colored washes to the background

7

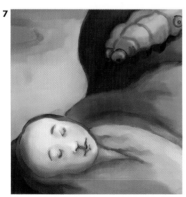

Detail of the pupa face and the caterpillar in the completed image

variants of the Blenders. She used soft, short strokes to blend the lines into the existing color.

6 Painting deeper color and tones on the background. With the foreground completed and dried, Benioff started building up the color and tones on the background. She painted wide strokes with the Soft Broad Brush. Then, she continued to apply color with her Dry Grainy Brush, and Thick Clumpy Dry Brush. To clean up overlapping brush strokes on the completed dried foreground elements, she used the Gentle Wet Eraser. For the large areas of the water and sky, she used her Soft Wash Brush. To add color and depth to areas of the water, she painted washes with her Dry Grainy Brush with the Wet Fringe setting reduced to zero. This softened the edge of the stroke. To soften the edges in the background, Benioff used her Fine Tip Blender brush (which is described in the tip below). She dried the background wet layer, and then she added thin washes of complementary color using her Glaze Brush. When she was happy with the colors, she dried the entire image.

7 Glazing to add depth. In order to achieve the level of richness that she wanted, Benioff added thin washes of complementary color. As a last step, she added details with the Tapered Artist Chalk variant of Chalk: for instance, she painted a few small highlights on the caterpillar and the pupa. 🖌

MORE CUSTOM DIGITAL WATERCOLOR BRUSHES

For the four other custom brushes used in her *Pupa* illustration, Carol Benioff used the Brush Controls (Window, Brush Controls) to make changes to default Digital Watercolor brushes in Painter IX. Beginning with the Dry Brush variant of Digital Watercolor, she built the

Brush strokes from the four custom brushes: 1. Thick Clumpy Dry Brush, 2. Soft Wash Brush, 3. Fine Tip Blender, 4. Extra Fine Tip

Thick Clumpy Dry Brush (1), the small size brush that is full of color, and shows both bristle marks and grain. The altered settings are as follows: General section, Expression, Pressure; Grain, 20%; Size section, Size, 23.6, Minimum Size, 58%; Bristle section, Thickness, 40%, Clumpiness, 65%; and Hair Scale, 468%. Next, Benioff created the *Soft Wash Brush (2),* which was based on the Broad Water Brush. A painting and blending brush that paints short broad strokes, the Soft Wash Brush will easily pick up the underlying wet colors. The setting changes for this brush are as follows: Size section, Minimum Size, 28%; Expression, Pressure; Digital Watercolor section, Diffusion, 5, Wet Fringe, 0; Well section, Resaturation, 20%; Spacing section, Spacing, 15%; and Minimum Spacing, 1.5. From the Fine Tip Water brush, Benioff built two custom brushes. She built the *Fine Tip Blender (3)* to paint long, thick-to-thin strokes (with grain) that easily blend with the underlying wet paint. The changed settings are General section, Grain, 79%; Size section, Size, 11.1; Well section, Resaturation, 8%; and Bleed, 90%. She built the *Extra Fine Tip Water (4)* to be a smaller and stiffer version of the Fine Tip Water brush. The changed settings are Size section, Size, 3.5, Minimum Size, 34%.

Sculpting a Portrait

Overview *Make a sketch; block in color with Chalk variants; build a custom Distortion brush; blend and sculpt the forms; refine the composition.*

RICHARD BIEVER

The sketch on a warm-toned paper color

Loosely blocking in mid-tone color

Sculpting the facial features

RICHARD BIEVER LOVES THE EXPRESSIVE FREEDOM he enjoys while working with Painter and a pressure-sensitive tablet and stylus—the natural brushstrokes, the sensitivity, the happy accidents of two colors blending together or a bit of canvas showing through. Biever's painting *The Parable,* a portrait of Jesus Christ, was painted using Painter's Chalk and custom Distortion variants.

1 Sketching on a colored ground. To begin the portrait with a warm tone, Biever began a new file (about 3000 x 3500 pixels) with a sand-colored paper color. He chose the Sharp Chalk variant of Chalk in the Brush Selector Bar, a dark neutral color in the Colors picker and Basic Paper in the Paper Selector. Using the Sharp Chalk, he sketched loosely, indicating the general position of the facial features and shape of the head.

2 Blocking in color and blending. Next, Biever blocked in the base tones using the Square Chalk variant (Chalk). Using the Size slider on the Property Bar, he enlarged the Square Chalk to make thicker strokes. Using broad strokes of color, he established the planes of the face and set the general tone of the painting and the angle and color of light on the face. (Biever wanted the feeling of natural sunlight, outdoors.) He worked from dark to light, roughing in general shapes using mid-toned color to sculpt the facial structure, letting his brushstrokes follow the direction of the forms. (He planned to add the highlights last.)

3 Blending and sculpting with a custom brush. Biever built a custom brush that is based on the Marbling Rake. This custom Marbling Rake gives an illusion of oil paint texture. To build

4a

Roughing in the left hand

4b

The left hand and more canvas added

5

The completed face after the contrast was adjusted

his brush, which paints a smoother stroke than the default Marbling Rake, reduce the Size and Opacity of the brush using the sliders in the Property Bar. For more smear, lower the Resaturation using the slider in the Well section of Brush Controls. Next, in the Rake section (Brush Controls), reduce the Brush Scale to between 75%–100%. Save your new variant and give it a name. You can lose the paper texture with the Rake, but through careful stroking Biever left bits and pieces of the canvas showing through. He continued to refine the face using the Large Chalk (Chalk), while mixing and pulling color with his custom Marbling Rake.

USING PAPER COLOR

Painter lets you specify Paper Color in the New dialog box (File, New) by clicking the Paper Color icon and choosing a color in the Colors window. You can change it midway through the painting process by selecting a color in the Colors picker and then choosing Canvas, Set Paper Color to apply the color. The color of the existing background doesn't change, but if you make a selection and delete an area of the image or choose an Erasers variant (Bleaches don't work) and erase an area of the image, the new color appears.

4 Painting the hands and emphasizing the face. To emphasize the telling of a story, Biever roughed in the hand on the left. To balance the composition and give the picture more room, he added to the canvas using Canvas, Canvas Size. After he had rendered the right hand also, he selected them using the Lasso tool, floated them (Select, Float) and repositioned them using the Layer Adjuster tool. Then, he dropped the layer by choosing Drop from the Layer Commands menu on the bottom of the Layers palette. (To learn about using selections and layers, turn to Chapters 5 and 6.)

Using lighter colors, Biever brought out highlights in the face and hands using small Chalk variants. To emphasize the face even more, he painted over the tunic with the Large Chalk and lighter color, again blending with the Marbling Rake.

5 Adding final details and more texture. To enhance the highlights and shadows in the portrait, Biever increased the contrast using Effects, Tonal Control, Brightness/Contrast.

Then for *more* atmosphere, he added a papyrus texture from an Art Beats CD-ROM, copying and pasting the texture into the file as a layer. Using the pop-up menu on the Layers palette, he set the Compositing Method to Soft Light. He blended the texture into the hair and beard, creating a dusty feel. To blend a texture into your painting, target the texture layer in the Layers palette; then click on the Layer Mask button. The new Layer Mask will appear in the Channels palette. Choose the Digital Airbrush (Airbrushes) and black color. Spray over the area of the image that you want to hide. (To read more about working with masks and layers, see Chapters 5 and 6.) 🖌

Painting with Pastel and Oils

Overview *Create a sketch with a custom Pencils variant; block in color using a custom Artist Pastel Chalk; blend and pull color with the New Totally Oils Brush from the Painter IX Wow! CD-ROM.*

Orlando's pencil drawing

Creating color activity while painting the water

DENNIS ORLANDO

INSPIRED BY NATURE'S DESIGN—spectacular driftwood on a beach with a restless tropical sea—artist Dennis Orlando created a dynamic composition. In *Barbados Driftwood*, the strong intersecting diagonal and vertical thrusts lead the viewer's eye to follow the composition around the image. Orlando's sensitivity to light and shadow all combine to give the composition its power.

1 Sketching with a custom Pencil. Orlando set up a new 11 x 15-inch document with a resolution of 300 ppi and a white Paper Color. He modified a Pencils variant and used it to create a drawing. To create his custom variant, select the Thick and Thin Pencil variant of Pencils. (So that you begin with the same settings that Orlando used, choose Restore All Default Variants from the pop-up menu on the Brush Selector Bar before beginning to build the brushes.) Next, open the Brush Controls (Window, Brush Controls). In the General section, change Method to Cover and Subcategory to Grainy Soft Cover. Save your new variant by

2b

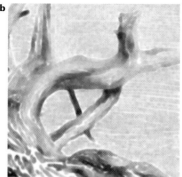

Laying in color using the Pastel variant

3

The in-progress pastel image

4

Choosing the IX Wow! Oils library from the Brush Libraries dialog box

5a

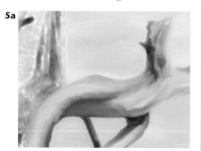

Blending and pulling paint using the New Totally Oils brush

choosing Save Variant from the pop-up menu on the Brush Selector Bar, and give it a descriptive name, such as *Soft Cover Pencil*. After saving your custom variant, return the original Thick and Thin Pencil to its default setting by choosing Restore Default Variant from the pop-up menu on the Brush Selector Bar. Switch back to your new Soft Cover Pencil and select the Artists' Canvas texture in the Papers Selector. Choose a color in the Colors picker (Orlando started with a dark gray) and begin sketching.

2 Underpainting with a custom Pastel. To define the shapes in his composition, Orlando roughed in the water and beach with a favorite custom Pastel. Select the Artist Pastel Chalk variant of the Pastels brush. To build his Pastel, change the Subcategory in the General section to Grainy Soft Cover—this gives softer brushstrokes than Grainy Hard Cover. Save the custom Soft Grainy Pastel by choosing Save Variant from the menu on the Brush Selector Bar.

One of Orlando's trademarks is activity in the color, achieved by adjusting the Color Variability settings for certain brushes. To re-create the active color look in the water, start with the same Pastels brush that you created for the beach. Choose a blue-green and then open the Color Variability section of Brush Controls (Window, Brush Controls, Show Color Variability) and adjust the Color Variability sliders: set Hue (±H) to 13%, Saturation (±S) to 3% and Value (±V) to 6%. On the Brush Selector Bar, choose Variant, Save Variant, enter a descriptive name and click OK. Begin painting. Orlando painted a creamy tan on larger areas of the beach and around the edges of the wood. He changed to a smaller brush size when working close to the driftwood to preserve its shapes.

3 Establishing values and adding details. Use a smaller version of the same Pastel brush to rough in color and value details on the driftwood. Keep the same Color Variability settings. Orlando used blue-gray colors to paint the dark, recessed areas inside the driftwood, and he used lighter values of a warm, creamy color to paint the sunlit areas on the wood.

4 Loading a new brush library. To get a look similar to pushing conventional oils around on a canvas, Orlando used the *New Totally Oils Brush* from the IX Wow! Oils library located on the *Painter IX Wow!* CD-ROM. (This brush was inspired by a brush that shipped with an early version of Painter, the Total Oils.) To load the brushes, locate the IX Wow! Oils folder. The folder contains a category folder and a category JPEG. Copy the folder with its contents to the Brushes folder within the Painter application folder. From the pop-up menu on the Brush Selector Bar, choose Load Brush Library. The new library will appear in the Brush Selector Bar.

5 Simulating traditional oils. Choose the New Totally Oils Brush. **A word of caution:** The New Totally Oils Brush incorporates the Liquid method (in the General section of Brush

5b

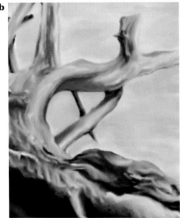

Finessing the highlights and shadows on the wood

5c

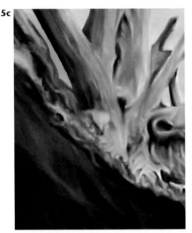

Painting the reflected light on the wood using the New Totally Oils Brush

6

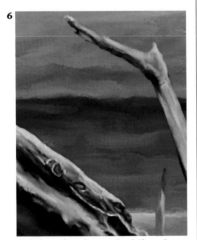

Defining a few edges on the driftwood using a small default Artist Pastel Chalk

Controls), which allows the moving of paint. As of this writing, brushes that employ the Liquid method work best on the Canvas and may have problems when painting on layers. Orlando created his entire painting on the Canvas without the use of layers, as he might have done with traditional materials. As he painted, he varied his brush size slightly. With the Dropper tool, sample a color from the area you want to paint, or hold down the Alt/Option key while using a brush to temporarily switch to the Dropper tool.

To maintain the modulated color of the underpainting, give the New Totally Oils Brush the same Color Variability settings that were described in step 3. Save this variant by choosing Save Variant from the Brush Selector Bar, giving it a descriptive name.

Use this brush and short strokes to pull color from one area of your painting into another. Orlando switched between this brush and his custom Pastel (described in step 2) to work over the entire surface of the painting, including the shadow areas on the sand and the modeling on the wood. He painted the reflected light on the wood by sampling color from the water and painting into some of the mid-tone areas using the New Totally Oils Brush.

6 Defining the details. So that the arms of the driftwood stood out from the sky and water, Orlando used a small default Artist Pastel Chalk to define the surface edges on the driftwood and to add more color details to the wood and to the beach.

7 Softening the horizon and water. The Grainy Water variant of the Blenders brush is useful for blending and softening areas if you want to preserve some of the paper texture as you blend. Orlando used the brush to soften the horizon, making it appear to recede into the distance. He dabbed this brush on the water, using short, curved strokes to suggest a stormy, restless sea. He was careful to preserve the modulated color in the water as he worked.

7

Softening the horizon and water with the Grainy Water variant of Blenders. The delicate shading and reflected light is also visible in this detail.

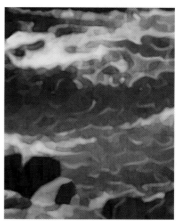

■ For *Monterey Bay,* **Dennis Orlando** used a process similar to the one that he used for *Barbados Driftwood,* but for this painting, he carefully painted details to depict the swirling water and to highlight the form and texture of the rocks in the foreground.

Orlando began the painting by sketching with a modified version of the Thick and Thin variant of Pencils. To build his custom pencil, he chose the Thick and Thin variant of Pencils, and in the General section of Brush Controls, he changed the Method pop-up menu to Cover and the Subcategory pop-up menu

to Grainy Soft Cover. The Grainy Soft Cover subcategory helped the pencil to feel softer, and it allowed him to paint light colors over dark ones (when drawing over the dark tones). Next, he roughed in color using the Artist Pastel Chalk variant of Pastels. To achieve activity in the color, Orlando opened the Color Variability section of Brush Controls and chose these settings: Hue (±H) 13%, Saturation (±S) 3% and Value (±V) 6%. Then he laid in more brush strokes. Next, he pulled and blended colors into one another using the Grainy Water variant of the Blenders.

For the look of wet paint, Orlando used the *New Totally Oils Brush* (a custom brush from the IX Wow! Oils brush category on the *Painter IX Wow!* CD-ROM in the back of this book). The New Totally Oils Brush allowed him to add color and to blend as he painted. To finish the painting, Orlando added a few grainy strokes using the Artist Pastel Chalk. This brushwork is most noticeable on the foliage and on the rocks in the foreground.

■ An award-winning cartoonist whose work has been published in *Newsweek, The New York Times, The Washington Post, USA Today,* and *The Chicago Tribune,* **Nick Anderson** is the chief editorial cartoonist at *The Louisville Courier-Journal* in Louisville, Kentucky. Anderson is the recipient of the 2005 Pulitzer Prize for editorial cartooning. This cartoon was in his prize-winning portfolio.

Anderson begins each cartoon by drawing a rough sketch on traditional tracing paper. Then, he creates a black-and-white drawing using Sakura Micron Pigma pens on smooth bristol board. The thin, felt tip pens allow him to create drawings with sensitive line and tone. After completing a drawing, he scans it and then uses a variety of Painter brushes to add color and texture. Anderson

isolates elements in his images by creating selections that he saves as alpha channel masks. For more information about his masking process, see page 213.

Anderson describes his inspiration for *Bush Crosses:* "Bush had just won re-election. The exit polls showed that 22% of the voters had said that moral values were the most important issue in their vote. Bush's Texas cowboy image lent itself well to this metaphor." For most of the *Bush Crosses* cartoon, Anderson used a low-opacity version of the Soft Charcoal variant of Charcoal, building the color and values from light to dark. After laying in the basic colors, Anderson added highlights and shadows using the custom *Bristle Wet 60%* variant from the Painter IX Wow! Wet Brushes category, which can be found on the *Painter IX Wow!*

CD-ROM. Then he used the *Tiny Air Spatter Custom* variant from the Cher's Building Brushes category (also on the *Wow!* CD-ROM) to add the speckled texture effect to the ground and the saddle. Anderson has found that painted texture reproduces better in the newspaper when there is greater contrast between the texture and the underlying colors. To complete his cartoon, he used the Spatter Water variant of the Digital Watercolor brush to paint the larger spatters. For crisper edges on the spatter droplets, he increased the brush's Wet Fringe by using the slider in the Property Bar. Then, to achieve looser splatters, he opened the Brush Controls by choosing Window, Brush Controls, Show Random, and in the Random section, he increased the Jitter setting.

■ Artee's Island Designs commissioned **Keith MacLelland** to create *Pink Cadillac* as part of a classic car line of teeshirt graphics. MacLelland began his illustration by using Pencils variants to draw a sketch of the Cadillac and palm trees. He drew the car and the trees, each on a new empty layer so that he could adjust the opacity of the elements as he worked.

To give his black-and-white line work more energy, MacLelland built a custom brush called *Scratchboard Fuzzy* that is based on the Scratchboard Tool variant of the Pens. He chose the Scratchboard Tool in the Brush Selector Bar. Then, he opened the Brush Creator (Ctrl/⌘-B), clicked on the Stroke Designer tab, and in the General section, he set the Dab Type pop-up menu to Line Airbrush.

When his final inking was complete, MacLelland softened the lines by selecting them and adjusting their value. He chose the Magic Wand tool, set the Tolerance at 32 in the Property Bar and unchecked the Contiguous box. Then, he clicked on the black lines to select the center of the ink lines. Next, he chose Effects, Surface Control, Dye Concentration using Uniform Color, set the Maximum to 16% and clicked OK.

Now MacLelland was ready to paint with color. He added another new layer and began to paint using his own *Oil Pastel Clumpy* custom brush. This brush is based on the Oil Pastel variant of Oil Pastels. To build the brush, he chose the Oil Pastel and in the Stroke Designer tab (Brush Creator), he opened the General section and set the Subcategory pop-up menu to Grainy Soft Cover. In the Angle section, he set Angle to 132, Angle Range to 139,

and left the other settings at their defaults. Next, so that he could use the Wacom Intuos Airbrush Fingerwheel to achieve a scumbling effect, he set the Expression pop-up menu to Wheel so that he could control the Jitter, using the Fingerwheel.

To begin painting the palm trees, he added another new layer and used the Coarse Bristle variant of Sumi-e to paint loose strokes for the trees. Then, to create depth in his illustration, he lowered the Opacity of this layer to 70%, and he did not add an ink outline. As a final step for this illustration, he used the Text tool to add his grandfather's name, "J CLARK," to the license plate. He converted the Text layer to pixels (by choosing Convert to Default Layer from the Layers palette menu), and then to position the name onto the license plate, he chose Effects, Orientation, Distort.

■ Artist **Terrie LaBarbera** painted
Nimbus Portrait. Her painting was
inspired by a photograph of the Arabian
mare Nimbus that was taken by Lark
Baum. LaBarbera began the painting by
choosing Italian Watercolor Paper in the
Paper Selector. She opened the photo in
Painter and created a clone copy (File,
Quick Clone). Then, she added a new
layer for her sketch by clicking the New
Layer button on the Layers palette, and
drew a tight black-and-white sketch
using a custom Soft Cover Pencil variant.

LaBarbera built several custom Digital
Watercolor brushes that she used as
cloning brushes so that she could paint
using color from the photograph. Her

DWC Wet Soft and *DWC Wet Large*
brushes are described here. To build the
DWC Wet Soft brush, LaBarbera began
by choosing the Simple Water variant of
Digital Watercolor in the Brush Selector
Bar. To begin, she enabled the Clone
Color button on the Colors picker. In the
General section, she changed the Dab
Type pop-up menu from Circular to
Static Bristle, and then reduced the
Opacity to 5%. In the Size section of
Brush Controls, she set Size to 20 and
Min Size to 23%. In the Bristle section,
she set Thickness to 50%, Clumpiness to
50% (for a smooth look), Hair Scale to
200% (for finer bristles) and Scale/Size to
0. In the Well section, she set

Resaturation to 100% and Bleed to 90%.
Then, she saved the variant. Next, she
built the DWC Wet Large brush, a
variation of the DWC Wet Soft. In the
General section, she set the Opacity to
52%; in the Well section, she set
Resaturation to 25%, leaving Bleed at
90% and then saved her new variant.

LaBarbera added another new layer to hold
the first washes of colored paint. Then, she
used the DWC Wet Soft brush to paint light
washes over the entire image. For the detail
on the horse's mane, jaw and lower face,
she added another new layer, and then
painted with the DWC Wet Large brush.
She changed the sizes and opacity of her
brushes as she worked.

■ *Whiskey Shoals* is a member of the series *Mendocino* by **Cher Threinen-Pendarvis**. The series focuses on landscape and architectural subjects from the Mendocino area in northern California. Pendarvis began the painting by making conventional colored pencil sketches on location. Later, she scanned the sketch, opened it in Painter and used the custom *Soft Captured Oils Brush* variant of the IX Wow! Oils category (from the *Painter IX Wow!* CD-ROM in the back of the book) to paint colored washes onto the sketch. The instructions for building the Soft Captured Oils Brush are described on page 159 in the introduction to this chapter.

Working over the underpainting, Pendarvis used the Lasso to make selections of the major elements (the hills, ocean and sky) and then saved them as masks in the Channels palette. To try out color variations in her composition, she used the selections to isolate areas of the composition while previewing variations in color. For instance, she loaded the "ocean" selection and used Effects, Tonal Control, Adjust Color to increase the saturation, deepening the blue in the water. She also loaded a selection of the distant hills and used Adjust Color to lower its saturation, making the hills recede farther. To blend the color adjustments into the image and to modulate the color, she used a custom *Soft Bristle Rake* brush that incorporated Color Variability (also from the IX Wow! Oils). This brush work is most noticeable on the rocks and water in the midground of the painting. To paint dappled light on the distant water, she painted short dabbing strokes using a small Soft Bristle Rake brush. For the trails of the breaking waves, she used a small *Soft Dry Flat* brush, from the IX Wow! Oils brushes, also described on page 159. For the grass, she used the Soft Captured Oils Brush, which incorporated the Rake stroke type (with the Spread Bristles box enabled in the Rake section of Brush Controls). As she completed each stroke and lifted the stylus, the strokes ended by showing the spread bristles. This can be seen on the blades of grass in the foreground. To finish, Pendarvis sharpened details with a small version of the Soft Captured Oils Brush.

SELECTIONS, SHAPES AND MASKS

Flame Throwing His Voice. *Artist Chet Phillips began by making a black-and-white drawing with the Scratchboard Tool variant of the Pens. Next, Phillips turned the entire scratchboard drawing into a separate layer by choosing Select, All and then Select, Float, and set its Composite Method to Gel. Then, working on top of the scratchboard drawing, he used the Lasso tool to create a selection for the figures and other elements. Then he saved each selection as a mask (Select, Save Selection). Working on the now blank image canvas, he loaded each of his masks in turn (Select, Load Selection) and used various brushes to paint within the selections. To read more about the image, see "Coloring a Woodcut" on page 42.*

INTRODUCTION

TO GET THE MOST FROM PAINTER, you need to invest some time in understanding how the program isolates portions of images so you can paint them, apply special effects, or otherwise change them without affecting the rest of the image. Much of the program's power is tucked into the complex area of *selections*, *shapes* and *masks*.

WHAT IS A SELECTION?

A *selection* is an area of the image that has been isolated so changes can be made to the contents only, or so the area can be protected from change. There are two kinds of selections in Painter: outline-based and pixel-based. Like a cookie cutter, an *outline-based* selection sharply defines the area it surrounds. But unlike cookie cutters in the real world, an outline-based selection border in Painter can be freely scaled or reshaped. Outline-based selections can be made by dragging with the Lasso tool (for free-hand selecting), the Rectangular Selection tool or the Oval Selection tool.

If Painter's outline-based selections are like the outlines produced by cookie cutters, then *pixel-based* selections are more like painted resists. Pixel-based selections make the selected areas fully or *partially* available for change or copying, with the degree of availability determined by the nature and "thickness" of the "resist material." Pixel-based selections can be made by selecting based on the color or tone of pixels, rather than by an outline you draw. The Magic Wand tool makes pixel-based selections; they can also be made with the Auto Select and Color Select commands from the Select menu.

The perimeter of either kind of selection is indicated by an animated border, the selection marquee. A selection is temporary. If

The selection tools are located near the top of the Toolbox. Some tools share a space in the Toolbox with other tools, as shown here in pop-out view. (The Rectangular Selection, Oval Selection and Lasso are shown popped out on the left; the Magic Wand is shown on the right.)

The shape-drawing tools are the Pen and Quick Curve (left), which share a Toolbox space, and the Rectangular Shape and Oval Shape (right), which also share a space.

USING ANTIALIASING

Antialiasing renders a smooth selection edge, preventing jagged, pixelated edges. All of Painter's selection tools make smooth-edged selections. The Magic Wand is the one tool that gives you a choice—just uncheck the Anti-Alias checkbox on the Property Bar if you want to make a jaggy-edged selection.

To isolate an area of the canvas for filling with blue, the Oval Selection tool was used. This extreme close-up shows the antialiasing of the edge after filling. At normal magnification, the antialiasing makes the edge look smooth.

you choose Select, None (Ctrl/⌘-D) or accidentally click outside the selection marquee, the selection will be lost, unless you have stored it in the Selection Portfolio palette or saved it as a mask in the Channels palette or converted it to a shape. (The Selection Portfolio is described on page 183, the Channels palette is covered on page 191 and shapes are described next.)

WHAT IS A SHAPE?

A *shape* is similar in construction to an outline-based selection, but it has stroke and fill characteristics. (This chapter tells about how to draw shapes and how they are related to selections. The stroke and fill attributes of shapes, their layering capabilities and their relationship to layers, are covered in Chapter 6). Shapes can be created with the Rectangular Shape, Oval Shape, Pen or Quick Curve tool. As soon as a shape is drawn, it is automatically stored in the Layers palette. (The Layers palette can be used to control how shapes are used in the image, as described in Chapter 6.)

Shapes can be used as independent elements in an illustration, or a shape can be converted to a selection and then used to isolate an area of the image. When you convert a shape to a selection (Shapes, Convert to Selection), its name disappears from the Layers palette and an animated selection marquee appears on the image. **Beware:** If you convert a shape to a selection, it will be permanently lost if you deselect it before you either convert it back to a shape, store the selection you made from it, or choose Edit, Undo (Ctrl/⌘-Z) or Select, Reselect (Ctrl/⌘-R).

WHAT IS A MASK?

Unlike a shape, which is stored *outline* information, a *mask* is stored *pixel-based* information. Masks can store 8-bit grayscale information, which means that complex image information such as a painting, a photo or a graphic can be saved and then loaded

RESTORING A SELECTION

If you've made a selection and have deselected it—either by accident or to work outside of it—and then want to use it again, choose Select, Reselect (Ctrl/⌘-R).

CONTEXT-SENSITIVE MENUS

Painter offers context-sensitive menus that allow access to helpful commands. For instance, click within an active selection while pressing the right mouse button on the PC (or the Ctrl key on the Mac) to display a list of commands that are useful for working with selections.

The context-sensitive menu for an active selection appears at the spot where you right/Ctrl-click.

The Property Bar for each of the selection-drawing tools has buttons for access to the other selection-drawing tools. It also has a button for converting the current selection to a shape.

The Property Bar for each of the shape-drawing tools has buttons for access to the other shape-drawing tools. It also has a button for transforming the current shape to an outline-based selection. This button will work only if the shape is closed—that is, if it has no gaps.

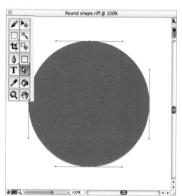

This shape has been selected with the Shape Selection tool (shown chosen in the Toolbox) and shows its control points and handles.

as a selection. Painter's 8-bit masks allow 256 levels of opacity. When a mask is loaded as a selection, in areas where the mask is black, the selection completely protects the pixels of the image from change; where the mask is white, the pixels are fully selected and exposed to brushstrokes; gray areas of the mask result in partially selected pixels. The protective mask can be "thinned" or even completely removed pixel by pixel. Masks allow complex image information to be used as a selection. Another way to use a mask, besides loading it as a selection, is to choose it when applying the functions in the Effects menu, such as Tonal Control, Adjust Colors and Surface Control, Apply Surface Texture. Masks also provide a way of permanently storing selection information until you need to use it. The Channels palette not only stores masks but also controls operations such as turning them on and off so they can be used as selections. (The Channels palette is described on page 191.)

CREATING OUTLINE-BASED SELECTIONS AND SHAPES

You can make an outline-based selection or a shape in a number of ways. One way, as mentioned earlier and described in more detail here, is to draw it with one of the selection or shape tools:

Rectangular and Oval Selection tools. Drag to make selections with these tools. To constrain the Oval or Rectangular Selection tools so they select perfect squares or circles, begin dragging and then hold down the Shift key to complete the drag.

Lasso tool. The Lasso tool is good for making quick, freehand selections. Choose the Lasso and carefully drag around the area that you want to isolate.

Rectangular and Oval Shape tools. Drag with these tools to create rectangular and elliptical shape layers. Hold down the Shift key as you drag with the tool to draw a perfect square or circle shape.

Pen tool. Choose the Pen tool for precise drawing using a combination of straight lines and curves. Click from point to point to create straight line segments; to draw curves, press to create a curve point and drag to pull out handles that control the curves. To complete an outline drawn by the Pen, close the shape by connecting to the origin point or by pressing the Close button on the Property Bar.

Quick Curve tool. Drag with the Quick Curve tool to draw freehand shapes. Like the Pen, the Quick Curve has a Close button on its Property Bar.

WHERE'S THE PATH?

If you switch from the Pen to another tool (such as the Brush), and your paths seem to disappear, you can bring them back into view by choosing the Pen, the Quick Curve tool, the Shape Selection tool or a shape-editing tool (Scissors, Add Point, Delete Point or Convert Point).

PRECISION DRAWING SETUP

If you're drawing shapes and you find that the stroke and fill obscure your view and make it hard to see the outline, simply uncheck the Fill and Stroke boxes in the Property Bar.

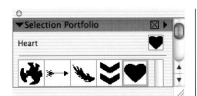

Choosing a heart-shaped path in Painter's Selection Portfolio palette, opened by choosing Window, Show Selection Portfolio

These type shapes were set with the Text tool and converted to shapes (choose Convert Text to Shapes from the pop-up menu on the right side of the Layers palette). They were then selected with the Layer Adjuster tool (top), converted to a selection (Shapes, Convert to Selection) and then used to fill areas of the image canvas by choosing Effects, Fill (bottom).

When this bird, drawn in Adobe Illustrator, was copied and pasted into Painter, it came in as a compound shape. To read about how the drop shadow was added turn to page 349.

In addition to drawing them by hand, here are some other ways of making an outline-based selection or a shape:

Transforming a pixel-based selection. Change a pixel-based selection to an outline-based selection by choosing Select, Transform Selection. (See page 188 for information about converting soft-edged pixel-based selections to outline-based.)

Using the Selection Portfolio. Drag a stored selection from the Selection Portfolio palette into your image. (If you use a lot of custom paths in your work, you may want to create custom libraries as described in the "Libraries and Movers" section of Chapter 1.)

Converting text. Convert a text layer to shapes by choosing Convert Text To Shapes from the Layers palette's pop-out menu. (For more information about type, turn to Chapter 9, "Working with Type in Painter.")

AI IMPORTING ALERT!

There may be problems with importing Illustrator files created in early versions of Freehand and Illustrator (prior to version 7 of the programs). So if you have an older file you want to use, open it in version 7 or later and resave it for version 7 compatibility. When working in Illustrator 10 or CS, for best results, save the file in AI format with Illustrator 7 or 8 compatibility.

Importing PostScript art. Import EPS paths as shapes from a PostScript drawing program. Painter supports two ways to import shapes, such as preexisting EPS clip art or type set on a curve and converted to outlines in a PostScript drawing program. The first option (File, Acquire, Adobe Illustrator File) creates a new file, importing the EPS outlines—with their strokes and fills—into Painter as shapes. To add the shapes to an existing Painter file, copy and paste the shapes from the new file into your working composition.

The second option allows you to copy outlines with strokes and fills from a PostScript program to the clipboard and paste them into your Painter file. The outlines will be imported into your document as shapes and will appear in the Layers palette. Objects such as the converted letters "O" and "A" that have a *counter,* or hole, in them will come into Painter as compound shapes, preserving the holes.

MOVING SELECTIONS AND SHAPES

For both pixel-based and outline-based selections, you can move the selection boundary without moving the pixels it surrounds. This gives you a great deal of flexibility in positioning the selection boundary before you use it to change the image. To move a selection boundary without moving any pixels, choose the Selection Adjuster tool and put its cursor inside the animated selection boundary; dragging will move the selection boundary. This works for both pixel-based and outline-based selections. To move the

Use the arrow keys on your keyboard to move selections or shapes by one screen pixel at a time. (Before attempting to move a selection, choose the Selection Adjuster tool; prior to moving a shape, choose the Layer Adjuster tool.) Since the distance moved is a screen pixel and not a fixed distance, zoom out from the selection or shape if you want to make coarse adjustments and zoom in for fine adjustments. Arrow-key nudging is especially useful for kerning type that has been converted to shapes.

Alt/Option-dragging a selection to make a copy

Dragging a side handle to scale horizontally

Shift-dragging one of the corner handles to scale proportionally

Using a corner handle and the Ctrl/⌘ key to rotate

selection's contents, drag with the Layer Adjuster tool instead of the Selection Adjuster; this turns the selected area into a new layer. The Layer Adjuster can also be used to move shapes: Click the name of the shape in the Layers palette and then use the Layer Adjuster tool to drag the shape.

RESHAPING SELECTIONS

Painter allows an outline-based selection border or a shape to be transformed—scaled, skewed or rotated—without altering the image. It can also be expanded, contracted, smoothed, or made into a selection of its border area only. Selections made with the Lasso or Rectangular or Oval Selection tools, as well as selections converted from shapes, are automatically outline-based and thus can be transformed. Selections made with the Magic Wand or loaded from masks must be converted to outline-based information before they can be scaled, skewed or rotated. To convert a pixel-based selection to an outline-based selection, choose Select, Transform Selection. To convert a selection stored as a mask in the Channels palette to an outline-based selection, load the selection (Select, Load Selection) and then transform it.

Whether it was outline-based from the beginning or it was made by transforming, a selection needs to be displaying its bounding box handles in order to be transformed. To display the handles for the currently working selection, the Selection Adjuster tool has to be chosen. Once the bounding box handles are visible, you can move the selection, or scale, skew, or rotate its outline, or change it using commands under the Select, Modify menu to widen, contract or smooth it, or make a selection around its border.

Since outline-based selections are based on mathematical information, they can undergo all of the following transformations, carried out with the Selection Adjuster tool, with no loss of edge quality. (These transformations don't work on pixel-based selections; a pixel-based selection has to be converted to an outline-based selection first, as described above.) Display the eight bounding box handles as described above and then:

To duplicate, hold down Alt/Option (a tiny "plus" will appear next to the cursor); drag and release to add a copy to the selection.

To scale, position the tool over one of the corner handles; when the cursor changes, drag the handle. To *scale proportionally,* hold down the Shift key as you drag. If you want to *resize only horizontally or vertically,* drag on the center handle of the top, the bottom or a side.

To rotate, use a corner handle, adding the Ctrl/⌘ key as you position the cursor. Be sure you see the curved arrow cursor around the handle before dragging to rotate. **Be careful:** Don't

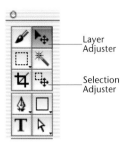

Layer
Adjuster

Selection
Adjuster

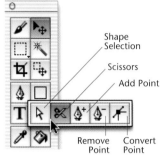

Shape
Selection

Scissors

Add Point

Remove   Convert
Point   Point

The Layer Adjuster and Selection Adjuster tools can move, rotate, scale and skew shapes and outline-based selections, respectively. The shape-editing tools that share a space on the Toolbox are used for reshaping shapes in a more detailed way.

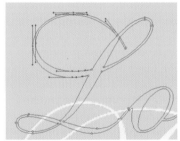

This path has handles showing and is ready to be manipulated with the Shape Selection tool.

start dragging until you see the curved arrow cursor, because the Ctrl/⌘ key is also used to temporarily turn the Selection Adjuster tool into the Layer Adjuster tool—the pointing-finger cursor. If you're trying to rotate the selection boundary, don't drag with the pointing finger! If you do so accidentally, the contents of the selection will be moved, but you can recover by pressing Ctrl/⌘-Z.

To skew, press Ctrl/⌘ while positioning the cursor over a center handle on the side, top, or bottom and then drag. **Be careful:** Don't start dragging until you see the slanted arrow cursor across the handle. If you're trying to skew the selection boundary, don't drag while the cursor is a pointing finger! If you do so accidentally, you can recover by pressing Ctrl/⌘-Z.

RESHAPING SHAPES

The Layer Adjuster tool can scale, rotate and skew shapes in much the same way the Selection Adjuster works with outline-based selections. In addition, shapes can be modified in more detail with the shape-editing tools, which share a space in the Toolbox. The Shape Selection tool (hollow arrow) and the other shape-editing tools allow you to adjust individual anchor points and control handles to modify shapes.

The Shape Selection tool works much like its counterpart in Adobe Illustrator, by clicking the outline of a shape to show its control points, then dragging a point or path segment to change its position. You can also use it to click on an individual point so it will show its handles, and then drag a handle to adjust the curve.

The Scissors, Add Point, Remove Point and Convert Point tools will also be familiar to Illustrator users. For instance, the Scissors tool allows you to cut a path segment. To add a new anchor point, click with the Add Point tool. To delete an anchor point, click on it with the Remove Point tool.

Because it's so easy to convert an outline-based selection to a shape and vice versa (see page 188), you can easily modify an outline-based selection by converting it to a shape, editing it with the shape-editing tools and then converting it back to a selection.

SELECTING AND MASKING BY COLOR

In addition to the selection-outlining tools described on pages 182–183, Painter also offers useful tools and procedures for making selections and masks based on the color in your image rather than on an outline you draw.

Magic Wand. Painter's easy-to-use Magic Wand is a real production time-saver. The Magic Wand lets you select an area of your image based on color similarities of contiguous (touching) or noncontiguous pixels. This is especially useful for selecting a uniformly colored element in an image, without having to draw

The Property Bar for the Magic Wand lets you set the Tolerance, or size of the color range, you want the Wand to select. You can also choose whether to select only those pixels that are connected as a continuous patch of color that touches the pixel you click; for this option, Contiguous should be turned on (checked in the Property Bar). To select all pixels within the color range, both touching and not touching, turn off the Contiguous option.

around the area with the Lasso or Pen tool. To select a wider range of color, increase the Tolerance number in the Property Bar before you use the Wand. To make a smooth-edged selection, make sure the Anti-Alias box is checked before you make the selection.

To add areas of similar adjacent color to the selection, reset the Tolerance higher; then hold down the Shift key and click inside the existing selection. To shrink your selection by reducing the range of the colors it's based on, Alt/Option-click within the selection on the color you want to eliminate (you may want to set the Tolerance lower first). To remove a range of colors from a selection, Alt/Option-drag in the area. To add areas of similar color that are not adjacent (like Select, Similar in Photoshop), turn off the Contiguous check box in the Property Bar, and continue adding areas of non-contiguous color by Shift-clicking on other areas of the image. To turn off the nonadjacent mode, turn on Contiguous again.

Once the Magic Wand has produced the pixel-based selection you want, you can store it as a mask by choosing Select, Save Selection or by clicking the Save Selection as Channel button at the bottom of the Channels palette.

Color Select. Painter also offers an automated procedure for isolating parts of images based on color. It does something similar to the Magic Wand in non-Contiguous mode. In one way you have more control than with the Magic Wand because "Tolerance" is separated into three components (hue, saturation and value) and you can choose to partially select colors outside the range. The difficulty with this selection method is that it's hard to control the smoothness of the edges, and they tend to be somewhat rougher than an antialiased Magic Wand selection. To generate a rough-edged pixel-based selection based on a range of color, choose Select, Color Select. When the Color Select dialog box opens, click in the image on the color that you want the range to center around. In the Color Select dialog box adjust the H (Hue), S (Saturation) and V (Value) Extents sliders to control the range of each of these properties sampled in the image. Experiment with adjusting the Feather sliders to partially select the other colors in the image. To reverse the mask to a "negative," enable the Inverted check box. Click OK to complete the selection.

Our goal was to generate a selection for the sky in this photo. We chose Select, Color Select and clicked in the image to sample the color we wanted to isolate. We adjusted the H, S and V sliders until the red mask covered only the sampled color in the preview window, and then clicked OK to activate the selection. Alternatively, you can use New from Color Range (from the pop-out menu of the Channels palette) to accomplish the same thing, except as a mask rather than a selection; the mask is automatically stored in the Channels palette.

To save your Color Select selection, you can use Select, Save Selection or click the button in the Channels palette as described above for the Magic Wand. But the Channels palette also provides a way to make and store a color-based mask directly, as described in the New from Color Range, below.

New from Color Range. In the Channels palette's pop-out menu, choose New from Color Range. In the Color dialog box (which works the same as the Color Select box described above), you can then make the same Extents, Feather and Invert choices.

Killdeer by Mary Envall. To create this wildlife illustration—featuring a black-and-white ink drawing floating on top of colored, textured paper—Envall began by making a black-and-white scratchboard drawing in Painter. To drop the white background out behind the drawing she made an automatic selection, choosing Select, Auto Select, using Image Luminance. She floated the active selection by clicking on it with the Layer Adjuster. Next, she filled the background (the Canvas) with a colored texture, using Effects, Surface Control, Color Overlay using Paper and Dye Concentration.

Susan LeVan used Painter's New From, Current Color feature to make rough-edged masks for brushstrokes shown in this illustration Covering Home, *created for* Becoming Family *magazine.*

OTHER PIXEL-BASED SELECTING AND MASKING OPTIONS

Two powerful functions—Auto Select and New From (short for "New Channel From")—create a selection or mask based on color or on tonality (brightness values, or shades of light and dark). When you choose Select, Auto Select or choose New From from the Channels palette's pop-out menu, a dialog box opens that gives you a choice of Paper, which bases the selection or mask on the tonality of the currently selected Paper texture; 3D Brush Strokes, which is useful when you are "cloning" a painting from an image; Original Selection, which can be used to copy a selection from one file to another; Image Luminance, which bases the selection or mask on the lights and darks in the current image; Original Luminance, which is useful for importing an image into a channel so it can serve as a mask; or Current Color, which creates a selection or mask based on the current primary color. The dialog boxes for Auto Select and New From are identical, with the exception that Auto Select creates a pixel-based *selection,* whereas New From creates and stores a *mask.* Both have an Invert check box for reversing the selection or mask, as described in the "Doing the Opposite" tip below.

To practice generating a mask based on the brightness values in an image, try this: Create a new file (Ctrl/⌘-N) with white as the Paper Color. Double-click the primary (forward) color square in the Toolbox and when the Color Picker opens, choose black. From the Brush Selector Bar (opened by choosing Window, Show Brush Selector Bar), choose the Scratchboard Tool variant of the Pens. Make a sketch, and then generate a mask for your sketch by choosing New From (Ctrl/⌘-Shift-M) using Image Luminance; click OK. The mask will appear in the Channels palette, targeted and with its eye icon turned on, and you will see the mask as a red overlay. You can edit it by painting on it with a brush. Current Color is the only option for Auto Select or New From that produces a completely jagged selection or

To vignette this photo, we began by making an Oval selection. We scaled the selection using the Selection Adjuster tool, and then applied a feather of 15 pixels (Select, Feather) to soften the edge. Next, we reversed the selection by choosing Select, Invert. We chose Edit, Clear to delete the background, leaving the vignetted edge against white.

MIDDLE OF THE ROAD

When you use the Select, Transform Selection command on a soft-edged selection, Painter draws an outline-based selection using the 50%-transparency boundary. For instance, if you make a hard-edged selection with the Rectangular Selection tool, then feather it (Select, Feather) and transform it (Select, Transform Selection), the result will be a hard-edged selection, but with rounded corners.

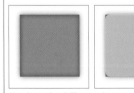

To show the difference between a hard-edged and a feathered selection, the original rectangular selection was filled with blue, then feathered 20 pixels and filled with a rose color (left). Then the selection was transformed to an outline-based selection and filled with yellow, revealing the new rounded hard edge (right).

mask, with no edge-smoothing or antialiasing at all. For an example of Auto-Selecting using Current Color, turn to "Auto-Selecting with Current Color" on page 207.

FEATHERING

Feathering a selection softens its edge. This is useful for vignetting an image or for blending a selected area into a background. To see feathering at work, drag a selection from the Selection Portfolio into your image. Choose Select, Feather, and type 20 into the field to define the extent of the feather; click OK. Now choose Effects, Fill, then select one of the options and click OK. Note the soft edges of the filled selection. The feather is always built both inward and outward from the selection boundary. Applying the Select, Feather command to an outline-based selection changes it to a pixel-based selection.

CONVERTING SELECTIONS, SHAPES AND MASKS

Outline-based and pixel-based selections have entirely different origins, but there is some degree of interchangeability.

To convert a pixel-based selection into an outline-based selection so you can transform the outline (scale, skew or rotate) using the Selection Adjuster tool, choose Select, Transform Selection. To convert a mask into an outline-based selection so you can transform it, first load the mask as a selection: In the Channels palette, click the Load Channel As Selection button at the bottom of the palette. In the Load Selection dialog box, choose the appropriate mask, make sure the Replace Selection button is chosen and click OK. This turns the mask into an active selection. Then you can choose Select, Transform Selection. (When a selection is loaded from a mask and transformed, the mask in the Channels palette remains unmodified unless you replace it using the Save Selection, Replace Mask command.)

To convert an outline-based selection into a mask and save it in the Channels palette as pixel-based information instead of outline information, choose Select, Save Selection or click the Save Selection As Channel button at the bottom of the Channels palette. (You might want to make this kind of conversion in order to edit the mask by painting on it, and then load the modified mask as a selection again.)

To convert a shape to a selection so can you use it to isolate an area of the image canvas, select the shape by highlighting its name in the Layers palette, and choose Shapes, Convert to Selection. (The tools that draw and edit shapes and selections have a Convert to Selection button on the Property Bar, allowing quick conversion of a shape you make or edit with one of these tools.)

Remember: If you convert a shape to a selection, the shape is no longer stored in the Layers palette, and it will be lost when you

We set this Adobe Woodtype Ornament using the Text tool. We Alt/Option-dragged with the Layer Adjuster tool to make a copy of the text ornament. To convert it to shapes, we chose Convert Text to Shapes from the Layers palette's pop-out menu. Next, we converted the copy into an active selection (Shapes, Convert to Selection) for treating the image canvas. To add the colored texture, we chose Effects, Surface Control, Color Overlay, Using Paper, Hiding Power with a pavement-like texture.

A QUICK INVERT

When you want to *paint* inside or outside of a selection, you can use the Drawing icons to quickly invert the selection without forcing the whole image to redraw every time you switch. However, *to invert the selection if you are applying a special effect*, you must use Select, Invert, which forces a complete screen redraw.

deselect—unless you have stored it in the Selection Portfolio (described in "Saving Selection Outlines" below) or in the Channels palette as a mask (as described earlier in this section), or unless you convert it back to a shape (as described next).

To convert the current selection into a shape so you can store it in the Layers palette, or edit its outline (using anchor points and control handles), or fill and stroke it (using the Shapes, Set Shape Attributes dialog box), choose Select, Convert to Shape. Alternatively, all of the selection tools have a Convert to Shape button on the Property Bar for quick conversion when one of these tools is active.

SAVING SELECTION OUTLINES

Use the Selection Adjuster tool to drag outline-based selections to the Selection Portfolio to store them. If you want to save shapes into this library, first convert them to selections (Shapes, Convert to Selection) and then drag them to the Selection Portfolio. If you're very organized, you might create multiple selection libraries for different jobs. To swap outlines between libraries or to set up a new, empty palette, you can use the Selection Mover, accessed by clicking the triangle in the top-right corner of the Selection Portfolio palette, to open the palette's pop-out menu.

Use File, Export, Adobe Illustrator™ File to export shapes to PostScript drawing programs. We successfully exported simple shape objects as well as more complex objects that included blends and compounds, opening them in Illustrator 7, 8 and 9.

SELECTIONS AT WORK

Once you've made or loaded a selection, you can choose to draw outside of it instead of inside, or use it to isolate areas of the image canvas or a layer when applying special-effects procedures found in the Effects menu.

Inverting a selection. If you want to apply a fill or effect to the *outside* of your active selection, use Select, Invert beforehand. This procedure reverses the current selection. It's often useful to save a selection as a mask in the Channels palette, and then save the inverse of it; for instance, save an element, and then save the background, also as a mask. This inverting process can also be used for painting outside a selection, but there's a more efficient way to control painting, described next.

Using the Drawing icons. The Drawing icons are found in the bottom-left corner of an active document's window. Take the name "Drawing icons" literally; they affect *drawing and painting actions only,* not fills or other effects. A fill or effect is always constrained to the inside of an active selection, regardless of which Drawing icon you choose. Several of the techniques in this chapter demonstrate how these icons work, and you can refer to

PHOTO: CORBIS IMAGES

To make a selection isolating the large dahlia in this photo, we used Select, Color Select, and then used the Lasso to "clean up" the selection border—pressing the Alt/ Option key to subtract from the selection— to exclude the smaller flower.

To create a light-valued border for an image, make a rectangular selection where you want the inner edge of your border; then choose Select, Modify, Border and set the width for the border large enough so it reaches all the way to the edge of the image. Then choose Effects, Tonal Control, Adjust Colors and move the Value slider to the right to lighten the border area.

PHOTO: CORBIS IMAGES

"Selecting a Drawing Mode" in the Selections section of Painter IX's online help for a detailed explanation.

Stroking a selection. In Painter, you can use any brush variant *to stroke an outline-based selection.* Begin by making an outline-based selection, either with one of the outline-based selection tools described earlier in this chapter or by transforming a pixel-based selection to outline-based. The effect is more fun to observe if you choose one of Painter's grain-sensitive brushes. In the Brush Selector Bar, choose the Large Chalk variant of Chalk. Next, open the Papers palette (Window, Show Papers) and choose a texture from the Paper Selector near the upper-right corner of the palette. With the selection still active, press the Drawing icon in the bottom-left corner of the image window and choose from the three options: You can choose to have your stroke inside the selection border (Draw Inside), outside of it (Draw Outside), or centered directly on top of it (Draw Anywhere); then go to the Select menu and choose Stroke Selection.

TRANSFORM FIRST. . .

If you'd like to stroke the outline of a pixel-based selection, use Select, Transform Selection to convert it to an outline-based selection before attempting to use the Select, Stroke Selection command.

EDITING SELECTIONS

Painter offers methods for finessing outline-based and pixel-based selections that will be familiar to Photoshop users. (To read about editing masks, see "Using the Channels Palette," on the facing page.)

Adding to a selection. To add to an existing selection marquee, choose a selection tool, and then click the Add to Selection button in the Property Bar and click or drag outside of the existing marquee. (A keyboard shortcut for using the button is to hold down the Shift key as you click or drag.) The Add to Selection operation is also useful—it is described on page 192.

Subtracting from a selection. To remove a portion of a selection, press the Subtract from Selection button in the Property Bar (or hold down the Alt/Option key) and drag with a selection tool. The Subtract from Selection and Intersect operations are also useful; they are described on page 192.

The Modify menu. Four commands under the Select, Modify menu—Widen, Contract, Smooth and Border—allow you to change outline-based selections. Widen and Contract allow you to change the size of a selection by a specified number of pixels. The Smooth command is useful for rounding corners and softening jaggedness in a selection. The Border function selects a border area (based on a specified number of pixels) outside the existing marquee.

Multiple applications of the Smooth function can turn a perfectly good typeface (Stone Sans, left) into a trendy, avant-garde one. Set type with the Text tool, convert the characters to shapes (choose Convert Text to Shapes at the bottom of the pop-up menu of the Layers palette), convert the shapes to selections (Shapes, Convert to Selection), apply the Smooth operation (Select, Modify, Smooth) and fill them with a color (Effects, Fill). If the characters aren't "smooth" enough yet, undo the fill (Ctrl/⌘-Z), smooth again, and fill again.

The Channels palette. Several useful commands are found in the pop-out menu.

Five buttons at the bottom of the Channels palette offer shortcuts to important commands: From left to right, Load Channel As Selection, Save Selection As Channel, Invert Channel, New Mask and Delete.

MASKS

You can create masks in Painter in several ways: by making a selection and saving it in the Channels palette, by painting directly onto a new blank channel with brushes, by generating masks with procedures such as New From or New from Color Range in the Channels palette's pop-out menu, or by using Boolean operations to calculate new masks from existing ones. To read about New from Color Range, turn to "Selelcting and Masking by Color" on page 185, and for more information about calculating masks, turn to "Calculating and Operating" on page 192.

USING THE CHANNELS PALETTE

The Channels palette lists all the masks you've made and stored. A Painter file can contain a maximum of 32 of these stored masks. If you'll be doing a lot of work with masks, it's a good idea to get on friendly terms with this palette. Here are some basics:

To view a mask as an overlay on top of the RGB image canvas, open the eye icon to the far left of the mask's name.

To hide a mask, click its eye icon shut.

To view a mask alone in black and white, without the RGB Canvas, open the mask's eye icon and close the RGB eye icon.

To view a mask as an opaque overlay, choose Channel Attributes from the pull-down menu of the Channels palette, and move the Opacity slider to 100%. Viewing a mask as an opaque overlay can often help you see defects in the mask, and it may be less confusing than using partial opacity. Adjusting the Opacity slider changes the overlay's onscreen appearance only, and does not affect the actual density of the mask.

To edit a mask, click the mask's name to activate it (the mask's name will then be highlighted). Open the eye icon to the far left of the mask's name.

TARGETING A MASK

In the Masks section, make sure to click on the mask's *name*—not the eye icon—to target it.

INVERT CHANNEL BUTTON

The Invert Channel button at the bottom of the Channels palette makes a negative of a mask or a part of the mask that you select. To use this function, target a mask in the Channels palette and click the Invert button. If you want to invert only part of the mask, make a selection of that part before clicking the Invert button.

MASKS FROM PHOTOSHOP

When you open a file in Painter that contains a mask created in Photoshop, the area that was masked in Photoshop now seems to be exposed in Painter. Don't despair: Although the mask appears inverted, it's functionally the same as it is in Photoshop. If you need to reverse the mask, highlight its name in the Masks section of the Channels palette, and click the Invert Channel button at the bottom of the palette.

To change the mask overlay to a color easier to see while making a mask for an orange Garibaldi fish, we changed the overlay color from the default red to yellow by choosing Channel Attributes from the Channels palette's pop-out menu and clicking the Color swatch in the Channel Attributes dialog box.

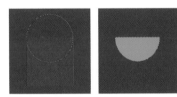

We used Intersect with Selection to create the filled half-circle (above right). To repeat what we did, begin by making a square selection with the Rectangular Selection tool and Shift key and save it by choosing Select, Save Selection, or clicking the Save Selection As Channel button at the bottom of the Channels palette. View the mask as an overlay (above left) by clicking its eye icon open in the Channels palette, along with the eye for RGB (at the top of the palette). Click the RGB name to target the image canvas, and make a new selection partially overlapping the square with the Oval Selection tool. With this oval selection active, click the Load Selection from Channel button at the bottom of the Channels palette. In the Load From pop-up menu, choose the square mask, click the Intersect with Selection button and click OK. Now you can fill the selection (choose Effects, Fill).

You can edit the mask by painting on it with any brush except a Water Color or Liquid Ink brush.

To apply a paper grain to a mask, click the mask's name to activate it and use Effects, Surface Control, Express Texture, using Paper. Watch the Preview as you experiment with the Gray Threshold, Grain and Contrast sliders.

To blur a mask so that loading it as a selection will produce a feathered selection, select the mask and choose Feather from the pop-out menu, type a number in the field and click OK.

CALCULATING AND OPERATING

Painter offers Boolean operations, useful functions that help generate new masks that fit perfectly against existing ones. Skillful use of these techniques will save time and effort. To see these functions at work, turn to "Making Masks for Embossing" on page 193.

To edit a mask using a selection, create a selection marquee, and choose Select, Save Selection or click the Save Selection As Channel button at the bottom of the Channels palette. In the Save Selection dialog box, choose the mask you wish to edit from the Save To pop-up menu, and choose the operation you wish to perform.

To replace a mask with the active selection, in the Save Selection dialog box, from the Save To menu, choose the mask you wish to replace, and then click the Replace Mask button. This choice "throws away" the original mask.

To edit a selection using a mask, create a selection marquee and choose Load Selection, or click the Load Channel As Selection button at the bottom of the Channels palette. In the Load Selection dialog box, choose the mask you want to use and click a button to add, subtract or intersect; then click OK. The Intersect with Selection button makes a new selection from the intersection of the existing selection and the mask, selecting only the area where the two overlap.

PAINTER AND PHOTOSHOP

To save Painter masks and use them in Photoshop, save a Painter file in Photoshop format. When you open the file in Photoshop, the named masks will automatically appear in the Channels palette. To learn more about using Painter masks and paths with Photoshop (and vice versa) turn to Chapter 10, "Using Painter with Photoshop."

Making Masks for Embossing

***Overview** Open a new file with a colored background; set type; convert the type to a shape and the shape to a selection; save the selection as a mask; use the selection to build bevel and background masks; apply special effects to create three-dimensional looks.*

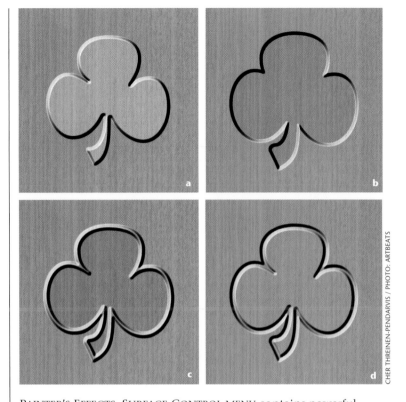

CHER THREINEN-PENDARVIS / PHOTO: ARTBEATS

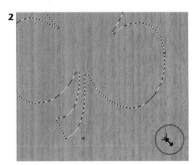

The shape before converting to a selection

Using the Selection Adjuster to scale the selection

PAINTER'S EFFECTS, SURFACE CONTROL MENU contains powerful features for creating three-dimensional artwork needed for an embossed look or for interactive buttons. These features are most effective when combined with a skillful use of selections and masks. To create these tooled wood reliefs, we began with a graphic shape for the face of the graphic. Then we created a series of masks based on the original graphic—a widened face, a bevel and a background—to isolate areas for special effects applications. Preparing the masks up front allowed quick previewing of a variety of effects.

1 Setting a shape and converting it to a selection. Create a new file with a light background color, or open a textured background image (we chose Beechwood from the ArtBeats *Wood and Paper* CD-ROM). Choose black (Colors palette), click in the image with the Text tool, and type a letter. (Using a 500-pixel-wide file, we set an ornament using the Adobe Wood Type Ornaments font.)

Before you can use the graphic character to isolate areas of the image canvas, you'll need to convert it to a shape, and then to a selection. Target the Text layer in the Layers palette and choose Convert Text to Shapes from the bottom of the palette's pop-out menu. Now from the main menu choose Shapes, Convert to Selection.

Typing a descriptive name for the mask

Viewing the widened face mask along with the RGB image

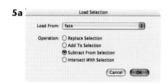

Subtracting the "face" mask from the "widened face" selection

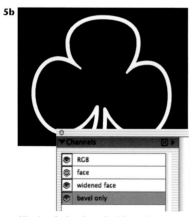

Viewing the bevel mask without the canvas

2 Moving and scaling. Choose the Selection Adjuster tool from the Tools palette. Press inside the selection with the Selection Adjuster tool; you can safely move your selection without distorting it. To scale, drag on one of the selection handles; to scale proportionately, press Shift and drag one of the corner handles (a two-headed diagonal arrow).

3 Saving and naming the selection. Saving a selection permanently stores it in the Channels palette as a mask. The first selection will be the top face of the bas relief, and we will use it to create three masks. To save the selection, choose Select, Save Selection, or click the Save Selection As New Channel button at the bottom of the Channels palette. When the Save Selection dialog box appears, accept the default in the pop-up menu—Save to New. Click OK. The selection is converted from outline-based to mask information. To rename the mask, double-click its name in the channels palette. We named ours "face."

4 Widening the selection. With the "face" selection still active, choose Select, Transform Selection. You can now expand the selection to create a wider boundary around the graphic. Choose Select, Modify, Widen and set the radius by typing a number in the field (we used 10 pixels). Save this new widened selection into the Channels palette, naming it "widened face."

5 Creating new masks using calculations. Next, we created a bevel mask describing the thin area between the outside widened boundary and the original face boundary. Painter offers Boolean operations, calculations in the Save Selection and Load Selection dialog boxes to make the job easier. To build a mask for the bevel (with the "widened face" selection still active), click the Load Channel As Selection button at the bottom of the Channels palette and choose "face" from the pop-up menu and under Operation, click the Subtract from Selection button to subtract the original face area from the widened face area, and click OK. Then click the Save Selection As Channel button and name the channel "bevel only."

We also built a mask isolating the image area outside of the widened face mask. To do this, load a selection using the "widened face" mask, and then choose Select, Invert. We saved this selection as a mask, naming it "background."

QUICKER LOADING

To save a visit to the Select menu or Channels palette when you'd like to load a selection, press Ctrl/⌘-Shift-G to display the Load Selection dialog box.

MODIFYING SELECTIONS

Only outline-based selections accept commands from the Select, Modify menu such as Widen and Contract. To convert a mask-based selection to path-based information so you can modify it, choose Select, Transform Selection. For more information, turn to "Editing Selections" on page 190.

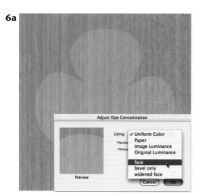
Using Dye Concentration in conjunction with the "face" mask

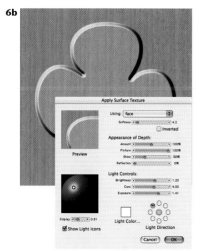
Using the "face" mask to apply Surface Texture to create the embossed face

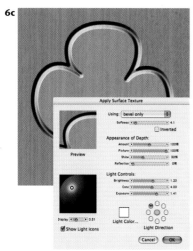
Using the "bevel only" mask to apply Surface Texture for the cut bevel effect

6 Putting the masks to work. Many operations available under the Effects menu in Painter—for instance, Tonal Control, Adjust Colors; Surface Control, Apply Surface Texture; and Focus, Glass Distortion—offer a pop-up menu allowing you to apply the effect using any mask saved in the Channels palette.

MAC OS X GLITCH

In the first release of Painter IX, the "Using" function for the Effects, Surface Control, Dye Concentration doesn't work right. Channels are listed as choices for the Using function, but when you try to choose a channel, it doesn't "load"; instead, the Original Luminance choice is used. Because of this, step 6 of the "Making Masks for Embossing" technique doesn't work with Mac OS X. Until Corel fixes this problem, you can use a different method for step 6:

Load the face channel as a selection by choosing Select, Load Selection and choosing the channel. Then apply Effects, Surface Control, Dye Concentration Using Image Luminance. (Experiment with the settings in the Dye Concentration dialog box until you get the result you want.)

To **emboss** the face, creating the bas-relief look in image **a** at the top of page 193, you can use the "face" mask to isolate an area of the image to lighten and "raise" above the surrounding surface. Lightening the face of the graphic will enhance the illusion of relief. With no selection active (Ctrl/⌘-D deselects all) click the RGB channel in the Channels palette and the Canvas in the Layers palette. Then choose Effects, Surface Control, Dye Concentration. In the Using pop-up menu, choose the "face" mask; to lighten the area, set the Minimum slider below 100% (we used 80%) and click OK. Now, for the relief effect: To "pop" the graphic face out (creating a convincing 3D effect), choose Effects, Surface Control, Apply Surface Texture. In the Using menu choose "face." Set Softness (we used 4.3), reduce the shine (we used 30%), click the top-left Light Direction button and click OK.

To **deboss** the face of the graphic as in image **b** at the top of page 193, you can use the same process described above for embossing, except that for Dye Concentration, darken the face area by setting the Minimum slider higher than 100% (we used 125%). And for Apply Surface Texture, click the Inverted check box to turn it on.

To create the **beveled** look in image **c** at the top of page 193, use the embossing process described above, but use the "bevel only" channel instead of the "face" channel.

To **carve the beveled area *in***, leaving the face and background flat (image **d** at the top of page 193), use the debossing process described above, except use the "bevel only" channel instead of the "face" channel. 🖐

Working with Bézier Paths and Selections

Overview Use the Pen tool to create paths of straight and curved lines; convert the paths to selections; use a custom pencil to draw inside and outside of the selections.

JOHN FRETZ

1

The logo sketch, including a rough grid

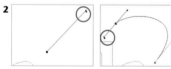

2

Pulling a handle from an anchor point to prepare for a curved path segment, then pressing and dragging to create the curve

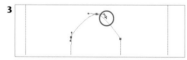

3

Dragging on a control handle to change the path's shape

CHANGING DIRECTION

While drawing with the Pen, click a second time on an anchor point to create a *cusp* and establish a new direction for the next curve. A cusp is a corner point between two curved line segments, such as the "dent" at the top of a heart shape.

TO DESIGN A LOGO FOR THE 100-YEAR-OLD Bethany Church in Seattle, John Fretz used a custom pencil to draw inside and outside of selections to create a hard-edged, graduated look similar to his conventional, colored-pencil illustration style.

1 Sketching the logo. Fretz created a 4 x 4-inch pencil drawing of the logo that included a rough grid aligning the roofs of the houses. He scanned the sketch at 300 ppi and opened it in Painter to use as a template.

2 Creating a path with Bézier curves. The most efficient way to create a combination of curve and straight-line path segments is with the Pen tool. You can set up shape attributes (with no fill or stroke) to produce a skeletal line that will help you see precise lines and curves while you draw: Choose the Pen tool from the Toolbox. In the Property Bar, make sure the Stroke and Fill boxes are *not* checked. Now click to place anchor points for straight-line segments, and press, hold and drag to create anchor points with handles that control curve segments. When you want to close a path, place the cursor over the starting anchor point, and click when you see a small circle designating the origin point, or press the Close Shape button in the Property Bar.

3 Changing the path shape. You can use the Shape Selection tool to fine-tune a path. First, if the anchor points are not showing, click the shape with the Shape Selection tool to show them; to show the control handles for an anchor point, click the point. Move the Shape Selection tool over an anchor point, a control handle, or a curve segment and drag to reposition it. (While drawing with the Pen tool, you can temporarily change from the Pen to the Shape Selection tool by pressing the Ctrl/⌘ key.)

4 Changing the path to a selection. Paths must be turned into selections before you can use them to control where paint is applied on the image. You can convert a path drawn with the Pen

4a

Click on the Convert to Selection button to change the shape into a selection.

4b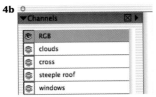

Selections stored as masks in the Channels palette

5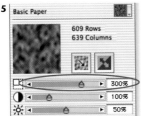

Scaling the Basic Paper texture

6a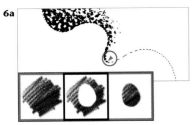

Painting outside of the cloud selection using the custom black pencil

6b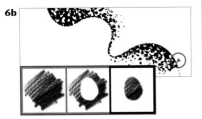

Painting inside of the cloud selection

7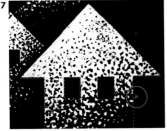

The subtracted selection of the windows protected those areas, keeping them black when Fretz filled the house with white. He used his custom pencil to add black texture over the white fill.

or Quick Curve tool to a selection immediately after drawing it by pressing the Convert to Selection button in the Property Bar. You can also change a path into a selection by selecting the shape in the Layers palette and choosing Shapes, Convert to Selection. In your image, the Bézier curves will turn into a selection marquee. To save and name the selection as a mask in the Channels palette for future use, choose Select, Save Selection. Type into the Name field and click OK. To return to the image canvas, click on RGB in the Channels palette.

5 Creating the pencil and surface. To re-create the graduated effect he gets with conventional pencils on rough illustration board, Fretz built a heavy, grainy pencil. To build a grainy pencil similar to the one Fretz used, choose Window, Brush Control, Show General and then choose the Pencils and the 2B Pencil variant in the Brush Selector Bar. In the General section of the Brush Control palette, modify the variant by switching to the Cover method and Grainy Edge Flat Cover subcategory, and change the Grain setting to 10%. In the Size section, increase the Size to roughly 200 pixels. In the Spacing section, set the Spacing slider at 25% (so the dabs created by the larger pencil will overlap and paint continuous strokes). Now choose black in the Colors palette. In the Papers section, Fretz clicked the Paper Selection swatch and chose Basic Paper because of its even texture, scaling it to 300% using the Scale slider.

6 Drawing in and out of selections. Fretz used the Drawing Modes, three icons located in the bottom-left corner of the image window, to paint inside and outside of selections. Begin by loading a selection (Select, Load Selection) and choosing the Brush tool in the Toolbox. To protect the area inside an active selection, click on the middle Drawing button; to protect the area outside the selection, click on the far right Drawing button. Fretz switched back and forth between these two options as he rendered a graduated, even texture using his custom pencil. (You can also use the Select, Invert command to invert an active selection.)

7 Subtracting from a selection. To fill each house with white and leave the windows black, Fretz loaded each house selection and subtracted the window selection from it: Choose Load Selection again and in the Load Selection dialog box, choose a selection and click the Subtract from Selection button to subtract it from the original selected area. Fretz filled the resulting selection with white; then he added black texture to the house with his custom pencil. He continued to add textured, even tone with the black and white pencils until he completed the logo.

Fretz saved the finished image in TIFF format, and to eliminate all grayscale information, he opened the image in Photoshop and converted it from grayscale to a 600 ppi bitmap image.

Using Selections to Limit Paint

Overview *Make a sketch on a colored ground; draw paths, convert them to selections and store them as masks; paint and apply effects within the selections.*

RAY BLAVATT

Sketching with the Flattened Pencil variant

Adding bolder lines to the sketch

RAY BLAVATT LOVES THE ENERGETIC, EXPRESSIVE line work of fashion illustrators (notably Carl Erickson and Rene Bouche) and political cartoonists (including Jim Borgman and Pat Oliphant). His background is in traditional illustration, but today most of Blavatt's work is in animation. His procedure involves drawing in Painter and then saving the illustrations for animation in QuickTime format, importing them into Macromedia Flash and eventually exporting his work to VHS tape.

To create *Parisian,* Blavatt began by making a gestural drawing in Painter. Then he drew paths with the Pen tool directly on the sketch and converted the paths to selections so that he would have boundaries to limit paint when he painted fast. Artists familiar with drawing in a PostScript program (as Blavatt is) will like this method of drawing straight and curved line segments with the Pen, and then converting the shapes to selections. (To read more about different methods of making selections, turn to the beginning of this chapter.)

1 Sketching on a colored ground. Blavatt opened a new file measuring 1900 x 2100 pixels with a newsprint-colored background. He chose the Brush tool from the Toolbox and chose the Flattened Pencil variant of the Pencils in the Brush Selector Bar. He chose a gold color in the Colors picker and Pavement texture in the Paper Selector (loaded from the Extras, Paper Textures, Painter 6 Textures library on the Painter IX CD-ROM). Envisioning a young woman on a fictitious street in Paris, he sketched quick, gestural strokes to lay out the drawing. He changed the

3a

Drawing the path around a building

3b

The Property Bar showing the Convert to Selection button

4

The painting with textured chalk strokes added to the sky, street and figure

5a

Using Dye Concentration to apply a darker tint to the selected background

size of the pencil as he worked using the Size slider on the Property Bar. The Flattened Pencil incorporates the Buildup method, which allows color to be applied with transparency (overlapping strokes will darken); its Grainy Hard Buildup subcategory creates crisp-edged strokes that are affected by the current paper texture.

2 Emphasizing the line work. Next, Blavatt added darker color and textured, thick and thin lines to the drawing using the Graphic Paintbrush variant of the F-X brush. (The Graphic Paintbrush reminds Blavatt of the Rough Out brush, a favorite he liked using in earlier versions of Painter, although by default the Graphic Paintbrush reveals more paper texture along the edges of the strokes, due to the Grainy Edge Flat Cover method it uses in the Stroke Designer tab of the Brush Creator.) To lay bold strokes over your pencil sketch, choose the Graphic Paintbrush and a dark color in the Color picker. For finer line work, Blavatt sized the brush smaller (to 7.3) using the Size slider on the Property Bar.

3 Drawing paths and converting to selections. So that he could isolate areas of the drawing while painting and applying special effects, he created selections. Because his subject included straight lines (buildings) and smooth curves (the figure and street light, for instance), Blavatt chose the Pen from the Toolbox to draw a path around each building and the figure of the young woman. To draw precise paths, some artists prefer to draw the paths without a Stroke or Fill. But to make it easier to see the path as he was drawing it, Blavatt applied a Stroke. To set up the Pen to automatically stroke paths as you draw them, without filling: In the Property Bar, click as needed to make sure the Stroke check box is checked and the Fill box is unchecked; click the Stroke color swatch and choose a color that will show up well against your artwork. Click and drag with the Pen tool to draw a path. (For more information about drawing paths with the Pen tool, turn to "Working with Bézier Paths and Selections" on page 196.)

When the path was complete, Blavatt converted it to a selection. (Click the Convert to Selection button on the Property Bar.) To make a soft selection edge that would help to make transparent color on the edges when he painted or filled, he feathered the selection 8 pixels (Select, Feather). Then he saved the selection as a mask so he could use it later (Select, Save Selection). Each mask was saved in the Channels palette.

4 Adding color and texture. Painting with blues and golds, Blavatt used the Square Chalk variant of Chalk to quickly build up color over the entire image, using a light enough touch on his stylus to reduce opacity and preserve the texture.

5 Enhancing the figure as the focal point. Next, he added details to the blouse and more colored texture to the figure. He chose Select, Load Selection and chose the figure's mask from the

6a

Drawing a path for the beam of light

6b

Airbrushing within the active selection

6c

The completed beam of light

7

The Flattened Pencil variant (Pencils) and the Graphic Paintbrush variant of F-X were used to add final details to the face.

Load From menu. When the selection was active, he added highlights to the woman's blouse using the Bleach variant of Erasers. To deepen color and build shadows, he used the Darkener variant of Erasers. Then he chose a creamy pink color in the Colors picker, and with Pavement texture still chosen in the Paper Selector, he used the Square Chalk to gently brush textured highlights over the figure's face, neck and arms. When he'd finished the figure and clothing, he reversed the selection by choosing Select, Invert so he could work on the background while protecting the figure.

To further strengthen the focal point and to enhance the mysterious atmosphere of the city street, Blavatt added a dark burgundy "dye" to the background only, while leaving the focal point—the figure—in lighter colors. To add a "dye" to an area of your image, start by loading a selection. To re-create Blavatt's effect, make sure Pavement is the current texture in the Papers Selector. (When Paper is chosen in the Using menu, the luminance of the current texture chosen in the Papers section is used as the means to apply the transparent dye effect.) Then choose a deep red in the Color picker and choose Effects, Surface Control, Dye Concentration, Using Paper. Experiment with the settings. (Blavatt set a Maximum of 488% and a Minimum of 50%.) To scroll around your image in the Preview window, drag in the Preview window. Click OK when you have an effect you like.

6 Airbrushing a beam of light. To balance the composition, Blavatt added a gold beam of light shining from a street light on the left side of the image. First he created a selection to limit the paint: Using the Pen tool from the Tools palette, he drew a path to define the beam of light; he converted the path to a selection by using the Convert to Selection button on the Options bar. For a smooth edge, he feathered the selection to 8 pixels (Select, Feather), and then he stored the selection as a mask for safekeeping (click the Save Selection As Channel button at the bottom of the Channels palette). To ensure that the color of the light matched existing color in the illustration, he used the Dropper tool to sample a gold color from the image. Next, he chose the Fine Spray variant of the Airbrushes and used firmer pressure to spray denser color near the light source, and then used lighter pressure to fade the spray of color as he painted lower within the selection.

7 Final details. To complete the painting, Blavatt went back over the image and added details: With the Flattened Pencil and a dark color he touched up the woman's eyes; with the Graphic Paintbrush he added more tiny strokes of white at the top of the light beam; and he strengthened highlights on the woman's hair and blouse collar. Finally, he used the Bleach variant of the Erasers to brighten the highlight on the roof of the background building.

Selections and Airbrush

***Overview** Create a pencil sketch; create PostScript outlines in a drawing program; import outlines and sketch into Painter; add texture and gradient fills within the selections; use the Airbrush to create a metallic look.*

JOHN DISMUKES, CAPSTONE STUDIOS

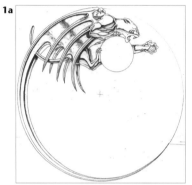

The original pencil sketch

The selected and grouped panther outlines were copied to the clipboard in Illustrator.

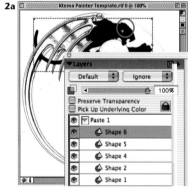

The pasted shapes selected with the Layer Adjuster tool on the image, showing their names in the expanded group in the Layers palette

ARTISTS USING TRADITIONAL AIRBRUSH techniques cut friskets out of paper, film or plastic to protect portions of their artwork as they paint. For complex jobs this can become quite a task. That's one of the reasons why John Dismukes of Capstone Studios traded in his traditional tools for electronic ones. For this logo for Ktema, a manufacturer of promotional clothing for the entertainment industry, he started with a pencil sketch, added PostScript paths and brought both into Painter. He turned the paths into selections and used them as friskets.

1 Organizing the elements. Dismukes had a scanned pencil sketch and a PostScript drawing created in Adobe Illustrator, which fit the sketch. The paths included the panther, the wing ribs and membrane, the large and small globes, and the Ktema nameplate. (If you need to import type from Illustrator into Painter, first convert the type into outlines.) Painter has the capability to recognize fill and stroke attributes and groups when PostScript art is imported. To prepare a document for importing into Painter, save a version in Adobe Illustrator 5 (or later) or EPS format.

2 Importing, positioning and scaling. Dismukes opened the original pencil sketch in Painter and began importing the paths into the document. There are two reliable ways to import PostScript outlines into a Painter file: using File, Acquire, Adobe Illustrator File (which creates a new file) or copying from the PostScript program to the clipboard and then pasting into an open file in Painter. For the second method to work, both applications have to be running at the same time. Importing the outlines through the clipboard is fairly fast and always reliable. To do this, select the outlines in Illustrator and copy; then switch to Painter and paste. You'll see a closed group of shapes appear in the Layers palette. Move this shape group into position on the template using

2b

The Layer Adjuster tool changes to an arrow cursor when scaling shapes.

3

The named masks in the Channels palette

4

Cloning texture into the membrane selection

5

Airbrushing highlights on the panther

6a

Applying the drop shadow

6b

The shadow and lens flare are shown in this detail. The 40 MB logo was output as a 4 x 5-inch color transparency at 762 ppi.

the Layer Adjuster tool or the arrow keys on your keyboard. To scale the shapes proportionally, choose the Layer Adjuster tool, hold down the Shift key and drag on a corner handle.

3 Converting, saving and naming. If you have a complex graphic with overlapping shapes, you may want to ungroup the shapes before converting them to selections. This will enable you to save each selection as a mask in the Channels palette so it can be used individually or added to or subtracted from the other selections. To ungroup, first make sure the group is closed (not expanded) in the Layers palette. Then at the bottom of the Layers palette, click the Layer Commands button and from the menu choose Ungroup. To convert a shape to a selection so you can paint or fill it, click on its name in the Layers palette and choose Shapes, Convert to Selection. The shape will disappear from the Layers palette and will become an active marquee on the image canvas. Store the selection in the Channels palette as a mask by choosing Select, Save Selection and then typing a Name and clicking OK.

4 Filling selections. Dismukes created texture within the membrane selection using a Cloners brush and a modified paper texture from a second document. He filled the large globe with a maroon gradient and the small globe with a green gradient. To read more about cloning, turn to "Cloning, Tracing and Painting" in Chapter 3.

5 Airbrushing. Dismukes's template showed good shadow and highlight detail. Using it as a guide, he began by laying down dark colors, gradually building forward to the white highlights. He used the Digital Airbrush variant of Airbrushes, adjusting only the Size and Min Size in the Size section of the Brush Creator window as he worked.

6 Adding a shadow. Dismukes used a layer to create the panther's drop shadow on the maroon globe. To use the Create Drop Shadow command to do this, you first need to load the selection: Click the Load Channel As Selection button at the bottom of the Channels palette and choose a channel. To load more than one mask at a time as a single selection, load the first selection, and then click the Load Channel As Selection button again; in the Load From menu, choose a second selection and for the Operation choose Add to Selection. Continue to Load and Add to your selection until you have all of the elements active. Store this complex selection as a new mask by clicking the Save Selection As Channel button at the bottom of the Channels palette.

To create the shadow, turn the new selection into a layer by clicking on it in your image with the Layer Adjuster tool. Choose Effects, Objects, Create Drop Shadow. Use the default settings or experiment with other settings, and then click OK.

As a final touch, Dismukes opened the image in Adobe Photoshop and applied the Lens Flare filter to the green globe. 🖌

Using Hand-Drawn Selections

Overview *Create a drawing; select areas of the image using the Lasso; use selections to constrain brushstrokes, fills and effects.*

DON STEWART

Stewart's drawing in brown line drawing

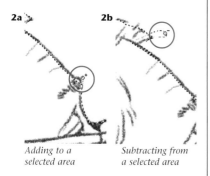

Adding to a selected area   *Subtracting from a selected area*

To create *You're Fired*, an illustration for *Physician* magazine, Don Stewart began by making a drawing in Painter while referring to photo references. In preparation for painting, he drew freehand selections using the Lasso tool (just as he would use friskets with conventional airbrush) so that he could isolate portions of the image as he painted.

1 Developing the composition. Stewart discussed the assignment with the designer at *Physician* magazine, and then he rendered a rough thumbnail sketch in Painter. Upon approval of the thumbnail sketch, he shot photos for reference. Then he created a new Painter file that measured 8 x 10 inches at 300 ppi. He used the Sharp Pencil variant of Pencils to draw a brown pencil sketch on top of a fine paper texture (similar to Fine Grain).

2 Creating selections. To isolate areas of his image, Stewart built a selection for each element in his drawing. To select with the Lasso tool, drag carefully around the area you want to select, ending at your origin point. You may find it helpful to zoom in on your image while making detailed freehand selections. Press M to switch to the Magnifier tool; then click to zoom in, or press Alt/Option and click to zoom out. (Press L to switch back to the Lasso.) You can also zoom in and out of your image by using the

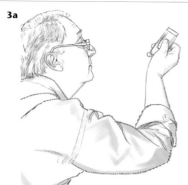

3a

Painting inside the selection for the shirt

3b

The in-progress underpainting painted with the Wash Camel (Watercolor)

4a

Adding deeper color and splatter texture

4b

The type has been added to the image

Scale slider in the lower-left corner of the image window.

Painter's Lasso tool lets you add to or subtract from the currently active selection. To add to the currently selected area, click the Add to Selection button on the Property Bar or hold down the Shift key and then drag with the Lasso. To subtract from the currently selected area, use the Subtract from Selection button on the Property Bar or hold down the Alt/Option key and then drag to cut away part of the active selection. Saving the completed selection as a mask will store it permanently with your image in the Channels palette. To save a selection, choose Select, Save Selection or click the Save Selection As Channel button at the bottom of the Channels palette. For straight line selections, such as the glass of the door, Stewart used the Pen tool and then converted the shapes to selections. For information about this method, see "Working with Bézier Paths and Selections" on page 196.

3 Painting inside selections. With the selections and masks built, Stewart was ready to start painting. He chose Painter's Big Canvas texture (from the Paper Textures 2 library in the Paper Textures folder, Extras folder on the Painter IX CD-ROM). After loading the selection for the area he wanted to isolate and paint (Select, Load Selection), he used the Wash Camel variant of Watercolor to brush on color.

4 Painting richer color and texture. After he finished the underpainting for the image, Stewart loaded selections to isolate each area again, one at a time. This time he used the Digital Airbrush variant of Airbrushes to darken shadows and to smooth areas.

For the texture on the glass of the door, he loaded a selection to isolate the area. Then, he chose a custom paper (similar to the Pavement texture from the Painter 6 Textures library) that he built to achieve the look of frosted glass. He used the Large Chalk variant of Chalk to paint a white-to-lavender gradation within the isolated area. Next, Stewart added more texture interest by spraying a subtle splattered paint look on the entire image by using a combination of the Pepper Spray and Coarse Spray Airbrushes.

Adding final details. Stewart switched back to the finer texture he used for his drawing, and then he used both the Sharp Chalk (Chalk) and Round Camelhair (Oils) to add details to the image; for instance, the man's hair and the edges on the door. As a last step, Stewart used the Text tool to set the words on the door glass.

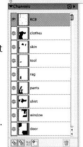

Making a Color Mask

Overview *Use New From Color Range and brushes to mask an area of an image; convert the mask to a selection; use Adjust Color to shift the color of the selected area.*

PHOTO: CAROL BENIOFF

The original photo

The default Color Mask dialog box

Adjusting the sliders to isolate the light portion of the background water

COLOR MASK IS ONE OF PAINTER'S most powerful features, letting you create a mask based on a specific color in an image. In the example above, we used a combination of the New From Color Range command and edited with brushes to create masks for individual leaves. We saved the masks in the Channels palette, and then used Adjust Color to change the hue and saturation of the individual leaves and the background.

1 Sampling color and adjusting the mask. Open an image and then open the Channels palette. Click the triangle in the top-right corner of the palette and choose New From Color Range. When the Color dialog box appears, click in your image (*not* in the preview window) on the color you want to sample (the "center color" of the range of colors to be selected). We selected a color in a lighter portion of the water in the center of the image. To narrow the range of selected colors, drag the H (Hue) Extents slider to the left (we set ours to 60%). Press and drag to scroll the image in the Preview window so you can see how your settings are affecting selection in other parts of the image. Experiment with the S (Saturation) and V (Value) Extents sliders; we got the best results when we set the V Extents to 123% to isolate the lighter portion of the water from the shadows in the background water. You may also want to move the three Feather sliders to the left to create harder transitions in your mask. When you're satisfied with the preview of your mask, click OK. Painter will generate a mask based on the sampled color. The mask will automatically appear in the Channels palette.

2 Cleaning up the mask. To view the mask as a red-tinted overlay on top of the image canvas, in the Channels palette make sure the eye icons are open for both the mask and the RGB channel. To edit the mask, click on its name in the palette and choose the Scratchboard Tool variant of Pens in the Brush Selector Bar (it allows smooth painting with opaque "paint"). Choose black for the primary color and paint to add to your mask; paint with white to remove portions of the mask.

The interior of your mask will need to be opaque to completely select your subject. You'll need to view the mask at full opacity to

2a

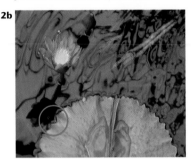

Using the Scratchboard tool and white paint to erase an area of the mask

2b

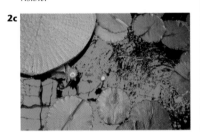

Using the Scratchboard tool to erase the mask from shadow areas in the water. The mask is viewed at a reduced opacity, making both the mask and the image beneath it visible.

2c

The finished mask of the center leaf viewed at 100% opacity

2d

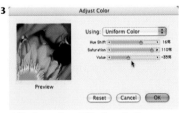

Replacing the original mask

3

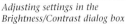

Adjusting color within the selection

identify areas where coverage is not complete so you can paint over any thin spots. To adjust the opacity of the mask overlay, display the Mask Attributes dialog box by double-clicking the mask name in the Channels palette. Move the Opacity slider to 100%; this will have no effect on the actual density of the mask—it's for viewing only.

As a final check for your mask, turn off the eye icon for the mask, and then load the mask as a selection by clicking the Load Channel As Selection button. To edit the selection, use the Lasso, clicking the Add to Selection button or the Subtract from Selection button in the Property Bar to draw around the area you want to add or remove. If you edit your selection like this, make sure you replace the original mask in the Channels palette with the edited one: Choose Select, Save Selection; in the Save To menu, choose the mask name, select the Replace Mask option, and click OK.

3 Colorizing with Adjust Color. To make changes to the color within a selection, begin by loading a selection (as above or by choosing Select, Load Selection). With the selection active, choose Effects, Tonal Control, Adjust Colors, Using Uniform Color. Use this feature to change the hue, saturation or brightness in the selected area. If you prefer more radical changes, you can also paint within your selection or apply any of the commands under the Effects menu. 🖌

COLOR MASK HINTS

You'll save time if you mask less of the image with New From Color Range and paint more of the mask with a brush rather than masking more and trying to erase. Aim for good edges with New From Color Range, though, since edges are difficult to touch up with a brush.

CLEANING UP MASKS WITH BRIGHTNESS AND CONTRAST

Here's a method for cleaning up masks that can save time and effort when the color of the subject you want to mask also occurs in the surrounding image. Start by making a mask using New From Color Range, clicking to sample the color you need to mask and adjusting the H (Hue), V (Value) and S (Saturation) Extents sliders to create the best mask you can for your subject. Then click OK. To select the mask so you can view it in black and white, and manipulate it using commands under the Effects menu, click on the mask name in the Channels palette and click the RGB channel's eye icon closed. Click on the name of the mask, and then use Effects, Tonal Control, Brightness/Contrast to bump up the contrast and adjust the brightness to make the gray areas solid black or white. To avoid losing antialiasing in the mask, use moderate settings and check the edges of the mask closely.

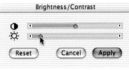

Adjusting settings in the Brightness/Contrast dialog box

The mask before (left) and after (right) adjusting Brightness/Contrast

Auto-Selecting with Current Color

Overview *Use the Auto Select command to generate a selection based on a specific color; paint into the selection with various brushes.*

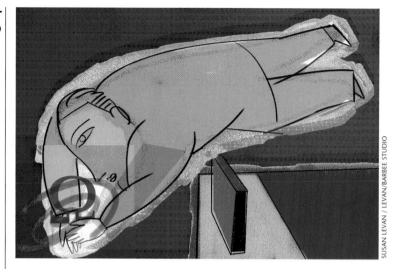

SUSAN LEVAN / LEVAN/BARBEE STUDIO

The black-and-white sketch

Painting the gray-purple strokes using the Square Chalk variant of Chalk

WITH PAINTER'S AUTO SELECT, USING THE CURRENT COLOR command, you can isolate an area of an image by automatically generating a selection based on color. After the selection has been created, you can fill the area with color or paint into it.

"What I like about using the Current Color Auto Select feature with Chalk is the random residue of the original color that is left behind. This creates a natural, subtle texture within the masked areas of color," says Susan LeVan of LeVan/Barbee Studio. When LeVan created *Goal Leap*, she used brushes to paint within selections. She used the Current Color setting of the Auto Select command to create jaggy white "halos" around the elements in her image, giving her piece texture, lightness and air.

1 Establishing the composition. LeVan began a new document that measured 1200 x 800 pixels, with a white paper color. She drew a sketch on a new layer using the black color. To sketch as LeVan did, choose Basic Paper from the Paper Selector near the bottom of the Toolbox. From the Brush Selector Bar, choose the Hard Colored Pencil variant of Colored Pencils, and then choose black in the Colors picker. (If the Layers palette is not open, choose Window, Show Layers.) To create a new layer, click the New Layer button near the bottom of the Layers palette. For more information about using Layers, see Chapter 6, "Using Layers."

2 Adding colored brushwork. Next, LeVan clicked on the Canvas layer and added loose, grainy strokes using the Square Chalk and a gray-purple color. She loves the look of Painter's grainy Chalk brush strokes. Pick a color, choose the Square Chalk variant of Chalk, select the Canvas layer in the Layers palette, and then paint loosely. Don't worry about staying inside the lines of your sketch. Then merge your drawing with the colored chalk on the Canvas. When you have your colored brush strokes as you

3a

The Invert button is checked.

3b

The figure is floated to a layer.

4

Painting within the active selection using the Square Chalk

5a

LeVan added the Omega symbol, and sketched the field

5b

The added yellow square, the field with its irregularly textured edges, and the beginning of the blue background

like them, drop the sketch layer to the Canvas by clicking on it in the Layers palette list, and then choosing Drop from the pop-up menu on the right side of the Layers palette. Merging the sketch with the chalk strokes will add more texture richness in the next step when you do further auto-selecting and painting on the figure using the Square Chalk.

3 Auto-selecting using Current Color. LeVan lifted the figure to a layer so that she that could paint the playing field behind it. To put your painted figure on a layer using LeVan's technique, begin by selecting the background color (white) using the Dropper tool. Choose Select, Auto Select, Using Current Color. Then to reverse the selection and select the figure, enable the Invert box.

4 Floating, selecting and painting. To cut the selected figure to a layer, click on the layer's name in the Layers palette, and then choose Select, Float. LeVan sampled purple color on the figure using the Dropper tool, and again used the Auto Select, Using Current Color command. With the new selection active, she painted textured gray strokes onto the figure. Click on a colored area on your figure using the Dropper tool; then choose Select, Auto Select, Using Current, Color. So that the purple will be selected, this time uncheck the Invert box. Now choose the Square Chalk and a new color (LeVan chose a medium gray), and paint loose strokes into the selection.

5 Building the symbol and playing field. For the Omega symbol, LeVan typed with the Text tool. (Typing created a Text layer.) Next, she chose the Canvas layer in the Layers palette and added the playing field, by using the same painting and masking technique that she used for the figure, sketching the orange and green areas using the Square Chalk.

To build the square area under the Omega symbol, she began by making a selection on a blank area of the Canvas by using the Rectangular Selection tool. To make a layer from this selected area, she chose Edit, Copy, and then Edit, Paste in Place. After enabling Preserve Transparency in the Layers palette, she filled the rectangular area with yellow color, using Effects, Fill with Current Color. Then, to have the yellow area blend with the color on the Canvas, she selected Colorize as the Composite Method in the Layers palette.

For the blue-purple background, again, LeVan sampled color from the Canvas using the Dropper tool, and built another selection for the background area. Then using the Square Chalk, she painted a dark blue-purple onto the selected areas of the Canvas.

6 Adding a pattern and more color. LeVan wanted to strengthen the concept for *Goal Leap* while adding more interest to the background, so she built a pattern using + and = symbols. She started a new, separate file and typed the symbols using the Text tool.

6

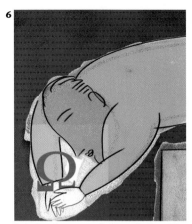

Painting the orange chalk on the face. The subtle background pattern is applied.

7a

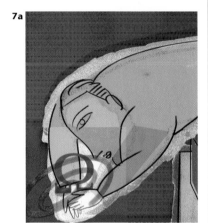

LeVan added texture to the spiral, as shown in this detail. You can see subtle shaded areas above the figure.

7b

The details and textured elements are nearly complete.

She dropped the layers to the Canvas, and then using the Rectangular Selection tool, she selected the area with the type and captured the pattern. (See "Creating a Seamless Pattern" in Chapter 8 for more information about creating patterns.) Next, she used her Current Color method to select the blue areas around the figure. She copied this selection, and pasted it in place (Edit, Paste in Place). LeVan filled this layer with her custom Pattern. Then she dropped it to the Canvas. The pattern was only partially visible because the auto-selecting created a textured look. Next, using the Current Color method, she also selected an area of the man's face and then painted orange chalk strokes on his face, and then she painted more orange color onto the area with the yellow rectangle.

7 Adding final elements and details. To create a subtle shaded edge on the top of the figure and field, she reselected the blue-patterned background area, and copied and pasted it (Ctrl/⌘-Shift-V) to create a new layer. Using the Layer Adjuster, she shifted the layer so that it was slightly out of register with the background, and then she reduced its opacity. She created the barrier wall, the spiral, and the transparent gray patch on separate layers, as described above, and then dropped them onto the Canvas. As a final touch, she used her masking technique to add more rich texture to the face, the wall, and the spiral. 🖌

To create Coffee Alone, *Susan LeVan used much the same process as she used for* Goal Leap. *She sketched with the Fine Bristle variant of Gouache. Then, to create the halos around the lines, she used her Auto Select, Current Color technique to select the drawing, and then she painted with Chalk brushes. For the texture on the pants, she used the same selection method, and then painted with the Chunky Oil Pastel (Oil Pastels).*

■ **Don Stewart** specializes in book illustration. For many years he worked on gessoed illustration board with airbrush and colored pencil. Today he draws on the computer, using Painter's tools and brushes that match his traditional ones.

Library Teacher (above) was commissioned by *Liberty* magazine as a cover illustration. Stewart began the illustration by sketching in Painter using the Sharp Pencil variant of Pencils on a Fine Grain paper. Then, he isolated areas of his image by making freehand selections with the Lasso (for example, the buttons and other elements on the clothing) so that he could limit the paint as he added color with the Wash Camel variant of Watercolor. He used the Digital Airbrush to paint smoother areas (the skin, for instance) and to begin to build up deeper values. Stewart drew the detailed highlight texture on the suit fabric using the Sharp Chalk. For subtle texture in a few areas, he used the Fine Spray and Coarse Spray variants of Airbrushes. When the figure was modeled the way he wanted, he added a few final highlights and details using the Sharp Chalk.

■ **Don Stewart** was commissioned to create *Nature Center*, an illustration for a children's reader textbook published by *Oxford University Press.* Stewart began the illustration by making a tight drawing in Painter using the Sharp Pencil variant on Fine Grain paper. Next, so that he could protect areas while he painted, he isolated the important elements in his sketch by making selections with the Lasso (for example, the children's clothes,

their skin, and the crystals in the foreground). He loaded a selection for an element (Select, Load Selection) and then he chose a medium-grained canvas texture and laid in colored washes using the Wash Camel variant of Watercolor. Next, he loaded each selection again, and then he added richer color and values to each element with Painter's Airbrushes. He used the Digital Airbrush to paint smoother areas (the skin, for

instance). When the subjects were modeled, he added highlights and details using the Sharp Chalk variant of Chalk (the sketchy white strokes on the quartz crystals and the highlights in the hair, for instance). To add texture to the shadows on the tabletop, he painted with subtle colors using the Wash Camel and Sharp Chalk brushes over the medium-grained canvas texture.

■ **James D'Avanzo** was a young man with a lot of artistic talent and little physical mobility. He began with very basic computer graphics programs and then moved to CorelDraw, which allowed him the opportunity to create some very sophisticated images. However, it was with Painter that he blossomed as an artist. Using Painter with the Wacom tablet and a multi-button mouse, D'Avanzo painted still lives and imaginary landscapes. The National Muscular Dystrophy Association chose his image **Woods** for their Christmas card for 1996.

For *Woods*, D'Avanzo chose a limited palette of deep colors to depict a haunting moonlit night. He blocked in broad areas of color using Airbrushes and Chalk variants. Then he blended paint by using the Grainy Water and Just Add Water variants of Blenders. To protect the shapes of clouds and moon from paint, he used the Lasso to make selections. To reverse the selected moon (so that he could paint on the sky while protecting the moon area), he chose Select, Invert. After painting the sky, he dropped the selection (Ctrl/⌘-D). To finish, he added more texture to the moon and clouds by painting a few lighter-colored brushstrokes using the Artist Pastel Chalk variant of Pastels.

THE *other* AXIS of EVIL...

MURDEROUS REGIMES

HUNGER

AIDS

AFRICA

■ **Nick Anderson** is the chief editorial cartoonist at the *Louisville Courier-Journal* in Louisville, Kentucky. His award-winning cartoons have been published in *Newsweek, The New York Times, The Washington Post, USA Today,* and *The Chicago Tribune.* Anderson is the recipient of the 2005 Pulitzer Prize for editorial cartooning. This cartoon was in his prize-winning portfolio.

Anderson begins each cartoon by doing rough sketches on conventional tracing paper. When a concept is approved, he creates a black-and-white drawing using Sakura Micron Pigma pens on smooth bristol board. The thin felt tip pens allow him to create sensitive line work. Then, he scans his drawing and uses a variety of Painter brushes to add color and texture. Anderson always creates several masks for the elements in each cartoon. He usually paints directly on the alpha channel masks by using the Flat Color variant of Pens and black and white paint. To begin each mask, he created a new empty

channel by clicking the New Channel button on the Channels palette. By default, this command creates a mask that is filled with black, which can be viewed on the working image as a red overlay. With the red overlay in place over his drawing, Anderson paints directly onto the channel using white or black paint. Creating channels can become tedious, but when they are complete, they allow him to paint freely within isolated areas.

For *The Other Axis of Evil,* Anderson was inspired by a *New York Times* story about how AIDS has ravaged villages in Africa, killing people in the prime of their life, leaving the elderly and children to contend with the aftermath. "Combined with the constant threat of famine and the murderous regimes of Sudan, Congo and others, I was moved to draw attention to their plight," says Anderson.

He opened his scanned drawing in Painter and cut it to a layer by choosing

Select All, and Select, Float. So that the white areas of the drawing would appear transparent, he set the Layer Composite Method to Multiply in the Layers palette. Working on the Canvas, he used the Wet Acrylics variant of Acrylics to lay down most of his basic colors. Then, he reduced the opacity of the brush and built up subtle, colored glazes. He kept all the paint on the canvas so that as he painted the background colors of red, orange and yellow, he could push, pull and distort some of the colors from the foreground elements. The working of the paint gave the image a more dramatic, haunting look. To make the border of the image irregular, he blended in a little bit of white paint around the edges of the image. As a final touch, Anderson added a random spatter texture to the reapers, the foreground and the sky, using the Tiny Spatter and Variable Spatter variants of the Airbrushes, varying the opacities of the brushes as he painted.

■ Creative use of saturated color, loose illustrative strokes and an eclectic mix of brushes and paper textures let **Susan LeVan**, of LeVan/Barbee Studio, create a strong emotional quality in her work.

When LeVan created the illustrations *Subway* (above) and *Nonconformity* (right) she used brushes to paint within selections. To build rough (not anti-aliased) edges on line drawings and around the shapes, and to give her work more texture, she repeatedly used the Auto Select command using the Current Color setting, and then she painted back into her image.

For *Subway,* LeVan was inspired by her memories of riding the "T" subway when she lived in Boston. To begin, she used the Fine Bristle variant of Gouache and black color to make a loose line drawing of the main elements. Next, she made selections for the line drawing by choosing Select, Auto Select, Using Current Color, and then she used the Square Chalk variant of Chalk and the Chunky Oil Pastel variant of Pastels to paint grainy strokes within each selection. For the larger areas, she selected them using her auto-select technique and then painted color into each selection with the Coarse Spray variant (Airbrushes). For more depth and interest in a few areas, LeVan painted transparent washes using the Simple Water variant of Digital Watercolor.

■ **Susan LeVan** created *Nonconformity* for her portfolio. She began the illustration by sketching with the Hard Colored Pencil variant of Colored Pencils and an earthy green color. She created an irregularly edged selection for the background behind the lines by sampling green color from the lines using the Dropper tool and then choosing Select, Auto Select, Using Current Color. Then, she added color and brush work to the area using the Oil Pastels. For the angular areas outside the central figure, she used the Pen tool to build a path, which she then converted to a selection (Shapes, Convert to Selection). With the selection active, she used the Coarse Spray variant of Airbrushes to add speckled textures. Next, she painted the bright colors onto the figure using the Fine Bristle (Gouache). She gave the edges of the brightly colored figure texture by repeatedly auto-selecting and painting into the area. To finish, she added details using the Chalk brushes.

■ Artist **Martha Jane Bradford** has developed a technique for using masks to not only constrain paint, but to build tones in her paintings. She began *The Lupine Letters* series with two goals: She wanted to create a very stylized image with flat tones and pen line-work that would have the look of an aquatint or hard-ground etching, and she wanted to see how many variations she could create using one set of masks. The black-and-white drawing *An Oblique Way* and two of the colored images in the series—*To Keep a Connection* and *At the End of the Day*—are shown here.

Bradford began by working at the final size, a 2300 x 3440 pixel file, because

masks can get fuzzy edges when resized. She put her reference photo on a layer to use as a guide. Bradford decided that the basic image would have 10 values from white through gray to black. To make the first mask, she clicked the New Mask button on the Channels palette, filled it with black and then renamed it Value One. So that she could get very sharp, clean edges, she customized a Flat Pen to use the Grainy Edge Flat Cover Subcategory in the Brush Controls: General section. Then, she drew with white on the black mask wherever she wanted Value 0 (the white of the Canvas) to show. Then, she carefully made masks for the remaining nine values.

Next, Bradford created the black-and-white drawing *An Oblique Way* (far left) using the set of masks. To paint, she began by creating a layer for Value 0, which she left empty everywhere except for the sky. She loaded a selection using the Value 0 mask by choosing Select, Load Selection. Then, she used the Pixel Spray variant of Airbrushes on Synthetic Superfine paper on the sky to create a glow along the horizon. Next, she created a layer for Value 1, where she used the Value 1 mask to lay in the lightest tones, drawing with a combination of large-sized Pixel Spray and Charcoal brushes on Synthetic Superfine Paper. She continued the process to paint her values 2–9.

■ To create the colored images *To Keep a Connection* and *At the End of the Day*, **Martha Jane Bradford** created two colored versions of the black-and-white drawing *An Oblique Way* (described on page 216). For the daytime version, *To Keep a Connection* (on the facing page), she wanted colors that would suggest a hazy, golden August afternoon, similar to the reference photograph. For *At the End of the Day* (above), she wanted a palette of blues, greens and purples that would suggest a clear night with a full moon rising.

To begin coloring her image, Bradford copied the black-and-white drawing file twice, one copy to be the clone source and one to be the colored daytime version of the drawing *To Keep a Connection*. On the clone source, she applied a Two-point Gradient with the foreground color black and the background color a pale yellow with the Left-to-Right Gradient Order button selected. This gave the black-and-white drawing a yellow tint, which she cloned into the sky area by using a combination of Soft and Straight Cloner brushes. Then, she reverted the Clone Source

drawing to its original state by choosing File, Revert, and then she applied a new Gradient using black and a red-violet color. On the color drawing, she loaded the mask for Value 1 and then she cloned the red-violet into the edges of the buildings and trees along the horizon. She repeated the process using different colored gradients to add colors through Value 9, sometimes using multiple colors within one value mask. Bradford finds that seeing the gradients as she applies them provides her with new ideas for coloring her working image and for new images.

■ Artist and designer **Judy Miller** loves the way the Wheel Airbrushes in Painter allow her to paint with the ease of a conventional airbrush. Miller modifies the settings for the Wheel Airbrushes so that she can use the stylus wheel to adjust the width of the spray and the pressure to control the amount of spray. When creating *Beauties*, she built a series of masks that she used to constrain paint while she developed her image.

To begin, Miller shot a reference photograph at Halifax Gardens in Nova Scotia. Back at her studio, she opened the photograph in Painter. She created a custom color set from the photograph by choosing New Color Set from Image from the pop-up menu on the Color Sets palette.

Next, so that she could paint quickly and loosely in the first stages of her painting, Miller used the Lasso and Pen tools to create selections. Working over the photo reference, she created a selection for each petal, and then she saved each one

as a mask in the Channels palette by choosing Select, Save Selection. For the more complex petals, Miller used the Pen tool to create a shape path, and then she converted it to a selection by choosing Shapes, Convert to Selection. She saved these selections as masks into the Channels palette as well. To keep her file organized, she created each mask and named it logically, beginning from the center petals and working toward the outer petals.

When painting the flower petals and leaves, Miller used the same techniques. She added a new layer by clicking the New Layer button on the Layers palette. Then, she loaded a selection for one of the petals, for instance, and using her Airbrush, she laid in the base color paint. Gradually, she built up the values to establish the forms of the petals and leaves.

Next, she decreased the Size of her Airbrush to 6–10 pixels, and she used a very light touch on her stylus as she added stronger shadows in the deeper areas of the flower and brighter highlights to the

areas that were catching the light. Then, she used an even smaller brush to paint the fine veins on the leaves.

Miller also stroked the edges of the flower petals with light colors to give the petals the appearance of more depth. This is most easily done by painting outside of a selection, allowing just a hint of the color to come within the edge of the selection. It is much easier to paint the fine edges using a selection than attempting to paint a fine line along the edges. Miller wanted a smoother look for the leaves, so to blend areas, she used the Soft Blender Stump variant of Blenders to smooth the colors on each leaf.

For the background, she created a new layer at the very bottom in the layer stack and filled it with a blue color. Then, using very soft strokes, she added color using the Airbrush and blended it with the Soft Blender Stump. As a last touch, to create the illusion of more depth, she used the Detail Airbrush to paint darker colors around a few of the flowers and leaves.

■ Award-winning illustrator **Michael Bast** has worked with conventional art tools for many years. Since 1990 he has painted digitally using Painter's brushes and art materials. Bast loves Painter because it allows him to capture the warmth and texture of his favorite conventional media.

To begin *Keebler Tray,* Bast assembled elements to use for reference. His client wanted him to use items that he had created for earlier illustrations, as well as draw new ones. He created a composition drawing that included all of the food items by using conventional pencils and paper; then he scanned the drawing.

Bast created selections, masks and vector shapes to make his work easier as he painted the *Keebler Tray.* Working over his drawing, Bast built selections for each element in his illustration—the bowl rim, and the purple grapes and peppers, for instance. For safekeeping, he saved each selection as a mask in the Channels palette by choosing Select, Save Selection. For the geometric shapes, such as the tray, he used the Pen tool and then

saved the shapes into the Layers palette. He also converted a copy of the shapes to selections and then saved them into the Selection Portfolio. To store a selection in the Selection Portfolio as Bast did, choose Window, Show Selection Portfolio. Make a selection using one of the selection tools or load a selection by choosing Select, Load Selection. Then, use the Selection Adjuster tool to drag the active selection into the Selection Portfolio. When you want to use the selection on your image, use the Selection Adjuster to drag a stored selection from the Selection Portfolio palette into your image. (Read more about using the Selection Portfolio on page 183 in the beginning of this chapter.)

To paint, Bast primarily used the New Simple Water variant of Digital Watercolor to lay in colored washes within selected areas. Bast likes this brush because it is easy to build up areas of color. Using a process similar to glazing in conventional watercolor, he paints washes of color, dries them by

choosing Dry Digital Watercolor from the Layers palette menu, and then adds more color with the New Simple Water brush. (Read more about Digital Watercolor on pages 90–95.) When he wanted to pull color out from an area of wet paint, he used the Gentle Wet Eraser. To add opaque brush work, he used the Variable Flat variant of Oils. To add finer detail to areas, such as the strawberries, he used the Detail Opaque variant of Gouache. For the speckled texture on the crackers, he loaded a selection for the area and then used the Pepper Spray variant of the Airbrushes.

6

USING
LAYERS

Working in separate source files, we painted elements—the turtle, the fish, and the paint can and brushes—for this Emerald City *illustration. Then we painted a mask to silhouette each element. We loaded the selection from each element's mask in turn and used the Layer Adjuster to drag and drop the element into the final composite. After dragging the items in, we used the Layer Adjuster to position them. To create a transparent look on the bottom of the paint can, we created a layer mask for the paint can layer and used the Digital Airbrush variant of the Airbrushes and black paint to paint on the layer mask; the effect was to softly "erase" lower areas of the can as they were hidden by the layer mask.*

CHER THREINEN-PENDARVIS

INTRODUCTION

LAYERS ARE ELEMENTS THAT HOVER above Painter's image Canvas, or base layer, providing a great deal of flexibility in composing artwork. You can move, paint on, or apply a special effect to a layer without affecting other layers or the background canvas. So when building images you can try several possibilities by manipulating or repositioning the various elements. Then, when your layers are as you like them, you can drop them onto the canvas, blending them with the background.

In addition to *image* (or pixel-based) *layers,* Painter incorporates other types of "layers": *floating objects, reference layers, shapes, dynamic layers, text layers,* and two *media layers—Watercolor and Liquid Ink.* The controls for naming, stacking, compositing and grouping all of these kinds of layers are found in the Layers palette, as described in "Organizing with the Layers Palette" on page 230. Each layer in a layered file has a Composite Method that affects how it interacts (or blends) with other layers and with the Canvas.

You can preserve layers by saving your file in RIFF format. Saving in most other formats requires *dropping,* or merging, the layers.

A TIFF-TO-RIFF LIFESAVER

If you save a layered file in TIFF format (a format in which Painter doesn't support layers and floating objects), Painter is smart enough not to automatically drop the layers in your working image. A dialog box will appear, and when you click OK, the program will save a closed copy of your document with layers dropped in TIFF format, but the layers will stay alive in your open working image. Make sure to save in RIFF format before quitting in order to preserve the image layers, floating objects, reference layers, dynamic layers, text layers, shapes, and Watercolor and Liquid Ink layers.

Recognizing items in the Layers palette: Image layers are designated by a stack of rectangles, a floating object by a star, a shape by a circle and triangle, a reference layer by a dotted rectangle with handles, a dynamic layer by a plug icon, a Text layer by a capital "T," a Watercolor layer by a blue water drop and a Liquid Ink layer by a black drop of ink. In the Layers palette shown here, the document's Canvas is selected.

USING DRAG-AND-DROP

Here's a quick way to copy a layer or shape into a composite file from a source image. Open both images. In the source image, select the layer or shape by clicking its name in the Layers palette and then drag the item into the composite image using the Layer Adjuster tool.

For this flower illustration, the Wash Bristle and Runny Wash Camel variants of Watercolor were used to paint washes on Watercolor layers.

However, if you'd like to be able to open a Painter image in Photoshop with layers intact, save the file in Photoshop format. All layers and shapes will be converted to Photoshop layers, with their names and stacking order intact. To read more about working with Photoshop, turn to Chapter 10, "Using Painter with Photoshop."

An *image layer* can hold pixels or transparency. When you add a new layer by clicking the New Layer button at the bottom of the Layers palette or by choosing New Layer from the palette's pop-up menu, it's completely transparent until you paint on it. See "Working with Image Layers," below.

A *layer floating object* is an area of an image layer that has been isolated and lifted from the layer, to create a kind of sublayer. Each layer can have only one floating object at a time. See "Working with Layer Floating Objects" on page 223.

Reference layers can be helpful for assembling large images from several separate source files. A reference layer is a 72 ppi screen proxy (or "stand-in") for an image layer in the current image, or for a placed image that's linked to an image file outside of the document. (See "Using Reference Layers" on page 224.)

Shapes are essentially a resolution-independent kind of layer that can be reshaped or resized without degradation. As described on page 225, shapes are outline-based elements with attributes such as stroke, fill and transparency. Shapes and their attributes are PostScript-based objects. To be able to paint on a shape, adding pixel information, you have to first convert it to an image layer.

Dynamic layers are special hovering devices that allow you to make adjustments to an existing image (by adding an Equalize layer or Brightness and Contrast layer, for example), or to create entirely new effects (for instance, a Liquid Metal layer). You can create a dynamic layer by clicking the Dynamic Plug-ins button at the bottom of the Layers palette and choosing a plug-in from the pop-up menu (see page 227).

Painter's *Text layers* are described on page 229.

Media layers are special layers that allow startling, realistic painting effects. Read about Watercolor and Liquid Ink layers on page 229.

All layers take up extra disk space and RAM. You can minimize the need for extra space by floating only what's necessary, and by dropping and combining layers whenever it makes sense.

WORKING WITH IMAGE LAYERS

You can make an image layer by activating the Canvas layer, selecting part of it, and then clicking on the selected area with the Layer Adjuster tool. This process cuts the selected area out of the Canvas and turns it into the new layer, leaving behind a hole that

LAYER OR FLOATING OBJECT?

New *image layers* can be made by selecting an area of the *Canvas* and cutting or copying. But if you select and cut or copy *from a layer other than the Canvas*, you produce a *layer floating object* associated with the layer you used to make it.

To make a new layer by copying an active selection on Painter's image Canvas (similar to choosing Layer, New, Layer Via Copy in Photoshop), make or load a selection in your image, hold down the Alt/Option key, choose the Layer Adjuster tool, and click or drag inside the selected area. To *cut* from the image canvas and turn the selected area into a new layer, click or drag with the Layer Adjuster without pressing the Alt/Option key.

PHOTO: CORBIS IMAGES

If you don't hold down the Alt/Option key when you drag a selection with the Layer Adjuster, you'll leave a hole behind in the Canvas if you then move the newly created layer. Occasionally this is desirable, but most of the time you'll want to use the Alt/Option!

In Painter there can be only one active selection at a time. You can use a selection to edit a portion of any image layer, reference layer, Watercolor layer or Liquid Ink layer listed in the Layers palette.

you can see if you drag the new layer with the Layer Adjuster. Alt/Option-click to *copy* an active selection or to duplicate the entire Canvas. This creates a new layer from the copy but also leaves the original pixels in place on the Canvas. The selection that defines the area to turn into the new layer can be made with any of the selection processes described in Chapter 5.

There are other ways to create an image layer. For instance, all elements pasted into a Painter document come in as image layers, and you can also drag an image layer from the Image Portfolio palette into your image.

An image layer automatically includes a *Transparency mask;* when the layer is active (clicked in the Layers palette) its Transparency mask is available to be loaded to select all the nontransparent areas of the layer (Select, Load Selection). An image layer can also include a *layer mask,* created by clicking the Create Layer Mask button at the bottom of the Layers palette. The layer mask determines what parts of the pixel information on the layer are shown or hidden. You can load the layer mask for the active layer as a selection (Select, Load Selection), just as you can the Transparency mask described above. In contrast to the transparency mask, the layer mask can be directly modified to hide or reveal parts of the layer or to blend layered images with exciting transparency effects.

Here's how to work with image layers once you've created or imported one:

To activate a layer, click its name in the Layers palette. Or choose the Layer Adjuster in the Toolbox, and then turn on Auto Select Layer in the Property Bar and click on a visible area of the layer. Either way, the name will be highlighted in the Layers palette to show that the layer is active.

To deactivate a layer, click on another layer. Or choose the Layer Adjuster tool, turn on Auto Select Layer in the Property Bar and click somewhere in the image where the current layer has no pixels.

To apply a special effect to a layer, make sure it's active (highlighted in the Layers palette, as described above). Then choose from the Effects menu. (Of course, an effect applied to a transparent layer with no pixels on it has no effect.)

To paint on a layer, make sure it's active (highlighted in the Layers palette, as described above). Choose any brush (except a Watercolor or Liquid Ink variant) and paint brushstrokes onto the layer. (Watercolor and Liquid Ink can paint only on appropriate media layers, which will automatically be created if you try to use these brushes on image layers.) For more information, turn to "Painting on Layers" on page 68 in Chapter 3.

To erase paint you have applied to a layer, making the area "clear" again, you can choose the Eraser variant of the Erasers (in the Brush Selector Bar) with 100% Opacity set in the Property Bar, and paint on the layer to "erase."

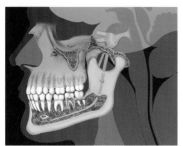

When creating Neural Pathway, *a detail of which is shown here, David Purnell used many layers and shapes. See the complete illustration and more of Purnell's work in the gallery at the end of this chapter.*

A QUICK CANVAS COPY

To quickly float a copy of the Canvas to a layer, choose Select, All (Ctrl/⌘-A); then hold down Ctrl-Alt (Windows) or ⌘-Option (Mac) and click on the Canvas with the Layer Adjuster.

RESTACKING LAYERS

When you create a new layer, it appears at the top of the layer stack. To reposition it in the stack, simply drag its name to the appropriate level in the Layers palette.

To hide part of a layer without permanently erasing it, begin by choosing black in the Colors picker. Click on the layer in the Layers palette. If the layer doesn't already have a layer mask, click the Create Layer Mask button at the bottom of the palette. Then click the mask thumbnail that will appear next to the image thumbnail for the layer; this activates the mask rather than the layer's image. Choose a brush (such as the Pens, Scratchboard tool) and paint on the mask with black where you want to hide the layer. If you want to *reveal* parts of the image that you have hidden with the layer mask, paint the mask with white.

The most foolproof way to move a layer is to click the layer's name in the Layers palette to activate the layer, and then choose it with the Layer Adjuster tool (make sure the Auto Select Layer check box is turned off in the Property Bar), and drag anywhere in the image window. To adjust a layer's position a screen pixel at a time, activate the layer and use the arrow keys on your keyboard.

To merge a layer with the Canvas, activate the image layer in the Layers palette and click the Layer Commands button (far left at the bottom of the palette) and choose Drop from the pop-up menu, or click the triangle in the upper-right corner of the palette and choose Drop from that menu. If you want to merge all of your layers onto the Canvas—much like using Photoshop's Flatten Image command—simply choose Drop All from the menu in the upper-right corner (this command is not available through the Layer Commands button). Another option, if you want to keep a layered version but also create a "flattened" one, is to choose File, Clone; a duplicate of the image will appear with all layers merged.

To scale, rotate, distort or flip a layer, activate the layer and choose the appropriate command under Effects, Orientation.

To change the opacity of a layer, click its name in the Layers palette and use the Opacity slider near the top of the palette.

WORKING WITH LAYER FLOATING OBJECTS

To reposition a portion of an image layer, Painter uses a *layer floating object*. Only an image layer can have a floating object, and each layer can have only one floating object at a time. Besides moving part of a layer, you can also use a layer floating object to isolate part of a layer for editing. The advantage of using a floating object (rather than simply selecting an area of the layer and changing it) is that a floating object can have its own layer mask, which you can use to hide or reveal part of the floating object.

To create a floating object that's cut out from a layer, make a selection, click on a layer's name in the Layers palette and choose Select, Float, or click inside the selection with the Layer Adjuster tool. The floating object will be listed below its parent

If you'll be making several transformations (such as rotations or scaling) to a single layer, like rotating it into place and then scaling it to fit your layout, you need to know that the quality of an image layer can be degraded with every transformation. Instead of using a series of individual transformation commands (such as Effects, Orientation, Rotate and then Effects, Orientation, Scale), consider converting the layer temporarily to a reference layer by selecting it and choosing Effects, Orientation, Free Transform. You can then rotate, scale and skew the reference layer as many times as you like. When you arrive at the result you want, choose Effects, Orientation, Commit Transform. The effect is to transform the actual pixels only once and thus preserve quality.

A reference layer, ready to have Free Transform applied, has eight handles around it.

You can merge several layers at once with the Canvas by Shift-selecting their names in the Layers palette before clicking the Layer Commands button and choosing Drop from the pop-up menu.

layer in the Layers palette, indented to show the relationship. (If you turn off visibility for the floating object by clicking its eye icon, you'll see the hole where it has been cut from the parent layer.)

To make a floating object copy of information on the parent layer (without cutting out), make a selection, press the Alt/Option key and then choose Select, Float, or Alt/Option-click with the Layer Adjuster tool. The floating object "copy" will be listed below its parent layer in the Layers palette.

To recombine a floating object with its parent layer, activate the floating object by clicking its name in the Layers palette and click the Layer Commands button (far left at the bottom of the palette) and choose Drop from the pop-up menu. The floating object will also recombine with its parent layer if you do any of the following: paint or make another selection while either the layer or its floating object is active or paste into the document or drag an item from the Image Portfolio while the floating object is active.

USING REFERENCE LAYERS

If you work with large files and your computer slows to a crawl when you try to reposition a big image layer, consider converting image layers to *reference layers*. Reference layers are 72 ppi proxy, or "stand-in" images. They let you manipulate high-resolution images faster, instead of dragging huge images around your screen. Because you are working with a proxy—and not the actual pixels—you can perform multiple rotations, scaling, skewing and repositioning very quickly. When you've finished all your manipulations, convert reference layers back to image layers; Painter will remember all the manipulations you've made and will carry them out as a single change, with much less loss of quality than if you had made them one by one on the high-resolution file.

To make a reference layer, select an image layer and choose Effects, Orientation, Free Transform. To get ready to operate on the layer, choose the Layer Adjuster.

To scale a reference layer proportionately, press the Shift key and drag on a corner handle with the Layer Adjuster tool to resize as many times as needed to get just the result you want.

To rotate a reference layer interactively, press the Ctrl/⌘ key and drag a corner handle with the Layer Adjuster.

To skew a reference layer interactively, press the Ctrl/⌘ key and drag one of the original four middle handles with the Layer Adjuster tool.

If you're compositing large files, you may want to work with each component file separately, and then make a reference layer by importing the image (with its layer mask, if you like) into your composite file using File, Place. When the positioning and transformations of the imported layer are complete, convert the reference layer to an image layer by choosing Effects, Orientation, Commit Transform.

Rick Kirkman created Postal Cat *by drawing shapes, and then converting them to image layers so that he could paint on them. Turn to page 233 to read about his technique step by step.*

The opacity of a shape's fill can be set in the Set Shape Attributes dialog box (Shapes, Set Shape Attributes).

WHOLE SHAPE SELECTION

To select an entire unfilled shape path, choose the Shape Selection tool (hollow arrow), press the Ctrl/⌘ key to put it in Whole Shape Selection mode and click on the shape's outline to select all of its anchor points at once, making it possible to move the shape to a new location, undistorted, by dragging anywhere on its outline.

To scale, rotate or skew a reference layer numerically, choose Effects, Orientation, Set Transform, and type specifications into the fields. (The skew is set as the Slant, which is found in the Rotation section of the dialog box.)

To turn a reference layer back into an image (pixel-based) layer, choose Effects, Orientation, Commit Transform, or paint or apply an effect to the reference layer, clicking the Commit button when prompted. If you drag a reference layer into the Image Portfolio palette, the full-resolution version is stored in the Portfolio.

WORKING WITH SHAPES

Shapes can be drawn with the Rectangular or Oval Shape tool, or the Pen or the Quick Curve tool. Or they can be made from a selection (converted from a selection using the Select, Convert to Shape command) or imported from a PostScript drawing program such as Adobe Illustrator (this process is described in Chapter 5).

Before modifying a shape, you need to make it active. You can activate a shape just as you would a layer—by clicking its name in the Layers palette or by clicking it with the Layer Adjuster tool, with Auto Select Layer turned on in the Property Bar. Or use the Whole Shape Selection tool (solid arrow, the Shape Selection tool with the Ctrl/⌘ key held down) to select the entire shape so you can move it as a unit, without distorting it, by dragging anywhere on its outline.

To drag off a copy of a shape, you can select the shape with the Layer Adjuster tool, and then press Alt/Option and drag.

To scale a shape proportionately, click it with the Layer Adjuster, hold down the Shift key and drag a corner handle.

To rotate a shape, click it with the Layer Adjuster, press the Ctrl/⌘ key and drag a corner handle.

To skew a shape interactively, click it with the Layer Adjuster, press the Ctrl/⌘ key and drag a middle handle.

To scale, distort, rotate or flip a shape, select it in the Layers palette and use one of the choices from Effects, Orientation.

To duplicate a shape and transform the copy, choose Shapes, Set Duplicate Transform. Set up specifications in the Set Duplicate Transform dialog box and click OK. Now when you choose Shapes, Duplicate, the transformation will be applied to the copy.

To modify the stroke and fill attributes of a shape, select it and open the Set Shape Attributes dialog box by choosing Shapes, Set Shape Attributes or by double-clicking on the name of a shape in the Layers palette. To change the fill or stroke color of a shape, click once in the Stroke or Fill color field and choose a new color in the Colors picker. (This method lets you select the current color

For this restaurant logo, we drew black calligraphy letters on the canvas using the Calligraphy variant of the Calligraphy brush. We made a luminosity mask by choosing the New From command from the Channels palette's triangle pop-out menu and choosing Image Luminance in the New From dialog box. Then we loaded the selection (Select, Load Selection, Alpha 1), and converted the selection to shapes (Select, Convert to Shape). The client planned to use the logo in a variety of ways, so we appreciated that Painter automatically created compound shapes to make the counters transparent for the letter "O," the two descending "g" shapes and the "e." Seen here are the selected filled shapes (top), and the logo applied onto Koa wood texture (bottom) from an ArtBeats Wood and Paper CD-ROM (bottom). To read more about compound shapes, turn to "Making a Compound," on the next page or to "Using Shapes," in the Painter IX Help.

without displaying the color wheel. To use the wheel instead, simply *double*-click the Stroke or Fill color swatch in the Set Shape Attributes dialog box.) **A word of warning:** If you paint on, or apply an effect to, a shape—rather than simply changing its stroke and fill—it will be automatically converted into an image layer when you click the Commit button. When this happens, shape attributes (such as resolution independence and control of stroke and fill) are lost.

To convert several shapes into individual image layers, you can Shift-select multiple shapes in the Layers palette and convert the shapes to image layers all at once—as long as they are stroked and filled—using Shapes, Convert to Layer.

To make a single image layer from several shapes, first Shift-select the shapes, and then click the Layer Commands button on the left at the bottom of the Layers palette to access the pop-up menu, and choose Group. With the group closed (controlled by the arrow to the left of its name in the Layers palette), choose Shapes, Convert to Layer.

To duplicate, move or transform a group of shapes, you can select the group by clicking its name in the Layers palette and then move or transform it as you would a single shape. (See "Organizing with the Layers Palette" on page 230 to read more about groups.)

To move an individual shape within a group, expand the group by clicking the arrow to the left of the group's name in the Layers palette. Then choose the Layer Adjuster tool and drag the shape; or click it and move it using the arrow keys.

Blending between shapes. To create intermediate shapes between two shapes, Shift-select both shapes in the Layers palette

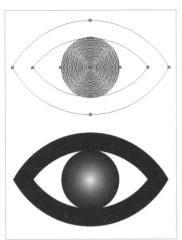

Viewing shape paths (top) and finished objects (bottom). For this filled compound outer object with blended interior object, we began by making a blend. To blend the blue circle with a very small white circle in its center, we selected both circles in the Layers palette, and then chose Shapes, Blend and specified 50 steps. To build the compound of the two outer shapes, we Shift-clicked in the Layers palette to target them both and chose Shapes, Make Compound. The Make Compound command cut a hole with the smaller eye shape, allowing only part of the outer fill to be visible.

Detail from Hot Beveled Metal. *Beginning with a text layer, we used a Bevel World dynamic Plug-ins layer to commit the live text to an image layer and to create a 3D effect. Then we layered two more copies of the bevel—we painted on the first copy and we created the glow using the second copy. To learn more about type effects using Bevel World, turn to Chapter 9.*

and choose Shapes, Blend. Make choices in the dialog box and click OK. Painter IX Help contains a complete explanation of the Blend dialog box.

Here's a useful application for Painter's Blend command: If you've imported an image created in Illustrator that has blends but they don't make the transition successfully into Painter, zoom in and count and then delete the interior objects inside the blend using the Shape Selection tool and Delete key. Shift-select the two remaining outside objects in the Layers palette, and then choose Shapes, Blend and specify the number of steps to regenerate the blend.

Making a compound. To cut a hole in a shape and reveal the underlying image, make a compound using two shapes: Move a small shape on top of a large one, Shift-select both of them in the Layers palette and choose Shapes, Make Compound. The top shape will cut a hole in the bottom shape to reveal the underlying image. Compounds are made automatically to create counters in letters when type is set or when type outlines are imported, and also when selections with holes are converted to shapes.

USING DYNAMIC LAYERS

Dynamic layers are special devices that allow you to create a variety of effects. To keep dynamic layers "live" (allowing changes to be made and previewed on the image without becoming permanent), the file can be saved only in RIFF format. Saving in Photoshop format converts the dynamic layers to image layers, freezing the effects in their current state.

Dynamic layers, which are indicated by a plug icon in the Layers palette, fall into three basic categories. The first kind is similar to an adjustment layer in Adobe Photoshop. It allows you to set up a procedure such as a brightness-and-contrast correction or a posterization of the underlying image, without permanently changing the pixels of the image itself. Image correction tools such as Equalize, Brightness and Contrast, and Posterize, as well as special

Cool Water Drops. To add a water droplet effect to this photo (simulating water drops on a camera lens), we used the Liquid Metal dynamic plug-in. First we made a clone of the image (File, Clone). Then we clicked the Dynamic Plug-ins button on the Layers palette and chose Liquid Metal from the menu. We chose the Clone Source Map type and a high Refraction setting to make the "water" translucent with a blue reflection. Then we clicked and dragged with the Circle tool from the Liquid Metal dialog box to place the drops. A drop can be extended simply by starting to drag with the Circle tool inside the edge of the existing drop.

Clicking the "plug" icon on the Layers palette will reveal the Dynamic Plug-ins menu.

effects layers such as Glass Distortion, Kaleidoscope and Liquid Lens fall into this "adjustment" category. To generate a Posterize layer, for example, click the Dynamic Plug-ins button at the bottom of the Layers palette and choose Posterize from the pop-up menu. Click OK to apply it. The posterization will apply to all image layers, reference layers, shapes and dynamic layers listed below the Posterize dynamic layer in the Layers palette, so if you want it to apply to only certain layers, you can drag it down in the Layers palette. (To read more about Painter's image-correction layers, turn to Chapter 7. For information about creating special effects with this series of dynamic layers, refer to Chapter 8.)

For a second kind of dynamic layer, you choose an image layer and apply a special effect procedure to the selected image layer, the "source image layer," *turning it into* a dynamic layer. The dynamic layer is "live," so you can preview changes and then modify the effect and preview again, or even return the source image layer to its original condition if you choose. Three of the dynamic layers—Bevel World, Burn and Tear—require a source image layer to perform their magic. To make this kind of dynamic layer, activate a layer in the Layers palette (you can select only part of the layer with any selection tool if you like) and choose Bevel World, for instance, from the Dynamic Plug-ins menu. Make adjustments to the settings and click OK. (If you start with a selection on the image Canvas, clicking Apply will automatically generate a new dynamic layer from the selection.) Read more about these dynamic layers in Chapter 8.

The third type of dynamic layer allows you to build special-effects imagery on a new layer. Liquid Metal falls into this category. To read about exciting techniques using Liquid Metal, turn to Chapter 8, "Exploring Special Effects," and to "Painting with Ice" on page 350 in Chapter 9.

To change a dynamic layer's appearance, double-click its name in the Layers palette, make changes to the settings in the dialog box and click OK.

To convert a dynamic layer to an image layer, so you can add a layer mask or convert the image layer into a reference layer (to scale it using Free Transform, for instance), click the triangle in the Layers palette's upper-right corner and choose Convert to Default Layer from the menu. The following actions will also convert a dynamic layer to an image layer: transforming using Effects, Orientation (to scale, rotate or distort); applying an effect from the Effects menu (such as Effects, Surface Control, Apply Surface Texture); painting on the layer; applying a dynamic layer special effect (such as applying the Tear special-effect layer to an active Burn layer) or merging a group that includes a dynamic layer.

For this text design, we began by setting small colored text on a layer. Then we made several duplicates by Alt/Option-dragging with the Layer Adjuster. We repositioned the text layers using the Layer Adjuster, and set a large black "W" above the other layers. To achieve the inside-out color effect, we set the Composite Method for the large "W" to Reverse-Out in the Layers palette.

The Layers palette showing the pop-up menu that includes important commands for use with Liquid Ink and Watercolor layers.

Watercolor layers and their special brushes were used to paint the illustration Maui North Shore 2.

USING TEXT LAYERS

When you select the Text tool in the Toolbox and begin to set type on your image, the type is set on a new layer that appears in the Layers palette, designated by a "T" icon. Controls for specifying text settings are located in the Property Bar. For in-depth information about using Text layers, turn to Chapter 9, "Working with Type in Painter."

WORKING WITH MEDIA LAYERS

Painter includes two media layers, Watercolor and Liquid Ink. Special brushes must be used to paint on each kind of media layer. When the Canvas or an image layer is selected in the Layers palette and you attempt to paint with a Watercolor brush or Liquid Ink brush, a new Watercolor or Liquid Ink layer is automatically generated. Chapter 3 includes in-depth information about Watercolor and Liquid Ink, including "A Painter Watercolor Primer" and "A Painter Liquid Ink Primer" as well as step-by-step techniques for using both media.

Using Watercolor layers. Painter offers Watercolor layers and special Watercolor brushes, making it possible to add wet color on separate layers. Watercolor layers can be edited using selections to restrict the changes to the selected area. A Watercolor layer can also have a layer mask, which can be edited by clicking on the layer mask thumbnail in the Layers palette and targeting the mask in the Channels palette, and then editing the mask. (You'll have to choose a different brush to edit the mask, because Watercolor brushes don't work on masks.) For a step-by-step technique for using selections with Watercolor layers, turn to "Mixing Media on Layers" on page 242.

Using commands found under the triangle pop-out menu on the right side of the Layers palette, you can stop paint from diffusing on a Watercolor layer by choosing Dry Watercolor Layer, and you can re-wet a Watercolor layer by choosing Wet Entire Watercolor Layer. Or you can add the content of the Canvas to an existing Watercolor layer as wet paint, or create a new Watercolor layer from the Canvas content, also by choosing from this Layers palette menu.

Using Liquid Ink layers. Liquid Ink is a thick, viscous ink medium. A Liquid Ink layer is not pixel-based but resolution-independent. To paint on a Liquid Ink layer, you must use special Liquid Ink brushes found in the Brush Selector Bar. (Choosing a Liquid Ink brush and painting automatically creates a new Liquid Ink layer except when a Watercolor layer is active.) A Liquid Ink layer can have a layer mask. To constrain paint to a specific area, make a selection and then target the Liquid Ink layer before painting.

John Derry created Capitola *using Liquid Ink layers.*

For the ultimate in management using the Layers palette, see how Rick Kirkman did it in "Working with Shapes and Layers," on page 233.

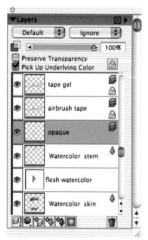

In the Layers palette (above), for Delro Rosco's Apple *illustration, he organized some layers in groups and locked other items so he wouldn't accidentally select them with the Layer Adjuster.*

ORGANIZING WITH THE LAYERS PALETTE

In the Layers palette, Painter assigns sequential names to layers and shapes (such as Layer 1, Layer 2 and so on) in the order they were created. Rename them by double-clicking on a name (or select the name and press the Enter key) to bring up the appropriate dialog box. Enter the name and click OK. So that you can more easily work with underlying items, you can hide layers or shapes by clicking to close the eye icons next to their names. Click the eye open to show an item again.

To lock an item (making it impossible to select it in the image window, even with Auto Select Layer turned on), target the layer in the Layers palette and click the lock icon near the top of the palette. To unlock, click the lock icon again.

Using groups. Grouping layers or shapes is an ideal way to organize related elements in the Layers palette so the palette doesn't take up so much space on the screen. To group layers or shapes, Shift-select the elements in the Layers palette, and then click the Layer Commands button at the bottom of the Layers palette and choose Group, or press Ctrl/⌘-G. To ungroup, click the Layer Commands button and choose Ungroup, or press Ctrl/⌘-U. If you want to apply effects (other than Scale, Rotate, Flip or Create Drop Shadow) to a group of layers or shapes, you'll need to open the group, select individual items and then apply the effect. Like individual layers, groups can be hidden or made visible by clicking the eye icon, and they can also be locked.

Using the Image Portfolio. Open the Image Portfolio palette by choosing Window, Show Image Portfolio. To store a copy of an element for later use or for use in another file, hold down the Alt/Option key and use the Layer Adjuster tool to drag it from the image window into the Image Portfolio palette.

PRESERVE TRANSPARENCY

By turning on the Preserve Transparency check box in the Layers palette, you can confine your painting and editing to those areas of an image layer that already contain pixels. Turn Preserve Transparency off if you'd like to paint or edit outside the existing pixels—for instance, to feather the edge by applying the Effects, Focus, Soften command, which would spread pixels outside of the original area. Preserve Transparency is not available for Liquid Ink or Watercolor layers.

AUTO-SELECTING A LAYER

By choosing the Layer Adjuster tool and turning on Auto Select Layer in the Property Bar, you can click on the visible portion of any layer to select the layer and drag to move its contents.

READY TO COLLAPSE

If you've finished making changes to a group of layers but you still want to keep the group separate from the Canvas, consider clicking the Layer Commands button at the bottom of the Layers palette and choosing Collapse. This feature merges a selected group of default layers into a single default layer and can be a real memory-saver.

Create an empty image portfolio by opening the Image Portfolio palette (Window, Show Image Portfolio) and choosing Image Mover from the pull-down menu, opened by clicking the triangle on the right side of the Image Portfolio palette bar. In the Image Mover, click the New button to create an empty portfolio, name it and then save it into the Painter application folder. Drag items from the current Image Portfolio into your new Image Portfolio. (To learn more about using Painter's movers and libraries, turn to Chapter 1.)

ERASING AND RESTORING

Caution: Using the Eraser variant of the Erasers brush permanently removes the erased information from the layer. But adding a layer mask and editing it using black paint is much more flexible, because you can also restore the image by painting the layer mask with white. Use *black* on the mask to *hide* the layer, and use *white* on the mask to *restore* the layer's visibility.

(To remove the element from the current file as you store it in the Portfolio, use the Layer Adjuster without the Alt/Option key.)

LAYERS AND THEIR MASKS

Layer masks allow for transparent effects. You can edit layer masks using either brushes or special effect commands (such as Effects, Surface Control, Express Texture, with which you can apply a texture to a mask). To view a layer mask, target the layer in the Layers palette; then target the Layer Mask in the Channels palette. For more information, see the "Dropping and Saving a Layer Visibility Mask" tip on this page.

Importing a source file with an alpha channel. Because it's faster to work with fewer layers, many artists assemble pieces of artwork in source files and then import the pieces into a final composite file. Consider preparing a mask in a smaller source file that you plan to import into a composite (using File, Place) and storing the mask in the Channels palette. When you import the file, in the Place dialog box, check the Retain Alpha check box, and click OK to place the source as a reference layer in your document. The imported layer will include the transparency created by the alpha channel mask. To turn the reference layer into an image layer, select it in the Layers palette and choose Effects, Orientation, Commit Transform. (For more information, see "Using Reference Layers" on page 224.)

COMPOSITE CONTROLS

Painter's composite controls can give you nifty special effects with very little effort. With a layer selected in the Layers palette, choose from the Composite Method pull-down menu on the Layers palette. The list includes many of the same blending modes found in Adobe Photoshop, which are listed below the

A VERSATILE MASK EXCHANGE

If you'd like to use a layer mask to make a selection on another layer or on the background Canvas to constrain paint or effects there, here's a way to trade masks back and forth: To copy a layer mask so it becomes a separate mask in the Channels palette, target the layer in the Layers palette, and then in the Channels, target the layer mask. Choose Duplicate from the Channels palette's pull-down menu. In the Duplicate Channel dialog box, choose "New" to create a new mask based on the layer mask, and click OK. Now you can activate any layer in the Layers palette and use Select, Load Selection to use the new mask on that layer.

DROPPING AND SAVING A LAYER VISIBILITY MASK

To merge the visible part of an image layer so it becomes part of the image Canvas but at the same time preserve its transparency mask, choose Drop and Select from the Layers palette's pull-down menu. A selection will be made from the transparency mask, and you can save it as a mask in the Channels palette by choosing Select, Save Selection.

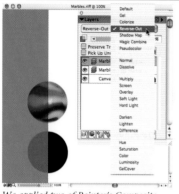

We applied two of Painter's Composite Methods to these marbles floating over a blue-and-white background. The top marble uses Gel and the bottom one uses Reverse-Out.

ones that are unique to Painter. (Not included are Photoshop's Color Dodge, Linear Dodge, Color Burn, Linear Burn, Exclusion, Vivid Light, Linear Light and Pin Light.) "A Visual Display of the Composite Methods" below shows these controls in action.

You'll find Painter's *Composite Depth* pull-down menu near the top of the Layers palette, to the right of the Composite Method menu. Painter's Composite Depth controls work only on impasto paint (see "A Painter Impasto Primer" on page 123 and "Working with Thick Paint" on page 127 for more information about Impasto). The default Composite Depth method is *Add*. If you paint with an Impasto brush on a layer, *Add* raises the thick paint. *Ignore* turns off the thickness for the paint on the layer, and *Subtract* inverts the paint thickness on the layer, making brushstrokes on this layer excavated rather than raised on the surface. *Replace* changes the paint depth of Impasto on the underlying layer to the applied layer's depth wherever the layers overlap.

A VISUAL DISPLAY OF THE COMPOSITE METHODS

Painter's Composite Methods (from a menu at the top of the Layers palette) change how a layer interacts with the image underneath. Here a leaf floats over a two-part background. The Default and Normal methods give the same results, as do Shadow Map and Multiply. For complete descriptions of what the modes are doing, refer to Painter's Help, and *The Photoshop CS Wow! Book* or Adobe Photoshop's *User Guide*.

 Default / Normal

 Gel

 Colorize

 Reverse-Out

 Shadow Map / Multiply

 Magic Combine

 Pseudocolor

 Dissolve (50%)

 Screen

 Overlay

 Soft Light

 Hard Light

 Darken

 Lighten

 Difference

 Hue

 Saturation

 Color

 Luminosity

Gel Cover

Working with Shapes and Layers

Overview *Draw Bézier shapes in Painter; fill and name the shapes; convert the shapes to layers; paint details on the layers with brushes; add and edit layer masks to achieve transparency; apply textured special effects with Color Overlay, Surface Texture and Glass Distortion.*

RICK KIRKMAN

Kirkman's scanned pencil sketch

Setting the Shapes preferences

SHAPES BRING POWER AND VERSATILITY to Painter, saving many illustrators a trip to a drawing program to create Bézier paths for import. With Painter's Pen tool (now similar to Illustrator's) you can completely create and edit Bézier paths, add a stroke and fill, name them and organize them in the Layers palette. After you draw shapes, you can convert them to layers and add paint and special effects. Rick Kirkman created the illustration above—one in a series of editorial illustrations for *Professional Speaker* magazine—entirely within Painter.

1 Setting up a template. Kirkman began by scanning a pencil sketch, saving it as a TIFF file and opening the scan in Painter. The file measured 2374 x 3184 pixels.

2 Creating shapes. To create your outlines, you can work either in Painter or in a PostScript drawing program. If you plan to trace a template—as Kirkman did—set up shape attributes so that you can draw with a precise skeletal line. For Windows, choose Edit, Preferences, Shapes, or for Mac OS X choose Corel Painter IX, Preferences, Shapes, and choose these settings: Under "On Draw," uncheck the Fill and Stroke check boxes; under "On Close," uncheck the Stroke check box and check the Fill check box. Using the Pen tool to draw Bézier shape paths, Kirkman carefully traced

2b

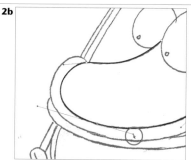

Dragging with the Direct Selection tool to adjust a control handle on a path

3a

Preparing to fill the selected "nose" shape with a flesh color

3b

Applying the flat color fills

4

Painting the shadow on the fish's body using the Digital Airbrush variant

5

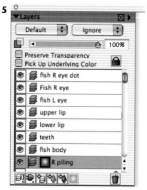

The layer mask for the "R piling" layer is targeted in the Layers palette. The heavy black border around the thumbnail shows that the mask, not the image, is targeted.

his sketch. To make adjustments on the fly while drawing a path with the Pen tool (like adjusting a control handle or anchor point), press the Ctrl/⌘ key to temporarily switch to the Shape Selection tool.

3 Coloring, naming and converting. Before he started drawing each shape, Kirkman clicked the Fill swatch in the Property Bar and chose a color close to the color he would finally use, so the shape would fill with the color when he completed the path. As soon as he had created each shape, he double-clicked its default name in the Layers palette and renamed it. As he worked, he adjusted the opacity of the shapes (using the Opacity slider near the top of the palette), so he could see the layers below more clearly. After he had filled the shapes with color, Kirkman Shift-selected them in the Layers palette and chose Shapes, Convert to Layer.

4 Shading individual layers. To paint on an individual layer, target it in the Layers palette. To create a nice grainy look (similar to colored pencil on kid-finish illustration board), Kirkman chose Basic Paper texture in the Paper Selector and added shading to the clothing using the Fine Spray variant of the Airbrushes. For a smoother look on the man's skin and eyes, he added strokes with the Digital Airbrush variant. Overlapping elements on the layers helped Kirkman create the cast shadows. For example, to paint the shadow under the fish's lips, he targeted the underlying body layer and then airbrushed the shadow directly on it.

5 Editing layer masks. Kirkman added and edited a layer mask on the layer he called "R piling" to achieve a transparent look. To achieve transparency—like Kirkman's—on your layer: Target the layer in the Layers palette, and then click the Create Layer Mask button at the bottom of the palette. Click on the new layer mask's thumbnail to target the mask. Next, choose black in the Colors palette, choose a soft Airbrush variant (such as the Digital Airbrush) and carefully paint into the mask to partially hide the layer. (See "Melting Text into Water" on page 244 for a more detailed description of this technique.)

6 Adding details, texture and an irregular edge. Kirkman added the pattern to the tie using Effects, Surface Control, Color Overlay, Using Paper to apply the Op texture (Painter IX application

> **NAMING AND FILLING SHAPES**
>
> To name and add a colored fill (or stroke) to a shape, with the Colors picker open (Window, Show Colors) double-click on the shape's name in the Layers palette. Rename the shape in the Set Shape Attributes dialog box and check the Fill (or Stroke) check box. With the Fill (or Stroke) color swatch active (outlined by a black and gold box), click in the Colors picker. (You can use the Color Sets palette instead of the Colors picker if you like.)

> **PRESERVING TRANSPARENCY**
>
> To constrain your painting to stay within the edge of the element on a layer, turn on Preserve Transparency in the Layers palette.

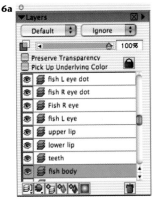

6a

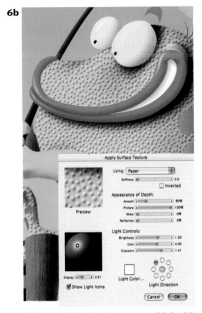

Kirkman targeted the "fish body" layer in the Layers palette before choosing Apply Surface Texture to add texture to the fish's body.

6b

Using Apply Surface Texture to add the 3D texture to the fish

6c

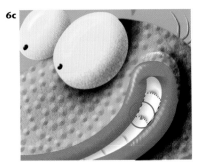

Adding dimension to the fish's teeth by airbrushing along a selection edge

folder, Extras, Paper Textures, Crazy Textures). To add details to the water, he used Color Overlay to apply a colored texture using Globs from Wild Textures2 (Painter IX application folder, Extras, Paper Textures), scaling it larger using the Scale slider on the Papers palette. To add more interest to the water, he added Effects, Focus, Glass Distortion, Using Paper with the Blobular texture from Molecular Textures (Painter IX application folder, Extras, Paper Textures).

Using Effects, Surface Control, Apply Surface Texture, Using Paper, he added a 3D texture to the fish with Random Bubbles (Molecular Textures). He used these approximate settings: Softness, 1.0; Amount, 50%; Shine, 0; leaving other settings at their default values.

The final embellishments he added were the man's mouth, the fish's teeth and the separation of the man's pant legs. To paint these details, Kirkman drew on his many years of experience as a traditional airbrush artist using a technique very similar to traditional airbrush friskets. Using the Pen tool, he drew a shape for each element and converted each shape to a selection by choosing Shapes, Convert to Selection. To save each selection as a mask in the Channels palette after he had converted it, he chose Select, Save Selection. When he wanted to use a selection as a frisket, he chose Select, Load Selection and then chose the appropriate mask from the Load From pop-up menu. When loaded, each active selection acted like a traditional airbrush frisket. For instance, to paint the fish's teeth, he selected the layer containing the teeth, loaded a selection and then airbrushed along the edges of the selection, letting the selection create the hard edge where he needed it. He let the spray from the Airbrush fade out across the selected area. This technique added more dimension and created a rounded, cushiony effect.

Finally, Kirkman created an irregular edge for the background. He used the Lasso to make a loose, freehand selection on the background canvas and turned the selected area into a layer. (Drag with the Lasso and click with the Layer Adjuster.) After the area was on its own layer, he reselected the canvas (click on the Canvas name in the Layers palette) and deleted the unneeded background (Ctrl/⌘-A, then Delete), leaving a white border area. Then he clicked on the layer and dragged it to the bottom of the layer hierarchy to serve as a background element, and he renamed it Sky. To give the sky layer a smooth edge, he added a layer mask (using the process described in step 5) and feathered the mask 3 pixels by targeting the layer in the Layers palette, then targeting the layer mask in the Channels palette, and choosing Feather from the palette's pull-down menu (accessed by clicking the triangle in the top-right corner of the Channels palette). After he had feathered the edge, he added a drop shadow based on the Sky layer by choosing Effects, Objects, Create Drop Shadow. To flatten the image, he dropped all layers (choose Drop All from the Layers palette's pull-down menu). 🖌

Painting on Layers

Overview *Make practice sketches; set up a reference layer and build a canvas "ground;" sculpt the forms of the head on a layer using tone and color; add transitional tone and detail; apply a canvas texture to the painted layer.*

RON KEMPKE

1

One of the "practice" digital charcoal sketches

2a

The Layers palette with the reference layer active and at a lower opacity

2b

The reference layer at low opacity (left), and the sketch on "canvas" made with the Captured Bristle variant of Acrylics (right)

YOU CAN USE PAINTER'S LAYERS, BRUSHES AND TEXTURES to create a realistic simulation of oil or acrylic paint. Ron Kempke painted *Portrait of Cindy* by painting on layers on top of a canvas "ground."

1 Assembling references and making practice sketches. Kempke clamped a reference photo to his monitor, so he could easily refer to it when he needed to. He prefers not to clone or to do too much tracing because drawing by hand using the stylus keeps his brushstrokes freer and more expressive. Carefully studying his reference photo, Kempke drew several charcoal sketches in Painter just as a "warm up," working until he had achieved a good likeness of his subject.

2 Setting up layers and a canvas "ground." Kempke began his painting much as a portrait painter might do. But instead of projecting his painting onto a working canvas, he used a 1200 x 1400-pixel scanned photo at reduced opacity in Painter. To set up your onscreen reference, open your scanned image and open the Layers palette (Window, Show Layers). To reduce the opacity of the photo, choose Select, All, and then Select, Float. This lifts the image to an image layer, leaving a white canvas underneath. By moving the Opacity slider near the top of the Layers palette, you can fade the reference photo.

Next, Kempke used the Raw Silk texture to add the look of canvas before he started to paint. To build a canvas "ground," target the Canvas in the Layers palette. Apply the Raw Silk paper texture

The shadow shapes are blocked in over the sketch.

The shadow and midtone shapes are more developed in this example.

The image with most of the transitional tones and details added

to the image as follows: Open the Paper Selector by clicking the top-left square in the group of six at the bottom of the Toolbox. Then find the Raw Silk texture in Painter 7 Textures (loaded from the Painter IX Application Folder, Extras, Paper Textures). Choose Effects, Surface Control, Apply Surface Texture, Using Paper. For a subtle canvas effect, reduce the Amount to approximately 20% and Shine to about 10% and leave the other settings at their defaults (Softness, 0; Picture, 100%; Reflection, 0; and Light Direction, 11:00).

Kempke created his painting on a layer above the reference so he could rework certain areas without disturbing the reference. (To add a new layer, click the New Layer button at the bottom of the Layers palette.) He planned to apply surface texture to the brush work on the layer when he finished it, using the settings above to match the texture on the Canvas. When the painting was finished, the final texture application would perfectly match the existing texture on the image canvas.

Kempke chose a neutral gray in the Colors picker and sketched using a modified version of the Captured Bristle variant of Acrylics. He mapped out the proportions of the head with perpendicular lines to locate the eyes, nose and mouth. He occasionally compared the proportions of his drawing with the reference photo on the layer below, toggling the visibility of the reference layer on and off as he worked by clicking the "eye" icon to the left of the layer name. After he was satisfied with the proportions, he deleted the reference layer by targeting it in the Layers palette and clicking the Delete button. (The photo clamped to his monitor was still available for reference if he needed it.)

3 Adding color and shadow. Kempke sculpted the solid form of the head with simplified shapes of the shadow colors using the Captured Bristle variant. He painted midtones, and then blocked in shadow colors in flat tones for the larger masses.

Next, he added transitional tones in the areas between light and shadow. He painted these in flat tones, also, resisting the temptation to blend them with the shadow colors. These transitional tones are among the most intense colors in the portrait.

4 Refining the portrait and adding texture. Kempke added the highlight areas in the face and hair, using broad strokes of color to loosely indicate the features. To bring the head forward by suggesting the space behind it, he added a medium-dark background. Then he added depth and sheen to the hair and loosely suggested the teeth. In areas where he felt there was too much contrast, he added transitional tones and softened edges using a low-opacity brush. (Move the Opacity slider, popped out from the Property Bar, to the left to reduce opacity.) Kempke also added brighter highlights to the eyes and nose. To complete the painting, he added "canvas" to the painted layer using the Apply Surface Texture process described in step 2.

Collage with Cloning and Brushes

Overview *Create a collage image from a variety of source photos; use point-to-point cloning with multiple brushes; paint portions of a source image on its own layer.*

1

The source photographs and scans

2a

Capturing the photograph of the lily pond to use as a paper texture

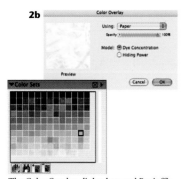

2b

The Color Overlay dialog box and Benioff's Custom Color Set

CAROL BENIOFF

FOR *WISH*, A NARRATIVE COLLAGE, Carol Benioff combined photographic elements by painting on layers using Cloners brushes and custom brushes that incorporate Clone Color.

1 Gathering elements. Benioff began by assembling digital photographs and scanned elements that touched on her childhood—her grandmother Nana at 18, the lily pond from the San Francisco Conservatory of Flowers near her childhood home and wishbones saved from family Thanksgiving dinners. After you have assembled your photos, open a new file (Benioff's measured 4 x 4 inches at 300 ppi). Save the image in RIFF format.

2 Capturing and applying a colored texture. Benioff wanted the lily pond image to be monochromatic, so that it would sit behind the other collage elements and help to unify the elements. To accomplish this, she captured the pond photo as a paper texture that she could use when applying a monochromatic color effect. Choose a photo that you want to use as a texture, and then use the Crop tool to crop a square area of the image. Choose Canvas, Resize to resize it to the same size as your working composite file. Next, select the entire photo image (Select, All). Click the Papers Selector button in the Toolbox, and then click the right triangle to open the pop-up menu and choose Capture Paper. Leave the Crossfade setting at the default of 16. Crossfade blurs the transition between the tiles of the paper texture. Name

2c

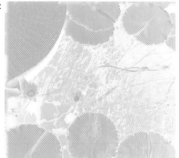

The captured paper texture applied as a Color Overlay to the image Canvas

3a

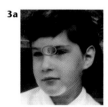

Starting point indicator for point-to-point cloning on the source file (left) and starting point indicator for point-to-point cloning on the target file (right)

3b

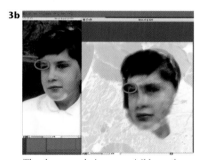

The clone crosshair cursor visible on the clone source file (left) and the brush cursor visible on the target file (right)

4

The Glazing Acrylic 20 brush transformed into a cloning brush by clicking on the Clone Color button (rubber stamp) in the Colors palette

your texture (Benioff named the paper texture *Lily Pond*). Select it from the list of papers in the Paper Selector. To apply the new paper texture to your image using transparent color, choose Effects, Surface Control, Color Overlay. From the Using menu choose Paper, leave Opacity at 100% and click the Dye Concentration button. (Benioff applied a blue color from her custom Color Set.) Then, to lift the image to a layer, choose Select, All and then chose Select, Float.

3 Using point-to-point cloning. Point-to point cloning is an intuitive way to use a brush to clone. With this technique, you select a starting point on your source file and on your target file. As you paint, with your brush on your target file, a crosshair cursor follows, pinpointing where you are painting from in your clone source file. First, create a new layer by clicking on the New Layer button in the Layers palette. Benioff planned to create a layer for each new element in the collage. To keep track of the layers, give each layer a distinct name. Double-click on the layer in the Layers palette to open Layers Attributes, where you can type in a new layer name. Next, Benioff opened a black-and-white scan of a portrait of herself that was taken when she was a child. To clone as Benioff did, select the Soft Cloner variant of Cloners in the Brush Selector Bar. Arrange the two images on your monitor so that both are visible, along with Painter's palettes. With the source image active (the black-and-white photo), press the Alt/Option key and click on a point in the source image. A green circle with a number 1 appears, indicating where Painter will start to clone information from this source image. Next, make the target image active by choosing it from the Window menu and clicking on the new layer to make it active. Holding down the Shift and the Alt/Option keys, click in the target file where you want to begin painting. A red circle with a number 1 appears, indicating the starting point. As you paint on the target file with the Soft Cloner brush, a crosshair cursor moves in sync on the source file. Benioff carefully watched the crosshair cursor to make sure that she picked up only the information she wanted from the source file. This allowed her to paint selectively from her clone source image to her target image *Wish*.

4 Changing an Acrylics brush to a cloning brush. Next, Benioff selected the Glazing Acrylic 20 variant of the Acrylics and changed it into a cloning brush. In the Colors palette, choose Clone Color by clicking on the rubber stamp button. With Clone Color enabled, the Colors picker will gray out. You can now use Clone Color (color from a clone source) with the Glazing Acrylic 20 brush. It's a good idea to save your new variant. Choose Save Variant from the pop-up menu on the Brush Selector Bar and then restore the Glazing Acrylic 20 to its original settings by choosing Restore Default Variant from the menu on the Brush Selector Bar.

Point-to-point cloning with the custom Glazing Acrylic Cloner brush

Point-to-point cloning with the Glazing Acrylic 20 brush and Soft Cloner brush

Point-to-point cloning with the Pencil Sketch Cloner brush

Targeting the wishbones layer to move it below all the other layers in the file

5 Cloning images. Now choose the new Glazing Acrylic Cloner brush in the Brush Selector Bar, establish the two cloning points, one from the source and one on the target image, and then paint into your target image. Benioff

USING ITERATIVE SAVE

The new Iterative Save feature in Painter IX adds a sequential number after the filename and is useful when saving a file in stages. (Choose, File, Iterative Save.)

used Glazing Acrylic Cloner to create light, sweeping strokes that followed the contours and shapes of the clone source photo. To bring out some of the detail from the clone source photograph, she used the Soft Cloner Brush, moving in a light circular motion. Then, she used the Iterative Save function (File, Iterative Save) to save the file in progression. After she completed painting from one clone source, she used the Iterative Save function, saving the file in sequential steps. She created 14 iterative saves.

When you have your first image painted into your working file, close the first clone source and open your second source image. Benioff opened her next source photo, Nana, a photo of her grandmother. Repeat the process in step 3 to add your new image. Use the same two cloning brushes, the Soft Cloner and the Glazing Acrylic Cloner, and the point-to-point cloning technique to softly paint from the source photograph. As you paint, follow the contours and shapes of the forms. Benioff created a new layer in the target file *Wish*. She made sure both the source photo file and the target file were visible on her screen, and that the new Nana layer was active. Then she painted to bring the second photo into her composition.

For the wishbones, Benioff created a new layer, which she named Wishbones. She opened her photograph of multiple wishbones on a painted background. This time, she chose the Pencil Sketch Cloner variant of the Cloners brushes. Using point-to-point cloning, Benioff carefully drew with short strokes to paint in one of the wishbones from the source file onto the new layer in her target file. Then, she switched to the Soft Cloner variant of the Cloners to add more detail from the wishbones photo.

6 Duplicating and arranging layers. Benioff envisioned the wishbones fading in and out of the two figures and the pond, so she added an additional wishbone image. To achieve this, she moved the wishbones layer underneath all the other layers of the image. Then, in the Layers palette, she selected the Wishbones layer and dragged it below the Pond layer. The wishbone image was now hidden by the pond image. To "see through" the pond image without changing its opacity, she changed the Composite Method of the Pond layer to Multiply in the Layers palette. Next, she selected the Layer Adjuster tool and with the Wishbone layer active, she repositioned it to overlap both of the figures. To create a second wishbone, Benioff duplicated the Wishbone layer (Layers, Duplicate Layer), and then she named the layer *Wishbones 2*. With

Changing the Composite Method of the pond layer to Multiply

6c

Detail of the image with the second wishbones layer in place

7a

Drawing the outline of the orchid with the Sharp Pastel Pencil Cloner (top) and adding detail with the Soft Cloner (bottom)

7b

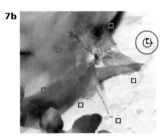

Rotating the orchid layer using the Free Transform feature

8

Point-to-point cloning using the Chalk Cloner variant of the Cloners

9

Two layers with the applied lighting effect

the Wishbones 2 layer active, she used the Layer Adjuster to reposition the second wishbone so that it overlapped the lower half of the woman's dress. Then, she enlarged the second wishbone image to 115%, using the Effects, Orientation, Scale dialog box.

7 Transforming layers. To paint in the orchid blossom, she opened the photograph that contained the orchid. She chose the Sharp Pastel Pencil variant of Pastels, enabled Clone Color on the Colors palette, and used it with the point-to-point cloning technique to draw the outline of one of the blossoms. To paint with more detail, she used the Soft Cloner.

To duplicate the orchid layer, Benioff repeated the same duplicating and arranging steps that she used for the layers in step 6. Then, she selected the Layer Adjuster to move the Orchid 1 layer under the ear of the girl. To make the orchid transparent, she set the opacity of the Orchid 1 layer to 90% in the Layers palette. Then, she duplicated the orchid layer (Layers, Layer, Duplicate). She named the duplicate layer Orchid 2 and selected Effects, Orientation, Free Transform, so that she could rotate and scale the image simultaneously.

The Free Transform function retains the quality of an image so that it does not degrade with the transformations. There are eight handles surrounding an image that is in the Free Transform mode. To rotate the image, press the Ctrl/⌘ key. To constrain the aspect ratio when scaling the image, press the Shift key as you click and drag on the corner handles. When Benioff was happy with the size and angle of the Orchid 2 layer, she fixed the changes by selecting Effects, Orientation, Commit Transform. Then, she used the Layer Adjuster to position the second orchid into place at the bottom portion of the women's dress.

8 Adding the blue flower. For the final layer, Benioff opened the photograph of a blue flower. She chose the Chalk Cloner (Cloners), which revealed the paper grain. For her paper texture, she selected Basic Paper from the Paper Selector. In the Wish image, she created a new layer and named it Blue Flower. With both the source photo and the target file visible, she used point-to-point cloning to draw in the blue flower. She painted with short, quick strokes and varied the brush size as she worked. If she picked up some of the photo background, she used an Eraser variant to clean up the edges. She used the Free Transform function to rotate and scale this final layer and then she moved the Blue Flower layer to the lower-right corner of her image.

9 Applying lighting for more depth. As a last step, Benioff used lighting to give her image more depth. She clicked on the Pond layer in the Layers palette and then chose Effects, Surface Control, Apply Lighting. In the Apply Lighting dialog box, she clicked on the Library button and loaded her custom lighting library. Then, she chose the Soft Globe light and clicked OK. She applied the same light to the Blue Flower layer to complete her image *Wish*. 🖌

Mixing Media on Layers

Overview *Scan a pencil sketch; make masks to constrain paint; lay in color with Airbrushes; paint transparent Watercolor glazes on layers; add final details.*

DELRO ROSCO

The scanned pencil drawing

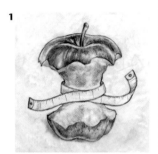

The apple masks in the Channels palette

The airbrushed color within the active selection for the apple

ILLUSTRATOR DELRO ROSCO WAS COMMISSIONED to create this book cover illustration for the *3 Apple-a-Day Plan*, published by Random House. Rosco's work has been honored by the Society of Illustrators of New York and Los Angeles, American Illustration, the National Watercolor Society, and *Print Magazine*.

Rosco built selections and masks to limit the paint, and then he airbrushed smooth paint. To add glazes and interesting paint texture, he painted diffused washes on Watercolor layers above the airbrushed paint. "The Watercolor layers make my work look more like my traditional wash and dry brush paintings, which are done using conventional watercolor on Arches hot press water-color paper with very fine sable brushes," says Rosco.

1 Sketching and scanning. The art director gave Rosco a pro-posed layout to use as a starting point for the illustration. Rosco began by sketching using traditional pencil on tissue paper. He scanned the sketch at 100%, at 350 ppi, saved it as a TIFF file and then opened the scanned drawing in Painter.

You can scan a sketch or create a drawing in Painter using the Pencils variants. When your drawing is complete, put it on a layer by choosing Select, All and then Select, Float. To keep your image organized, name the layer. Double-click its name in the Layers palette and when the Layer Attributes box appears, name the layer *Sketch*. So that he could use it as a guide while painting, Rosco lowered the opacity of the Sketch layer to about 30%.

2 Making selections and masks. Rosco used selections and masks to limit paint, just as he used friskets with conventional airbrush. Next, he built hand-drawn selections and masks for ele-ments in his image. Choose the Lasso tool (Toolbox) and use it to trace the outline of the drawing. When your selection marquee is complete, save it as a mask into the Channels palette (Select, Save

4a

Watercolor washes on the apple's center

4b

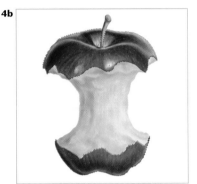

Textured Watercolor washes on the skin within the active selection

4c

The Watercolor skin layer selected in the Layers palette

5

The final details on the skin and stem

Selection). For detailed information about freehand selections see "Using Hand-Drawn Selections" on page 203. With the mask chosen in the Channels palette, Rosco used the Scratchboard tool (Pens) to refine the shape of the mask. He used the color white to erase from the mask and black to add to the mask. (See "Masks" on page 191 in the beginning of Chapter 5 for information about editing masks.) When he was satisfied with the mask, he named it *Apple Skin* and saved it. He repeated this process for various parts of the illustration.

> **RUNNING OUTSIDE**
>
> If the Wind Force is set high in the Water section of the Brush Controls (Window, Brush Controls, Show Water), a runny wash (painted with the Runny Wash Bristle, for instance) may creep outside a selection.

3 Airbrushing on layers. Rosco added a new layer to his image and then used Airbrushes to lay in base colors within selected areas. To make a new layer, click the New Layer button in the Layers palette. To load a selection based on your mask, choose Select, Load Selection and choose your mask. Using the Digital Airbrush variant of Airbrushes, lay in base colors, render the form and depth of your subject, and then save your image as a RIFF file.

4 Painting on Watercolor layers. When the airbrush layers were complete, Rosco built up more color, form and texture by using Watercolor brushes and layers. He moved the sketch to the top of the Layers palette and used the eye icon to toggle the sketch on as he worked. Load a selection for the area that you want to paint. To lay in soft, smooth washes, use the Wash Camel variant of Watercolor. Brush lightly, following the directions of the forms. For more textured brushstrokes, paint with the Diffuse Bristle, Dry Camel or Dry Bristle variants of Watercolor.

5 Adding final details. To paint over rough areas of color, add details and define areas, Rosco used the Opaque Round variant of Oils. As he worked, he varied its size and opacity using the sliders on the Property Bar.

When the details were complete, he saved his working image as a RIFF file to preserve the wet Watercolor paint and layers. Then, he used the Digital Airbrush to paint a cast shadow. First, he saved a copy of the image and dropped the layers. (Choose Drop All from the Layers palette menu.) Then, he used the outline mask described in step 2 to limit paint as he created the drop shadow. Choose Select, Load Selection to load a selection based on the outline mask. The Drawing Modes enable you to paint outside the selection and save the time of creating another mask. In the lower left of the image window, click the Drawing Mode icon and choose Draw Outside. Finally, for the tape measure, Rosco used the Text tool with the Curve Style option to set type on a path. Then, he converted the text to shapes and saved them as selections so that he would use them to limit paint.

Melting Text into Water

Overview *Use the Text tool to set type over a background; convert the text to selections; float two copies of the type, one to be used as a drop shadow; use feathering, Dye Concentration and a fill to add dimension to the type; add layer masks and paint on them to "melt" the bottoms of the layers.*

CHER THREINEN-PENDARVIS

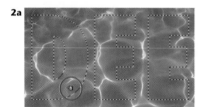

Converting the Text layer to a default layer

2a

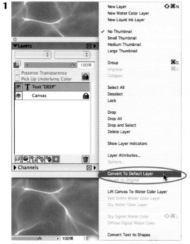

Alt/Option-clicking with the Layer Adjuster on the selection to make a layer

2b

The Layers palette after naming the layers

YOU CAN ACHIEVE A DRAMATIC TRANSLUCENT EFFECT using Painter's brushes to paint on a layer mask of a layer. In the image above, we used the Digital Airbrush variant (Airbrushes) on the lower part of two layers—the type and the feathered shadow behind it—to create the illusion of type melting into water. You can get a similar result using other backgrounds such as clouds, stone or wood.

1 Setting text and converting it to selections. Open an image to use as a background; our photo was 3 inches wide at 225 pixels per inch. Choose the Text tool and select a font and point size in the Property Bar. Procedures such as feathering can erode a thin font, so we chose a font with thick strokes—90-point Futura Extra Bold Condensed. Open the Layers palette (Window, Show Layers). With the Layers palette open, you'll be able to see the text layer appear there when you type. Click the Text tool in the image to place the cursor and begin typing.

To achieve the result in the above image, using the text outlines to float portions of the background, it's necessary to convert the text to a default layer, then to selections. With the Layer Adjuster tool chosen and the text layer targeted in the Layers palette, choose Convert to Default Layer from the pop-out menu on the right side of the Layers palette. Next, reduce the layer's opacity to 0% using the Opacity slider near the top of the Layers palette; the converted text layer will disappear from your image. Choose Drop and Select from the pop-out menu on the right side of the Layers palette; the type will reappear in your image as animated marquees.

To save your selection as a mask so you can use it later, choose Select, Save Selection. Open the Channels palette to see the new mask (named Alpha 1).

With the marquee still active (in preparation for making the soft shadow layer), choose Select, Feather; we used 15 pixels. Click OK. Now save this selection as a mask by choosing Select, Save Selection. This mask (named Alpha 2) will appear in the Channels palette.

2 Using selections to make layers. To make the two layers needed for this technique, begin with the active feathered shadow

3a

Selecting the text layer mask in the Channels palette

3b

Using Dye Concentration to lighten the text (left) and filling the Shadow layer with a dark blue (right)

3c

The Layers palette showing the Composite Method for the shadow layer set to Multiply

4

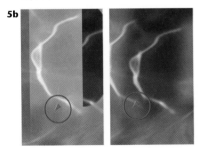

Skewing the shadow to add a look of depth

5a

The text layer mask is selected in the Layers palette.

5b

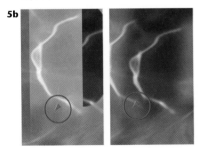

Using the Digital Airbrush variant on the text layer's mask (left) and the shadow layer's mask (with the text layer hidden) to reveal the underlying image

selection (if it's no longer active, you can load Alpha 2 by clicking the Load Channel as Selection button at the bottom of the Channels palette). Choose the Layer Adjuster tool, press the Alt/Option key and click on the active text selection to create Layer 1. (Holding the Alt/Option key makes a copy of the selected area, leaving the background intact.) Click on the Canvas name to deselect Layer 1. Now load the text selection (New Mask 1) by choosing Select, Load Selection; when it appears, Alt/Option-click on it with the Layer Adjuster tool. In the Layers palette, you'll see two items named Layer, followed by a number. Double-click on the Layer 2 name and rename it "text" in the Layer Attributes dialog box. Do the same for the Layer 1, naming it "shadow."

3 Distinguishing the layers. Next, you'll make the text layer stand out from the background. In the Layers palette, click once on the text layer to make it active. Now, change the color of the layer by choosing Effects, Surface Control, Dye Concentration, using Uniform Color and dragging the Maximum slider to 53%. Click OK.

To create a soft, saturated shadow, select the shadow layer in the Layers palette and enable Preserve Transparency (near the top of the palette). Using the Dropper tool, sample a dark color from your image and choose Effects, Fill, Current Color at 100% Opacity. Set the Composite Method of the layer to Multiply in the Layers palette.

4 Offsetting the shadow. Give a greater illusion of depth to the type by nudging the shadow up and to the right using the arrow keys on your keyboard. To make the type appear to stand at an angle to the background, as we did, skew the shadow: With the shadow layer selected, choose Effects, Orientation, Distort. Drag the top center handle of the bounding box down and to the right, check the Better box and click OK. There's no preview of this effect, so it may take a few tries to get the look you want.

5 Painting into the layer masks. To "melt" the lower portions of the letters into the water, you can add layer masks to both text and shadow layers and use a brush to partially erase the layer masks.

To add each layer mask, target the layer in the Layers palette and click the Create Layer Mask button at the bottom of the palette. Choose the Digital Airbrush variant of the Airbrushes. For more sensitivity, check to make sure the Opacity in the Property Bar is set to 9%. Choose black in the Colors palette. Now click the text layer's mask in the Layers palette to target the mask. A dark border will appear around the mask when it is selected. Brush along the bottom of the letters to make the lower part of the text layer disappear. If you need to restore part of the text, switch to white paint. Then complete the effect by targeting the shadow layer's mask in the Layers palette and brushing black along its bottom. You may find it easier to work on the shadow layer if you hide the text layer temporarily: In the Layers palette, click the text layer's eye icon to close it. When you're finished working on the shadow, click the text's eye icon open again.

■ Artist **Jan Smart** enjoys creating wildlife portraits. She created *Pelican* with the Digital Watercolor and Pens variants using several layers.

Smart began by taking a digital photo of the pelican on a wooden deck. So that she could trace the shapes, she opened the photo in Painter and made a clone of the photo by choosing File, Clone and deleted the contents of the clone image by selecting All (Ctrl/⌘-A) and pressing Backspace/Delete. She saved the clone image by choosing File, Save As, and gave it a unique name. Smart kept the original photo open and turned on Tracing Paper in the clone by pressing Ctrl/⌘-T.

Next, she chose French Watercolor Paper from the Paper Selector in the Toolbox. After adding a new layer to her file, she drew a sketch using the Thick n Thin Pen variant of Pens and a light brown color. When the drawing was complete, she set the Composite Method for the sketch layer to Multiply.

At this point, Smart toggled off Tracing Paper (Ctrl/⌘-T), but she kept her reference photograph on the screen next to her artwork so that she could refer to the colors in the photo. For the first washes of color, Smart added a new layer and set its Composite Method to Multiply. Then, she used the Simple Water, Soft Diffused Brush and Tapered Diffuse Water variants of Digital Watercolor to paint the feathers and body of the pelican. She applied thin glazes of subtle colors to give the feathers a rich look.

For the boardwalk, Smart added another new layer and set its Composite Method to Multiply. Then, she used the Soft Broad Brush to paint shades of pale greenish-gray. To create the grain pattern and the deep grooves between the boards, she used a small Thick n Thin Pen. To soften some of the lines, she used the New Simple Diffuser (Digital Watercolor).

So that she could edit the wet Digital Watercolor paint with Erasers variants, she chose Dry Digital Watercolor from the menu on the Layers palette. For the stains and whitening effects on the deck, she used the Gentle Bleach variant of the Erasers. To add the finishing touches to her pelican, Smart used the Gentle Bleach to paint the spikes of hair on his head, to lighten a few areas on the feathers, and to create more intense highlights.

For the varied shades of green and gray on the water, Smart added another new layer and then applied subtle color using the Wash Brush (Digital Watercolor). After the washes were laid in, she dried the Digital Watercolor, and then she used the Pointed Stump variant of Blenders to soften and smooth the paint. As a final touch, she used the Gentle Bleach to touch up areas on the bird's feathers.

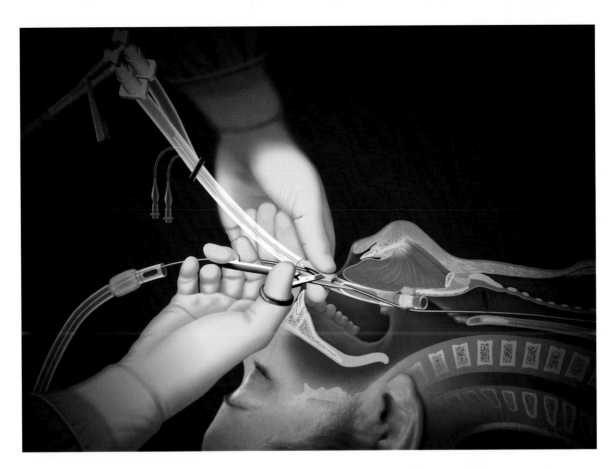

■ Medical illustrator **David Purnell** is the proprietor of the New York West Medical Illustration Studio.

Purnell began *Endotube* by rendering conventional pencil sketches, at the request of the surgeon, during a surgical procedure that involved a special technique for placing an endotracheal tube in the patient's bronchus. Using his pencil sketches for reference, Purnell drew a black-and-white illustration with pen and ink. Later, Purnell re-created the image in full color to use as a promotional piece. To begin, he scanned the black-and-white illustration, and then he used it as a template while building the color version of the image.

To begin the color illustration, Purnell photographed a lateral view of a human face, mouth open, with the head tilted to approximate the angle of the head and neck in the pen-and-ink illustration. He opened the photo image in Painter, chose Select, All, and then copied and pasted it into his working image as a layer above the black-and-white line drawing. Using Effects, Orientation, Free

Transform, he scaled the Head Photo layer to fit the line illustration. With the Head Photo layer selected, he clicked the Create Layer Mask button on the Layers palette to add a mask to the layer, and then he used the Digital Airbrush variant of Airbrushes and white paint to hide portions of the Head Photo layer. Then he hid the Head Photo layer by toggling the eye icon to the left of its name.

Next, Purnell used the Pen tool to draw shapes for every anatomical feature in the image, and then he filled them with flat colors. When he had created all of the shapes, he grouped them and moved the group to a level below the Head Photo layer. Then, he toggled the visibility of the Head Photo layer back on so that the line illustration, the shapes, and the photo layer were displayed. Next, he converted each shape to a layer by choosing Shapes, Convert to Layer.

Then, he painted using various brushes, including the Digital Airbrush and the Variable Spatter variant of Airbrushes. Purnell also used a custom tapered version of the Variable Splatter Airbrush to paint

the texture of the bone cross-sections (cancellous bone). After he was satisfied with the splatter on the bone, he used the Distorto variant of Distortion to gently push and pull areas of the splatter to make it appear more natural. To add three-dimensional highlights and shadows to the bone, he used Effects, Surface Control, Apply Surface Texture, Using Image Luminance, with subtle settings.

As a last step, Purnell enhanced the lighting in his image. He created a new layer and set it to the Gel Composite Method in the Layers palette. Then, he created a dark-to-light effect by using the Effects, Fill command to apply a Two-Point circular gradient fill to the layer. He chose black as the Main Color and White as the Additional Color in the Colors palette. Then, he opened the Gradients palette (Window, Library palettes, Show Gradients) and clicked the Circular Gradient button, which made the gradient white in the center and black on the edges. The Gel Composite Method made the white on the layer appear transparent, so the gradient fill appeared as a translucent gradient from black to clear over the entire image.

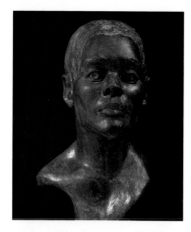

■ A beautiful terra cotta sculpture provided inspiration for *Woman of Colors* by artist **Joyce Ryan**. The image is a collage that incorporates a photograph of the sculpture with painted brush work, textures and special effects. Ryan began by photographing a life-sized sculpture that she had modeled in terra cotta clay. The sculpture had been fired, and a patina had been applied for a metallic finish.

Ryan likes using experimental color for emotional impact. She created a new file in Painter and drew rough sketches of the sculpture, playing with lines and then combining the drawings with textures. To build rich texture on the painting, she used the versatile Apply Surface Texture feature. She likes to create custom textures using Painter's Papers and Patterns functions. Ryan built complex textures and then applied them to layers in her composite file. (For information about creating and applying custom paper textures, see "Applying Paper Textures" on page 117 in Chapter 3.)

To add a mysterious mood to her painting, she chose Effects, Surface Control, Apply Lighting and applied a custom lighting effect.

When she was happy with her painting, she opened the photograph of the sculpture. With her painting image active, she added a new layer. Then, she chose File, Clone Source and defined the sculpture photo as the Clone Source. Using Cloning brushes (including the Soft Cloner), she painted the photo image onto the new layer in her painting. To complete her image, Ryan used a variety of brushes to bring out the features. Finally, to enhance the depth of the image, she added a few accents by drawing over the painting with small brushes.

■ For more than 16 years, artist **Delro Rosco** has created illustrations for product packaging and print advertising. His work has been honored by the Society of Illustrators of New York and Los Angeles, *American Illustration*, the National Watercolor Society and *Print Magazine*.

Rosco created *Olive Grove*, a Tuscan hillside scene as feature art on the packaging for a new line of olive oil by Mazola. The goal of this illustration was to portray an olive tree basking in the warm glow of a hillside town in Tuscany. Rosco began by drawing several sketches of the composition using conventional pencil on tissue paper.

When the final design was approved by the client, he scanned the sketch into Photoshop and saved it as a TIFF file. Opening the sketch in Painter, Rosco put the sketch on a layer by choosing Select, All and then Select, Float. He lowered the opacity for the sketch layer using the slider on the Layers palette. Then, he laid in base colors using the Digital Airbrush variant of Airbrushes. To create more depth and interest, he varied the opacity of the airbrush as he worked, using the Opacity slider in the Property Bar.

When the general areas of color were established, Rosco used Painter's Watercolor layers and brushes to paint glazes and to build up natural-media textures that would enhance the scene. When

creating the groves of olive trees, Rosco found the copying, pasting and layer features helpful. For instance, he painted one small tree and then selected it, copied it and pasted it back into the image as a new layer. He positioned the layer and dropped it by choosing Drop from the Layers palette menu. Then, he added more paint to blend the tree with the painting.

Rosco added final details to the painting using the Opaque Round variant of Oils, again varying the opacity to simulate transparent and opaque painting with conventional watercolor and gouache. The client was thrilled with the final illustration and requested the artist to sign limited edition prints.

■ Artist **Michela Del Degan** creates illustrations for educational books and multimedia projects, and she exhibits fine art work.

Africa and Life is a series of six images; the first image in the series is shown here. The works were inspired by a story that takes place in Africa. In the story, there are three parallel situations: the growth of a tree from a small seed, the growth of love, which brings to life a new being, and the attraction between the sun and the moon. Four main elements—Earth, Wind, Fire and Water—are important in the story. Del Degan began the images using traditional materials. She painted with conventional acrylic on canvas using thick white paint and she chose a piece of watercolor paper and painted bright-colored washes over the background and figures. To define the elements, she used a dark pencil to draw an outline rendering for each composition. Next, she scanned the canvas and the watercolor and pencil studies using a flatbed scanner and saved each scan as a TIFF file. Working in Painter, she opened the scan of the acrylic on canvas and each scanned watercolor and then assembled the pieces as layers in six separate files. To combine the acrylic brush work with the watercolor images, she used Multiply Composite Method in the Layers palette, and then she dropped the layers by choosing Drop All from the Layers palette menu. She increased the saturation of the image using the Effects, Tonal Control, Adjust Colors dialog box. She also bumped up the luminosity by using Image Luminance in the Adjust Color dialog box. Then, Del Degan strengthened the outline drawings using the Soft Charcoal. To retouch areas of the scanned art, she sampled color from the image and used the Soft Charcoal to paint color over the areas. To add a rough paper texture to areas of her images, she used the Grain Emboss variant of Impasto. Finally, to complete the works, she touched up the black outlines using a small Soft Charcoal variant.

■ *The Green Room* was created by artist **Donal Jolley** as a life drawing exercise. Jolley began the painting by drawing sketches from life using conventional soft leads on paper. He also shot a photograph to use for reference. Later, back at his studio, Jolley used his sketches and photo for reference. He opened the photo and cloned it by choosing File, Quick Clone to create a clone of the image, deleted the contents of the clone image and enabled Tracing Paper.

Jolley saved the clone image by choosing File, Save As and renamed the file *Green Room*. He kept the original photo open. Next, Jolley added a new layer, on which he would rough in the composition. He

sketched in color on the layer using the Square Chalk variant of Chalk, varying the size and opacity as he worked. To smooth areas, he used the Just Add Water variant of Blenders.

When the figure and room were blocked in, Jolley toggled off Tracing Paper (Ctrl/ ⌘-T). He arranged his reference photo next to his painting on the screen so that he could refer to it while he developed the values of the forms on the figure and drapery.

Next, Jolley added a new layer to his image and set its Composite Method to Multiply in the Layers palette. The Multiply method allowed him to create rich depth in the shadows. As he painted, he

used several brushes, including the Round Camelhair and Smeary Round variants of Oils, and he varied their size and opacity as he worked.

When the basic composition was complete, Jolley added another new layer (leaving this one set at the Default Composite Method), and he used low-opacity brushes to paint glazes over the entire image to brighten color and add more contrast and texture. To finish, he added a few opaque brushstrokes to the figure and the bench with the Smeary Round variants of Oils. Then, he chose the Square Chalk, enabled Clone Color in the Colors palette and then blended and refined a few areas.

■ *Squirrel Whistle* was created by artist **Chet Phillips** for *Say Goodnight to Illiteracy,* a compilation of bedtime stories sponsored by Half Price Books. Phillips began by making a stylized drawing using the Scratchboard Tool variant of Pens. Then, he floated the entire scratchboard drawing to a layer by choosing Select, All and clicking inside the active selection with the Layer Adjuster tool. Before deselecting the layer, he set the Composite Method to Gel in the Layers palette.

Next, Phillips selected the Canvas in the Layers palette and used the Airbrushes, Chalk and Pastels brushes in varying sizes to color the background. He brushed textured strokes onto the noses of the foreground squirrels using light cream colors with the Artist Pastel Chalk variant of Pastels. Then, he painted the fur using grainy strokes of varied browns.

For the acorn wallpaper, Phillips began by creating a separate illustration of an acorn, and then he copied and pasted the acorn into his working illustration. He created the repeat effect by pressing Alt/Option and clicking on the layer with the Layer Adjuster to create copies. Then, he used the Layer Adjuster to position the acorn images. When he had settled on the position, he grouped the acorn layers and reduced the opacity of the group to 50% to integrate the wallpaper into the blue wall.

Next, Phillips created an atmospheric feeling that would separate the foreground group of squirrels from the background. He added a new layer and made a soft-edged selection of the background area, and then he airbrushed white into both the black-and-white drawing and the color on the Canvas to fade them into the background.

When the coloring was complete, Phillips merged the layers by clicking on the black-and-white drawing layer's name in the Layers palette and choosing Drop from the pop-out menu on the right side of the Layers palette. To see more of Chet Phillips's work, turn to "Coloring a Woodcut" in Chapter 2.

■ Artist **Michael Bast** creates illustrations for commercial products and packaging.

To begin *Chipotle Salsa,* Bast assembled elements to use for reference. He sketched the food items conventionally using pencils and paper, and then he scanned the drawing. Bast created selections, masks and vector shapes to make his work easier. Working over his drawing, he created selections for the elements in his illustration, such as the chili peppers, tomatoes and wood. As he built each selection, he saved it as a mask in the Channels palette by choosing Select,

Save Selection. (For detailed information about working with selections and masks, see Chapter 5.)

To paint the illustration, Bast began by using the New Simple Water variant of Digital Watercolor to lay in colored washes within selected areas. Using a process similar to glazing in conventional watercolor, he painted washes of color and then dried them by choosing Dry Digital Watercolor from the Layers palette menu. Then he added more color with the New Simple Water brush. (Read more about Digital Watercolor on pages 90–93.)

When Bast wanted to pull out color from an area of wet paint, he used the Gentle Wet Eraser variant of Digital Watercolor. To add final opaque brush work to the image, he used the Variable Flat variant of Oils. For finer details to areas (such as the tomato seeds and detail on the lime), he used the Detail Opaque variant of Gouache. Finally, to paint the speckled texture on the wood, he loaded a selection for the area and then used the Pepper Spray variant of the Airbrushes.

■ **Bill Hall** has completed paintings for sporting events that include the Special Olympics, the Cleveland Grand Prix and the Virginia Slims Master's Tourney. Prior to working in Painter, Hall created his illustrations with conventional oil paint. Painter's brushes and other natural media tools allow Hall to successfully re-create his conventional oil painting style.

Hall created *Nascar* for the Texas Motor Speedway in Fort Worth, Texas. To begin the image, he took reference photos of the car. Later, back at his studio, he opened a new file in Painter and clicked the New Layer button on the Layers palette to add a new transparent layer. He referred to the photographs as he sketched with the Pencils variants. When he was satisfied with the drawing, he

added a new layer directly below the pencil drawing so that the pencil drawing would still be visible when he added colored paint. Next, he used the Lasso tool to make loose, freehand selections for elements in his drawing, and then he used the Effects, Fill, Fill with Current Color command to quickly fill each selection with a flat mid-tone color.

For the modeling of the forms, Hall added another new layer and positioned it above the Flat Color layer and below the Pencil layer. Working on the new layer, he used the Loaded Palette Knife variant of Palette Knives to model the forms, varying the size and opacity of the brush as he worked. When he had the modeling as he liked it, he painted speed blurs on the car. He opened the

Color Variability section of the Brush Controls (Window, Brush Controls, Color Variability) and adjusted the Value slider to increase the streaky quality of the Loaded Palette Knife. So that he could pull up color from the layer below, he enabled Pick Up Underlying Color in the Layers palette. As he worked, he varied the opacity of the brush to achieve the color blending that he desired.

To emphasize the horizontal movement of the car, Hall painted textured, transparent washes. He added a new layer, and he positioned it above the modeling layer and below the pencil sketch. After choosing a canvas texture in the Paper Selector, he used grainy Digital Watercolor brushes to paint textured, horizontal strokes.

■ For the dynamic illustration **Women's Soccer**, **Bill Hall** used Painter's brushes and Palette Knives to paint exciting color and dramatic motion that captured the action of the game. Hall created the image for a mural at a soccer park in Irving, Texas.

Hall began by taking photographs to use for reference. To design the composition, he opened a new file, added a transparent layer to his image and then sketched directly in Painter using Pencils variants. When the drawing was complete, he created a new layer below the pencil drawing so that he could view the pencil as he added colored paint. Next, he made hand-drawn selections with the Lasso tool, and then he filled each selection on the layer with a flat mid-tone color by

choosing Effects, Fill, Fill with Current Color (Ctrl/⌘-F).

Next, Hall added another new layer, and he positioned this layer below the Pencil layer and above the Flat Color layer. So that he could pull color from the Flat Color layer below, he enabled Pick Up Underlying Color in the Layers palette. Working on the layer, he used the Loaded Palette Knife variant of Palette Knives to model the forms. Hall painted brushstrokes that followed the forms and the direction of the motion that he wanted to express. To blend and pull paint without adding new color, he used the Palette Knife variant of Palette Knives.

When he was satisfied with the modeling, Hall added a new layer and painted blurs on the players to show movement and

speed. He also smudged paint in a few areas of the background. Using a method similar to the one he used for *Nascar*, he adjusted the Value slider in the Color Variability section of Brush Controls to increase the streaky quality of the Loaded Palette Knife. As he worked, he varied the size and opacity of the brush using the sliders in the Property Bar.

When Hall was satisfied with the way the painting looked, he selected the Pencil layer and used an Eraser variant to erase lines that were not needed, and he used a small Palette Knife to subtly blend other lines into the colored paint.

■ **Mike Reed** takes an approach to digital illustration that avoids the slick look sometimes seen in art created on the computer. To re-create the traditional look of pastel and paint on a richly textured surface, in *Dan* (above) and *Freshman* (opposite), Reed sensitively layered textured color with the Chalk variants on top of a captured paint texture and the Wood Shavings paper texture (loaded from Wow! Textures on the *Painter IX Wow!* CD-ROM).

Dan is an illustration for an upcoming children's book called *Cowboy Camp,* for Sterling Publishing. To begin the illustration, Reed painted using acrylic paint on illustration board, and then he scanned the painting and opened it in Painter.

Reed also built a richly textured surface. He painted thick acrylic paint on another illustration board, and then he scanned it. He captured the scan as a paper texture by selecting it (Select, All), and then clicking the Paper Selector (Toolbox) and choosing Capture Paper from the pop-up menu on the right side of the paper list menu.

To smooth the original paint texture while retaining the interesting surface, Reed applied rich layers of color using the Square Chalk variant of Chalk on a layer, over the captured paper. Reed found the captured paper to be best for broader strokes, but when he wanted to paint precise details, he switched to the Wood Shavings paper.

When the underpainting was complete, Reed added a new layer for the shadows and then set its Composite Method to Gel in the Layers palette. Using the Square Chalk, he built up rich tones in the shadows. Next, he added another new layer and set it to Gel, and then he glazed the edges of the painting and added more saturation and tonal complexity. Finally, Reed switched to the Wood Shavings paper and applied highlights and a few brightly colored accents with the Square Chalk.

■ **Mike Reed** created *Freshmen* for the School of Visual Arts at Saint Paul, Minnesota. Using a pen with a flexible quill, Reed painted washes of thinned India ink on 140 LB Arches cold press watercolor paper. When the drawing was complete, he scanned it. Then, he used the Magic Wand to select the white areas in the drawing, inverted the selection, and saved it as a mask in the Channels palette.

Next, Reed put the entire drawing on a layer (Select, Float) and set the layer Composite Method to Gel in the Layers palette. He loaded the saved selection and then, using flat color, he colored areas of the Canvas layer that showed through the Gel layer. The selection

marquee was so complex that it obscured the image, so he chose Select, Hide Marquee. As he worked, he toggled between painting inside and outside the selection using the Drawing Modes at the lower left of the Painter image window. Next, he made a copy of the Gel layer and then used Effects, Tonal Control, Brightness/Contrast to increase the contrast, which left only a dense black line drawing with very few grays remaining in the copy. He toggled the layer visibility icon (the eye) off to make the copied layer invisible and returned to working on the other layers. Reed selectively painted out some of the grays on the Gel layer so that more of the color on the Canvas would show through.

To apply interesting texture to the Canvas, Reed used Effects, Surface Control, Dye Concentration, Using Paper with Woodshavings paper texture. Then, he washed out areas of the color on the Canvas using the Dodge Variant of the Photo brush. Then, he darkened a few edges of the color areas using the Burn variant of the Photo brush. This gave the painted surface a remarkable resemblance to conventional watercolor. He continued to remove gray and black from the Gel layer until he was pleased with the color values. As a last step, Reed added a new layer and then painted details of opaque color using the Square Chalk variant of Chalk over the Woodshavings paper.

ENHANCING
PHOTOS,
MONTAGE
AND COLLAGE

Michael Campbell created Frances with Hat. *See more of Campbell's work in "Creating a Photo-Painting" on page 274 and in the gallery at the end of this chapter.*

INTRODUCTION

ALTHOUGH PAINTER BEGAN as a painting program, the features that have been added over the years have turned it into a powerful image processor as well. Many tools are designed *just* for photographers— for instance, dynamic layers that allow you to adjust brightness and contrast, perform posterization, apply glass distortion effects and more! (For the basics of how to work with dynamic layers such as Glass Distortion, turn to page 262.) Painter boasts color reduction features that are useful for working with photographs: *woodcut* and *distress*. (See "Creating a Woodcut from a Photo" on page 280 and "Distressing a Photo" on page 277). Painter also includes brush variants specifically designed for photographers, such as the Scratch Remover and Saturation Add brushes found in the Photo brush category in the Brush Selector Bar. And, of course, when it comes to achieving painterly effects with photographs, Painter has no peer. If you're a photographer, a photo-illustrator or a designer who works with photos and you want to get the most out of Painter, you'll want to pay attention to the following areas of the program.

The Effects menu. Most of Painter's image-altering special effects can be found in the Effects menu. The features under the subheads Tonal Control, Surface Control and Focus are loaded with creative promise for the adventurous photographer.

Selections and masks. To alter only a portion of an image, you'll need to become acquainted with Painter's shapes and its selection and masking capabilities. If you're not familiar with the Pen and Lasso tools, turn to "Working with Bézier Paths and Selections" and "Working with Hand-Drawn Selections" in Chapter 5.

Painter's powerful automatic masking features—located in the Channels palette—give you a big jump on the tedious process of creating masks to isolate parts of your image. And a bonus: All of

To enhance this portrait, we began by painting a mask to isolate the dancers. To create a shallow depth of field, we used Effects, Tonal Control, Adjust Colors to desaturate the background and Effects, Focus, Soften to blur it.

PHOTO: CORBIS IMAGES

PHOTO: CHER THREINEN-PENDARVIS

Equalize

Black and White Points

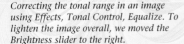

Black 95.6%   White 3.1%

Brightness ───────────────●── 70.2%

☑ Apply to Entire Image

Cancel   OK

Correcting the tonal range in an image using Effects, Tonal Control, Equalize. To lighten the image overall, we moved the Brightness slider to the right.

Painter's brushes except Watercolor and Liquid Ink and the Plug-in method brushes (such as the Add Grain variant of the Photo brush) can be used to paint directly on a mask. For a detailed description of combining Painter's automatic and painterly masks, turn to "Making a Color Mask," in Chapter 5.

Layers. Chapter 6 gave you an overall look at techniques using layers; this chapter focuses on using layers and masks for photo-compositing and other photo effects—for example, in "Simulating Motion," "Selective Coloring" and "Creating a Montage Using Masks and Layers," later in the chapter.

Dynamic layers. Painter offers dynamic layers that are useful for making adjustments to images. They are: Brightness and Contrast, Equalize, and Posterize. To find these tools, access the Dynamic Plug-ins pop-up menu by clicking the plug icon at the bottom of the Layers palette. Several of the techniques described later in this chapter use dynamic layers. To read more about dynamic layers and how they relate to other elements in Painter, turn to the beginning of Chapter 6.

Cloning. A very powerful and versatile feature, cloning (File, Clone) lets you make multiple copies of an image, alter each copy and then recombine them in various ways while preserving access to the original. Several of the techniques described in this chapter use this or another kind of cloning method.

IMAGE-PROCESSING BASICS

With its strong focus on *creative* image manipulation, Painter has left some *production*-oriented tasks such as color-correcting CMYK images to Adobe Photoshop. But there's no need to move an image from Painter to Photoshop to perform basic image-processing tasks such as sharpening and adjusting brightness and contrast, because Painter has tools that are similar to many of Photoshop's.

Equalizing. Choosing Effects, Tonal Control, Equalize (Ctrl/⌘-E) produces a dialog box with a histogram similar to Photoshop's Levels dialog, which allows you to adjust the tonal range in an image—the difference is that in Painter the image is automatically equalized (an effect similar to clicking on the Auto button in Photoshop's Levels). Move the triangular sliders toward the ends of the histogram to decrease the effect.

Painter also features an Equalize dynamic layer that operates like Effects, Tonal Control, Equalize, but on a copy of your image so you can easily try out different tonal adjustments. To make an Equalize layer, open an image and choose Equalize from the Dynamic Plug-ins pop-up menu at the bottom of the Layers palette. Choose Equalize to generate the dynamic layer. When the Equalize dialog box appears, set the controls as you would for Effects, Tonal Control, Equalize. Using an Equalize dynamic layer you can preview as many changes as you like: Click the Reset button to return your image to its original condition and then apply a new correction.

PHOTO: CORBIS IMAGES

Using a feather setting of 15 pixels, we created a textured edge for this 500-pixel-wide photo. (To make a soft-edged vignette around an image, turn to page 188 in Chapter 5.)

To create a vignette with a textured edge, begin by making a selection with the Oval Selection tool. Use the Selection Adjuster tool to position and scale the selection. Next, apply a feather (Select, Feather). Save the selection (Select, Save Selection). Now for the textured edge: In the Channels palette, select the mask, open its eye icon and close the RGB-Canvas eye icon to view the mask in black-and-white. Select a rough paper texture in the Paper Selector (such as French Watercolor), and choose Effects, Surface Control, Express Texture. Adjust the sliders to confine the texture to the soft edge. Click OK. In the Channels palette, click the channel eye icon shut and select RGB. Load the selection (Select, Load Selection). Next, reverse the selection (to select the area outside the oval) by choosing Select, Invert. To clear the background, press the Backspace/Delete key.

Adjusting brightness and contrast. Painter offers two ways to change image brightness and contrast. The first—Effects, Tonal Control, Brightness/Contrast—applies a correction directly to an open image or selection. But if you'd like to preview several Brightness and Contrast options, consider making a Brightness-and-Contrast dynamic layer. Click the plug icon at the bottom of the Layers palette to access the Dynamic Plug-ins menu and select Brightness and Contrast. When the Brightness-and-Contrast dialog box appears, continue to adjust the settings as you preview the corrections in your image. To read more about a Brightness-and-Contrast dynamic layer, see "Making a Selective Correction" on page 268.

Stripping color from an image. There are several ways to turn a color image into a grayscale one in Painter. The quickest way is to desaturate the image using the Adjust Color dialog box. Choose Effects, Tonal Control, Adjust Colors and drag the Saturation slider all the way to the left.

Changing color. While you're using the Adjust Color dialog box, experiment with the Hue Shift slider to change the hue of all of the colors in an image (or a layer or selection). You can get greater control in altering specific colors (turning blue eyes green, for instance) by using Effects, Tonal Control, Adjust Selected Colors. Click in the image to select a color; then drag the Hue Shift, Saturation and Value sliders at the bottom of the dialog box to make the changes. Fine-tune your color choice and the softness of its edge with the various Extents and Feather sliders.

To repair a white scratch on this photo we used a two-step process, beginning with Painter's useful Scratch Remover brush (located in the Photo category, in the Brush Selector Bar). Open a photo you'd like to repair, choose the Scratch Remover variant and for the best results, use a small brush size (we used a 1.7-pixel brush on this 350-pixel-wide image) and a low Opacity setting in the Property Bar (we used 9%). Zoom in to a magnification where you can see the scratch in detail, and carefully paint to blend the scratch into the image. This first step is usually sufficient for images with even color. But the sky in our image was graduated and required more repair. Next, we used

PHOTO: CORBIS IMAGES

a Soft Cloner variant of the Cloners with a small brush size and a very low Opacity, set in the Property Bar. Alt/Option-click to set the clone source to a point near the repair; then gently paint over the repaired area to bring back appropriate colors.

The scratched image (left) and the repaired image (right)

Using the Saturation Add brush from the Photo brush library to "pop" the color on the red raincoat, umbrella and reflection

PHOTO: CORBIS IMAGES

We applied Fine Hard Grain (chosen from the Papers Selector near the bottom of the Toolbox) to this photo with Effects, Surface Control, Dye Concentration Using Paper with the Maximum slider set to 200%.

PHOTO: CORBIS IMAGES

To "age" this photo, we painted with the Add Grain variant of the Photo brush using the Dry Cracks texture for a crackled look.

PHOTO: CORBIS IMAGES

The image above was sharpened to produce the result on the right using these settings: Amount, 2.15; Highlight, 90%; Shadow, 80%. A larger image can accept a higher Amount setting.

PHOTO: CORBIS IMAGES

Painting saturation with brushes. To "pop" the color in a specific area, use Painter's Saturation Add brush, located in the Photo brush category in the Brushes palette. For a more subtle look, lower the Opacity to about 10%.

Adding film grain. Photoshop's Noise filter is a good way to emulate film grain. To get a similar effect in Painter, open the Papers palette by choosing Window, Show Papers and choose an even-textured Paper grain, like Basic Paper or Fine Hard Grain. Next, choose Effects, Surface Control, Dye Concentration, Using Paper. Scale the texture in the Papers palette until the grain in the Preview window of the Adjust Dye Concentration dialog box is barely visible—try 50% as a starting point. Try minor adjustments to the Maximum and Minimum sliders.

Adding grain with a brush. Painter offers an exciting pressure-sensitive brush—the Add Grain Brush—that allows you to paint grain onto your images. To begin, choose the Photo brushes icon in the Brush Selector and select the Add Grain variant. Choose a texture in the Paper Selector, scale it if necessary and brush lightly onto your image. For a more subtle effect, reduce the Opacity of the brush in the Property Bar. The Grain Emboss variant of Impasto is also useful for adding a textured, embossed look to an image.

Creating a shallow depth of field. By softening the background of an image, you can simulate the shallow depth of field that you'd get by setting your camera at a low *f*-stop. Select the area you want to soften and feather the selection by choosing Select, Feather to avoid an artificial-looking edge. Then choose Effects, Focus, Soften.

Smearing, smudging and blurring. To smoothly smear pixels in the image, choose the Just Add Water variant of Blenders in the Brush Selector; vary Opacity in the Property Bar between 70% and 100%. To smudge the image, while bringing out the texture chosen in the Paper Selector, choose the Smudge variant of Blenders. For a "wet oil" effect, try the Distorto variant of Distortion. To softly blur an area of the image, use the Blur variant of the Photo brush set to a low Opacity (about 20%).

Sharpening. Painter's Sharpen feature (Effect, Focus, Sharpen) gives you control equivalent to unsharp masking on a drum scanner. (Unsharp masking sharpens the edges of elements in an image.) Use it to give definition to a selected area of interest, or to an entire image as a final step in preparing for output. To sharpen an area in an image using a brush, choose the Sharpen variant of the Photo brush. This brush puts sharpening (very similar to the Effects, Focus, Sharpen command) on the tip of a brush.

Retouching. The Straight Cloner and Soft Cloner variants of the Cloners brush work like Photoshop's Clone Stamp tool (with the Aligned function turned on) to reproduce imagery; use the Alt/Option key as you would Photoshop's Alt/Option key to sample

To add a mysterious gold spotlight to this woman's portrait, we used Effects, Surface Control, Apply Lighting. We modified the Center Spot by changing the Light Color from white to gold. To make the spotlight softer, we decreased the Exposure from 1.00 to .85.

an area (even in another image); then reproduce that image (centered at the point of sampling) wherever you paint. The Straight Cloner variant reproduces imagery without changing it; to clone imagery with a soft edge and low opacity (like an Airbrush) use the Soft Cloner.

ADVANCED TECHNIQUES

It often takes a lot of time and trial-and-error to get cool effects in-camera or in the darkroom. Some third-party plug-in filters do an adequate job of replicating these effects, but Painter gives you more control than you can get with filters alone.

Here's a short guide for using Painter to re-create traditional photographic techniques, starting with simpler, in-camera ones and progressing to more complex darkroom procedures.

Motion blur. You can use the camera to blur a moving subject by using a slower shutter speed or jittering (shaking) your hands while you hold the camera, or you can blur the background by panning with the subject. (See "Simulating Motion" on page 266 to read about a versatile motion-blur technique that involves using an additional layer.)

To create the look of "camera jitter," just as if you had moved the camera while taking a picture, choose Effects, Focus, Camera Motion Blur. When the dialog box appears, drag in the image (not the Preview) to specify the camera's direction and distance of movement. Dragging farther in the image will create a wider blur. To move the origin of the movement along the path of motion, adjust the Bias slider.

Lens filters and special film. To re-create in-camera tinting effects achieved with special films or colored filters, use Effects, Surface Control, Color Overlay. If you want to mimic the effect of a graduated or spot lens attachment (partially colored filters), choose a gradation and fill your image (Effects, Fill) with the gradation at a reduced opacity. (You may need to add contrast to your image afterwards with Effects, Tonal Control, Equalize.)

To get the effect of a line conversion, a straight-line screen was applied to a photo with Effects, Surface Control, Express Texture Using Paper and a Line texture set to an angle of 40. (For directions for setting up a Line texture, see Line Screen on the next page.)

Shooting through glass. With Painter's Glass Distortion effect or Glass Distortion dynamic layer you can superimpose glass relief effects (using a paper texture or any other image) on your photo. A small amount of this feature adds texture to an image; larger amounts can make an image unrecognizable! To apply the effect directly to your image choose Effects, Focus, Glass Distortion. To make a Glass Distortion dynamic layer for your image, click the plug icon at the bottom of the Layers palette to open the pop-up menu, and then choose Glass Distortion. (See Phil Howe's work with Glass Distortion in the gallery at the end of Chapter 8.)

Lighting effects. Use Painter's Apply Lighting feature (under Effects, Surface Control) to add subtle or dramatic lighting to a scene.

For this graphic effect, we applied Painter's Woodcut feature to a photo. See "Creating a Woodcut from a Photo" on page 280 for a step-by-step demonstration of a similar technique.

We posterized this Craig McClain photo using a custom Color Set of "desert" colors and the Effects, Tonal Control, Posterize Using Color Set command.

The original photo of a kelp frond had strong contrast, contributing good detail for this embossed image.

Multiple exposures. Whether created in camera (by underexposing and shooting twice before advancing the film) or in the darkroom (by "sandwiching" negatives or exposing two images on a single sheet of paper), it's easy to reproduce the effect of multiple exposures by using layers or clones in Painter.

Solarization. Painter's Express Texture (Effects, Surface Control) command is a great way to re-create darkroom solarization. Read about a Painter version of a "custom" solarization on page 278.

Line screen. Instead of developing your image in the darkroom onto high-contrast "line" or "lith" paper, try getting a similar effect in Painter. Open the Papers palette by choosing Window, Show Papers, click the right arrow on the Papers palette to access the pop-up menu, and choose Make Paper. In the Make Paper dialog box, choose the Line option and set the Spacing to approximately 10. (You can also adjust the Angle slider if you like.) Store your new texture in the current Paper library by naming it in the Save As field and clicking the OK button. With your new paper chosen in the Papers palette, choose Effects, Surface Control, Apply Screen, Using Paper to get a two- or three-color effect with rough (aliased) lines. Or try Effects, Surface Control, Express Texture, Using Paper to get a broader range of value and smoother, anti-aliased lines. You can also apply screens using Painter's Distress feature. See "Distressing a Photo" on page 277 for a step-by-step demonstration of this technique.

Posterizing an image. Painter lets you limit the number of colors in your image via posterization. To apply a posterization directly to your image choose Effects, Tonal Control, Posterize and enter the number of levels (usually 8 or fewer for best results). You can also perform a posterization using the Posterize dynamic layer. At the bottom of the Layers palette, click the plug icon to open the Dynamic Plugins menu and select Posterize from the menu. Click Apply and enter the number of levels. Because the Posterize plug-in layer is dynamic, you can experiment and preview the effect on your image until it's the way you like it.

You can get creative posterization effects by making a Color Set (see "Capturing a Color Set" in Chapter 2) and selecting Effects, Tonal Control, Posterize Using Color Set. This is a great way to unify photos shot under a variety of conditions.

Embossing and debossing. To emboss an image, raising its light areas, choose File, Clone; then Select All and Delete, leaving a blank cloned image. Now choose Effects, Surface Control, Apply Surface Texture, and choose 3D Brush Strokes from the Using pop-up menu. To raise the dark areas instead of the light, click the Invert box or change the Using menu choice to Original Luminance. Images with a lot of contrast give the best results, and busy images work better if less important areas are first selected and softened using Effects, Focus, Soften.

Selective Coloring

Overview *Open a color photo and copy it to a layer; desaturate the layer; paint with a brush to erase areas of the layer mask and reveal the underlying color photo.*

CHER THREINEN-PENDARVIS / PHOTO: PHOTOSPIN

The color photo

Using the Adjust Color dialog box to desaturate the layer to black-and-white

Painting on the layer mask to reveal the color image underneath

IF YOU WANT TO FOCUS ATTENTION on a particular element in a color photo, you can turn the photo into a black-and-white image and then selectively add color back into it for emphasis. Here's a way to use Painter's layers and brushes to "paint" color on an image.

1 Copying the image. Open a color photo and choose Select, All (Ctrl/⌘-A). Press the Alt/Option key and choose Select, Float. This creates a layer with an exact copy of the original image, in register with the original.

2 Desaturating the layer. Now use the layer to make the image appear black-and-white: Choose Effects, Tonal Control, Adjust Colors, Using Uniform Color, drag the Saturation slider all the way to the left and click OK.

3 Revealing color in the underlying image. To allow parts of the color image to show through, use a brush to hide portions of the "black-and-white" layer. Target the layer in the Layers palette and add a layer mask by clicking the Create Layer Mask button on the Layers palette. Click on the layer mask thumbnail to target it—you'll see a dark outline around it when it is active. In the Brush Selector Bar, choose a Fine Tip Soft Air variant of Airbrushes and choose black in the Colors picker. (To view the layer imagery while editing the layer mask, keep the layer mask eye icon shut.) As you paint with black on the layer mask to hide that area of the mask, the color will appear. If you want to turn a color area back to gray, choose white from the Colors picker and paint on the area.

FINE-TUNING YOUR MASK

It's difficult to tell if you've completely covered (or erased) areas when working on a mask with a brush. To view a layer mask in black-and-white, click on the layer mask icon in the Layers palette, and in the Channels palette, open its eye icon. Choose a Fine Detail Air (Airbrushes), and paint directly on the mask to clean it up. (Black creates an opaque mask that hides the layers below; pure white creates no mask, allowing the layers below to show through; shades of gray create a semi-transparent mask.) To switch back to color view, click the layer mask eye icon shut.

Painting on the layer mask using a Fine Detail Air variant of Airbrushes

Creating a Sepia-Tone Photo

***Overview** Use gradient features to tint a color or black-and-white image; adjust the image's contrast and saturation.*

CHER THREINEN-PENDARVIS

1a

The original photo

1b

Choosing Express in Image

2a

Applying the Sepia Browns gradient

2b

Adjusting the contrast

3

Neutralizing and warming up the browns

TYPICALLY FOUND IN IMAGES CREATED at the turn of the last century, sepia-tones get their reddish-brown color cast in the darkroom when the photographer immerses a developed print in a special toner bath. You can use Painter's gradation and tonal control features to quickly turn color or grayscale images into sepia-tones.

1 Tinting the image. Open a grayscale or color photo. In the Gradients palette (Window, Show Gradients), select the Sepia Browns gradient from the picker. Choose Express in Image from the triangle pop-up menu at the right end of the Gradients section bar. (Read more about gradients in Chapter 2.) Click OK in the dialog box to tint your image with shades of brown. (You can also use a similar procedure to turn a color image into shades of gray, but make sure the back and front Color rectangles in the Colors picker are black and white, respectively, and choose Two-Point in the Gradients palette.)

2 Adjusting the white and black points. If you're working with an image that has poor contrast, you can adjust the white and black points by choosing Effects, Tonal Control, Equalize (Ctrl/⌘-E). When the dialog box appears, the image will be automatically adjusted so that its lightest tones are pure white and its darkest ones are pure black. The automated contrast was too dramatic for our taste, so we lightened the image by moving the Brightness slider to the left.

3 Desaturating the image. We wanted to emulate the mild tinting effect usually used for traditional sepia-tones, so we desaturated the image using Effects, Tonal Control, Adjust Colors, dragging the Saturation slider to the left to –40. Set the Hue Shift at 0% and experiment with the Saturation slider until you see the effect you want in the Preview window. We also adjusted the Hue a slight amount (to 2%) to warm up the browns in the image. 🖌

Simulating Motion

Overview *Open a color photo and copy to a layer; apply Motion Blur to the copy; add a layer mask to the layer; paint with a brush to erase areas of the layer mask and reveal the original photo.*

The original photo

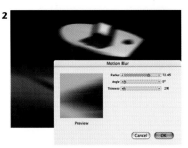

Applying Motion Blur to the layer

Painting the layer mask to hide a portion of the blurred layer

Adjusting the opacity of the blurred layer

CREATING A SENSE OF MOVEMENT for a subject *after* the film is out of the camera is easy with Painter's layers and Motion Blur command. We blurred a layer, and then used a layer mask to hide some areas to reveal the untouched image underneath. The benefits of this method over applying effects to selections are that you can control the amount of the effect by adjusting opacity of the layers; you can simultaneously add effects other than a blur (such as lighting and texture); and you are altering a copy while leaving the original intact, and this makes it easy to correct errors.

1 Copying the image. Open a color photo and choose Select, All (Ctrl/⌘-A). Using the Layer Adjuster tool, Alt/Option-click on the image. This creates a layer that's an exact copy of the original image.

2 Blurring the layer. Select the layer by clicking on its name in the Layers palette and choose Effects, Focus, Motion Blur. To get a dramatic blur on our 1500-pixel-wide image, we set Radius to about 72.45, Angle to 5° (to complement the direction the table was moving) and Thinness to 2%. Experiment with different Angle settings for your particular image.

3 Painting on the mask. To allow parts of the original image to show through, target the layer in the Layers palette and add a layer mask by clicking the Create Layer Mask button on the Layers palette. Click on the layer mask to target it—you'll see a dark outline around it when it is active. Use a brush to paint on the layer mask. In the Brush Selector Bar, choose the Digital Airbrush (Airbrushes) and choose black in the Colors picker. As you paint the layer mask in the area you wish to hide, the underlying image will appear. If you want to restore an area of the blurred layer, choose white in the Colors picker and paint on that area of the layer mask. For an illusion of speed we hid the frontal blur on the table and laptop, leaving trails of motion blur behind them.

4 Adjusting the opacity. To reduce the blur we clicked on the layer (instead of the mask) and made it slightly transparent by lowering the Opacity of the layer in the Layers palette to 75%.

Zooming and Solarizing

Overview *Float a copy of the image; use Painter's Zoom Blur feature to zoom in on an area of the layer; paint the layer mask to accentuate the focal point; make a solarization by changing the Composite Method.*

CHER THRENEN-PENDARVIS / PHOTO: CORBIS IMAGES

1

The original photo of the volleyball players

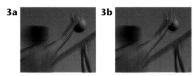

2

The Zoom Blur dialog box after clicking in the image

3a **3b**

The zoom-blurred layer (left) and the mask retouched to reveal the sharp underlying image of the hand and ball (right)

4

The Opacity and Composite Method settings for the solarization

WITH PAINTER'S ZOOM BLUR feature you can create zoom and pan effects that rival results you can achieve when shooting with a zoom lens. Here we used Zoom Blur to elongate the subjects, adding to the excitement and illusion of speed during a volley. Afterwards, to add more drama we changed the photo into a mysterious "night scene."

1 Copying the image. Open a color photo and choose Select, All (Ctrl/⌘-A). Choose the Layer Adjuster and Alt/Option-click on the image. This creates a layer with an exact copy of the original image.

2 Blurring the layer. Select the layer by clicking on its name in the Layers palette and choose Effects, Focus, Zoom Blur. To get a moderate blur on our 600-pixel-wide image, we set the Amount to 31%. Set the focal point of the zoom by clicking in the image (not in the Preview). To create the elongated, distorted effect of zooming in, check the Zoom In box. Click OK.

3 Painting on the mask. To enhance the focal point of the image, we painted areas of a layer mask to reveal the underlying image, for instance, the ball and hands. Target the layer in the Layers palette and add a layer mask by clicking the Create Layer Mask button on the Layers palette. Click on the layer mask thumbnail to target it—you'll see a dark outline around it when it is active. In the Brush Selector Bar, choose a Fine Tip Soft Air variant of Airbrushes and choose black in the Colors picker. (To view the layer imagery while editing the layer mask, keep the layer mask eye icon shut.)

4 Making a solarization. Next, we created a solarized "night scene" from the image by selecting the layer in the Layers palette, choosing the Layer Adjuster tool and changing the Composite Method to Difference in the Layers palette. To make the layer slightly transparent, allowing the original colored image to show through, we also lowered the Opacity of the layer to 85%.

Making a Selective Correction

Overview *Use a dynamic layer to adjust the brightness and contrast of an image; convert the dynamic layer to an image layer; make a selection; use the selection to remove a portion of the layer.*

The original photograph

Making a Brightness and Contrast dynamic layer

Increasing the Brightness by moving the lower slider to the right

HERE'S A USEFUL IMAGE-EDITING TECHNIQUE that combines a dynamic layer Brightness-and-Contrast adjustment and a selection. Using a dynamic layer has the advantage of being able to make a correction and dynamically preview the changes on the image without harming the image. To enhance the focal point of this image—shining more light onto the faces—we selectively lightened the shaded window area.

1 Editing brightness and contrast with a dynamic layer.
Open a grayscale or color photo. To make a Brightness and Contrast dynamic layer for your image, click the Dynamic Plug-ins button at the bottom of the Layers palette and from the pop-up menu, choose Brightness and Contrast. A Brightness and Contrast dynamic layer will cover your entire image. (Turn to "Using Dynamic Layers" on page 227 in Chapter 6 to read about the basics of using dynamic layers.)

When the dialog box appears, adjust the sliders and preview the correction in your image. To see more detail on the faces, we moved the Brightness (lower) slider to the right, making the image lighter. We also slightly increased the contrast by moving the Contrast slider (upper) to the right.

We only wanted the Brightness-and-Contrast adjustment to affect the shaded area within the window, so we planned to make a mask and load a selection that we could use to isolate a portion of the layer. To use a selection on a dynamic layer, the layer must first be converted to an image layer. When you've finished making adjustments, convert the dynamic layer to an image layer as follows: Click the right triangle on the Layers palette bar to open the pop-up menu and choose Convert to Default Layer. Next, hide the layer temporarily: In the Layers palette, click the layer's eye icon shut; then click on the Canvas layer's name.

The active selection around the window

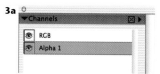

Selecting the mask to view it as a red overlay

Viewing the mask as a red overlay before editing and feathering

The completed mask

Detail from the final corrected image with more detail in the shaded areas

2 Making a selection and saving it as a mask. In our example, when we were satisfied with the Brightness-and-Contrast adjustment in the window area, the blue wall was too light and flat. In preparation for using only the window area of the adjusted layer, we made a selection of the window area on the image canvas and saved it as a mask. In the Toolbox, choose the Pen tool or Lasso and make a selection. (We drew a shape with the Pen tool and converted it to a selection using Shapes, Convert to Selection.) When you've completed the selection, choose Select, Save Selection to save it into the Channels palette. (For more information about using the Pen tool to create paths with which you can make selections, turn to the beginning of Chapter 5, "Selections, Shapes and Masks" and to "Working with Bézier Paths and Selections" on page 196.

3 Editing and feathering the mask. To get a clear view of the mask as we edited and feathered it, we worked back and forth between viewing it as a red overlay (on the image) and as a black-and-white mask. We used the Digital Airbrush variant of the Airbrushes and white paint to spray soft edges along the top of the window and added a 3-pixel feather to the entire mask to give it a soft transparent edge. If your mask needs editing, select its name in the Channels palette. To view your mask as a red overlay, click both the mask eye icon and the RGB eye icon open. To view the mask in black-and-white, click the RGB eye icon closed. With the mask active you can give it a soft edge by applying feathering as follows: Click the right triangle on the Channels palette bar to open the menu and choose Feather. Type a feather width in the field and click OK. Now shut the mask eye icon and click on RGB in the Channels palette to prepare for the next step.

4 Using the selection to edit the layer. In our example, we used the selection to remove the area on the Brightness-and-Contrast layer outside the window. Now that your mask is complete, load the selection from the mask, as follows: In the Layers palette, click on the Brightness-and-Contrast layer name to select it, and also open its eye icon to display the layer. Now choose Select, Load Selection and choose the mask that you saved (Alpha 1) to isolate the area on the layer. To remove the unwanted portion of the layer, choose Select, Invert and press the Backspace/Delete key.

USING SELECTIONS WITH LAYERS

You can have several masks saved in the Channels palette and choose any one of them to load as a selection to then isolate paint or effects on any image layer. Choose Select, Load Selection and pick the selection you need from the menu. In the Layers palette, click on the name of the layer with which you want to work.

Hand-Tinting a Photo

Overview *Retouch a black-and-white photo; color the image using Tinting brushes and several layers set to Gel Composite Method.*

CHER THREINEN-PENDARVIS

Using Equalize to adjust the tonal range of the black-and-white photo

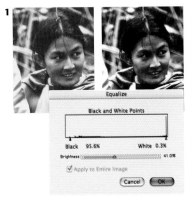

Repairing scratches with the Soft Cloner variant of Cloners

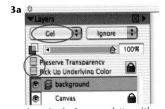

The new layer in the Layers palette, with Composite Method set to Gel

HAND-TINTING IS A GREAT WAY to give an old-fashioned look to a black-and-white print. It also gives the sensitive artist plenty of opportunity to add depth to an image using hues, tints and shades. For this example, *Rell with Bird's Nest Fern,* we hand-colored a portrait of Hawaiian friend Rell Sunn using Painter Tinting brushes, applying transparent color to layers above the image, so we would not disturb the existing photo.

1 Equalizing the image. To preserve shadow detail during tinting, choose a light image without solid shadows, or correct the tonal range after scanning as described below. Because we no longer had the 35mm slide, we scanned an 8 x 10-inch print at 100%, 150 pixels per inch. The print was slightly overexposed, so we darkened it, taking care to preserve detail in the shadows. If your image needs tonal correction, select Effects, Tonal Control, Equalize (Ctrl/⌘-E). Your image will be automatically adjusted when the dialog box appears. For a more subtle result, experiment with spreading the triangular sliders on the histogram, or move them closer together for more contrast. Use the Brightness slider to make the gray tones brighter or darker overall.

2 Retouching scratches. To touch up scratches, use the Magnifier tool to enlarge the area that needs retouching. Now choose the Soft Cloner variant of Cloners in the Brush Selector Bar. Establish a clone source by Alt/Option-clicking on your image near the area that needs touch-up, then begin painting. A crosshair cursor shows the origin of your sampling. If necessary, re-establish a clone source as you work by Alt/Option-clicking again.

3b

Coloring the "background" layer with the Basic Round variant of the Tinting brush

4a

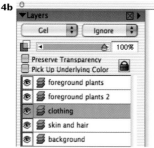

Flat, transparent washes on the "clothing" and "skin and hair" layers

4b

The Layers palette showing the "clothing" layer selected

5a

Bringing out highlights on the shirt using the Soft Eraser variant of Tinting

3 Making a new layer and coloring the background. Create a new layer by clicking the New Layer button on the bottom of the Layers palette. So the paint will appear transparent, in the Layers palette, set the layer's Composite Method to Gel. Also, disable Preserve Transparency (so you can add pixels to the layer) and turn off Pick Up Underlying Color, so the Tinting brushes will not pick up gray from the Canvas as you paint. Choose a color in the Colors picker and the Basic Round variant of the Tinting brush from the Brush Selector Bar. Begin to brush color onto your image. If the color looks too strong, reduce the opacity of the Basic Round variant using the Opacity slider in the Property Bar. For grainier brushstrokes, try the Soft Grainy Round variant.

4 Coloring elements on separate layers. It's often helpful to color areas of the image (such as the skin, clothing and background) on separate layers to make it easy to edit a specific element. Add more layers as needed by clicking the New Layer button on the Layers palette. Remember to set each new layer to Gel Composite Method before you start to paint. We added new layers for each of these elements: the skin and hair, clothing, and the foreground plants.

5 Emphasizing the area of interest. After you've painted color washes, look at the overall balance and color density of your image. Add more or brighter color to the areas that you want to emphasize and apply less saturated colors to make other areas appear to recede. For detail work, reduce the size of the Basic Round variant using the Size slider on the Property Bar. To remove color from oversaturated areas or to clean up edges, use the Soft Eraser variant of Tinting, adjusting its Opacity setting in the Property Bar as you work. The Blender and Softener variants are useful for making color or value transitions smoother.

We used the Blender variant to smooth the brush work in the face and shirt, by softly brushing over the areas using a low-opacity version of the brush.

Saving the image. If your coloring extends for more than one work session, save your image in RIFF format to preserve the layers set to Gel Composite Method. If you'd like import your image into

5b

We used the Blender variant of Tinting to smooth areas in the face and shirt.

Adobe Photoshop, you'll want to flatten a copy of the image first, because Gel method is not available in Photoshop and the color on your tinted layers may change if you open the layered file in Photoshop. Choose File, Clone to quickly make a flattened copy; then save the image as a TIFF file.

Blending a Photo

Overview *Open a photo and clone it; use the Just Add Water variant of Blenders to smear pixels in the image; restore a portion of the original with the Soft Cloner variant of Cloners.*

ANDREW HATHAWAY

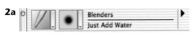

Hathaway's original photo of the dogs

Choosing the Just Add Water variant of the Blenders

Making loose strokes with the Just Add Water variant at 40% opacity

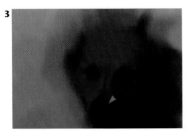

Partially restoring the dog's face using a low-opacity Soft Cloner variant of Cloners

TO CREATE THE EXPRESSIONISTIC *DOGS OF THE SURF*, Andrew Hathaway used Painter's Just Add Water brush to paint directly onto a clone of one of his photographs, transforming it into an intense, emotionally charged abstract painting. He gave the piece a touch of realism with a Cloners brush, using it to restore a hint of the original photo to the clone.

1 Choosing a subject and making a clone. Open your photo in Painter; then choose File, Clone to make a copy of your image to alter. Hathaway chose one of his own photos—an image of two dogs running toward him on the beach—and then cloned it.

2 Blending with a Water brush. Hathaway used the Just Add Water variant of Blenders; since it uses the Soft Cover submethod and doesn't show paper texture, it's the smoothest of the blending brushes. For a more subtle smearing effect, you may want to reduce the Opacity in the Property Bar. To make more expressive strokes, with the brush size changing as you vary pressure on the stylus, choose Window, Brush Controls, Size, and in the Size section, move the Min Size slider to about 15%. Now, make some strokes on your clone. Hathaway painted energetic, angled, smeary strokes on the clone to emphasize the focal point and perspective in the foreground; then he smeared the background into more abstract shapes. He modified his brush as he worked, varying the Size between 10 and 30 pixels, and lowering the Opacity to 30%–40% using the sliders in the Property Bar.

3 Partially restoring from the original. As a last step, Hathaway used the Soft Cloner variant of the Cloners brush with a very low opacity (5%) to subtly restore the foreground dog's face. Try this on your clone. Use the Soft Cloner brush to bring the original back into the blurred areas of your image. Experiment with the Opacity slider in the Property Bar until you find a setting that suits your drawing style and pressure. 🖌

Cloning a Portrait

Overview *Retouch a photo and soften background detail; clone the image with brushes; paint details by hand; add texture.*

The original photograph

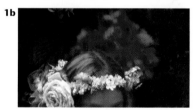
Using darker colors to paint over the busy flowers in the background

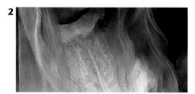
Adding hand-painted details to the hair

Adding relief to the brush work with Apply Surface Texture Using Image Luminance

LAUREL BECKER

PAINTERLY CLONING IS A GREAT WAY to add natural atmosphere to photos. To create *Flower Girl,* Laurel Becker began by retouching a photo. Then she enhanced a clone of the photo by painting expressive brushstrokes and adding texture. When cloning, after blocking in the image, add hand-painted details, highlights and shadows.

1 Scanning, adjusting and retouching. Becker scanned an 8 x 10-inch photo at 100% and 150 ppi. Then she bumped up the image contrast using Effects, Tonal Control, Brightness/Contrast. To focus attention on the girl, she selected the background and "played down" the busy foliage details. If your background is busy, consider making a selection and using Effects, Focus, Soften to blur details or paint over areas with darker colored brushstrokes, as Becker did. (For information about making selections, turn to Chapter 5.)

2 Cloning and painting. Next, Becker cloned the photo (File, Clone). For this portrait, she chose Basic Paper in the Paper Selector and the Captured Bristle variant of Acrylics from the Brush Selector Bar. Before beginning to paint, she checked the Clone Color box in the Colors palette to sample color from the original image. Then she painted over the entire clone. As she worked, she sized the brush using the Size slider on the Property Bar. She used a larger brush while painting loose strokes behind the girl and a tiny brush to paint the details on the face, dress and hair. She turned off Clone Color, and then painted brighter highlights on the cheeks, nose, eyes, chin and lips, her brush following the contours of the forms.

3 Adding texture. After she was finished painting, Becker added relief and texture to her brush work using two applications of Effects, Surface Control, Apply Surface Texture: The first, Using Image Luminance, Amount 20% and Shine 0%; the second, Using Paper, Amount 20% and Shine 0%. She left other settings at their defaults. 🖌

Creating a Photo-Painting

Overview *Open a retouched photo in Painter; paint a loose abstract background; clone and paint the image with brushes; add surface texture.*

MICHAEL CAMPBELL

The original photo shot by Campbell

The clone filled with a tan color (left) and the loose brush work painted over the tan fill (right)

FOR *PORTRAIT OF PATRICE*, Michael Campbell combined photography with painting. Campbell is a professional photographer who specializes in portraits. He began the work by choosing a photo from a shoot and retouching it using Photoshop, and then saving it as an RGB TIFF file. In Painter, he used cloning and paint applied with various brushes to combine the photograph with expressive brush work and texture.

1 Opening a photo and making a clone. To begin the image, Campbell opened his photo in Painter. The file was approximately 10 x 14 inches, at 150 pixels per inch. He made a clone of the image by choosing File, Clone. (Campbell left the original photo open so that he could sample color from it later using the Dropper, or clone from it later using the Cloners brushes.) He saved the cloned image, giving it the name *Step 1* to keep versions of his image organized.

2 Building a painted background. For a colored background that would provide a base for more tightly rendered brushstrokes,

3

Loosely cloning the photo into the painted background

4a

Building the forms and colors

4b

Using smaller brushes to refine the forms and background

Campbell used the Dropper tool to sample a light tan color from the original photo. Then he filled the clone canvas with the color by choosing Effects, Fill (Ctrl/⌘-F), choosing Current Color and clicking OK. Next, he applied loose brush work to this background using various Oils brushes (for instance, the Opaque Round variant of Oils), applying colors that he had sampled from the photo with the Dropper. At this point, he had not cloned imagery from the photo yet. He saved and named the painted background image *Step 2*.

3 Beginning to clone in the photo. Next, Campbell added more loose brushstrokes to his image using a large cloning brush based on the Camel Oil Cloner variant of Cloners. (During this step in his process, he doesn't like to use Painter's Tracing Paper function much, because he feels that it hides the look and color of his brushstrokes).

4 Building form and color. As Campbell continued to paint the figure and basket, his brushstrokes followed the contours of the forms as they do when he uses conventional oil paints. While he worked, he often changed the Size of the brush using the Size slider popped out of the Property Bar. Sometimes he turned off the Clone Color button in the Colors palette and painted freehand to retain a loose painterly feeling in the image. He saved this version of the image as *Step 3*.

5

The final painted stage is shown in this detail.

5 Refining the painting. Campbell wanted to create a looser painted look in the clothing, flower basket and background, and more realistic detail in the model's face. To paint the dress, flowers and basket, he used a small version of the Camel Oil Cloner variant. He softly refined the detailed parts of the face, especially the eyes and mouth. In areas where he wanted even more realism, he switched to a small Soft Cloner variant of the Cloners and with the original photo as the clone source, he carefully restored the model's eyes, nose and lips. When Campbell was pleased with this stage, he saved it and named this version of the image *Step 4*.

6a

The complete painted and cloned image before texture was added

6b

Detail of the face showing the Surface Texture applied to the paint

6c

Detail of the image showing the second Surface Texture application using the canvas texture

6 Applying two kinds of texture. Next, Campbell added three-dimensional highlights and shadows to his brushstrokes by choosing Effects, Surface Control, Apply Surface Texture, Using Image Luminance, with subtle Amount and Shine settings of approximately 30%, leaving other settings at their defaults. He named this textured image *Step 5*.

He wanted to try a canvas-like texture, so he opened his "Step 4" image, and chose File, Clone again. With this image active, he chose Effects, Surface Control, Apply Surface Texture, this time Using Paper. He chose the Raw Silk texture from the Painter 7 texture library, loaded from the Painter IX CD-ROM. He named the clone with the canvas texture *Step 6*.

7 Cloning imagery from different versions. To hide the canvas in some areas as if it were thick paint covering up the canvas of a real painting, Campbell used various sizes of the Camel Oil Cloner variant to clone imagery from the *Step 5* clone into the *Step 6* clone. (To designate another image as a clone source, open it; then choose File, Clone Source and select its name in the menu.) After he was satisfied with the look of his image, he saved it as *Step 7*, and as an RGB TIFF file for printing on a high-resolution inkjet printer using archival inks. The final image can be seen on page 274. 🖌

7

Detail of the final image showing areas of the first Apply Surface Texture application that accentuated the brushstrokes ("Step 5") cloned into the "Step 6" clone that included the Apply Surface Texture application Using Paper

Distressing a Photo

Overview *Open a photo; copy the image to a new layer; use Distress to make it black-and-white and texturize it; combine the layer and the canvas using a transparent Composite Method.*

CHER THREINEN-PENDARVIS

1a

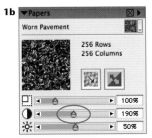

The original photo of Ludwig Palace

1b

Increasing the Contrast of the paper texture

2

Applying the Distress effect

3

The image showing the layer set to Screen Composite Method before reducing Opacity

BY DEFAULT, THE DISTRESS FILTER IN PAINTER adds texture and changes a color image to black-and-white. In this example, we used custom settings to apply the filter to a layer and then set its Composite Method to Screen, so the effect would combine with the colored photo beneath it.

1 Choosing a photo and a texture. Open a photo with good contrast and color. A bold image with a strong focal point will respond best to this technique. Choose a high-contrast texture that will complement your photo. We opened the Papers palette (Window, Show Papers) and chose Worn Pavement from the Papers picker menu. To achieve a more dramatic texture in the final image we increased the contrast to 190%.

2 Making a layer and applying the effect. The Distress process is easier to control when the filter is applied to a copy of the image on a layer, and then the filtered and original versions are combined. To put a duplicate of the image onto a layer in the Layers palette, choose Select All (Ctrl/⌘-A); then press the Alt/Option key and choose Select, Float.

With the layer active, access the Distress dialog box by choosing Effects, Surface Control, Distress. Leave the Using menu set to paper. Experiment with the settings in the dialog box to suit your taste. We increased the Edge Size to 20.39 to bring out the highlights; lowered the Edge Amount to 36% to darken the shadows; reduced Smoothing to 1.00 so the filter would not "round" the edges and reduced Threshold to 43% to lighten the image. When you've achieved a texture with the amount of white you want, click OK.

3 Blending the treated layer with the original photo. In the Layers palette, to drop out the black areas of the layer to reveal the photo underneath, change the Composite Method to Screen. For a more subtle effect, we also lowered the opacity of the layer to 80% using the Opacity slider in the Layers palette.

Making a Custom Solarization

Overview *Use Express Texture on positive and negative clones of an image; merge the images by filling with a Clone Source.*

1

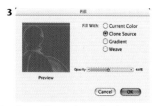

The original image after equalizing (left), and the negative clone

2

Creating black-and-white positive (left) and negative versions of the clones using Express Texture

3

Merging the positive and negative images

4

Adjusting the image's brightness and contrast

IN THE DARKROOM, SOLARIZATION OCCURS when a negative or print is exposed to a flash of light during the development process, partially reversing the photo's tonal range. To achieve this effect digitally, we tested other image-processing programs and filters, and found that we got the most control and detail using Painter's Express Texture feature. This technique gives you a lot of control over the image's value contrast and it frequently creates a glowing edge-line effect where contrasting elements meet.

1 Making positive and negative clones. Open an image with good value contrast; then choose Effects, Tonal Control, Equalize (Ctrl/⌘-E) to increase its tonal range. Choose File, Clone twice. Make one of the clones into a color negative by selecting Effects, Tonal Control, Negative.

2 Making black-and-white separations. Use Painter's Express Texture feature to convert both clones to black-and-white: Choose Effects, Surface Control, Express Texture, and select Image Luminance from the pop-up menu. Experiment with the sliders and click OK. Repeat the process for the second clone. We set Gray Threshold to 85%, Grain to 85% and Contrast to 113%. These settings helped emphasize the gradient effect in the sky.

3 Merging the two exposures. Choose File, Clone Source and choose the positive clone. Now fill the negative image with a percentage of the positive (the "flash of light"): With the negative window active, choose Effects, Fill, Clone Source. Set the Opacity slider between 40% and 60%.

4 Pumping up the tonal range. To achieve a broader tonal range while maintaining a silvery solarized look, we selected Effects, Tonal Control, Brightness/Contrast. We increased the contrast (the top slider) and decreased the brightness slightly.

Melting with Watercolor

Overview *Posterize the image to create flat areas of color; build a soft border; lift the Canvas to a Watercolor layer; apply effects; enhance the image using a Composite Method.*

CHER THREINEN-PENDARVIS

1

The color photograph

2

The posterized photo with soft edge added

3a

The Watercolor Layer set to Screen

3b

The photograph melted into watercolor

WITH PAINTER'S WATERCOLOR LAYERS, a photograph on the Canvas layer can be melted into a watercolor painting.

1 Choosing an image. For the best results, open an image with good value contrast and color. Our image was 1200 x 900 pixels.

2 Posterizing and making a layer. To build flat areas of bright color that will aid in simulating watercolor paint, choose Effects, Tonal Control, Posterize. Choose a setting that complements your photo. (We chose 12.) Now give your image a soft vignette. (For information about building a vignette, see page 188 in Chapter 5.) Next, put a copy of the Canvas on a new layer by choosing Select, All, pressing Alt/Option and then choosing Select, Float. Hide this layer by toggling its eye icon closed in the Layers palette.

3 Creating a watercolor effect. Now, select the Canvas, and from the pop-up menu on the Layers palette, choose Lift Canvas to Watercolor Layer. Choose a texture in the Paper Selector. (We chose French Watercolor Paper.) Now choose a Watercolor brush whose characteristics you'd like to apply to your image when you "wet" the Watercolor layer. We used the Diffuse Grainy Camel variant of Watercolor.

To melt the image with watercolor, choose Wet Entire Watercolor Layer from the pop-up menu on the Layers palette. In the Layers palette, when the animated water drop next to the Watercolor layer name stops dripping, the watercolor effect is complete.

We wanted a brighter, high-key look, so we dragged the posterized photo layer under the Watercolor Layer and then opened its eye icon. Because the default Composite Method of the Watercolor Layer is Gel, the image looked dark. To lighten it, we changed the Composite Method for the Watercolor Layer to Screen in the Layers palette. Then we lowered its opacity to 80%.

Creating a Woodcut from a Photo

Overview *Open a photo and clean up the background; copy the Canvas to make a new layer; create a color woodcut plate on the Canvas; create a black woodcut plate on the new layer; retouch the black plate; add clouds and texture.*

JOHN DERRY

The original digital photo of the pagoda

2a

Setting the Tolerance for the Magic Wand in the Property Bar

WITH PAINTER'S WOODCUT FILTER you can start with a photo and achieve a look similar to a conventional wood block print. You can simply use the color arrived at by the Woodcut filter defaults, or you can enjoy complete control over choosing the colors.

The traditional wood block printing process involves simplification of detail in the lines and color areas. Inspired by Japanese wood block prints from the 1800s, John Derry created *Pagoda*, which is based on one of his own digital photos. Painter's Woodcut filter helped him to reduce the number of colors in the image and to fine-tune the colors for the final artwork.

1 Choosing a photo. Open a photo with good contrast and color. A bold image with a strong focal point will work best for this effect.

2 Cleaning up the sky. To focus more attention on the pagoda, Derry simplified the sky by selecting it and applying a blue fill. Choose the Magic Wand in the Toolbox and click in the sky. Adjust the Tolerance in the Property Bar until most of the sky is

2b

The Image viewed with the mask eye icon open (left), and the active selection with the blue fill applied (right)

3

The visibility of Layer 1 is turned off and the Canvas is selected.

4a

Increasing the Color Edge to make simpler, smoother shapes (left) and brightening the gold color (right)

4b

The color woodcut plate

selected; at this point, edges are most important, since you can clean up any small internal "debris" by painting on the mask later. Save the selection as a mask in the Channels palette by choosing Select, Save Selection. In the Channels palette, open the eye icon to the left of the mask's name. Choose *black* in the Colors picker and paint on the mask where you need to *add* more mask; use *white* to *remove* areas of the mask (for instance, to remove debris). To use the mask to isolate the sky, choose Select, Load Selection. (See Chapter 5 to read more about working with masks and selections.) Next, fill the selection with blue by choosing Select, Fill with Current Color.

3 Setting up layers. The Woodcut process is easier to control when the color elements are on a separate layer from the black elements. Derry started his layering by making a duplicate of the original image. To put a duplicate of the image canvas onto a layer, choose Select, All (Ctrl/⌘-A), press the Alt/Option key and choose Select, Float. In the Layers palette, turn the new layer's visibility off by toggling shut the eye icon to the left of its name.

4 Cutting the color "wood block." In the Layers section, click the canvas name to activate it for the colors. To access the Woodcut dialog box, choose Effects, Surface Control, Woodcut. When the dialog box appears, disable the Output Black check box. The options for Black Output will now be grayed out. In the lower portion of the window, accept the default number of colors (16), and smooth out the edges of the color blocks by adjusting the Color Edge slider to the right. (Derry set it at approximately 11.46.)

When the edges were as he liked them, Derry fine-tuned a few of the colors. For instance, he chose a tan color swatch (at the bottom of the dialog box) and made the color brighter. Click on a color square to select it; a red outline will appear around it. Now that it's selected, you can choose a new color in the Colors picker and the swatch will change to the new color. To sample a color directly from the image Preview window, press the Ctrl/⌘ key and click on the Preview. To change the color, choose a new color in the Colors picker.

To see other areas of your image in the Preview window, drag with the grabber hand cursor to move around the image

WOODCUT PREVIEWS

It's possible to view two previews in the Woodcut dialog box: the working woodcut image and the original image. By default the woodcut image is visible. To see the original image, drag the Grabber hand in the Preview window. When you release, the preview of the woodcut will be visible again.

The Woodcut dialog box with the standard preview showing a color woodcut image (left) and dragging with the Grabber hand to reveal the original image (right)

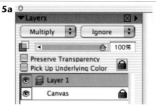

5a

Setting the Composite Method for Layer 1 to Multiply

5b

To achieve more detailed black edges, the Black Edge slider was adjusted to the left.

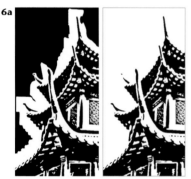

6a

The black plate (shown with the Canvas hidden) with black in the sky (left), and with the sky retouched (right)

6b

The in-progress woodcut with both color and black plates in place

preview. When you're satisfied with the colors, click OK to accept.

5 Cutting the black plate. To begin making the black plate, target Layer 1 by clicking on its name in the Layers palette and open its eye icon. At the top of the Layers palette, set its Composite Method to Multiply so the white that will be generated on the layer by the Woodcut effect will disappear. Now, choose Effects, Surface Control, Woodcut and turn on Output Black and turn off Color Output in the dialog box. For more detailed edges, adjust the Black Edge slider to the left. (Derry set it to approximately 25.75.)

6 Cleaning up the black plate. The settings that worked well for the detail in the pagoda left too much black in the sky. Using the Scratchboard variant of Pens and white paint, Derry removed the black by painting white over the sky. He chose the Scratchboard tool because it paints with a crisp edge. An Eraser variant would have produced a softer edge.

7 Adding clouds and texture. Next, Derry painted simple cloud shapes on a new layer using a large Scratchboard Tool and white paint. (To add a new layer, click the New Layer button near the bottom of the Layers palette.) Increase the size of the Scratchboard Tool using the Size slider in the Property Bar (Derry adjusted his to about 25.4). Paint loose brushstrokes that complement your composition. Then he dragged the layer below the black plate layer in the Layers palette so the black would appear to be "printed" on top.

For added realism, Derry completed the woodcut by adding a subtle paper texture to the colored layer. To add texture, click on the colored layer in the Layers palette. Select Basic Paper in the Paper Selector; then choose Effects, Surface Control, Dye Concentration, Using Paper. In the dialog box, try moving the Maximum slider to the right until a subtle paper texture effect is visible. Adjust the settings to your taste and click OK.

7

The clouds and texture have been added.

Creating a Montage Using Masks and Layers

Overview *Create masks for the component photos in Photoshop or Painter; copy them into a single document; use a brush to edit the layer masks when compositing them; paint on the final image.*

JOHN DISMUKES / CAPSTONE STUDIOS

1

The original photos

2

The cut-and-pasted comp ready to be scanned and used as a template

WHEN CONTINENTAL CABLEVISION asked John Dismukes of Capstone Studios to illustrate a direct-mail piece, he and his team turned to Painter. He combined photographs and splashy color with loose airbrush and chalk brushstrokes to illustrate the theme "Can Summer in California Get Any Better?"

1 Gathering illustration elements. Begin by collecting all of the individual elements that you'll need for your illustration. Dismukes and his associates photographed separate images of clouds, a pair of sunglasses, ocean foam, palm trees, and a television on the sand. The team scanned the photo negatives at 762 ppi.

2 Making a template from laser prints. Dismukes's team created a traditional comp by printing the individual elements, and then photocopying them at different scales and assembling them using scissors and adhesive. They turned the completed comp into a template by scanning it at 72 ppi, opening it in Painter and sizing it to the final image size of 4 x 5 inches at 762 ppi, using Canvas, Resize. The template would act as a guide for Dismukes to accurately scale and position the various elements. If you choose to include this step, don't be concerned about the "bitmapping" that occurs when scanning the comp at a low resolution; when the composition is finished, the template will be removed from the file. For flexibility, put your template on a layer by choosing Select, All and then Select, Float.

3

Three of Dismukes's Photoshop masks

4a

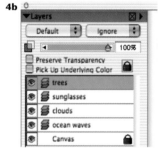

The glasses source file with active selection, ready to copy and paste or drag and drop into the background image

4b

Bringing the layers into the composite file

5

Selecting the layer mask in the Layers palette and opening its eye icon in the Channels palette

6a

Using the Digital Airbrush variant and black paint to paint on the layer mask and hide the portion of the cloud layer that covers the TV

3 Masking unwanted portions of the source images.

Working in Photoshop, Dismukes used the Pen tool in Paths mode to cut masks for the sunglasses, ocean foam, palm trees and television on the beach. He converted each path to a selection, saved the selection as an Alpha Channel, and then saved each image as an RGB TIFF file, including the alpha channel. You can accomplish the same result in Painter. Open one of your source photos and use the Pen tool (Toolbox) to draw a shape around the desired portion of the image. When you're done, choose Shapes, Convert to Selection; then to save the selection as a mask, choose Select, Save Selection. View the selection as a mask by opening its eye icon in the Channels palette. You should see your image covered by a red overlay—the default color for the mask. To view only the mask in black-and-white, click the RGB eye icon shut in the Channels palette.

FEATHERING A MASK

To add softness around a hard-edged mask, select it by clicking on its name in the Channels palette. Click the right triangle on the Channels palette bar and choose Feather. Type in the amount of feather in pixels and click OK.

4 Compiling the source files.

When you've finished masking the images, bring them into a single document. Open the template if you have one, or the photo that will become your background image. Choose the Layer Adjuster tool and if the Layers palette is not open, choose Window, Show Layers. Then open each of the source images and choose Select, Load Selection and Alt/Option-click on each selection to make a layer. Loading the selection and making a layer prepares Painter to export the item from the source image with its mask.

There are three ways to import source images into a composite file: Copying and pasting through the clipboard, performing a drag-and-drop, or using the File, Place command to bring the source image in as a reference layer. To paste using the clipboard, select the layer in the source image with the Layer Adjuster tool, choose Edit, Copy, and then make the background image active and choose Edit, Paste. If your component images are approximately the right size, the easiest way is probably to drag and drop: Select the layer in the source image with the Layer Adjuster. Now use the Layer Adjuster to drag the masked item to the background image.

If you're working with large files, positioning and scaling can be accomplished much more quickly using reference layers. To import an image as a reference layer with a mask, save the source file in RIFF format (to preserve its mask); then choose File, Place, navigate to the source image and choose Open. In the Place dialog box check the Retain Alpha check box and click in the image to place the layer. (For more information about reference layers, see "Using Reference Layers" on page 224 in Chapter 6.)

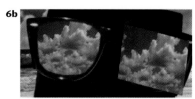

Compositing the clouds inside the glasses

Revealing the cloud layer around the tree

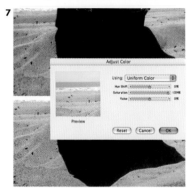

Using Adjust Colors to increase saturation in the image

Adding squiggles and lens glare (top) and smudges and blurs

5 Adding layer masks and putting them to work. To add a layer mask to a layer, select the layer in the Layers palette and click the Create Layer Mask button at the bottom of the Layers palette. To view the mask in black and white, open the layer mask's eye icon in the Channels palette. To switch back to color view so you can edit the layer mask while viewing the image on the layer, shut the layer mask's eye icon.

6 Positioning the layer and painting on its layer mask. First scale, rotate and position one layer on top of another and make sure that the top layer is selected in the Layers palette. Now, fit the top element inside the element below it by using a brush and black color to paint a portion of the top layer's mask, as follows: Begin by targeting the layer name in the Layers palette, and then click on the layer mask's thumbnail to the right of the layer. (A dark outline will appear around the thumbnail when it is targeted.) Choose the Digital Airbrush variant of Airbrushes and choose black in the Colors picker. Begin painting around the edge of the top layer to hide part of the layer imagery, making it appear "inside" of the layer beneath it. Paint with white to restore the layer.

When you've completed all compositing, turn off visibility for the template layer in your file by selecting its name in the Layers palette and shutting its eye icon. Then make a copy of your image with the layers merged with the background by choosing File, Clone. This step gives you a lot of flexibility—you have an "original" with layers intact, and a "working image" (the clone) on which you can paint and make other adjustments.

7 Shifting colors. To make the image "pop" a bit more, Dismukes increased the color saturation. Choose Effects, Tonal Control, Adjust Colors, and experiment with the Hue Shift, Saturation and Value sliders to modify the colors in your image.

8 Painting on the photo montage. To transform the television into a lively caricature in vivid color, Dismukes first used the Digital Airbrush variant to add details such as glare on the glasses. He switched to the Impressionist variant of the Artists brush to paint on the sand and water, and then painted spontaneous, textured squiggles around the TV and on the sand and water with the Artist Pastel Chalk variant of Pastels using the Big Canvas paper (loaded from the More Paper Textures library, in the Paper Textures folder on the Painter IX CD-ROM). As a final touch, Dismukes switched to the Grainy Water variant of Blenders. To smear while revealing texture, he changed the subcategory to Grainy Hard Cover in the General panel of the Stroke Designer (Brush Creator) and added the smudges and blurs on the sand and television.

Finishing the job. Using the same style, technique, tools and colors, Dismukes created similar illustrations on a smaller scale that were used throughout the brochure, as well as a border around the edge of the piece. 🖌

■ For *Under the Bridge*, fine artist and photographer **Helen Golden** began by capturing a colorful digital photograph on a rainy night. To capture this shot, she deliberately moved the camera slightly to get a blurred effect. Back at her studio, Golden noticed that the original photo lacked detail, so she explored techniques to create a photographic image with a painterly feeling. She opened the photograph in Photoshop and used the Photoshop LucisArt plug-in on the digital photo. The filter extracted hidden details and color information. Then, she used Photoshop to combine pieces of the image using layers with different blending modes, including Overlay, Multiply, Soft-light and Color. Golden also created new image elements to balance the composition. When she was pleased with the collage, she saved it in Photoshop format and then closed it.

Next, Golden opened the layered image in Painter. She cloned the image (File, Clone) and then selectively used Cloners brushes to add to the watery look. To enhance the brush work in the image, she applied textured highlights and shadows. She chose Effects, Surface Control, Apply Surface Texture, Using Image Luminance, with subtle settings. Then she saved the enhanced image as a Photoshop file.

Golden wanted to print the image at a large size, so she increased the pixel size of the file using Genuine Fractals PrintPro. Then she opened the file in Painter again to give it an overall unifying treatment of subtle texture. She used Effects, Surface Control, Apply Surface Texture, this time using Paper. Finally, Golden printed the image as a variant edition on Hahnemuhle's Digital Fine Art paper, using a Hewlett-Packard DesignJet 5000PS printer with archival UV inks.

©Helen Yancy

■ An internationally acclaimed portrait photographer and artist, **Helen Yancy** has been honored by the Professional Photographers of America, the British Institute of Photography, the United Nations and other organizations. For more than 40 years, Yancy has created exquisite images that portray people with sensitivity and realism. Working with Painter has helped Yancy to break down creative boundaries and to enjoy great artistic freedom.

Yancy began *In His Presence* by taking a photograph of a friend and his wife in an old Italian church in Tuscany. She saw her friend deep in thought, gazing at a crucifix above the altar, and there in the shadows was his wife, gazing at him. Yancy knew that it was a spiritual moment for both of them, and therefore the title has a double meaning.

She decided to rework the photograph as a painting in Painter that would retain the ambiance of the location. As she worked with the image, she used colors that would enhance the rich earthtones in the photograph. The original photograph was grainy and soft, because it had been shot in a dark church with very little light, so Yancy painted over the entire image to create the look of an oil painting. She made a clone of the photo by choosing File, Clone. She left the original image open, and then saved the clone, giving it a new name. Working in the clone, she used the Artist Pastel Chalk variant of Pastels (with the Clone Color option enabled in the Colors palette) to brush on expressive, colored strokes, and she blended areas using the Grainy Water variant of Blenders. She subdued the strongly lit edge of the pillar by painting over it with slightly darker colors to bring out the subtle rim light on the man's face. She also brushed over areas of the masonry to enhance its textures. When the image was complete, Yancy printed *In His Presence* on both photographic paper and on canvas using a large format inkjet printer with archival inks.

■ Photographer and artist **Marilyn Sholin** was commissioned to create *Remember When Your Brother Was Your Best Friend*. The painting is part of Sholin's *Remember When* series, which is devoted to precious childhood memories.

Sholin began by shooting photographs of the children at a Key Biscayne beach (Florida) at sunrise, using her Hasselblad 500C with a 150 mm lens and Kodak 400NC film. She captured the exquisite light of the early morning, and the warm relationship that the twins shared. After the film was processed, she ordered a high-resolution scan of the negative, and then she enhanced the saturation of the photo using Photoshop.

Sholin opened the edited photograph in Painter and cloned it by choosing File, Clone. Then, she deleted the contents of the clone image by choosing Select, All (Ctrl/⌘-A) and then pressing Backspace/ Delete. She saved the clone image by choosing File, Save As, and gave it a new name. Sholin kept the original photo open and enabled Tracing Paper in the clone by pressing Ctrl/⌘-T. Working in the clone, she used Cloners brushes to paint the image into the clone Canvas.

After establishing the image in the clone, she toggled Tracing Paper off and on as she worked. To enhance the mood in the painting, she added warmer, soft colors by using a variety of Acrylics brushes.

Then, to smooth and blend areas, she used the Wet Sponge variant of Sponges and various Blenders brushes. As she worked, Sholin was careful to retain the highlights and the contrast in her portrait. Next, she added details to the children's eyes and faces.

At last, to give the image an irregular border, Sholin extended the size of the Canvas by choosing Canvas, Canvas Size, and then she added more width and height. Then, she used the Acrylics, Blenders and Sponges to paint around the border to create a soft edge. When her image was complete, Sholin printed it on Red River Lux Art watercolor paper.

■ Artist **Ad Van Bokhoven** works both traditionally and digitally. To create the photo-painting *Old Men*, he used Painter to emulate the brushstrokes and style that he achieves with traditional oil paints. Van Bokhoven began by capturing a digital photograph to use for reference.

Later, back at his studio, he opened the photo in Painter. He chose File, Quick Clone to clone the image, delete the contents of the clone Canvas and enable Tracing Paper. He left his original image open, targeted the clone and chose a custom Oil brush, and then he enabled Clone Color in the Colors palette. He painted broad brushstrokes to bring elements of the photo into the clone Canvas.

To take advantage of being able to apply paint and blend it as he worked, he worked directly on the Canvas, without the use of layers. To mix and pull color, he used modified Blenders brushes, similar to the Round Blender Brush and the Grainy Blender variant of Blenders.

As he worked, Van Bokhoven focused on the figures. To de-emphasize the background, he simplified it by using larger, looser brushstrokes and less saturated colors.

Van Bokhoven painted expressive, dynamic brush work. He suggested the shapes of the figures and architecture, rather than painting a lot of details.

Finally, to add a subtle canvas texture to his image, Van Bokhoven chose a canvas texture in the Paper Selector and then chose Effects, Surface Control, Apply Surface Texture, Using Paper, with subtle settings. To avoid a filtered look, he painted back into areas of his image with a Blenders brush.

■ When artist **John Derry** created *A Slice of Ward Parkway*, his intent was to create a photo-illustration from an illustrator's viewpoint, rather than a photo-realistic look. With his Sony DSC-707 digital camera, Derry shot 12 digital photos of a series of homes on Ward Parkway. These homes exemplify the architectural style of early Kansas City developer N.W. Dible. Derry was inspired by the artist Ed Ruscha, who had created amazingly long panoramic images, one of which is called "Every Building on Sunset Strip."

To begin the panorama, Derry shot photos of the colorful, quaint homes. To create a planar panorama of the street, he repositioned the tripod to be directly in front of each house and driveway for each shot. If trees obscured important architectural details, Derry took additional photos to provide him with enough source imagery so that he could piece together a complete view of the home. "It is critical that each photo have some overlap with the previous shot, says Derry. "The repetitious data becomes important later when 'stitching' the image pieces together."

Back at the studio, he assembled the photos into a wide panoramic montage. Derry imported each of the source files into a composite file in Painter. Keeping the images on separate layers allowed him to reposition elements easily. To align the images precisely, he lightened their opacity and moved them into place. When they were aligned, he blended the images into one another at their edges using layer masks, which he painted using the Digital Airbrush variant of Airbrushes. Derry also used Cloners brushes to retouch a few artifacts. The final composite shows each house and driveway interleaved with the next, as if they are each viewed head on.

When the composition was complete, Derry flattened a copy of the image and saved it as a TIFF file, which he opened in Photoshop for printing. He printed the image on his six-color Epson 1270 using Epson's archival ink set on 13 x 19-inch sheets of Epson Radiant White Watercolor paper.

"Although the program is called Painter," says renowned photographer **Pedro Meyer**, "it's important not to exclude photography from its repertoire, given that the program can also be used effectively in that medium." Meyer's keen photographic eye—and a Nikon digital camera—captured the initial photo for the image above in Glendale, California. "One of the aspects that I do find intriguing with the tools that we have at hand today, is that we can explore after the image is taken, what works to our best advantage in making the image more effective," says Meyer.

Meyer had taken the photograph straight. To create an impression of dynamic motion, he tilted it slightly, and then used focus and blur effects (for instance, Camera Motion Blur) to help the viewer concentrate on the most significant areas in the image. The stores in the background were not as important as the single figure, so Meyer turned them into more general texture elements. Meyer says, "Before digital photography it was very hard to make credible images which had these traits, for instance, the special focus and blur effects which are used in *Glendale*. It was quite complicated and time-consuming. These days, almost all it takes is the imagination to use the tools in ways that are more about the ideas than about showing off the virtues of the tools themselves."

■ An internationally acclaimed studio portraitist, **Phillip Stewart Charris** has created elegant and timeless likenesses of celebrities, individuals and families for more than three decades. Known for his life-sized portraits, which are printed and then mounted on canvas, Charris has drawn inspiration from artists such as John Singer Sargent, Raphael and Rembrandt. The portrait *Pretty Little Girl* was photographed in his studio in Southern California. Then, a transparency was scanned, saved as an RGB TIFF file and opened in Painter. To

protect the figure while he worked on the background, Charris made a mask.

Then, using expressive brush work, he painted over the image background with the Sable Chisel Tip Water variant of Brushes (loaded from the Painter 5.5 Brushes library from the Brushes folder on the Painter IX CD-ROM). To smooth some areas, he painted finer strokes with a low-opacity Just Add Water variant of Blenders. He used the brushes not to apply color, but to blend and smear pixels in the image in a painterly way.

For the figure and clothing, Charris used smaller versions of the same two brushes. When brushing over the face and hair, he carefully painted with a small brush to preserve the important details. "The photographer must seek out the personality of the sitter, which lies beneath a veil that subtly alters the surface of the face. Piercing that veil to reveal the subject's character is something that, after the posing is taken care of, can only be done for a fraction of a second," says Charris.

■ An innovative master photographer and artist, **Michael Campbell** specializes in portraits and also excels in painting. When creating *Mandolin Player*, Campbell combined photography with painting using Painter brushes. He began the work by choosing a photo from his shoot and retouching it using Photoshop.

In Painter, he used cloning and paint applied with the Oil Pastels and Artists' Oils to build expressive brush work and texture. He opened the photo in Painter and chose File, Quick Clone to clone the image, delete the contents of the clone Canvas and enable Tracing Paper. He left his original image open, and targeted the clone image. Next, he built a custom Oil Pastel that incorporated Clone Color. He chose the Soft Oil Pastel variant of Oil Pastels and then enabled Clone Color in the Colors palette. He saved the image and then began to model the forms of the figure and clothing, using the Oil Pastels and Artists' Oils brushes.

Campbell alternated between painting with Clone Color turned on and off in the Colors palette. With Clone Color turned on, he could sample color from the original, and with it turned off, he could paint with color he chose in the Colors palette. He gradually built up details in the focal areas of the image (for instance, the model's face and hands), and he painted looser brush work to suggest folds in the clothing. To smooth areas, Campbell used the Blenders brushes. He printed the image on water-resistant canvas with an Epson 7600 using UltraChrome inks.

■ To create the richly textured photo-collage *Orange Bike 3,* renowned artist and photographer **Laurence Gartel** began by taking photographs at Bike Week in Daytona Beach, Florida. Later, back at his studio, he scanned each of the transparencies into Photoshop, where he made selections to isolate the subjects from their backgrounds. He opened a large new blank file, copied each component image, and then pasted it onto its own layer in the composite. After saving the layered file in Photoshop format and closing it, he opened it in Painter and then used the Layer Adjuster tool to position the elements to create a balanced composition.

To build a flashy, textured look that would enhance the motorcycles, Gartel added layers to his image that he filled with custom patterns, textures and effects. For the rock-like texture in the red areas of the bike, Gartel began by

building a selection. He gave the selection a subtle feather and then saved it as a mask in the Channels palette. Next, he added a new layer, loaded the selection, and with a rock texture chosen in the Papers palette, he increased its size using the Scale slider. He chose black color in the Colors picker and then he chose Effects, Surface Control, Color Overlay, Using Paper, with strong settings to apply the texture to the selected area.

For the brightly colored drops of paint, Gartel selected an orange color in the Colors picker. Then, he added a new layer, used the Lasso tool to select the area, and chose Effects, Esoterica, Blobs. The Blobs effect randomly placed organically shaped spots of paint within the selection. To integrate some of the edges of this layer with the image, he deselected, and then brushed over areas with Blenders variants and the Coarse Distorto variant of Distortion.

Gartel painted brush work using the Smeary Round and Smeary Bristle Spray variants of Oils. To blend and pull paint, he used Distortion variants. For instance, in the middle right of the image, where the pink blends with yellow, he created interesting texture by smudging paint with the Coarse Distorto brush. For the thick, pink paint in the middle right, he used the Distorto variant of Impasto. To give the image glazes of colorful translucency in areas, he used the Watercolor brushes.

Gartel wanted to add relief to a few of the patterned areas, so he selected each one and chose Effects, Surface Control, Apply Surface Texture, Using Image Luminance, with subtle settings. To complete his image, Gartel changed the Opacity and Composite Method in the Layers palette for a few of the layers (for instance, the bikes in the upper left and the light purple patterned areas in the middle area).

■ Artist **Fay Sirkis** created the engaging portrait *Ashlie*, using a photograph captured by the late **Don Blair** and sensitive Painter brush work. Sirkis has a background in traditional painting and uses this experience to create paintings from photographs. "I am inspired by the fact that I can turn cherished photos into timeless portrait paintings, thereby helping people keep their special memories alive," says Sirkis.

Sirkis wanted to paint the young teen using high to medium key colors with a dramatic background. To begin, she opened the image in Photoshop and adjusted the Curves and the Hue and Saturation to obtain the skin tones that she desired for her painting. In Painter, she used cloning and paint applied with various brushes on layers.

She opened the photo in Painter and chose File, Clone to clone the photo. She left the original photo open and selected the clone image. Next, she added a new transparent layer to the clone image, and then she enabled Pick Up Underlying Color in the Layers palette.

She painted using a soft brush, the Digital Airbrush variant of Airbrushes and a hard-edge brush, the 2B variant of Pencils. First, she chose the Digital Airbrush and enabled Clone Color in the Colors palette, and then she painted on the layer, right over the photo on the Canvas below. She used a very small brush to outline the image, and then she added broader strokes. As she painted colors for the portrait onto the layer, she turned Clone on and off as she worked. She

alternately added color with the Airbrush, and then blended it with the Smudge and Grainy Water variants of Blenders.

For the background, Sirkis painted deeper tones using the Palette Knives, and she also used the Palette Knife to define crisper edges on the girl, making the portrait seem three-dimensional. Finally, she added the smaller details on the sweatshirt seams and hood strings with a tiny 2B Pencil brush.

When the painted layer was complete, Sirkis merged it with the Canvas by choosing Drop from the Layers palette pop-up menu. The photo acted as a foundation for her brushstrokes, and the painted brush work blended with the photograph perfectly so that no details were lost.

EXPLORING
SPECIAL
EFFECTS

An innovative artist, Steve Campbell combines drawing and painting with special effects, as shown here in his tribute to Woody Guthrie, This Machine. *He used Apply Surface Texture and other effects to add texture and interest to the work. To view more of Campbell's work, turn to the gallery at the end of this chapter.*

INTRODUCTION

PAINTER'S SPECIAL EFFECTS ARE SO NUMEROUS and complex that an entire book could be written about them alone. Because they're so powerful, there's much less need for third-party filters than with Photoshop or other image processors. But with that power comes complexity; some of these effects have evolved into "programs within the program." This chapter focuses on five of Painter's most frequently used "mini-programs"—Apply Surface Texture, Apply Lighting, Patterns, Glass Distortion and Mosaics. It also covers several special-effects dynamic layers—including Bevel World, Burn, Tear and Liquid Metal—and a handful of other exciting effects.

ADDING EFFECTS WITH SURFACE TEXTURE

One of the most frequent "haunts" of Painter artists is the Effects, Surface Control, Apply Surface Texture dialog box. You'll find it used in a number of places throughout this book. The Apply Surface Texture dialog box contains intricate, powerful controls, allowing you to apply paper textures to images, build realistic highlights and shadows for masked elements, and more. First, the Softness slider (located under the Using pop-up menu) lets you create soft transitions, such as smoothing the edge of a mask or softening a texture application. Adding Softness can also increase the 3D effect produced when you apply Surface Texture Using Mask (when working with an image that contains a mask). And with the Reflection slider (bottom Appearance of Depth slider), you can create a reflection in your artwork based on another image or the current pattern.

Another very important Surface Texture control is the preview sphere, located below the image Preview. Think of the sphere displayed as a dome supporting lights above your image. Although the preview sphere seems to show a spotlight effect, any lights you set are applied evenly across the surface of your image.

Creating textured, dimensional brushstrokes with Apply Surface Texture Using Image Luminance

Creating the illusion of type under water (top), with Apply Surface Texture using Original Luminance and a reflection map. We applied the reflection using a clone source image of a cloudy sky (tinted red to match the color in the type by using Effects, Tonal Control, Adjust Color).

Experiment with adding more lights by clicking on the sphere. Adjust an individual light by selecting it and changing its color, and adjusting its Brightness and Conc (Concentration). Use the Exposure slider to control ambient light in the environment.

You can get some interesting effects by changing your color choices for the lights. For instance, if the area to be lit contains a lot of blue, you can add more color complexity by lighting with its complement, an orange-hued light.

Applying a reflection map. Reflections can add interest to shiny type and to other surfaces like glass or metal objects in your illustrations. The Reflection slider allows you to apply an image that you designate as a clone source to your illustration as a reflection. Open an image and make a selection or mask for the area where you'll apply the reflection. You can use a pattern as a source for a reflection map or you can open an image the same size as your working file (the current Pattern is applied automatically if you don't choose another image as clone source). (Turn to "Making an Environment Map" and "Applying an Environment Map," later in this chapter, to read about how Michelle Lill builds custom-made reflection maps and applies them to her images. And for more inspiration, check out Michelle Lill's E-Maps folder on the *Painter IX Wow!* CD-ROM, and in Painter IX's application folder, Extras, Patterns for more Pattern libraries.)

Creating 3D effects. You can use Apply Surface Texture to enhance the surface of your image and give dimension to your brushstrokes. Image Luminance, in the Using pop-up menu, adds depth to brushstrokes by making the light areas appear to recede or "deboss" slightly. If you want to bring the light areas forward, check the Invert box. Experiment with the sliders to get the effect you desire. You can get a stronger 3D effect by clicking to add a second light (a bounce or a fill light) to the preview sphere with a lower Brightness or a higher Concentration (Conc) setting.

RETURN TO DEFAULT SETTINGS

Painter remembers the last settings you choose in effects dialog boxes such as Effects, Surface Control, Apply Surface Texture and Color Overlay. This is helpful when designing scripts (see "Automating Movie Effects" in Chapter 11). To revert to Painter's default settings, save your image and quit Painter to clear the program's Temp file settings.

REFLECTING ANOTHER IMAGE

To use a separate image as a reflection map, bend it using Effects, Surface Control, Quick Warp to achieve a spherical or rippled look. (Quick Warp is applied to the entire image, not just to selections or to a single layer.) Open the reflection image and designate it as the clone source (File, Clone Source). Then (in the original image, not the map image) choose Effects, Surface Control, Apply Surface Texture Using Original Luminance to apply the effect to an entire image. To see the reflection, move the Reflection slider to the right, or distort the reflection effect by moving the Softness slider to the right. Experiment with the other settings.

In Still Life, *Chelsea Sammel created drama in her image using Effects, Surface Control, Apply Lighting. Then she painted over some areas with Brushes variants. She finished the image with an application of Apply Surface Texture Using Paper and a rough paper texture.*

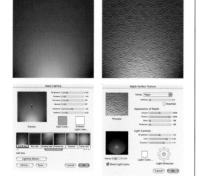

When you use Surface Texture together with Apply Lighting, you'll get more dramatic results if you choose similar lighting directions for both commands.

Combining Surface Texture with other effects. Apply Surface Texture works especially well when combined with other Painter tools. "Creating an Impressionist Look," on page 309, uses a Glass Distortion dynamic layer and Surface Texture to add paint-like texture to a photo. "Draping a Weave," on page 319, uses a powerful Glass Distortion displacement in combination with Surface Texture to achieve the look of draped fabric. And Steve Campbell used Surface Texture and Apply Lighting together to add gradations to textured areas while creating the illustration "Coffeehouse" on page 233 in the gallery.

ADDING DIMENSION WITH LIGHTING

Painter's *Help* gives a good description of how to adjust the controls under Effects, Surface Control, Apply Lighting. Here are some tips and practical uses for the tool.

Applying Lighting to unify an image. Like most of the Surface Control effects, applying lighting across a composite image can help to unify the piece. (If the lighting effect is too dramatic, try using Edit, Fade immediately afterward to reduce it.)

Preventing hot spots. You can avoid "burnout" of lit areas by increasing the Elevation of the light, reducing the light's Exposure or Brightness, or giving the light a pastel or gray color.

Lighting within selections or layers. Add instant dimension to a selection or a layer by applying lighting within it.

Creating subtle gradient effects. To achieve colored gradient effects in an image, some artists prefer lighting with colored lights instead of filling with a gradient; they prefer the Apply Lighting command's smooth luminosity shifts over the more "mechanical" result usually achieved when using gradations.

Painting back into lit areas. For artists who want to achieve a more painterly effect, the Apply Lighting command can look a bit artificial. In creating *Still Life* (left), Chelsea Sammel used Apply Lighting and then she broke up the lit area with brushstrokes, sampling color from the image as she worked.

Creating softly lit backgrounds. On a white background, start with the Splashy Colors light effect. Increase the Brightness and Elevation and reduce the Distance on both colored lights until they form very soft-edged tinted circles on the background. Click in the Preview to add another light or two and change their colors. Move the lights around until the color, value and composition are working. Save and name your settings and click OK to apply the effect. Repeat this process two or three times, returning each time to your saved effect and making minor adjustments in light color, light position and other settings.

Painter's F-X brush variants are capable of creating many subtle or dramatic effects such as fire, glow, and shattered, to name a few.

For Caterpillar, *Matt Dineen used the Furry Brush variant of the F-X brush to paint the caterpillar's colorful hair. See the gallery at the end of this chapter for other examples.*

Grunion Run *is an illustration for a calendar designed and illustrated by Kathleen Blavatt. She used several special-effects brushes to paint the image. Beginning with a black-and-white pen drawing, she modeled the hills using the Pixel Dust variant of Pens (loaded from the Ver 5 Brushes library in the Painter IX application folder, Extras, Brushes). She added sparkling texture to the sky using the Fairy Dust variant of the F-X brush. Blavatt painted the water with the Piano Keys variant of the F-X brush. She added textured brushstrokes to the sun's head using the Grain Emboss variant of Impasto.*

EXPLORING PATTERNS

On the Patterns palette, there are commands that let you make seamless wrap-around pattern tiles. (To access the menu, click the right triangle on the Patterns palette.) Once a pattern has been defined and is in the Patterns section, it becomes the default Clone Source when no other clone source is designated. You can apply a pattern to an existing image, selection or layer with Cloning brushes, with the Paint Bucket tool (by choosing Fill with: Clone Source in the Property Bar), with any of the special effects features that use a clone source (such as Original Luminance or 3D Brushstrokes), or by choosing to fill with a pattern or clone source (Ctrl/⌘-F). (The Fill dialog box shows a Pattern button if no clone source image is designated; if a clone source *is* available, a Clone Source button appears.) Use the pattern feature to create screen design backgrounds, textile design, wallpaper—anywhere you need repeating images. (For step-by-step techniques, see "Creating a Seamless Pattern" and "Applying Patterns" later in this chapter.)

To turn off a clone source so you can fill an image with the current pattern (if the clone source is another image), close the clone source image. If you've cloned from one place to another in the *same* image, click on a pattern in the Patterns section of the Toolbox to clear the clone source.

Capturing a Pattern. To make and store a pattern image in the Patterns section, select an area of your document with the Rectangular Selection tool (or press Ctrl/⌘-A to select the entire image) and on the Patterns palette, click the right triangle and choose Capture Pattern. To offset your pattern use the Horizontal and Vertical Shift options and the Bias slider to control the amount of the offset. Experiment with these settings to get nonaligned patterns—for example, to create a brick wall look, wallpaper or fabric.

Using Pattern wrap-around. Painter creates a wrap-around for the pattern tile you create. Here's a great way to see it work. Select a pattern in the Patterns palette. From the pop-up menu on the right side of the Patterns palette, choose Check Out Pattern; a pattern tile image will appear. Choose the Image Hose category in the Brush Selector Bar. Select an Image Hose nozzle from the Toolbox's Nozzles section. Begin spraying across your image and beyond its edge. Notice how the hose images "wrap around" the edges of the pattern tile (so that when the pattern is captured and an area is filled with these pattern tiles, the edges will match seamlessly).

Making a Fractal Pattern. Choosing Make Fractal Pattern from the Patterns palette menu automatically creates a pattern as a new file when you click OK in the Make Fractal Pattern dialog box. Some of the textures you can create with Make Fractal Pattern make very cool paper textures: Select the area of the fractal pattern

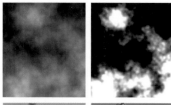

The evolution of a fractal pattern. The original pattern was made by choosing Make Fractal Pattern from the Patterns section menu (top left), and then a hard edge was added with Effects, Surface Control, Express Texture Using Image Luminance (top right). We loaded the Earthen gradient from the Painter 6 Gradients library in the Gradients folder in the Extras folder inside the Painter IX application folder, and applied it via Express in Image—chosen by clicking the right triangle on the Gradients section bar (lower left). To change the color, we adjusted the Bias to 46% in the Express in Image dialog box (lower right).

that you want for your texture (or choose Select, All) and on the Papers palette, click the right triangle and choose Capture Paper.

Enhancing Fractal Patterns. You can add any special effect to fractal (or regular) patterns and they still remain patterns. Here are two creative applications of fractal patterns.

To create a hard-edged fractal pattern with wild color, make a Fractal Pattern, setting Power to –150%, Feature Size to 75% (for a relatively coarse pattern) and Softness to 0. Click OK. Select Effects, Surface Control, Express Texture Using Image Luminance. Adjust the Gray Threshold and Grain sliders to about 80%, and set the Contrast slider at 200% for a contrasty effect. Click OK. Now color the pattern by choosing the Spectrum gradation from the Gradients palette and clicking the right triangle of the Gradients palette and choosing Express in Image. Experiment with shifting the distribution of color in the image by dragging the Bias slider. Choose Select, All and capture the pattern.

To make an abstract topographical map image with color and relief, create a new pattern using Fractal Pattern's default settings: Power, –150%; Feature Size, 100%; Softness, 0%; Angle, 0°; Thinness, 100%; and Channel, Height As Luminance, click OK. Give the image a "topographical" look by choosing Effects, Surface Control, Apply Surface Texture, Using Image Luminance (Amount, 200%; Picture, 100%; Shine, 0% and Reflection, 0%). Tint the image with Express in Image and the Earthen gradation, loaded from the Painter 6 Gradients library, in the Painter IX application folder, Extras, Gradients folder. Now, add a little relief by applying a second pass of Apply Surface Texture, Using Image Luminance (Amount, 100%; Picture, 100% and Shine, 0%). To add a swirl to your "map" choose Effects, Surface Control, Quick

After creating this topographic map using Make Fractal Pattern, we added clouds for more atmosphere by copying our original Fractal pattern file and pasting it into the map image as a layer. We changed the Composite Method in the Layers palette to Screen to apply only the light parts of the clouds to the topographic map image. Then we adjusted the Opacity slider for the clouds layer to 90%.

CREATING REPEATING TEXTURES WITH MAKE PAPER

Using the Make Paper dialog box, accessed by clicking the right triangle on the Papers palette, you can make seamless repeating textures to apply to your images. For the image below, Corinne Okada created her own repeating texture that resembled a grid of pixels to represent the digital output process. She created the grid of beveled squares with Make Paper using the Square Pattern, then chose her new paper from the list on the Papers palette and applied the texture to the central portion of her image using Effects, Surface Control, Color Overlay.

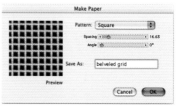

Left: Detail from a package design created by Corinne Okada for The Digital Pond. Above: Okada's settings for the grid of beveled squares.

Conventional diffuser screens attach to the camera lens, breaking up or softening the image as it refracts through the screen. Painter's Glass Distortion layer works the same way but with more variety. To make a Glass Distortion layer for your image, select Glass Distortion from the Dynamic Plug-ins menu at the bottom of the Layers palette. Choose Paper from the Using menu and experiment with refracting your image through different textures chosen in the Papers palette. On this photo, we used Diagonal 1 from the Paper Textures 2 library (in the Paper Textures folder in the Extras folder in the Painter IX application folder).

Warp and click the Swirl button. Experiment with different Angle Factor settings in the dialog box.

CREATING EFFECTS WITH GLASS DISTORTION

Try using another image as a "refractor" for your main image. With Painter's Glass Distortion features you can superimpose glass bas-relief effects (using a paper texture or another image). You can apply the procedure directly to your image by choosing Effects, Focus, Glass Distortion. Or you can use a Glass Distortion layer, which lets you preview the effects on a copy of your image without changing the original image; however, the Effects, Focus, Glass Distortion command features a dialog box with more controls. (To learn more about using Effects, Glass Distortion turn to "Diving into Distortion" and "Draping a Weave" later in this chapter. To read about using a Glass Distortion layer, turn to "Creating an Impressionist Look.")

WORKING WITH MOSAICS

Tile mosaics became a popular medium at about 200–300 B.C. in the Roman Empire, Greece, Africa and Asia; floors and walls of many buildings were decorated with mosaics made of small pieces of glass, stones or shells. They were most often built to celebrate a historic event or for religious purposes.

Inspiration for mosaics. You can build mosaics using Painter's Mosaic brush and dialog box in any of three ways: by drawing them from scratch, by basing them on a line drawing that you've scanned, or by creating a clone-based mosaic using an existing piece of art or a photo. Keep in mind that because of the nature of

To change the hue of an image, use Effects, Tonal Control, Adjust Color and then drag the Hue Shift slider. Use Uniform Color to shift the hue of the entire image, or use Image Luminance to change color properties only in the lighter (but not white) areas.

Highpass (under Effects, Esoterica) acts like a color filter. It looks for smooth transitions in dark areas (as in a sky or shadowed background) and replaces them with abrupt edges or halo effects. Keep the Radius slider to the left for a more pronounced halo effect. To further enhance Highpass, try using Effects, Tonal Control, Equalize.

The initial, unaltered photograph

PHOTO: CHER THREINEN-PENDARVIS

Adjust Colors, Uniform Color: Hue Shift, –44%; Value, 25%

Adjust Colors, Image Luminance: Hue Shift, 20%; Value, 25%

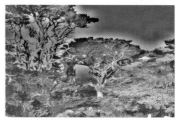

Highpass: Amount, 26.05

To create Pencil and Brush, artist John Derry built a mosaic in Painter beginning with white grout.

A colored pen-and-ink sketch was used as reference for this mosaic. Top: The cloned sketch (with Tracing Paper turned on) shows the mosaic in progress with recently applied tiles. Bottom: The same stage with Tracing Paper turned off. Click Tracing Paper on and off without closing the Make Mosaic dialog box by using the check box.

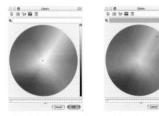

The default grout color is white, shown here (left) in the Colors dialog box. Dragging the Lightness slider to the bottom darkens the color of the grout. The Colors dialog is accessed by clicking on the Grout Color button in the Mosaic dialog box.

the Mosaic tool, your decorative design or photo reference should have a strong compositional focal point. If you want to use a photo that has a busy background, consider simplifying it first by desaturating or blurring. (For tips on neutralizing busy backgrounds, see "Creating a Shallow Depth of Field" on page 261.)

Laying down tiles. Here's a way to try out Painter's Mosaics. Open a new blank file, or a reference on which to base your mosaic. Visualize the forms in your design before you begin laying down the tiles, and rotate your page by dragging with the Rotate Page tool (nested with the Grabber tool in the Toolbox) to accommodate your drawing style so you'll be able to make smooth, controlled strokes to describe the forms.

Open the Colors picker by choosing Window, Color palettes, Show Colors. (If the Colors picker is *not* open, you cannot open it while the Mosaic dialog box is open.) Then choose Canvas, Make Mosaic to open the Make Mosaic dialog box. Opening the dialog box will turn the background of the currently active image white, the default grout color. To change the grout color in the Colors dialog box, click in the Grout box, and choose a new color. Then choose a contrasting color in the Colors picker to paint some tiles. Switch colors again and continue to make tiles. Once you have tiles in place, you can sample color from an existing tile by pressing the Alt/Option key as you click on it. You can undo an action without closing the Mosaic dialog box by pressing Ctrl/⌘-Z. To erase a tile, click the Remove Tiles button and stroke with the Mosaic brush over the tile. While working on a mosaic, save it in RIFF format to preserve the resolution-independent nature of the mosaic. (Because mosaic tiles are mathematically described, a mosaic can be resized without loss of quality.) See the *Painter IX Help* for an in-depth explanation of Painter's mosaic-building tools. And to read about using a photo reference for a mosaic, turn to "Building a Clone-Based Mosaic," on page 314.

SPECIAL EFFECTS USING DYNAMIC LAYERS

Painter features seven kinds of dynamic layers (plug-ins) that allow you to create exciting special effects quickly. They are Glass Distortion, Kaleidoscope, Liquid Lens, Burn, Tear, Bevel World and Liquid Metal. In the paragraphs below, we focus on special-effects applications for several of these plug-ins. (To read more about working with plug-in layers turn to the introduction of Chapter 6; see Chapter 6 to see how dynamic layers apply to image correction and photography. Turn to "Creating an Impressionist Look" later in this chapter to read about using the Glass Distortion dynamic layer in combination with Apply Surface Texture. And the *Painter IX Help* contains good descriptions of each of these dynamic layers.)

Painting with metal and water. Painter's versatile Liquid Metal dynamic layer allows you to paint with bas relief and give it the look of chrome, steel, ice, water and other materials. The Liquid

Hiroshi Yoshii painted Bird with Painter's Liquid Metal. He used colored environment maps and multiple Liquid Metal layers to sculpt the bird's outline and body.

©CDM-F.LLI MAGRO (ITALY)

Athos Boncompagni used the Liquid Metal Brush tool to draw trees and falling stars for this wrapping paper design.

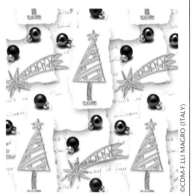

We used the Kaleidoscope plug-in to make a seamless tile from a Corbis Images photo. To read a step-by-step description of the technique, turn to "Making a Seamless Tile" in Chapter 12, "Using Painter For Web Graphics."

BURNED AND TEXTURED

By checking the Use Paper Texture box in the Burn Options dialog box you can apply the current Paper texture to the burned edge of a layer.

Metal layer works in an existing file to make a layer on which you create the metal. To make a dynamic layer, open an image, click the Dynamic Plug-ins icon at the bottom of the Layers palette and choose Liquid Metal from the menu. To paint with chrome, select the Brush in the Liquid Metal dialog box and choose Chrome 1 or Chrome 2 from the Map menu. Drag in the image with the Brush. For thin lines, try a Size of 8.0 and a Volume of 25%. For thick lines, increase Size to 50 and set Volume over 100%.

If you'd like to paint with bubbles or water drops that reflect your image, begin by making a clone of the image (File, Clone). On the clone, make a Liquid Metal layer. From the Map menu choose Clone Source, choose the Circle or Brush and drag to paint on the layer. For fairly flat drops use an Amount of 0.5 to 1.5. For the look of 3D water drops on a camera lens, move the Amount slider to between 3.0 and 4.0. For bubbles use an Amount of 5.0.

You can color the objects on a Liquid Metal layer based on a clone source (as above) or on the current pattern. Begin by making a Liquid Metal layer. In the Liquid Metal dialog box, choose Clone Source from the Map menu. Select a pattern in the Patterns palette or open an image and define it as the clone source (File, Clone Source). Now use the Circle or Brush tool to apply metal to the layer.

Tearing, burning and beveling. The Tear, Burn and Bevel World layers require a selected "source image layer" to perform their effects. To Tear or Burn an image's edges, begin by opening a file. You can select a layer in the image and apply the plug-in to it or you can reduce the image canvas to accommodate the torn or burned edge to come: Choose Effects, Orientation, Scale—we scaled our image at 80%. The Scale command will automatically create a "source layer." With the layer still selected, click the Dynamic Plug-ins icon at the bottom of the Layers palette and choose the Tear or Burn plug-in from the menu. To change the color of the torn (or burned) edge, click in the Color box and choose a new color. Bevel World allows you to create complex bevels quickly. You can apply a bevel to a "source layer" in an image or make a unique beveled frame for an image. Open an image you'd like to frame, choose Select, All and choose Bevel World from the Dynamic Plug-ins menu on the Layers section. Choose your settings and click OK. To read more about Bevel World, turn to "Creating Beveled Chrome," in Chapter 9 on page 348.

To design this striking beveled button Michelle Lill captured a custom-made environment map as a pattern, and applied it to the button graphic using the Reflection slider in the Bevel World dialog box. To learn more about reflection maps, turn to "Making an Environment Map" and "Applying an Environment Map," later in this chapter.

Creating a Seamless Pattern

Overview *Set up and capture a basic pattern layout; check this pattern out of the library; add more elements, shifting the pattern as needed; capture the final pattern; save it in a pattern library.*

ARENA REED

Reed's basic pattern layout image with peach fill and spiral "doodle"

Setting up the Vertical Shift in the Capture Pattern dialog box

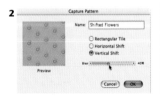

Choosing Check Out Pattern from the Patterns palette

PAINTER'S AMAZING PATTERN-GENERATION tools make it easy to build even a complex pattern tile. You can capture a very basic layout for your tile into a Pattern library and then "check it out" of the library to add complex elements. The new elements will automatically wrap from one edge of the pattern to the opposite edge as you paint, to make a pattern that tiles seamlessly! *Shifted Flowers* is a pattern created by Arena Reed. See "Applying Patterns" on page 306 to see how Reed used this and other patterns.

1 Setting up your pattern layout. To start the pattern files, choose File, New, and in the New dialog box, set up a small image. Reed's image was 240 x 400 pixels. In the Colors picker, choose the basic background color you want for your tile, and then choose Effects, Fill, Fill with Current Color to fill the new image Canvas. To create the base color for her pattern tile, Reed filled the image with a light peach color.

To show how the process works, we'll create a test pattern with a quick doodle, which we can later use as a template. Then we'll describe the steps that Reed used in creating Shifted Flowers.

2 Capturing the pattern. With your basic pattern layout (solid-color background and stand-in pattern element) complete, capture the layout as a pattern tile: From the pop-up menu on the Patterns palette's bar, choose Capture Pattern. In the Capture Pattern dialog box, set up any Horizontal or Vertical Shift that you want for your pattern, and watch how your stand-in element repeats as you

Pressing Shift-spacebar and dragging in the image to shift the pattern

3c

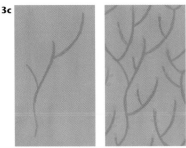

The painted background with the first branch (left) and the completed branches, leaves and flowers (right)

3d

The nearly completed seamless pattern with most of the flower buds and details in place

4

Saving the completed pattern using the Capture Pattern dialog box

5

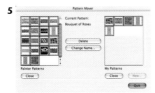

Dragging and dropping new patterns into the newly created My Patterns library

experiment with the Bias slider. Reed chose a Vertical Shift and set the Bias slider to 40%. Name your pattern and click OK to accept. The working pattern will be saved to the current Patterns library.

3 Embellishing the tile. To access Painter's automatic seamless tiling feature for developing the pattern tile, make sure that your new pattern is selected in the Patterns library and choose Check Out Pattern from the pop-out menu on the right side of the Patterns palette bar. A new Painter window will open with the pattern tile in it.

By working in this "checked-out" pattern window, you'll be able to embellish your tile without having to do a lot of retouching at the edges. Notice that you can shift the pattern tile and view the repeating element: If you press the spacebar and Shift keys, the cursor will change to a hand, and you can drag in the image window to shift the pattern so you can see the offset that you built into it in step 2.

Now you can paint to embellish your basic layout, turning it into your final pattern tile. Reed used the Smeary Round variant of the Oils to paint a deep pink color over the background. Because of Painter's seamless wrap-around feature for checked-out patterns, her brushstrokes automatically wrapped around, and there were no obvious tile edges as the pattern repeated.

As you paint, shift the pattern continually (with the Shift key and spacebar) to check the design and make sure it's balanced. Reed shifted the pattern as she used the Variable Colored Pencil variant of the Colored Pencils to draw the branches and their flowers, and to add the details.

4 Capturing the final pattern. When your pattern is complete, add the final tile image to the Patterns library: Choose Capture Pattern from the pop-out menu on the Patterns palette bar. In the Capture Pattern dialog box, leave the Shift and Bias settings as they are, give the pattern a new name (Reed named hers "Shifted Flowers") and click OK.

5 Saving your patterns in a library. Continue to make more patterns if you like, following the instructions in steps 1 through 4. Then store your new pattern(s) in a library for safekeeping: Click the right triangle on the Patterns palette bar to open the pop-out menu and choose Pattern Mover. When the dialog box appears, the currently loaded pattern library, with the pattern(s) you created, will appear on the left of the mover. To create a new library, click the New button, and then name and save the new empty pattern library. To copy an item from the current pattern library, click on the pattern thumbnail and drag and drop it into the new library. If you leave all of your custom patterns in the default Painter Patterns library, the library can become very large, taking up a lot of disk space. So after you've copied your new patterns to the new library, it's a good idea to delete the original(s) from the default library: For each one, click on the pattern swatch and then click the Delete button. 🖌

Applying Patterns

Overview *Make selections and fill them with patterns; add stitching on a new layer; give the stitching highlights and shadows; add clouds that have stitching and Surface Texture.*

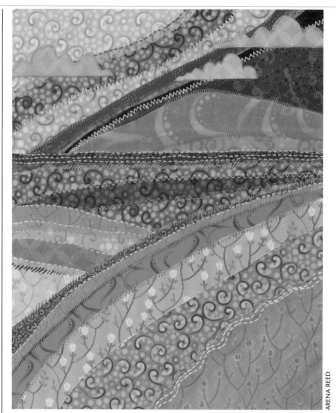

ARENA REED

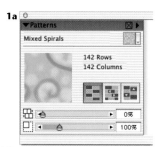

The Mixed Spirals pattern is chosen in Reed's pattern library.

Reducing the opacity to 60% for a translucent fill

Here the Mixed Spirals and Spirals in Blue patterns have been applied to the sky.

YOU CAN APPLY A PATTERN TO AN EXISTING IMAGE, selection or layer with Cloning brushes, with the Paint Bucket tool (by choosing Fill With: Clone Source in the Controls: Paint Bucket palette), with any of the special effects features that use a clone source (such as Original Luminance or 3D Brushstrokes) or by choosing Effects, Fill, Fill with Pattern (Ctrl/⌘-F).

Arena Reed built the colorful landscape image above, *Dreams in Distant Lands*, by filling selections with several illustrated patterns she created, and then drawing stitching with pattern pens.

1 Setting up a new image, selecting and filling. Create a new image by choosing File, New. (Reed's image was 1200 x 1500 pixels.) For practice in using a pattern library, you can follow along with the process Reed used for the image above. Or you can create your own patterns and store them in a pattern library, and then use them to create an image. (See "Creating a Seamless Pattern" on page 304 for more information.)

Reed's pattern library is located on the *Painter IX Wow!* CD-ROM, in the Arena Reed's Patterns folder. Begin by copying the library from the *Painter IX Wow!* CD-ROM to your Painter IX application folder. Then, click on the right triangle on the Patterns palette bar, and choose Open Library. Navigate to the Painter application folder, select Patterns_arenaReed and click the Open button.

1d

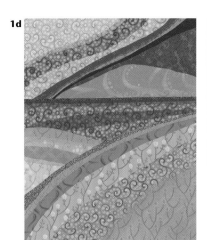

The quilt with basic fills completed

2

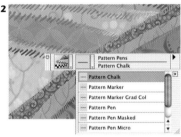

Reed created the stitching using the Pattern Chalk and custom patterns.

3

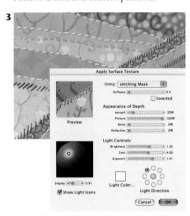

Apply Surface Texture was used to add highlights and shadows to the stitches.

4

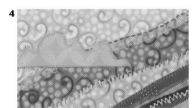

The completed clouds with "embossed" stitching

For each area you want to fill with a pattern, make a selection (with the Lasso, for instance); then click in the Patterns palette to choose a pattern from the library and choose Effects, Fill, Fill with Pattern. As you fill, you can vary the scale of the pattern using the Scale slider on the Patterns palette. Reed made selections and filled them to create a landscape design, varying the scale and the opacity of her fills. The top of the sky was filled with her Mixed Spirals pattern at a reduced opacity of about 60% so the pattern would appear lighter in the sky than it would be in the foreground, where she planned to apply it at 100% opacity.

2 Making stitching on a new layer. Next, Reed created stitching on a separate layer using custom patterns that were applied with the Pattern Chalk variant of the Pattern Pens. To try out the Pattern Chalk, make a new layer on your image by choosing New Layer from the menu on the right side of the Layers palette bar. Click with the Magnifier tool to zoom in on your image. Choose a color in the Colors picker and choose the Pattern Chalk variant of Pattern Pens in the Brush Selector. For wiggly-line style stitching, choose the stitching_luminance3 pattern in the Patterns section, and paint stitching along the edges of the filled areas. For smaller stitches, reduce the size of the Pattern Chalk using the Size slider in the Property Bar. Try out the other stitching patterns in Reed's library.

3 Adding highlights and shadows to the stitches. First select the stitching layer in the Layers palette. Go to Select/Load Selection and load the stitching layer's transparency mask. With this selection active, go back to Select and choose Save Selection, and name the mask. Next choose Effects, Surface Control, Apply Surface Texture and in the dialog box, set Using to the stitching layer's mask and use these approximate settings: Amount, 15%; Shine, 0; Softness, 2; and leave the other settings at their defaults.

4 Making clouds. Reed created a new layer for each cloud so they could be arranged and scaled independently. Add a new layer, draw a cloud shape with the Lasso tool and fill the selection with the Overlapping Circles pattern. After filling, adjust their color: Choose Effects, Tonal Control, Adjust Colors and in the dialog box, increase the Value and change the Hue to create contrast with the background. Use the Layer Adjuster tool to reposition the cloud layers. To scale them, choose Effects, Orientation, Free Transform, and then choose Effects, Orientation, Commit Transform to accept. Choose one of the stitching patterns and stitch the edges of the clouds. After the clouds are as you like them, you can group them in order to make it easier to add dimension to the stitches. Shift-select their names in the Layers section and Group them (Ctrl/⌘-G). Then Collapse them by clicking the Layer Commands button on the bottom of the Layers section palette and choosing Collapse from the menu. Now, add highlights and shadows to the clouds by choosing Effects, Surface Control, Apply Surface Texture, using the same settings as in step 3. 🖌

Diving into Distortion

***Overview** Use Glass Distortion to displace an image using a clone source; then combine a dramatic distortion with a subtle one to create a water-stained effect.*

1a

The original photograph

1b

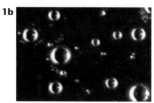

The water image displacement map

2a

Settings for the subtle distortion

2b

The Extreme clone (left), and the Subtle clone (right)

3

Cloning in a dramatic water drop

PAINTER'S GLASS DISTORTION can move pixels in an image based on the luminosity of another image. We used it here to simulate water drops on a camera lens.

1 Choosing images and making clones. Choose an image for a displacement map (the water drops in this case) that has good contrast; both crisp and soft-focus images can give good results. Because you'll be applying the displacement map image to the original image as a clone source, you'll need to size the map image to the same pixel dimensions as the image you want to distort. (Our images were 883 x 589 pixels.) Make two clones of the image you want to distort by choosing File, Clone (twice). Save the clones, naming them Extreme and Subtle; then size and position them on your screen so that you can see both of them.

2 Applying the distortion. Open the displacement map image. Now, click on the Extreme clone, and designate the displacement image as the clone source (File, Clone Source). With the Extreme clone active, choose Effects, Focus, Glass Distortion, Using Original Luminance, and choose the Refraction Map model. (Refraction works well for glass effects; it creates an effect similar to an optical lens bending light.) Our settings were Softness, 2.3 (to smooth the distortion); Amount, 1.35; Variance, 6.00. We left Direction at 0, because it has no effect when using a Refraction map, and clicked OK. Click on the Subtle clone, and apply Glass Distortion with subtler settings. (Our settings were Softness 15.0; Amount, 0.07; and Variance, 1.00.) We wanted the diving board to curve, while preserving smoothness in the image.

3 Restoring from the Extreme clone. We added several dramatic water drops from the Extreme clone to enhance the composition of the Subtle image. Click on the Subtle clone to make it active and choose the Extreme clone as clone source. Use the Soft Cloner variant of the Cloners brush to clone dramatic effects from the Extreme clone into your Subtle image. 🖌

Creating an Impressionist Look

Overview *Combine Glass Distortion and Surface Texture special effects to transform a photo into a painting, creating brushstrokes and building up paint.*

1

The original photograph

2

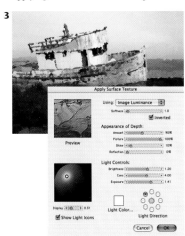

Applying Glass Distortion to the photo

3

Adding highlights and shadows to the distorted image with Apply Surface Texture

BY COMBINING TWO POWERFUL EFFECTS, Glass Distortion and Apply Surface Texture, you can create an Impressionist look with textured highlights and shadows—turning a photo into a painting. This effect can be applied to an entire image, a selection or a layer, giving you much more flexibility than you would have in the darkroom working with diffuser screens and masks.

1 Choosing an image. Choose an image with a strong focal point and good highlights and shadows. You can achieve good results with either crisp or soft-focus images.

2 Initiating strokes. Choose a coarse paper texture—large organic textures with a broad tonal range help to emulate the look of paint on canvas. We chose River Map from the Branched Textures library (located in the Paper Textures folder on the Corel Painter IX CD-ROM). Then we used the Paper Scale slider on the Papers palette to scale it to 60% to complement our 1200-pixel-wide image. To diffuse or break up the image into paint-like strokes on paper, apply the Glass Distortion dynamic layer: In the Layers palette, click the Dynamic Plug-ins button and choose Glass Distortion from the pop-up menu. In the Using menu select Paper. Choose subtle settings—our settings were Amount, 0.77; Variance, 1.00; and Softness, 0. Click OK to apply your settings.

3 Adding texture and shadows. To add realistic relief, choose Effects, Surface Control, Apply Surface Texture. (If the Commit dialog box appears asking you if you'd like to convert the dynamic layer to an image layer, choose Commit.) In the Using menu choose Image Luminance. Use subtle-to-moderate Surface Texture settings to avoid a harsh look and to preserve the original image. We used Amount, 90%; Picture, 100%; Shine, 10%; Softness, 0 and Reflection, 0. (To raise the highlights, we turned on the Inverted check box.) Choose a light direction that complements the light in your photograph, and click OK.

Making an Environment Map

Overview *Choose a file and resize it; make a selection; use Quick Warp to bend the image into an environment; capture it as a pattern.*

MICHELLE LILL

YOU CAN USE PAINTER'S QUICK WARP FEATURE to bend any image into a useful environment map, an image that shows an environment as if it were seen through a fish-eye lens or reflected in a shiny metal sphere. Multimedia designer Michelle Lill creates her own environment maps—like the one above on the left—and uses the maps to enhance images by applying them as she did in the image on the right.

1 Opening an image and making a selection. Open the image that you want to use as the basis for your reflection map. To conserve disk space and optimize performance, Lill recommends that a reflection map image be a square that is 256 pixels or fewer. Using the Rectangle Selection tool, make a 256-pixel-square selection (holding down the Shift key as you drag to constrain the selection to a square), as you check the Width in the Info palette. If you need to move or scale the selection, use the Selection Adjuster tool. (Turn to "Transforming Selections" in the beginning of Chapter 5 for more about manipulating selections.) Copy the selected area (Edit, Copy), and paste it into a new file by choosing Edit, Paste into New Image.

Michelle Lill's original photo

Making a square selection on the image

2 Bending the image. To get the "fish-eye lens" effect that adds realism to the map (since most surfaces that reflect their environment are not flat), Lill chose Effects, Surface, Control, Quick Warp and selected the Sphere option. She used the default settings of Power 2.0 and Angle Factor 2.0. The effect was applied to the entire canvas.

Applying the Quick Warp Sphere option

3 Saving the image as a pattern. To save the map into the current Pattern library, capture it as a pattern: With the environment map image open, select all, click the right triangle on the Patterns palette bar and choose Capture Pattern from the menu. Name the map when prompted and click OK. The environment map is now a permanent member of the library. Now you can use the map to enhance special effects—as Lill did in her water illustration above. To read a step-by-step description of how Lill used a custom environment map to enhance an image, see "Applying an Environment Map" on the next page. 🐾

Naming the water map in the Capture Pattern dialog box

Applying an Environment Map

Overview *Open a file and set type shapes; convert the shapes into a layer; add an environment map, dimension and a soft drop shadow to the type; add a border to the image.*

MICHELLE LILL

1a

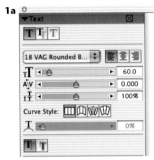

Choosing a font and size in the Text palette

1b

The text set on a layer over the image

1c

The selected Text layer in the Layers palette

2

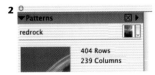

Choosing Lill's custom-made environment map in the Patterns palette

TO CREATE THE TITLE DESIGN *RED ROCK*, designer Michelle Lill used a custom-made environment map in combination with one of Painter's most powerful and versatile tools, Apply Surface Texture.

1 Opening an image and setting the type. For this example, Lill began by setting 60-point VAG Rounded Bold text on top of a photo. Begin by opening a background image (Lill's image was 889 pixels wide). Select the Text tool and choose a font in the Property Bar. For the best results, choose a bold font with a broad stroke and rounded corners. Position the cursor in your image and type the text.

When you're finished setting the text, select the Layer Adjuster tool and drag to reposition the text layer to your taste. (To read more about using Painter's text features see Chapter 9, "Working with Type in Painter.")

2 Selecting the reflection map. Load the Reflection Map pattern from Painter 8's Patterns by clicking on the right triangle of the Pattern Selector, chose Open Library, navigate to the Painter IX application folder, Extras, Patterns. Lill used her own pattern, made from the same Red Rock photo she used for the background. (To read about how to make your own environment map, check out Michelle Lill's method in "Making an Environment Map," on page 310.)

PROPERTY BAR TEXT CONTROLS

You can format your type without opening the Text Palette. As soon as you select the Text tool, most of the controls you will need to format your text will be available in the Property Bar.

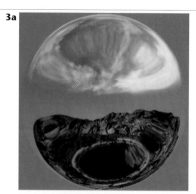

3a

Michele Lill's Red Rock environment map

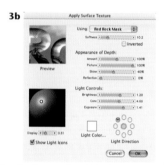

3b

Settings for the second Apply Surface Texture application showing dimension on the type

4a

Setting up an automatic drop shadow

4b

The Red Rock image with the drop shadow applied to the text layer

3 Adding reflection and dimension to the type. To achieve a strong reflection in the type and a realistic 3D look, Lill used two applications of Apply Surface Texture. First select the text layer in the Layers palette to make it active. Then click on the right arrow of the Layers palette and select Convert to Default Layer from the menu. Next, choose Select, Load Selection and load the transparency mask for the text layer. Then choose Effects, Surface Control, Apply Surface Texture. To reflect the environment map onto your type, use these settings: In the Using menu choose the text mask to restrict the reflection to the type. Move the Reflection slider to 100% (so the environment map shows up) and move the Softness slider to the right (to scale the reflection map). Adjust the other settings to suit your image. The Apply Surface Texture dialog box is interactive, so you can scale your pattern while viewing the reflection map in the Preview window. When the reflection looks good, click OK in the Apply Surface Texture dialog box. Lill's Apply Surface Texture settings for the first application are as follows: Softness 40.0; Amount 200%; Picture 100%; Shine 40%; and Reflection 100%.

Now add a realistic 3D look to the text by choosing Apply Surface Texture a second time. This time, check the Inverted box (to add a second light source); decrease the Reflection slider to 0% by moving it all the way to the left; and decrease the Softness to about 10. Lill's second Surface Texture application settings are as follows: Softness, 10.0; Amount, 100%; Picture, 100%; Shine, 40%; and Reflection, 0%. Click OK. The image with Apply Surface Texture can be seen at the beginning of this story.

4 Adding a shadow and a soft black border. Next, Lill added a black drop shadow to her text, adding to the 3D look and giving her image more contrast. To generate the shadow, she chose Effects, Objects, Create Drop Shadow. In the dialog box, she specified settings for the X and Y coordinates to fit her image, increased the Opacity of the shadow to 80%, left the other settings at their defaults and checked the Collapse to One Layer box to combine the text and shadow.

Then, to finish the image with a more graphic look that would complement the shadow, Lill added a softly feathered black border to her image. To create her border effect, begin by choosing Select, All. Then from the Select menu choose Select, Modify, Contract. In the Contract Selection dialog box, type in 12 pixels. Now choose Select, Feather and set the feather to 24 pixels. Finally, Lill filled the selected, feathered edge with black. Begin by choosing black in the Colors picker. Choose the Paint Bucket, and in the Property Bar make these choices: Click the Fill Image button, and from the Fill menu choose Current Color. Click inside the active selection with the Paint Bucket tool.

Building a Terrain Map

Overview Create a terrain map from elevation data; make a custom gradient; color the map; use Apply Surface Texture to give it realistic dimension.

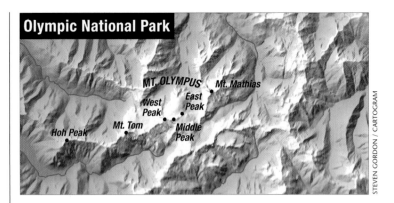

Olympic National Park

MT. OLYMPUS   Mt. Mathias
West   East
Peak   Peak
Hoh Peak   Mt. Tom   Middle
Peak

STEVEN GORDON / CARTOGRAM

The grayscale image representing elevation

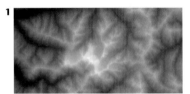

Edit Gradient

☑ Linear

Cancel   OK

Building a custom gradient for the map

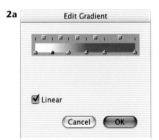

The map with the custom gradient applied using Express in Image

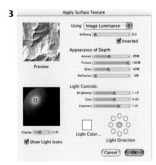

Gordon's settings in Apply Surface Texture, used to produce the terrain map

TO CREATE THIS REALISTIC MAP of Mount Olympus, Washington, Steven Gordon built a color terrain background from real data. As principal cartographer and owner of Cartagram, Gordon produces custom maps for electronic and print publication, specializing in tourism maps with relief renderings of the terrain.

1 Making a grayscale-to-height image. To begin the map, Gordon downloaded a digital elevation model (DEM) file from the USGS (www.usgs.gov). He processed it using a shareware DEM reader he found by searching for the keyword "DEM" in an Internet search engine. The resulting PICT image contained grayscale values mapped to elevation values, which Gordon could then use in building the image.

2 Coloring the image. Gordon opened the grayscale PICT file in Painter and built a custom gradient to color the map. To make your own gradation, open the Colors and the Gradients palettes; in the Gradients palette choose the Two-Point gradation. Now open the Edit Gradient dialog box by clicking the right triangle on the Gradients palette bar and choosing Edit Gradient. Using the dialog box, you can create a new gradation with color control points representing elevation zones (as Gordon did). Add control points to the center of the gradient by clicking in the Gradient bar. Click each control point and then click in the Colors section to choose a color for that point. Gordon's gradation progressed from dark blue-green valleys to white mountain crests. When the gradient looks good, click OK and then save it by choosing Save Gradient from the Gradients palette's menu. Apply the gradient to your image by choosing Express in Image from the Gradients section's menu.

3 Building Terrain. To add realistic relief to your map, choose Effects, Surface Control, Apply Surface Texture, Using Image Luminance. Click the Inverted box to make the light areas in the map "popup." To blur undesirable detail, move the Softness slider to the right. Adjust the Amount to build dimension and shadow. Gordon decreased the Amount to 85% to keep the shadows from being too dark and prominent. He used the default 11:00 light direction setting and left the Shine at the default 40%. 🖌

Building a Clone-Based Mosaic

Overview *Choose a photo reference and retouch it if needed; make a clone of the retouched photo; use the Make Mosaic dialog box to design and lay down colored tiles in the clone.*

1

The original photograph

2a

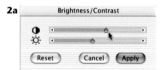

Increasing the contrast in the source image

2b

Detail of the retouched source image

MOSAICS HAVE BEEN USED AS A NARRATIVE and decorative art form since Hellenistic and Roman times. Because of its graphic nature, the mosaic is a medium that can be used to express strong emotion. S. Swaminathan created the digital mosaic *Soul of Homelessness*, based on his photograph of a homeless man. His vision was to create an abstracted mosaic portrait of the man that would portray the dignity he projected.

1 Selecting a source image. Choose a photo with a strong focal point and meaningful content, so the mosaic technique does not overpower the image. The photo should also have a broad tonal range and good color detail to help build value and color complexity into the tiles. Swaminathan began with a 675 x 920-pixel photo.

2 Retouching and cloning. To separate the subject from the background, Swaminathan used a modified Digital Airbrush variant of Airbrushes to simplify the background of the photo, adding soft blue and white strokes. He also increased the contrast in the image using Effects, Tonal Control, Brightness/Contrast.

When he was satisfied with the retouching, he cloned the image. Choose File, Clone to make a clone of your source image. In preparation for laying down colored tiles in the clone based on the color of the clone source image, enable the Use Clone Color button (the rubber stamp) in the Colors picker.

3a

Designing a horizontal tile to use on the face

3b

Using Tracing Paper to view the clone source while positioning tiles on the clone

4a

Erasing a course of tiles in the hair

4b

Adding new irregular tiles in the hair

3 Laying tiles. With the clone active, open the Make Mosaic dialog box (Canvas, Make Mosaic), and enable the Use Tracing Paper box so you can see the source image while laying down the tiles. To change the Grout from the default white to black, click the Grout square in the Colors dialog box and move the Lightness slider all the way to the bottom. To design a custom tile, begin by setting Dimensions for the tile; choose a Width, Length and Grout size. Make a stroke on your image to test the settings. Press Ctrl/⌘-Z to Undo a test stroke without closing the Make Mosaic dialog box. Experiment with the settings until you get just the look you want.

Swaminathan began with the face, which would become the focal point of the mosaic portrait. As he worked, he varied the size of the tiles, using larger tiles for the broader areas of the face (the forehead and cheeks), and smaller tiles to render detailed areas (the shadowed right side of the man's nose, eyes and eyebrows).

Generally, he worked from the center out, beginning with the face and hair and then rendering the shirt, shoes and background. To depict the long hair (and to contrast with the more uniform shapes of tiles on the subject's jacket) he designed narrow, irregularly shaped tiles. To vary the tile shapes and grout (as Swaminathan did), choose Randomness from the Settings pop-up menu to access the sliders. Begin by moving the Cut slider to the right to increase Randomness in the shape of the tile ends. To vary the spacing between tiles, move the Grout slider to the right. Experiment with each of the sliders individually until you arrive at the look you want.

SAMPLE WITH A CLICK

To sample color from an existing tile in your mosaic (with Clone Color turned off in the Colors picker), press the Alt/Option key and click on a tile. You won't see the Mosaic brush's crosshair cursor change to the Dropper when you're working with the open Make Mosaic dialog box, but you *will* be able to sample the color.

CORRECTION SHORTCUT

To remove tiles without clicking the Remove Tiles icon, press the Ctrl-Shift/⌘-Shift keys and drag the Mosaic brush over the tiles that you want to remove.

4 Completing the image. To refine the tile design, Swaminathan sampled color from existing tiles and applied the color to new tiles. (Before sampling color from a tile, click the Clone Color button in the Colors picker to toggle it off; then press the Alt/Option key and click on a tile.) To erase tiles, click the Remove Tiles icon and drag the cursor over the tiles that you want to remove. Click back on the Apply Tiles icon and drag to add new tiles.

Adding highlights and shadows. Finally, Swaminathan used Apply Surface Texture to add realistic highlights and shadows like those you would see on the slightly uneven surface of handmade tiles. Choose Effects, Surface Control, Apply Surface Texture Using Image Luminance. Try these subtle settings: Softness, 0; Amount, 20; Picture, 100; Shine, 25; and Reflection, 0. Click OK. 🖌

Creating a Circular Panorama

Overview *Shoot a series of photos for a panorama and stitch them together; capture a pattern; use a Pattern Pen to stroke a circular selection; touch up areas and add clouds to the sky.*

JOHN DERRY

1a

The original photographs

1b

Arranging the horizon of the photographs

1c

The completed linear panorama

2a

The flipped linear panorama

WITH THE GROWING POPULARITY of digital photography, it's become easier to create panoramic imagery. By combining a linear photographic panorama with the Pattern Pen, you can create a very unique variation—the circular panorama.

John Derry has been passionate about photography for more than 30 years. He enjoys creating panoramas; however, he wanted to give some of his imagery a new twist, as shown here in *Bonfante Gardens*. After a lot of experimentation, he discovered how to create a circular panorama using the Pattern Pen in Painter.

1 Creating a panorama. A digital panorama is created by stitching together several photos that have been carefully shot as a set of overlapping images. Stitching refers to the process of matching up image elements in the overlapping areas of the adjacent photos. Derry manually stitched the images together in Painter, with each photo element on an individual layer. He used layer masks, cloning and Airbrushes to match up the edges. When it was complete, he flattened the file. For more information about layers and layer masks, see Chapter 6, "Using Layers."

2 Converting a panorama to a pattern. When the panorama is ready, you can capture it into the Pattern library so that it can be used by the Pattern Pens. (A Pattern Pen uses the Current Pattern as its media.) Open the Patterns palette by choosing Window, Library Palettes, Show Patterns. Now, make a selection

2b

Capturing the original panorama into the Patterns palette

2c

Naming the panorama pattern and using the default settings

3

Test strokes painted with the Pattern Pen, using the original panorama pattern (left) and the flipped image (right)

4a

The Drawing Mode buttons with the Draw Anywhere button being selected

4b

The stroked circular selection painted with a 500-pixel Pattern Pen, using the original panorama pattern (left) and the flipped image (right)

around your image by choosing Select, All and then choosing Capture Pattern from the pop-up menu on the Patterns palette. Give your new pattern a name and accept the default settings. The selected image will appear in the current Patterns library.

Derry also created a second version of his linear panorama with the sky at the bottom so that he could try them both out with the Pattern Pen and then decide which image worked the best. To flip your panoramic image, choose Select, All and then Select, Float to put it on a layer. Then, choose Effects, Orientation, Flip Vertical. Now, make a selection around the panorama (Select, All), choose Capture Pattern from the pop-up menu on the Patterns palette and name the pattern. The new pattern will appear in the current Patterns library as before.

3 Making practice strokes. With both versions of the panorama captured as patterns, you are now ready to test the patterns using the Pattern Pen. Open a large, new file about 3000 pixels x 3000 pixels. Select the Pattern Pens category and then choose the Pattern Pen variant. Draw a few practice strokes with both versions of the pattern image.

4 Stroking a circular selection with the Pattern Pen.
Next, open a new 3000 x 3000 pixel image. In this step you will create the circular selection that the Pattern Pen will follow when you use the Stroke Selection feature. Select the Oval Selection tool in the Toolbox and press Shift, and then draw a circular selection. (Derry made the circle about one third of the width of the image.) Now, use the Oval Selection tool to reposition the active selection into the center of your image. (For more information about selections, see Chapter 5.)

Before stroking the selection with the Pattern Pen, you must first set the Drawing Mode (the buttons at the bottom-left corner of the Painter image window) to Draw Anywhere, because the Draw Inside mode will automatically be chosen when you make a selection, and it will constrain the media to the inside of the selection. Draw Anywhere will allow the media to be painted on both sides of the selection border. Now choose Select, Stroke Selection, and marvel as the linear panorama flows from the Pattern Pen in a continuously repeating stroke.

The final size of the circular panorama is controlled by a combination of the circular selection's diameter and the current size of the Pattern Pen. The goal is to make adjustments until the linear

5

Using the Soft Cloner variant of Cloners to complete the unfinished area

6a

The airbrushed sky added to the center

6b

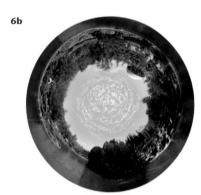

The clouds added to the sky

7

The final rotated image with the soft edge

panorama is wrapped around the circle with the two ends slightly overlapped. You will need to experiment to find the desired settings.

If the linear panorama imagery repeats, try increasing the size of the Pattern Pen using the Size slider in the Property Bar. It's a good idea to adjust the size value in regular increments. Derry started with a 500-pixel brush. When he needed to adjust the brush up or down in size, he did so using increments of 50 pixels. For instance, his resized brush increments varied like this: 1050, 1100, 1150 pixels and so on.

You might also want to adjust the size of your selection. By doing this in regular increments, you can estimate your additional adjustments more accurately. Open the Info window (Window, Show Info) and select the Selection Adjuster tool (Toolbox). Hold down the Shift key and click and drag on one of the corner handles outside of the selection to adjust the selection's size. Watch the Info palette, noting the numeric Width and Height readout as you adjust the selection. Derry repeated the Stroke Selection and Undo commands (using a combination of brush and selection sizing adjustments) until he arrived at the result he desired.

5 Hiding the flaws. When the linear panorama is correctly wrapped into a circle, there will be a flaw where the two ends meet. This flaw can be repaired in a variety of ways. You can use Painter's cloning features to clone bits of imagery over the flaw. You can also use the Lasso tool to draw a freehand selection around a bit of imagery and then copy and paste it into an area to cover the flaw.

6 Painting the sky. To complete your circular panorama, you'll need to paint over the blank area inside. Derry created a layer, sampled a blue color in the sky with the Dropper tool and then used a large airbrush to feather in a completed sky area. To complete the effect, he painted a few faint clouds.

7 Making final adjustments. Take a good look at your final circular panorama and decide whether there is a subject element that you'd like to position at the bottom of the composition. Derry wanted to position the tower element at the bottom. Use the Rotate Page tool (located in the Toolbox under the Grabber hand) to preview the various degrees of image rotation. Then, for the actual rotation, use the Oval Selection tool to select the panorama and copy the image. Choose Edit, Paste in Place to put the copy of the panorama on a new layer and then choose Effects, Orientation, Free Transform. Press the Ctrl/⌘ key and drag a corner handle to rotate the layer and then choose Commit Transform. Finally, drop the layer by choosing Drop from the Layers palette menu. To add a soft edge treatment to your image as Derry did, use the Magic Wand (Toolbox) to select the white background, and then choose Select, Feather (using about 30 pixels). Finally, press the Backspace/Delete key to clear the area and leave a soft edge. 🖌

Draping a Weave

Overview *Paint a grayscale file that will be your source image; fill a clone of that file with a weave; use a combination of Glass Distortion and Surface Texture to wrap the weave around the source image.*

CHER THREINEN-PENDARVIS

The grayscale form file with strong values

YOU CAN USE PAINTER'S WEAVES, located in the Weaves palette, to fill any selection or document, using either the Fill command or the Paint Bucket tool. Weaves can be used in fashion design and they make good backgrounds for scenes, but their flat look can be a drawback. To create the appearance of fabric—to hang behind a still life, for instance—we added dimension to a weave by "draping" it over a painted form using a powerful Glass Distortion displacement effect along with Apply Surface Texture.

1 Making the form file. Think of the form file as a kind of mold—or fashion designer's dress form—over which you'll drape your fabric. Create a grayscale form file that has strong value contrast and smooth dark-to-light transitions. As a reference for our 500-pixel-square form file, we draped fabric over a chair and sketched it in Painter, and then cleaned up the sketch with the Digital Airbrush variant of Airbrushes. Since any hard edges in the form file would make a noticeable break in the weave's pattern, we softened the image with Effects, Focus, Super Soften. We used a 7-pixel Super Soften setting on our file.

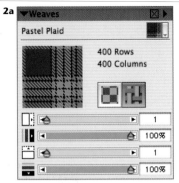

2a

The Pastel Plaid in the Weaves palette

2b

Filling the clone with the weave

3

Applying Glass Distortion to the weave

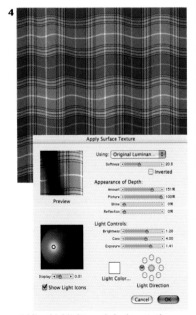

4

Adding highlights and shadows to the distorted image using Surface Texture

If you don't want to paint the form file, here's a fast, but less "organic" way to create it. Open the Make Paper dialog box by clicking the Paper Selector on the Toolbox and then choosing Make Paper from the pop-up menu (to the right of the paper list). In the Make Paper dialog box, choose Line from the pop-up menu. Use a high spacing setting to make vertical lines and set Angle at 90˚. In the Save As field, type a name for the new paper. Choose your new paper in the Paper Selector and then choose black in the Colors picker. To apply the new paper, choose Effects, Surface Control, Color Overlay, Using Paper, at 100% Opacity and then click the Hiding Power button. To blur the image, use Super Soften as described above.

2 Making a clone and filling it with a weave. Choose File, Clone to make a duplicate of the form file with identical dimensions. Now choose a weave from the Weave Selector. (We chose the Pastel Plaid weave.) Fill the clone file with your weave (Ctrl/⌘-F; Weave, 100%).

3 Initiating the distortion. Here's where the movement begins. Choose Effects, Focus, Glass Distortion, Using Original Luminance. Now let Painter know the direction that you want the fabric to go when it overlies the form file. When a clone image is displaced by Glass Distortion using Original Luminance, the distance each pixel moves is based on the luminance of each pixel in the source file. We chose Vector Displacement to move pixels in a specific direction, and used the Amount slider to get a moderate "ripple" effect in the Preview (we chose 1.55), leaving Variance at 1.00. To establish the direction (and make the light areas move up and to the right, and dark areas move down and to the left—based on the form file), we moved the Direction slider to 90°. We added a Softness of 20.9 to smooth any rough edges that might be caused by the distortion of the weave. Experiment with your settings; the Softness, Amount and Direction may change based on the size of your file.

4 Adding highlights and shadows. Using Apply Surface Texture adds to the illusion of folded fabric by contributing highlights and shadows based on the form file. Choose Effects, Surface Control, Apply Surface Texture, Using Original Luminance. Experiment with your settings—paying special attention to how the lighting controls affect the look—and click OK. We set Softness to 20.3 (to smooth the image and slightly increase the depth of the folds), Amount to 151%, Picture to 100% (to make the image lighter while maintaining weaving detail), and Shine to 0% and then chose the 9 o'clock Light Direction button. 🖌

Creating Art for Glass Sculpture

Overview *Draw freeform images to capture as paper textures; use the custom textures to build background surfaces and to add texture to motifs; add embossing and texture effects; transfer the final images onto a glass block.*

MARY ANN ROLFE

FOR HER GLASS SCULPTURE *Petroglyphs,* Mary Ann Rolfe developed iconic southwestern images using texture, dimension and lighting effects in Painter. She used Painter to create the images and to preview them prior to output. She superimposed five panels in Painter: two background panels and three motif panels with figures. Then, she output the images and transferred them onto the glass using techniques that she teaches in her Digital Stretch workshops (www.digitalstretch.com). All of the panels combine to emphasize the transparency and depth of the glass.

Getting organized. Rolfe enjoys the freeform, playful aspect of her digital art. She also carefully documents her processes as she works, which takes discipline but serves her well. On her computer, she creates a project folder to save all the Painter files that she uses to create a piece. Careful organization allows her to re-create all or part of these effects on future works.

Before beginning to draw the pieces featured here, Rolfe created a custom color set from an earlier image so that she could incorporate its color scheme. (To read about color sets, see Chapter 2.)

1 Drawing patterns and capturing paper textures. First, Rolfe needed to create the textures that she would use to create the water-like background image, and to texturize the three overlaid motifs. She created a new file that measured 6 x 6 inches at 200 ppi. Keeping her strokes loose, she used the Flat Color variant of Pens to draw multiple patterns. Then, she captured each pattern as a paper texture. To build a paper texture, use the Rectangular Marquee tool to make a selection around an image, leaving plenty of white space around it. Click the triangle on the right side of the Paper Selector (in the Toolbox) and choose Launch Palette to open the Papers palette. Now, choose Capture Paper from the pop-up menu on the Papers palette. (Rolfe used the default Crossfade setting of 16. Crossfade blurs the transition between the tiles of the captured paper texture.) Save and name your paper. Rolfe saved all of her textures into her own paper library. (For more information on working with paper libraries, turn to page 17 in Chapter 1.)

Three-quarter view of the final sculpture

1

Drawn patterns that were captured and turned into paper textures

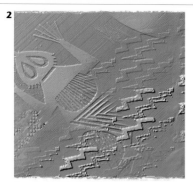

Detail of Background2 after Rolfe used the Apply Surface Texture effect using Image Luminance

Rolfe started with a basic shape for each of the three motifs and she colored them.

She added paper textures to the figure using Apply Surface texture.

She applied Surface Texture to the figure using Image Luminance.

2 Embossing the background. For the background panel, Rolfe created an empty new file, *Background2*. She used a two-point color gradient that had a diagonal axis and filled the entire Canvas. (See Chapter 2 for more information about using gradients.) To add interest to the color transitions in the gradient, she used the Turbulence variant of the Distortion brushes. Next, to apply an emboss effect using the lights and darks of her image, she chose Effects, Surface Control, Apply Surface Texture and chose Image Luminance from the Using pop-up menu.

To soften the edges of the background, Rolfe began by adding space around the outside of the image. She selected the entire Canvas (Select, All), chose Effects, Orientation, Scale and scaled the image to 96%. Then, she blended the colors into the white of the Canvas using the Oily Blender variant of the Blenders.

Next, Rolfe built up textured layers of color using the Square Chalk variant of Chalks. She picked colors from her custom color set and papers from her custom library of paper textures. As she worked, she changed the opacity and grain settings of the Square Chalk (using the sliders in the Property Bar) to vary the amount of texture and color that she applied with each stroke. To add dimension and an embossed effect to the brush work, she chose Effects, Surface Control, Apply Surface Texture, Using Image Luminance. She set Softness to 0% and under Appearance of Depth, she set the Amount to 28%.

3 Developing the motifs. Rolfe opened a black-and-white figure motif and added colors using the Oils Pastel variant of Pastels. To create your own motif, open a new image and add an empty new layer by clicking the New Layer button on the Layers palette. Choose the Flat Color variant of Pens and draw a motif or figure. When your motif is complete, turn on Preserve Transparency in the Layers palette. Preserve Transparency will protect the pixels outside the motif from new paint. Now, you can add color using the Oil Pastel variant of Oil Pastels.

Next, Rolfe added custom paper textures to selected areas of her motif. She used the Magic Wand tool to select a colored area of the motif; then she chose Effects, Apply Surface Texture, Using Paper and applied a custom paper texture. She repeated this step multiple times to add a variety of textures to her motif. Then, to add more depth to the texture, she chose Effects, Surface Control, Apply Surface Texture, this time using Image Luminance. She experimented with the Softness and Amount sliders to achieve the desired depth and roundness. Then, she added a drop shadow for more depth (Effects, Objects, Create Drop Shadow) and accepted the default settings.

4 Building the panels. Next, Rolfe created three beveled panels that would appear behind the figures. She selected the Canvas layer in the Layers palette and filled the canvas with the same style of gradient that she had used in step 3. To add texture to the gradient

4a

The completed Canvas layer for one of the three motifs

4b

One of the three completed motif panels

5a

▼ Papers ⊠ ▶

Starry Sky

256 Rows
256 Columns

□ ◄ ▲ ► 100%
◑ ◄ ▲ ► 100%
☼ ◄ ▲ ► 50%

Starry Sky paper in the Papers palette

5b

Front Layer image with gradient fill and Apply Surface Texture using Starry Sky paper

5c

Front Layer with Bevel World effect applied

fill on the Canvas, first choose a paper texture from the Paper Selector in the Toolbox. Choose Effects, Surface Control, Apply Surface Texture and then select Paper from the Using pop-up menu. Adjust the controls for Softness, Amount, Shine, and Reflection in the Apply Surface Texture dialog box to achieve the look you desire and then click OK. To create the illusion of a raised panel to go behind your motif (as Rolfe did), select the entire image (Select, All), and make an exact copy of the Canvas layer by pressing Alt/Option and choosing Select, Float. Click on the new layer in the Layers palette to select it and reduce its size to 90% by choosing Effects, Orientation, Scale. To add the drop shadow to the new layer choose Effects, Objects, Create Drop Shadow and use the default settings. When Rolfe had completed all these steps, she dropped all of the layers and saved her file.

5 Adding dimension to the background. The last panel Rolfe created was the top portion of the background that would fit behind the three motif panels and in front of Background2. Create a new file with the same dimensions as Background2. (Rolfe named hers *Front Layer*.) Fill the canvas with the same type of gradient you used in step 3, but pick two different colors. Next choose Effects, Surface Control, Apply Surface Texture, Using Paper. Rolfe used the Starry Sky texture from the Paper Textures library. To load the texture that she used, choose Open Library from the pop-up menu on the Papers palette. Navigate to the Painter Application folder, Extras folder, Paper Textures folder, choose the Paper Textures library and then choose the Starry Sky texture. To give the image a beveled edge, choose Select, All, click the Dynamic Plug-ins button on the Layers palette and then chose Bevel World. Adjust the Bevel Width and the lighting direction. When you have the settings as you like them, click OK.

6 Visualizing and printing. To help visualize how the elements would look together on the glass, Rolfe created a new file that contained a copy of each of the panels on its own layer. To build a layered file like Rolfe's, open each image and choose Select, All and then copy and paste each image into the new file. Rolfe reduced the opacity of each layer in the Layers palette so that she could see through each image to preview how it would look after it was embedded in the glass.

Rolfe printed the three motif panels using Painter and her Epson 2000P printer onto Epson Enhanced Matte paper. She also used the Epson 2000P to output the two other panels onto a specialty paper that she uses in her unique transfer process. When the prints were complete, she was ready to assemble and apply the images onto her digital glass sculpture titled *Petroglyphs*. 🖌

6

Details of a motif transferred onto the glass

Creating a Color-Adjustable Leaf Brush

Overview *Paint a background, tree and branches; draw leaf elements using values of gray; capture them as an Image Hose Nozzle; load the Nozzle and adjust it; decorate the tree with colored leaves.*

JOHN DERRY

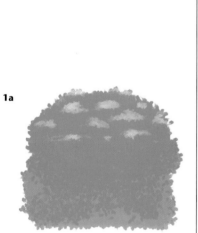

1a

Painting the sky using an Artists' Oils brush

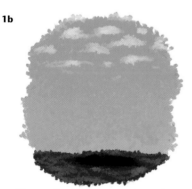

1b

The completed landscape background

THE IMAGE HOSE IS A UNIQUE BRUSH that uses multiple elements as its medium. Small painted elements or masked photographic elements can easily be captured into an Image Hose Nozzle file. John Derry and Mark Zimmer invented the Image Hose. They received a patent for it, and the Image Hose made its debut appearance in Painter 3. As Painter has evolved, Nozzle files have become easier to build.

Many kinds of illustrations employ similar visual elements. Illustrating a tree, for example, can require the rendering of many small leaves. When painted using conventional media, the leaf elements must be individually created, and this can be a tedious, time-consuming process. For the fanciful illustration *Tree*, John Derry created a set of leaves and then used them to quickly decorate the branches of the tree. He was also able to use the Nozzle that he had built on future illustrations.

1 Setting the stage. Derry wanted to create a stylized illustration of a tree in a landscape. He painted the background using two layers, and he used a modified Clumpy Brush variant (Artists' Oils) to paint the grass and sky.

Open a new 1200 x 1000 pixel file, and choose a bright blue color in the Colors picker. Now, choose the Clumpy Brush variant of the Artists' Oils. Add a new layer to your image by clicking the New Layer button on the Layers palette. Use quick, loose brushstrokes to paint the sky. As you work, vary the value of the color by

2

The painted tree trunk and branches

3a

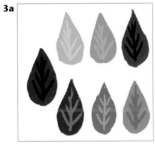

The painted leaves

3b

Grouping the selected layers

3c

Choosing the Make Nozzle from Group command

3d

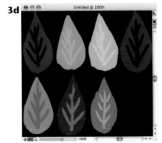

The Nozzle file created by the Make Nozzle from Group command

choosing subtly lighter or darker values in the Colors picker. When the sky is as you like it, add a new layer, choose a green color and then paint the grass using loose strokes. To suggest the shadow patterns on the grass, vary the value of the color as you did for the sky.

2 Painting a bare tree. With the background finished, Derry used the Scratchboard Tool variant of Pens to draw the tree's trunk and branches. Then, he painted the bark and the shadows.

Next, add a new layer for the tree. Choose a rich brown color, and use the Scratchboard Tool variant of Pens to paint the trunk and branches. When you have completed the base color for the tree, enable the Preserve Transparency check box in the Layers palette so that the new paint that you apply will appear only within the existing tree shape. Use varied brown colors to paint the bark and shadows on the trunk and branches.

3 Creating the leaf nozzle. Now that the stage was set, Derry was ready to build the leaf Nozzle. He began the Nozzle by creating six leaf elements that would form a layer group that could be incorporated into an Image Hose Nozzle. To match the brush work on the tree, he used the Scratchboard Tool to illustrate the leaves, with each leaf on its own layer. Derry drew the leaf elements using values of gray, rather than color, so that later he could take advantage of the Image Hose feature that allows you to add variable color to the Nozzle elements.

Begin by opening a new file (Derry's measured 500 x 500 pixels). Add a new layer for your first leaf. Disable Preserve Transparency in the Layers palette and then use the Scratchboard Tool to paint the leaf with values of gray. Repeat the process of adding a new layer and then painting each leaf on its own layer. When the leaf layers are complete, Shift-select them in the Layers palette and group them using the Group command found in the Layers palette pop-up menu. Next, convert the layer group into a Nozzle. Click the Nozzle Selector on the Toolbox, and from the pop-up menu choose Make Nozzle from Group. This command organizes the layer group into a grid that can be used by the Image Hose to read the individual elements. Save the Nozzle file in RIFF format. Now you are ready to load your new nozzle into the Image Hose.

4 Loading and adjusting the Image Hose. To load the newly created leaf nozzle into the Image Hose, click the Nozzle Selector on the Toolbox, choose Load Nozzle from the pop-up menu and navigate to where you saved the file. Now, select the Image Hose in the Brush Selector Bar and choose the Spray-Size-P Angle-D variant. This variant uses pressure (P) to vary the Nozzle's element size and the direction the stroke is painted to express the angle (A) of the element. When Derry tried out the variant on a test image, he found that the leaf elements were incorrectly angled for the tree. He corrected this by experimenting with the Angle of the

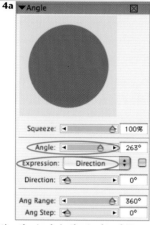

4a

Adjusting the Angle in the Angle palette. The Expression menu is set to Direction.

4b

The leaves pointing outward

5a

Adjusting the Grain slider in the Property Bar

5b

The dark green color chosen as the Additional Color and the dark green leaves

5c

The lighter green color chosen as the Additional Color and the light green leaves

6a

Painting the shaded leaves

brush using the Angle section of Brush Controls. When he arrived at a setting that he liked, the pointed ends of the leaves were positioned away from the brushstroke direction as it was drawn. This enabled drawing the leaves from the outer periphery into central areas of the tree, with the leaves pointing outward. Open the Angle section of Brush Controls (Window, Brush Controls, Show Angle) and experiment with the Angle slider.

5 Controlling the nozzle color. Because Derry chose to create the leaf elements using values of gray, he could mix any color with his Nozzle elements. He used the Grain slider in the Property Bar to mix color with the luminosity of his nozzle elements. Click on the Additional Color (back color square) in the Colors palette and choose a dark green hue. In the Property Bar, experiment with the Grain Setting (Derry used 39%).

6 Painting the leaves. When he painted the leaves, Derry wanted to create highlights and shadows in areas of the leaves. To accomplish this, he painted the leaves on three separate layers, using a variety of greens that would simulate the variations in highlights and shadows.

   Paint each series of leaves on its own layer so that you will be able to adjust their opacity or make tonal adjustments later. Add a new layer for the shadowed lower leaves. Choose a dark yellow-green in the Colors picker and spray these leaves onto the layer. When you have the lower leaves as you like them, follow the same process. Use a new layer and lighter greens to build each of the remaining levels of tone.

   With the three leaf layers painted, Derry was now ready to make final adjustments. He selected the top leaf layer and adjusted its tonal values using the Effects, Tonal Control, Brightness/Contrast command. The final image on page 324 shows his hand-rendered illustration. He dramatically reduced the tedious process of leaf creation by using the Image Hose.

6b

The leaves painted and adjusted

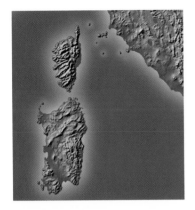

■ This richly textured map of Italy was created by **Steven Gordon** and commissioned by ArtService in Rome, Italy. The map is one of five maps Gordon produced for the "Alitalia for you" section of Alitalia Airlines's in-flight magazine. To make the maps distinctive and different, Gordon turned to Painter's brushes and Auto Clone command to transform terrain images into faded watercolor landscapes.

Gordon began by constructing color terrain images from elevation data in Digital Wisdom's MapRender3D. He used the same color-to-elevation scheme so that all five terrain images would result in a consistent color appearance. After exporting TIFF files from MapRender3D, Gordon opened each image in Photoshop, where he cropped it and set its resolution to 300 ppi.

For the map of Italy, Gordon opened the Photoshop file in Painter. He cloned the image (File, Clone) and in the cloned file, chose Select, All and then pressed the Backspace/Delete key to clear the image from the clone Canvas. To begin

auto-cloning the Italy map, Gordon selected the Impasto Soft Oil brush (loaded from the *Painter IX Wow!* CD-ROM). He enabled the Clone Color button in the Colors palette and in the Property Bar, he set Size to 100 and Opacity to 10%. (For all of the brushes, Gordon set Grain to 20.) Then, he chose Effects, Esoterica, Auto Clone and let it run for one minute, which filled the image with light brushstrokes based on the source image.

Next, Gordon selected the Soft Diffused Brush variant of Digital Watercolor in the Brush Selector Bar; then he enabled Clone Color in the Colors palette. He set the brush Size to 40 and Opacity to 10% in the Property Bar. He chose Effects, Esoterica, Auto Clone again, and let it run for 12 seconds, which filled in gaps between the brushstrokes laid down by the first Auto Clone and darkened the clone with more of the source image. He ran Auto Clone with the same brush for 12 seconds again, but this time changed its Size to 5 to bring out more detail.

To complete the Italy image, Gordon selected the Impasto, Soft Oil brush again, enabled Clone Color in the Colors palette, and set the Size to 5 and Opacity to 10% in the Property Bar. He chose Effects, Esoterica, Auto Clone again, running the effect for 12 seconds. Some parts of the image appeared to be diffused or too light, so Gordon selected the Soft Cloning variant of Cloners, and set its Size to 200 and Opacity to 3% in the Property Bar. He manually stroked over light areas to make them darker and into better focus. When he had finished retouching, Gordon selected the image, copied it and then selected the source image and pasted the cloned image into it as a layer. He set the resulting layer at 65% Opacity and with a Normal blending mode in the Layers palette. This allowed the clone image to be combined with the original source image. Finally, he saved the image as a TIFF file.

■ *Purple Cow* by **Steve Campbell** began as a low-resolution color sketch drawn during a trade show demo. Campbell wanted to create a whimsical illustration that had rich color and three-dimensional texture. He began the illustration by sketching, with a variety of brushes to create an underpainting.

Next, Campbell isolated the figures and background elements by making selections using the Lasso tool and floating the elements to layers. (Alt/Option-click on an active selection with the Layer Adjuster tool to copy it to a layer.) Campbell painted and sketched using several Oils variants and smudged using the Just Add Water variant of Blenders on the cow, figure, moon and

background. He used the Digital Airbrush variant of Airbrushes to add more subtle color to the sky and to paint the cast shadows under the moon and the figure. Then, he painted the figure's bright balloon by using Oils variants.

When he was satisfied with the composition, Campbell applied lighting and rich texture effects within selected areas. For instance, to add lighting to the cow, he selected its layer by clicking on it in the Layers palette; then he chose Effects, Surface Control, Apply Lighting and applied a custom light (based on the Splashy Colors light). For the three-dimensional texture on the cow, he chose a bold seamless texture from his custom library and applied it to the cow layer by choosing Effects, Surface

Control, Apply Surface Texture, Using Paper. To add relief texture to the moon, he chose a custom texture and again chose Apply Surface Texture, Using Paper.

When he finished working on the layers, Campbell flattened the image by choosing Drop All from the pop-up menu on the Layers palette. Next, he created a copy of the Canvas by choosing Select, All and then Alt/Option-clicking it with the Layer Adjuster tool. He used Effects, Surface Control, Apply Lighting on the layer and then adjusted the strength of the lighting effect on the image by reducing the Opacity of the "lighted" layer. Finally, to complete the image, Campbell used the Chalk and Oils variants to paint bright colored accents.

■ Illustrator **Philip Howe** was commissioned by the Harvey and Daughters agency to create this richly textured photo-collage painting for H & S Bakery. The completed illustration was used for a trade show mural that was more than 18 feet wide.

First, Howe built a photographic composite using several photos that his team had shot of the breads. Then, he tightly rendered the stands, windows, walls, floor, oven and other elements to give the illustration the look of an old world bakery. At this point, Howe's client decided that he wanted more of a painted look, so

Howe used Painter to create the illusion of a painting. He made a clone of the photo-illustration by choosing File, Clone. To create brushstroke effects, he used a smeary custom cloning brush (similar to the Oil Brush Cloner variant of the Cloners) to paint over every inch of the image, building expressive brush work. Then, he enhanced the brush work using special effects.

Howe began the process of building relief on the image with distortion. He applied Effects, Focus, Glass Distortion Using Image Luminance and the Refraction Map Type. Then, to give the relief highlights and shadows, he applied Effects, Surface

Control, Apply Surface Texture, Using Image Luminance.

The combination of powerful effects created a heavy-looking texture, which he wanted to subdue in a few areas. Howe saved the painted, textured image as a Photoshop file. Then, he copied and pasted the image as a layer over the tightly rendered photo-illustration. He added a layer mask to the texture layer (click the Create Layer Mask button on the Layers palette), and he softly airbrushed areas with black paint to hide portions of the texture layer so that the breads would appear more photographic, because they were revealed through the texture layer.

■ Artist and teacher **Jinny Brown** painted the intriguing still life *Posies* from her imagination, without the use of references. She used her own custom brush and Painter's cloning features to paint each brushstroke by hand.

Brown began by opening an image that she had painted as a texture experiment. The colorful texture image is shown on the left. Then, she opened another new image the exact same size as the texture image and filled it with a dark reddish-brown color. The dark color would contrast with the lighter colors that she planned to paint in from the clone source. She specified the textured image as the Clone Source by choosing File, Clone Source and then choosing the filename from the list. Next, she chose a custom brush variant that incorporated a painted rose petal as its captured dab. Then, she clicked the Clone Color button on the Colors palette and began to paint the flowers. For each flower, Brown painted a circle using light pressure. At the end of a stroke, she lifted the stylus with a flip of the hand. For the softer looking flowers, she applied lighter pressure while she painted around in a tighter circle. When the flowers and vase were complete, she enhanced her painting by applying a watercolor texture. From the pop-up menu on the Layers palette, she chose Lift Canvas to Watercolor Layer. Then she selected the Dry Camel variant of Watercolor in the Brush Selector Bar and choose Wet Entire Watercolor Layer from the Layers palette menu.

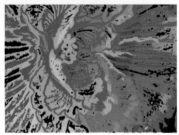

■ To create a series of elegant, sophisticated images that would be printed on cards and calendars, artist **Anne Syer** transformed several of her close-up flower photographs using the Woodcut effect in Painter.

Syer began *Coral Begonia Woodcut* by opening a photograph of a begonia flower in Painter. She selected Effects, Surface Control, Woodcut. In the Woodcut dialog box, she set the Black Edge slider to about 9% and kept the Heaviness at 50%. The lower Black Edge setting brought out the detail and delicate

texture of the begonia petals in the black portion of the effect. For a posterized effect, she limited the number of colors to about 14 in the colors area of the Woodcut dialog box.

To clean up some of the lines and to add detail to the black areas, Syer used the Opaque Round variant of the Oils brushes. For more depth in the color areas, she added a new Watercolor layer by clicking the New Watercolor Layer button on the Layers palette, and then she painted washes of similar hues using the Simple Round Wash and Wet Flat

variants of the Watercolor brushes. When Syer had completed her washes, she merged the Watercolor layer with the Canvas by clicking on the right arrow on the Layers palette and selecting Drop from the pop-up menu.

Next, Syer added more rich color to her image. She selected solid areas of color using the Magic Wand and Lasso tools. Then, she applied a custom linear gradient that she had built using two colors from the image. She repeated this process several times until she achieved the harmonious colors that she desired.

■ Inspired by the music of the late, great Ray Charles, **Jeremy Sutton** created the expressive portrait *Ray*. "I have always been deeply moved by his music. There is something so raw and honest in his songs, so moving," says Sutton.

Sutton began by searching for a photograph of Ray Charles. Eventually, he found a photo, taken by Ira Schwartz, that captured the exuberance of Charles's personality and his joy of life. Sutton purchased the rights from the Associated Press to do a derivative work based on the photograph.

He cropped and resized the photograph to the resolution and size that he wanted to use for a printed image (40 x 40 inches at 150 dpi). Then, he made a clone of the photo by choosing File,

Clone. Next, he chose the Big Wet Luscious variant of the New Paint Tools library (located in the Brushes folder within the Extras folder on the Painter IX Application CD-ROM) and painted a loose, colorful painting that he refers to as his "muck-up" stage. Then, he saved two copies of the painting so that he could apply a different set of effects to each. For the first copy, he applied a Zoom Blur that emanated from the center by choosing Effects, Focus, Zoom Blur. With the second copy, he created a woodcut version by choosing Effects, Surface Control, Woodcut. Then, he pasted both of the variations into the original photograph as layers, with the Woodcut version on top. To blend the information on the layers, he adjusted the Composite Methods, setting the Woodcut layer to Overlay and

the Zoom Blur layer to Magic Combine. When he was satisfied with the image, he flattened it and then used Canvas, Canvas Size to add a white border around the image. For the explosive effect with paint emanating out from the center, he used the Smear variant of Blenders and the Big Wet Luscious brush to add diffused brush work.

Finally, Sutton printed the image using an Epson 9600 on Epson PremierArt Water Resistant Canvas with Epson UltraChrome inks. To protect the ink, he sprayed several coatings of Krylon Acrylic Crystal Clear protective non-yellowing finish, and then he stretched the canvas on stretcher bars. As a final touch, Sutton added accents of acrylic paint and gels.

■ An innovative artist, **Steve Campbell** began *Coffeehouse* by sketching a cafe scene using conventional pencils and paper. The color theme was inspired by the work of traditional artist Yoshiro Tachibana.

When his sketch was complete, Campbell scanned the drawing and opened it in Painter. He cleaned up the drawing using a low-opacity Eraser variant, and then he smudged areas using the Just Add Water variant of Blenders. Next, he brushed on translucent color using the Diffuse Bristle variant of Watercolor. To complete the underpainting, he added opaque paint using the Square Chalk variant of Chalk.

So that he could limit paint as he refined the image, he isolated the figures and areas of the background by making hand-drawn selections using the Lasso tool and then floating the elements to layers. (Alt/ Option-click on an active selection with the Layer Adjuster tool to copy it to a layer.)

Campbell used numerous custom textures during the development of the piece, including textures from the *Painter IX Wow!* CD-ROM. For instance, the texture on the table in front of the Bird Girl (left foreground) was created from a scan of a checkered Japanese paper, and another was built using a scan of a musical notation by Beethoven.

To model the foreground figures and other areas, he used the Square Chalk and then blended areas with the Just Add Water variant of Blenders.

To add to the rich texture, Campbell used pieces of manipulated photographs. He pasted bits of his own photos into the working image, for instance, a shot taken at Golden Gate Park, a crowd scene and another of a sax player. Then, to give the photos an aged, textured look, he chose Effects, Surface Control, Distress. To subdue the images and merge them with the composition, he adjusted the opacity and the Composite Method for the photo layers.

As a last step, Campbell set type on paths in Adobe Illustrator and then he pasted the text into his Painter image as layers. He adjusted the opacity and Composite Method for each layer to blend the text phrases with the image.

■ **Mary Beth Novak** creates textile designs that are used in a variety of products—from bedsheets to bath accessories. From concept to production art, Novak uses Painter IX, Adobe Photoshop and Macromedia FreeHand. Using Painter gives her greater flexibility and the ability to create hand-drawn textured looks in her textile designs.

Incorporating Painter into her process has pushed her textile designs to a whole new level. Novak says, "I use a lot of the different brushes, and I use the Distress feature all the time to give things a more hand-done look. Painter has really gotten us to a whole new plane with our prints. Usually, I am able to get a look that looks more hand-done than if we had painted all the layers on paper and scanned them in."

For the *Sakura* print (above right), Novak first sketched the branches, leaves and flowers in pencil. She scanned her pencil sketches at the scale they would be in the final print. Novak opened the scans in Painter, creating a new, separate layer for the leaves, branches and flowers. On the new leaves layer, using her scanned pencil sketch as a template, Novak used the Gouache brushes to paint the basic leaf shapes, and she repeated this process for the branches and flowers layers.

Then, she duplicated the branches layer and checked the Preserve Transparency button in the Layers palette. With this layer active, Novak added brush work by using a variant of the Gouache brushes over a custom paper texture. Using Preserve Transparency kept her brushstrokes within the shape of the branches. She repeated the same process for the leaves and flowers. Novak then distressed the three textured layers by choosing Effects, Surface Control, Distress. In the Using pop-up menu, she selected Paper, and then she chose a custom paper that looked like an irregular water texture. The Distress effect converted her image into black and white. She repeated this same process for the leaves and flowers. Then, she repeated this process to add another layer of texture to the leaves.

Because textile prints cannot have any random additional colors, the colors Novak used in the Painter file were for visual reference only. Textile prints consist of 6 to 12 spot colors (Pantone textile colors), each of which may consist of multiple elements. At this point, Novak saved the layered Painter file in Photoshop format, opened the image in Photoshop and saved each layer as a separate TIFF file. Using FreeHand, she

imported each of the files (as layers) into one FreeHand file so that she could reassemble the branches, leaves and flowers in the correct order and then color them using the Pantone textile colors that she had selected to use in the design.

To build the background of the print (above left), Novak used Painter to clone scans of Japanese paper patterns. She used the Splattery Airbrush and Cloners brushes to paint the Japanese patterns, leaving open areas and rough edges to create an irregular, stamped look. She brought the finished, cloned images into Photoshop and saved them as black-and-white TIFF files. Next, Novak imported the TIFF files into FreeHand, with each image on its own layer. She arranged them into a pleasing pattern and colored each layer to create the finished background image (shown on the top right). The ability to pull out elements, scale, rotate and change colors easily is essential to Novak's creative process.

To complete the *Sakura* print, Novak combined the final background layers that included the final leaves, branches and flower layers in FreeHand. She created her final pattern for printing as a 28" or 36" repeat design in FreeHand.

■ Artist **Susan Thompson** created *Pettus Home*, a mosaic portrait of the historic Pettus family home, in Elm Hill, Norwich, England. Originally, she was commissioned to create an enlarged, hand-colored version of a pencil drawing of the home, which dated back to the 1500s. The client provided colored photographs of the street for her to use for reference. Thompson colored the image in Photoshop using several tinted layers.

A year later, Thompson decided to use the *Pettus Home* image as a reference for a mosaic that she created in Painter. To begin the mosaic, she opened the final colored *Pettus Home* image, and then she created a clone (File, Clone). She chose Canvas, Make Mosaic, enabled the Use Tracing Paper button and then clicked the Apply Tiles button. She applied tiles along the most important shapes first,

following the design of the composition; for instance, the perimeters of the building, the flow of the street and the perimeter of the entire image. Then she applied tiles to the interior areas. To build perspective, she used larger tiles in the foreground of the street and then gradually reduced the size of the tiles as the street receded into the distance. Thompson made notes of the tile sizes and other details so that she could return to certain areas, if needed. When she was happy with the mosaic, she gave the tiles three-dimensional highlights and shadows by choosing Effects, Surface Control, Apply Surface Texture. The mosaic, which contains more than 77,000 tiles, took a few months for Thompson to complete. Her delighted client purchased the mosaic rendition, as well.

■ Filmmaker, painter and printmaker **Elizabeth Sher** traveled to the Crusaders Palace in Rhodes, Greece, where she saw a mosaic of the Medusa. Inspired, she created *Me Dusa*, an installation piece that she exhibited at the Oliver Art Center, C.C.A., in Oakland, California. Sher has used Painter in her teaching at C.C.A. and in her own work since Painter 4.

Sher began by scanning a photograph of the Medusa mosaic and a 4 x 6-inch portrait of herself, using the same scale and resolution. She opened the scan of the portrait in Photoshop and used the Quick Mask function to isolate her face from the rest of the photograph. Then, Sher opened the scan of Medusa in Painter,

and she created a Color Set from the image. She chose Create Color Set from Image in the pop-up menu on the Color Set palette. Next, Sher opened and made a Clone (File, Clone) of her face image. Then, she chose Canvas, Make Mosaic and enabled the Use Tracing Paper button to keep the image of her face visible. She selected a tan grout color to blend with the face tiles. Then she mapped the size, shape and tone of the tiles to the contours of her face as she carefully built the mosaic.

With the face mosaic completed, Sher copied and pasted it as a layer over the Medusa mosaic photograph. She reduced the opacity of the layer in the Layers palette so that she could see underneath it

to align the two images. When the alignment was complete, Sher used a variety of brushes to add translucent glazes of color to integrate the two images. To smooth out the rough transitions, she used a variety of the Blenders brushes.

The circle image was printed with an Iris printer onto treated canvas at the Lightroom in Berkeley, California. Sher cut and mounted the printed piece onto cotton canvas, and then she painted the marble floor with acrylic paints to complement the 4 x 6-foot canvas. The final piece was shown on the floor with rocks and sand covering parts of the image, as a re-enactment of the uncovering of the mosaics in Petra, Jordan.

(c) GARTEL 2000

■ To create the surreal photo-collage *Clown Cuzin,* renowned and innovative artist **Laurence Gartel** combined his own photos with Painter brush work and special effects, and conventional acrylic paint. Gartel is delighted when unexpected surprises happen during his creation process. He enjoys painting gestural brush work in Painter.

Clown Cuzin is a member of Gartel's *Cousins* series. Each of the works in the series blends the real and the unreal—a portrait and a cybernetic hand. He began the work by scanning several of his photographic transparencies, including the background image of Coney Island shot in 1992. Then, he added acrylic paint and glitter to other photos and scanned

them. He opened all of the scanned images in Painter and assembled them into a composition. He painted brushstrokes using a variety of brushes, including the Smeary Round and Smeary Bristle Spray variants of the Oils. To blend areas of the image, he used Distortion variants. For instance, in the lower left of the image, where the gold blends with the red and pink, he created an interesting smudged texture using the Coarse Distorto variant of Distortion. To give the image levels of colorful translucency, he painted using Watercolor brushes. When he was happy with the composition, Gartel printed the image on a large-format Kodak printer using light-fast inks. The height of the final print was more than ten feet.

■ Artist **Ad Van Bokhoven's** works are sold in fine art and commercial markets. *Blue Woman* reflects his background in conventional intaglio printmaking and painting. For *Blue Woman*, he built a rich composite that includes custom patterns, paper textures, pieces of digital photos and drawing using Chalk brushes.

He began the image by using a Nikon Coolpix 990 to photograph a container of rusty pieces. Back at the studio, he copied the photo and pasted it into a new blank image as a layer and then set the Composite Method of the layer to Gel in the Layers palette.

Van Bokhoven loves to create custom paper textures using photographs. His children enjoy drawing with chalk on the street stones, and the drawings have a beautiful texture. He shot close-up photos of their drawings and then captured them as custom papers. (For information about creating custom paper textures, see "Applying Paper Textures" on page 117 in Chapter 3.) For the drawing of the blue woman, he used the Square Chalk variant of Chalk over the rich custom texture of the children's drawings. For the connecting lines between the figures in the image, he used the Pens variants to sketch the line drawings on a new layer.

Next, he created a custom pattern for the handwriting, which is overlaid on the image. (For information about making a custom pattern, see "Creating a Seamless Pattern," earlier in this chapter.) To blend the handwriting with the image, he added a new layer, filled it with the pattern and then set the layer's Composite Method to Gel.

For the image border, he opened a new image and drew a rectangular area of blue squares, which he captured as a custom pattern. To build the frame for the image, he applied it by adding a new layer and then one by one, he filled four overlapping rectangular selections with the pattern.

To complete the work, Van Bokhoven wanted to achieve a worn, aged look. From his image library he chose a photograph of stained paper, and then he copied and pasted it into the image and set the layer's composite method to Gel. When the image was complete, Van Bokhoven printed *Blue Woman* on German Etching paper using an Epson 7600, in a limited edition of 50 pieces.

■ "I am interested in how we can connect with the world beyond our own individuality—how we can connect with the past and with each other living in the present," says artist **Cynthia Beth Rubin**. *Senegal Textures* was created by Rubin based on photographs that she had taken while visiting Africa.

Although she does most of her compositing in Photoshop, Rubin uses Painter extensively to bring out textures in her images and to enhance the color and lighting. When an image is complete, she saves a copy of the image as a TIFF file and opens it in Photoshop for printing.

She printed *Senegal Textures* in two sizes, one large (about 22 x 36 inches) and the other small (on 13 x 19-inch paper). The large print was done on a Roland HiFi Jet printer with pigmented inks in the Faculty Research Lab at the Rhode Island School of Design. For the Roland print, Rubin set up the image with an Adobe RGB color profile embedded in Photoshop on a Macintosh, and then ported it over to the ripping PC for the Roland. The Roland color choice software does the final color conversion from RGB to CMYK. After running a few tests at 20% size, she subtly color corrected the image. For the smaller print, Rubin used

her studio Epson 1280 printer, using Jon Cone's system (inkjetmall.com). She bought paper, inks and color profiles from him, and followed his instructions. Again, she printed out of Photoshop.

In *Senegal Textures*, Rubin captures the grass houses that are still in use, playing the architecture against the textural illusions in the fabric of the clothes that are still worn by so many in Senegal. To add highlights and shadows to the foliage and the homes, making them look more three dimensional, she used the versatile Apply Surface Texture feature.

WORKING WITH TYPE IN PAINTER

Susan LeVan created Goal Leap *for her agents Bruck and Moss. A detail of the image is shown here. LeVan used Painter's Text layers to build elements for her illustration. See "Auto-Selecting with Current Color" on page 207 for step-by-step technique featuring the image.*

INTRODUCTION

PAINTER IS A POWERFUL TOOL FOR DESIGNING creative display type and for special effects. With Painter you can set type and put an image inside it; add texture to type; rotate type, stretch it and paint on it; fill and stroke type for a neon look; add type with special effects to your illustration (for a book cover design, for example); and create three-dimensional chrome type for a logo. You can set text on a path, fill the type with a color, add a shadow and much more. This typography primer will help you get the most out Painter's type tools.

A TYPOGRAPHY PRIMER

Painter is not recommended for setting large amounts of text—it's a good idea to leave this task to your favorite page layout program, such as InDesign, QuarkXPress or PageMaker. Instead, we'll focus on type as a design element using display type, because this is where Painter's tools shine. Display type is generally set in sizes 14-point or larger; it's usually used for feature headlines in magazines, for book covers, for posters and billboards and for Web page headers, to name a few applications.

Fonts and font families. A *font* is a complete set of characters in one size and one typeface. The characters usually include uppercase and lowercase letters, numbers, punctuation and special characters. A *font family* is all of the sizes and style variations of a typeface (for instance, Roman and italic styles in light, medium and bold weights).

Serif and sans serif. One way typefaces differ from one another is in the presence or absence of *serifs,* the small cross-strokes on the ends of the strokes that make up the letters. Serif faces were the first typefaces designed for printing. The serifs help our eyes to recognize the shape of a letter sooner and to track horizontally

The letter "E," showing the City font family, which includes upper- and lowercase City Light and City Light Italic, City Medium and City Medium Italic and City Bold and City Bold Italic

Serif fonts have small cross-strokes at the ends of the strokes. The letter "G" is shown here in a serif font, Goudy (left), and a sans serif font, Stone Sans Semibold (right).

The letter "T," demonstrating examples of several type classes. From left to right, top row: Black Letter, Fette Fraktur; Roman, Century Old Style; Slab Serif, City Bold. Bottom row: Script, Reporter Two; Sans Serif, Stone Sans; and Novelty, Arnold Böcklin.

from one letter to the next across a page, which makes these faces typically easier to read than sans serif faces.

The term *sans serif* refers to type without serifs. Usually sans serif fonts have a consistent stroke weight. Because of this quality, they can be ideal for display type because they look good in larger sizes and are good candidates for graphic treatments such as beveling and edge texture application. A sans serif font with very broad strokes has plenty of weight to work with when you apply special effects!

Classes of fonts. Fonts can be further grouped into several classes: Black Letter, Roman, Slab Serif, Sans Serif, Script and Novelty. *Black Letter* type resembles the style of hand-lettering that was popular during the time of Gutenberg's first printing press in 1436; Fette Fraktur is an example. These faces are usually used for an old-fashioned, formal look. Many typefaces fall into the *Roman* classification, including Old Style (for instance, Caslon and Century Old Style), Transitionals (Times Roman), and Modern (Palatino). The Old Style fonts have angled serifs, while the Modern Roman faces have straight vertical or horizontal serifs. *Slab Serifs* are also known as Egyptians, and they are characterized by even stroke weights and square serifs (examples are City Bold and Stymie). *Sans Serif*, mentioned earlier, is also considered a classification of type. Examples are Helvetica, Franklin Gothic, Futura and Stone Sans.

Designs for *Script* type were originally inspired by penmanship. Script fonts with dramatic thick-and-thin strokes (such as Linoscript) are often not good candidates for special effects because many techniques

We set type using two script fonts, Linoscript (top) and Monoline Script. Our example shows the original typeset word above the type with textured edges. As you can see, the Monoline type kept its integrity of design through the special-effects application because of its thick, even stroke weight, while the thick-and-thin Linoscript did not.

Each typeface has its own aesthetic and emotional feel, as shown in this example. With Painter's text you can easily set type in different faces and colors. Shown here, from left to right are Fenice Ultra, Brush Script, Vag Rounded Black and City Medium. In this example, each letter was set on a separate layer so the different fonts could be applied.

Jeff Hull created The Crossing Guard storyboard for a Miramax Films movie title and trailer. He began with a black background and set individual letterform shapes in Painter using Mason from the Emigré font library. After converting the shapes to layers, he filled them with color and erased portions of the letters by painting the layer masks with white paint. He also used Effects, Orientation, Scale on the layers to vary the size of the elements.

involve blurring of the edges or beveling, which can destroy the thin strokes. If you'd like to try special effects and still preserve the script typeface, find a font with thick strokes, such as Kaufmann Bold, Monoline Script or Reporter Two.

Finally, the *Novelty* category is diverse and graphic. These faces are often used to communicate emotion in special projects like poster designs (Arnold Böcklin and Stencil are examples).

Legibility. Have you ever driven past two billboards and noticed that one was easy to read as you drove by, and the other was not? The easier-to-read one was more *legible* than the other. When it's easy to recognize the words so you can absorb their meaning quickly, the type is legible. Legibility was important when you drove by the billboard, or when you were able to efficiently scan the headlines on the front page of a newspaper this morning.

When you set type in Painter, choose fonts carefully if you intend to manipulate them with special effects. Are you using the typeface simply as an element in a collage, where the letters are employed for graphic purposes only and content is not as important? Or do you plan to set an important, legible headline and enhance it with beveling? If the latter is the case, make sure to choose a font with strong enough strokes to withstand the bevel effects, such as a bold sans serif face. Turn to "Creating Beveled Chrome" on page 348 for a step-by-step example of a three-dimensional chrome effect applied to sans serif type with Painter's Bevel World plug-in.

> **TWO COMBINED INTO ONE**
>
> Since Painter 7, the functionality of dynamic text and type shapes from earlier versions has been combined into one solution for text. If you like to use type shapes, it's easy to convert a text layer to shapes by choosing Convert Text to Shapes from the menu on the right side of the Layers palette.

DESIGNING WITH PAINTER'S TYPE TOOLS

Each type element that you design has its own purpose: a Web page header, a food advertisement in a magazine, a billboard, the headline for a feature story in a magazine or a signage design. Know your client and research the style aesthetics needed for the design. This knowledge will help you choose the tools to use for the project.

Painter's Text is editable, which means you can easily change the size, color, font or content of the text, until you decide to convert the text layer into an image layer so you can paint on it or add special effects, or convert it to shapes so you can edit the outlines or do hand-kerning of the individual letters. Painter can display TrueType or Adobe Type 1 fonts if the printer font is installed. Painter can't display bitmap fonts because it needs the printer font's outline information to render the text. Each text layer can display a single font.

This Frutiger Black text was set using the Text tool from the Toolbox. It shows the bounding box around the selected type and the insertion point crosshair.

When the Text tool is clicked in the image window, a new Text layer represented by a "T" icon is generated in the Layers palette.

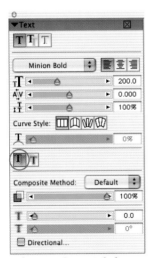

The Text palette contains controls for specifying the appearance of the type, including putting type on a curve and specifying an angled blur for a shadow.

Setting text in your image. Begin by choosing the Text tool in the Toolbox. Using controls in the Property Bar, you can specify a font and the size, alignment, color, opacity and shadow attributes. Click the cursor anywhere on the image and enter your text. The type will be displayed on a special new Text layer in your image. Using controls in the Text palette (Window, Show Text), you can also add a shadow and apply a curve style to the baseline of the type. Any changes that you make will be applied to the entire text layer.

In the Property Bar or Text palette: To specify the size, adjust the Point Size slider or click on the number to the right of the slider and enter a numerical value. Adjust the Tracking slider in the Text palette to globally change the spacing between the letters. To specify the alignment of the text, click the Align Left, Align Center or Align Right icon.

<table>
<tr><td>

TEXT LAYER TO IMAGE LAYER

To convert a text layer to an image layer, choose Convert to Default Layer from the menu on the right side of the Layers palette. The text will be converted to a pixel-based layer so that you can paint on it or apply effects; the text layer's name will be preserved in the Layers palette.

</td></tr>
</table>

If you'd like to set more than one line of text, press the Return key (without moving the cursor), and Painter will begin a new line of type. To remove the last letter you typed, leave the cursor where it is and press the Backspace/Delete key. To adjust the spacing between multiple baselines of the Text, adjust the Leading slider, or enter a numerical value.

Applying a new color. The current color chosen in the Colors picker will automatically be applied to the text as you set it. If you'd like to change the color of the text, make sure that the Text Attributes button is chosen in the Text palette. Choose a new color in the Colors picker and the text will update to display the new color.

Adding a shadow. When you'd like to add a shadow to your type, click the External Shadow or Inside Shadow icon on the left side of the Property Bar or in the Text palette. By default, a black shadow will be applied and the Shadow Attributes button will automatically be chosen. To adjust the opacity or the softness of a shadow, use the Opacity and Blur sliders. To blur the shadow

SPECIFYING TEXT ATTRIBUTES USING THE PROPERTY BAR

When the Text tool is chosen in the Toolbox, you can specify a font as well as the point size, alignment, color, opacity, shadow and a Composite Method in the Property Bar.

Choosing 200-point Minion Bold in the Property Bar

This type was set along a path using the Curve Perpendicular style.

more on one edge than on the opposite edge, enable the Directional Blur check box and adjust the Directional Blur slider. For a colored shadow, choose a new color in the Colors picker.

Setting type on a curve. The Text controls in Painter include the capability to create a Bézier path for the type baseline right in the Text palette. (The Curve Style controls are in the Text palette underneath the sliders, as shown in the illustration on page 343.) To begin, enter your type on the image. To place the type on a curve, click on a non-straight Curve Style icon. The first icon is Curve Flat, which will not create a curve. The other three icons will generate a curved baseline and allow you to edit the baseline using Bézier curves: the Curve Ribbon style specifies that the vertical strokes of the type will be straight up, and Curve Perpendicular places each character perpendicular to the curve, without distorting the letters. The fourth option, Curve Stretch, distorts the shape of individual letters to fit the space created by the bend of a curve. Use the Centering slider on the Text palette to move the type along the baseline curve. See "Setting Text on a Curve" on page 346 for a step-by-step description of the process.

Converting Text to Shapes. After you set type with Painter's Text tool, you can convert each letter that you set to an individual vector object on its own layer by choosing Convert Text to Shapes from the triangle pop-up menu on the right side

SELECTING A WORD

To select an entire word on a text layer so you can edit it, begin by clicking on the Text layer's name in the Layers palette, and then double-click on the word with the Text tool to select it.

Double-clicking with the Text tool

MOVING A SHADOW

After adding a shadow to type, if you'd like to move the shadow, click on the shadow with the Layer Adjuster tool and drag in the image.

We dragged the shadow slightly down and to the right.

SLANTING OR ROTATING TYPE

In Painter you can skew or rotate type easily. After you've completed setting the type, choose the Layer Adjuster tool in the Toolbox. To rotate it, press the Ctrl/⌘ key and drag on a corner handle. To slant the type, press the Ctrl/⌘ key and drag on the top or bottom handle.

This Futura Extra Bold type was slanted by pressing the Ctrl/⌘ key and dragging the bottom handle to the left.

The Curve Ribbon style chosen in the Text palette allowed us to rotate this text set in the Bauer Bodoni Italic font around a path. We set text and clicked the Curve Ribbon button to place the text on the curve. Then we used the Add Point tool to add an anchor point near the center of the path and used the Shape Selection tool to manipulate the path.

of the Layers palette. Shapes have certain advantages over type: They have editable Bézier curve outlines and unique transparency

We created this clear, embossed look by setting text in the Machine Bold font, converting it to a default layer, and then using Apply Surface Texture and Composite methods.

To create this painted text, we began by setting type in the Sand font and converted it into an image layer by choosing Convert to Default Layer from the menu on the right side of the Layers palette bar. The Opaque Round variant of Oils was used to add colored brushstrokes.

To make the type break up into sharp ice shards, we set type on a Text layer using Futura Extra Bold, and then painted on the type with the Shattered variant of the F-X brush, clicking the Commit button when the warning dialog box appeared.

capabilities. You can stroke and fill them, and then change fill and stroke. As with type, you can rotate them without loss of quality. Because each letter is a separate element, it's easy to do custom kerning of the individual letterforms, which isn't possible with text.

Convert text to shapes when setting small amounts of type, when you want to pay special attention to spacing between individual letters, or when you want to edit the outline shape of the letters. Also, shapes are useful when you want to make a quick selection or mask from type (Shapes, Convert to Selection)—for instance, when you want to put an image inside of the type. (For more information about shapes, turn to "Working with Shapes," in the beginning of Chapter 6.)

When to convert text to pixels. If you'd like to paint on type, add special effects such as Apply Surface Texture or manipulate a layer mask on the type layer to erode the edges of the type, you'll need to convert the text layer to an image layer. To convert a text layer to an image layer, choose Convert to Default Layer from the triangle pop-up menu on the right side of the Layers palette. If you attempt to paint on a text layer without converting it, a Commit dialog box will appear, asking if you would like to convert the text layer to an image layer. Click Commit to convert it.

AN ORGANIZATIONAL GROUP

When you convert text to shapes, Painter sets each character's shape on a separate layer and automatically groups the text on the layer into one group. The group makes it possible to move individual characters or to move the type as a unit. As a bonus, the group will be named after the text it was derived from. For more information about working with shapes, turn to the beginning of Chapter 6.

GO FOR CONSISTENT-LOOKING LETTER SPACING

Kerning is the process of removing or adding space between pairs of letters so that the spacing is *visually* consistent. To kern type visually, train your eye to see the negative spaces *between* the letters. After kerning, the spacing should appear balanced. To hand-kern individual letters in Painter, you must convert the text layer to shapes by choosing Convert Text to Shapes from the menu on the right side of the Layers palette bar. Using the Layer Adjuster tool, select each shape in the Layers palette and move it using the arrow keys on your keyboard.

This text was set in Meta Bold. The original text had "uneven" letterspacing (top), so it was converted to individual shapes and kerned to tighten the spacing and to make it more consistent (bottom).

Setting Text on a Curve

Overview *Set the text; choose a Curve Style; use the Shape Selection tool to finesse the length and shape of the path; adjust the text on the path.*

1a

We set type using the Sand font and used the Tracking slider to tighten letterspacing.

1b

Choosing the Curve Stretch style

2a

Using the Shape Selection tool to pull an end point and lengthen the curve

2b

With two more points added, the curve is taking shape.

IT'S A SNAP TO SET TEXT ON A CURVE in Painter. The Text controls in Painter IX enable you to create a Bézier path for the type baseline right in the image window. Here's a quick method, applied to a comp for an advertising layout:

1 Setting the type and applying it to a curve. For this technique you can begin with a new blank image, or start with a photo, as we did. Choose the Text tool in the Toolbox and open the Text palette by choosing Window, Show Text. Choose a font and size and set your type. We chose the typeface Sand, because its organic shape and playful feel would work well with the Curve Stretch curve style we planned to use.

Click on the Curve Stretch button in the Text palette (the button farthest to the right in Curve Styles), and you'll see the text curving around the baseline of a newly generated path in your image. The Curve Stretch curve style distorts the letters to fit the spaces in the curve. The slight distortion adds to the ripply underwater effect. To reposition the text layer on the image, use the Layer Adjuster tool.

2 Adjusting the path. To change the shape of the path, choose the Shape Selection tool in the Toolbox (it's the hollow arrow), select the text layer in the Layers palette and click on an end point. Pull on the end point to lengthen the path. To change the shape of the curve, drag a control handle in the direction that you want the curve to go. As you manipulate the path, aim for gentle curves so the type will flow smoothly.

To add more anchor points (for instance, to make a gentle wavy line, like we did), choose the Add Point tool (it's nested under the Shape Selection tool in the Toolbox) and click the baseline curve. To remove a point, choose the Delete Point tool (it's also nested under the Shape Selection tool in the Toolbox) and click the anchor point. Use the control handles on each anchor point to finesse the curve. To adjust the position of the text on the path, use the Centering slider in the Text palette. We set Centering at 2%. 🐾

A Spattery Graffiti Glow

Overview *Use the Text tool to set text over a background; convert the text to an image layer, then to selections; stroke the selections using the Draw Outside mode to spatter the background outside the type.*

The text set in City Bold Italic

The selection marquee created from the layer

Choosing the Pixel Spray variant of the Airbrushes in the Brush Selector Bar

Selecting the Draw Outside mode and stroking outside the active selection

WITH THE HELP OF PAINTER'S TEXT LAYERS, selections and Draw modes, you can stroke around the edges of type with an Airbrush to create this fast, fun title solution.

1 Choosing an image and setting type. Open an image to use as a background; our photo was 864 x 612 pixels. Choose the Text tool in the Toolbox, and then select a font and size in the Property Bar. (We chose 200-point Berthold City Bold Italic.) Click in the image and begin typing. If the Layers palette is open, you'll see a text layer appear when you begin typing. To adjust the spacing between the letters, open the Text palette (Window, Show Text) and adjust the Tracking slider.

2 Converting the text to selections. To achieve the result at the top of this page, it's necessary to convert the text to an image layer, then to selections. Select the text layer in the Layers palette, click the right triangle on the Layers palette bar and choose Convert to Default Layer from the menu. Now reduce the opacity of the layer to 0% using the Opacity slider in the Layers palette and choose Drop and Select from the menu on the right side of the Layers palette bar. The layer will disappear from the list in the Layers palette and will reappear as animated marquees. To prepare the selection for stroking, choose Select, Transform Selection.

3 Stroking outside of the selection. With the help of Painter's nifty Drawing Modes in the bottom left of the image window, we used a brush to stroke around the edge of the selection. The Drawing Modes allow you to use a selection just as you would a traditional airbrush frisket, to paint inside or outside of the selection. From the Drawing Modes pop-up in the bottom-left corner of the image window, choose the Draw Outside (center) icon. In the Brush Selector Bar choose the Pixel Spray variant of the Airbrushes. (We increased the size of the brush to 60 pixels, using the Size slider on the Property Bar.) Choose white in the Colors picker; then choose Select, Stroke Selection and watch as Painter gives your type a fine-grained, spattery glow. Try stroking your selection with other Airbrushes such as the Coarse Spray or the Variable Spatter variant. 🖌

Creating Beveled Chrome

Overview *Open a file and apply lighting to build a background; set text; convert the text to shapes and then to a layer; bevel the forms and apply a reflection; add a shadow.*

CHER THREINEN-PENDARVIS

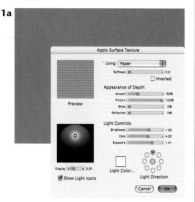

1a

Applying a woven texture to the background

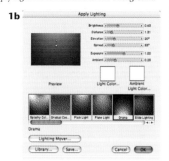

1b

Creating an overhead spotlight based on the Drama light

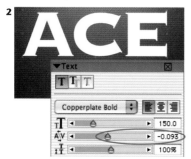

2

The selected type and the background with lighting after the spacing was adjusted between the letters

PAINTER'S BEVEL WORLD DYNAMIC LAYER allows you to try an endless variety of custom bevels on a selected layer quickly, without time-consuming masks and channels. To create this three-dimensional chrome title, we applied effects that included custom lighting, a complex bevel with a reflection map and a shadow.

1 Creating a textured background with lighting. Begin by creating a new file with a medium blue background (our file was 1000 x 700 pixels). To add a woven texture to the background, choose Gessoed Canvas in the Paper Selector and then choose Effects, Surface Control, Apply Surface Texture. Set Amount to 50%, Shine to 0% and click the 12 o'clock light direction button. Leave the other settings at their defaults.

To add depth to the background, we applied overhead lighting that would complement the bright, shiny chrome to come. Choose Effects, Surface Control, Apply Lighting and in the dialog box, click on the Drama choice. To shine the light from overhead, click the small circle and drag it so that it points upward. Increase Brightness to 0.63 and decrease the Distance to 1.31. To save your new light, click the Save button and name it when the Save Lighting dialog box appears.

2 Setting the type and adjusting the tracking. Now that the backdrop is finished, you're ready to create the type. Choose a color that contrasts with the background in the Colors picker. This will automatically fill the text with color as you type. The contrasting color will make it easier for you to see your type as you adjust the spacing between individual letters. Select the Text tool in the Toolbox and in the Property Bar, choose a font and size. Click in the image with the Text tool and enter the type. We set 150-point type using Copperplate Bold. (If you don't have the typeface we used, choose a bold font with broad strokes to accommodate the beveling effect to come.) So that you can tighten the spacing between the individual letters, open the Text palette by choosing Window, Show Text and move the Tracking slider to the left to decrease it.

3 Beveling the type. With the layer still selected, click the Plug-ins button at the bottom of the Layers palette and choose Bevel World from the menu. When the Commit dialog appears, click Commit

3a

The rough bevel generated by the Bevel World layer default settings

3b

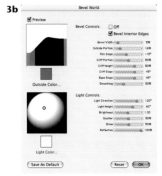

Our settings in the Bevel World dialog box

4

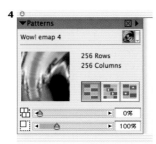

We used "Wow! emap 4" from the Wow! Patterns on the Painter IX Wow! CD-ROM.

5

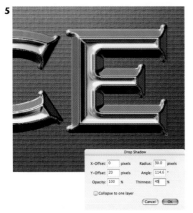

The Drop Shadow dialog box with settings for casting the shadow directly below the chrome type

to convert the Text layer to a default layer. To build a 3D effect with a smooth stamped shape that would show off the reflection map we planned to add, we used these settings: Bevel Width slider to 5% (for narrower sides and a broader top); Outside Portion, 16% (for a small bevel outside of the original pixels on the layer); Rim Slope, -15° (for a recessed top); Cliff Portion, 50% (the vertical distance between the base and rim); Cliff Height, 50% (the height of the sides); Cliff Slope, 45° (the angle for the middle of the bevel); Base Slope, 45° (the angle of the outermost portion); and Smoothing, 30% (to smooth any ridges, while retaining the tooled shapes). Ignore the outside color, because it will disappear when the reflection is applied. Leave the dialog box open.

4 Achieving the chrome effect. The secret to achieving this chrome effect is choosing a bright, shiny environment map in the Pattern Selector, and then going back to the Reflections slider in the lower part of the Bevel World dialog box. We chose an environment map that included shiny metal reflections and bright colors. To apply the reflection map that we used, you'll need to load the "Wow emap" library. Locate it in the Wow! Patterns folder on the *Painter IX Wow!* CD-ROM and copy it into the Painter IX application folder. To load this library, click the Pattern Selector on the Toolbox and choose Open Library from the triangle menu. Navigate to the "Wow emap" library in the Painter application folder, select it and click Open. Back in the Pattern Selector, choose "Wow! emap 4" from the triangle menu. Now move the Reflection slider in the Bevel World dialog box to the far right (we used 100%). Your type will magically change to bright shiny chrome! Click OK to close the Bevel World dialog box.

5 Adding a shadow. To increase the depth of our image, we added a drop shadow using Painter's automatic drop shadow feature. To build your shadow, select the beveled layer and choose Effects, Objects, Create Drop Shadow. In the dialog box, we set X-Offset to 0 pixels, Y-Offset to 20 pixels and increased the Opacity to 100%. For a softer shadow, we set Radius to 30.0 pixels, and we left the Angle (114.6°) and Thinness (45%) at their defaults. (A low Thinness setting creates a streaked look similar to a motion blur.) 🐾

Painting with Ice

Overview *Set Text to use as a template for "hand-lettering"; paint icy script on a Liquid Metal plug-in layer; composite a copy of the layer to enhance the design.*

The original photograph

The Text palette with settings for our title, including the tighter Tracking

The image with the Text set and in position

YOU CAN CREATE TEXT EFFECTS QUICKLY with dynamic layers. To begin this cover comp for an online travel agency catalog, we set type on a Text layer. Using this text as a template, we "hand-painted" new 3D letters onto a Liquid Metal dynamic layer using a tablet and stylus. Then we applied special settings to give the liquid letters a clear, frozen look.

1 Choosing an image. We began by selecting a photo that measured 768 x 512 pixels. Although the final art used online would be smaller, we preferred to work at a larger size so we could zoom in and finesse the details, and then reduce the size later. We chose a photo with a Mediterranean theme and refreshing colors that would complement the "ice" or "glass" title.

2 Setting Dynamic Text. To make it easier for you to see the type over the image, choose a contrasting color in the Colors picker to automatically fill the text with color as you type. Select the Text tool in the Toolbox. In the Property Bar, choose a font and size and set the type directly on the image. (We set our text using the Reporter Two font.) Open the Text palette by choosing Window, Show Text, and adjust the spacing between the letters, using the Tracking slider in the Text palette. To interactively resize the type, use the Size slider in the Property Bar or Text palette. To use the Layer Adjuster tool to resize the type, position it over a corner of the text, and when the arrow cursor appears, drag on the text. Drag the text with the Layer Adjuster to reposition it in your image.

3 Drawing with crystal-clear ice. Using the text as a template, we drew new letters using a Liquid Metal plug-in layer. Set up your Liquid Metal layer as follows: Open the Layers palette, click the Dynamic Plug-ins button at the bottom of the Layers palette and choose Liquid Metal. Painter will generate an empty, transparent Liquid Metal dynamic layer, and the Liquid Metal

3a

The settings in the Liquid Metal dialog box for the icy look

3b

Beginning to hand-letter the Liquid Metal type using the dynamic text as a template

3c

The underlying template layer is visible through the "ice."

3d

The icy type with text layer removed

4

Detail of the icy type showing the underlying layer's Composite Method set to Darken

dialog box will appear. With the title as an underlay, we used a stylus to trace the text with the Liquid Metal brush tool. To begin, move the Refraction slider all the way to the right (so you can paint with crystal-clear ice). Choose the Brush tool in the Liquid Metal dialog box and carefully paint your title.

Adjust the Amount, Smooth, Size and Volume settings to your liking. To select all of the Liquid Metal so that you can apply new settings, choose the Liquid Metal Selector (arrow) and drag a marquee around what you've painted. Our settings were Amount, 1.1; Smooth, 90%; Size, 16.3; Volume, 97%; Spacing, .331; Map, Standard Metal, with Surface Tension checked. We reduced the Refraction setting to 90%, because it helped the type stand out from the photo.

After completing your letters, click OK to close the Liquid Metal dialog box. Then delete the Text layer you used as a template: Select its name in the Layers palette and click the Delete (Trash can) button.

A Liquid Metal dynamic layer is *live*, which means you can continue to finesse the dialog box settings. To keep a layer dynamic, do not "commit" the layer (change it into an image layer), and make sure to save the file in RIFF format. For more information about dynamic layers, turn to Chapter 6, "Using Layers."

4 Compositing a second layer. As you can see in your image, Painter's Liquid Metal dynamic layer "refracts" an underlying image. To give the ice more texture and make it look shinier, we set up another layer between our ice layer and the image beneath. To begin, make a copy of the Liquid Metal layer (Alt/Option-click with the Layer Adjuster tool in the image). To enhance the copy of the Liquid Metal layer using tonal effects, choose Effects, Tonal Control, Brightness/Contrast and slightly increase the contrast. When the Commit dialog box appears, asking if you'd like to convert the dynamic layer to an image layer, click Commit. To add more texture and bring out the highlights in the icy type, we changed the underlying layer's Composite Method in the Layers palette to Darken. 🖌

So many options! When you have the underlying layer in place, experiment with changing the Composite Method in the Layers section to different settings. We experimented with Gel (left), and Pseudocolor (right). Control the effect with the layer's Opacity slider.

■ **Keith MacLelland** designed this colorful cover illustration for *Summertime Fun Bunch Comics*, a self-published zine that he creates with several other artists.

MacLelland started by creating a new file and filling it with a medium-toned brown for the background. Then he added colored squares to the background by making constrained rectangular fills with the Paint Bucket as follows: He chose the Paint Bucket tool and clicked and dragged with the Paint Bucket to "sketch" the area where the fill would be applied. He repeated this process until the background was covered with small squares of varying color. When he was happy with the background, he built the Tiki character using his typical working process, which includes sketching with the 2B Pencil variant of Pencils, making a back-and-white ink drawing using the Scratchboard Tool variant of Pens, and adding color by painting with the Airbrushes, Chalk, Pastels and Oils brushes.

To apply paper textures to areas in his image (for instance, the Tiki's head) he used the Square Chalk variant of Chalk. For the three-dimensional texture on the bathing suit, he made a selection of the bikini with the Lasso tool, and then he loaded a custom floral texture in the Paper Selector and chose Effects, Surface Control, Apply Surface Texture, Using Paper, with subtle settings.

To draw the wood grain effect on the Tiki, he used the Scratchboard tool. Working on a separate layer, he drew the wood grain, and then he set the Composite Method for this layer to Gel and made the layer partially transparent using the Opacity slider in the Layers palette.

MacLelland created all of the text in Painter. For the list of contributors, he chose a color and size in the Property Bar and set the text. To adjust the angle of the text to match the sign under it, he chose the Layer Adjuster tool, positioned it over a corner point on the Text layer and pressed the Ctrl/⌘ key to rotate the layer. For the title, he set the type, and then duplicated it five times. He experimented with the color of each title layer (finally choosing yellow, orange, pink and magenta colors), and used the Layer Adjuster tool to finesse the position of each one to achieve the effect shown in the final illustration.

■ **Keith MacLelland** was chosen by *Philly-Tech* magazine to create the illustration *Seeds* for an article on job searching. The image was created using several layers for the sketch, ink drawing, coloring and text. Working on layers allowed him to keep elements separate, so he could reposition them and independently adjust the Opacity and the Composite Methods. MacLelland began by clicking the New Layer button on the Layers palette to add a new empty layer, where he drew a rough pencil sketch. He added a second layer and used the Scratchboard Tool variant of Pens to create an ink drawing with flowing black lines. After adding another new layer, he blocked in the basic color areas using the Chalk,

Pastel and Oil Pastels brushes, and then MacLelland refined the color using his own custom variants of the Oils. Now that he had the line drawing and color as he liked them, MacLelland wanted to enhance the lines, so he selected each ink stroke by clicking on it with the Magic Wand and painted it using a custom brush based on the Smeary Round. He used the Square Chalk variant of Chalk to apply more texture around the elements on the basic color layer (for instance the shaking hands, gloves and laptop computer). MacLelland also painted textures onto areas of the bags, gloves and a few other elements using the Square Chalk. Then he used his custom Smeary Round brush to paint the water pouring from

the watering can (a wet paint smear effect) and to paint more soft reflections onto the laptop screen. MacLelland added the type using Painter's Text tool. So he could paint, erase and apply effects to some of the type elements, he converted them to image layers by selecting each Text layer in the Layers palette, clicking the triangle on the right side of the Layers palette and choosing Convert to Default Layer from the menu. Besides adding brushstrokes and texture to many of the converted Text layers, he also erased areas of some of them (such as the Seed House text in the lower right) where the text covered areas of the plant and the water pouring from the can.

■ **John Dismukes** of Capstone Studios is well known for his creative logo design and hand-drawn typography. He used similar processes to design and airbrush the three images on these pages. Dismukes begins each design by drawing many sketches, and when the direction is established, he draws a tight visualization of the typography on paper. The approved pencil sketch is then scanned and used as a template in FreeHand to create Post-Script outlines. He imports the outlines into Photoshop and builds elements on layers. Then he opens the file with layers in Painter for the airbrushing. In Painter, some of the layers are duplicated and used to make selections (via Drop and Select from the Layers palette bar menu), and they are then saved as masks. (Alternatively, outlines can be imported directly into Painter as shapes via File, Acquire, Adobe Illustrator File and then converted to layers.) Dismukes uses selections to limit paint as he airbrushes using the Digital Airbrush variant of Airbrushes. For a step-by-step description of a similar technique using Painter, turn to "Selections and Airbrush," in Chapter 5.

The *Grand Margarita Metallic Cactus* illustration (top) was commissioned by Alcone Marketing Group and art-directed by Liliana Marchica. Dismukes began with a tight sketch, but he wanted a rough look for this logo, so he did not import outlines. He painted masks for the type, and then converted them to selections he could use to limit the paint. Using the Digital Airbrush, Dismukes airbrushed the lettering. To add texture to the leaf, he cloned texture onto a layer from another file: He opened a texture file with the same dimensions as the logo file, defined it as the clone source by choosing File, Clone Source and used a Cloning brush variant to softly brush the texture onto the layer.

■ **Susan LeVan** used several layers when she created *Going Global* for her agents, Bruck and Moss. She began by drawing the figures on separate layers with the Smooth Ink Pen variant of Pens and the Square Chalk (Chalk) and Oil Pastel variants, and added their drop shadows using Painter's Effects, Objects, Create Drop Shadow command. For the background behind the figures, LeVan used two patterns that she had made in separate source files. To build the "text" pattern, she used Futura, Bubble Dot and a few other fonts to set letters and symbols using the Text tool and sized them using the Size slider in the Property Bar. She positioned them with the Layer Adjuster tool. When the text elements were complete, she dropped the text layers to the Canvas by choosing Drop All from the triangle pop-up menu on the right side of the Layers palette. Then she captured the text design as a pattern in the Patterns palette by choosing Capture Pattern from the triangle pop-out menu on the right side of the Patterns palette. (See "Creating a Seamless Pattern" and "Applying Patterns" in Chapter 8.) Now working in the final image, she added new layers and filled each one with the type or globe pattern by selecting one of the custom patterns in the Patterns section and choosing Effects, Fill, Fill with Pattern. To make the white areas of the layers transparent, she set the Composite Method to Gel in the Layers palette. LeVan wanted to add more color and texture interest to the background, so she adjusted the size of each pattern using the Scale slider in the Patterns palette and filled two more new layers with them. She selected white areas on the new layers and deleted them. Next, she colored one of the layers gold and the other green by turning on Preserve Transparency in the Layers palette and filling the layers with new color. Finally, she set their Composite Method to Colorize and adjusted the Opacity of each layer.

10

USING
PAINTER
WITH
PHOTOSHOP

When creating Star, Pamela Wells used Painter and Photoshop. To see the complete image, turn to page 371.

When creating Star, Pamela Wells used Painter and Photoshop. To see the complete image, turn to page 371.

MASK MAXIMUMS

A Painter file can contain up to 32 masks in the Channels palette, plus one layer mask for each layer. Photoshop 7's maximum is 24 channels in an RGB file, but three of the channels are taken up by the Red, Green and Blue color channels (leaving room for 21 masks). If you attempt to open a file with 32 masks in Photoshop 7, you will be greeted by a polite dialog box asking if you would like to discard the extra channels (numbers higher than 21 will be discarded). In Photoshop CS the maximum number is 50 channels, in addition to the RGB channels.

INTRODUCTION

IT'S EASY TO MOVE FILES back and forth between Painter IX and Photoshop. And what does Painter have to offer the Photoshop user? Fantastic natural-media brushes that give your images warmth, a multitude of textures and fabulous special effects! In addition to the work showcased in this chapter, several of the other artists whose work appears in this book have used both Painter and Photoshop in the development of their images. If you're an avid Photoshop user and would like to see more examples of how others have combined the use of the two programs, check out the work of these artists for inspiration: Jeff Burke, John Dismukes, Donal Jolley and Pamela Wells. The index in the back of the book lists page references for each of their names.

PAINTER TO PHOTOSHOP

Here are some pointers for importing Painter IX files into Photoshop:

- To preserve image layers when moving an image from Painter IX into Photoshop, save a file in Photoshop format. Photoshop will open the file and translate the layers with their names and the layer hierarchy intact. (Photoshop rasterizes any dynamic layers such as Text, Liquid Metal and Water Color, as well as Shape layers.)

- If a Painter file contains layers that extend beyond Painter's live image area, and that document is opened in Photoshop 4 and later versions, the areas outside of the live area are retained. (Photoshop 3 clipped the layer information outside the live area.)

- Painter offers most of the Photoshop Blending modes; some exceptions are Color Dodge, Color Burn and Exclusion. And Painter has seven additional Compositing Methods of its own. Photoshop converts Magic Combine to Lighten mode, Gel to Darken mode, Colorize to Color mode and Shadow Map to Multiply. When Photoshop

Marc Brown used Illustrator, Photoshop and Painter when building Iron Casters, *a detail of which is shown here. See the entire image on page 366.*

DYNAMIC LAYERS

When a Painter file that includes a Dynamic Layer such as Liquid Metal is opened in Photoshop, the layer is preserved but the dynamic capabilities are lost. To retain the dynamic properties for further editing in Painter, save a copy of your file with live dynamic layers in RIFF format.

A PATH TO PHOTOSHOP

You can store path information with a selection in Painter for import to Photoshop, and it will appear in the Photoshop Paths palette. When you make a selection with Painter's Lasso or Rectangular or Oval Selection tool, or set text and convert it to shapes and then to a selection in Painter (by choosing Convert Text to Shapes from the triangle pop-out menu on the Layers palette and then choosing Shapes, Convert to Selection), path information is automatically stored in the file. Then if you save the Painter file in Photoshop format, these kinds of outlines will appear in Photoshop's Paths palette. If you save a selection as a mask in the Channels palette you can build path information back into the file: Choose Select, Load Selection to create a selection based on the mask; then convert this mask-based selection to outline information using Select, Transform Selection. (Painter's Transform Selection command adds vector information to the selection border.)

encounters a Painter-native Composite Method it can't convert (such as Pseudocolor or Reverse-out), it converts that layer to Normal.

- To preserve the alpha channels (masks) in Painter's Channels palette and use them in Photoshop as channels, save a Painter file in Photoshop format. When you open the file in Photoshop, the named masks will automatically appear in the Channels palette.

PHOTOSHOP TO PAINTER

Here are some pointers for importing Photoshop files into Painter IX:

- If you prefer to begin your file in Photoshop, and the file contains layers, Painter can open Photoshop format files saved in RGB, CMYK and Grayscale modes.

- Although Painter IX will open CMYK files in both Photoshop and TIFF formats, keeping files in RGB color mode when porting files from Photoshop to Painter will make the best color translation, because RGB is Painter's native color model.

- If you save your Photoshop image (version 4 or later) with layers in Photoshop format, Painter IX will open it and translate the layers with their names intact. If you are using Photoshop 3, save the file in Photoshop 3 format.

- Photoshop type layers will be rasterized by Painter. However, shape layers, layer clipping paths and clipping groups will not translate.

- Photoshop layer masks translate consistently into Painter.

- A Photoshop document made up of transparent layers only—that is, without a Background layer—will open in Painter as layers over a white-filled background in the Canvas layer.

- Painter can recognize most of Photoshop's Blending modes when compositing the layers (some exceptions are Color Dodge, Color Burn, Vivid Light, Linear Light, Pin Light and Exclusion). Painter converts blending modes that it doesn't recognize to the Default Compositing method.

- Layer sets created in Photoshop will be recognized by Painter, and the layers within them will translate.

- A layer with a live layer style will disappear when the file is opened in Painter. You can try this work-around: Convert a "styled" layer to a series of rasterized layers (Layer, Layer Style, Create Layers) before attempting to open it in Painter. But this often doesn't work either, since the conversion often involves a clipping path group, and clipping groups don't translate to Painter.

- Photoshop Alpha Channel masks are recognized by Painter IX. The channels will appear in Painter's Channels palette.

- Photoshop layer masks will also convert to layer masks in Painter. (They will be listed in the Layers palette, as they are in Photoshop.) To view a layer mask in black and white, select the layer in the Layers palette, click the layer mask thumbnail and in the Channels palette, open its eye icon.

Compositing, Painting and Effects

Overview *Scan a drawing and a sheet of paper and composite the scans; add color and texture with brushes; add a colored lighting effect; open the image in Photoshop and convert it to CMYK.*

JOHN FRETZ

1a

The sheet of speckled Oatmeal paper

1b

The pencil-and-charcoal drawing on paper

2

Compositing the scans of the Oatmeal paper and the sketch

JOHN FRETZ COMBINED TRADITIONAL DRAWING materials and digital ones in Photoshop and Painter to build the composite illustration *AM Exercise* for an American Lung Association calendar.

1 Drawing and scanning. As a basis for his illustration, Fretz drew a black-and-white study using pencil and charcoal on a rough newsprint paper. Then he used a flatbed scanner to scan the drawing and a sheet of Oatmeal paper into Photoshop using RGB mode.

2 Compositing the scans. Fretz built the image in Photoshop because he was more familiar with Photoshop's compositing procedures. (His compositing process, which follows, can be accomplished almost identically in Painter.) Fretz copied the drawing and pasted it as a new layer on top of the Oatmeal paper background. To make the white background of the drawing transparent, he applied Multiply blending mode to the drawing layer using the triangle pop-up menu on the Layers palette.

For the soft, irregular edge on the background layer, Fretz first used the Lasso to draw a selection around the perimeter of the image. He reversed the selection by choosing Select, Inverse and feathered it 30 pixels (Select, Feather); then he filled the border area with 100% white. He saved the file in Photoshop format to preserve the layers for import into Painter.

3 Modifying brushes. At this point, Fretz opened the composite drawing in Painter, where he planned to add color and texture. Before beginning to paint, he made two custom Soft Charcoal brushes. The first, for adding soft values, used the Soft Cover subcategory; the second, for subtly darkening color, used the Grainy Soft Buildup subcategory and a low opacity. To make Fretz's

Building up color on the faces using the custom Soft Charcoal brushes

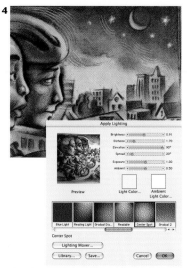

Creating a colored glow in the sky using Apply Lighting

Painting details on the foreground

"darkener," in the Brush Selector Bar, choose the Soft Charcoal variant of Charcoal. In the General section of the Brush Control Palette, change the method to Buildup and the subcategory to Grainy Soft Buildup. A lower opacity will give you more control when building up color, so in the Property Bar, change the Opacity to about 15%. Save your new variant by choosing Save Variant from the Brush Selector Bar's triangle menu. Name it and click OK.

Adding color and texture in Painter. Fretz chose Basic Paper texture in the Paper Selector. To enlarge the texture to complement the grain of the Oatmeal paper background, he used the Scale slider on the Papers palette (Window, Library Palettes, Show Papers). He brushed color onto his drawing using two grain-sensitive brushes, the Large Chalk and Square Chalk variants of Chalk, and used his custom Charcoals to deepen color saturation in some areas. Choose a Chalk brush and begin painting color onto your image background; switch to the custom Soft Charcoal variant using Grainy Soft Buildup to darken color. To change the brush size and the opacity while you work, use the Size and Opacity sliders in the Property Bar.

4 Emphasizing the sky with lighting. For a warm glow in the sky that faded across the people's faces, Fretz applied a colored lighting effect within a soft-edged selection. Begin by choosing the Lasso tool and making a loose freehand selection. Now give the selection a soft edge by applying a feather: Choose Select, Feather, type in a feather width and click OK. Now apply the lighting effect to make the sky glow as Fretz did: Choose Effects, Surface Control, Apply Lighting. In the Lighting dialog box, choose the Center Spot light. To give the light a colored tint, click on the Light Color box to open the Select Light Color dialog box. Then choose a color by clicking on it in the Colors picker. (If the circle is black, move the slider up to the top.) Click OK. To move the spotlight to a new location in the Preview window, drag the large end of the light indicator. To save the custom light, click the Save button and name the light when prompted; then click OK to apply the light to your image, and deselect (Ctrl/⌘-D).

5 Painting final details. To make the layer and image canvas into one surface on which he could paint details, Fretz merged all the layers. (Click the right triangle on the Layers palette bar to open the menu and choose Drop All.) Then he chose the Scratchboard Rake variant of Pens, and modified it by reducing the number of bristles. To build a similar brush, open the Rake section of the Brush Control Palette. Reduce the number of Bristles to 5. Fretz added finishing strokes in various colors to several places in the foreground, the grass and highlights on the cars. He also used a smaller brush and more subtle colors to add textured strokes to areas of the background.

Fretz saved a copy of the image as a TIFF file. He opened the file in Photoshop and converted it to CMYK for use in the calendar.

Illustrating with Soft Pastel

Overview *Shoot photos; build a rough composite in Photoshop to use for reference; paint with Pastels in Painter.*

Four of the reference photos

The composite image

PAMELA WELLS

PAMELA WELLS USED PHOTOSHOP AND PAINTER to create *Sun*, which is a member in her series of works inspired by Tarot cards. "The Sun card represents happiness, contentment and joyful living," says Wells. She built a composite to use for reference, and then working in Painter, she created a colorful illustration that has the look of blended pastel.

1 Shooting photos. Wells set up her model, the flowers and other elements using a white background; then, she photographed them with a digital camera.

2 Building a composite. To begin the illustration, Wells built a composite that included several elements. She made masks for the images in Photoshop using the Lasso tool, and then she dragged and dropped the elements into a composite file. Wells could have brought a layered Photoshop file into Painter with layers, but she wanted a flat document with all of the elements merged together.

Using the Soft Pastel to paint color over the simple pencil outline

Achieving a soft, blended pastel look. The Paint Bucket fills can be seen on two flowers.

Building color and tones on the foliage and flowers

3 Tracing, sketching and coloring. Wells opened the flat composite file in Painter, and then she made a clone copy of the image to use as a guide while she created the sketch.

Open your reference image and choose File, Quick Clone. The default Quick Clone feature is set up for tracing. It creates a clone copy of your image, removes the contents of the clone copy document and then turns on Tracing Paper. Save your clone image and give it a descriptive name. Leave your original open. (For more information about cloning, see "Cloning, Tracing and Painting" in Chapter 3.) To sketch as Wells did, choose the Soft Pastel Pencil variant of Pastels and draw a black-and-white sketch on the Canvas of the blank clone image. Make sure to create solid lines so that you can use the Paint Bucket to fill areas with base colors, in preparation for modeling the forms.

When her sketch was complete, Wells used the Paint Bucket to fill areas of the sun with a yellow-gold color directly over the drawing on the Canvas. Then, using the Soft Pastel variant of Pastels, she began to develop the forms. As she worked, she mixed color using the Colors picker, occasionally sampling colors from her reference collage using the Dropper tool. Wells works completely on the Canvas without the use of layers. She likes the paint interaction that is possible when working on the Canvas because it is more similar to traditional painting, working on a conventional surface. When the sun's basic forms were blocked in, she used the Paint Bucket to fill a few of the flowers with their base colors.

Choose the Paint Bucket (Toolbox) and fill an area of your drawing with its base color in preparation for painting. Then, use Soft Pastel (Pastels) to build the highlights and shadows. As you work, vary the appearance of the grain by adjusting the Grain slider in the Property Bar. For a grainier look, move the Grain slider to the left, and for a smoother look, move the Grain slider to the right. For a softer look similar to blended traditional pastels, continue to work over areas with the Soft Pastel until they are smooth. (For more information about the Grain slider and grain penetration, see the "Grain Penetration" tip on page 58.)

4 Modeling the forms. When she had most of the color for her composition laid in, Wells began to gradually develop more three-dimensional form and color on the flowers and other elements in her composition. Carefully observe your reference, and then use the Soft Pastel to refine the forms in your composition.

Wells recommends cloning or painting directly over photo references *only* to gain practice with how to develop color and anatomy. After creating a drawing, she prefers to work from scratch, referring to the reference, rather than cloning in color from her reference. As she models the forms, she leaves the reference composite open on the screen to the left of her working painting so that she can refer to it. For Wells this approach is less confining than cloning (or continuing to trace over a photo).

Collage Using Cloning and Layers

Overview *Scan photos into Photoshop and retouch; use Painter's brushes and textures to build a background image and add textured brush work to source files; build the composite image in Photoshop; add blending and airbrushed highlights in Painter.*

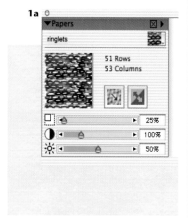

1a

Burke's custom Ringlets texture was used for the background.

1b

The test file with tonal variations

ART DIRECTION AND IMAGES: BURKE / TRIOLO PRODUCTIONS / DESIGN: BOB MARRIOTT, MARRIOTT & ASSAY
CLIENT: ACAPULCO RESTAURANTS

WHEN JEFF BURKE AND LORRAINE TRIOLO—owners of Burke/Triolo Productions—were commissioned to create new menus for Acapulco Restaurants, they turned to Photoshop for image compositing and to Painter for a textured, painted look. The final composed menu pages are filled with unique, stylized graphics that reflect the texture and style of Old Mexico and suggest the qualities of handmade food and old-world service.

Burke began by exploring techniques in Painter, settling on a rough-edged, textural look with lively brushstrokes, which he presented to the client and the designer. After approval, he built the interior menu pages using several elements: a background paper texture image, textured food images and border graphics. The source files were all composed into a single image file in Photoshop and then opened again in Painter, where more texture and brush work were added. Later, in QuarkXPress, the type and the dingbat illustrations were placed on top of the composed image as EPS files. The folded menu was composed of several panels, each built using the same process. The steps that follow use panel 3 as an example. Turn to page 365 in the gallery to see the front cover of this menu.

1 Building a textured background. The partners realized that a textured feel would contribute to the old-world atmosphere they wanted to achieve. To accomplish this, Burke created a new

The retouched food photograph

Using the Chalk Cloner variant of Cloners to paint a rough edge around the elements

Refining the texture around the edge of the plate and beverage

The food photograph with brush work nearly complete

document in Painter that matched the page size of the menu, measuring 9 x 14.5 inches at 300 pixels per inch. He created a custom paper texture in Painter, called Ringlets. (To read about making a custom paper texture turn to "Applying Paper Textures" in Chapter 3, on page 117.) Then, using a warm-colored Oil Pastel variant of Oil Pastels, he brushed the texture over the surface of the page, using light pressure on the stylus. He saved this master texture image for use on each panel of the menu.

Burke converted the light, delicate paper texture to CMYK and created a test file with tonal variations. He sent the test file to his service bureau for a Fuji ColorArt film proof, and when the proof came back, the partners chose the darkest, yellowest variation.

2 Scanning and retouching the images. The team at Burke/ Triolo scanned the food images on a Scanview ScanMate 5000 drum scanner, and then converted them to RGB. Burke used Photoshop's Rubber Stamp tool to lightly retouch scanning imperfections and to improve details, such as stray rice grains, sauce smears on the plates and dark areas in the food. To whiten most of the background, he made a loose selection completely outside of the elements and reversed it by choosing Select, Inverse. Then he pressed the Delete key.

3 Texturizing the source images. Burke opened each food image in Painter and created a clone by choosing File, Clone. He chose Big Grain Rough paper texture in the Paper Selector (loaded from the Painter 6 Textures library on the Painter IX application folder, Extras, Paper Textures). Using the Chalk Cloner variant of Cloners, with brush sizes varying between 20 and 100 pixels, he gently painted over the image in the clone file along the edges of the plates, the base of the glasses and the stone surface material, in varying densities. This produced a painterly quality in the images reminiscent of painting by hand. By constantly varying the size of the brush and by using a light touch on the stylus, he changed the amount of chalk texture applied. His goal was to add texture to the original without obscuring it completely. As specialists in food styling and photography, Burke and Triolo know that it's important to avoid obscuring the food products in an image.

To add subtly colored brush work to the edges of the elements, Burke used an Oil Pastel variant (Oil Pastels). He sampled the color from the image (using the Alt/Option/⌘ key) and then painted diagonal strokes. He likes using the Oil Pastel when applying dark colors over a light background or light over dark, because the brush smears color slightly, making the strokes appear to bleed. He carefully applied the treatment consistently over the photo.

Wherever the image became too obscured with brush work, Burke used the Soft Cloner variant of Cloners to gently bring back detail from the original, after designating the original retouched

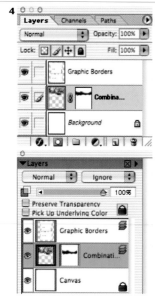

The named layers in the composite file, shown here in the Layers palette in Photoshop (above) and the Layers palette in Painter (below)

Burke painted with the Just Add Water variant to blend the border elements into the page.

A detail of the final image with airbrush highlights added

photo as the Clone source by choosing File, Clone Source. After completing each individual food image, he saved it for later.

4 Compositing the menu elements. Because the layout also included border graphics created in Adobe Illustrator, these elements were rasterized (converted from CMYK PostScript elements to bitmapped RGB graphics) so they could be blended into the final page composition. To do this, the designer's QuarkXPress document was modified to remove all of the elements except certain borders (and some headline type, which was retained for position, but later removed). Burke saved the page individually as a separate EPS file from QuarkXPress.

Burke built each panel of the menu as a single image file in Photoshop. However, the elements could have been combined in Painter in almost exactly the same way. He opened the master paper-textured background and the treated food image in Photoshop and dragged and dropped the food image file on top of the background into the position specified in the designer's layout. To blend the images softly into the paper background, he added a layer mask to the food element layer.

Finally, Burke opened the QuarkXPress EPS file and dragged and dropped it into position. To create the illusion of plates and other objects overlapping the graphic elements, he added layer masks for the graphic elements where they appeared to go "behind" the food objects. He also removed the headline type at this point. Because he wanted to use Painter to add brush work that would blend elements that were currently on separate layers, he merged the layers in the file. Then he saved the file as an RGB TIFF.

5 Adding final details in Painter. Burke opened the file in Painter and prepared to add texture and brushstrokes throughout the image. For editing flexibility he began by creating a clone of the image by choosing File, Clone. To enhance and blend the graphic borders into the image, he used the Oil Pastel 30 variant, and roughly filled in the hollow borders with a warm-white color. Then, to gently blur the colored border graphics into the background paper, he used the Just Add Water variant of Blenders. Again, if he overdid the effect, he switched to the Soft Cloner brush (with the original image designated as the Clone Source) and restored detail and clarity.

6 Airbrushing highlights. To complete the menu panel, Burke wanted to embellish the bright highlights on the plate, glass and food. For optimal flexibility, he added a new layer for the highlights by clicking the New Layer button on the Layers palette (making sure that Preserve Transparency was turned off in the Layers palette). Using the Digital Airbrush variant of Airbrushes and a bright, warm-white color, he softly painted strong, yet natural brushstrokes to "blow out" the highlights.

■ When partners **Jeff Burke** and **Lorraine Triolo** were commissioned to create the new *Acapulco Restaurants menu cover,* several people played important roles: Photography and imaging, Jeffrey Burke; food and prop styling, Lorraine Triolo; art direction, Jeff Burke and Bob Marriott; Design Firm, Marriott & Assay; and client, Acapulco Restaurants.

To begin the menu cover, Burke built a composite that included several images of food and live models, shot in the studio against a white cove background. To add to the atmosphere, he incorporated a sky image from a recent Caribbean vacation, as well as an outdoor fountain photographed with a point-and-shoot digital camera. He made masks for several of the images in Photoshop using the Lasso and Pen tools and dragged and dropped elements into a composite file. After several preliminary compositions and the client sign-off on a final arrangement, he flattened the file and saved it in TIFF format. (Burke could have brought the file into Painter with layers, but he wanted a flat document with all of the elements merged together so that he could use Painter's brushes to paint over the entire image, completely integrating the elements.)

Burke opened the file in Painter and used much the same process as described in "Collage Using Cloning and Layers" on page 362. He cloned the file and used the Big Grain Rough texture (loaded from the Painter 6 Textures library on the Painter IX CD-ROM) and a pressure-sensitive tablet and stylus. He smudged the edges of some of the elements and added colored brush work to some areas using an Oil Pastel variant of Oil Pastels. By selectively blending areas in the image with the Just Add Water variant of Blenders, and leaving other edges in focus, Burke created a dynamic feeling of movement in the illustration. For instance, in the server's skirt and blouse, the leading and trailing edges are blurred with soft diagonal brush work, but the sash and ruffle are sharper. To lead the eye to the food tray, Burke airbrushed a glow under the tray and along the sleeve of the blouse. Because the food was the focal point of the composition, Burke avoided adding brush work here. To balance the design, he left the faces of the mariachis in clearer focus than most of the other elements. It was easy to restore the focus where it was needed by designating the original file as the clone source (File, Clone Source) and using the Soft Cloner.

Finally, Burke airbrushed highlight hints on the image on a separate layer (for editing flexibility), using the Digital Airbrush to "blow out" the highlights, while keeping the look natural.

■ Designer/illustrator **Marc Brown** was commissioned by Angie Lee, art director at Grindstone Graphics, to create *Museum Store* (above). He created *Iron Casters* (right) for Amanda Wilson, art director at The Evans Group Advertising. Brown employed similar techniques to create both illustrations. He started with a loose pencil drawing, and then scanned the drawing and placed it into Adobe Illustrator as a template. In Illustrator he drew the elements on individual layers and filled them with flat color. To rasterize the image, he copied each Illustrator layer and pasted it into Photoshop as a layer. (This process can also be accomplished in Painter by drawing shapes and filling them with color, or by importing Illustrator art into Painter. See Chapters 5 and 6 for more information about using and importing shapes.) At this point, Brown opened the layered file in Painter. He used Airbrushes and Chalk variants to add colored details to the faces and clothing, blending color with Blenders variants. After he had completed the composite, he merged the layers by choosing Drop All from the menu on the right side of the Layers palette bar. To finish, he broke up some of the smooth edges by painting them with the Just Add Water variant of Blenders.

■ **Phillip Straub** is the Senior Concept
Artist at Electronic Arts, and he illustrates
children's books. He is the co-author of
two books, *d'artiste* and *Otherworlds*.

For **Cohabitation**, Straub was inspired to
create a unique, futuristic city. He began
the image by making sketches to work
out the composition. In Painter, he used
the Pastels brushes to rough in the color
scheme. Then, he used the Thick Oil
Bristle variant of Oils to add more color
and to move paint around on the Canvas.

The brush work with the Thick Oil Bristle
is most evident on the sky and on the
large building that overshadows the city
in the distance. Straub painted without
using masks, because he wanted to avoid
a mechanical look. When working in
Painter, he emulates his favorite traditional painting practices.

To create the spaceship in the foreground, Straub added a new layer and
then worked on that layer with Pastels
brushes to build its design. When he was

satisfied with the basic forms for the
spaceship, he dropped the layer by
choosing Drop from the Layers palette
menu. Then, working on the Canvas, he
continued to model the spaceship using
the Pastels and Thick Oil Bristle brushes.

Finally, Straub opened the painting in
Photoshop, where he added fine details
with the program's brushes. For instance,
he painted the tiny people and added details to the piping around the building in
the foreground.

■ Graphic designer and artist **Donal Jolley** created *Winter Morning* and *Independent Baptist Church*, two of twelve images for the *Turning Point 2002 Calendar*. To begin the calendar, Jolley worked with his client David Jeremiah to select reference photos. Beginning in Photoshop, Jolley opened the reference photos for *Winter Morning* (shot by Robert Hayes) and *Independent Baptist Church* (taken by Jolley). He removed unwanted elements from the foreground, trees and skies by cloning using the Rubber Stamp tool. To achieve the mood he wanted in each image, he intensified the yellows and oranges in *Winter Morning* and the background greens in *Independent Baptist Church* using Photoshop's Hue and Saturation controls. So that he would be able to isolate areas of the images (for instance, the snow, sky and water in *Winter Morning* and the truck, wood buildings and sign in *Independent Baptist Church*), he made selections and saved them as alpha channels. Then he saved the image with its alpha channels in Photoshop format, so he could work on it in Painter. Jolley planned to use Painter's brushes for textured brush work that would add painterly movement to the images and break up the smooth photographic look. Using several layers and paying careful attention to the volume of the forms, he painted with the Artist Pastel Chalk variant of Pastels and the Square Chalk variants of Chalk (with a rough paper texture chosen in the Paper Palette). When he wanted to constrain paint to a particular area of a layer (such as the sky), he loaded a selection based on the alpha channel he had saved for that area by choosing Select, Load Selection and choosing it in the Load From menu. Then he painted within the area. When he wanted to sample color from the layers below, he enabled Pick Up Underlying Color in the Layers palette. To blend and pull color while adding texture in the sky, he used the Grainy Water variant of Blenders. To achieve a "salt" effect on the water reflections in *Winter Morning*, he used the Fairy Dust variant of the F-X brush. Then he added final colored details to the snow, church and water with a small Artist Pastel Chalk.

■ For *Independent Baptist Church*, **Donal Jolley** used Watercolor brushes in addition to the Chalk, Pastel and Blenders variants. Jolley appreciates the flexibility of painting on layers. When he wants to make changes to an area, he often paints the changes on a new layer so he can control the strength of the effect using the Opacity slider in the Layers palette. After establishing the overall brush work using the Square Chalk (Chalk) and Artist Pastel Chalk (Pastels) variants and then blending with the Grainy Water variant of Blenders, he painted transparent watercolor glazes onto the truck to create the look of shiny metal and glass. He also added light watercolor washes on top of

the pastel brush work on the wood buildings and street, and then painted subtle texture on the street and wood siding using a small Splatter Water variant of Watercolor. When the brush work on *Independent Baptist Church* was complete, Jolley added more texture as follows: First he saved a copy of each image using a different name and flattened the layers in the copies by choosing Drop All from the menu on the right side of the Layers palette bar. Next, he made two duplicates of each image by selecting all (Ctrl/⌘-A) and Alt/Option-clicking with the Layer Adjuster. On the top layer, he used Effects, Surface Control, Apply Surface Texture, Using Paper, with subtle settings, to add paper

also with subtle settings, to add paper grain. On the next layer, he used Effects, Surface Control, Apply Surface Texture, Using Image Luminance, with subtle settings, to "emboss" the brushstrokes. Then he adjusted the Opacity of both layers to his liking, using the slider on the Layers palette. He saved a duplicate of each of the final layered files in TIFF format, flattening the images. Because Jolley was more familiar with color correction and conversion in Photoshop, he opened both final TIFF files in that program, made color adjustments and then converted the images to CMYK for printing in the calendar.

■ The recent works of award-winning art-ist **Pamela Wells,** which focus on femi-nine archetypes, are sold in commercial and fine-art markets. *Abundance* is a member of Wells' *Apple* series. In her series, she used the apple as a symbol of feminine strength and power. "*Abundance* is about the moment when we are open to receiving all that the universe has to offer, good or bad, and how we become em-powered when we embrace all that is hap-pening in our lives around us," says Wells.

She began the image by shooting digital photos of a model to use for references. Wells opened the photos in Photoshop

and built a rough collage to use for inspi-ration while working in Painter. She drew a tight line drawing using the 2B Pencil variant of Pencils and a dark neutral color. Because she wanted to begin the coloring of the sketch by filling areas with flat color, she made sure to create solid lines to enclose the areas she wanted to fill. She could then apply color fills to the woman and clothing, for example, using the Paint Bucket from the Toolbox. To model the forms of the figure and her clothing, she carefully painted over the filled areas. Wells used the Soft Charcoal variant of Charcoal to apply layers of color using a light pressure on the stylus.

To blend areas, she laid subtly different colors over existing ones. For instance, to render the skin, she brushed the areas with a light tan color, and then covered them with a darker orange and finally, with a peachy red. To add texture to the fabric and brighter colors to the foliage, she used more contrasting values and a tiny Soft Charcoal variant. When she finished painting the illustration, Wells saved it as a TIFF file and opened it in Photoshop, where she applied a few minor color and brightness adjustments. To read about how Wells made a fine-art print of her image, turn to the beginning of Chapter 13, "Printing Options."

■ **Pamela Wells** created *Star*, a member of her *Tarot* series. The Star card is meant for mediation on "generosity, wisdom and understanding," says Wells. "The stars represent the universe and all of its mystery and potential for growth."

Wells began the image by shooting digital photos to use for reference. She opened the photos in Photoshop and made a collage; then she merged the layers and saved the file in TIFF format. Wells opened the flattened collage file in Painter and made a clone by choosing File, Clone. She wanted to use Tracing Paper so that she could see her reference as she sketched, so she deleted the

contents of the clone by choosing Select, All and then pressing the Backspace/ Delete key. To turn on Tracing Paper, she pressed Ctrl/⌘-T. Then she drew a detailed line sketch with the 2B Pencil variant of the Pencils. Wells created solid lines that would completely enclose areas in the drawing because she wanted to use the Paint Bucket to fill the areas with flat color. She began the coloring process by applying colored fills to the figure, clothing and other elements. Then, using the Soft Pastel variant of Pastels and a light pressure on the stylus, she carefully painted over the filled areas to model the forms. Wells brushed subtly different

colors over existing colors. To render the fabric, she painted areas a light-gold base color and then covered them with a darker gold. To finish an area, she painted with deeper tones. For the texture on the background hills, she sampled color from the image using the Dropper tool, and then adjusted the color in the Colors picker to a lighter value and used small Pastels variants to add grainy textures. To smooth areas of the water, she used Blenders variants. When the illustration was complete, Wells saved it as a TIFF file and opened the image in Photoshop, where she applied color and tonal adjustments.

■ An innovative professional photographer, **Michael Campbell** specializes in digital photography and portraiture. When creating *Girl on the Beach*, Campbell began the work by shooting the model against a gray paper background. He also painted a sheet of rough paper with acrylic paints in pastel colors, and then scanned both images into Adobe Photoshop. In the scanned photo file, he chose Select, All and placed the portrait on a layer by choosing Layer, New, Layer Via Cut. Then he used the program's Extract function to isolate the figure and drop out the background. After retouching the figure, Campbell

adjusted its color and tones using Photoshop's Hue/Saturation and Levels features. Next, he copied and pasted the scan of the painted paper into the portrait file below the figure, and then saved the composite image as a PSD file that he could import into Painter with the layers intact. In Painter, he used cloning and paint applied with various brushes to paint over the photograph, adding expressive brush work and a canvas-like texture. He made a clone of the image (File, Clone), and roughed in a loose, ocean scene for the background using the Chalk Cloner variant of Cloners. He saved the

image and then began to gradually build up basic forms of the figure and clothing using the Oil Brush Cloner. To gradually build up details in the focal areas of the image (for instance, the girl's face) he used a small Camel Oil Cloner, and he used a larger version of this brush to paint the looser brush work on the clothing. Finally, he used Effects, Surface Control, Apply Surface Texture to add three-dimensional highlights and shadows to the brush work and canvas texture. Turn to "Creating a Photo-Painting" on page 274 to see a similar step-by-step technique featuring Campbell's work.

■ The color and vibrant energy of the Caribbean radiates in *Phoenix.* Artist **Ileana Frometa Grillo** was inspired to create the image after a visit to the Dominican Republic; this image celebrates the reconnecting with her father's roots. While traveling, Grillo took photographs of places she had visited as a child.

Back at her studio, Ileana began the image by making a pencil drawing to work out the composition. After scanning the drawing into Photoshop, she created collage elements from her photographs. Next, she opened the composite in Painter and added brush work to areas using the Chalk variants. To blend, she used the Blenders brushes. The blended pastel brush work is most noticeable in the woman's skin and hair. For more texture in a few of the blended areas, she brushed lightly with a Soft Chalk, which was based on the Large Chalk variant of Chalk.

ANIMATION AND FILM WITH PAINTER

Award-winning film artist Ryan Church created Balloon Battle *using Painter's brushes and effects. To see more of Church's work, turn to the gallery at the end of this chapter.*

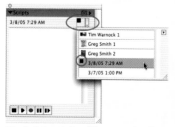

The Scripts palette with a current script chosen in its menu. The most recent current script has a small rectangle to the left of its name.

INTRODUCTION

WHETHER YOU'RE AN ANIMATOR, film artist, designer, or 3D artist, Painter's capabilities offer you dozens of practical techniques. Concept artists appreciate the creative freedom offered by Painter's brushes, textures and effects. If you're producing an animation or making a movie, many of the techniques and effects shown in this book can be applied to frames in a Frame Stack, Painter's native animation format, or to an imported movie clip. Although it isn't a full-featured animation or film-compositing program, Painter is good for making comps so you can preview motion. And Painter gives 3D artists a wide variety of choices for creating natural, organic textures to be used for texture mapping. In addition, the ability to record painting scripts lets you make tutorials to show others how your painting was built and even lets you batch-process a series of images.

WORKING WITH SCRIPTS

Painter's versatile Scripts feature lets you record your work, and then play the process back, either in Painter or as a QuickTime or AVI (video for Windows) movie. But if you use this feature a lot, you'll soon discover its limitations—for example, its inability to record some Painter operations can produce a different effect during playback.

There are two basic kinds of scripts—Painter's automatically recorded Current Script and scripts that are recorded by enabling the Record feature. Both kinds of scripts are visible in the Scripts palette when you install Painter: The white icon with a date represents the Current Script and the icons with pictures represent scripts that were manually recorded by artists while they worked, to demonstrate various

A CURRENT SCRIPT PREFERENCE

You can tell Painter how long to save current scripts by specifying the number of days in the Preferences, General dialog box. (The default is one day.) A word of caution: Saving several days of scripts can use a lot of hard disk space!

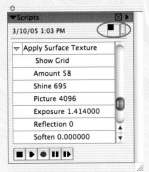

An open Current Script showing the instructions for an application of Apply Surface Texture. The white icon in the picker near the top right of the Scripts palette represents the Current Script. The tiny rectangle identifies the most current script.

You can use these buttons on the front of the Scripts palette to begin recording a single script (center red button) and to stop recording when you're finished (left square button).

Athos Boncompagni saved a series of scripts when creating La Luna e le Stelle, and played them back at higher resolution to build a larger image. For more information about using scripts in this way, see the tip "Increasing File Resolution with Scripts," on page 376.

kinds of images that can be created using Painter. If you record your own scripts they will also appear in the Scripts palette.

Understanding the Current Script. The Current Script starts when you launch Painter and closes when you quit the application. While you work, Painter transparently records your actions automatically, saving them as the Current Script in the Painter Script Data file in the Painter application folder. If you have launched and quit Painter several times during a 24-hour day, you'll notice several white icons in the Scripts menu list, with the dates and times for each work session listed in the pop-out resource list menu on the Scripts palette (for instance, "5/22/03 8:07 AM").

Playing back a complete Current Script in which you created and saved more than one image can cause problems. For instance, if you opened a file, added brushstrokes and saved it, playing back the Current Script may result in Painter finding the first file, redrawing your strokes over the image and then resaving over the file. A more practical way to use an automatically recorded script is to open it and copy a specific series of commands from it (a lighting and texture effect, for instance) to paste into a new script, which can then be played back on other images.

Using a portion of a Current Script. To use a portion of a current script, copy specific commands from it and paste them into a new script, begin by opening the Scripts palette (Window, Show Scripts). Click the right triangle on the Scripts palette bar and from the menu select Open Script. In the dialog box that opens, choose Current Script from the Painter Script Data file list and click Open. The Current Script cannot be edited, but to use only a specific set of instructions from it, you *can* copy them to the clipboard and paste the instructions into a new script. Then you'll be able to use your new script to re-create just that series of actions. To do this, open the Current Script, Shift-select the instructions that you want to use (you may want to start at the bottom of the list, where the most recent instructions are found), choose Copy from the Scripts menu, choose Close Script and then choose New Script from the menu. Type a name for your new script in the Script Name dialog box, and click OK. Now choose Paste from the Scripts menu, and then choose Close Script. To play your new script, select the new script by name from the pop-up list in the Scripts palette and click the Playback button.

Recording a planned script. To record a series of deliberate actions into a script (instead of copying and pasting from the automatically recorded script), click the right triangle on the Scripts palette bar to open the menu and choose Record Script to begin recording, or click the Record button (the red dot) on the Scripts palette. When you've finished working on your image choose Stop Recording Script (or click the square Stop button). Painter will prompt you to name your script. The new named script will appear

To add lighting and a paper texture to this Mediacom video clip, we played a special effects script (using Effects, Surface Control, Apply Lighting and Apply Surface Texture) on each of the frames.

in the pop-up list in the Scripts palette, available for later playback. To play the new script, select it from the list and click the Play (forward arrow) button.

Recording and saving a series of scripts. If you want to record the development of a complex painting (so you can use the script to demonstrate how you created the painting) but you don't want to finish the painting in one sitting, you can record a series of work scripts to be played back. First note the dimensions of your file by choosing Canvas, Resize, and then click OK to close the dialog box. Click the right triangle on the Scripts palette bar, and choose Record Script. Include a number in the name of your script (such as "01") to help you remember the playback order. Then begin your painting. When you want to take a break, stop recording (Scripts palette bar, Stop Recording Script). When you're ready to continue, choose Record Script again and resume working on your image. Record and save as many scripts as you need, giving them the same basic name but numbering them so you can keep track of the order. To play them back, open a new file of the same dimensions as the original, and then choose Playback Script from the menu on the Scripts palette bar. Choose the "01" script, and when it's done playing, choose the next script: It will play back on top of the image created by the first script. Continue playing back scripts in order until the image is completed. (You can also record a script so that it can be played back on a canvas of a different size; see the tip below.)

QUICKTIME CAN'T CONVERT

Scripts that contain Painter commands that QuickTime cannot convert can't be turned into QuickTime movies. It's not possible to use the Record Frames on Playback function with scripts that contain commands such as File, New, or File, Clone (an Illegal Command error message will appear).

INCREASING FILE RESOLUTION WITH SCRIPTS

You can use Painter's Scripts function to record your work at low resolution, and then play it back at a higher resolution. This technique gives you a much crisper result than simply resizing the original image to a new resolution. Here's how to do it: Start by opening the Scripts palette (Window, Show Scripts). Click the right triangle on the Scripts palette bar to open the menu and choose Script Options. In the Script Options dialog box check the Record Initial State box, and then click OK. Open a new file (File, New) and choose Select, All (Ctrl/⌘-A). From the Scripts palette menu, choose Record Script (or press the round red button on the Scripts palette) to begin recording. Then begin painting. When you're fin-ished, from the menu on the Scripts palette bar, choose Stop Recording Script (or click the square black button on the Scripts palette). Open a new document two to four times as large as the original (this technique loses its effectiveness if your new file is

Choosing Script Options from the menu on the right side of the Scripts palette bar

much bigger than this). Again press Ctr/⌘-A to select the entire Canvas. Then choose Playback Script from the menu, or click the black triangle button (to the left of the red button) on the Scripts palette. Painter will replay the script in the larger image, automatically scaling brushes and papers to perfectly fit the new size. A word of caution—scripts can be quirky: Your higher-resolution image may not match the lower-resolution one if you use imported photos, complex selections, shapes or the Image Hose, for instance.

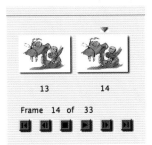

The Frame Stack palette for Donal Jolley's animation Rattlesnake *showing the movement in frames 13–14.*

To record the painting process of Mill Valley *(720 x 540 pixels, painted with Pastels and Blenders brushes), we made a movie using Save Frames on Playback and an interval of 10. The resulting movie was 110.6 MB with 120 frames.*

Automating a series of operations. Recording a series of actions can save you a lot of time when you need to apply the same effect to several images. Test a combination of operations (such as a series of choices from the Effects menu) until you get something you like. Choose Record Script from the menu on the Scripts palette bar (accessed by the right triangle), and repeat the series of choices that produces the effect you want. After you've stopped recording and have saved your script, you can apply the operations to a selection, a layer or a still image by selecting your script in the Scripts palette and clicking the forward arrow button on the front of the palette.

You can also apply your script to a Frame Stack. Turn to "Automating Movie Effects" later in this chapter for a detailed explanation of this technique.

Saving a script as a movie. This is a great option if you'd like to "play back" a painting for someone who does not have Painter. QuickTime movies can be played on Macintosh and PC/Windows computers with a freeware QuickTime projector such as Movie Player. First you'll record your work as a script, then you'll play it back on a new file, and then you'll save it as a QuickTime/AVI movie.

Begin by clicking the right triangle on the Scripts palette bar and choosing Script Options. In the Script Options dialog box, turn on Record Initial State (otherwise Painter will play back the first few commands or brushstrokes of your script using whatever colors, brushes and textures are active, instead of the ones you actually used during the recording of the script). Check Save Frames on Playback. You can leave the time interval Painter uses to grab frames from your script at 10, the default, but you may want to experiment with lower settings instead, to get a smoother playback result.

Next, open a new file of the dimensions you want for your eventual movie file. Click the right triangle on the Scripts palette bar, choose Record Script from the menu, and make your drawing. When you've finished, from the same menu, choose Stop Recording Script; name your script and click OK to save it. Now Painter will

A storyboard frame from the MGM *movie* Stargate. *Peter Mitchell Rubin used Painter to build digital storyboard illustrations for the movie, saving them as numbered PICT files and animating them with Adobe Premiere.*

convert the script to a movie. First, watch your recorded script played back as a Painter Frame Stack by opening a new file (same dimensions) and choosing Playback Script from the menu, choosing your script from the list and clicking the Playback button. Painter will prompt you to enter a name for your new movie file. Name it, click Save and then specify the number of layers of Onion Skin and color depth by clicking on the appropriate buttons. (For most uses, select 2 Layers of Onion Skin and 24-bit color with 8-bit alpha.) Click OK, and your script will unfold as a Frame Stack. When it's finished playing, save it in QuickTime/AVI movie format by choosing Save As, Save Movie as QuickTime. The QuickTime/AVI file will be smaller than a Frame Stack (if you use a Compressor choice in the Compression Settings dialog box) and will play back more smoothly. (Because most compression degrades quality, compress only once—when you've completed the project. Film artist Dewey Reid suggests using Animation or None as the Compressor setting.) To read more about preserving image quality when working with movies, turn to "Importing and Exporting," on page 380.

Making movies using multiple scripts. You can save a series of successive scripts, and then play back the scripts as frame stacks and save them as QuickTime movies without compression to preserve quality. Then you can open the movies in a program such as Adobe Premiere or Adobe After Effects and composite the movies into a single movie.

ANIMATING WITH FRAME STACKS

If you open a QuickTime or AVI movie in Painter, it will be converted to a Frame Stack, Painter's native movie format. Frame Stacks are based on the way conventional animators work: Each frame is analogous to an individual transparent acetate cel. You can navigate to any frame within a stack and paint on it or apply effects to it with any of Painter's tools (see "Animating an Illustration" on page 383).

Artists accustomed to specialized animation and video programs such as Adobe After Effects and Adobe Premiere will notice the limitations of the Frame Stack feature (there are no precise timing or compositing controls, for instance). If you use one of

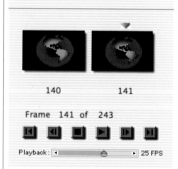

140   141

Frame 141 of 243

Playback: ◄   ▲   ► 25 FPS

To change the continents from brown to green in this Cascom video clip, we recorded a script while performing the New from Color Range procedure and Color Overlay tinting process on one frame, and then stopped recording and saved our script. After undoing the effects applied to the first frame, we chose Movie, Apply Script to Movie and took a break while Painter completed the masking and tinting process on all 243 frames. Above: The Frame Stack palette shows frame 140 with the operations applied, and frame 141 as yet untouched.

A frame from an animation based on a video clip. We began by using Painter's Watercolor brushes to illustrate the frames, which created a Watercolor Layer. Because a Watercolor Layer sits on top of the entire Frame Stack, we copied the layer to the clipboard, and then dropped it to the Canvas when we had finished painting the frame. We advanced to the next frame and pasted in the copied watercolor and added new brushstrokes, repeating this copying, dropping, pasting and painting process until the frames were complete. As a final touch, we applied an effects script (with Apply Surface Texture, Using Paper) to complete the piece.

these programs, you will probably want to work out timing and compositing in the specialized program, and then import your document into Painter to give it an effects treatment.

When you open a QuickTime or AVI video clip in Painter or start a brand-new movie, you'll specify the number of frames and color bit depth to be used in the Frame Stack. You will be asked to name and save your movie. At this point the stack is saved to your hard disk. A Frame Stack will usually take up many more megabytes on your hard disk than it did as a movie (depending on the kind of movie compression used), so have plenty of space available. Each time you advance a frame in the stack, Painter automatically saves any changes you have made to the movie. When you choose Save As, Painter will ask you to name the movie again. This is not a redundant Save command, but an opportunity to convert the file to another format: Save Current Frame as Image, Save Movie as QuickTime or AVI format, or Save Movie as Numbered Files (to create a sequence of frames to edit in another program such as Adobe Premiere).

USING A VIDEO CLIP REFERENCE

Painter's cloning function allows you to link two movies—a video clip and a blank movie of the same pixel dimensions—and use the video as a reference on which to base an animation. Open a video clip that you want to use as a reference (File, Open), and then make a blank movie (File, New Movie) of the same pixel dimensions as your video clip. (The second movie doesn't need to have the same number of frames.) Under File, Clone Source, select the video clip. In the blank movie frame, turn on Tracing Paper (Ctrl/⌘-T). Using the clone source as a guide, choose a brush and paint on the frame. To use the Frame Stacks palette to advance one frame in the original, click the appropriate icon (circled in the palette shown below), or press Page Up on your keyboard. Do the same to advance the clone one frame. Use Movie, Go to Frame to move to a specific frame in either the clone or original. You can also apply special effects such as Effects, Surface Control, Apply Surface Texture and Color Overlay, or Effects, Focus, Glass Distortion (all using Original Luminance), to your new movie using the clone source.

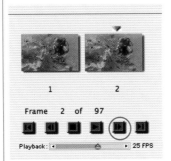

We opened a video clip (shown here in the Frame Stack palette) and a new Frame Stack, both using two layers of Onion Skin to show the position of the diver in both frames. Click on the circled button to advance one frame in the Frame Stacks palette.

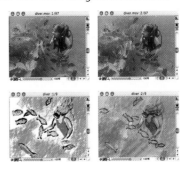

Frames 1 and 2 of the Diver video clip (top row), and corresponding frames in the animation (bottom row), painted with the Sharp Chalk variant of Chalk. Tracing paper is active on the bottom-right image.

Artist Dewey Reid advises using Effects, Surface Control, Apply Lighting to add cohesiveness and to smooth out transitions in a movie. For instance, using Apply Lighting with the same setting on all frames will smooth color transitions between clips and make elements from different sources blend together more successfully.

Reid used Apply Lighting and Apply Surface Texture (using Paper Grain) on the animated character Yuri the Yak for Sesame Street (produced by Children's Television Workshop).

When you record a drawing as a script, all of your actions are captured. Keep this in mind if you plan to play back your script as a movie. Plan to storyboard your movies so that you'll be able to execute the operations as smoothly as possible. If, in spite of your best efforts, you need to edit your movie, here's how to do it: After you Record Frames on Playback, look at the frame stack carefully and make changes to individual frames you want to edit. If you want to remove frames choose Movie, Delete Frames. Or you can save the Frame Stack as a QuickTime/AVI movie and edit it in iMovie or Adobe Premiere.

Creating animated comps. Painter provides a good way to visualize a rough animation. An animatic (a comp of an animation, consisting of keyframe illustrations with movement applied) can be comprised of images drawn in Painter, scanned elements, or numbered PICT files created in Painter, Photoshop or even object-oriented programs that can export PICT files (such as Illustrator). (See "Making an Animated Comp" on page 386, featuring Dewey Reid's illustrations in a demonstration of an animatic technique.) You can also alter individual frames in a movie with Painter's effects or brushes. For a demonstration of frame-by-frame painting, see "Animating an Illustration" on page 383.

Rotoscoping movies. There are numerous ways to rotoscope (paint or apply special effects to movie frames) in Painter. Many of the techniques in this book can be used for rotoscoping—brush work, masking, tonal adjustment or filters, or Effects, Surface Control, Apply Lighting and Apply Surface Texture, or Effects, Focus, Glass Distortion, for example.

Basing an animation on a movie. You can use Painter's Tracing Paper to trace images from a source movie to a clone to create an animation. This feature lets you shoot video and use it as a reference on which to base a path of motion. This process is described in the tip "Using a Video Clip Reference" on page 379.

IMPORTING AND EXPORTING

With a little planning and understanding of file formats, still and animated files can easily be imported into Painter and exported out of Painter to other programs.

Preserving image quality. Because compression can degrade the quality of image files, when you obtain source files to bring into Painter, choose uncompressed animation and video clips. And because quality deteriorates each time you compress (the degree of degradation depends on the compression choice), save your working files without compression until your project is complete. If you plan to composite Painter movies in another application, such as Adobe Premiere, After Effects or Final Cut, save them without compression. For an in-depth explanation of compressors for QuickTime or for AVI, see the *Painter IX Help*.

Importing multimedia files into Painter. Painter can accept QuickTime and AVI movies from any source, as well as still image PICT files and numbered PICT files exported from PostScript drawing programs, Photoshop and Premiere. To number your PICT files so that they're read in the correct order by Painter, you must use the same number of digits for all the files, and you must number them sequentially, such as "File 000," "File 001," "File 002" and so on. With all files in a single folder, choose File, Open and check the Open Numbered Files option. Select the first

Jon Lee of Fox Television used Painter's brushes and effects to progressively modify the logo for the comedy Martin, creating numbered PICT files for an animated sequence. The modified files were animated on a Quantel HAL.

numbered file in your sequence and, when prompted, select the last file. Painter will assemble the files into a Frame Stack.

IMPORTING AND EXPORTING MOVIES WITH MASKS

You can create a mask in a Painter movie and use it in your Frame Stack, or export it within a QuickTime movie to another program such as Premiere or After Effects. To make a movie with a mask, choose File, New, click the Movie button and enter the number of frames desired and click OK. In the New Frame Stack dialog box, choose one of the options with a mask: for instance, 24-bit color with 8-bit Alpha. (You can also make a Frame Stack from a sequence of numbered PICT files in which each file includes its own mask.) To export the movie from Painter as a QuickTime movie and include the mask, choose Save As and select the Save Movie as QuickTime option. When the Compression Settings dialog box appears, in the Compressor section, choose Animation or None from the top pop-up menu to make the mask option available, and then choose Millions of Colors+ in the lower pop-up menu. Click OK.

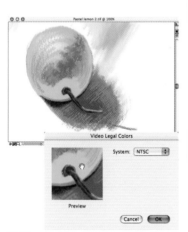

Highly saturated colors can smear when output to video. Choose Effects, Tonal Control, Video Legal Colors to make the colors in your file compatible with NTSC or PAL video color. In the Preview, press and release the grabber to toggle between the RGB and Video Legal Colors previews; click OK to convert the colors in your file.

Exporting Painter images to film editing applications.
Since most animation work is created to be viewed on monitors and the standard monitor resolution is 72 ppi, set up your Frame Stacks and still image files using that resolution. Most files that use film editing have a 4 x 3 aspect ratio: 160 x 120, 240 x 180, 320 x 240 or 640 x 480 pixels. Television also has a 4 x 3 aspect ratio, but for digital television the pixels are slightly taller than they are wide. Artists and designers who create animation for broadcast usually prepare their files at "D-1 size," 720 x 486 pixels. Digital television uses a ".9" pixel (90% the width of standard square pixels). The narrower pixel causes circles and other objects to be stretched vertically. To create a file for D-1 maintaining the height-to-width ratio (to preserve circles), begin with a 720 x 540-pixel image. When the image is complete, scale it non-proportionally to 720 x 486. This will "crush" the image slightly as it appears on your computer screen, but when it's transferred to digital television it will be in the correct proportions.

QuickTime movie files can be exported from Painter and opened in film editing programs such as Premiere and After Effects. If you're using one of these programs to create an 8-bit color production, you'll save processing time if you start with an 8-bit Frame Stack in Painter: Choose the 8-bit Color System Palette option in the New Frame Stack dialog box (after choosing File, New and naming your movie). If you don't set up your file as 8-bit in Painter, you should consider using Photoshop or Equilibrium DeBabelizer—both offer excellent color-conversion control.

We used a modified photo to create this repeating pattern. To generate seamless, tiled textures for 3D, use any of the commands in the menu of the Patterns palette. Turn to "Exploring Patterns" on page 299 in the beginning of Chapter 8 and to "Creating a Seamless Pattern" on page 304, for more about working with patterns.

Some experienced artists prefer to export their Painter images as PICT files rather than as movies because they can easily remove frames from the sequence if they choose. To export Painter still images to applications such as Premiere and After Effects, or to other platforms, save them as single PICT images or as a series of numbered PICT files. You can include a single mask in a Painter PICT file that can be used in compositing in Premiere or After Effects. See "Animating a Logo," on page 388, for a demonstration of exporting Painter images to another platform.

You can also import Painter-created QuickTime movies and still PICT images into Macromedia Director. A QuickTime movie comes in as a single linked Cast Member in the Cast Window, which means it will be stored outside the Director file, keeping file size manageable.

CREATING TEXTURE MAPS FOR 3D RENDERING

A *texture map*—a flat image applied to the surface of a 3D object—can greatly enhance the realism of rendering in 3D programs such as Bryce, Maya, LightWave 3D, 3ds Max and Strata Studio Pro. Many kinds of images can be used for mapping—scanned photographs, logo artwork or painted textures, for example. 3D artists especially like Painter's capability to imitate colorful, natural textures (such as painted wood grain or foliage). There are several kinds of texture maps: A *color texture map* is an image that's used to apply color to a 3D rendering of an object. Other types of mapping affect other qualities of the surface; for instance, a *bump map* (a two-dimensional representation of an uneven surface), a *transparency map* (used to define areas of an image that are transparent, such as glass panes in a window) and a *reflectance map* (used to define matte and shiny areas on an object's surface). If you're developing more than one of these texture maps to the same 3D object, you can keep them in register by using Save As or making clones of the same "master" Painter image to keep file dimensions the same. Remember to save your surface maps in PICT or TIFF format so the 3D program will be able to recognize them.

These floating globes were rendered by John Odam in Strata Studio Pro. He created a texture map in Painter using the Wriggle texture from the More Wild Textures library (located on the Painter IX Application CD-ROM, in the Paper Textures folder) and applied the texture to the objects as follows: color map (A), bump map (B), reflectance map (C) and transparency map (D). The Studio Pro document size was 416 x 416 pixels; the texture map size was 256 x 256 pixels.

Animating an Illustration

Overview *Create an illustration; open a new movie document; paste the drawing into the movie and onto each frame as a layer; copy an area you want to animate; position it and drop it as a layer into a precise position; advance to a new frame and repeat the pasting, moving and copying process; use brushes to paint on individual frames.*

DONAL JOLLEY

1a

Jolley's finished Painter illustration

1b

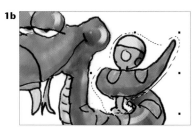

Making a selection of the tail and rattle

1c

The Layers palette showing the Tail layer selected

CREATING AN ANIMATION—whether you use Painter or draw on traditional acetate cels—is labor-intensive because of the sheer number of frames required to get smooth motion. But working digitally does have advantages. You can save a lot of time by copying and pasting a single illustration onto multiple frames. Corrections to digital art are easier to make than with conventional methods and, thanks to the Frame Stacks player, you can see results immediately.

To begin *Rattle Envy*, Donal Jolley painted and animated a comical snake with Painter's brushes. Once the basic animation was complete, Jolley composited some extra layers at a reduced opacity to add the feeling of movement, further enhancing the effect with painted speed blurs.

1 Planning the animation and illustrating. Create an illustration in Painter, choosing a file size no more than a few inches square at 72 ppi (Jolley's illustration was 3 x 3 inches at 72 ppi). Use Painter's brushes to paint just the essential image; you'll be adding the details to each individual frame later. To keep the animation process simple, choose a subject that you won't need to redraw in every frame, such as a character winking an eye. Jolley sketched a whimsical rattlesnake, and then copied the tail area, eyebrows and tongue elements to separate layers so that he could transform them later to create motion in the animation.

After sketching the snake using the Scratchboard Tool variant of Pens, Jolley added color and modeled forms using the Digital Airbrush variant of Airbrushes and the Square Chalk variant of Chalk. Then he added more linework and shadows using the Colored Pencil variant of Colored Pencils and blended color with the Grainy Water variant of Blenders.

He carefully selected each of the areas he planned to animate— three elements in the illustration—the tail area, the eyebrows, and the tongue—and pasted copies of them on separate layers as described below. In addition, he created a layer with a copy of only the stationary parts of the snake's body without the tail, eyebrows and tongue, so when he rocked the tail back and forth or moved the parts, the area underneath it would be white.

When you've finished your illustration, make a selection around an area that you want to animate (Jolley used the Lasso tool), press Alt/Option and choose Select, Float to place a copy of

2

Beginning a new Frame Stack, 3 x 3 inches, 72 ppi, with 33 frames

3

Pasting the base illustration into the movie

4a

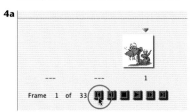

Clicking the Rewind button to return to Frame 1

4b

Frame 3 with Tracing Paper/Onion Skin (three layers) turned on

4c

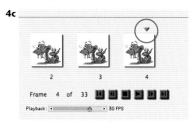

The red marker shows that Frame 4 is active.

it on a new layer. Repeat for any other parts that you want to animate. Also prepare a layer that includes everything that will *not* be animated. Now, click on the non-animated layer's name in the Layers section and choose Select, All, and copy it to the clipboard (Ctrl/⌘-Shift-C). It's now ready to be pasted into a movie. Leave the original illustration file open so you can copy elements from it into your movie.

2 Starting a new Frame Stack. To open a new movie file, choose File, New. Choose a small size so Painter will play the movie quickly; then click the Movie Picture Type, and enter enough frames to give you a smooth animation. Jolley created a 3 x 3-inch movie at 72 ppi (that matched the dimensions and resolution of his illustration), with 33 frames to start, though he added more frames as he needed them using Movie, Add Frames, so that his finished animation was 38 frames. Click OK; name and save your movie, and in the New Frame Stack dialog box, choose Jolley's options: three layers of Onion Skin (so you can see three frames back into the stack) and full 24-bit color with an 8-bit alpha.

> **MOVIE AUTO-SAVE**
>
> Painter saves your movie every time you advance a frame.

3 Pasting the illustration into the Frame Stack. Paste the non-animated part of your illustration from the clipboard into the movie file by choosing Edit, Paste in Place. It will come in as a layer. Now use the arrow keys on your keyboard to move it into position. Copy it in its new position, then drop it to the Canvas by choosing Drop from the triangle menu on the right side of the Layers palette. Because a layer sits on top of the entire frame stack, make sure that you've dropped it before you begin the next step. To advance the frame stack one frame, click the Step Forward

> **COPYING AND POWER-PASTING**
>
> You can greatly improve precision and productivity by copying an item and then *power-pasting* it: To copy an item from a frame press Ctrl/⌘-C, and then advance to the next frame and press Ctrl/⌘-Shift-V to paste it into the exact same position. You can also use this method to copy and paste between two single images that are exactly the same size.

icon on the Frame Stacks palette (or press the Page Up key on your keyboard). Paste the copied base illustration into a new frame in the same position (press Ctrl/⌘-Shift-V) and drop, repeating the paste and drop sequence for each frame of the movie.

4 Creating movement by offsetting layers. Then, to return to the first frame in the stack, click the Rewind button. Back in your original illustration file, choose the Layer Adjuster tool and select the layer for a part that you want to animate by clicking on its layer name in the Layers palette, and choose Ctrl/⌘-C to copy

4d

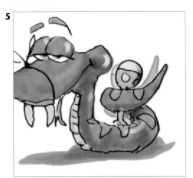

The frame stack palette, showing movement in Frames 30–32

5

Frame 29 shows a copy of the tail layer pasted in, rotated and at 58% opacity

6a

Frame 32 showing the Gritty Charcoal smudges and a low-opacity layer

6b

Frame 30 showing a speed blur painted with the Grainy Water variant

it. Now activate your frame stack file and choose Ctrl/⌘-Shift-V to paste it into exact position.

So that he would have an unmanipulated copy that he could use later, Jolley made a copy of the pasted tail area layer by Alt/Option-clicking on it in the image window with the Layer Adjuster tool. Then he hid the copy by shutting the eye icon to the left of its name in the Layers palette.

With the original tail section layer selected, he chose Effects, Orientation, Free Transform and used the feature to rotate the tail. When you choose Free Transform, an eight-handled bounding box will appear. Now choose the Layer Adjuster tool, press the Ctrl/⌘ key and position the tool over a corner handle. Drag to rotate the layer to a position that you like. So you can bring the layer in its new position into the next frame, store a copy of the layer in the clipboard by pressing Ctrl/⌘-C. Then choose Drop from the triangle menu on the right side of the Layers palette to drop the layer onto the current frame, and go to the next frame by pressing Page Up on your keyboard. Paste the copied illustration again (Ctrl/⌘-V), and use the Layer Adjuster tool to reposition the element in the frame; then drop it.

As you work, look at the Frame Stacks palette to check your progress. You can view previous frames "ghosted" in your main image—much like an animator's light box—by choosing Canvas, Tracing Paper (Ctrl/⌘-T). The number of previous frames displayed is determined by the number of Onion Skin layers you chose when you opened the movie. To change the number of layers, close the file, reopen it, and choose a new number of layers. Use Ctrl/⌘-T to turn the Onion Skin view on and off as you work. Click the Play button to play the animation, and take note of the areas that need to be smoother.

5 Making the animation smoother. After playing the animation, Jolley wanted to make the transition between some of the frames smoother and slower. So he used the tail area layer copy that he had hidden in the Layers palette (in step 4) as a basis to add several more low-opacity layers to a few of the frames. Then he replayed the animation again to check its smoothness. To blur a few of the edges, he used the Just Add Water variant of Blenders on some of the frames.

6 Adding more motion with brushstrokes. Now that he liked the way the animation played, Jolley added to the feeling of motion by painting more noticeable brushstrokes on the tail area. Using the Gritty Charcoal variant of Charcoal, he painted darker smudges on the tail—altering it slightly in each frame. He also added speed blurs by smearing the edges of the snake's tail and the rattle using the Grainy Water variant of Blenders. When the Frame Stack was completed, Jolley saved it as a QuickTime movie. (Turn to "Importing and Exporting" on page 380.)

Making an Animated Comp

Overview *Set up a layered illustration file; record the movement of a layer using scripts; play the script back into a movie.*

DEWEY REID

Reid's original street scene illustration

2a

The topmost layer (with the Canvas hidden) showing the dropped-out area that will reveal the background scene underneath

2b

The Dino character showing the painted mask (left), and with the background dropped out (right)

TO VISUALIZE MOTION in the early stages of creating an animation, Dewey Reid often makes an animated comp (a conceptual illustration with a moving element). Adding motion is a great way to help a client visualize a concept, and it's more exciting than viewing a series of still images. Reid's storyboard, above, shows frames from a movie created by recording a script of a moving layer.

Using scripts and the Record Frames on Playback feature, you can record a layer's movement. When you play the script back, Painter will generate a Frame Stack with the appropriate number of frames, saving you the tedious work of pasting in and moving the character in each frame. After you've made your Frame Stack, convert it into a QuickTime movie (or AVI/VFW on the PC) for easier and faster playback using a freeware utility like Movie Player.

1 Beginning with an illustration. Begin with an image at the size you want your final movie to be. Reid started with a 300 x 173-pixel street scene illustration from his archives.

2 Setting up a layered file. Like conventional animation where characters are drawn on layers of acetate, this animation technique works best when all elements in the image are on separate layers. You may want to create masks for the various elements in separate documents, and then copy and paste them into your main image. (For more about layers and masking, turn to Chapter 6.)

Reid envisioned three "layers" for this comp: a background image (the street scene) in the bottom layer, a copy of the street scene with a portion of the scene removed in the top layer, and a dinosaur positioned between the two street scenes that would move from left to right across the "opening" in the top layer. Reid made a duplicate layer from the Canvas by selecting all and Alt/Option-clicking on the image with the Layer Adjuster tool. To make it easier to see the top layer as you work, hide the Canvas layer by clicking its eye icon shut in the Layers palette. Select the top layer. To erase an area of the layer, choose a Pointed Eraser variant of the Erasers for most of the editing; for removing small

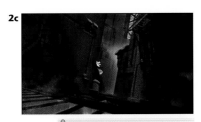

2c

The Dino layer, selected in the Layers palette and in starting position, ready to be moved by the arrow keys

3

Setting up the Script Options to Save Frames on Playback

4

Selecting the Dino script in the Scripts palette

5

Choosing the QuickTime button in the Save Movie dialog box

areas, you may want to try the 1-Pixel Eraser variant. To see the background layer again, click open the eye icon for the Canvas in the Layers palette. You'll see a complete background image, since the lower layer shows through the hole in the top layer.

In a separate file, Reid painted a mask to isolate Dino the dinosaur from the background and turned the mask into a selection by choosing Select, Load Selection. He copied Dino to the clipboard and pasted him into the street scene RIFF file. (An easy way to add a character is to drag an item from the Image Portfolio palette into your image—like the strawberry, the pumpkin or the lollipop, for example.) In the Layers palette, Reid dragged Dino down to a position between the two street scene layers. Using the Layer Adjuster and the arrow keys, Reid positioned the dinosaur so that only the red nose was visible behind the left front building, establishing Dino's starting position in the animation.

3 Recording the script. Click the right triangle on the Scripts palette to open the menu and choose Script Options; check Record Initial State, check Save Frames on Playback and enter a number for Every 1/10ths of a second (Reid chose 5), and click OK. Select the layer that will be moving by clicking on its name in the Layers palette (for Reid, the Dino Layer). Choose Record Script from the menu on the Scripts palette bar (or click the round red button on the front of the Scripts palette). Then hold down an arrow key to move the layer smoothly in the RIFF file. When you have completed the path of motion, choose Stop Recording Script from the Scripts palette menu (or click the Square button) and name the script. Return the character to its starting position by pressing Ctrl/⌘-Z.

4 Playing back the script into the movie. From the pop-up menu on the Scripts palette, choose Playback Script, choose your script from the list in the Apply Script to Movie dialog box and click Playback. When prompted, name your movie a different name than the RIFF file. Click the Save button and Painter will convert your RIFF image to a movie (leaving the original RIFF intact) and will add the movie frames needed. As the movie is generated, you will see the frames accumulating in the Frame Stacks palette. When Painter finishes generating the Frame Stack, turn off visibility for the layers that are above the Canvas by clicking their eye icons in the Layers palette. (If you don't hide the layers, you won't be able to see your movie, which is recorded on the Canvas.) Finally, press the Play button on the Frame Stacks palette to play your movie!

5 Converting the Frame Stack to QuickTime or AVI. To play the movie without having Painter loaded, convert the Frame Stack to QuickTime or AVI format: Choose File, Save As, and when the dialog box appears, choose Save Movie as QT/AVI. Give your movie a new name (such as "Dino movie.qtime"), click Save and in the Compression Settings dialog box, choose from the top pop-up menu (Reid recommends Animation or None).

Animating a Logo

Overview *Make a clone of existing artwork and modify it with Painter's brushes and effects; save it, make another clone and alter the new clone; continue to progressively make and alter clones, restoring the image when needed by pasting a copy of the original logo from the clipboard.*

JON LEE / FOX TELEVISION

1

Starting with the existing Martin logo

2a

Lee began manipulating the logo by selecting and scaling a portion of the cloned image (left). Then he selected and inverted a portion of the next clone in the sequence (right).

"IMPROVISATIONAL, FRESH, SPONTANEOUS, and very flexible!" says Jon Lee, Director of Art and Design for Fox Television, when describing his artistic experience with Painter. For the Fox TV program *Martin*, Lee built an animated title sequence like a painting, saving frames at different stages of development. He created a wild, hand-done, organic look to express the comedic street sensibility of the TV show.

Lee created a series of 35 keyframes in Painter (keyframes are the frames that establish essential positions in an animated sequence), eight of which are shown above. When he finished, he moved them from his Macintosh to a lightning-fast Quantel HAL system, where he added dissolves to blend one frame into the next. (Dissolves can also be achieved on the Macintosh desktop in Adobe After Effects or Adobe Premiere.)

1 Beginning with existing art. Lee began by opening the existing Martin logo in Painter. He copied and pasted it into a new file measuring 720 x 486 pixels (the aspect ratio of the Quantel HAL) with a black background, and then merged the layers by clicking the right triangle on the Layers palette bar, and choosing Drop from the menu.

2b

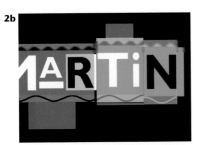

Adding colored boxes to Frame 05 with the Rectangular Selection tool and the Effects, Fill command

2c

Using Distorto variants (Distortion) to pull paint onto the background in Frame 07

2d

A motion blur effect applied in 14 (left), and then cloned and filtered in Frame 15

3a

Adding hand lettering and colored brush strokes to a clone of Frame 15 in Frame 16

3b

Restoring readability with a layer in Frame 17

Choose an image that you want to manipulate in your animated sequence and open it in Painter. Save your file in PICT format, naming it "01." In order for a numbered sequence of files to automatically play in numerical order, the files must be named using the same number of digits, such as 01, 02. . . 10, 11 and so on.

2 Manipulating progressive clones. After planning how many keyframes you'll need and how the artwork will progress through the frames, begin your manipulation. Clone the first document (File, Clone) and use Painter's tools and special effects on your clone. If you don't like the result of a brushstroke or applied effect, undo it and try something else. When you're satisfied with the result, save the file, name it "02," and make another clone from it. The new clone will become the next canvas for your experimentation. Working quickly and intuitively, Lee treated the logo with a wide variety of brushes, filters and effects from the Effects, Surface Control menu, saving progressive versions in a numbered sequence.

3 Restoring the logo. After a few progressively altered clones, your image may become unrecognizable. To restore the original to some degree, go to your original file, select all and copy, and then paste it into your current clone. Adjust the Opacity using the slider in the Layers palette and drop the layer by choosing Drop from the triangle menu on the right side of the Layers palette bar. Lee used this technique to periodically restore the readability of the type, working the original logo back into the progressive image.

Outputting the Painter files. When Lee was finished with the series of PICT frames, he used Electric Image Projector (a subprogram within Electric Image) to automatically shuttle the files over to the Quantel HAL platform for compositing and output to Beta videotape for broadcast. The workstation is set up with the Quantel HAL and Mac systems side-by-side; they're connected with an Intelligent Resources card that helps convert the digital imagery from one platform to another. Part of the translation process involved converting RGB color to the NTSC video color system for television.

On the HAL, Lee "stretched" the 35 original frames to 90 frames; the HAL added the appropriate number of frames to achieve the dissolves between each pair of keyframes, keeping the animation even and smooth. To create a 10-second title sequence at 30 frames per second, Lee needed 300 frames total. He made a loop of the 90-frame sequence and let it cycle until it filled the necessary frame count. ❧

Automating Movie Effects

Overview *Open a video clip; test a series of effects on a single frame; undo the effects; repeat the effects while recording a script; apply the script to the entire clip.*

CTP / VIDEO: MEDIACOM

WITH PAINTER'S SCRIPTS FEATURE, you can automate any series of recorded effects and apply them to each frame of an entire movie.

1 Starting with a video clip. Tests will be processed faster if you begin with a small video clip like the one we used—320 x 240 pixels with 67 frames. When you open a video clip (a QuickTime or AVI movie), Painter converts it to a Frame Stack. (When you save the Stack, give it a new name so the original clip isn't replaced.)

2 Testing a series of effects on a frame. Before you test a sequence of effects on a single frame, open General Preferences (Ctr/⌘-K) and set up multiple Undos so that you can return the clip to its original state. Enter a number of Undos that exceeds the number of effects you plan to use. Choose a rough paper texture (we chose Thick Paint from the Painted Effects 3 library on the Painter IX Wow! CD-ROM) and apply it to Frame 1 in your movie with Effects, Surface Control, Apply Surface Texture, Using Paper (we settled on Amount 22%, Picture 90% and Shine 12%). Next, we added a look of cloud-filtered sunlight by choosing Effects, Surface Control, Apply Lighting. We customized the Slide Lighting, named it "sunlight," and saved it. (See Chapter 8 for more about lighting techniques.) When you've finished testing, undo the effects you applied to Frame 1. (Painter will remember the last settings you used in the dialog boxes.)

1

Frame 1 of the original video clip

2

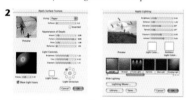

The Apply Surface Texture and Apply Lighting settings chosen for the movie

3

Choosing Movie, Set Grain Position to create a "live" texture on the movie

4a

The Stop button (left) and the Record button (center)

4b

Detail of effects on Frames 35 and 50

HI-RES MOVIE EFFECTS

If you want to apply effects to a broadcast-quality (640 x 480 pixels) video, use an editing program (such as After Effects) to create a low-resolution version on which to test a combination of effects. Because it takes a higher setting to get results in a larger file, plan to adjust the settings before treating the larger file.

3 Moving paper grain in the movie. To add subtle interest to your movie, you can change paper grain position on a frame-by-frame basis by choosing Movie, Set Grain Position. We chose the Grain Moves Linearly button and a 2-pixel horizontal movement.

4 Recording and playing back the session on the movie. Begin recording the effects by clicking the Record button in the Scripts palette; then repeat your sequence of effects. When you're finished, click the Stop button. Give your script a descriptive name, and undo your effects again. To apply your script to the movie, choose Movie, Apply Script to Movie. When the dialog box appears, find your new Script in the list, click the Playback button and watch as Painter applies the recorded series of effects to each frame.

■ **Dewey Reid** of Reid Creative, illustrated the 30-second animation *Yuri the Yak* for Sesame Street, a production of Children's Television Workshop. In the story segment, Yuri travels the countryside eating yellow yams and yogurt, and teaching the letter "Y." Reid stresses the importance of preproduction planning in animation. He created the *Yuri the Yak* animation with a total of only 35 drawings (it could have taken hundreds). His background in conventional animation helped him determine which drawings to make, and which to generate by tweening in an animation program, saving time and a lot of work. Reid used Painter to create individual parts of the Yak, such as the head, body and arms. He opened the illustrations in Photoshop and created a mask for each image, and then saved the illustrations as PICT files in a numbered sequence. (He prefers using PICT files rather than QuickTime movies, since PICT files allow higher quality. Also, a sequence of PICT files allows for more flexibility—it's easier to remove a frame or two, if necessary.) He imported the masked files into Adobe After Effects, created animation cycles for each of the Yak parts, and then joined animation cycles together. A virtuoso with effects, Reid completed his artistic vision by adding subtle lighting and texture. He opened the animation in Painter as a Frame Stack. After recording a script of Effects, Surface Control, Apply Lighting and Apply Surface Texture, he chose Movie, Apply Script to Movie to add the effects to the frames.

■ *Snuffy 1 and 2* are two compositional layout illustrations by **Cindy Reid** of Reid Creative for a proposed Sesame Street production of Children's Television Workshop. The animation was conceived to accompany the children's song "I Wish I Were Small." In Frame 1, Snuffy (who is normally mammoth-size) becomes small enough to fit into a bird's nest; in Frame 2, small enough to fit in a buttercup. To create both frames Reid shot photos of a bird's nest, a bee, the sky and clouds, foliage and buttercup flowers for "scrap." She scanned the photos into Photoshop and pasted the images onto layers to build two composite files. When the elements were in place, she opened the layered composite file in Painter, where she added painterly brush work to each layer using the Grainy Water variant of Blenders. She added details using a small Sharp Chalk variant (Chalk). When the brush work was complete, she flattened the image by choosing Drop All from the Layers palette bar menu.

■ Award-winning concept artist **Ryan Church** creates cinematic environments. He is the Concept Supervisor for *Star Wars III* and a senior art director at Industrial Light and Magic.

Before designing a two-dimensional concept for a scene, Church meets with the director to review the script, and then he does research for the elements he needs. When creating the scenes, he takes advantage of his background in conventional design and painting, and the flexibility of working on the computer with Painter and a Wacom tablet.

Church created *Pirate Catamaran* for his portfolio. He began by making rough sketches in Painter using Pens variants that included the Croquil Pen and Scratchboard tool. When the elements were as he liked them, he added a new transparent layer and then created a tighter line drawing.

European master artists such as Da Vinci, Michelangelo and Velasquez often worked over a midtone background because it made developing the highlights and shadows easier, and it helped them to create drama. With a similar goal in mind, Church selected the image Canvas and then applied a midtone brown by choosing Effects, Surface Control, Color Overlay, Using Uniform Color and Dye Concentration.

Then, Church developed the ship, water and clouds using translucent brushes that included the Detail Airbrush variant of Airbrushes. When the basic values were laid in, he painted opaque color on areas (including the gold sky) using a modified Square Chalk (Chalk). He increased the Grain setting in the Property Bar so that the brush would cover more grain and thus paint smoother strokes. Then, he smoothed areas of the water and sky using Blenders variants. His expressive

blending is most noticeable on the clouds and in water splashing the front of the boat. For more drama in the sky, Church added richer gold and rust colors with the Square Chalk and then smudged areas using the Diffuse Blur (Blenders).

At this point, he copied the Canvas onto itself by choosing Edit, Copy and then Edit, Paste in Place. Working on the layer, he used the Glow variant of F-X to add light to the windows and to the brightest sunlit areas on the clouds. To refine forms, Church painted translucent strokes on the sails and a few other areas with the Wash variant of Digital Watercolor. Then, he dropped the layer to the Canvas.

For the details, Church added a new, empty layer and then used the Detail Airbrush to refine areas and to paint a few orange accents on the boat. Finally, he deepened the shadows in areas that needed more contrast.

■ For the futuristic scene *Catamaran City*, **Ryan Church** began by making sketches in Painter with the Pens. To set the mood for the painting, he used a similar technique as *Pirate Catamaran.* He applied a warm, midtone gray to the Canvas by choosing Effects, Surface Control, Color Overlay. From the Using menu, he chose Uniform Color, and he clicked the Dye Concentration button.

Next, Church began to develop the atmosphere and architectural elements in his painting. He set up guides (Canvas, Show Guides) for the important vertical and horizontal elements in his composition. Working over his sketch, he made selections for the large buildings and then saved them as masks in the Channels palette.

Then, working on a layer over his sketch, he loaded each selection and then laid in broad areas of translucent color using the Digital Airbrush variant of Airbrushes. When the general values were roughed in, he added strokes of more opaque color using a modified Square Chalk (Chalk), and then he blended areas using the Grainy Water variant of Blenders.

So that he could refine areas of the image without disturbing the existing paint, he copied the Canvas onto a new layer by choosing Edit, Copy and then Edit, Paste in Place. Working on the layer, he used Broad Water Brush variant of Digital Watercolor to paint transparent glazes and refine forms. To make corrections to the Digital Watercolor washes, he used

the Wet Eraser. Next, Church added brightened areas of the illuminated buildings and street lights in the foreground using the Glow variant of F-X. When he was satisfied with the forms and lighting, he dropped the layer to the Canvas.

For the final details, Church added a new, empty layer. Then, he used the Detail Airbrush to add more contrast and deepen a few of the shadows. He also brightened areas, for instance, a few of the lights on the foreground buildings. As a last step, Church added soft strokes of bright blue and purple (with the Detail Airbrush) to suggest the lights on the speeding vehicles.

■ **Jean-Luc Touillon's** passion for drawing shows in *Endormie*, a page for an animated sketchbook that was created in Painter and Adobe After Effects. The animation shows the process of the drawing and then the addition of layers of color being added to the completed black-and-white drawing. Touillon prefers to draw with his pressure-sensitive tablet and stylus, watching the drawing develop on-screen, without the use of photographs. After opening a new file with a white background, he used various Liquid Ink brushes to draw a series of Liquid Ink drawings, the woman, pen, bath, teapot and movie camera. Liquid Ink is resolution-independent, so Touillon could sketch quickly and expressively using a tiny file size, and then increase the file size using Canvas, Resize. (For more information about Liquid Ink, turn to "A Painter Liquid Ink Primer" on page 130.) After all the black-and-white sketches were complete, he colored them using separate layers for each color. Then he converted each black-and-white drawing and its colored areas to shapes as follows: Touillon targeted each Liquid Ink layer and converted it to a default layer by clicking the right triangle on the Layers palette and choosing Convert to Default Layer from the pop-up menu. Next, he made a selection for each drawing and its colored elements by choosing Select, Auto Select, Image Luminance, and converted each selection to shapes by choosing Select, Convert to Shape. Finally, he exported the shapes from Painter by choosing File, Export, Adobe Illustrator File. He used the Adobe Illustrator-format vector files to create an animation in After Effects.

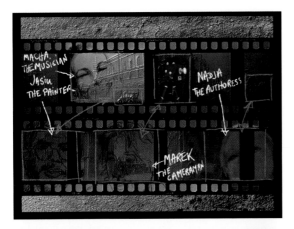

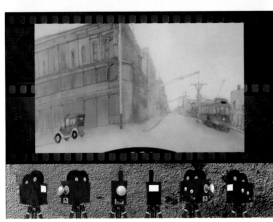

■ **Jean-Luc Touillon** also known as "**Jasiu**" created the illustrations for *L'histoire digitale évolutive d'une ville imaginaire*, an interactive mystery story on CD-ROM, while working with the team at LA F@KTORY in Paris. Touillon built the frames for the story entirely within Painter. QuickTime VR was used to produce the panoramic environment.

With QuickTime VR, the viewer can manipulate the camera by zooming in and out and scrolling 360° to the left and right as they tour the imaginary city. To begin, Touillon created a new frame stack and painted on the individual frames using the Artist Pastel Chalk (Pastels) and the Basic Crayon variant of Crayons. To blend the paint, he used the Grainy

Water variant of Blenders, creating a dreamlike atmosphere. When the images were complete, he saved them as a series of PICT files. Touillon later assembled the frames using Metropolis and Macromedia Director software. For information about using QuickTime VR, see http://www.apple.com/quicktime/qtvr and http://www.iqtvr.org.

■ An innovative storyboard artist, **Peter Mitchell Rubin** used a variety of Painter's brushes and compositing controls to create the storyboards for the MGM movie *Stargate.* The Giza, Egypt, sequence is shown here. Rubin outputs his illustrations from Painter as numbered PICT files, and then animates them in Adobe Premiere. Rubin's love of drawing shows in his storyboards. He works very quickly, in gray, at 72 ppi. His document size depends on the amount of detail needed, but is usually under 600 pixels wide. The aspect ratio depends upon how the film will be shot. Rubin organizes the thousands of drawings that he creates for a film in folders according to scene. He sets up QuicKeys macros to automate actions wherever possible, automating the processing of all the files in a folder. When Rubin adds other elements to an image, he pastes the element, drops it, and then paints into it to merge it seamlessly into the composition. He also uses Painter's Cloners brushes. For example, he created the texture in Frame 15 (left column, third frame down from top) by photographing the actual set sculpture used in the movie, scanning it and cloning the scan into his drawing.

■ Art Director and animator **John Ryan** employs an expressive approach when creating his animations. Ryan is co-owner of the Dagnabit! animation studio with Joyce Ryan and Robert Pope.

Black & Decker commissioned Dagnabit! to create *Mo Skeeter*, a 30-second animation spot for their Mosquito Halo product.

Ryan produced all of the original drawings for the *Mo Skeeter* character using a conventional 4B Derwent sketching pencil on animation bond paper. Then, he scanned the drawings in sequence into Softimage Toonz ink and paint software. Working in Toonz, he cleaned up the images and built mattes (alpha channels), which would help later with compositing the critter into the background scene. Then, Ryan saved the files as a series of sequentially numbered Targa files, and then he opened the numbered files in Painter as a Frame Stack.

Using the Soft Camel variant of Watercolor, he added color to the mosquito. As he worked, Ryan paid careful attention to the Grain setting in the Property Bar and the Paper Scale in the Papers palette because these settings influence the texture of the brush work. "I'll change the grain size or type of paper every few frames to mimic what would happen if I was actually painting on different sheets of paper and photographing them under a camera," says Ryan. While building the animation, he switched between French Watercolor Paper, Italian Watercolor Paper and Hot Press papers.

Ryan usually keeps a small version of the finished character design to use for reference, to keep the transparency densities in check. He also usually works through the Frame Stack, painting one color at a time whenever possible. Because he created mattes earlier to constrain the paint, he was free to make expressive brushstrokes without worrying about staying within the lines.

■ Artist and multimedia designer **Ted Larson** created the images for an educational CD-ROM about the book of Revelation in the Holy Bible. The pictures were designed as both large-format digital prints and PowerPoint-ready digital slides for seminary and church presentation aids. *Door to Heaven* is shown here.

Larson began by sketching in Painter to establish a composition. Then, working in Formz (a 3D modeling program), he built the doorway for the *Door to Heaven*.

Larson wanted to show the grand scale of the door by contrasting it with a human figure, so he shot photos of a friend posing as the apostle John. Inside the doorway, he used sunshine and clouds to give the feeling one was leaving the known universe and stepping into another dimension. He assembled a black-and-white composite image, which included the decorated door. Next, he made a new empty layer for the coloring, and to make the layer like a transparent color overlay on top of the gray image, he set the Composite Method of the layer to Color. Then, using warm colors, he painted over the clouds, and he colored the figure and the door using low-opacity Airbrushes variants. He also used Watercolor brushes to paint transparent details. Finally, he brightened the edge of the door and areas of the clouds using the Fire and Glow variants of the F-X brush.

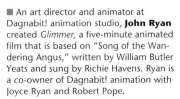 ■ An art director and animator at Dagnabit! animation studio, **John Ryan** created *Glimmer,* a five-minute animated film that is based on "Song of the Wandering Angus," written by William Butler Yeats and sung by Richie Havens. Ryan is a co-owner of Dagnabit! animation with Joyce Ryan and Robert Pope.

Throughout the story, the Angus character is bedeviled by an elusive female. Ryan rendered the drawings using conventional media and then later, he painted them in Painter.

To design the male and female characters and express two distinctly different per-

sonalities, he employed two contrasting art styles on animation bond paper. For Angus, he drew broad India ink brushstrokes that were shaded with scratchy ballpoint pen marks. Then, he drew the female character with a smaller handmade brush and India ink. **Joyce Ryan** built reference sculptures (based on John Ryan's original design of the two key characters) that he could use for reference as he animated them. (A photograph of the sculpture of Angus is shown above.) When the sequential illustrations were complete, Ryan scanned the drawings into Softimage Toonz ink and paint software. He used Toonz to clean up the

images and to build mattes (alpha channels), which would help later with compositing the characters into the background. Next, Ryan saved the files as a series of sequentially numbered Targa files and then he opened the numbered files in Painter as Frame Stacks. Working in Painter, he painted the frames using a combination of the Sargent Brush variant of the Artists category and the Palette Knife variant of Palette Knives to achieve the desired effect. Ryan also created an intriguing animated background in Painter that had the feeling of a hand-held camera.

12

USING PAINTER FOR WEB GRAPHICS

Ben Barbante created Efolio, *an illustration for his Web site's index page. To see the entire image, turn to the gallery at the end of this chapter.*

INTRODUCTION

WHAT DOES PAINTER OFFER AN ARTIST who designs graphics for the World Wide Web? In addition to its powerful natural media brushes, compositing tools, mosaics and other effects, Painter can help you prepare images for Web pages. For example, you can set type for titles with the Text tool, use shapes to draw polygons, convert the shapes to layers and define the polygons as clickable regions for use on your Web page. Use the Image Slicer to segment an image into smaller parts so the viewer can see pieces of the image as they load, and then export some of the slices with JavaScript rollovers. You can open source video in Painter as a Frame Stack and grab stills to use as graphics or as references for your Web illustrations, or export the Frame Stack directly from Painter as a GIF animation. (If you need help with the painting techniques or compositing methods referred to in this chapter, you can find more information in Chapters 3, 5 and 6. Turn to Chapter 11 for information on scripts and Frame Stack animations. And see Appendix C for recommended books relating to Web design.)

CREATING GRAPHICS FOR THE WEB

Painter has tools that make it easy to adapt graphics for the Web. For instance, you can save in GIF and JPEG (the two most popular image formats used on the Web). And you can tell Painter to do some of the coding to help you set up image maps or linked graphics. Here are some tips for creating Web graphics in Painter.

First, there are two basic uses for images on a Web page. One is an in-line graphic or "static" image embedded in a page without a link to another location—for example, an embedded background graphic. The second use for graphics is as "hot spots," or "buttons." A hot spot is a clickable region on your artwork that will allow the user to hyperlink (or travel) to another location on the Web, either within the same Web site or at another site. There are two general types of hot

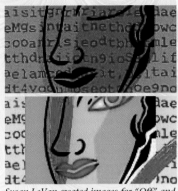

Susan LeVan created images for "Off" and "On" button states, for the Nichole Shoes Web site. To see the entire set of buttons, turn to the gallery at the end of this chapter.

spots. The simpler one is a *button* that links to one location (URL, or Uniform Resource Locator) such as www.peachpit.com. The second is an *image map*—an image that has been divided into regions, each of which lets you link to a different URL.

Making an image map. You can choose any kind of graphic as an image map: title type, a photograph or an illustration you've painted. Define an image map by selecting all or part of an image (by dragging around it with a selection tool and copying it to make a layer). Then double-click on the new layer's name in the Layers palette to access the Layer Attributes dialog box. Use the check box to make it a WWW Map Clickable Region. In the Save As GIF Options and JPEG Encoding Quality dialog boxes, you can choose to export a client-side image map (directions for the image map are included in the HTML for the page) or server-side image map (directions for the map are stored on the server) by telling Painter to create an image map definition file with dimensions for the hot spots. Client-side image maps are more efficient to use when designing for newer browsers, but if you want your image map to work with older browsers as well, consider including both client-side and server-side directions in the HTML for the image map. For more information, see "Building an Image Map for a Web Page" on page 409.

Using Web-friendly file formats. The JPEG and transparent GIF formats that Painter supports are two of the most popular file formats used in Web page design. Transparent GIF files make use of the mask you've saved with the file, allowing a graphic to be placed on the page with an irregular edge or with holes cut into it to reveal the background underneath. You can make a transparent GIF by choosing File, Save As, GIF, and then using the Output Transparency check box in the Save As GIF Options dialog box. You can pan around the Preview area to preview the transparency. We suggest using GIF format to save simple line art and flat-color graphics without gradations and soft edges. Save photos and painted artwork in 24-bit JPEG format.

Building small files that load fast. Web-savvy designers recommend making graphics files small, between 20 and 30K, because most Web visitors will not wait for images that take a long time to load. Typical modem speed is 56,600 bps and graphics of 20–30K will download within 1–3 seconds. To make GIF images small, use Painter's Save As GIF Options dialog box to compress the number of colors from millions to 256 (8-bit) or fewer. Save as GIF in the exact pixel dimensions needed for the page design. When you use JPEG format to preserve the 24-bit color of an image, experiment with the JPEG Encoding Quality settings to determine how much compression an image can withstand. JPEG is a lossy compression (it removes information, which can't be restored), so make sure to use File, Save As to create the new

TO QUANTIZE OR TO DITHER?

Painter offers two methods for reducing the number of colors in the Save As GIF dialog box: Quantize to Nearest Color and Dither Colors. Quantize to Nearest Color uses areas of solid color, picking the colors in the current palette that are the closest match to the color you're trying to convert. Dither Colors converts colors using a random pattern in the same color range (giving a less banded result or a better visual color match), but it generates a file that can't be compressed as small as one with solid colors.

i-potato

www.i-potato.net

*Arthur Steuer and Even Steven Levee,
principals of i~potato production company, commissioned artist/animator
Sharon Steuer to create the i-potato logo
for the cover of their pop music CD and
Web site. Steuer used Painter's Watercolor Brushes variants, Oils variants and
Airbrushes variants to paint the image.
Steuer created an animation of the eye
blinking for the launching of the Web site
(www.i-potato.net). She created the cels
for the eye-blink in Painter, using a separate layer to draw each stage of the animation. So the animation would load
quickly, her client chose to use only two of
the three stages. (See a QuickTime movie
with music that includes all three stages
in Steuer's folder on the* Painter IX Wow!
*CD-ROM.) To read about creating a GIF
animation step by step, turn to "Making a
Slide Show Animation" on page 412.*

JPEG file with a different name,
preserving your master file.

**Creating a subdued back-
ground.** Painter has tools for
creating exciting backgrounds,
but a busy, contrasty background can take attention away
from the subject of the screen
and overwhelm your audience.
Here are two suggestions that
will help you make a background more subtle: Turn down
the contrast using Effects, Tonal
Control, Brightness/Contrast, or desaturate the background (using
Effects, Tonal Control, Adjust Colors) to call attention to brighter-
colored content. To desaturate, move the Saturation slider to the
left. Click OK when you see the look you want in the Preview
window.

Adding movie stills and video to your page. You can open
a movie in Painter and capture frames to use as static images or
hot spots. And you can save a QuickTime or AVI movie using
effective compression such as Cinepak, so it can be played within
a Netscape or Internet Explorer browser.

Exporting a movie as a GIF animation. Painter makes it
easy to add movement to your Web pages with GIF animations.
You can open a QuickTime/AVI movie as a Frame Stack (or create
your own animation in Painter) and export it directly from
Painter as a GIF animation. Here are some tips to help you make a
GIF animation that loads quickly and plays smoothly on your
Web page: Make movies with a small frame size (such as 160 x 120).
(Painter doesn't permit movies to be resized. So if you plan to
import video into Painter, reduce the frame size in a video editor
such as Adobe Premiere before opening it in Painter.) Use as few
frames as possible. (You can use the Movie, Delete Frames dialog
box to remove any unnecessary frames.) Reduce the number of
colors—using black-and-white or just a few colors, for instance,
will help to make a smaller animation file.

To save a completed Frame Stack as a GIF animation, choose
File, Save As, Save Movie As GIF Animation. In the Save As GIF
Options box, make the choices you need. To read about making a
GIF animation step-by-step, turn to "Making a Slide Show Anima-
tion" on page 412. ⓦ

WEB-FRIENDLY COLOR

Painter ships with several color sets
built for Web graphics. To load a
Web-friendly color set, open the
Color Set palette, click the right
arrow and from the menu, choose
Open Color Set. Navigate to the
Painter IX application folder and
open the Color Sets folder. Select
one of the seven choices, the
Netscape 216, the Macintosh
default 256 or the Windows Default
256 Color Set and click Open.

SHRINKING A COPY

If you're doing detailed painting or retouching to be displayed on the Web at
72 ppi, you may want to create your art at a higher resolution so you can zoom
in and paint the details. Then use Canvas, Resize to shrink a copy of your image
down to 72 ppi. Sharpen areas that become soft (Effects, Focus, Sharpen).

Reducing Color Using Apply Screen

Overview *Choose an image; reduce color using Apply Screen; edit the color to make it Web-safe; export the image.*

1

The original photograph with selection active and background sky made lighter

2a

To choose a Web-safe HTML color in the Select Screen dialog box on a Mac, first click on the icon for Color palettes.

2b

Scroll down the list to select a Web-safe HTML color or type in the hexadecimal number of the color desired.

2c

The Apply Screen dialog box with preview showing the new color choices

ORIGINAL PHOTO: PHOTOSPIN

REDUCING THE NUMBER OF COLORS is a frequently used method for making small files for faster downloading of Web graphics. To create this three-color image, we used Apply Screen—one of Painter's most efficient "color reduction" tools. It allows you to create images composed of only three colors without the antialiasing that creates many intermediate colors when it smooths edges.

1 Choosing a photo and making adjustments. Open an image that you want to convert to a three-color composition. In our first attempt to modify color using the Apply Screen function, the car merged with the magenta background because the background's value did not contrast enough with the car. We undid the Apply Screen, and before trying again, we isolated the background by making a selection, and then lightened the magenta background. To make a selection of an area like the background based on color, click on the area with the Magic Wand. To add areas of noncontiguous color to the selection, turn off the Contiguous check box in the Property Bar; expand or shrink the range of colors by adjusting the Tolerance. (To read more about the Magic Wand, turn to page 185–186 in Chapter 5.) Then we increased the value within the selected background using Brightness/Contrast (choose Effects, Tonal Control, Brightness/Contrast). After adjusting the Brightness, we chose Select, None.

2 Reducing color. To apply the color effect to your entire image choose Effects, Surface Control, Apply Screen, Using Image Luminance and choose a color by clicking the middle of the three color squares. In the Colors picker that opened, we settled on a dark blue color, in addition to the black and white. In the Colors picker, click on the icon for Color Palettes, on the top row of the window. Click on the drop-down list and select Web Safe Colors, and choose a color. If your computer does not have the HTML color option, choose a color to serve as a preview of the final

REDUCING COLOR USING APPLY SCREEN **403**

3a

The image showing active selection made with the Dropper and the Auto Select, Using Current Color dialog box

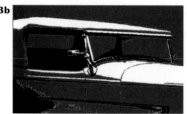

3b

Close-up of the image with selection. The original blue color shows dithering when viewed on a monitor with only 256 colors.

4a

The Netscape Navigator 216 Color Set, showing the new blue we used for the fill

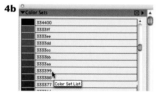

4b

The Hexidecimal Color Set, shown as a list

4c

Filling with the Web-safe color

5

Our settings in the GIF Options dialog box and the Color Set with three Web-safe colors

effect. It doesn't have to be a Web-safe color. In step 3 you can replace it. We adjusted the Threshold sliders to bring out important details in the car. The Threshold 1 slider controls the relationship between dark blue (the middle color) and white (the color on the right); the Threshold 2 slider controls the amount of black (the left color).

3 Making a selection. In Windows, Painter's Apply Screen dialog box does not let you directly apply color from a Web-safe color set (unless you have the option described in step 2). To replace our color with a Web-safe color when using our Windows machine, we first made a hard-edged mask. To make a hard-edged selection based on color, choose the Dropper and click on the colored area you want to mask. From the Select menu choose Auto Select, Using Current Color. Click OK; you'll see a selection marquee appear on your image.

4 Filling the selection with a Web-safe color. Now load the Web-safe Netscape Navigator 216 Color Set as follows: On the Colors Set palette, click the right triangle to open the menu and choose Open Color Set. Navigate to the Netscape Navigator 216 Color Set. This set can be found in the Color Sets folder, in the Painter IX application folder. Next, click on a Web-safe color that complements your design (we chose a dark blue). Choose Effects, Fill with Current Color, and click OK.

5 Making a color set and exporting a GIF file. To preserve the Web-safe colors that you used in your illustration, export a GIF that uses a custom color set that contains the three Web-safe colors in your image. (This process is similar to setting up an Indexed Color palette in Photoshop.) Before you make the Color Set, open the Color Variability palette, choose "In HSV" from the pop-up menu and set the ±H, ±S and ±V sliders to 0. Now choose the Dropper tool and click on one of the three colors in your image. The Colors picker will display the color. In the Color Sets palette, click on the right arrow and select New Empty Color Set from the pop-up menu. The Color Sets palette window will now be empty. Click on the Add Color to Color Set button to add the selected color to the Color Set. Sample and add the two remaining colors by using the Dropper and the Add Color to Color Set button. To save your colors, click on the right arrow in the Color Sets palette and select Save Color Set, name the set and Save. (For more information about making color sets, turn to "Capturing a Color Set" on page 44, in Chapter 2.)

To export a GIF from Painter to use on your Web page, choose File, Save As, GIF. When the Save As GIF Options dialog box appears, under Imaging method, turn on Quantize to Nearest Color and choose the Color Set button.

Posterizing with Web-Safe Colors

Overview *Open an image; load the Netscape Navigator 216 Color Set; posterize the image using the Color Set; retouch it using flat color fills and Painter's Web-safe brushes; export the file.*

ORIGINAL PHOTO: PHOTOSPIN

The original photo

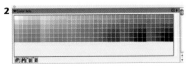

The Netscape Navigator 216 Color Set

POSTERIZING CAN ADD AN INTERESTING GRAPHIC LOOK to a photo, and at the same time simplify color for faster downloading. We posterized the image above using Painter's Netscape Navigator 216 Web-safe color set so the color would not dither on most monitors. Then we exported our GIF file with color constrained by the color set.

1 Choosing a photo. We opened a 616-pixel-wide photo. Select a photo or an illustration with a simple background, such as this runner image.

2 Posterizing using a Color Set. Begin by loading the Netscape Navigator 216 Color Set. On the Color Sets palette, click the right triangle to open the menu and choose Open Color Set. Navigate to the Netscape Navigator 216 Color Set. This set can be found in the Painter IX application folder, in the Color Sets

3

Making a selection with the Magic Wand

4

Painting with a Web-safe brush

5a

To constrain our GIF to Web-safe colors, we turned on the Quantize to Nearest Color and Color Set buttons in GIF Options.

5b

Detail of the final GIF shows no dithering when viewed using 256 colors

folder. Now choose Effects, Tonal Control, Posterize Using Color Set. The command doesn't allow you to have complete control over how color reduction is performed, but it does automatically constrain all of the colors in the image to the Netscape 216-color palette and can be a real time-saver.

3 Cleaning up the background. Posterizing with the Netscape Navigator 216 Color Set provided a close match for the important colors in our image (such as flesh tones), but it produced some distracting debris in the sky. We used the Magic Wand to select these areas. Click with the Magic Wand on the color you want to select. To select noncontiguous color, turn off the Contiguous check box in the Property Bar. If needed, adjust the Tolerance slider in the Property Bar. To read more about the Magic Wand, turn to page 185–186 in Chapter 5, "Selections, Shapes and Masks." After making the selection, we filled the area with blue sampled from the sky. To sample color in your image and fill as we did, choose the Dropper tool and click in your image. Then choose Effects, Fill, Fill with Current Color.

4 Touching up with a Web-safe brush. There was still some debris left after we applied the fill, so we painted the area using a "Web-safe" brush. To access the WebMedia Brushes, copy them from the Painter IX Extras folder inside your Painter IX Application folder to the Painter IX Brushes folder that also resides inside your Painter IX Application folder. Restart Painter. Load Painter's WebMedia Brushes library by selecting Load Brush Library in the pop-up menu of the Brush Selector palette. In the Brush Library dialogue, select the WebMedia Brushes and click the Load button.

Once the library was loaded, we chose the Calligraphic Winner brush variant of the W Thick-n-Thin brush. Then we used the blue, sampled from the sky, to paint over the remaining light blue and purple speckles and any of the grass stalks that no longer read clearly. The sky was now a solid blue.

5 Exporting the image. You can export a GIF from Painter, while retaining Web-safe colors from the Netscape Navigator 216 Color Set chosen in step 2, as follows: Choose File, Save As, GIF, and when the Save As GIF Options dialog box appears, under Imaging method, turn on Quantize to Nearest Color, and under Number of Colors, choose Color Set.

This function works similarly to the indexed color palettes supported by Equilibrium DeBabelizer, Macromedia Fireworks and Adobe ImageReady that allow Web-safe colors to be preserved. Our final image is at the top of the previous page. 🖌

Making a Seamless Tile

Overview *Select an image; use the Kaleidoscope plug-in to make a tile; edit its color; test the tile; save the tile in JPEG format.*

CHER THREINEN-PENDARVIS

PHOTO: CORBIS IMAGES

The original photograph of palm trees

The image with Kaleidoscope dynamic layer

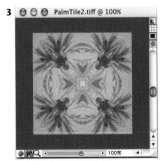

The new tile image

PAINTER HAS SEAMLESS TILE-CREATION TOOLS that are unequaled by other programs. To make this background for a Web site's welcome screen, we began by using the Kaleidoscope dynamic layer to create a symmetrical design based on a photo of palm trees. After making the seamless tile and testing it in Painter, we saved the finished image as a JPEG file for import into a Web page editor.

1 Choosing an image. For this nostalgic background design, we chose and opened a 768 x 512-pixel image with gold-to-brown colors.

2 Using Kaleidoscope as a lens. As you move it over your image, a Kaleidoscope dynamic layer distorts the underlying imagery into symmetrical designs that are ideal for perfect seamless tiles or fabric design. To make a Kaleidoscope layer, open the Layers palette (Window, Show Layers). Click the Plug-ins button at the bottom of the Layers palette and choose the Kaleidoscope plug-in from the pop-up menu. When the dialog box appears, it will reflect the default size of 100 x 100 pixels. We typed 200 into the field to make a larger "lens." Use the Layer Adjuster tool to move the Kaleidoscope layer around your image until you find a "tile" effect you like. (To read more about dynamic layers, turn to Chapter 6, "Using Layers.")

3 Making a tile image. Building a background by importing a single repeating tile into a Web page editor is much more efficient than importing an entire background image. That's because the smaller tile image downloads faster, and it can be repeated very quickly by the browser. Here's the quickest way to prepare your tile: With the Layers palette opened, choose the Layer Adjuster tool and select the Kaleidoscope dynamic layer by clicking the Dynamic Plug-Ins drop-down menu, on the bottom of the Layers palette. To capture the Kaleidoscope imagery, convert the dynamic layer into an image layer by clicking the right triangle on the Layers palette bar to open the pull-down menu and choosing Convert to Default

4

Lightening the color for a subdued look

5

Naming the pattern in the Capture Pattern dialog box

6

The Painter image filled with the Golden Palms pattern. The pattern can be found in the Palm Patterns library on the Painter IX Wow! CD-ROM in the Wow! Items folder.

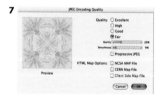

7

Saving the tile as a JPEG with Fair quality and a Smoothness setting of 5%

SOFTEN WITH SMOOTHNESS

When low-quality JPEG settings are used, square artifacts can appear in an image. The Smoothness setting in the JPEG dialog box can help to soften artifacts. Use Smoothness with care, however, because a setting that's too high can blur the image. A bonus: Smoothness can further reduce the size of the file.

layer. Copy the layer (Edit, Copy), and then choose Edit, Paste into New Image.

4 Lightening the tile image. We lightened the new image to make a background that would not compete with text and other elements on the page by choosing Effects, Tonal Control, Adjust Colors. To lighten, move the Value slider to the right. Our setting was 120%.

5 Making a pattern. Select the entire tile image by choosing Select, All. Now you can capture the tile as a pattern and test its tiling in Painter. On the Pattern palette, click the right triangle to open the menu and choose Capture Pattern. When the dialog box appears, name your pattern. For a Rectangular tile with no Horizontal or Vertical Shift (like ours), leave the other settings at their defaults and click OK. (See Chapter 8 for more information about working with patterns.)

6 Testing the tile. To see the overall effect of your pattern in Painter, create a new 800 x 800-pixel document. Now choose Effects, Fill, and in the dialog box, click the Pattern button. Click OK to fill the new document with the pattern.

7 Exporting the seamless tile. At this point we saved our 200 x 200 pixel full-color file (File, Save). Always remember to keep your original file in a format that preserves its image quality, such as TIFF, RIFF or Photoshop. Because the audience for this site would be viewing its images using millions of colors, we didn't want to limit the colors. So we saved a copy of the tile in JPEG format, to preserve the 24-bit color depth. If you have Photoshop, Photoshop Elements or Fireworks, consider using one of these programs to save your file as a JPEG since they all allow you to see the file size as well as the quality. In Painter, you can save a copy of your file as a JPEG. Choose File, Save As, JPEG, and remember to add the proper file extension (.jpg) to its name. To make the image small, we chose the Fair setting, and we applied a Smoothness of 5% in the JPEG dialog box to soften the JPEG artifacts. Our final background (viewed in Explorer) is shown at the top of page 407.

BRACKETING TO COMPARE JPEG IMAGE QUALITY

Most designers export continuous-tone images for the Web using JPEG format. Often, a low JPEG setting will provide adequate quality and a tiny file size. To

JPEG settings: Excellent (top left), High (top right), Good (bottom left) and Fair (bottom right).

know for sure in Painter, test the file by "bracketing," or saving it using several different quality settings. Begin by opening the image you want to compress. To duplicate the image, choose File, Clone, and save it using the lowest quality setting (Fair). Name the file so you can compare results later. Select your original file, choose File, Clone again and save the second image using Good quality. Repeat the process twice more using High and Excellent quality settings. Close the images, and reopen to compare the results. (JPEG compression artifacts are not visible until an image is closed and reopened.)

Building an Image Map for a Web Page

Overview Choose photos and other elements; fill with a patterned background; create layers and designate an image map in Painter; finish the HTML.

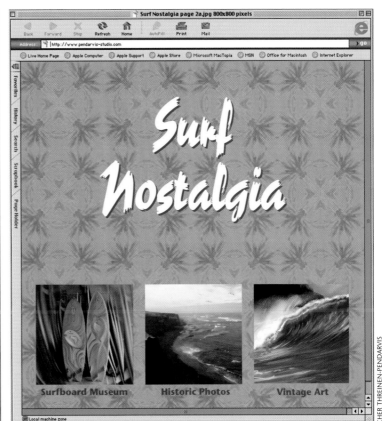

CHER THREINEN-PENDARVIS

Setting up the file in the New dialog box

Selecting the blue palm pattern

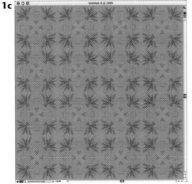

The new file showing the pattern

TO BUILD A PROTOTYPE WEB SITE for Surf Nostalgia, an ocean-related art and collectibles gallery, we used Painter to create a background pattern, graphics and image map buttons for the index page (including some of the HTML code for the image map). We designed the site to be viewed with any browser and used our own site, http://www.pendarvis-studios.com, to develop the prototype.

1 Setting up the page. This step sets up the home page for the Web site. There are no absolute size restrictions on Web pages. They can be any length, because the viewer can scroll. We set up an 800 x 800-pixel file that would easily accommodate viewers' screens with resolutions of 1074 x 768 pixels and larger.

To test how the background pattern would look on the image, we filled it with a blue version of the golden palms pattern, which was created step by step in "Making a Seamless Tile" on pages 407–408. (To load a blue version of the palm pattern, copy the Palm Patterns library from the Wow! Items folder on the Painter IX Wow! CD-ROM to your Painter IX application folder. Then choose Open Library from the right arrow from the drop-down menu on the Patterns palette.)

For your prototype Web page design, create a new file. To see how your pattern will look as a background, fill the image by

2a

The Text settings in the Text palette

2b

The centered white text set on top of the filled background

2c

The settings in the Property Bar and Text palette for the hard-edged shadow

2d

The shadow shows the color sampled from a dark area of the background.

choosing Effects, Fill, Fill with Pattern. The pattern will be removed from the file before the final export is done and a single pattern tile will be exported as a JPEG file to be repeated by the browser's tiling function for the finished page.

2 Creating a logotype and graphics. Using the Text tool with white as the current color, set large bold letters for a logotype. We typed "Surf Nostalgia" using the Reporter Two font and pressing the Enter/Return key after typing "Surf," to set the "Nostalgia" type on a second line. In the Property Bar, we clicked the center button to center the type, and then clicked the External Drop Shadow button to apply a solid, hard-edged shadow. The default color of the shadow is black. To change the shadow color, click on the color square and select one of the colors from the current Color Set. To load a new Color Set, hold down the right arrow and select Load Color Set. To adjust other shadow settings, open the Text palette.

3 Completing the layout. Now that the title type is complete, choose the Layer Adjuster and drag the type into position. Open the other element files that you'd like to add to your page, including those that you want to use as button graphics. Then copy and paste them into the file with the background and type. Use the Layer Adjuster to position them. Painter's Rulers and Guides are helpful with positioning. To use the Rulers and Guides, choose Canvas, Rulers, Show Rulers (Ctrl/⌘-R). When the Rulers appear, click on a ruler to create a guide; you can drag an endpoint to reposition the guide. The Effects, Objects, Align command is also useful when positioning a series of images or text blocks. To read more about these useful tools, turn to Chapter 1, "Getting to Know Painter." (After the three images were pasted in, we set small text in the dark color used for the shadow under each image.)

4 Making the image map. Painter allows you to define an image file as an *image map* (a document that's divided into non-overlapping clickable regions, each of which lets you link to a different URL, or location on the Web). In the finished layout, target one of the button picture layers that will become a clickable region. (Our file included three layers that would each be designated as a clickable region.)

Now it's time to tell Painter what to include in the image map definition file (ours included the picture buttons, but omitted the tiled background layer; it would instead be tiled in the browser). For each layer you want to include in the image map, double-click the layer name in the Layers palette to open the Layer Attributes dialog box. In the Name field, enter the name you want the layer to have on export. Use the check box to select WWW Clickable Map Region (the Region button will default to Rectangle Bounding Box), and type into the URL field the URL you want to link to. Repeat for the other buttons.

3

The in-progress layout with guides visible

4a

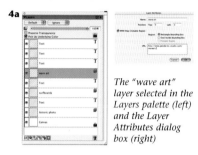

The "wave art" layer selected in the Layers palette (left) and the Layer Attributes dialog box (right)

4b

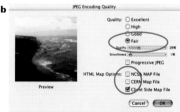

Setting the Quality and Smoothness, and then checking the Client Side Map File box to generate the map definition file for the client-side version of the image map

Painter can create image map definition files for both server-side and client-side image maps. We chose to create a client-side image map, which would be more efficient when viewed using newer browsers because the instructions for client-side image maps are included in the HTML for the page. To export a map definition file for a client-side version of the image map, click the Client Side Map File box in the JPEG Encoding dialog box. (We chose the JPEG file format because of the art and photos present on the page and because most people in the site's viewing audience use 24-bit color systems.)

5 Finishing the HTML. Painter will make the map definition file for you—which lists the name of each region, defines its position using *x* and *y* coordinates and lists the URL it links to. Instructions for client-side image maps are downloaded with the file when it is viewed in newer browsers. For server-side maps, which are important for much older browsers, ask your service provider where the CGI script for image maps is stored and how to use it (CGI is an acronym for Common Gateway Interface, and CGI script is the external programming script used by the Web server). Check out these URLs on the World Wide Web to learn how to set up programming for client-side and server-side image maps: http://www.ihip.com/cside.html and http://www.ihip.com. You'll also need additional HTML programming to make the links work. A Painter-generated image map definition file text can be copied and then pasted into the HTML for the Web page. 🖌

5

```
<map name="SurfNostalgiaMain">
<areas shape="rect" href="http://pendarvis-studios.com/waveart/html" coords= "295,500,
517, 722">
```

URL that hot spot links to   name of the hot spot   coordinates of upper left and lower right corners of the rectangle

The anatomy of one of the clickable regions in the client-side map definition file that Painter automatically generates

Making a Slide Show Animation

Overview *Choose images and resize them; create a new frame stack; paste each image into a frame; export the movie as a GIF animation.*

1

Resizing an image to 200 x 200 pixels for the GIF animation

2

Setting up a new frame stack with three frames and 24-bit color

3a

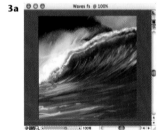

Pasting an image into Frame 1

3b

The Step Forward icon is circled here.

4a

Saving the Frame Stack as a GIF animation

4b

Our settings in the Save As GIF Options dialog box

IT'S EASY TO ADD MOVEMENT to your Web pages using a slide show created as a GIF animation in Painter.

1 Preparing the images. Open several images that you want to include in your slide show. Resize your images to 72 ppi (choose Canvas, Resize, disabling the Constrain File Size box and entering a new size), and then sharpen them (Effects, Focus, Sharpen). Save your resized and sharpened images under a unique name so that you don't accidentally destroy your originals. Keep the images open.

2 Making a new Frame Stack. To open a new Frame Stack, choose File, New and click the Movie button. Enter the dimensions and the number of frames you want to use. It's a good idea to make the movie a small size so that it will load and play quickly on your Web page. (We set up a 200 x 200-pixel Frame Stack with 3 frames and chose the 24-bit Color with 8-bit Alpha Storage Type.)

3 Pasting images into the frames. Activate the image you want in your first frame, choose Select, All (Ctrl/⌘-A) and then copy it to the clipboard (Ctrl/⌘-C). In the new Frame Stack, the first frame should already be selected. Paste the image into the first frame (Ctrl/⌘-V), and then drop it to the Canvas by pressing Ctrl/⌘-Shift-D. Because a layer sits on top of the entire Frame Stack, make sure that you've dropped it before advancing to the next frame. To advance the Frame Stack one frame, click the Step Forward icon on the Frame Stack palette (or press the Page Up key on your keyboard). Repeat the copy-paste-drop process to get the other images into the Frame Stack. (See Chapter 11 for more about working with Frame Stacks.)

4 Exporting the animation. To save the completed Frame Stack as a GIF animation, choose File, Save As, Save Movie as GIF Animation. Make sure to save your GIF animation under a new name so you don't accidentally replace your Frame Stack. (Painter will not open a GIF animation as a Frame Stack.) In the Save As GIF Options box, make the choices you need. (We chose 64 colors and Quantize to Nearest Color for the Imaging Method. Under Animation Options we chose a Frame Delay of 500 ms, Default Disposal Method and entered 3 times for the Loop.)

■ Art director **Ben Barbante** designed and illustrated *Efolio* for his home page using a combination of Painter, Illustrator and Photoshop. He used Painter's Image Slicer to separate the picture into both GIF and JPEG files for optimal file compression, and then he exported HTML code (including navigational buttons with JavaScript rollovers) and a GIF animation from Painter for the final page.

To begin the slicing and export process, Barbante opened the completed layered illustration, which included the efolio case with a light bulb (for the "off" state). He made a new layer and created a black screen on top of the light bulb as a placeholder, for the rollover "on" state. (Later, the "on" state graphic would be replaced by a GIF animation.) Then he hid the layer that would show the Mouse "on" state (the efolio with the black screen) by turning its eye icon off in the Layers palette. He targeted the image canvas and chose the Image Slicer from the Dynamic Plugins menu on the Layers palette. In the Image Slicer, Barbante used the Horizontal and Vertical tools to divide the image, and used the Select tool to group some of the slices. Then, using the Slice menu and the File Name field in the Image Slicer box, he named each slice that he planned to export and chose a compression method (File Type), choosing GIF format to save slices with

flat areas of color in the gray border outside the illustration, and JPEG format to save the slices within the illustration, which included airbrushed color gradations.

For most slices in the image, Barbante selected a slice that would not be exported and under HTML and JavaScript, he set the Rollover State to No Rollover. Next, he selected the efolio case slice that would be the Mouse "off" state, set the Rollover State to Mouse over-out and clicked the Export settings for Current Image State button. When the Export Settings dialog box appeared, he chose the Mouse out button, turned on Include JavaScript and clicked Export. He clicked OK in the Image Slicer, temporarily leaving the dialog box so he could turn on the hidden layer that would be the Mouse "on" state (when the cursor is over the button). He reopened the Image Slicer, selected the slice he wanted to export for the mouse "on" state and repeated the process he had used for the "off" state, but this time, he chose the Mouse over button in the Export Settings box. Painter saved the images and generated the JavaScript and the HTML.

For the final home page, Barbante substituted a GIF animation for the "on" state image (the black screen). After slicing the image and creating the JavaScript rollover, he noted the exact pixel dimensions of the mouse-over slice in the Image Slicer. He made a Frame Stack in Painter with five

frames (featuring his illustration portfolio) using the exact dimensions of the efolio screen with the light bulb. He exported a copy of the Frame Stack as a GIF animation and gave it the exact name of the "on" image so the HTML would replace it in the home page. The rollover displays the animated GIF when the cursor is placed over it. (For more information about using the Image Slicer tools in Painter IX, refer to the Painter IX Help.)

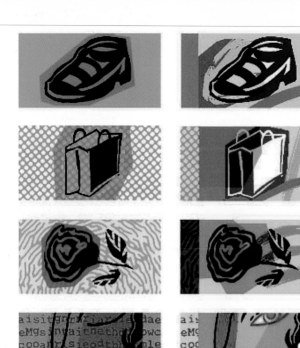

■ When **Karen Dodds** was looking for something lively and hip for the launch of a Web site Dodds Design had developed for *Nicole's Shoes*, she commissioned **Susan LeVan** of LeVan/Barbee Studio to create a series of colorful on-off buttons.

LeVan began by choosing a saturated color palette from Painter's default color set, including warm oranges and yellows, accented by blues and greens. (Painter's default color set is composed of Web-safe colors.) LeVan applied colorful textures to the backgrounds using a variety of favorite textures from earlier versions of Painter (such as the Simple Textures library from the Painter 7, CD_2 CD-ROM). She applied the textures with Effects, Surface Control, Color Overlay, Using Paper and Hiding Power. LeVan drew the shoes, flower and face with the Scratchboard Tool variant of Pens. For the abstract elements, she drew shapes using the Pen tool (Toolbox) and filled the shapes with color. When she was satisfied with the arrangement of colored shapes, she merged the layers by selecting their names in the Layers palette and Grouping them, by clicking the Layer Commands button at the bottom of the palette, choosing Group from the menu and then choosing Collapse. To finish, she set the layer's Composite method to Gel.

■ Designer and artist **Debi Lee Mandel** created *DT-Car* and *DT-Space* (top), two proposed animated banners for the Digital-Think Web site (left), and two screens for the DuraFlame Web site, titled *Campsite* (bottom).

Mandel began the banner animations by drawing the elements (the cars and buildings in *DT-Car* and the rocketship and planets in *DT-Space*) using the Pens variants, custom variants from the Oils category and Painter's Frame Stacks, finally adding the type with the Text tool.

For *Campsite*, she began by sketching in Painter with a custom "indigo-color crayon" (based on the Waxy Crayon variant) on a black background. Mandel began by painting elements for the animations (the comet and fire) using Painter's Frame Stacks. When she was pleased with the progression, she saved each Frame Stack as a GIF animation. After completing the crayon drawing, Mandel painted crisp-edged brushstrokes using flat color. To build up deep color saturation, she used custom variants from the Oils category with oval-shaped tips for a calligraphic feel.

■ Illustrator **Chet Phillips** built drawings for the *Funny Face Flip Book*, a game that is featured on his Web site. With the flip book, it's possible to change from one critter to another in a linear way, or to create unexpected combinations of faces.

To begin, Phillips used Painter to create an oval template with horizontal guidelines for the upper, middle and lower limits. The guides allowed him to line up the various facial parts and make sure that the eyes, noses and mouths would fall within the same general area. To stay within the parameters as he developed the faces, he used Painter's Tracing Paper feature. For instance, he opened the template file and then he opened a new, blank file exactly the same size. With the new file active, he designated the template file to be the Clone Source (File, Clone Source). Then, he drew the new face at the same size as the template. To create the illustrations, he used the Scratchboard variant of Pens. A similar technique describing his work, "Coloring a Woodcut," is featured in Chapter 2 on page 42.

When Phillips had created all of the faces, he copied them and then pasted the drawings into one file as separate layers using the Edit, Paste in Place command. Then, he separated each face by making a selection of each section, cutting and then pasting it back into place.

When the illustrations were complete, Phillips presented the layered Photoshop file to his Flash expert Todd Smith (www.saturatedpixels.net), who built an animation in Flash using the layers. You can try out the *Funny Face Flip Book* at www.chetart.com.

PRINTING
OPTIONS

Light in the Forest *is a part of the series* Fragile Beauty *by Dorothy Simpson Krause. The collage was based on a photograph by Viola Kaumlen. Using an Epson 9600, Krause printed onto Oce FCPLS4 clear film using Ultra Chrome ink. After coating a linen canvas with rabbit-skin glue and letting it set like gelatin, she transferred the image to the surface like a monoprint. To see more of her images in the series, turn to page 434 in the gallery.*

To see more of her images in the series, turn to page 434 in the gallery.

PAINTER AND CMYK TIFFS

Painter can open CMYK TIFF files, but in doing so, it converts them to RGB, Painter's native color space. You can also save a CMYK TIFF from Painter by choosing File, Save As, selecting TIFF from the Format menu and then clicking the CMYK button in the Export Options box.

INTRODUCTION

HOW WILL YOU PRESENT YOUR PAINTER ARTWORK to the world? Will it be as a limited-edition digital painting, printed on archival paper by a print studio or service bureau, and then matted, framed and hung on a gallery wall? Or as an illustration in a magazine, where it's part of a page layout that's output direct-to-plate, to be printed on an offset press? Or as a desktop color print? For each of these and other output options, there are things you can do to prepare your Painter file so the output process runs smoothly. We hope the tips that follow will help you as you plan your own project.

COLOR FOR COMMERCIAL PRINTING

Most types of printing involve the use of four-color process, or CMYK (cyan, magenta, yellow, black) inks and dyes. Painter's native color mode is RGB (red, green, blue), which has a larger color *gamut* (range of colors) than the CMYK color model. (An illustration that compares RGB and CMYK color gamuts is on page 8 in Chapter 1.) Although Painter doesn't let you specify CMYK color mixes as Adobe Photoshop and some other programs do, it does allow you to work in Output Preview mode, using only those colors within the RGB gamut that are realizable in CMYK. You can also output CMYK TIFF and EPS files for color separation directly from Painter.

Using Color Management. Before you turn a file over for output in a form that will be used for CMYK printing, consider using Color Management with Output Preview. With this system you can set up a monitor-to-printer calibration loop that will allow you to see an onscreen approximation of how your printed image

Click the Color Correction icon to toggle between RGB and the Output Preview.

Settings for Color Management to soft proof an image from our system. Internal RGB: Adobe RGB 1998, output profile: US Sheetfed Coated, monitor profile: Apple Cinema Display.

When you're preparing files to be printed on an offset press, ask what line screen will be used for printing so you can begin your file with a high enough resolution (ppi) to accommodate it. A factor of 1.5 to 2 times the line screen is typical. For example, to accommodate a 150-line screen, set up your file with the dimensions you need at a resolution of 225 to 300 ppi.

will look. (A word of caution: There are many variables besides the RGB-to-CMYK conversion that will affect how a color print will look—for instance, the color cast of your particular monitor and the color of your paper. Output Preview doesn't account for these factors.) Begin by choosing Canvas, Color Management to open the Color Management dialog box. In the dialog box, choose an Internal RGB color space, a Monitor Profile and an Output Profile depending on whether you'll be outputting to separations or to a composite printer in your studio such as an Epson 2200. When you perform a Painter Easy Installation, the program automatically installs a selection of Color Profiles into the Painter IX application folder. (If you don't see your monitor or printer profile in the list, it can often be obtained from the manufacturer.) To add profiles to your system, copy them to the following location: Macintosh OS X/Applications/Corel Painter IX/Color Profiles, and change the suffix from .icc to .cc. Windows users should copy profiles into the Windows\Color folder.

To toggle between the broader-gamut RGB image and the Output Preview, click the Color Correction icon above the right scroll bar. Remember to change the Color Management settings if you plan to print to another device. For more information about Painter's color management tools, see "Making a Color Managed Art Print" later in this chapter and "Color Management," in the *Painter IX User Guide.*

Making CMYK conversions in another program. Some Painter artists prefer to work in the broader RGB color gamut and convert their finished images to CMYK in another imaging program such as Photoshop or Equilibrium DeBabelizer, because these programs allow more control of how the conversion is made. There are several good resources that give detailed explanations of color conversion using Photoshop, including the *Adobe*

Using Color Management provides a preview only, and makes no permanent changes to the file. To include an embedded ICC profile in a saved file (so the file will look the same when viewed in another program), choose Canvas, Color Management and in the Color Management dialog box, click the Import/ Export icon (the page), and choose a profile in the Advanced Import/Export dialog box.

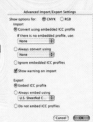

The Advanced Import/Export Settings dialog box with a profile chosen for export

As of this writing, we found that when we chose Canvas, Color Management, Style, Default Settings and then saved our file in PSD format, that Painter IX automatically embedded an RGB Kodak sRGB display ICC profile. Then when we opened the Painter PSD file in Photoshop, and chose to keep the embedded profile, the image looked almost identical from Painter to Photoshop.

Detail of Abundance, *by Pamela Wells. When making the fine art print of her image, Wells calibrated her computer system to the profile of the Iris inkjet printer at the service bureau she planned to send it to. Turn to page 370 in Chapter 10 to view the entire image.*

Bonny Lhotka created the digital file for Day Job *in Painter, by painting with brushes and using layers to composite several source files. Before printing the digital image, Lhotka prepared a one-of-a-kind surface using gold- and ochre-colored acrylics. She painted an abstract design on a nonporous surface to create a monotype that she could transfer to a piece of rag paper using a large roller. After drying and coating the surface of the monoprint with inkjet receiver to help it absorb the ink, she printed the image on top of it using an Encad NovaJet 3. A photograph of the final print is shown above.*

Photoshop User Guide and *The Photoshop CS Wow! Book* and *Photoshop in 4 Colors* (these last two are from Peachpit Press). Some printing studios—for example, Cone Editions—prefer to receive RGB files from artists and make the conversion themselves using custom color tables they create in Photoshop especially for that image. (See "Making a Fine Art Master Print" on page 428 for an explanation of Cone Editions's process.) Check with your printer to work out a conversion method.

FINE ART PRINTING AT A SERVICE BUREAU

Many artists prefer to choose a service bureau or master printer who specializes in output for fine art printmaking. Rather than attempt to print an edition in their studio, they rely on fine art service bureaus for high-quality equipment—for instance, an Iris inkjet printer is not affordable for most artists. (Iris prints are accepted by many galleries and museums; they are no longer thought of as "experimental prints.") The expertise needed for a fine art print studio differs greatly from that of a commercial service bureau accustomed to making film and proofs for offset printing. Choose a printer who has experience working with artists and who understands archival and editioning issues. (See Appendix B for a list of service bureaus that specialize in working with artists.)

Large-format inkjet printers. The Iris printer has played an important part in the history of digital printmaking because of its capability of producing images with luminous color and no visible dot, which made the output desirable for fine art printmaking. Unfortunately, Iris printers are no longer being manufactured and parts are difficult to obtain. Cone Editions and Nash Editions were among the first printers to pioneer printing techniques using the Iris; they moved back the printing heads, allowing 400-lb. watercolor paper, canvas or metal to be taped onto the drum.

Many more excellent choices are available for the artist who wants to order high-quality archival large-format prints of their work from bureaus. Some service bureaus offer prints from the Hewlett-Packard DesignJet 5500 CP series using the CP UV six-color archival ink set. These 1200 x 600 dpi printers can accept rolled watercolor paper and canvas and the largest model can print up to 60 inches wide. With these printers, sometimes images with very light, graduated tones can produce areas with tiny dots in a dither or scatter pattern. Printing on canvas can help hide these dots. Wilhelm Imaging Research, Inc. reports that the HP DesignJet CP ink systems' UV inks will hold true color for 150+ years.

High-quality prints from large-format Epson printers are also available from some service bureaus. The Epson 7600 (24 inches wide) and the 9600 and 10600 (both 44 inches wide) are 1440 dpi inkjet printers that use six-color archival inks. The Epson 4000 (17 inches wide) is a 2880 dpi inkjet printer that uses eight-color archival inks. They're capable of producing prints on a wide

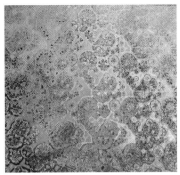

Robert Manning of Supersample Corporation / Lilika Productions designed this scarf using Painter's brushes, special effects and pattern features. Then the image was printed on cotton twill fabric with a 12-color Colorspan inkjet printer using Fiber Reactive dyes.

variety of media, including paper, canvas and posterboard with a thickness of up to 1.5 mm.

Large, high-quality prints from Roland printers are also available at service bureaus. The Roland HiFi or Pro V8 has a resolution of 1440 dpi and uses an eight-color archival ink set. The largest model can accommodate media widths to 64 inches.

Colorspan offers several large-format printers, even a model specifically designed to print fabric. There are three models that can be used for fine art printing that accommodate media up to 72 inches wide and up to 3 mm thick. The printers use either a set of eight-color or twelve-color light-fast dye inks.

Outputting to a digital positive. Major advances have been made in the area of direct digital photographic prints. In general, the three printing methods discussed below use a laser to image the digital file onto a photographic substrate.

Prints made from the Fujix Pictrography 5000 (up to 12 x 18 inches) offer permanency and natural color. The Fujix uses a laser to image the digital file onto a "donor" sheet, which is then printed onto photographic paper using a single-pass, silver-halide printing process. The appearance and permanency (about 20 years) of the Fujix are similar to those of a photographic Cibachrome (C-print). Prints can be laminated with a coating that includes an ultraviolet inhibitor, extending their life further. Additionally, the Noritsu 2701 produces high-quality Cibachrome-like prints up to 12 x 18 inches.

The Cymbolic Sciences LightJet 5000 also uses a laser, imaging the digital file to large-format archival photo paper and creating a continuous-tone print without visible dots, as large as 48 x 96 inches. Because the Lightjet 5000 uses 36-bit RGB color, the broad color gamut in these prints is comparable to that in photographic "R" prints. To prepare Painter files for the LightJet 5000, set up your file at its final output size, using a resolution of 150–200 ppi and save it as an uncompressed RGB TIFF file. The LightJet's software incorporates an interpolation algorithm that makes it possible to increase the resolution of the image while retaining its sharpness. Artist and photographer Phillip Charris often outputs his Painter-enhanced photographs using a LightJet 5000, and then carefully strips the print from its backing paper and mounts it on canvas.

Another recommended photo-slick, archival printmaking method is the Durst Lambda system. (Using a laser, it images to archival photo media, such as paper, color negative media or color reversal media.) It's also a 36-bit RGB system. The Durst Lambda 76 can print seamless 32-inch-wide images up to 164 feet long. Durst Lambda prints are reported to be lightfast for a minimum of 50 years. Some artists strip the prints, mount them on canvas, and then finish them with glazes of UV-protectant varnish (such as Golden Varnish, described on page 422) to protect the print from humidity and to add a hand-finished look.

To check color and detail before printing on a Hewlett-Packard DesignJet 5500 with the HP UV pigmented inkset, Cher Threinen-Pendarvis proofed Path to Water, North *as an 8 x 10-inch Fujix Pictrography print. (Fujix Pictrography prints are described in "Outputting to a Digital Positive" on this page.) The final print was made at 15 x 17 inches on Hahnemuhle Watercolor Paper and framed with UV-protective glass.*

John Derry printed Capitola, *shown here as a detail, on an Epson 1270 six-color printer using Epson's archival ink set.*

PHOTOGRAPHIC IMAGING OPTIONS

Many new technologies are available for Painter output at graphic arts service bureaus and photo labs that use digital equipment.

Imaging to transparencies using a film recorder. Small- and large-format film recorders are used to image digital files such as Painter artwork to transparencies ranging from 35mm to 16 x 20 inches. For output via a film recorder, images should be in landscape orientation (horizontal) to take advantage of the width of the film.

To avoid *pixelation* (a jaggy, stair-step look caused by lack of sufficient resolution) on transparencies generated by a service bureau's film recorder, here are some guidelines from Chrome Digital and Photodyne (San Diego) for creating or sizing your files. Most professional-quality 35 mm film recorders (such as the Solitaire 16 series) use a minimum resolution of 4000 lines; for this resolution, your image should be 4096 x 2732 pixels (about 32 MB). The minimum resolution for 4 x 5-inch transparencies is 8000 lines, requiring an 8192 x 5464-pixel (approximately 165 MB) file. For even more crispness, devices such as the Solitaire 16XPS will image at a resolution of 16000 lines (a 16384 x 10928-pixel file, of approximately 512 MB). Two powerful film recorders used to create 4 x 5-inch, 8 x 10-inch and larger-format transparencies are the LVT (from Light Valve Technology, a subsidiary of Kodak) and the LightJet 2080 (from Cymbolic Sciences, Inc.). Plan to create huge images (up to 15000 x 18000 pixels and approximately 800 MB) to take full advantage of the resolution capabilities of these machines.

Printing your images as Fujichrome. For fine art images, Fujichrome prints made from transparencies offer excellent detail and saturated color, and can be ordered with a high gloss. Prints can be made from 35 mm slides or 4 x 5-inch transparencies. To print to the maximum size of 20 x 24 inches, a 4 x 5 transparency is recommended. The permanency of the Fuji print is 40–50 years, and this can be extended by adding a lamination with an ultraviolet inhibitor. Diane Fenster, a noted fine artist and photographer, has produced much of her digital work as large-format Fujichrome prints.

FINE ART PRINTING IN THE STUDIO

Today, many exciting alternatives are available for artists who want to proof their images, or make fine art prints in their own studio using archival ink sets and papers.

Printing digital images with desktop printers. Desktop inkjet printers can deliver beautiful color prints if they are set up properly. The affordable HP printers (such as the DesignJet 30 or 130) and the Epson Stylus series (the 1280, for instance) are great printers not only for pulling test prints before sending images to a larger format printer, but also for experimental fine art prints. Most inkjet inks are water-soluble, so you can try painting into a print with a wet brush. There are exceptions: the Epson 2200 and 4000. The 2200 ships with a seven-color Ultrachrome pigmented

Flight, a mixed media painting by Carol Benioff. Benioff printed the image on an Iris printer, and then mounted the print on a panel. After painting it with a protective coating of clear shellac, she embellished it with oil paint and pencil.

Indigo, an experimental Fresco print by Bonny Lhotka. To view more of her work, turn to pages 438 and 439 in the gallery.

To view more of her work, turn to pages 438 and 439 in the gallery.

PAPER-AND-INK COMBOS

The correct paper-and-ink combination can contribute to the greater longevity of your prints. Check out Henry Wilhelm's Web site, www.wilhelm-research.com, for suggested paper-and-ink combinations.

inkset. The 4000 ships with eight-color Ultrachome pigmented inkset. They produce water-resistant prints. These prints will accept acrylic paint without smearing or running. Most desktop printers work best with slick paper, but archival-quality cotton papers produce excellent results on some machines. For example, the Epson 2200 and 4000 print on thicker acid-free papers, either the new enhanced art papers or traditional drawing or printmaking papers, if you feed the paper manually.

New inks and substrates for desktop art prints. With the increased interest in desktop art-making, new inks and papers keep coming out. Henry Wilhelm has done important research regarding the longevity of different ink and substrate combinations. A comparison of color gamut and longevity with the different inks is available through Wilhelm Imaging Research, Inc., on the Web at www.wilhelm-research.com.

New inks with better longevity and waterproof characteristics are becoming available for many inkjet printers. For information about products for use with the Hewlett-Packard printers, check out www.hp.com; for information about Epson products, visit its company Web site at www.epson.com. Also, InkJet Mall (a sister company of Cone Editions) is another good resource for information and you can buy sets of archival inks (such as Generation Enhanced Micro Bright Pigmented Inks) for several desktop printers; it's found on the Web at www.inkjetmall.com. Several other companies offer new archival inksets for desktop printers. One is Media Street, offering Generations Inks, among many other products, found on the Web at www.mediastreet.com. Another source is MIS ink, which manufactures and sell its own archival pigmented inks, as well as its own set of ultra chrome pigmented inks for many of the Epson printers, on the Web at www.inksupply.com.

Several traditional art papers are now manufactured for digital printmaking—for instance, Somerset Enhanced, Concorde Rag, Hahnemuehle's German Etching, William Turner or Photo Rag, all available from Cone Editions's InkJet Mall. And there are many canvases available for use with inkjet printers. For instance, check out the artist-grade canvases available from Sentinel Imaging, located on the Web at www.inkjet.com, and the pure-white artist-grade canvas from Dr. Graphix, Inc. at www.drgraphix.com.

Inkjet receivers and protective coatings. To seal custom substrates (like handmade papers), so the ink will hold better, paint thin rabbit skin glue onto the substrate with a brush and dry it thoroughly. Then make your print.

You can treat prints yourself so the color will last much longer. Several protective coatings are available at your local art supply store, from Daniel Smith via mail order, or from Media Street on the Web at www.mediastreet.com. One of our favorites is Golden MSA Varnish with UVLS (soluble with mineral spirits). Use a

Flint, *by Dorothy Simpson Krause,*
includes elements collected during a jour-
ney to Tibet. After the collage was com-
plete, Krause prepared the surface of the
substrate (dimensionally stable spunbond
polyester) for printing by painting it with
Golden Molding Paste. When the surface
was dry, she added a coat of gel medium
mixed with pearlescent pigment. To pro-
vide a receiver for the inks, she painted the
substrate with rabbit skin glue, dried it,
and then compressed it by running it
though a Coda laminator. The final print
was made on a Roland HiFi using the
Roland pigmented six-color inks.

Master printer David Salgado has
developed a process that combines
monotypes with archival digital
prints, using the 39 x 52-inch
Mailänder flatbed hand-fed offset
press at Trillium Press. After a
mylar-coated aluminum plate is
painted with lithography inks, the
plate is mounted on the press and
the press roller pulls ink from the
plate to transfer to the archival
digital print. Depending on the
image, seven to ten prints can be
pulled in what is known as an
edition variée. Some artists use an
archival digital print as a starting
point, while others use cutout
pieces of the print as elements in
collage work, after which the collage
is run through the press. Salgado
feels they've just begun to discover
the possibilities for this technique.
Trillium has printed editions of artwork that have combined archival
digital printing, silkscreen,
monotype and lithography in
edition numbers of 50 and more.

protective respirator and gloves
for the process because the fumes
from this coating are *very* toxic.
To minimize contact with danger-
ous airborne particles, dilute the
varnish and apply it with a brush.
Golden Varnish is also available
in a spray can, as is Krylon UV
Protectant spray. Make sure to use
a protective respirator when using the spray varnishes.

Caring for prints. After a UV-protective coating has been
applied, treat your print as you would a watercolor and avoid
displaying it in direct sunlight. Frame it using UV-resistant glazing (glass or Plexiglas) and preserve air space between the surface of the print and the glazing.

EXPERIMENTAL PRINTMAKING

In today's world of experimental printmaking, anything goes if
it works with your vision of the image you're printing. For
instance, many different substrates can be used successfully
with inkjet printers; among the favorites are archival-quality
papers with a high cotton content. Browse your local art store
for Saunders handmade watercolor paper, Arches hot-press and
cold-press watercolor paper, Rives BFK printmaking papers and
Canson drawing and charcoal papers. You can hand-feed these
papers into a studio desktop printer, or request that a fine art
print studio create an Iris print with paper that you supply. Fine
art print studios often keep special papers in stock—Cone
Editions, for instance, has hundreds of fine art papers on hand.
Some print studios also print on canvas, film or metal.

Mixing media. Prints from an Iris or another inkjet printer
can be modified with traditional tools and fine art printing processes, such as embossing, intaglio and silkscreen. (Turn to page
424 to read about Carol Benioff's technique of overprinting a
copperplate etching on top of an Iris print.) If you plan to
hand-work an inkjet print with media such as pastels, pencils or
oil paint, make the print on rag paper with enough body to
hold together when you apply the traditional media to the print.
Arches 140-pound watercolor paper and Rives heavyweight
printmaking paper are good choices.

Making Translite transfers. The Translite transfer technique
was pioneered by Jon Cone. First, a digital image is printed onto
Translite film using an Iris printer. Then a piece of archival-quality
paper (such as Rives BFK) is soaked in water, and when it is partially dry, the image is transferred from the Translite "plate" onto
the dampened printmaking paper using an embossing press—
producing a monoprint with softly graduated color.

If you plan to add another medium
(such as acrylic or pastel) to a digital print, keep in mind that different pigments and dyes can age at
different rates. So the strokes you
carefully hand-work into the print
may begin to stand out over time.

Bonny Lhotka creates a flexible waterproof decal using artist gloss acrylic medium and inkAID™ White Matte Precoat, which will be removed from a polypropylene carrier sheet printed on the Encad 880 with GO pigment inks. Other printers like the Epson 7500, 7600, 9500, 9600, 10600, Roland and Mutoh, can be used for this process if the polypropylene plate is thin enough. The decal can be glued to canvas, paper or wood using acrylic gel medium. The surface can be sealed with acrylic medium.

INKJET PRINT OR GICLÉE?

Some businesses in the fine art printmaking community have adopted the name Giclée (which can be loosely defined as *spray*) when referring to a fine art print made on a high-quality inkjet. Many artists who create their work digitally prefer to leave the Giclée term to the traditional fine art reproduction industry that originated it, thinking that it's important to maintain the distinction between an original print made from a digital painting or collage and a traditional reproduction. This is because each direct digital print has its own unique value and, in fact, is not a reproduction.

Overprinting a digital file onto a monotype. To create a surface that she would later use for printing *Day Job* (shown on page 418), Bonny Lhotka created a one-of-a-kind monotype "plate" by applying acrylic paint onto prepared acetate. She laid a piece of rag paper onto the "plate" and used a custom-made 40-lb. roller to transfer the painted image onto the paper. After transferring, she lifted the paper off the "plate" and allowed it to dry. Then she used a Novajet inkjet printer to overprint the digital file on top of the monoprint. She believes that the overprinting process produces a broader range of color than is possible if the entire image is composed and printed digitally. The result is a print with more depth.

FINE ART EDITIONS FROM DIGITAL FILES

Some artists scan finished, traditionally created artwork and then print it on an Iris or another high-quality printer (such as an Epson 7600 or a Roland HiFi). This process is actually *replicating* an original piece of work. However, when artwork *originates* as a digital file—using a program such as Painter—and is then output to a high-quality printer using an archival inkset, that print itself becomes an original. (Think of your Painter image as a kind of "digital printing plate" stored in your computer.)

Advantages of digital editions. Printing a digital edition has advantages over traditional, limited-run printing methods. Any number of multiple originals can be made from a digital file without loss of quality: The "digital plate" won't deteriorate. Also, the setup charge for the digital process is usually much less than when an edition is printed conventionally. And while an edition printed with traditional methods needs to be printed all at once, with digital editions, an artist may request prints from the fine art service bureau as needed.

CERTIFICATE OF AUTHEN

Title Swimmers 2

Image Size 12 x 18"   Edition # 2/50

Edition Size 50   Artist Proofs 5

Date Created July 1, 1995   Date Purchased July 14,

Art Media Iris print on Rives BFK

Uniqueness of this Print This print is hand-worked with pa

Artist

The above information contains all the information pertaining to this Edition. As y or watercolor, do not display this artwork in direct sunlight. Frame it under UV-3 pl

Detail of a sample certificate of authenticity. You'll find a PageMaker 6.5 file and a PDF of this sample certificate on the Painter IX Wow! CD-ROM.

Planning an edition. An edition should be carefully tracked and controlled, just as it would be if printed with traditional methods. It's wise to make a contract between the master printer and artist, stating the type of edition, the number of prints in the edition and that no more prints will be made. When an original is sold, the artist should give the buyer a certificate of authenticity that contains the name of the artist and the print, the date sold, the edition size, the print number, the number of artist proofs, the substrate, and any details of hand-working done on the print. Once the edition is complete, the artist should destroy the digital file, just as the screen would be destroyed after a silkscreen edition. (See "Making a Fine Art Master Print" on page 428.)

Combining Digital and Intaglio Printmaking

Overview *Make a print using a traditional printmaking method; scan the print and rough sketches; use the scans as a guide to create a colored image in Painter; print the digital file on an Epson 7600; overprint the traditional print on top of the Epson print in register.*

CAROL BENIOFF

1a

Photo of one of the four etched copperplates. The composition is created in reverse.

1b

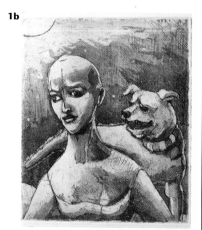

Grayscale scan of one of the four black-and-white intaglio prints

CAROL BENIOFF'S INNOVATIVE PRINTMAKING method combines classic intaglio techniques with digital printing. Currently, she works at Kala Art Institute, a traditional and digital printmaking studio and gallery in Berkeley, California, which has been in existence for more than 30 years. To create *Age of the Disturbed II*, Benioff overprinted four copperplate etchings on top of an Epson archival inkjet print made on Lana Gravure printmaking paper.

1 Making an intaglio print. Benioff planned the four 6 x 10-inch copperplates knowing that she would be adding color and depth with imagery created in Painter. She used a combination of hard ground, soft ground and aquatint etching techniques. Benioff drew lines with a stylus into the acid-resistant coating on the plate, exposing the metal underneath. Then, she soaked the plate in an acid bath to etch the drawing deep into the plate. To create the soft tonalities, she dusted the plate with a fine rosin and then fused it to the plate with heat. To keep areas of the plate white, Benioff painted an acid resist over certain areas. Then, she put the plate in an acid bath. The acid etched parts of the plate that were not fused with rosin or coated with the acid resist.

When the plate was etched, Benioff rolled dark sepia ink onto the plate, working it into the lines with a cardboard dauber. Then she rubbed off excess ink with tarlatan (starched, open-weave muslin). Next, she chose a piece of archival printmaking paper and soaked it so that it would absorb the ink better. After blotting the paper to partially dry it, she made a print using an etching press.

When the print was dry, Benioff placed tracing paper over it and made rough pencil sketches of the figures to be created in Painter. Next, she scanned the sketches and the four prints and created four

The completed figures and drop shadow for the Madness *section of* The Age of the Disturbed II. *The guides indicate the edges of the printing plate.*

2b

The completed color tint for the Madness *section of* The Age of the Disturbed II

2c

Detail of the completed image Madness *with Plate Layer visible*

3

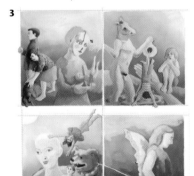

The final stitched-together images, ready to print on the Lana Gravure rag paper

composite files that included scans and sketches. She opened each print scan and floated its image canvas to a layer by choosing Select, All and Select, Float. Then she imported the sketches by choosing File, Place. So that the white in the layered images would appear to be transparent, she set the Composite Method for each layer to Multiply in the Layers palette.

2 Coloring and compositing. Benioff refined the rough drawings using the Dry Brush variant of Acrylics, and then she modeled the forms and added details using the Opaque Detail, Wet Acrylic, Wet Soft Acrylic and Glazing Acrylic variants of Acrylics.

To create a shadow layer for the figures, Benioff chose Effects, Objects, Create Drop Shadow. The command created a group layer of the figures and the drop shadow. So that she would have more control over the opacity and position of the drop shadow, she separated the shadow from the figures by selecting the group and choosing Ungroup from the Layers palette menu. She set the opacity of the shadow layer to 45%.

To keep the new paint separate from the print while hand-coloring it, she created a new layer below the print layer in the Layers palette and set its Composite Method to Multiply. Then, using Acrylics brushes, she painted pale colored washes. To soften some of the strokes, she used the Just Add Water variant of Blenders. For more drama, she applied a soft spotlight with warm tones to the Tint layer only (Effects, Surface Control, Apply Lighting) using a lighting effect from her custom lighting effects library.

3 Printing the image. When working at the Kala studio Benioff prints her images through Photoshop using the studio's Epson 7600. After opening all the files in Photoshop, she created two new files, each containing two of the four images. Then she printed each of the two files on a 22 x 30-inch sheet of Lana Gravure printmaking paper. To ensure accurate color and full range of tonalities, Benioff used a custom ICC profile from Chromix for the Lana Gravure paper and the Epson 7600 with Ultrachrome archival inks. (For more information, see "Making a Color Managed Print" on page 430.) Benioff brushed a light coating of shellac over the imaged portion of the paper and then she let it dry. So that the ink from the etching would adhere to the print, she lightly sanded it with very fine sandpaper.

4 Overprinting the etching. Benioff made an acetate template to register the image on the paper and plate. The elements in the Epson print needed to align perfectly with the copperplate, so she carefully traced the position of the figures onto the acetate. She soaked the printed paper in water for 30 minutes, placing it in blotters to keep it damp but not dripping. After preparing the copperplate with ink, she aligned the template, the plate and the paper (Epson print) on the press bed and pulled the print. When the prints were dry, Benioff glued the two sheets to complete the image.

Constructing a Lenticular Work

Overview *Build textured elements and layer them into a collage; set up multiple versions of the file for the lenticular; print the images on an inkjet printer; glaze the wood mat and embellish its surface.*

BONNY LHOTKA

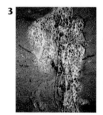

The handmade paper, the letterpress type block with the radio tower image and the tray filled with "lava"

The lava and paper elements with the Apply Surface Texture emboss added

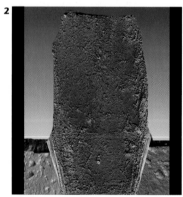

An impression of the photo of sand and foam was embossed into the working image.

"A LENTICULAR IMAGE SUSPENDS TIME, space and movement. It adds a level of ambiguity that engages the viewer's attention," says artist Bonny Lhotka. (A lenticular image is actually several images sliced into strips and alternated. A plastic sheet with a series of parallel lens strips, or lenticules, embossed into one surface is applied over the assemblage, so the different images are seen one at a time, as a viewer moves past the artwork.) To create *Ancient Echo*, Lhotka scanned elements, applied textural effects and then composited the source files into a collage. To build the lenticular, she created eleven variations of the file. As a viewer walks past *Ancient Echo*, the central portion of the image turns to black. At the same time, the background rotates through a rainbow of color shifts and the lower portion appears to recede. You may want to loosely follow Lhotka's process and also experiment with your own effects.

1 Preparing the source images. Lhotka chose squares of painted handmade paper from an earlier project, and a letterpress type block with a radio tower image. For one of the background layers, she built a surface using modeling paste and painted it with acrylics to look like lava. Lhotka scanned and touched up the source images. She created the rings in Painter and colored them with a gradient. To give the rings wire-like dimension, she used Glass Distortion.

2 Adding texture to elements. Lhotka likes to emulate the look of handmade paper, using Painter's Apply Surface Texture feature. For this work, she embossed several elements (including the lava and paper elements) with Apply Surface Texture Using Image Luminance and subtle settings.

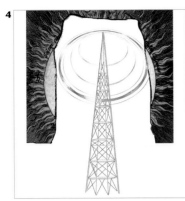

The composite in progress

Printing the images

Preparing the transfer board

Mixing the gel and applying it to the board

Preparing to transfer the mat print

Burning the mat surface to crackle the glaze

3 Giving the colored fields texture. She wanted to add texture to more colored areas in the image. So she opened an original photo of beach sand and used Apply Surface Texture, Using Original Luminance to emboss the pattern of the foam and sand into her image. To ensure that the emboss effect will apply to your entire image, choose as your clone source an image with the same pixel dimensions as your working file. Make the image that you want to emboss active, target a layer you want to emboss and designate the clone source by choosing File, Clone Source. Choose Effects, Surface Control, Apply Surface Texture, Using Original Luminance.

4 Assembling the composite. After all of the elements were embossed with Apply Surface Texture, Lhotka copied and pasted the elements into Photoshop, where she completed the composite. After the image was finished, she created 11 different color variations of the central portion of the file, which would become the lenticular.

5 Processing and printing the lenticular. For the next step, Lhotka used SuperFlip software. Using a sophisticated mathematical formula, the software sliced the images into linear strips and reassembled them according to the specifications for the lenticular that Lhotka had chosen. When the assemblage was complete, Lhotka printed it on a Roland HiFi. The six-color printer uses a CMYKOG archival pigment set with saturated colors. After the interlaced image was printed, it was aligned with the lens.

6 Setting up a gel transfer for the glaze. When building the fine art mat for the lenticular, Lhotka chose Baltic birch. As she planned to pour liquid onto the wood, to prevent the wood from bowing, she temporarily attached a one-by-three-foot board to the back of the birch mat. To hold the liquid, she placed duct tape around the sides to make a tray. Then she made a gel: She dissolved rabbit skin glue in water, warmed it, and allowed it to return to room temperature, and then added powdered pearlescent pigment to it. She used a strainer to remove undissolved colorant and large bubbles, and then poured the mixture onto the wood.

7 Printing the image for the mat. Lhotka printed the image for the mat on Rexam white film. After printing, she transferred it to the gel on the wood. Placing the printed film on the gel caused the image to transfer immediately without pressure. When the gel dried, the image was permanently bonded into the wood.

8 Embellishing the surface of the mat. To give the glaze a crackled effect, Lhotka used a torch to burn the surface of the mat after it was dry. This caused the glue to bubble, creating a crackled glaze surface. The completed presentation of *Ancient Echo* measures 34 x 28 inches; the 28 x 22-inch center of the image with the 3D animated lenticular sits inside a ½-inch recession on the glazed mat board. 🎨

Making a Fine Art Master Print

Overview *Make a custom color conversion of a Painter image; choose a textured, handmade paper that will enhance the image; after a first, light printing, paint an iridescent polymer onto some areas of the print; print the image a second time; apply a UV-protective coating to the print; document the edition.*

CHER THREINEN-PENDARVIS / PRINTED BY JON CONE, CONE EDITIONS PRESS

Cone at the Mac that's connected to the Iris system

JON CONE OF CONE EDITIONS PRESS has been making prints and editions for artists since 1980. In 1985, Cone Editions began using computers in printmaking, pioneering techniques such as digital gravure, digital silkscreen and various digital monotype techniques. The firm has made Iris inkjet prints since 1992 and has become a leader in printing technology, sharing methods, materials and techniques with other fine art service bureaus.

When he makes a fine art master print, Cone interprets the artist's image in a collaborative manner. Often the selection of a paper, a special color transformation or perhaps even an experimental printing method can enhance an image. Cone used all three of these to realize the Painter image above.

1 Resizing and converting the color mode. An image may need to be resized to take advantage of the Iris printer's resolution (300 dpi) and replication capabilities. The Iris achieves the look of a much higher resolution because of the way the ink sprays onto the paper. Although the optimal resolution for files that will be printed on the Iris is 300 ppi, the printer can interpolate resolutions of 150 ppi or 100 ppi to produce high-quality prints.

Cone prefers to use Adobe Photoshop for a monitor-to-output calibration loop. He has written a proprietary color transformation engine for Photoshop that he uses to convert images from RGB to CMYK. This interface also helps him calibrate the Iris, allowing the monitor to show a close approximation of the printed image. After converting this image, Cone used Photoshop's Image, Adjust,

IRIS FACTS

The Iris printer's drum spins at 110 inches per second; up to 1 million droplets of ink per second are sprayed at 90 mph through each of its four nozzles. Using only cyan, magenta, yellow and black inks, it can simulate millions of colors.

Positioning the paper on the Iris drum

Carefully painting the iridescent polymer coating on the print

Drying the iridescent solution

Stopping the printer to show how the cyan, magenta, yellow and black inks are printed in sequence on the substrate

Using a silkscreen process to add a protective archival coating

Curves dialog box to compensate for out-of-gamut blues that had been lost. (Since RGB has a broader color gamut than CMYK, out-of-gamut colors are dulled when an image is converted to CMYK.) The black plate was adjusted separately to bring out detail in the darkest areas of the image. Finally, a proprietary plug-in Iris format RIP (raster image processor) was used to save the image in a form that the Iris can use for printing.

2 Choosing a paper and setting up the Iris. Cone selected a sheet of heavy, handmade paper with a very soft, large surface grain and an exaggerated deckled edge that would complement the vivid color and lively brushstrokes in the image. He taped the paper to the drum of the Iris.

3 Printing, painting and drying. Cone used the Iris to print this particular image twice. For the first pass, he adjusted the ink tables in the Iris's RIP to print a faint version of the image. With the print still taped to the drum, Cone brushed an experimental iridescent solution (composed of titanium dioxide-coated mica and hygroscopic polymer) onto the lily only. Then he dried the hand-painted coating with a hair dryer.

4 Printing the image a second time. Cone loaded a new set of rich-printing color ink tables into the Iris's RIP and made a second printing pass. The transparent Iris inks adhered to the polymer coating on the lily as easily as they did to the uncoated paper; the iridescent polymer provided a subtle reflection, adding luminance to the lily.

5 Applying a protective coating to the print. Michael Pelletier, systems and production manager for Cone Editions, applied a silkscreen coating of hindered amine light stabilizers (HALS) and ultraviolet absorbers (UVA) to the finished print. This solvent-based coating developed by Cone carries the protective additives deep into the printed image where they fully encapsulate the dyes, helping to produce what Cone Editions says is "the longest-lasting archival Iris print available today."

Documenting the edition. The artist now signs the finished print to make it the "right-to-print proof" against which future prints in the edition will be compared. After the artist has signed approval, an edition can be printed on demand while the image file is stored safely on CD-ROM at Cone Editions. A documentation sheet signed by both master printer and artist details the size of the edition, number of proofs printed, methods used and dimensions. Most importantly, it specifies that no other proofs or prints can or will be made. (After completing an edition, Cone destroys all copies of the image file.) Each print will bear a unique print identification number and will be signed and numbered in pencil by the artist.

Making a Color Managed Art Print

Overview *Create a painting using a custom color set; use color management tools for consistent viewing between Painter and Photoshop; use a custom ICC profile for printing with archival inks on rag printmaking paper.*

CAROL BENIOFF

WHEN PRINTING ON DIFFERENT PAPERS or using different inks, custom printing profiles allow you to obtain more accurate color. Artist Carol Benioff has developed a useful color management system that includes color calibration and custom printing profiles. For the mixed media print *Waiting to Know,* Benioff combined three etchings, a painting created in Painter and a color pencil drawing to create a variation of her image. She printed the image on her Epson 4000 printer using UltraChrome inks on a sheet of Lana Gravure printmaking paper. After coating the print with shellac, she dried it. Then, Benioff soaked the print in water to soften the paper and blotted the excess water. After inking up the three etching plates, she placed them on the press bed, overlaid the damp print, and then ran the paper through the press to create the final image seen above.

1 Painting with printable colors. To begin, Benioff loaded one of her custom color sets. She has made a variety of color sets from images that have printed well using a commercial offset method or on her Epson 4000. To create your own custom color set from an image, first open the image in Painter, go to the Color Sets palette, click on the right triangle and select New Color Set from Image. A new Color Set will appear in the palette. Then click on the triangle again and choose Save Color Set, name your set, and save it to the Color Sets folder within the Painter IX application folder (or wherever you like).

2 Managing color. To ensure that her monitor displays colors accurately, Benioff calibrated her monitor using OptiCal, which includes both software and a sensor. (The calibration

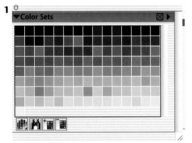

One of Benioff's custom color sets that she created from an image

Selecting the type of calibration sensor and mode of calibration in OptiCal, a monitor calibration software made by ColorVision

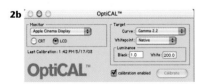

Selecting the monitor, curve and white point settings in OptiCal

COLOR MANAGEMENT

Color management is part science and part art. Some factors can be measured; some are subjective. CMM or Color Management Modules (ColorSync on the Macintosh, ICM on Windows) perform the calculations between the color profiles (the numerical description of the color) of your devices, such as your monitor and printer. For more information check out *Real World Color Management* by Bruce Fraser, Chris Murphy, and Fred Bunting, published by Peachpit Press.

2c

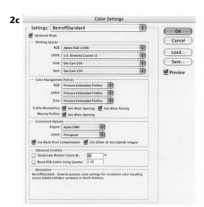

Benioff's custom color setup in Photoshop CS

3a

Choosing Leave as is (don't color manage) in the Missing Profile dialog in Photoshop

3b

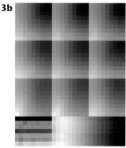

Target file provided by Chromix, which Benioff printed on Lana Gravure paper

4

To preview the custom print ICC profile, Benioff used Photoshop custom soft proof setup. Preview is on (top), and off (bottom).

sets the white point, the black point, the color temperature and the dynamic range or gamma of each monitor, and then generates an ICC profile based on the calibration.) To enable Color Management in Photoshop CS, go to Photoshop, Color Setting and select one of the preset color management settings or create your own custom settings. Make sure to choose Advance Mode so that you can set your Color Management Policies to display a warning dialog box when you open the file with no embedded color profile, or when the file has a color profile different from your own color working space.

PRINTING FROM PAINTER IX

Here's how to set up color management for printing from Painter IX: With the image open, choose Canvas, Color Management. Select the same internal RGB space with which you have been working. Click on the arrows from the internal RGB space to the Printer and to the Monitor icons. Select your printer and monitor ICC profiles. Click on the Plus button if you wish to save these settings. Choose your page setup, and in the print dialog box, select the media type, resolution or print style. Open the dialog box where color management is enabled in your printer driver and make sure that it is turned off.

3 Using custom ICC print profiles. Benioff purchased a custom ICC print profile from Chromix to ensure that she would achieve accurate color when printing on Lana Gravure rag paper. Chromix is a third-party company that specializes in color management and custom profiles, and they provide a downloadable profiling kit that includes instructions and profile target files (www.chromix.com). Open the profile target file provided in Photoshop. In the Missing Profile dialog box, select Leave as is (don't color manage). Print the file on the paper you wish to profile using non-color-managed settings. Make a note of the print settings, including the resolution, rendering intent and media type chosen. (The Media Type setting tells the printer how much ink to put down, not the color mix.) Make sure to use these same settings when printing with the custom profile. Next, inspect the printout to make sure you have a clean print and that all parts of the file have printed. Benioff sent the print to Chromix, and the company sent a custom profile via e-mail. In OS X for all users, load the custom ICC profile into the Library, ColorSync, Profiles; for a single user, choose User, Library, ColorSync, Profiles. In Windows, choose Program Files, Common Files, Adobe, Color, Profiles.

4 Making a soft proof. In Photoshop, Benioff chose View, Proof Set-up and Custom, and then she selected her new printing profile that Chromix had named: CB E4000 LGravure 9104.icc. For Intent she chose Relative Colorimetric (this was the same Rendering Intent used when printing the profile target file). Benioff did not check Simulate Paper White. She found that it does not correctly simulate the way inkjet ink sits on her paper. Next, she chose Proof Colors from the View menu to view the results. The "soft" (onscreen) proof is only an approximation. Benioff recommends keeping in mind

5a

Print with Preview dialog for Photoshop CS using the custom ICC print profile

5b

The Epson 4000 Print dialog boxes for Print Settings (top) and Color Management (bottom)

5c

Two details of the archival print on Lana Gravure paper

these critical factors: the effects of your lighting, ambient light, and angle of viewing on your perception of the color.

5 Printing from the desktop. Benioff opened her final image in Photoshop. In Photoshop's Print with Preview dialog box, she chose Page Setup, and then chose the paper dimensions and orientation for the Lana Gravure paper. Next, she chose the following settings: for the Source Space, she selected her internal RGB space, Adobe RGB 98; for Print Space she selected her custom ICC profile CB E4000 LGravure 9104, keeping the Intent as Relative Colorimetric. Next she selected Print, which opened the Print Settings dialog box, and from the Media Type menu, she chose Velvet Fine Art Paper. (She made these same selections when she printed the target profile file.) The Media Type setting tells the printer how much ink to put down. For glossy surfaces, the printer puts down less ink; for smooth soft papers, it puts down more ink. In the Color Management section of the Epson 4000 print dialog box, she selected No Color Adjustment. If you were to enable Color Management (at the printer driver level), there would be two layers of color management (one in Photoshop's Print settings and a second one in the printer driver settings), which would distort the colors in the print. Remember that each paper absorbs ink from your printer differently, just like any other painting or drawing medium. If you are using a printer's manufactured paper and ink, their off-the-shelf ICC printing profiles might be adequate. But when using different papers or different inks, custom printing profiles will allow you to easily obtain the most accurate color.

> **HOW DOES A PROFILE WORK?**
>
> An ICC color profile is a look-up table of color values that control a device such as a monitor, printer, scanner, or digital camera and its associated CIELAB color value. (CIELAB is the agreed-upon color values for device-independent color, created by the International Consortium on Color, or ICC.) The ICC color profile describes in numbers a particular device's color behavior. The profile for your monitor speaks to the profile for your printer through your computer's CMM (Color Management Module). On the Macintosh the CMM is ColorSync; on a PC it is called ICM or Image Color Management. There are different flavors of CMM; for instance, Apple, Adobe, Heidelberg, Agfa and Kodak. Make sure to select one of these on the OS level to make sure the color management calculations for all applications will be consistent for device-independent color. Color management makes it possible for your monitor and printer to speak the same color language.

The entire archival print on Lana Gravure paper

■ Artist **Carol Benioff** created *Waiting to Know, Variation 2,* using images that had been painted and drawn for different versions of the print series *And Then You Will Know*. Benioff enjoys playing with the same elements using different combinations to build new narratives with each variation. She developed the base image with two women in Painter using the Acrylic and Chalk brushes. To create depth and to paint the shadows, she used one of her own custom glazing brushes. She also used Painter's Apply Lighting effect to add warm graduated light on the image. Benioff photographed

a series of her own color pencil drawings to use in the series. She opened the two images of dolls in Painter and copied and pasted them into the file with the two women, with each figure of a doll on its own layer. She set the Composite Method of both of the doll layers to Multiply, which made the paper appear to be transparent. Benioff brought scans of the etchings into the working image so that she could play with the position of the elements. She copied and pasted them into the working composite file and set the Composite Method for each of the etching layers to Multiply. She experimented

with the scale and position of the etchings and the two doll images until she felt they all worked well together. Benioff would later print the etchings onto the digital print, so she deleted the two etching layers and flattened the remaining portion of the image. Next, she printed the flattened image on her Epson 4000 using a custom print profile on Lana Gravure printmaking paper. All the elements came together on the etching press. Benioff inked the two etching plates and printed them on top of the Epson print. The etching gave texture and depth to the final digital print.

■ With her series *Fragile Beauty*, fine artist **Dorothy Simpson Krause** transports us to treasured places where the impact of human existence has been kept at bay. Two images from the *Fragile Beauty* series, **Red Water** and **Reflections**, are shown here. Krause created each image for the series by digitally combining a conventional painting with a photograph. Then she printed these composite images using pigmented inks on various substrates including linen canvas, metal or film, depending on her vision for each work. Finally she embellished the final works on canvas with traditional art materials including oils, pastels, colored pencil and encaustic.

Red Water is a mixed media work on canvas and is an edition of one. Krause began the image by taking a digital photograph near her home, one evening at sunset. She also created a conventional oil painting of the marsh. After scanning it, she combined the scan with the digital photograph. To put *Red Water* on canvas she used a transfer process. First, she printed the image on Oce FCPLS4 clear film using her Epson 9600 and the UltraChrome inkset. Then she prepared a linen canvas by painting the canvas with a thick coating of rabbit-skin glue, which she allowed to set like a gelatin. (The rabbit-skin glue would receive the ink from the film.) Then she placed the image face down on the canvas, and transferred the image to the surface like a monoprint. The image melded with the canvas surface as the water evaporated from the rabbit-skin glue. The final stretched canvas measures 24 x 24 inches.

■ For the digital collage *Reflections,* a member of the *Fragile Beauty* series, **Dorothy Simpson Krause** began by taking a digital photograph of a pond near her home. Then, using her computer, she combined the photograph with a scan of a landscape painting that she had painted using conventional oil paint. Krause planned to print *Reflections* on aluminum. So she prepared a sheet of aluminum for printing by painting it with one coat of inkAID adhesive and two coats of inkAID clear gloss precoat. (The applications of InkAID allow the printing inks to adhere to the metal substrate.) When the coating was complete, Krause printed the image onto the pre-coated aluminum using an Epson 9600 with the Epson UltraChrome inkset. Reflections is an Edition of 4; the final print on aluminum measures 24 x 24 inches.

■ Artist **Helen Golden** achieves intriguing abstract spaces and three-dimensional textures in *The Explorer* (above) and *Waterdance* (right). When creating these exciting new images Golden used elements from two earlier works. She enjoys using Painter to bring out the texture in her images.

"*The Explorer* started its evolution many years ago as a faded out-of-focus photograph," Golden says. She had used this same source photo to create a favorite early work, *Ancestors.* She loved the forms, so years later, she created a monotype that incorporated the digital image for *Ancestors* and pieces of string and paper. To make an image file from the large monotype, Golden scanned it in six sections and then carefully reassembled it using Photoshop. When the

assembly was complete, she extracted hidden details by using the Photoshop plug-in LucisArt on the file. Then Golden copied the elements to layers and composited them using blending modes such as Multiply, Exclusion, Difference, Soft Light and Color. Next, she opened her Photoshop file in Painter, and used Effects, Surface Control, Apply Surface Texture, using Image Luminance to add dimension to the textures in the image. To unify the image, she added a custom paper texture over the entire image. She used Effects, Surface Control, Apply Surface Texture, this time using Paper. Golden printed *The Explorer* as a variant edition using a Hewlett-Packard DesignJet 5000PS printer and archival UV inks on Hahnemuhle Digital Fine Art paper.

■ For *Waterdance,* **Helen Golden** achieves playful movement within richly textured shapes. She was inspired to work over a large monotype that she had created earlier. Golden built a digital file by scanning the large monotype in several sections, and then painstakingly assembled them into a single image using Photoshop.

When the assembly was complete, Golden extracted details by using the Photoshop plug-in LucisArt on the file. Then Golden copied the elements to layers and composited them using blending modes such as Multiply, Exclusion, Difference, Soft Light and Color. Next, she opened her Photoshop file in Painter, where she removed some areas of the image and added painted brush work. Then she used Effects, Surface Control, Apply Surface Texture, using Image Luminance to add dimension to the textures in the image. She used Genuine Fractals PrintPro software to increase the pixel size of the file. Then, she added an overall light texture to the image, by choosing Effects, Surface Control, Apply Surface Texture, using Paper. Golden printed *Waterdance* as a variant edition using a Hewlett-Packard DesignJet 5000PS printer and archival UV inks on Hahnemuhle Digital Fine Art paper.

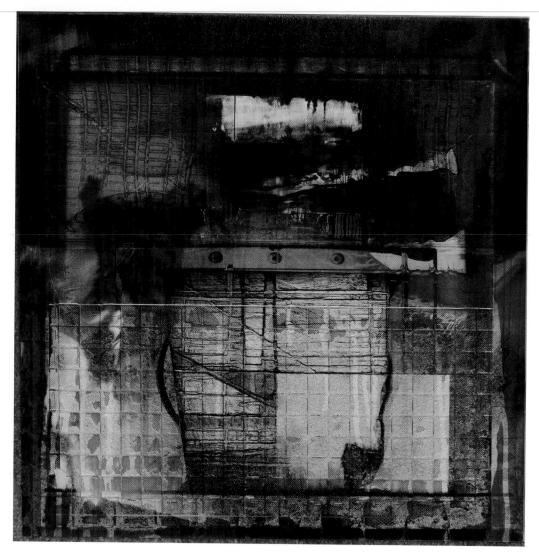

■ Digital Atelier artist **Bonny Lhotka** created *Bayside* using digital photographs and scans of objects that she had found at flea markets.

Lhotka built a surface to integrate with her digital image using wood, styrene ceiling tile, sand and acrylic paint. To create the illusion of white ink in the image, she brushed white gesso on parts of the substrate using varying levels of opacity. Then, she allowed the liquid to drip and run. She photographed the surface.

Next, Lhotka placed the digital file with the found objects over the photograph of the surface image. She lightened areas of the digital file and removed portions of the image so that the substrate and the image would blend into one another.

Lhotka printed *Bayside* using an OCÉ t220 flatbed printer. Before printing on the substrate, she measured a high test point for the collage and then used this information to set the head height of the printer. This feature is very useful when dealing with substrates made from collaged materials. The ability to print on anything up to two inches thick allows an artist to collage materials onto stretched canvas or panels.

During printing, if the print head senses a higher spot, the printer stops. Lhotka loves the flexible features of the OCÉ t220. She is able to move the carriage out of the way to compress or remove a higher spot on the substrate. When printing is resumed, the head finds where printing was stopped and then flawlessly completes the print.

The simplicity of substrate placement on the stationary bed makes this printer ideal for creating limited edition original prints on complex and varied surfaces.

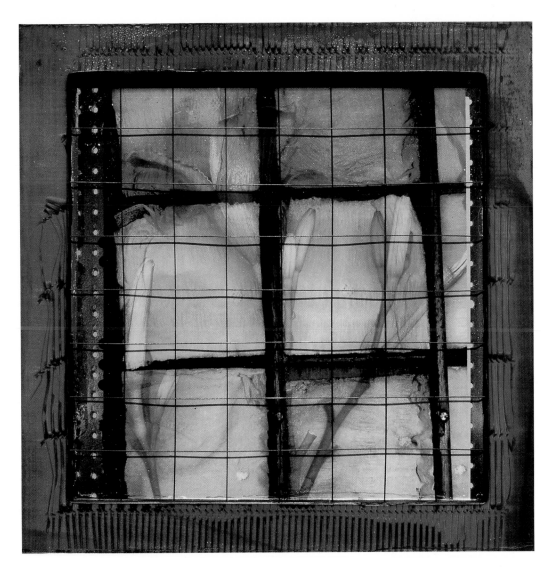

■ Inspired by flowers in her garden, artist **Bonny Lhotka** created the mixed media work *Lily*. Lhotka scanned a lily flower using a Microtek 9800XL scanner, and then she combined the lily scan with a digital photo that she had shot of a wooden antique tray.

Lhotka commissioned a woodworker to build a Baltic Birch frame with a recess in the center. She taped the outer edges of the 32 surround, or frame, to form a well that would hold the fresco mix. She made the mix from rabbit skin glue, pearl pigment, water and an inkAID adhesive; then she poured it into the taped area. As the mix cooled, it set up like Jell-O.

Then, she made the print for the frame on an Encad Novajet 880, using a film made by coating polycarbonate with clear inkAID inkjet precoat. After the gel set, she removed the tape. She rolled up the outer "frame" area of the film, aligned it with the edge and then carefully unrolled the film onto the surrounding wood. After five minutes she transferred the image onto the Baltic Birch. Then, she peeled off the film, leaving the image on the gel.

Lhotka mixed a batch of fresco mix, but this time, she added calcium carbonate to the fresco mix to make the image opaque white. She poured this mixture into the recess in the center.

Next, Lhotka printed the lily flower image on an Encad using GO pigment inks. She trimmed it to fit into the center and then rolled it down after the mix had cooled into a gel. After 5 minutes, she removed the film. Because of the calcium carbonate, the center dried to a chalky finish, in contrast to the transparent, iridescent border.

To complete the frame for the work, Lhotka had holes drilled into the inner lip of the surround. Then, she used rusty piano wire to create the laces over the frame.

■ Artist **Steve Rys** began *Crazy Horse* by making conventional sketches using pencils and paper. While sketching, he referred to source photographs. When he was happy with the sketch, he opened a new empty file in Painter and used brushes and a pressure-sensitive tablet and stylus to develop a color study. To build the large masses of color, he used the Round Camelhair variant of Oils, continually varying the size of the brush to achieve an expressive feeling with dynamic movement. He began with the lightest colors and then gradually built up darker tones as he developed the forms in the portrait. To blend areas, he used the Just Add Water variant of

Blenders, also varying the size of the brush, adding more color with Round Camelhair when needed for the look of wet paint.

Rys saved the final image as a 240 ppi RGB file in TIFF format and printed it using two methods—as a large inkjet print from a Roland printer, and as a series of unique monoprints. The inkjet print was printed on a Roland Hi-Fi Jet inkjet using an archival eight-color inkset on Concord Rag Bright White watercolor paper (which was manufactured with an inkjet receptive coating). Rys sealed the Roland print with a Krylon overcoat spray to protect the inks and paper from moisture and to

increase the light-fastness of the print. For a second series of prints, Rys created a series of monoprints using a hand transfer process that allowed him to create one-of-a-kind images. After making several 5 x 5-inch inkjet prints using water-soluble inks on paper, he used a burnishing tool to transfer each image onto a sheet of bristol board that had been dampened with Golden flow retarder solution. By varying the pressure and direction and the amount of dampness on the paper, and by burnishing onto inkjet prints that had been ghosted by previous burnishing sources, Rys created a variety of images. He ganged and matted these images in the order shown above.

■ Artist **Judi Moncrieff** created *Traditions* as a member of her series called *First Nation*, for a New York art exhibition. She began by taking photos of the people, artifacts and landscape surroundings at Spirit Days in Anchorage, Alaska. Spirit Days is a celebration of Native Americans from southeast Alaska to central and northern Alaska, and she had been invited to photograph people at the event. After the shoot, she used both Photoshop and Painter to create composite images from bits and pieces of many photographs, and then added textures, more color and brush work in Painter. "Nothing you see is real and, yet, *it is real*," says Moncrieff.

For the exhibition at the A.I.R. Gallery in SoHo, she created the main series as "one of a kind" (instead of members in an edition) because the images were presented using a complex printing, transfer and installation process that allowed Moncrieff to achieve a unique multidimensional look. To begin, the images were printed onto heat transfer paper on a Hewlett-Packard 2500CP with HP's pigment-based light-fast inkset. Then the resulting images on the heat transfer paper were applied to leather using heat and pressure. For the exhibition, the works were hung on the wall behind freestanding Plexiglas pieces on pedestals that were prepared with a black-and-clear image (printed onto a clear cling by the HP 2500CP). Placing the Plexiglas elements one-half-inch away from the leather created a multidimensional effect.

■ "For someone like me, who has both a painting studio and a digital studio, drawing with line is one of the options that bridge the gaps between media," says artist **James Faure Walker.** "What excites me is the continuing convergence of painting, photography and the digital."

Walker loves the immediacy with which he can create an image—taking digital photos, opening them in Painter, pasting them into a collage, manipulating the pieces of photos on their own layers and then painting on the image with brushes. He developed a method of digital painting that involved painting on cardboard constructions, photographing them from a variety of angles and reassembling them digitally.

In *Studio Chairs* there are two chairs: a small model Walker built using cardboard and another which is a straight-backed wooden chair. After photographing the chairs, Walker assembled the photo elements on layers. To color some of the photo pieces, he used Painter's Tonal Control effects, such as the Posterize feature. Then he added digital brush work, which he painted on transparent layers above and below the photo elements. He added the new transparent layers for the brush work by clicking the New Layer button on the Layers palette. Then he painted using several brushes, including the Opaque Round variant and other Oils variants to create loose strokes over and around the imagery of the chairs.

■ For *Blue Bowls*, **James Faure Walker** achieves a playful balance between the relaxed ease of physical paint and the snappiness of digital paint using Painter. "I had found three cardboard reels discarded by the road," says Walker. "They had been used in the manufacture of bracelets and watch straps. Then I did a sequence of large-scale blue gouache pictures that I composited digitally to build an interesting composition. Finally, I came across a fascinating bowl in ochres and reds in the Victoria and Albert Museum's English Decorative Arts section. The fluency of the foliage fascinated me, so I did a quick sketch." Walker photographed the blue gouache drawing constructions and his

sketch, and then he assembled the elements in Painter, where he also added more brush work drawn using his Wacom tablet and Painter. To give his image depth and to make the brush work layers stand out from the background, he applied soft drop shadows using the Create Drop Shadow command.

As he developed both *Studio Chairs* and *Blue Bowls*, he proofed them in his studio on an Epson 4000 inkjet printer. The final 17 x 22-inch prints for the edition of 20 were printed on Somerset Radiant Velvet White paper on an Iris printer using the Pinnacle Gold archival inkset.

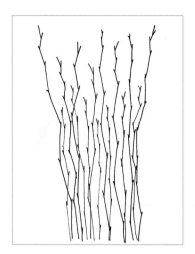

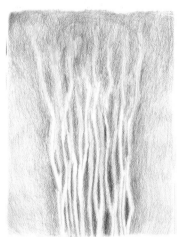

■ Digital Atelier artist **Karin Schminke** celebrates an interplay of shape and texture that is inspired by the natural world in her series *Form Inform*. Two images from her series are shown here, *Joy* (above) and *Tranquility* (right).

Schminke began *Joy* by creating a watercolor painting and colored-pencil drawings using conventional materials. When the painting and drawings were complete, she scanned them on a Microtek flatbed scanner. She opened a new file, and then copied and pasted the scans into the working file to build a layered collage.

Using an Epson Stylus Pro 9600 printer with Ultrachrome inks, she printed her layered image onto a black rag paper, Arches by Magic, which is precoated for inkjet printing. So that she could paint with conventional acrylics on her print, she applied inkAID Semi Gloss precoat. Then, she dried the surface.

She assembled a second combination of drawings to add another layer of imagery to her print. Schminke fed the precoated print into the Epson Stylus 9600 and printed it using the second combination of drawn forms.

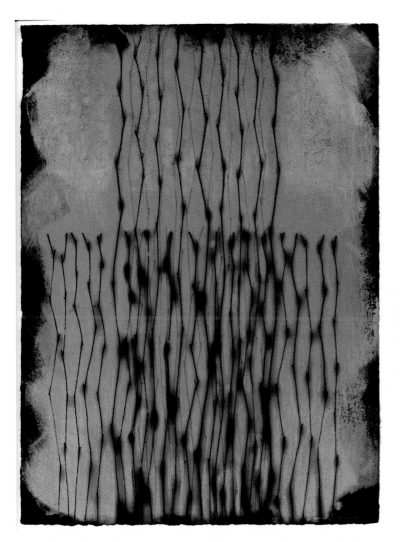

■ Artist **Karin Schminke** began the mixed media work *Tranquility* by sketching with colored pencils and paper. She also created a traditional watercolor study. Then, she scanned the paintings and drawings on a Microtek flatbed scanner and assembled the elements into a layered collage.

When the collage image was complete, she chose a piece of a black paper, Arches by Magic, an artist rag paper that was precoated for imaging on an inkjet printer. She printed the image using an Epson 9600 printer with Ultrachrome inks, and then she left the print to dry.

Schminke wanted to print over the image with another combination of drawn images, so she applied inkAID Semi Gloss precoat so that the ink would adhere to the acrylic paint. Then, she fed the print into the Epson 9600 and printed it using the new combination of scanned drawings. In the detail on the right, the rich texture of the white inkAID can be seen, along with the metallic gold paint.

Finally, Schminke mounted the finished prints for her series on half-inch thick board, and then she coated them with a protective varnish.

■ As the principal and creative director for Cinco de Mayo Design Studio, **Mauricio Alanis** conceived and built the *Shouting Bucket* vehicle graphics (bottom left) for Abigarrados, a service bureau in Monterrey, Mexico, which specializes in large-format printing. Using Painter, he created a layered image that included the paint can photo, the circular shapes around the can image and the exploding paint. To give the paint a dramatic three-dimensional look, he added a semi-transparent layer of Liquid Metal

brushstrokes. (For more information about Liquid Metal, turn to "Painting with Metal and Water" on page 302 in the introduction of Chapter 8 and to "Painting with Ice" on page 350.) To add realistic relief to other areas of the graphics, he used Apply Surface Texture with Image Luminance. The final 65 ppi image was output onto adhesive-backed vinyl media using a large-format inkjet printer, and then carefully mounted onto the Abigarrados van.

■ **Chet Phillips** created these larger-than-life-size vehicle graphics (top and middle left) for *Dallas Photo Imaging*, using the Scratchboard technique described on page 61. To make sure the three images would fit the truck exactly, he used a full-size template of the Suburban's shape (provided by the service bureau) to plan each panel. He created individual panels for the driver's side, passenger's side and the truck's back. Phillips built the original files at a resolution of 65 ppi; each file was over 100 MB. When the illustrations were complete, they were output on Dallas Photo Imaging's Idanit inkjet printer onto Avery fleet graphic vinyl with adhesive backing, and then attached to the truck.

Appendix A
Vendor Information

IMAGE COLLECTIONS

These vendors provided photos or video clips from their collections for the Painter IX Wow! *CD-ROM in the back of this book.*

Artbeats, Inc.
Myrtle Creek, OR
541-863-4429 541-863-4547 fax
www.artbeats.com

Corbis Images
Bellevue, WA
800-260-0444 425-641-4505 fax
www.corbis.com

Digital Wisdom, Inc.
Tappahannock, VA
800-800-8560 804-443-9000
804-443-3632 fax
www.digiwis.com

Fabulous Fonts
c/o PhotoSpin
Rolling Hills Estates, CA
310-265-1313 888-246-1313
310-265-1314 fax
www.photospin.com

Image Farm, Inc.
Toronto, ON, Canada
800-438-3276 416-504-4163 fax
www.imagefarm.com

Mediacom
Richmond, VA
804-560-9200 804-560-4370 fax

Getty Images / PhotoDisc
Seattle, WA
800-528-3472 877-547-4686 fax
www.gettyimages.com
www.photodisc.com

PhotoSpin
Rolling Hills Estates, CA
310-265-1313 888-246-1313
310-265-1314 fax
www.photospin.com

Visual Concept Entertainment
Sylmar, CA 91392
818-367-9187 818-362-3490 fax
http://www.vce.com

HARDWARE

Apple Computer, Inc.
800-767-2775

Color Vision / *Color Management*
Lawrenceville, NJ
609-895-7430
609-895-7447 fax
800-554-8688
www.colorvision.com

Epson America / *Desktop color printers*
Torrance, CA
800-289-3776 800-873-7766
www.epson.com

Encad, Inc. / *Desktop color printers*
San Diego, CA
800-453-6223
www.encad.com

Hewlett-Packard / *Desktop color printers*
San Diego, CA
858-655-4100
www.hp.com

Wacom Technology Corporation
Drawing tablets, Cintiq Interactive Pen Display
Vancouver, WA
800-922-6613
sales@wacom.com

SOFTWARE

Adobe Systems / *After Effects, GoLive, Illustrator, InDesign, Photoshop, Premiere*
San Jose, CA
800-833-6687

Auto F/X / *Photographic Edges*
Birmingham, AL
205-980-0056
205-9801121
www.autofx.com

Corel / *Corel Painter, CorelDraw*
Ottawa, ON, Canada
800-772-6735
www.corel.com

Macromedia / *Director, Dreamweaver, FreeHand, Fireworks, Flash*
San Francisco, CA
800-989-3762
415-252-2000

INKS AND SUBSTRATES

Charrette Corporation / *Substrates and Inks*
800-367-3729
www.inkjet.com

Digital Art Supplies / *Substrates and Inks*
877-534-4278
858-273-2576 fax
www.digitalartsupplies.com

Dr. Graphix Inc. / *Substrates*
www.drgraphix.com

Epson / *Substrates and Inks*
www.epson.com

Hewlett-Packard / *Substrates and Inks*
www.hp.com

ilab Corporation, Inc. / *Inks for Epson, Iris and Novaget*
Atkinson, NH
603-362-4190
603-362-4191 fax
www.ilabcorp.com

InkjetMall / *Substrates and Inks*
Bradford, VT
802-222-4415
802-222-3334 fax
Contact: Sarah Lyons

Luminos Photo Corporation / *Inks for Epson and other printers*
Yonkers, NY
800-586-4667
914-965-0367 fax

Media Street / *Substrates and Inks*
888-633-4295
888-329-5991 fax
www.mediastreet.com

MIS Associates, Inc / *Substrates and Inks*
248-391-2163
248-391-2527 fax
www.inksupply.com

TSS Photo / *Substrates and Inks*
801-363-9700
801-363-9707 fax
www.inkjetart.com
www.tssphoto.com/sp/dg/

Wilhelm Imaging Research, Inc. / *Ink and paper longevity information*
Grinnell, IA
515-236-4222 fax
www.wilhelm-research.com

Appendix B
Fine Art Output Suppliers

These bureaus specialize in making large-format prints for fine artists. More are listed on the Painter IX Wow! CD-ROM.

Cone Editions Press / *Fine Art Prints*
East Topsham, VT
802-439-5751
802-439-6501 fax
Contact: Sara Larkin

Chrome Digital / *Fujix Pictrography prints; film recorder output*
858-452-1588

Dallas Photo Imaging *LightJet 5000 prints; vehicle graphics*
Dallas, TX
800-852-6929
214-630-4351
www.dpitexas.com

Digital Output Corp. / *Fine art prints*
San Diego, CA
619-685-5800
619-685-5804 fax
www.digitaloutput.com

Durst Dice America / *Lenticular prints*
Tuxedo, NY
914-351-2677

High Resolution / *Fine art prints*
Camden, ME
207-236-3777

Lenticular Products / *Lenticular prints*
www.lenticulardevelopement.com

Photodyne / *Hewlett-Packard DesignJet CP prints; Durst Lamda prints; film recorder output*
San Diego, CA
858-292-0140

Trillium Press / *Fine art prints; monotypes; silk screen*
Brisbane, CA
415-468-8166
415-468-0721 fax

Appendix C
Reference Materials

Here's a sampling of recommended references for both traditional and digital art forms.

ART BOOKS

Art Through the Ages
Fifth Edition
Revised by Horst de la Croix and Richard G. Tansey
Harcourt, Brace and World, Inc.
New York, Chicago, San Francisco, and Atlanta

The Art of Color
Johannes Itten
Van Nostrand Reinhold
New York

Drawing Lessons from the Great Masters
Robert Beverly Hale
Watson-Guptill Publications
New York

Mainstreams of Modern Art
John Canaday
Holt, Reinhart and Winston
New York

Printmaking
Gabor Peterdi
The Macmillan Company
New York
Collier-Macmillan Ltd.
London

The Natural Way to Draw
Kimon Nicolaïdes
Houghton Mifflin Company
Boston

The Photographer's Handbook
John Hedgecoe
Alfred A. Knopf
New York

TypeWise
Kit Hinrichs with Delphine Hirasura
North Light Books
Cincinnati, Ohio

COMPUTER IMAGERY BOOKS

Designing Web Graphics.4
Lynda Weinman
New Riders Publishing
Indianapolis, IN

Digital Character Design and Painting
Don Seegmiller
Charles River Media
Hingham, MA

Non-Designers Web Book
Robin Williams and John Tollett
Peachpit Press
Berkeley, CA

The Illustrator CS Wow! Book
Sharon Steuer
Peachpit Press
Berkeley, CA

The Photoshop and Painter Artist Tablet Book
Creative Techniques in Digital Painting
Cher Threinen-Pendarvis
Peachpit Press
Berkeley, CA

The Photoshop CS Wow! Book
Linnea Dayton and Jack Davis
Peachpit Press
Berkeley, CA

Real World Color Management
Bruce Fraser, Fred Bunting and Chris Murphy
Peachpit Press
Berkeley, CA

PUBLICATIONS

Communication Arts
Menlo Park, CA
www.commarts.com

Design Graphics
Design Editorial Pty. Ltd.
Victoria, Australia
www.designgraphics.com/au

EFX Art and Design
Stockholm, Sweden
www.macartdesign.matchbox.se

How
Design Ideas at Work
New York, NY
www.howdesign.com

Graphis
New York, NY
www.graphis.com

Print
New York, NY
www.printmag.com

STEP Inside Design
www.dgusa.com

SBS Digital Design
www.dgusa.com

Appendix D
Contributing Artists

Mauricio Alanis
Monterrey, N.L., Mexico
malanis@mail.cmact.com

Nick Anderson
nanderson@courier-journal.com

Ben Barbante
San Francisco, CA
415-657-9844

Michael Bast
Brookfield, IL
708-485-4853
michael.bast@sbc.global.net

Laurel Becker

Carol Benioff
Oakland, CA
510-533-9987
carol@carolbenioff.com
www.carolbenioff.com

Richard Biever
Evansville, IN
812-437-9308

Kathleen Blavatt
San Diego, CA
619-222-0057

Ray Blavatt
San Diego, CA
619-222-0057

Athos Boncompagni
Arezzo, Italy
aramis@inwind.it
www.athosboncompagni.com

Martha Jane Bradford
Brookline, MA
martha@marthavista.com
www.marthavista.com

Jinny Brown
Cupertino, CA
jinbrown@pixelallery.com
www.pixelalley.com

Marc Brown
Denver, CO
303-758-9411

Jeff Burke
Culver City, CA
310-837-9900

Michael Campbell
San Diego, CA
858-578-8252
www.michaelcampbell.com

Steve Campbell
415-668-5826
steve_campbell@mindspring.com

Karen Carr
www.karencarr.com

Phillip Charris
San Juan Capistrano, CA
949-496-3330

Ryan Church
www.ryanchurch.com

James D'Avanzo
(11/2/73–5/28/96)
Family of James D'Avanzo
Fairfield, CT
203-255-6822

Linda Davick
Knoxville, TN
615-546-1020

Michela Del Degan
40131 Bologna, Italy
+31-339-58-99-741
mdegan@infinito.it
www.micheladeldegan.com

John Derry
Overland Park, KS
derry@pixlart.com

Matt Dineen
Santa Cruz, CA

John Dismukes
949-888-9911
www.dismukes.com

Mary Envall
Vista, CA
760-727-8995

John Fretz
Seattle, WA
206-623-1931

Laurence Gartel
Boca Raton, FL
561-477-1100
gartel@gate.net

Brian Gartside
beeegeee@clearnet.nz
www.gartside.info

Helen Golden
Palo Alto, CA
650-494-3461
hsgolden@aol.com

Steven Gordon
Madison, AL
256-772-0022
StevenGordon@cartagram.com

Ileana Frometa Grillo
949-494-3454
ileana@ileanaspage.com
www.ileanaspage.com

Bill Hall
www.billhall.com

Kathy Hammon
bouchedoree@wanadoo.fr

Andrew Hathaway
San Francisco, CA
415-621-0671

Fiona Hawthorne
+44 (0)20-8968-8889
fionahawthorne@beeb.net
www.portfolio.com/fionahawthorne

Philip Howe
Snohomish, WA
425-385-8426
www.philiphowe.com

Geoff Hull
Studio City, CA
818-761-6019

Donal Jolley
c/o Studio 3, Lilburn, GA
770-279-7753
www.studio3o.com

Andrew Jones
ajones@spectrum.net
www.androidjones.com
www.conceptart.org

Ron Kempke
217-278-7441

Rick Kirkman
Glendale, AZ
623-334-9199

Dorothy Simpson Krause
781-837-1682
www.dotkrause.com

Terrie LaBarbera
Reston, VA
portraits@tlbtlb.com
www.tlbtlb.com

Ted Larson
Seattle, WA
206-524-7640
theoneson@earthlink.net

John Lee
Los Angeles, CA
213-467-9317

LeVan/Barbee
LeVan/Barbee studio
Indianola, WA
lvbwa@earthlink.com
www.bruckandmoss.com

Bonny Lhotka
Bonny@Lhotka.com
www.Lhotka.com
www.inkAID.com

Michele Lill
Valparaiso, IN
219-531-4728
lill@netnitco.net

Keith MacLelland
617-953-9550
keith@yourillustrator.com
www.yourillustrator.com

Debi Lee Mandel
530-886-8910
www.catsprite.com

Robert Manning
Supersample Corporation
Lilika Productions
212-414-1680
meglartin@aol.com
www.supersample.com

Janet Martini
San Diego, CA
619-283-7895

Craig McClain
La Mesa, CA
619-469-9599

Pedro Meyer
Coyoacan, Mexico D.F., Mexico
011-525-55-54-39-96
011-525-55-54-37-30
pedro@zonezero.com
www.zonezero.com

Judy Miller
Fall River, NS, Canada
902-861-1193
www.creativeartist.com
www.forgetreality.com

Kramer Mitchell
rkm@starband.net
www.lair-wildcape.com

Judi Moncrieff
(10/25/41–4/06/01)
Family of Judi Moncrieff
Seattle, WA

Brian Moose
Capitola, CA
831-425-1672

Wendy Morris
wendydraw@aol.com

Richard Noble
Eagle, ID
208-429-1802
rnoble@mac.com
www.nobledesign.com

Mary Beth Novak
Riviera Van Beers
San Francisco, CA

John Odam
Del Mar, CA
858-259-8230

Dennis Orlando
215-355-1613
215-355-6924 fax
dennisorlando@comcast.net
www.dennisorlando.com

Chet Phillips
214-987-4344
chet@chetart.com
www.chetart.com

David Purnell
c/o New York West
Lonsdale, MN
507-744-5408
SkyOtter@aol.com

Arena Reed
617-945-2754
arena@visualarena.com
www.visualarena.com

Mike Reed
Minneapolis, MN 55403
612-374-3164
www.mikereedillustration.com

Cindy Reid
cindy@reidcreative.com

Dewey Reid
dewey@reidcreative.com

Lew Robinson
Photography and Digital Imaging
310-837-7009

Mary Ann Rolfe
520-399-2133
Green Valley, AZ
mrolfe1@cox.net
www.digitalstretch.com

Delro Rosco
Eva Beach, HI
delrorosco.com
delro@verizon.net

Cynthia Beth Rubin
New Haven, CT
http://CBRubin.net

Peter Mitchell Rubin
c/o Production Arts Limited
310-915-5610

John Ryan
Atlanta, GA
jryan@crawford.com
www.dagnabit.tv.

Joyce Ryan
Atlanta, GA
joyryan@mindspring.com
www.mindspring.com/~joyryan

Steve Rys
Trevor, WI
262-862-7090
steve@rysdesign.com
www.rysdesign.com

Chelsea Sammel
Oakland, CA
510-628-8474

Karin Schminke
Karin@schminke.com
www.schminke.com

Don Seegmiller
www.seegmillerart.com

Elizabeth Sher
510-528-8004
liziv@ivstudios.com
www.ivstudios.com

Marilyn Sholin
sparkle1@aol. com
www.marilynsholin.com

Fay Sirkis
fay@faysartstudio.com
faysartstudio.com

Jan Smart
jansmart@jansmart.net
www.jansmart.net

Nancy Stahl
nancy@nancystahl.com
www.nancystahl.com

Sharon Steuer
Bethany, CT
www.ssteuer.com

Don Stewart
336-854-2769
www.donstewart.com

Phillip Straub
straubart@aol.com
www.phillipstraub.com

Jeremy Sutton
415-626-3871
jeremy@.paintercreativity.com
www.paintercreativity.com

Anne Syer
Davis,CA
530-758-1949

S. Swaminathan
Capitola, CA
408-722-3301

Tom Tilney
tomt@belgiandiamonds.com
www.belgiandiamonds.com

Susan Thompson
Lindsay, CA
susan@sx70.com
www.sx70.com

Jean-Luc Touillon
jean-luc.touillon@wanadoo.fr
jasiu@lafactory.fr

Lorraine Triolo
Culver City, CA
310-837-9900

Ad Van Bokhoven
info@advanbokhoven.nl
www.advanbokhoven.nl

Stanley Vealé
zetar@yahoo.com

Pamela Wells
Cardiff, CA
artmagic1@cox.net
www.artmagic.com

James Faure Walker
London, UK
jamesfaurewalker@compuserve.com

Helen Yancy
helen@helenyancystudio.com
www.helenyancystudio.com

Hiroshi Yoshii
Tokyo, Japan
tel/fax 81-3-5491-5337
hiroshi@yoshii.com

Index

A

Acrylics brushes/variants
    Captured Bristle, 31, 236–237, 273
    Dry Brush, 94–95, 425
    Glazing Acrylic, 95, 239–240, 425
    Opaque Acrylic, 16, 61, 64, 157
    Opaque Detail, 425
    Thick Acrylic Round, 124
    3D paint look, 65
    Wet Acrylic, 94–95, 425
    Wet Soft Acrylic, 94–95, 425
Add/Delete Point tool, 11, 346
Additional colors (Colors Picker), exchanging Main and Additional colors, 27
Adjust Colors/Selected Colors features, 32–33
Adobe After Effects
    high-resolution effects, 390
    Painter movie scripts, 378
Adobe ImageReady, 406
Adobe Photoshop. *See* Photoshop
Adobe Premiere
    exporting files to Painter, 380–381
    Painter movie scripts, 378–379
Airbrushes brushes/variants, 402
    Coarse Spray, 204, 347
    dab type brushes, 155
    Digital Airbrush, 37, 41, 43, 114, 171, 202, 204, 220, 234, 243, 245, 266, 269, 284–285, 314, 319, 364, 383
    Fine Detail Air, 264
    Fine Spray, 63, 155, 200
    Fine Tip Soft Air, 264, 267
    Fine Wheel, 63
    Graffiti, 63
    media pooling, 155
    Pepper Spray, 204
    Pixel Spray, 63, 347
    redirecting spray, 155
    Variable Spatter, 347
Alanis, Mauricio, 446
aligning shapes/layers/text, 14, 343, 410
    Align to Path, 107
    for calligraphy, 62
    Snap-to-Path feature, 69
analogous color hues, 27
Anderson, Nick, 176, 213
animating illustrations
    copying and power-pasting technique, 384

Frame Stacks, 384
    movement by offsetting layers, 384–385
    movement with brushstrokes, 385
    planning, 383–384
animating logos, 388–389
animation
    animatic techniques, 380
    automating movie effects, 390
    basing on movies using Tracing Paper, 380
    comps, 380, 386–387
    with Frame Stacks, 378–379
        Frames Per Second (fps) timing, 378
    rotoscoping movies, 380
    slide show for Web pages, 412
    storyboarding, 380
    video clip references, 379
antialiasing
    selections, 181
    Web graphics, 401
Art Pen Brushes
    compatible with Wacom 6D Art Pen, 68
    Grainy Calligraphy, 68
    Square Grainy Pastel, 68
    Tapered Gouache, 68
    Thin Smooth Calligraphy, 68
ArtBeats, 193, 226
Artists brushes/variants
    Impressionist, 285
    Sargent Brush, 64, 66
    Van Gogh, 30
Artists' Oils brushes/variants, 65, 98, 109
    Blend, Bristling and Clumpiness settings, 99–100
    Blender, 103
    Blender Palette Knife, 99
    Clumpy Brush, 100, 324
    dab types, 156
    Dry Bristle, 104, 106–107
    Dry Brush, 10, 100, 106–107
    Dry Palette Knife, 99
    Flat, Flat Rake, Chisel and Wedge Profile, 99
    Flat Profile, 99
    Grainy Blender, 100
    Grainy Dry Brush, 99
    Oily Blender, 103
    Oily Bristle, 100, 103–104
    Pointed Rake Profile, 99
    Skinny Tapered, 107
    Smooth Dry Brush, 100
    Snap-to-Path feature, 69
    Soft Round, 99
    Soft Tapered Brush, 106
    Tapered Oils, 10, 106

Wet Brush, 106
    Wet Oily Brush, 106–107
    Wet Oily Impasto, 100
    Wet Oily Palette Knife, 103–104, 109
atmospheric perspective, with saturation and values, 28
AVI movie formats, 10
    converting Frame Stacks, 387
    saving scripts, 377–378

B

backgrounds, filled squares, 35
Barbante, Ben, 400, 413
Bast, Michael, 219, 253
Becker, Laurel, 273
Benioff, Carol, 69, 72–73, 92–95, 105–107, 115–118, 151, 166–169, 205–206, 238–241, 421–422, 424–425, 430–432, 433
Bevel World Dynamic Plug-in, 227, 302–303
    beveled-chrome effect, 348–349
beveled-chrome effects, 348–349
Bézier paths, Painter IX *versus* Photoshop, 8
Biever, Richard, 170–171
bitmap programs. *See* pixel-based programs
Black Letter font class, 341
Blair, Don, 295
Blavatt, Kathleen, 61, 63, 299
Blavatt, Ray, 198–200
Blenders brushes/variants, 56
    Add Water, 29
    Blender Brush, 64
    Camelhair Blender, 159
    Coarse Oily Blender, 116
    Coarse Smear, 66
    Coarse Smear Blender, 116
    Coarse Spray, 66
    Detail Blender, 116
    Fine Tip Blender, 169
    Grainier Water, 163–164
    Grainy Blender, 116
    Grainy Water, 29, 64, 66, 71, 77, 163, 168–169, 174, 285, 383, 385
    Just Add Water, 60, 163, 168–169, 261, 272, 364
    Oily Blender, 116, 322
    Round Blender Brush, 64
    Runny Blender, 116
    Smudge, 60, 64, 77, 163, 261
    Smudge Water, 29
BMP file format, 9
Boncompagni, Athos, 22, 52, 58, 303, 375
Borgman, Jim, 198

COREL® painter™ IX

Congratulations to author Cher Threinen-Pendarvis, a Corel Painter Master, for producing *The Painter IX Wow! Book*, the latest edition of this highly praised volume of techniques and inspiration. Her book is an invaluable resource for professional photographers, commercial designers, and artists at all levels. Cher has been widely recognized for her mastery of Painter and the Wacom® pressure-sensitive tablet, having used these electronic tools since they were first released. Exercising her passion for the artist tools in Corel® Painter™, Cher has worked as a consultant and demo artist for the Corel Painter development team. Thank you Cher and Peachpit Press for producing another fantastic edition in the *Painter Wow!* series.

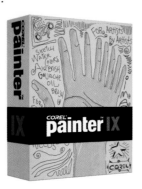

The introduction of Corel Painter IX—the world's most powerful Natural-Media painting and illustration software—reflects Corel's commitment to understanding and meeting the diverse needs of artists by providing a product that both delights and inspires.

Corel Painter IX features unique digital brushes, art materials and textures that mirror the look and feel of their traditional counterparts. It takes digital design to unprecedented levels with the revolutionary Artists' Oils Painting System, Snap-to-Path Painting, Quick Clone for photographers, and brushes that perform up to 10 times faster than in previous versions. Corel Painter enables some of the world's most accomplished creative professionals to extend their natural talents and techniques to create original works of breathtaking digital art.

While you enjoy Corel Painter as your digital art studio, you may also be interested to know about another Corel product, Paint Shop Pro, for your digital image-editing needs. Paint Shop Pro continues to set the standard for affordable, professional image editing. Version 9 builds on the Paint Shop Pro legacy of creative innovation, delivering a new suite of art media features, professional photo-editing tools, and precision graphic design capabilities.

To find out more about Paint Shop Pro, as well as Corel's other graphics products, please visit **www.corel.com**.

Nick Davies
General Manager, Graphics
Corel Corporation

Other graphics products available from Corel: